BE
GERMA

APPENDIX
II.1 ABOUT THE WORK

00:00 00:15 00:30 00:45 01:00 01:15 01:30

BELOW PROJECT
LOOKING NORTHWEST

00:00 00:15

PROJECT FROM RIVER

00.50m 00.60m

PERSPECTIVE
01:45
02:00
02:15
02:30
02:45
03:00
03:15
03:30
04:15
00:30
00:45
01:00
01:15
00.70m
00.80m

04:45
01:30
01:45
02:00
02:15
00.90m
01.00m
Dreyse
Stadtbad Tiergarten
Schule
Bf Bellevue
Lüneburger
Schloßpark Bellevue
Schloß Bellevue
Großer
Stern
Spree
Straße
T i e

Poststadion
Hamburg
Lehrter
Güterbahnhof
Friedhof
Senioren wohnhaus
Senioren heim
Heinrich Zille
Siedlung
Humboldthafen
Oberstufen zentrum
Washingtonplatz
Spree
Hamburg
Lehrter
Güterbahnhof
Moltke
Gen. Konsulat Schweiz
Herwarthstraße
Paul Löbe allee
Kongreßhalle
Platz der Republik
Deutscher Bundestag Verwaltung Berlin
Große Quer
Scheidemann
straße
Allee
CITY OF BERLIN
Platz vor dem Brandenburger Tor
des 17 Juni
Kleiner Stern
Garten
g a r t e n
Kemper platz
Bellevue
Lenné
Philharmonie
02:30
02:45
03:00
03:15
01.10m
01.20m

Volkspark
Rehberge
Humboldt
hain
Westhafen
Volkspark
Friedrichs
hain
Tiergarten
Platz d.
Republik
Kongreßhalle
Schöneberg
Volkspark
Hasenheide
Zentralflughafen
Berlin-Tempelhof
Neukölln
Tempelhof
Steglitz
03:30
03:45
04:00
04:15
01.30m
01.40m

RIVER
16
16
8
16
5
5
5
9
6
TIERGARTEN
9
5
6
7
8
6
25
26
2
1
6
5
2
23
04:30
04:45
01.50m
01.60m

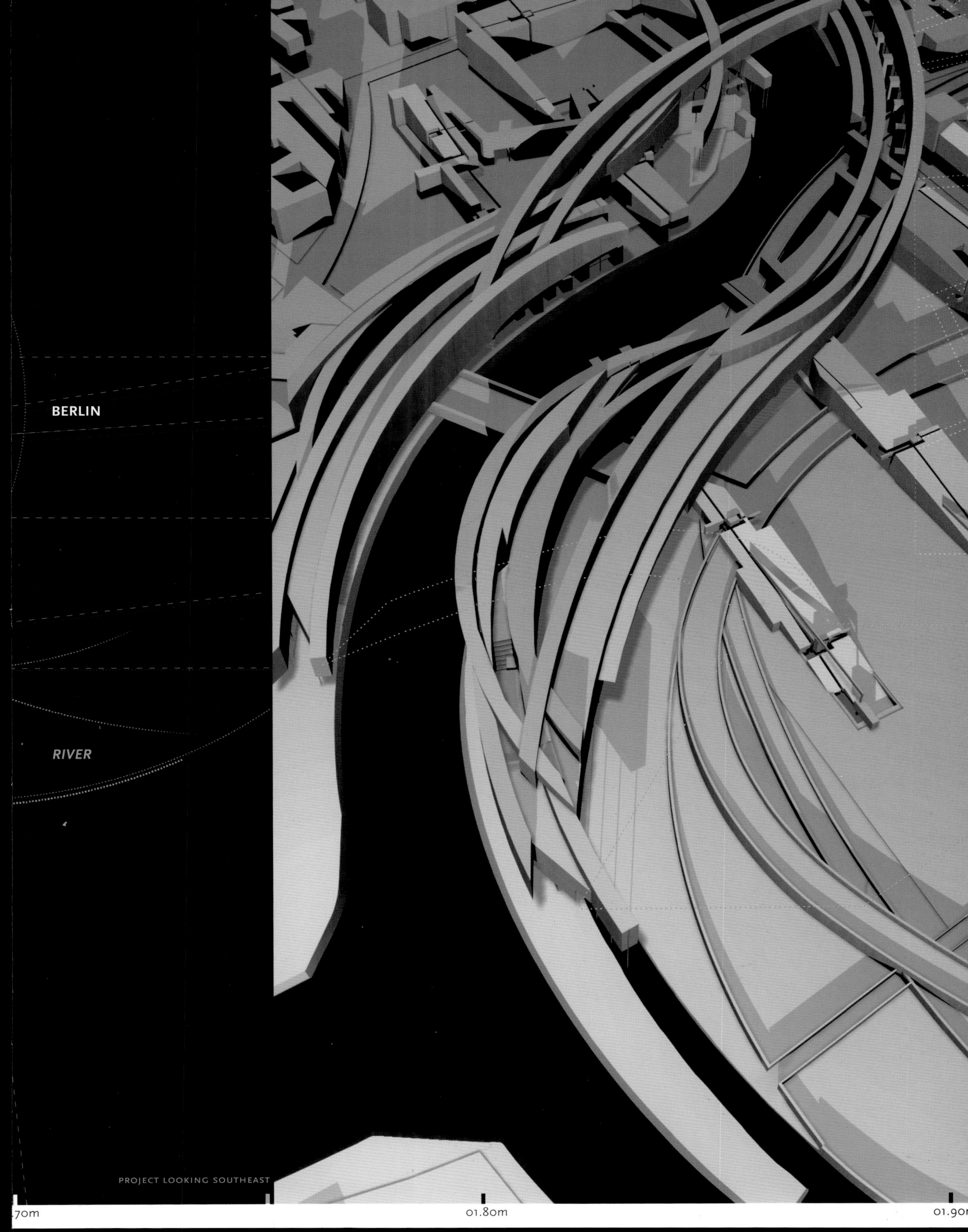
BERLIN
RIVER
PROJECT LOOKING SOUTHEAST
.70m
01.80m
01.90m

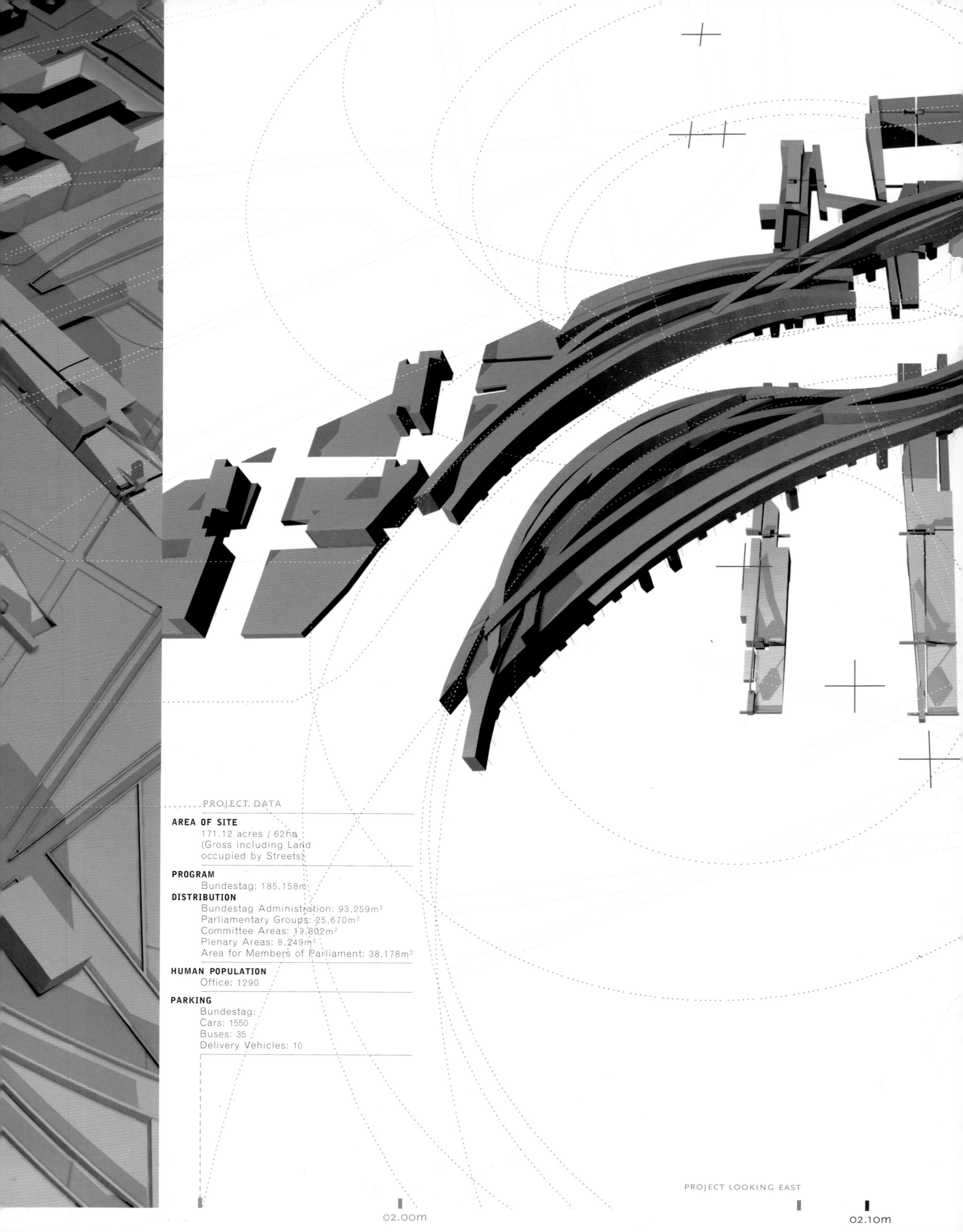
PROJECT DATA
AREA OF SITE
171.12 acres / 62ha
(Gross including Land occupied by Streets)
PROGRAM
Bundestag: 185,158m
DISTRIBUTION
Bundestag Administration: 93,259m²
Parliamentary Groups: 25,670m²
Committee Areas: 19,802m²
Plenary Areas: 8,249m²
Area for Members of Parliament: 38,178m²
HUMAN POPULATION
Office: 1290
PARKING
Bundestag:
Cars: 1550
Buses: 35
Delivery Vehicles: 10
PROJECT LOOKING EAST
02.00m
02.10m

PLAN **1.** Main Hall **2.** Parties **3.** Members **4.** Committees **5.** Administration **6.** Archives **7.** Cabinet Members **8.** Exhibition **9.** Diplomats **10.** Expansion **11.** Building Management **12.** Administration **13.** Equipment **14.** Official Apartments **15.** Security **16.** Government News Conference **17.** News Club **18.** German Government Society **19.** Main Hall **20.** Committees **21.** Offices **22.** Courtyards **23.** Exterior Parking **24.** Underground Parking **25.** Tunnel **26.** Raised Pedestrian Walkway **27.** Courtyard **28.** Future Apartment Development **29.** Future Commercial Development **30.** Boat Landing **31.** Metro **32.** Subway **33.** Helicopter Landing **34.** Central Energy Room
110.00m
00.00m
SITE PLAN
02.20m
02.30m

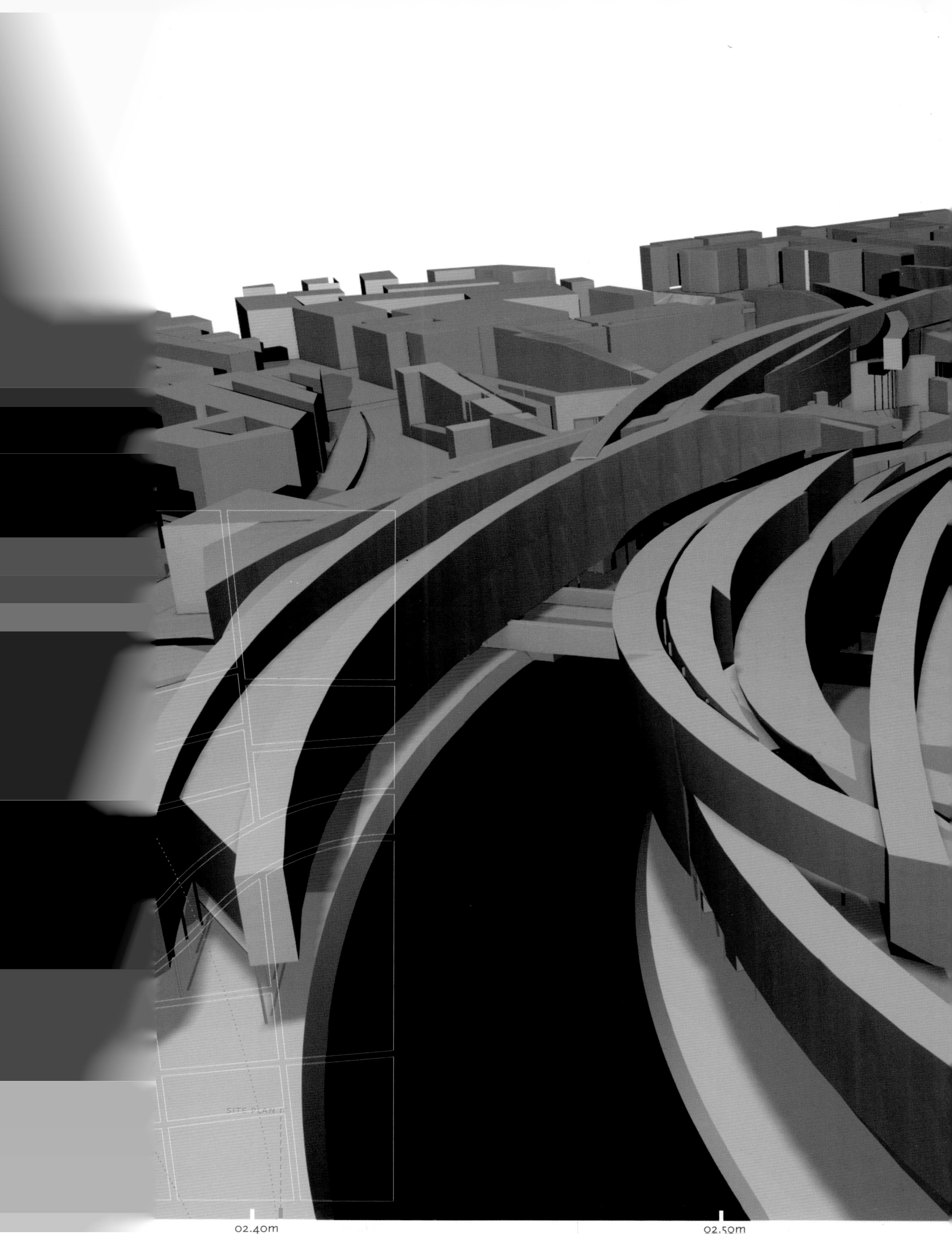
SITE PLAN 1
02.40m
02.50m

1997

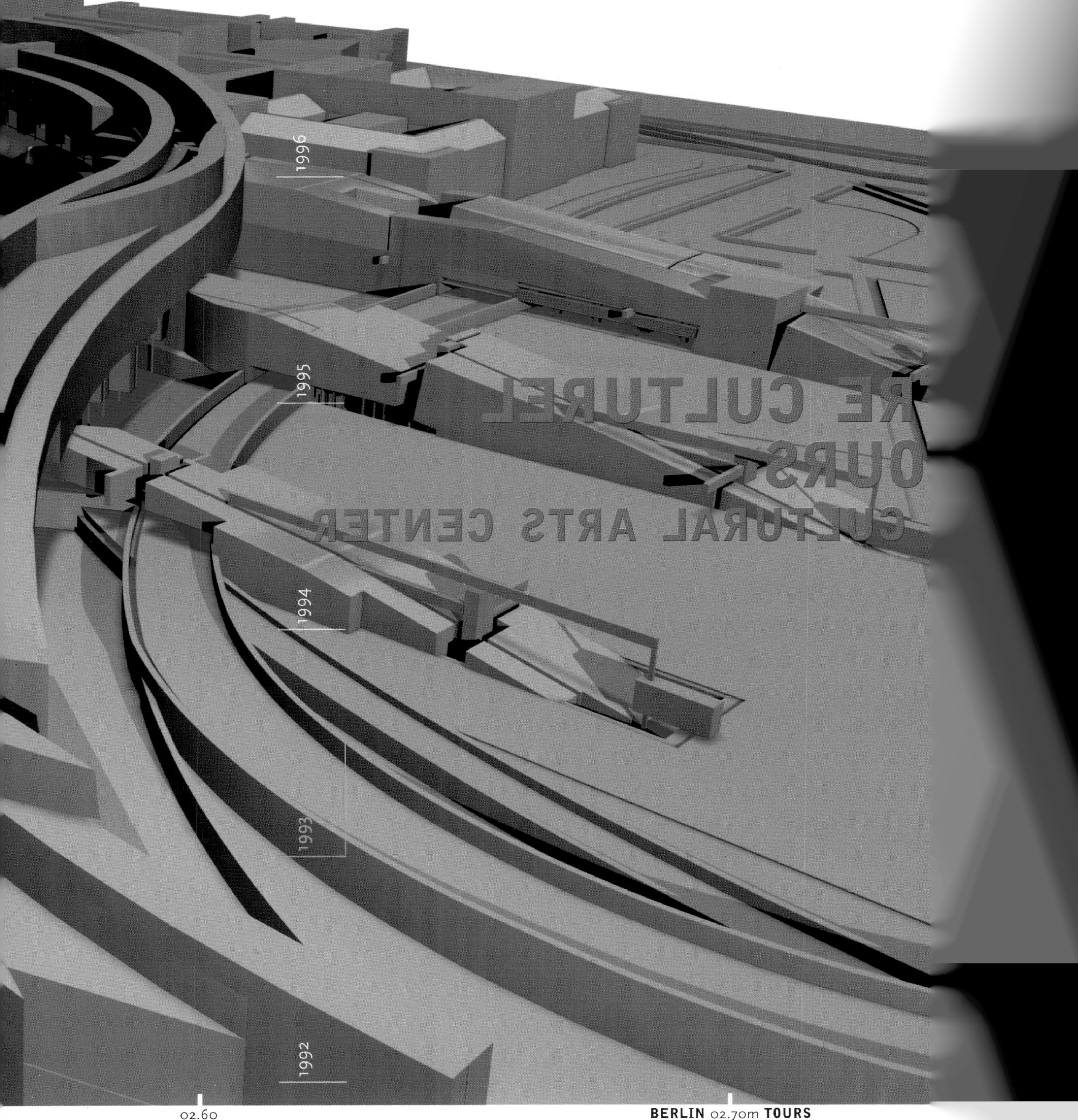

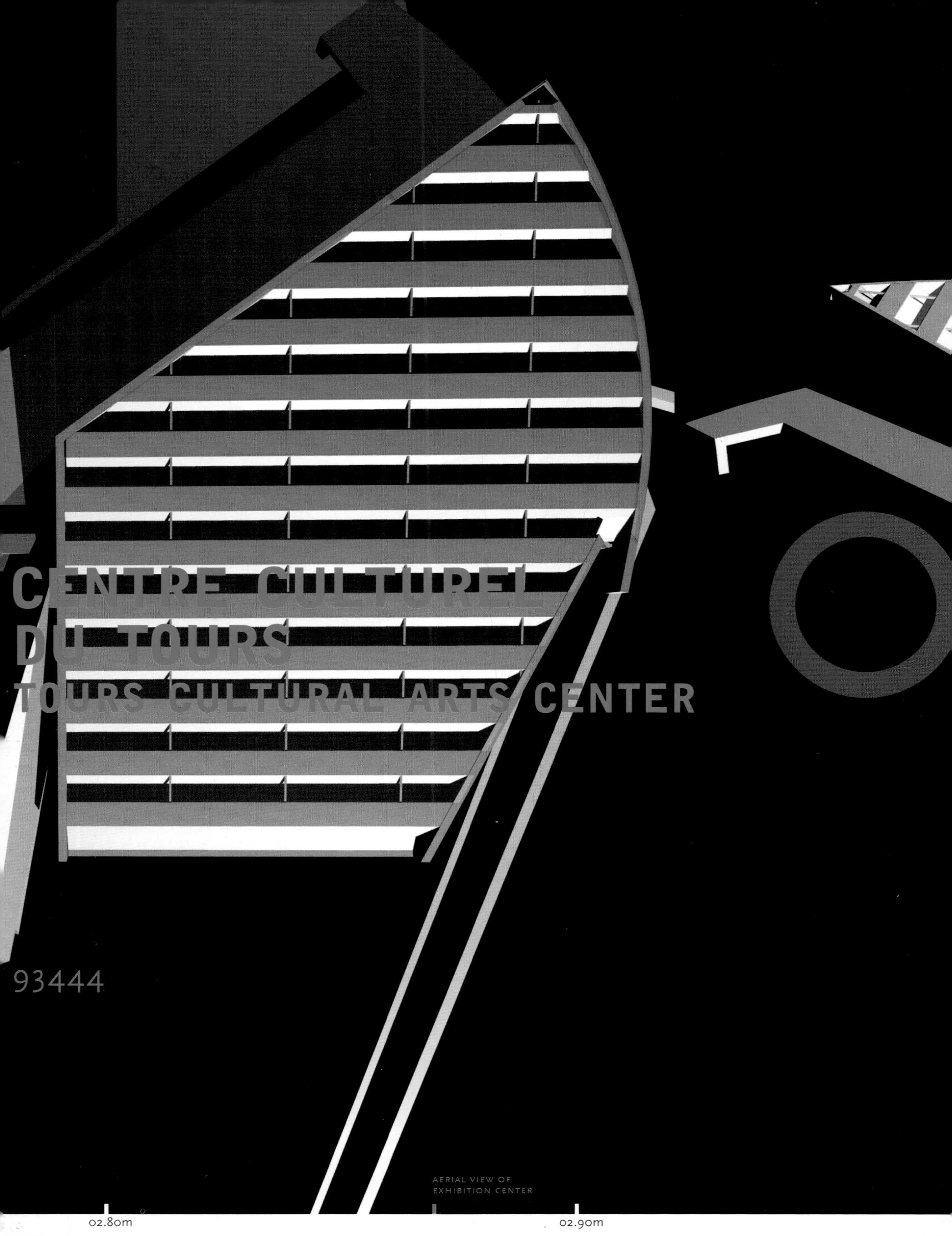

AERIAL VIEW OF
EXHIBITION CENTER

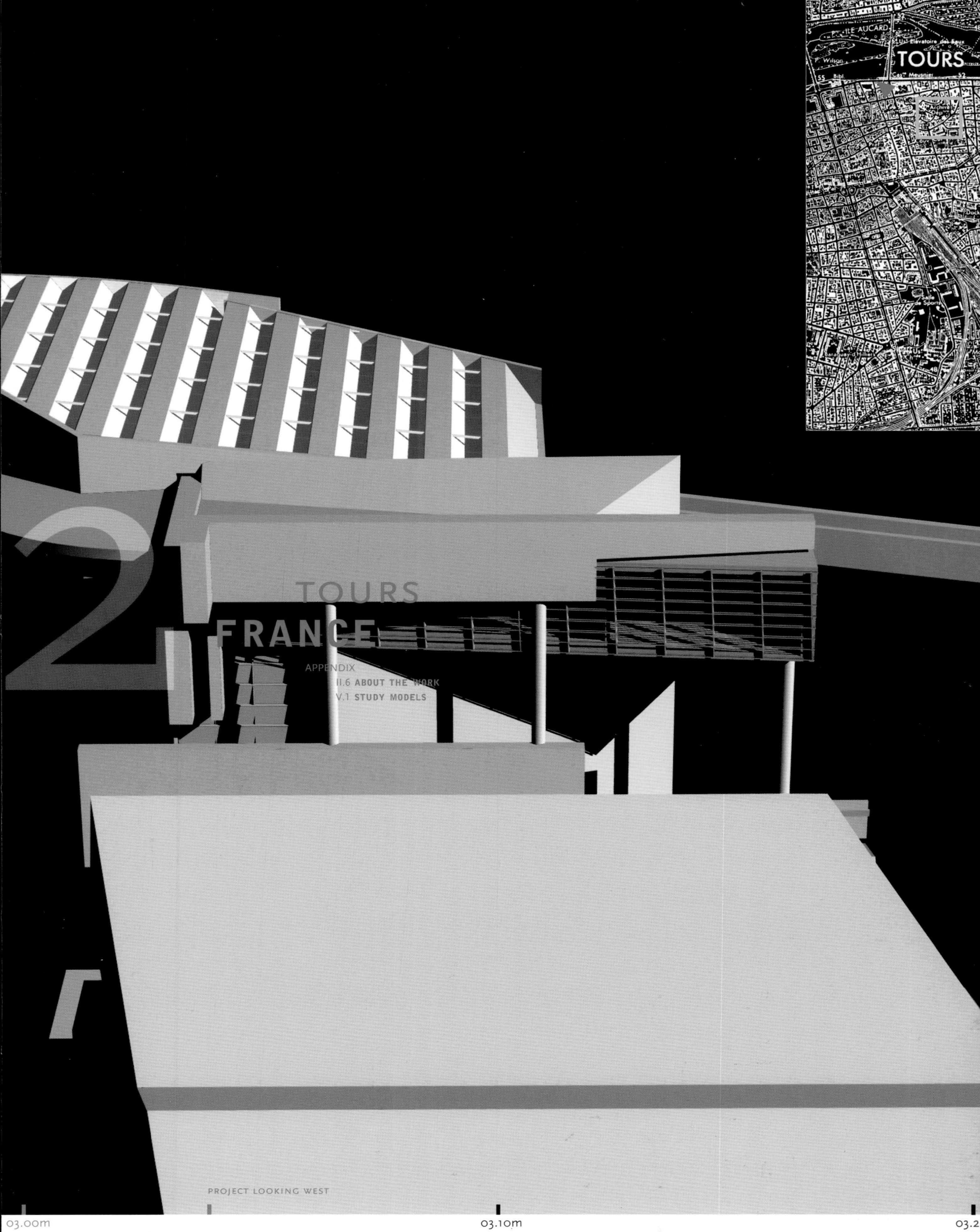
ILE AUCARD
TOURS
2
TOURS
FRANCE
APPENDIX
II.6 ABOUT THE WORK
V.1 STUDY MODELS
PROJECT LOOKING WEST

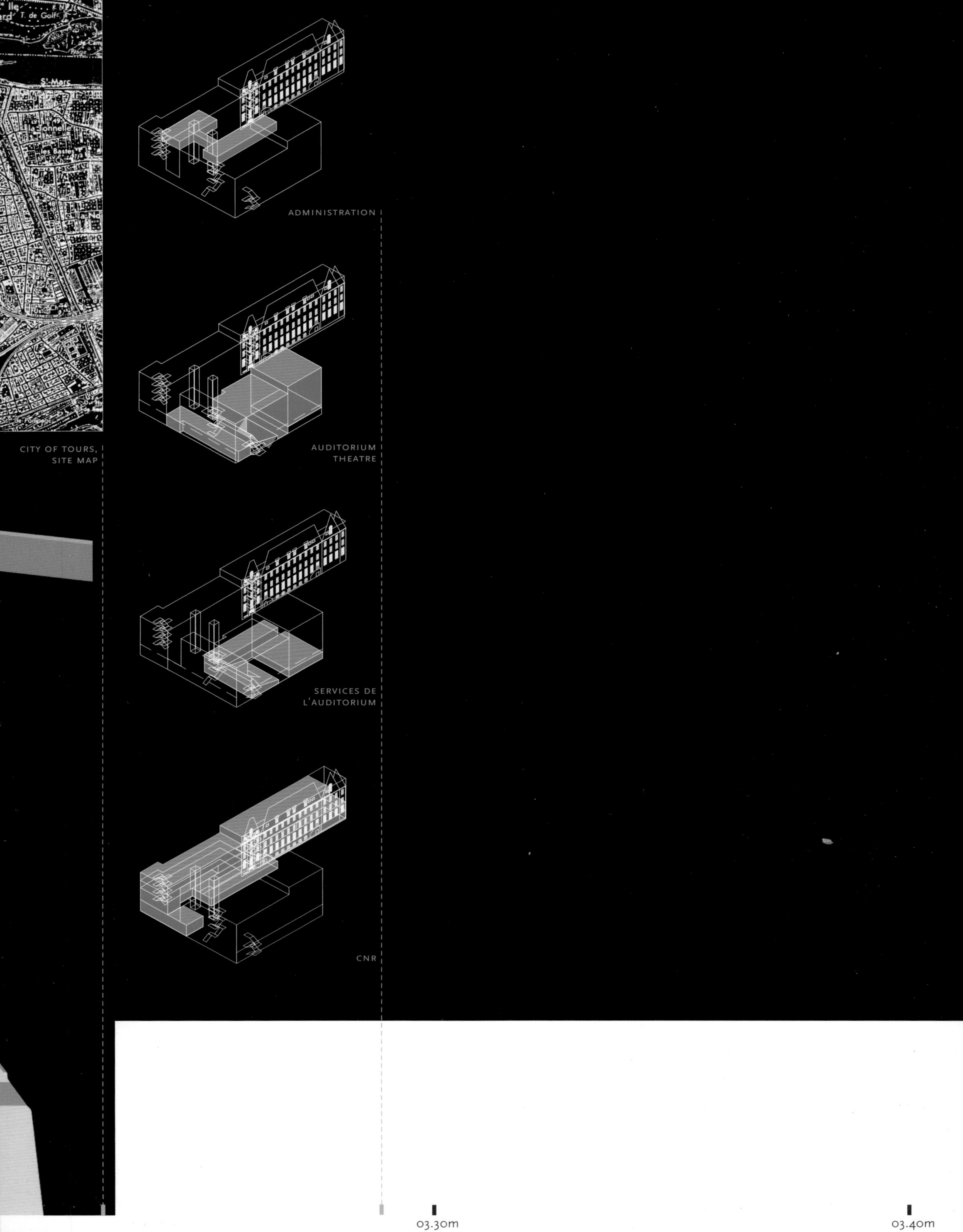

CITY OF TOURS,
SITE MAP

AERIAL SITE VIEW

SECTION 1

+16.00m

+08.00m

00.00m

−08.50m

−15.50m

+12.00m

+04.10m

−05.00m

−12.00m

03.50m

03.60m

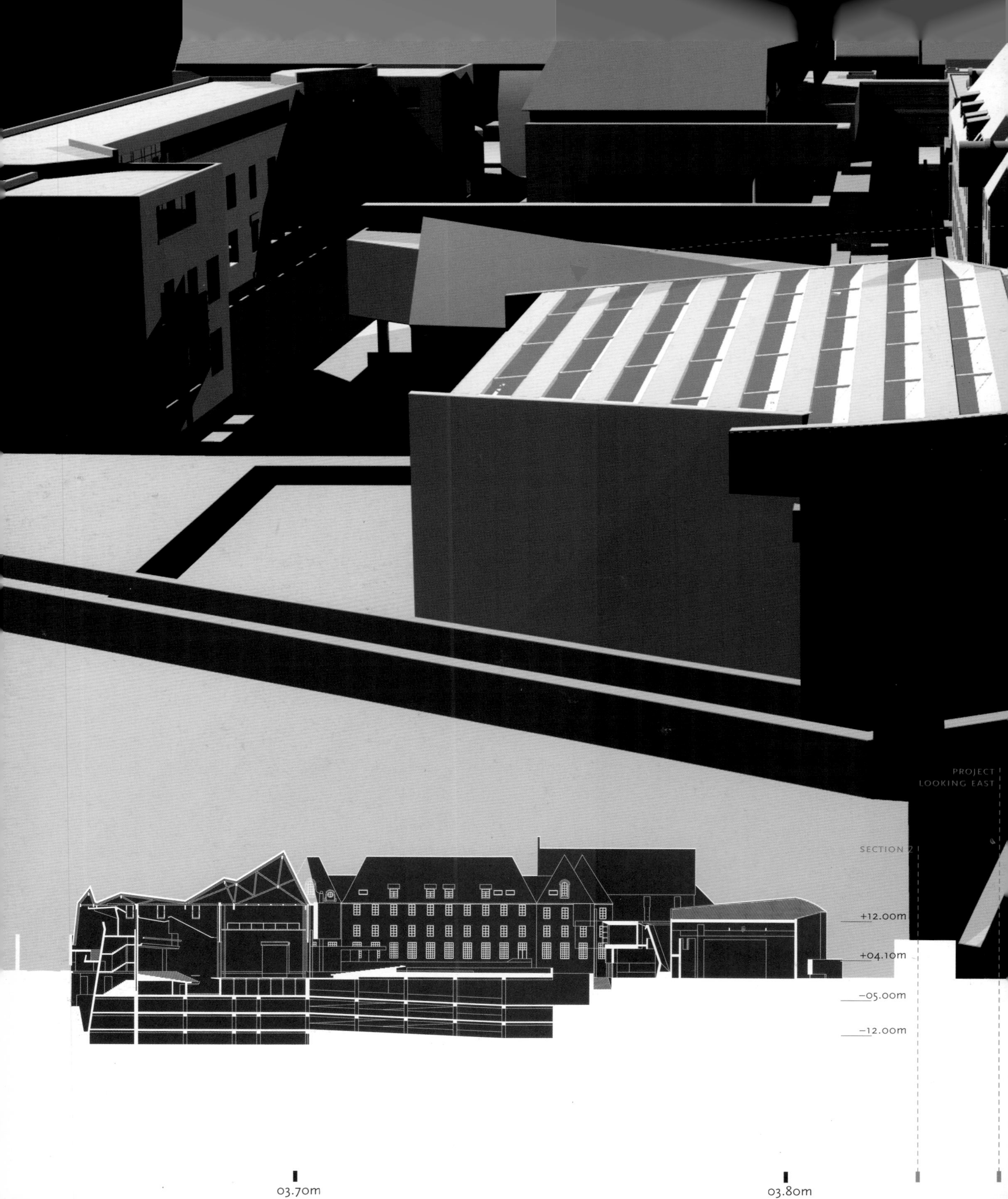
PROJECT
LOOKING EAST
SECTION 2
+12.00m
+04.10m
−05.00m
−12.00m
03.70m
03.80m

SECTION 3
+16.00m
+08.00m
00.00m
−08.50m
−15.50m
03.90m
04.00m

1
1
1
1
1
1
1
1
1
1
1
1
2
2
2
THIRD LEVEL
SECOND LEVEL
SECTION 4
+12.00m
+04.10m
–05.00m
–12.00m
04.10m
04.20m

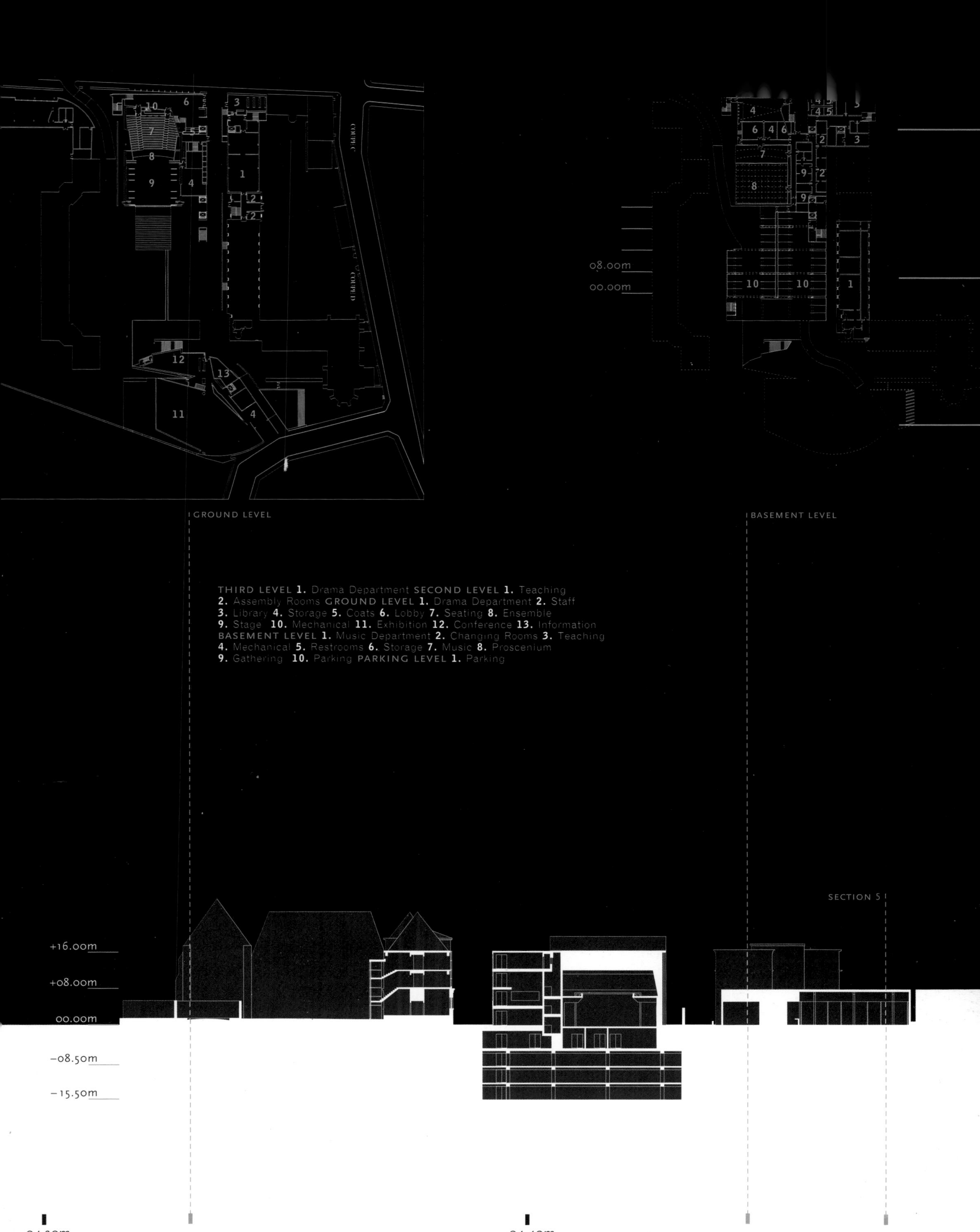

GROUND LEVEL
BASEMENT LEVEL
08.00m
00.00m
THIRD LEVEL 1. Drama Department SECOND LEVEL 1. Teaching
2. Assembly Rooms GROUND LEVEL 1. Drama Department 2. Staff
3. Library 4. Storage 5. Coats 6. Lobby 7. Seating 8. Ensemble
9. Stage 10. Mechanical 11. Exhibition 12. Conference 13. Information
BASEMENT LEVEL 1. Music Department 2. Changing Rooms 3. Teaching
4. Mechanical 5. Restrooms 6. Storage 7. Music 8. Proscenium
9. Gathering 10. Parking PARKING LEVEL 1. Parking
SECTION 5
+16.00m
+08.00m
00.00m
−08.50m
−15.50m
04.30m
04.40m

PROJECT DATA

AREA OF SITE
10000m²

PROGRAM
154825.755sf / 14385m²
Main Building:
57582.050sf / 5350m²
Garage:
83951.40sf / 7800m²
Reconversion of Exisiting Building:
13453.75sf / 1250m²

PARKING
Cars: 275

MECHANICAL SYSTEM
Air Condition

STRUCTURAL SYSTEM
Reinforced Concrete and Steel

1997

1996

1995

SCIENCE MUSEUM
SCHOOL

1994

1993

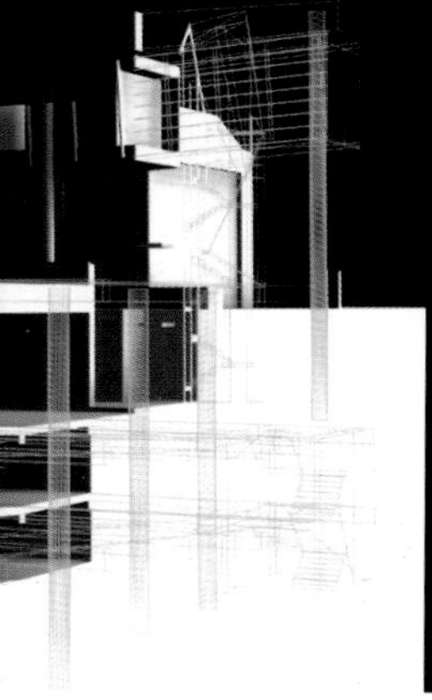

1992

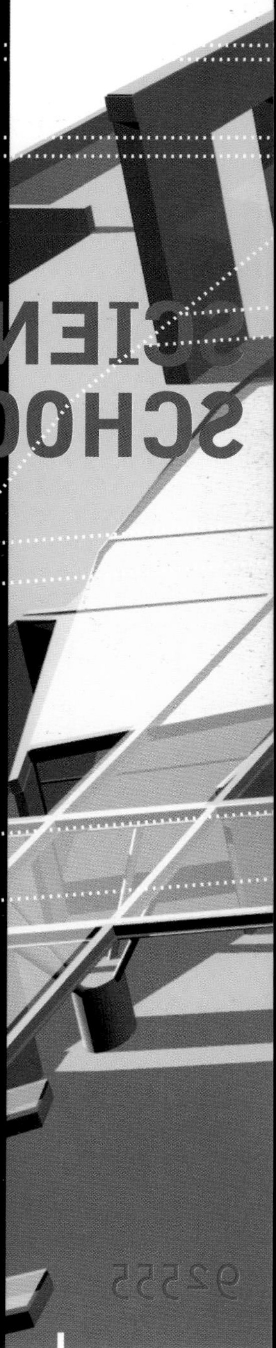

92555

SCIENCE MUSEUM
SCHOOL
92555
PROJECT
LOOKING NORTH

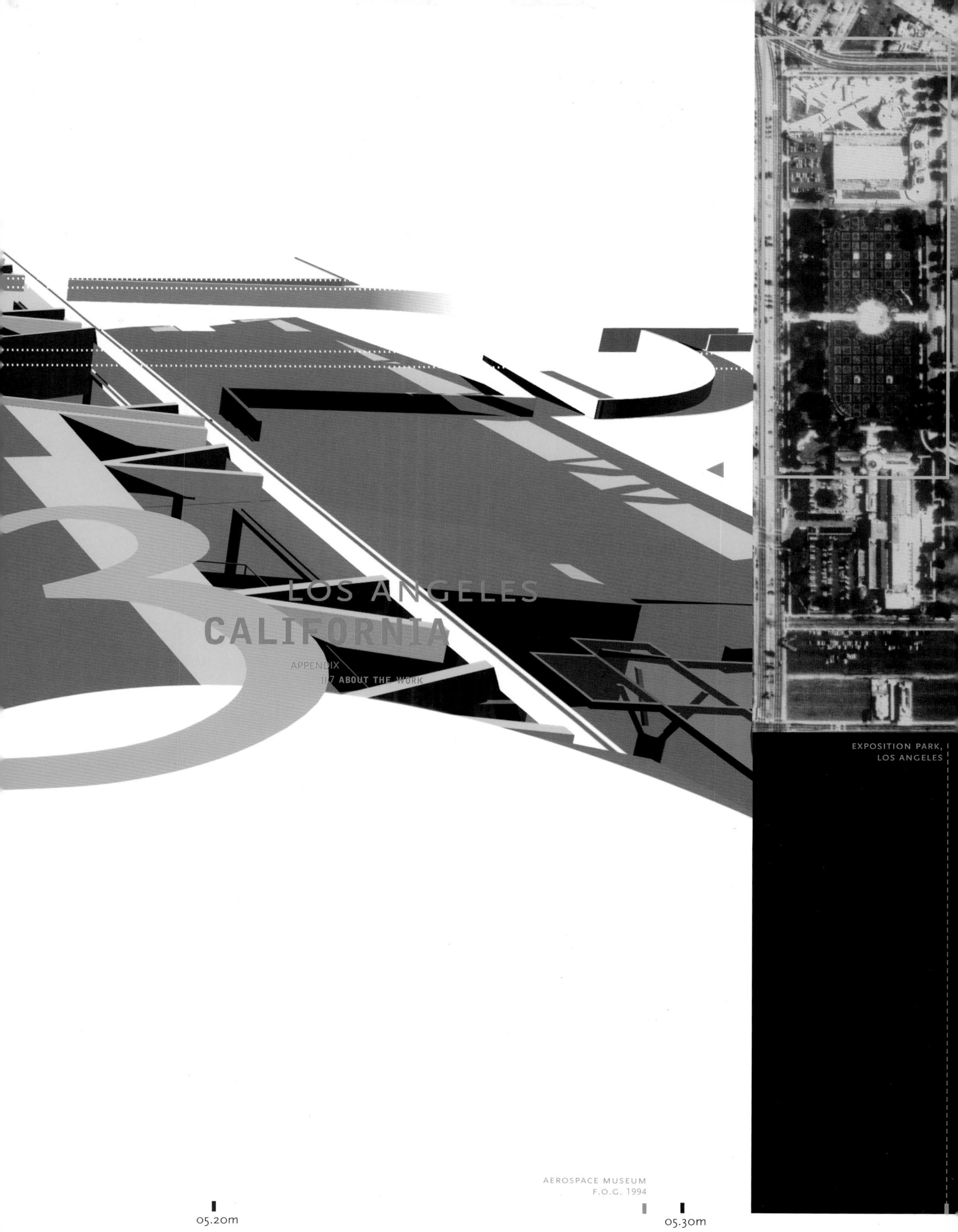
LOS ANGELES
CALIFORNIA
APPENDIX
117 ABOUT THE WORK
EXPOSITION PARK,
LOS ANGELES
AEROSPACE MUSEUM
F.O.G. 1994
05.20m
05.30m

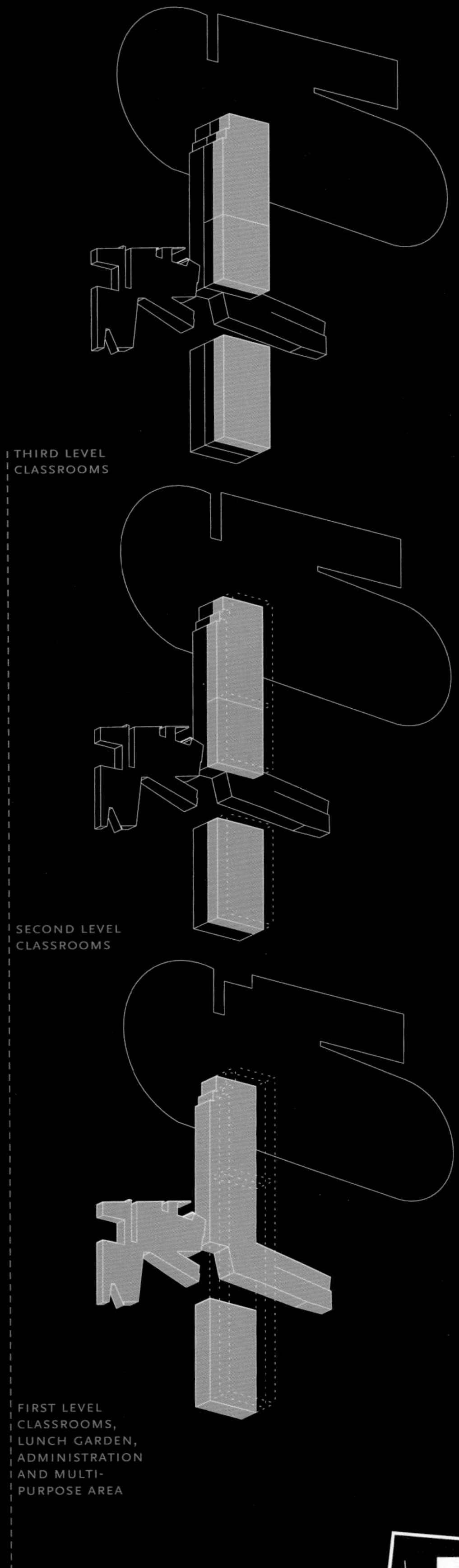

THIRD LEVEL
CLASSROOMS

SECOND LEVEL
CLASSROOMS

FIRST LEVEL
CLASSROOMS,
LUNCH GARDEN,
ADMINISTRATION
AND MULTI-
PURPOSE AREA

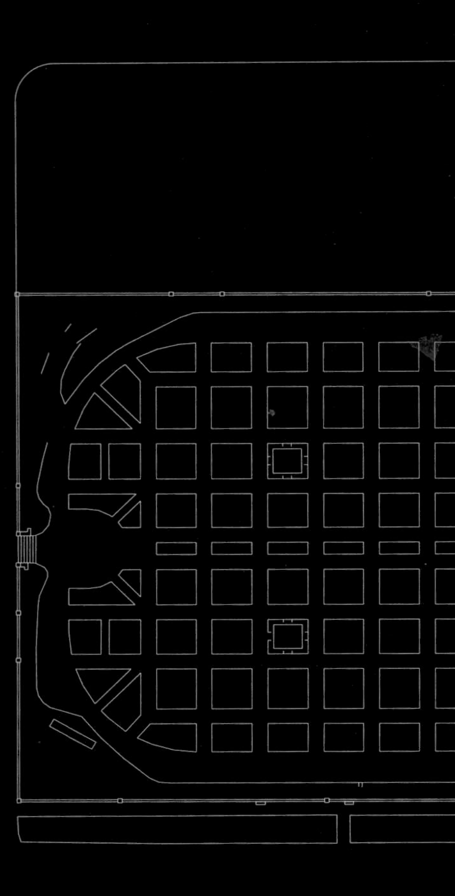

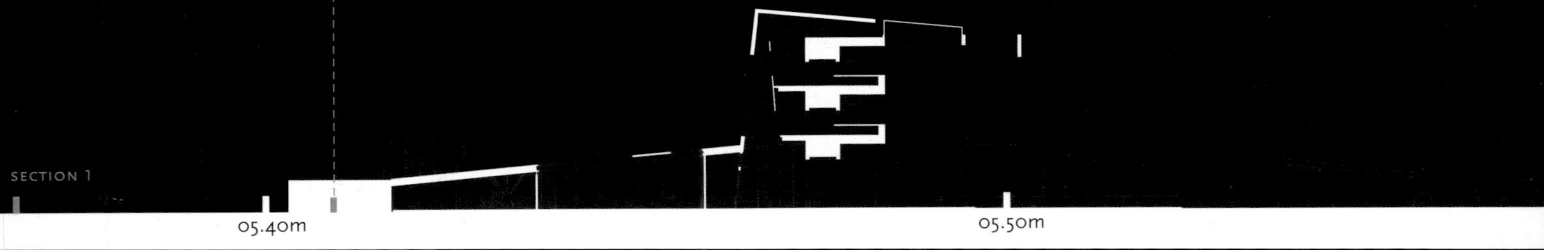

SECTION 1

05.40m

05.50m

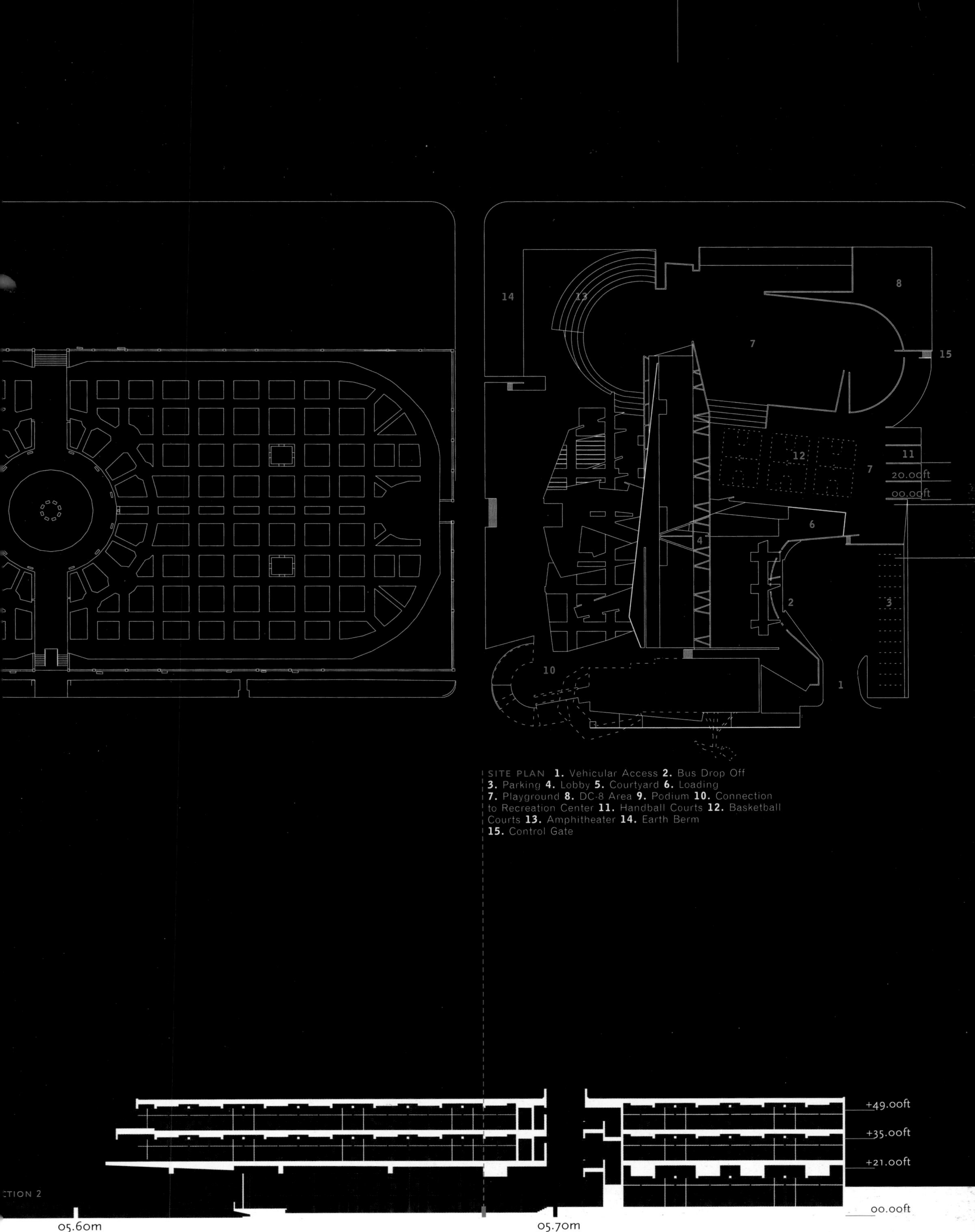

SITE PLAN **1.** Vehicular Access **2.** Bus Drop Off **3.** Parking **4.** Lobby **5.** Courtyard **6.** Loading **7.** Playground **8.** DC-8 Area **9.** Podium **10.** Connection to Recreation Center **11.** Handball Courts **12.** Basketball Courts **13.** Amphitheater **14.** Earth Berm **15.** Control Gate

GROUND LEVEL 1. Lobby **2.** Entry **3.** Public Reception Area **4.** Workroom **5.** Administrative Office **6.** Office **7.** Health Service Area **8.** Clerical Area **9.** Multipurpose Room **10.** Stage **11.** Student Lunch Shelter **12.** Kitchen **13.** Storeroom/Lockers **14.** Student Lavatory **15.** Kindergarten **16.** Kindergarten Lavatory **17.** Kindergarten Play Yard **18.** Storage **19.** Library **20.** Library Courtyard **21.** Bus Drop Off **22.** Loading **23.** Custodial **FIRST LEVEL 1.** Classroom Module **2.** Open Air Teaching Area **3.** Workroom **4.** Storage **5.** Lavatory **6.** Custodial **7.** Trellis Below **8.** Roof Below **9.** Armory Portico **SECOND LEVEL 1.** Performing Arts Module **2.** Classroom Module **3.** Technology Lab Module **4.** Open Air Teaching Area **5.** Workroom **6.** Storage **7.** Lavatory **8.** Stage **9.** Observation Room **10.** Custodial

SECOND LEVEL

FIRST LEVEL

GROUND LEVEL

AERIAL VIEW
06.10m
06.20m

PROJECT
LOOKING NORTH
WEST ELEVATION
06.30m
06.40m

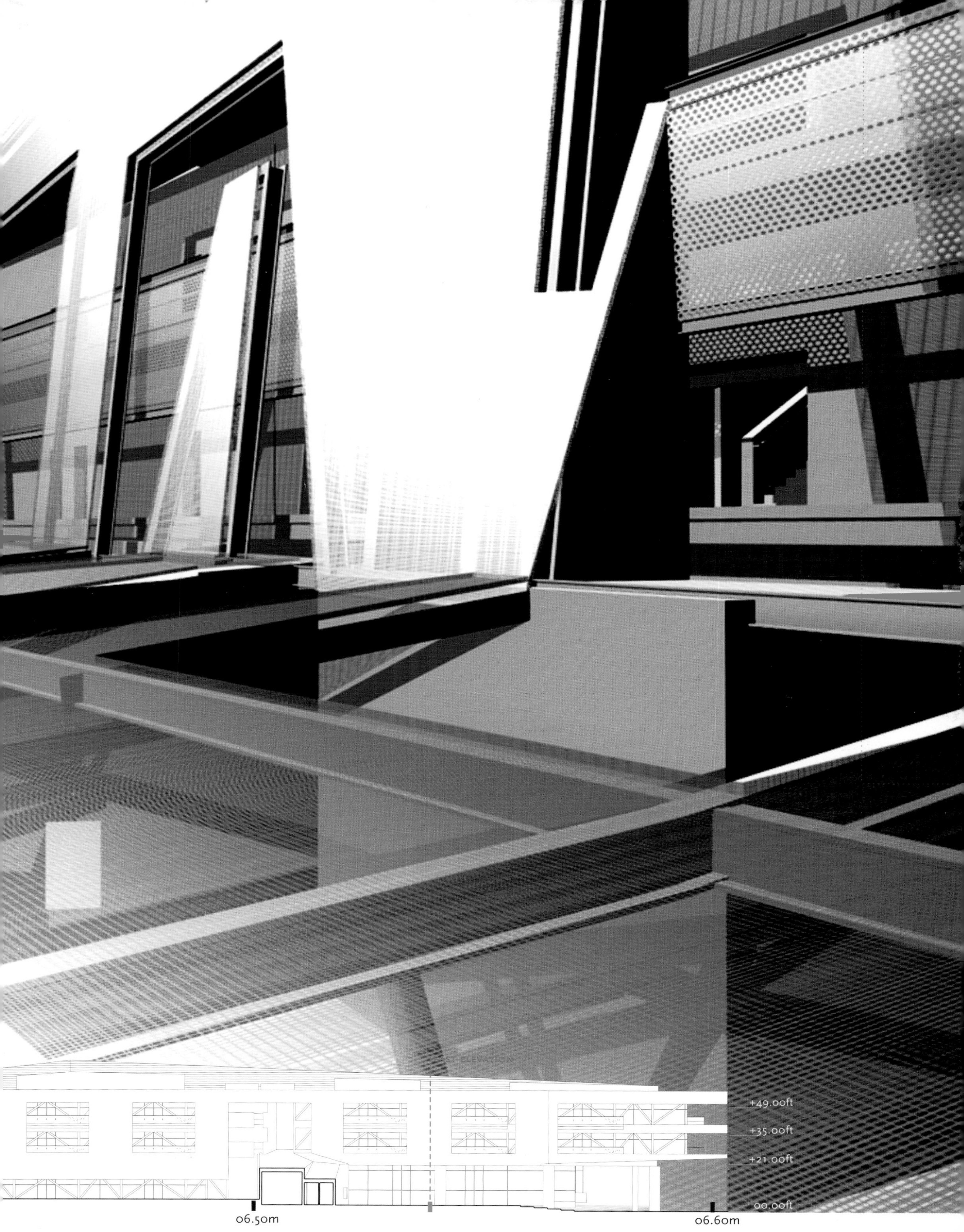
ELEVATION
+49.00ft
+35.00ft
+21.00ft
00.00ft
06.50m
06.60m

PROJECT DATA

AREA OF SITE
6.4 acres / 2.75ha

PROGRAM
New Building: 56,711sf / 4,955m²
Armory: 130,013sf / 12,079m²
Total: 186,724sf / 17,347m²

HUMAN POPULATION
Students: 900

PARKING
Cars: 61

MECHANICAL SYSTEM
Water Source Heat Pump

STRUCTURAL SYSTEM
Steel Frame

SALICK
ADMINISTRATIVE OFFICES
93100
1997
1996
1995
1994
1993
1992
06.90m
07.00m

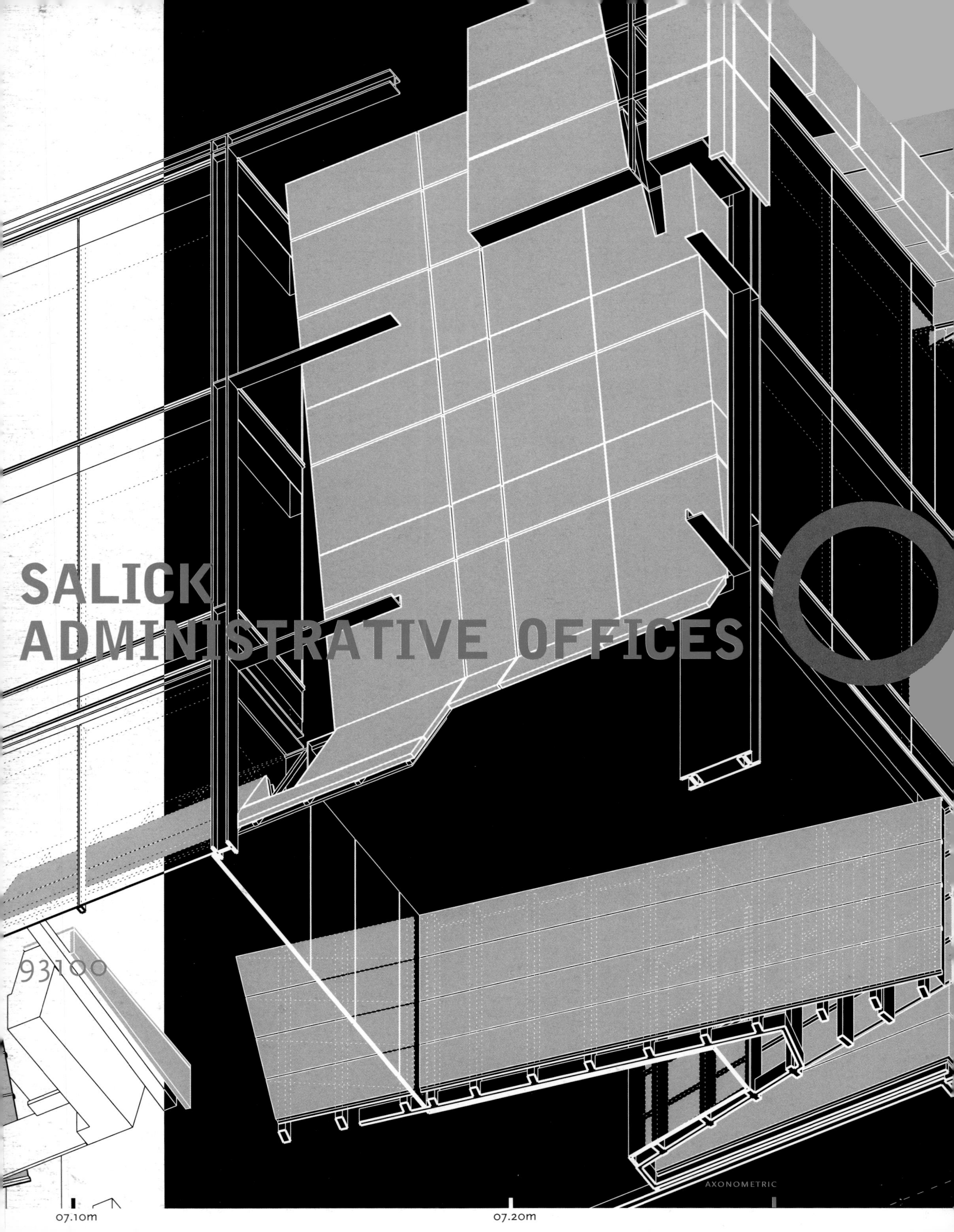
SALICK
ADMINISTRATIVE OFFICES
93100
AXONOMETRIC

4 LOS ANGELES CALIFORNIA

APPENDIX
II.9 **ABOUT THE WORK**
VI.8 **WORK IN PROGRESS**

02.08ft
00.00ft
PROJECT DATA
AREA OF SITE
0.2 acres / 0.0846ha
PROGRAM
19,600sf (3 floors) / 1821.5m2
HUMAN POPULATION
Staff: 100
PARKING
Cars: 20
MECHANICAL SYSTEM
Forced Air Units
STRUCTURAL SYSTEM
Existing Steel with Wood Frame, Concrete Block and Concrete Slab Floors and Roof
PARTIAL
FLOOR PLAN

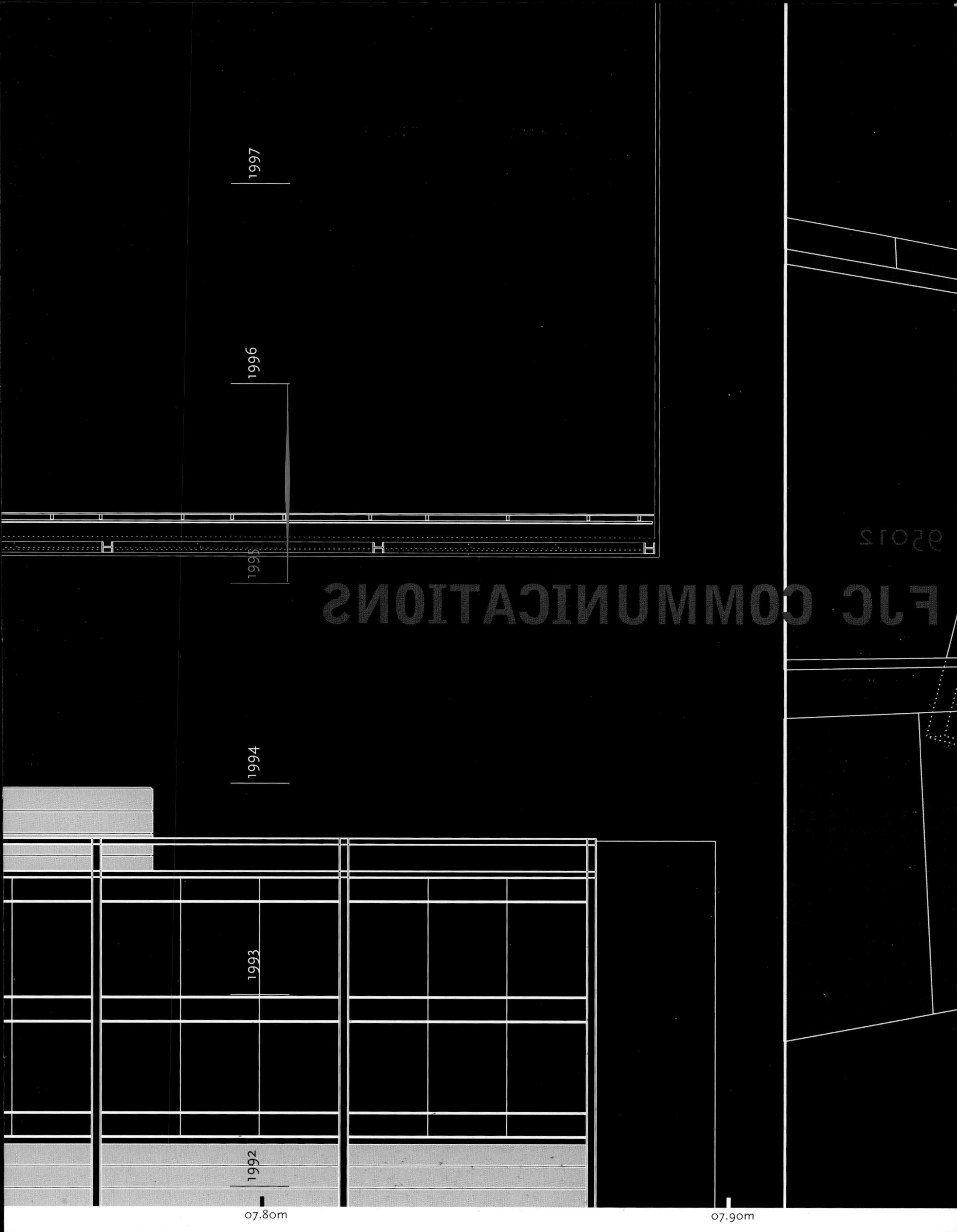
1997
1996
1995
1994
1993
1992
07.80m
07.90m

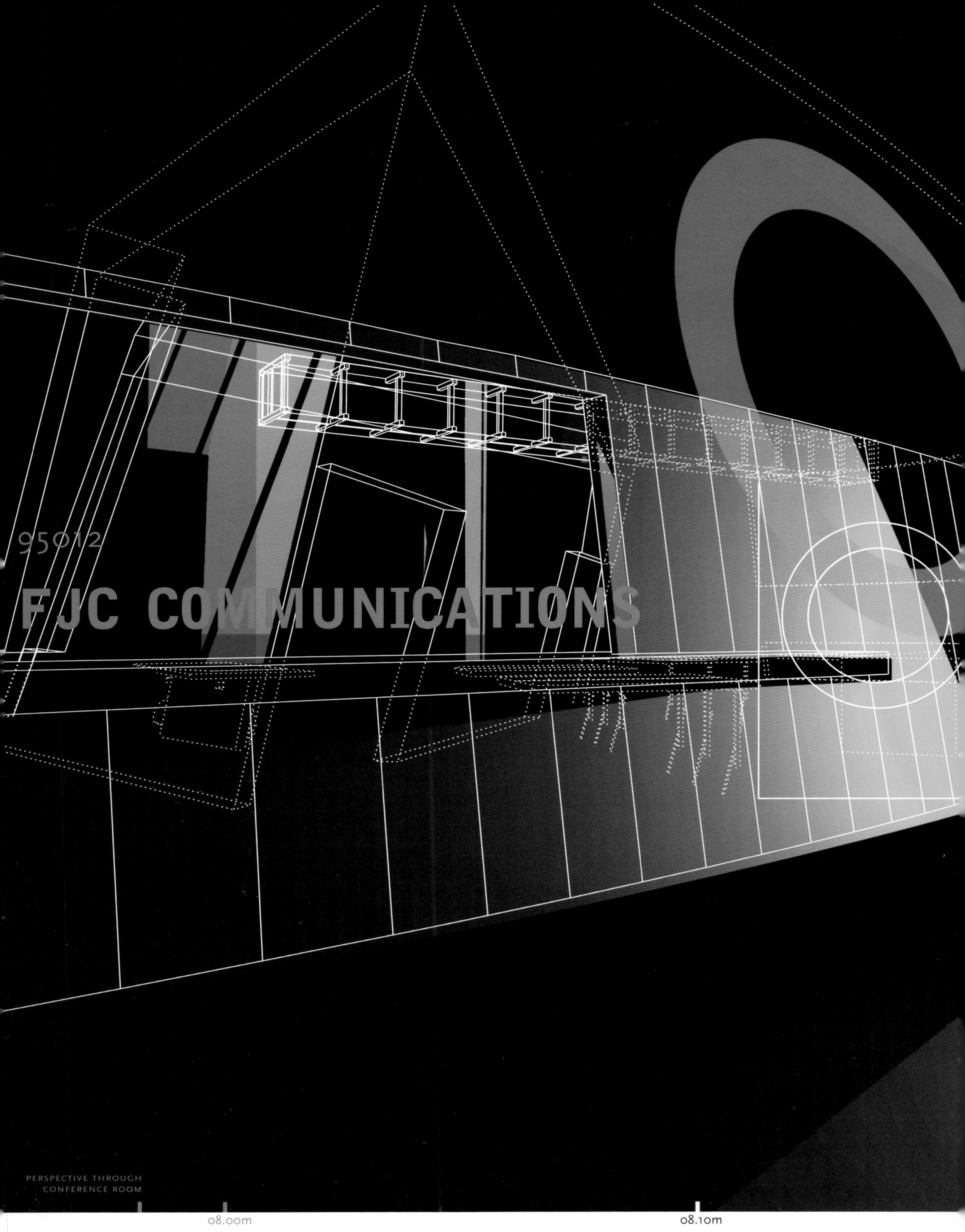

PERSPECTIVE THROUGH
CONFERENCE ROOM

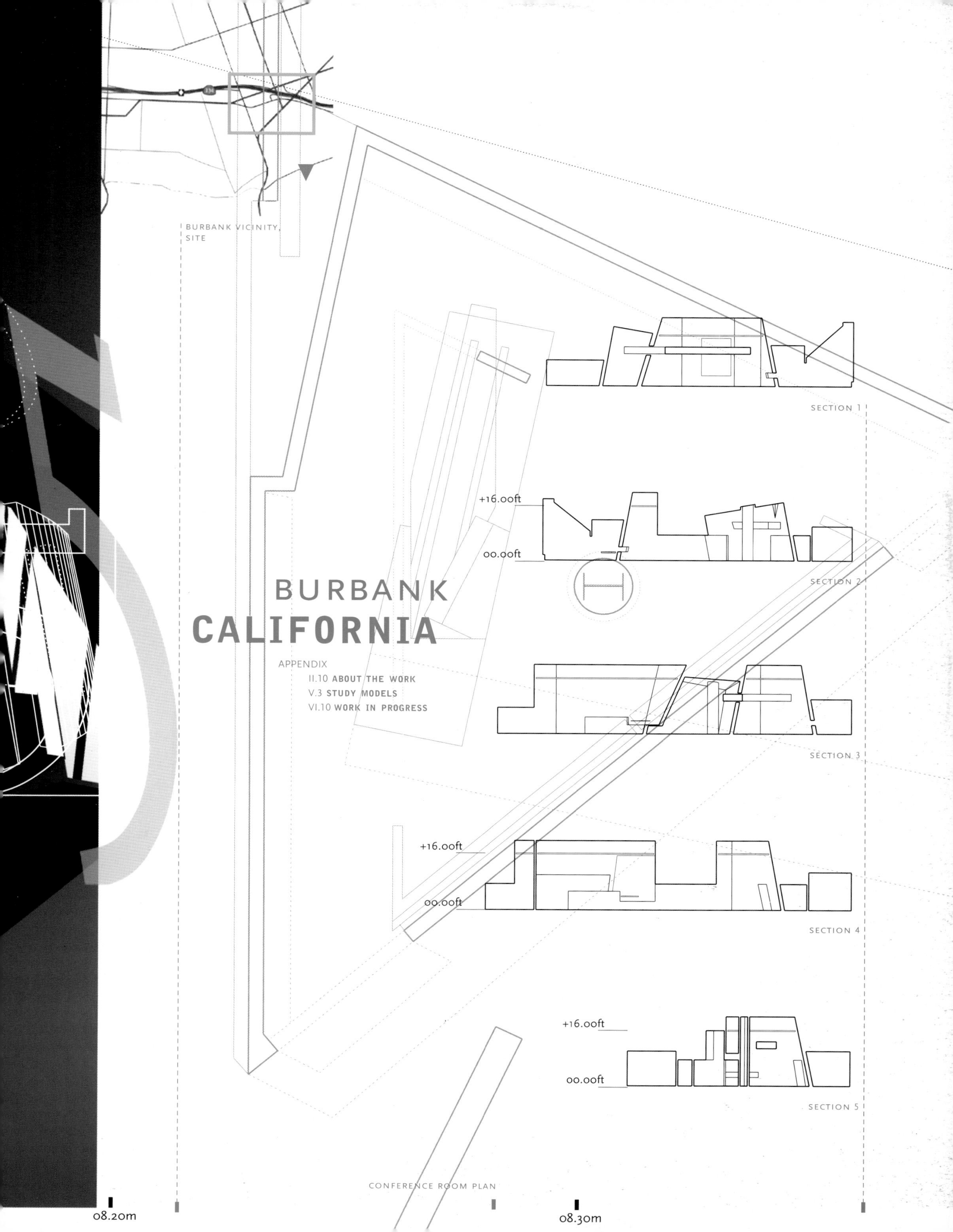

BURBANK
CALIFORNIA

APPENDIX

II.10 **ABOUT THE WORK**
V.3 **STUDY MODELS**
VI.10 **WORK IN PROGRESS**

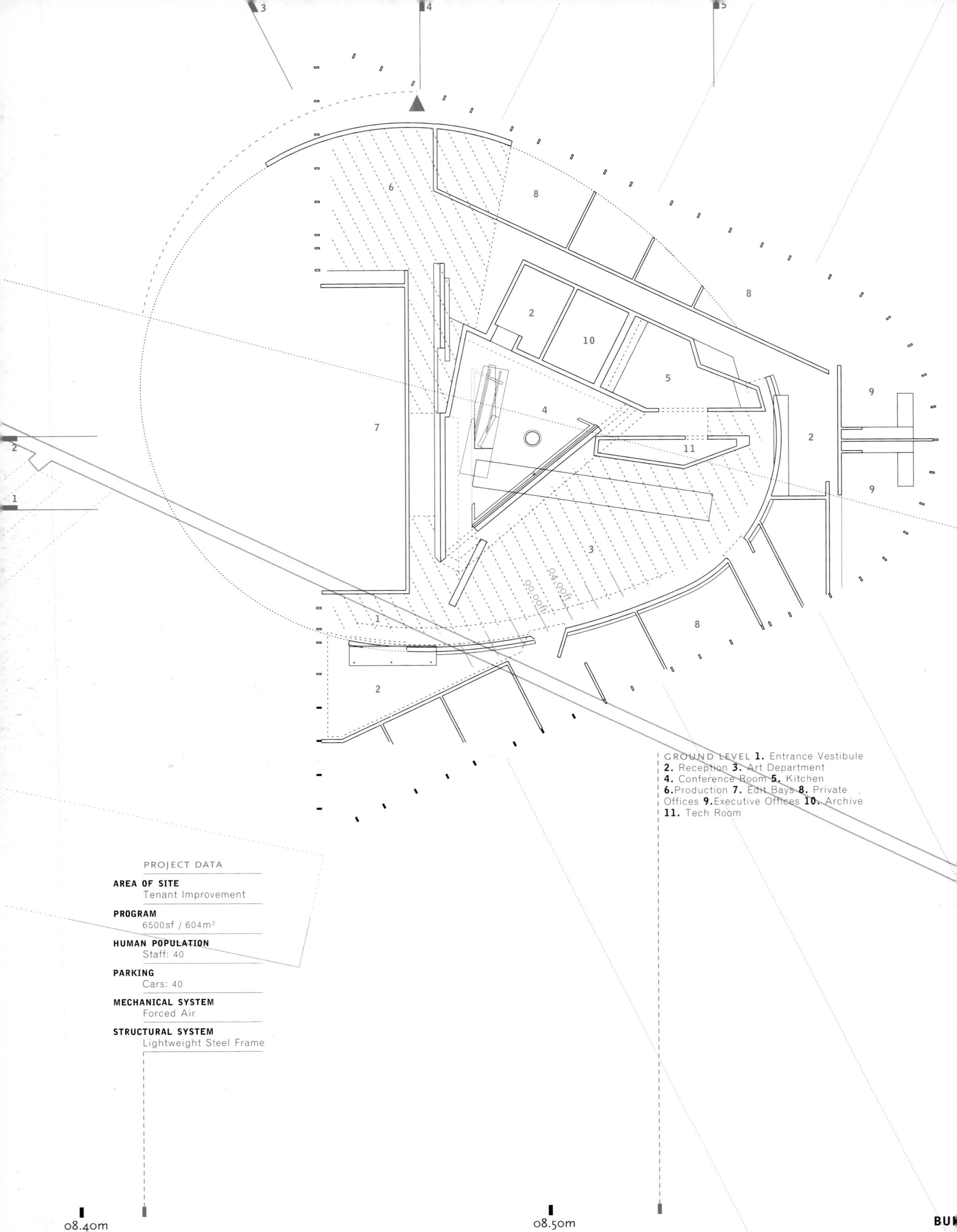

PROJECT DATA

AREA OF SITE
Tenant Improvement

PROGRAM
6500sf / 604m²

HUMAN POPULATION
Staff: 40

PARKING
Cars: 40

MECHANICAL SYSTEM
Forced Air

STRUCTURAL SYSTEM
Lightweight Steel Frame

1997

1996

1995

1994

1993

1992

92206

OVE ARUP & PARTNERS,
LOS ANGELES
BELOW GROUND
LOOKING NORTH
GROUND LEVEL
9
8
7
7
6
2
2
4
7
5
1
3
2
15.00ft
00.00ft
92206
GROUND LEVEL 1. Reception 2. Conference 3. Library 4. Kitchen 5. Administration 6. Office 7. Open Workstation 8. Work Tables 9. Storage
08.90m
09.00m

DIEGO
FRWY
BLVD
OLYMPIC
EXPOSI
PICO
GATEWAY
BLVD
10
LOS ANGELES
CALIFORNIA
APPENDIX
II.11 ABOUT THE WORK
VI.12 WORK IN PROGRESS
AERIAL VIEW
WITHOUT ROOF
09.10m
09.20m

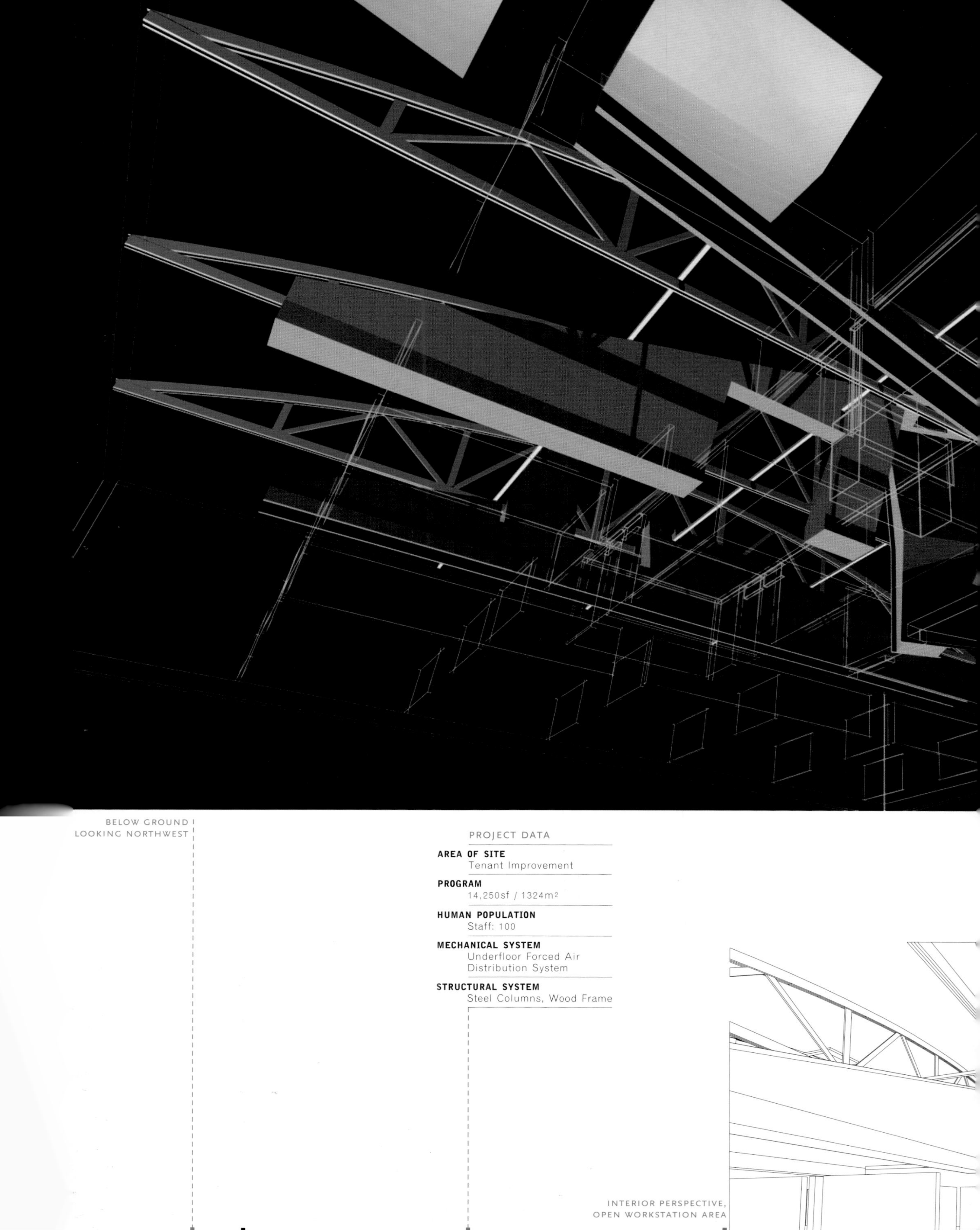

BELOW GROUND
LOOKING NORTHWEST

PROJECT DATA

AREA OF SITE
Tenant Improvement

PROGRAM
14,250sf / 1324m²

HUMAN POPULATION
Staff: 100

MECHANICAL SYSTEM
Underfloor Forced Air Distribution System

STRUCTURAL SYSTEM
Steel Columns, Wood Frame

INTERIOR PERSPECTIVE,
OPEN WORKSTATION AREA

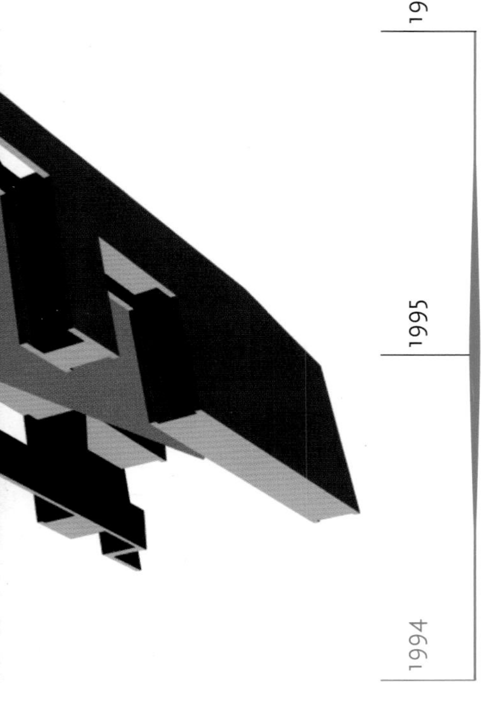

LANDA HOUSE

94111

1997

1996

1995

1994

1993

1992

LANDA HOUSE

94111

CITY OF MANHATTAN BEACH, SITE

DETAIL OF NORTH CORNER

MANHATTAN BEACH
CALIFORNIA

APPENDIX

II.12 **ABOUT THE WORK**
VI.14 **WORK IN PROGRESS**

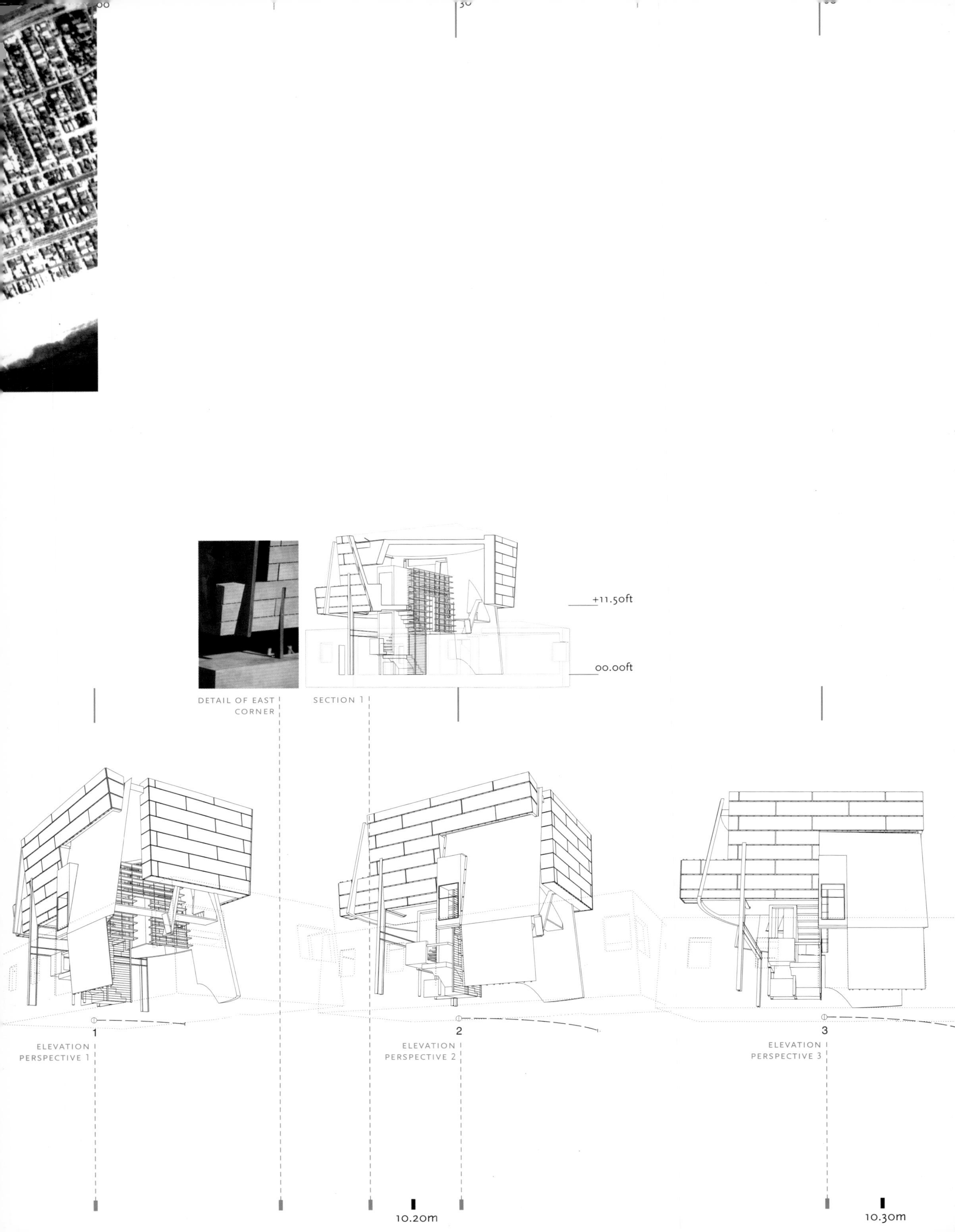
+11.50ft
00.00ft
DETAIL OF EAST CORNER
SECTION 1
1
ELEVATION PERSPECTIVE 1
2
ELEVATION PERSPECTIVE 2
3
ELEVATION PERSPECTIVE 3
10.20m
10.30m

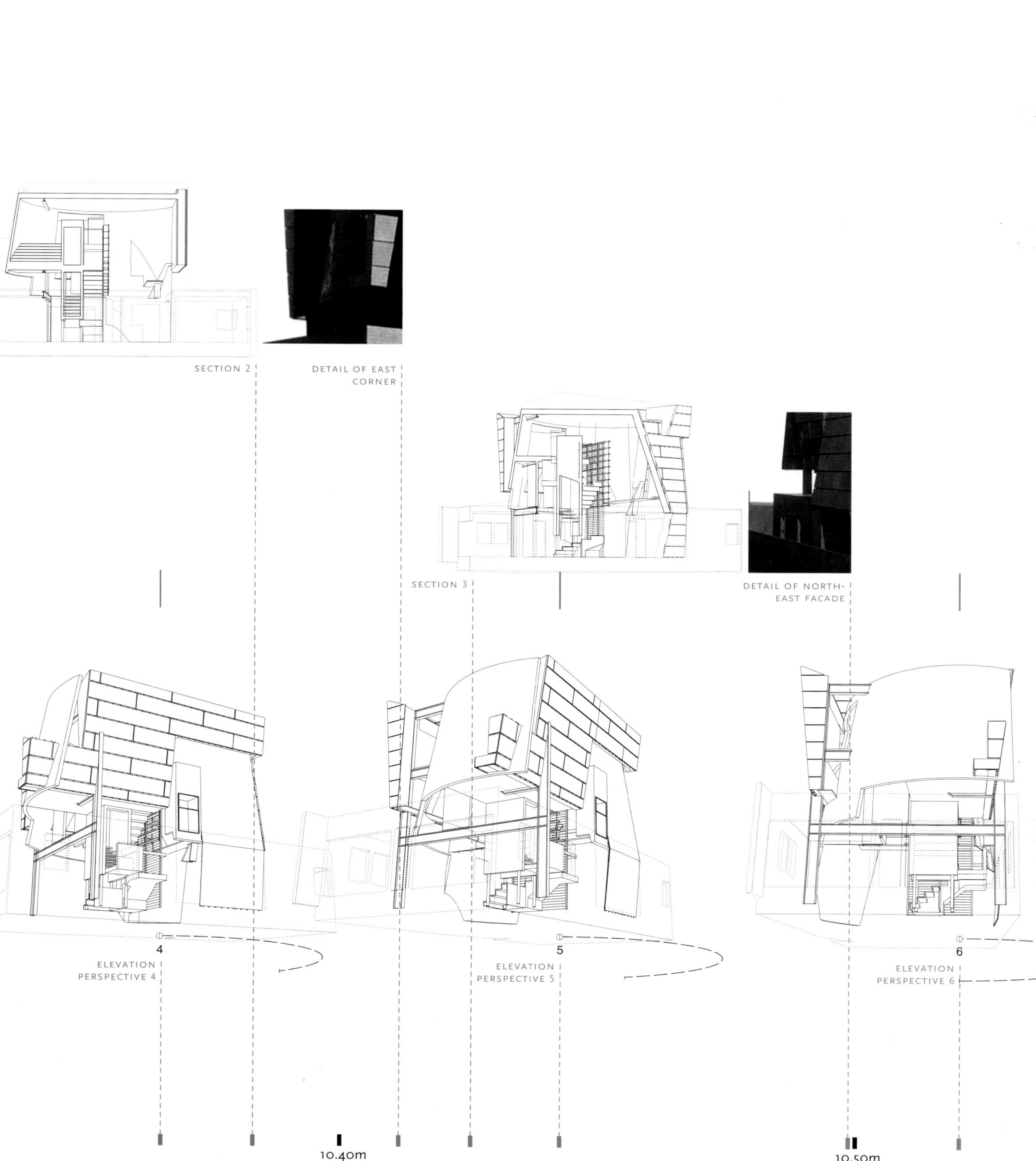
SECTION 2
DETAIL OF EAST CORNER
SECTION 3
DETAIL OF NORTH-EAST FACADE
4
ELEVATION PERSPECTIVE 4
5
ELEVATION PERSPECTIVE 5
6
ELEVATION PERSPECTIVE 6
10.40m
10.50m

PROJECT DATA

AREA OF SITE
0.0689 acres / 0.0279ha

PROGRAM
Addition: 683sf / 63m^2
New Garage: 576sf / 53.5m^2
Remodel of Existing: 1,050sf / 97.5m^2

HUMAN POPULATION
Residents: 3

PARKING
Cars: 2

MECHANICAL SYSTEM
Forced Air

STRUCTURAL SYSTEM
Wood Frame with Steel Moment Frame and Plywood Shear Walls

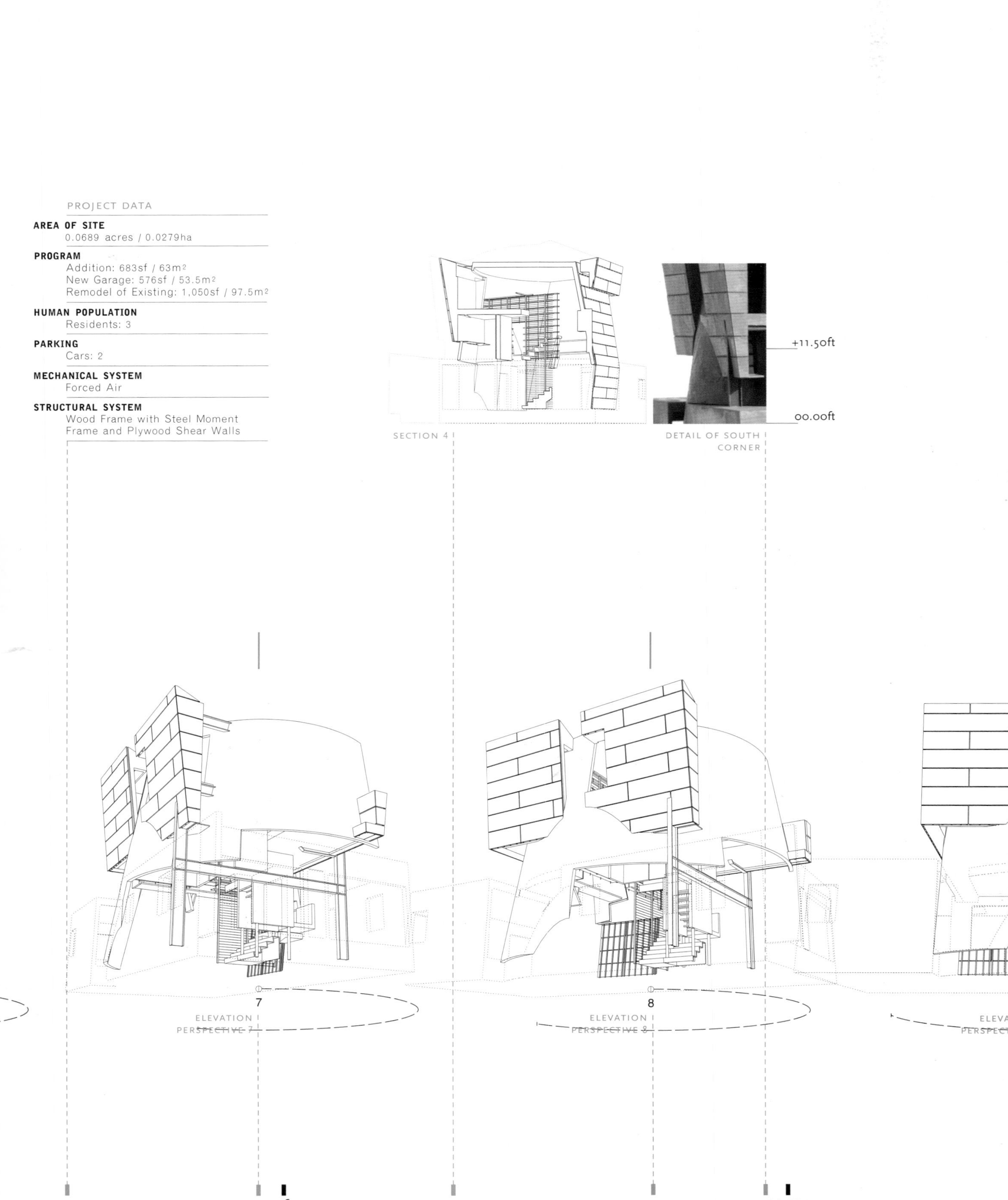

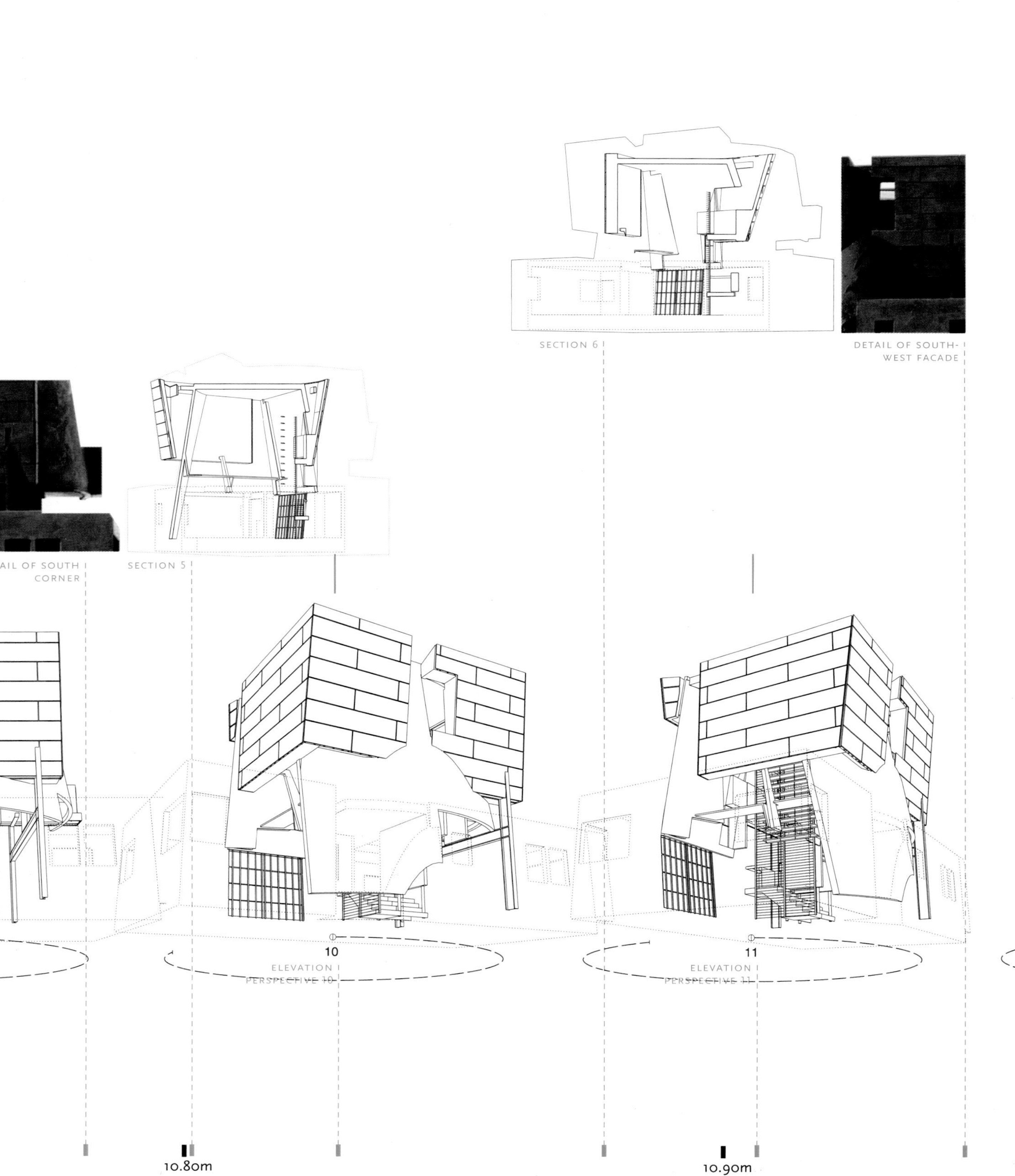
SECTION 6
DETAIL OF SOUTH-
WEST FACADE
TAIL OF SOUTH
CORNER
SECTION 5
10
ELEVATION
PERSPECTIVE 10
11
ELEVATION
PERSPECTIVE 11
10.80m
10.90m

8

3

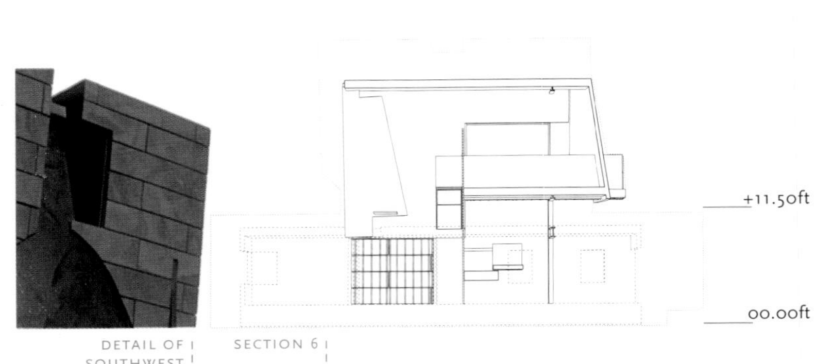

DETAIL OF SOUTHWEST FACADE

SECTION 6

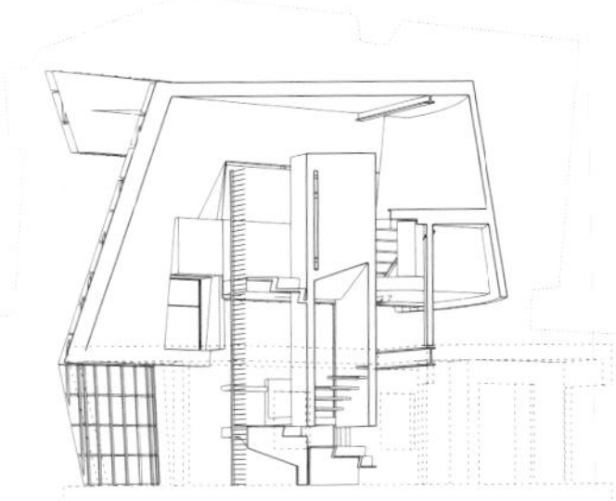

SECTION 7

DETAIL OF NORTH-EAST FACADE

EVATION
CTIVE 12

11.00m

11.10m

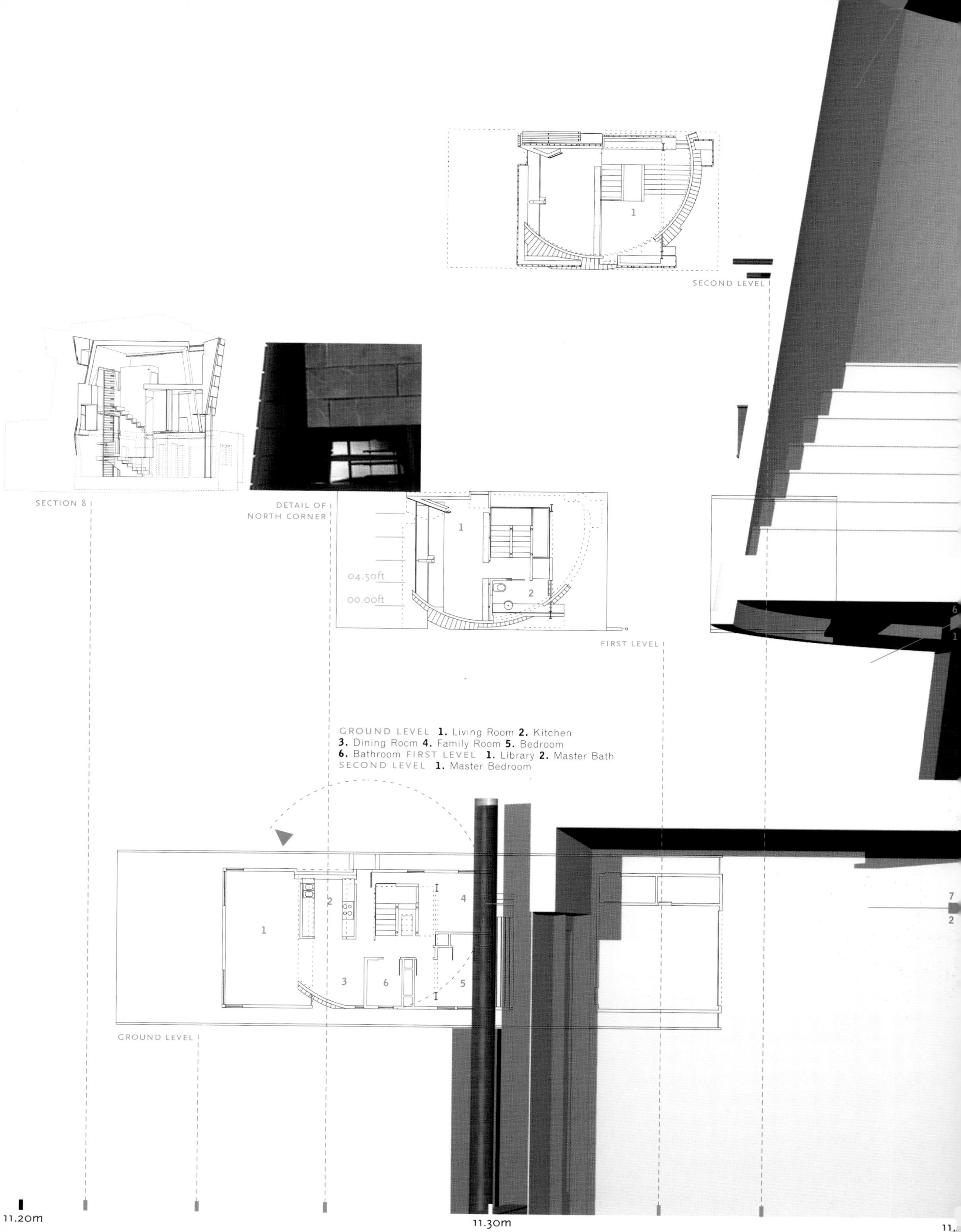

GROUND LEVEL **1.** Living Room **2.** Kitchen **3.** Dining Room **4.** Family Room **5.** Bedroom **6.** Bathroom FIRST LEVEL **1.** Library **2.** Master Bath SECOND LEVEL **1.** Master Bedroom

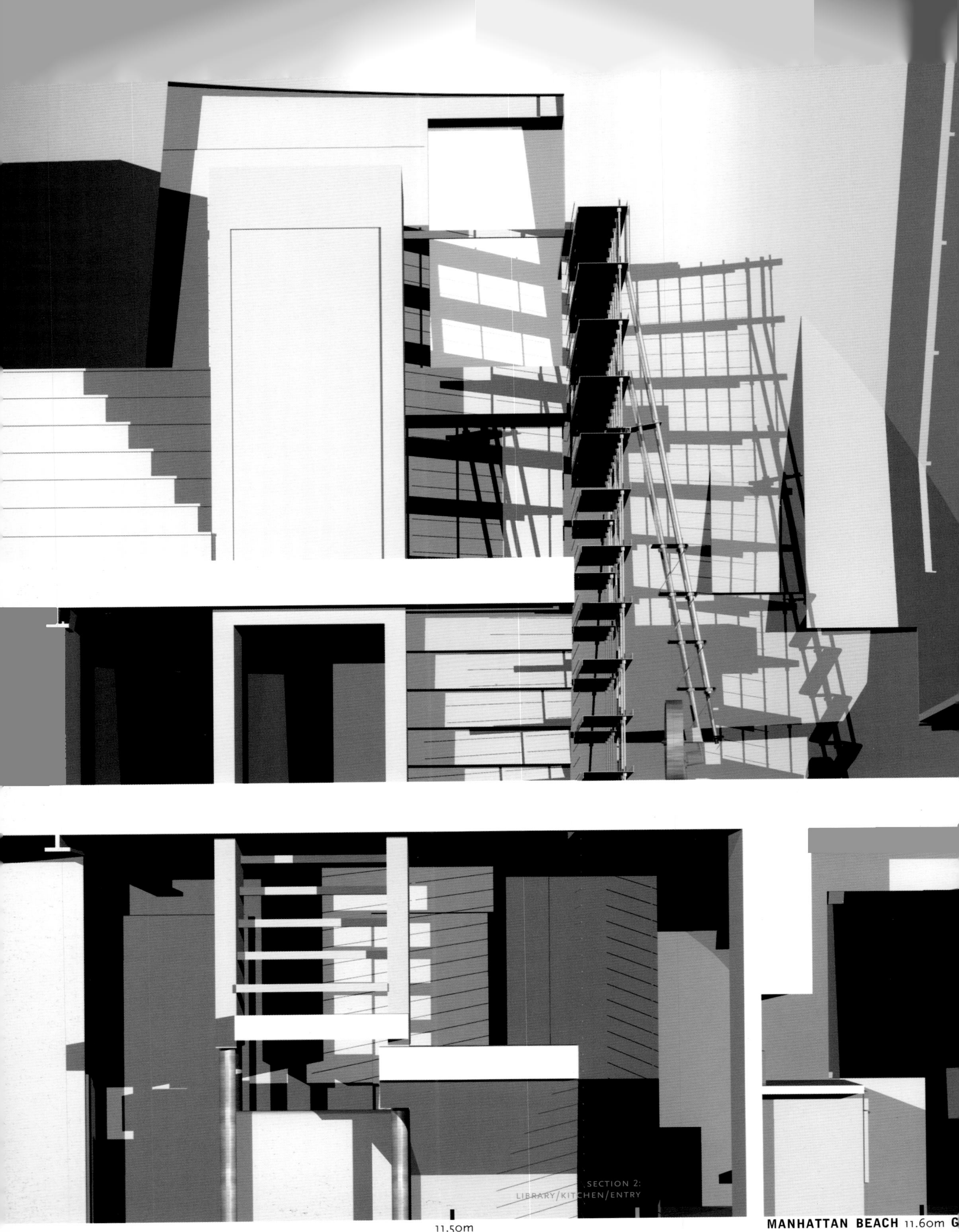
SECTION 2:
LIBRARY/KITCHEN/ENTRY
11.50m
MANHATTAN BEACH 11.60m G

BLADES HOUSE
92116
1997
1996
1995
1994
1993
1992
11.70m
11.80m

BLADES HOUSE

92116

LOOKING
SOUTHWEST

11.90m

12.00m

8

SANTA BARBARA
CALIFORNIA

APPENDIX
II.13 ABOUT THE WORK
VI.1 WORK IN PROGRESS

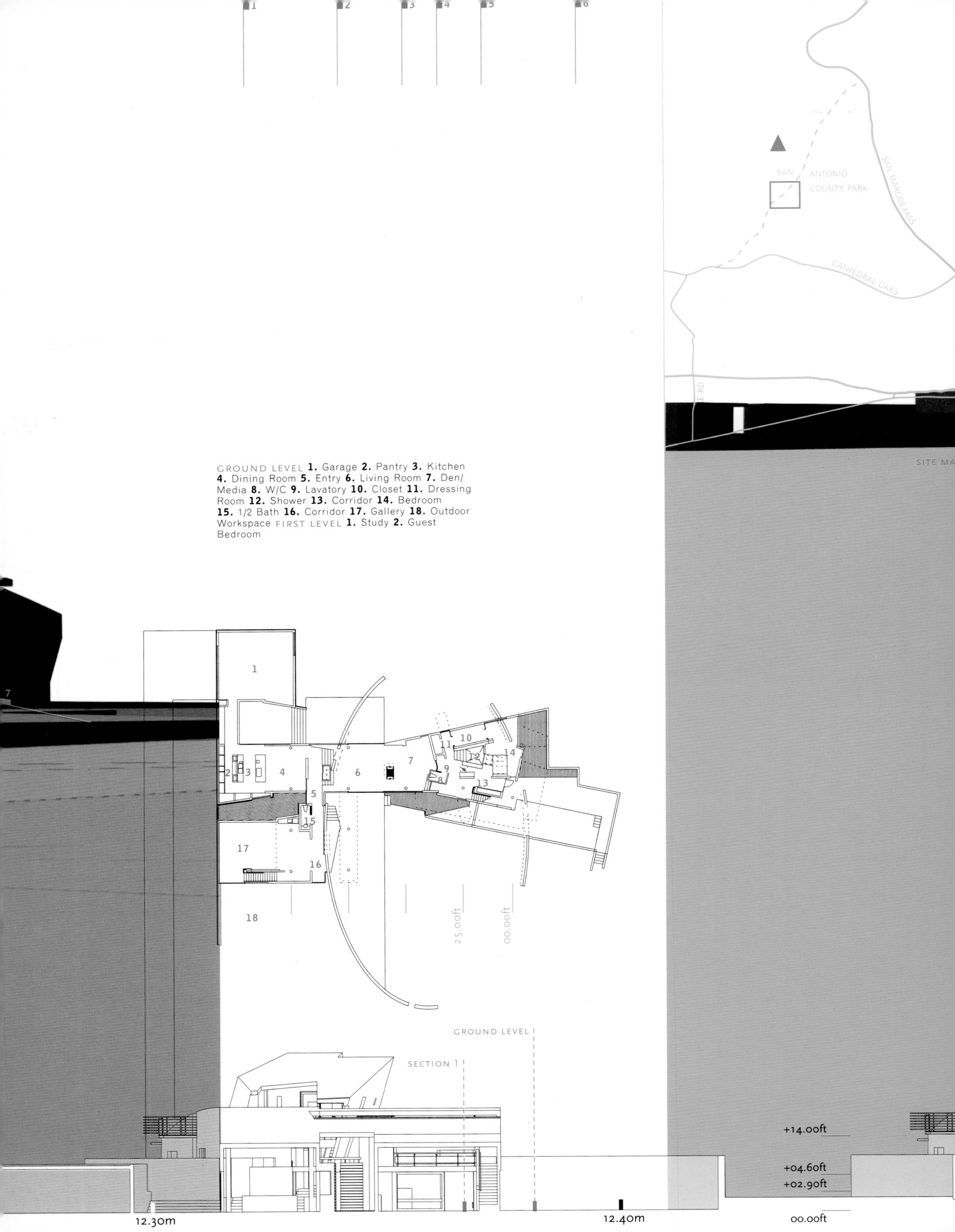

GROUND LEVEL **1.** Garage **2.** Pantry **3.** Kitchen **4.** Dining Room **5.** Entry **6.** Living Room **7.** Den/ Media **8.** W/C **9.** Lavatory **10.** Closet **11.** Dressing Room **12.** Shower **13.** Corridor **14.** Bedroom **15.** 1/2 Bath **16.** Corridor **17.** Gallery **18.** Outdoor Workspace FIRST LEVEL **1.** Study **2.** Guest Bedroom

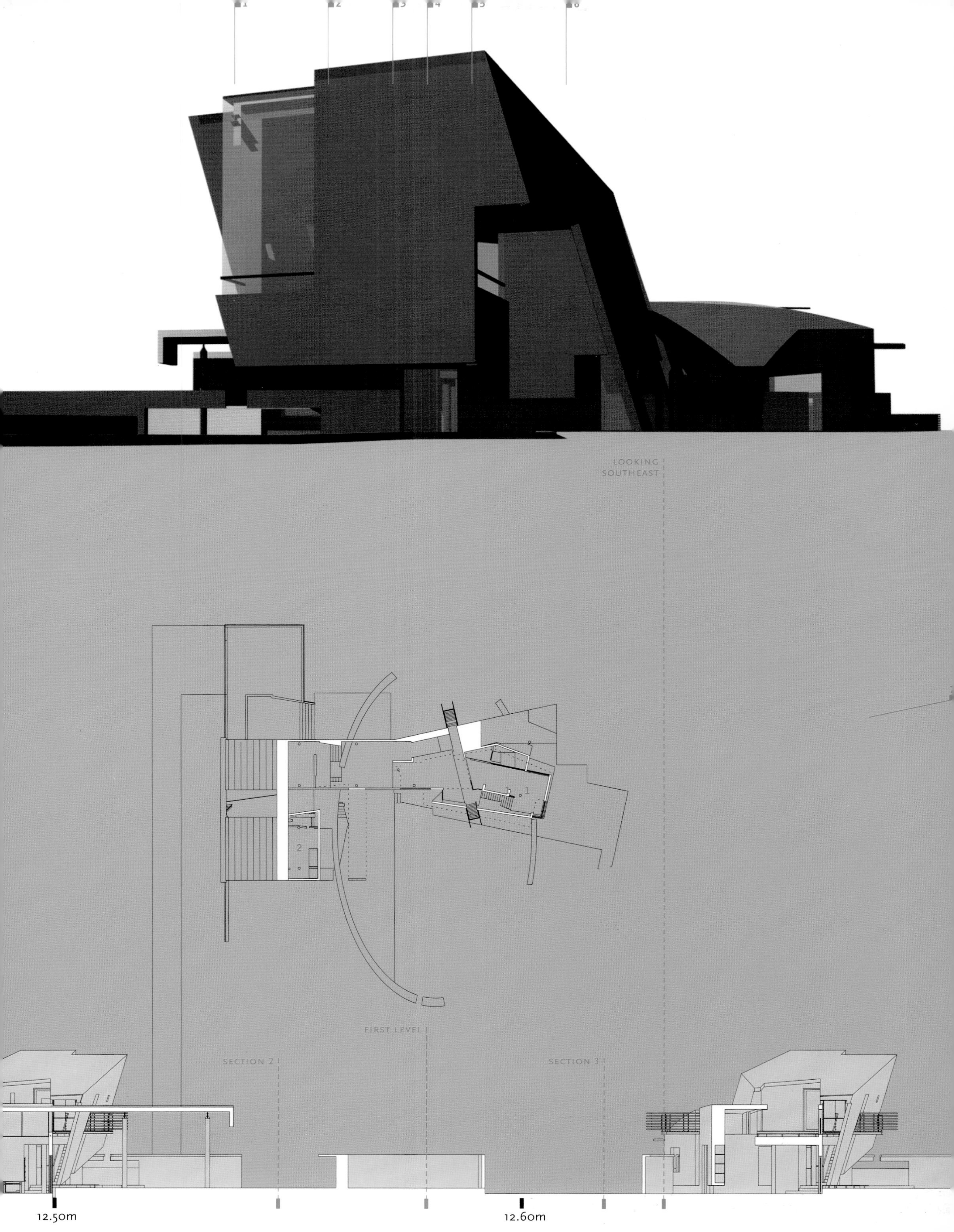
1
2
3
4
5
6
LOOKING SOUTHEAST
1
2
FIRST LEVEL
SECTION 2
SECTION 3
12.50m
12.60m

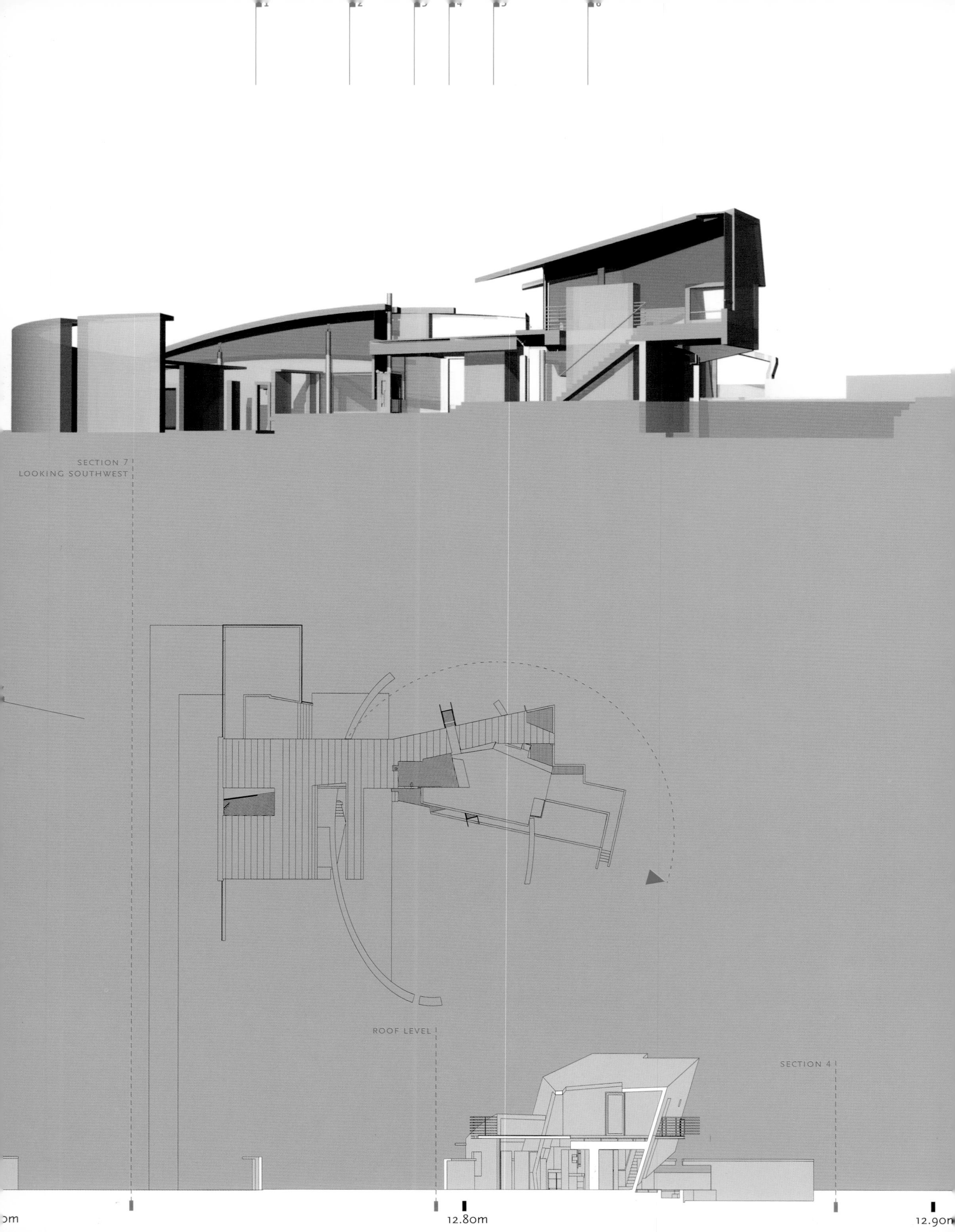
SECTION 7
LOOKING SOUTHWEST
ROOF LEVEL
SECTION 4
12.80m
12.90m

SECTION 2
KING NORTH
SECTION 5
+14.00ft
+04.60ft
+02.90ft
00.00ft
13.00m
13.10m

PROJECT DATA
AREA OF SITE
1.05 acres / 4259ha
PROGRAM
4,800sf / 446m²
HUMAN POPULATION
Residents: 2
PARKING
Cars: 2
MECHANICAL SYSTEM
Radiant Underfloor System
STRUCTURAL SYSTEM
Steel Column, Wood
Frame/Glue Lam Beams
SECTION 6
AERIAL VIEW
13.20m
GOLETA 13.30m FRANKFURT

1997
1996
1995
1994
1993
1992
MÜLLAUFBEREITUNGS-
ANLAGE FRANKFURT
WASTE MANAGEMENT FACILITY
13.40m
13.50m

MÜLLAUFBEREITUNGS-ANLAGE FRANKFURT
WASTE MANAGEMENT FACILITY

93302

PROJECT LOOKING NORTH

13.60m

13.70m

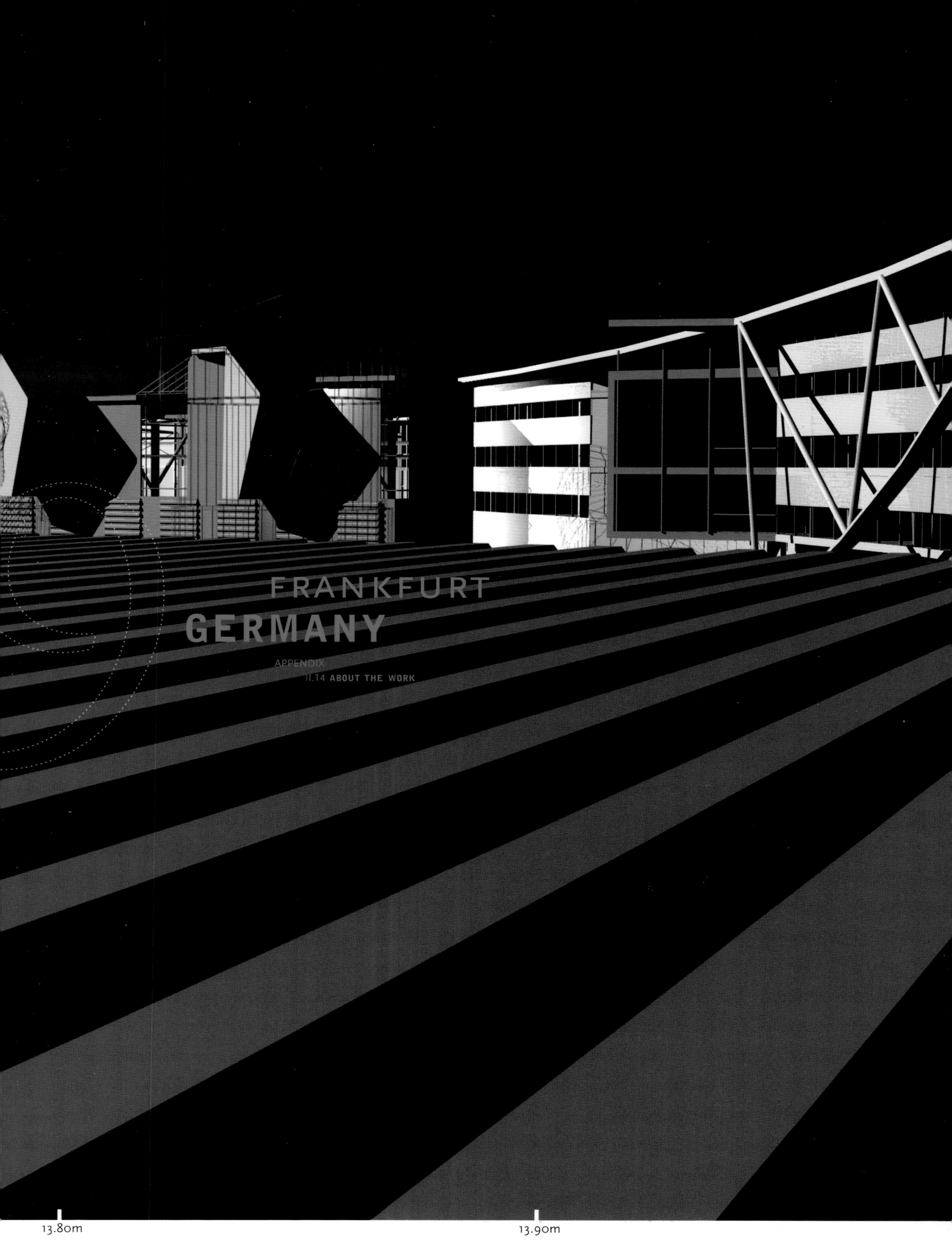
FRANKFURT
GERMANY
APPENDIX
II.14 ABOUT THE WORK

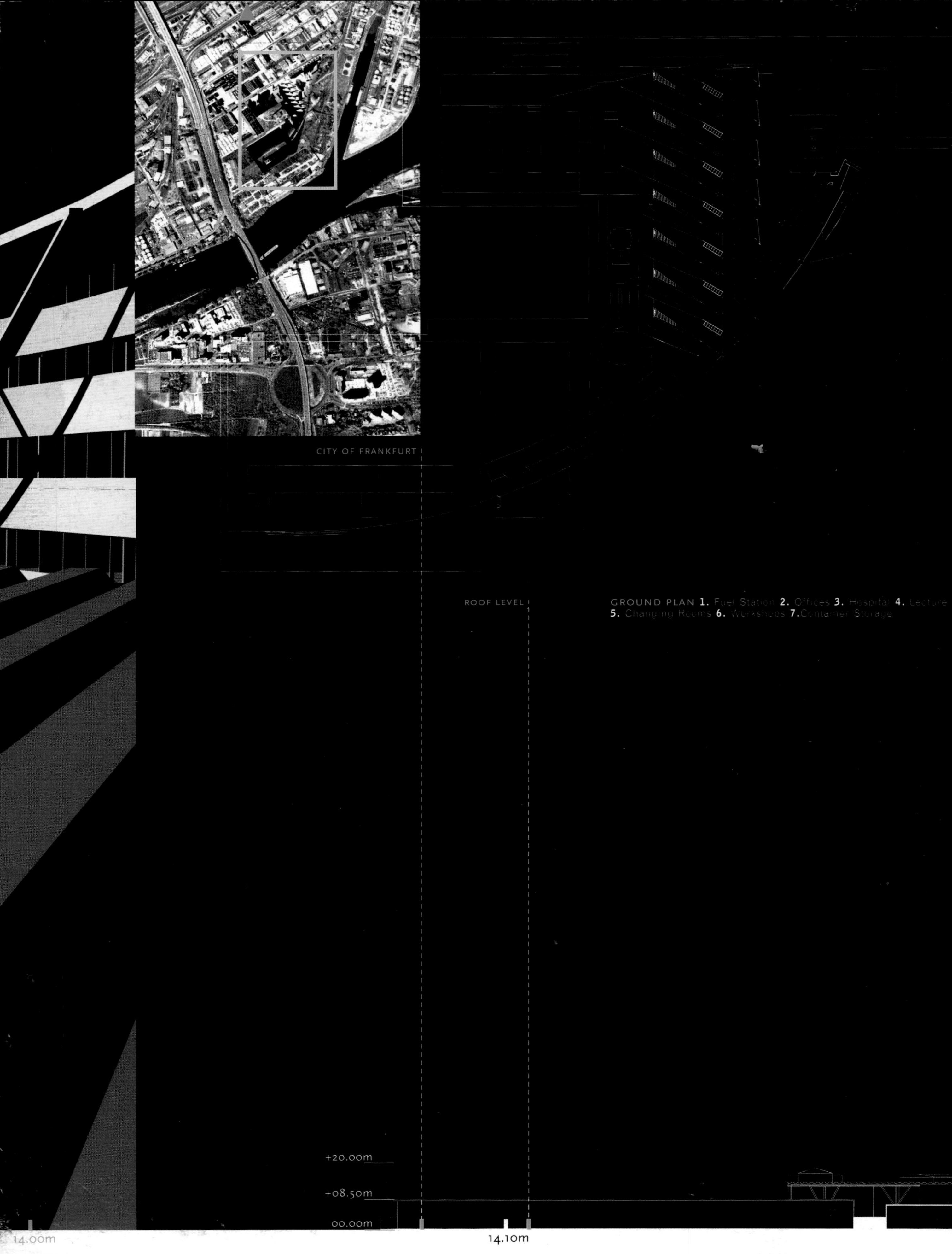
CITY OF FRANKFURT
ROOF LEVEL
GROUND PLAN **1.** Fuel Station **2.** Offices **3.** Hospital **4.** Lecture
5. Changing Rooms **6.** Workshops **7.**Container Storage
+20.00m
+08.50m
00.00m
14.00m
14.10m

6
6
6
7
07.80m
00.00m
3,4,5
2
1
1
2
GROUND LEVEL
+36.00m
+10.50m
+03.00m
14.30m
14.40m

SECTION 2
+20.00m
+08.50m
00.00m
14.50m
14.60m

ROOF
ABOVE
+36.00m
+10.50m
+03.00m
14.70m
14.80m
PROJECT LOOKING
SOUTHEAST

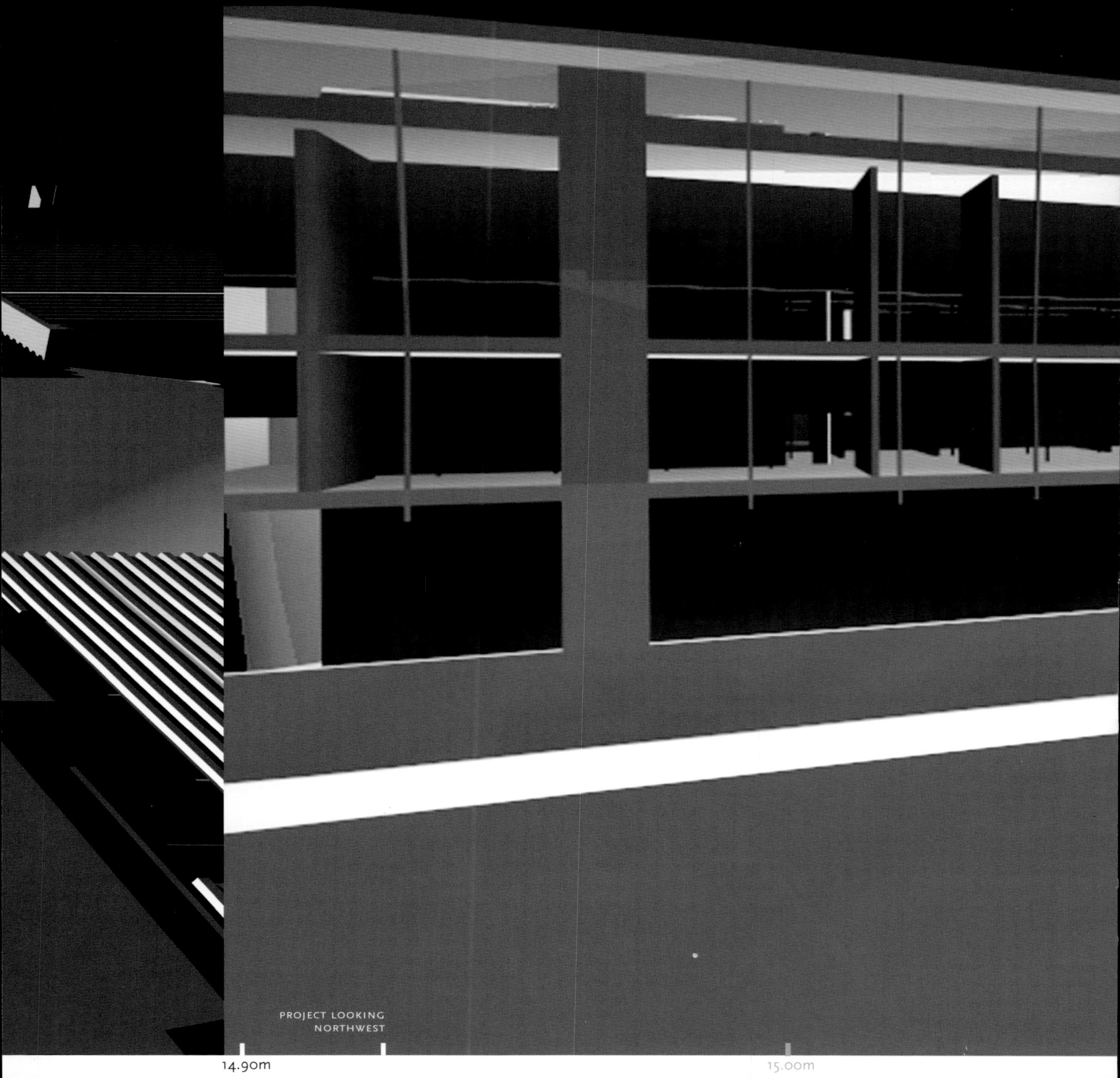
PROJECT LOOKING
NORTHWEST
14.90m
15.00m

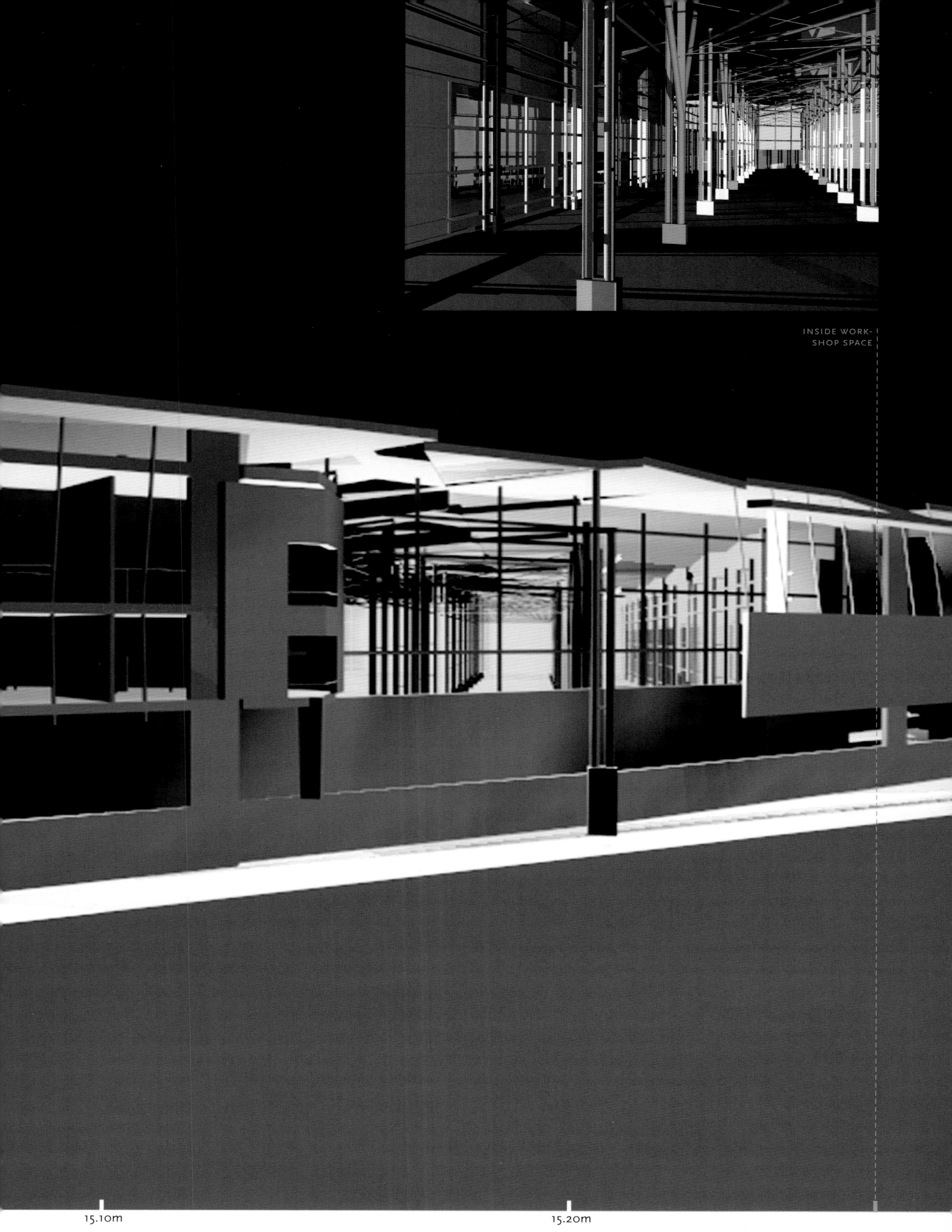

INSIDE WORK-
SHOP SPACE
15.10m
15.20m

PROJECT DATA

AREA OF SITE

EXISTING BUILDING

Instrumental Building: 14.732sf / 1369.18m^2
Social Building: 26.231sf / 2437.83m^2
Storage Building: 11.835sf / 1099.91m^2
Office: 9.996sf / 929.02m^2

PROGRAM

NEW BUILDING

Administration 48.420sf / 4500m^2
Shops 96.840sf/ 9000m^2
Parking 193,684sf / 18000m^2
Storage 59.180sf / 5500m^2
Social 37,660sf / 3500m^2
5 Apartments 5,380sf / 500m^2
TOTAL 378,375sf / 35.165m^2

HUMAN POPULATION

Staff: 400

PARKING

Cars: 230
Trucks: 180

MECHANICAL SYSTEM

Heat Pump

STRUCTURAL SYSTEM

Steel Frame

AMERICAN BUSINESS CENTER

1995

1994

1993

1992

ERLIN 15.60m 15.70m

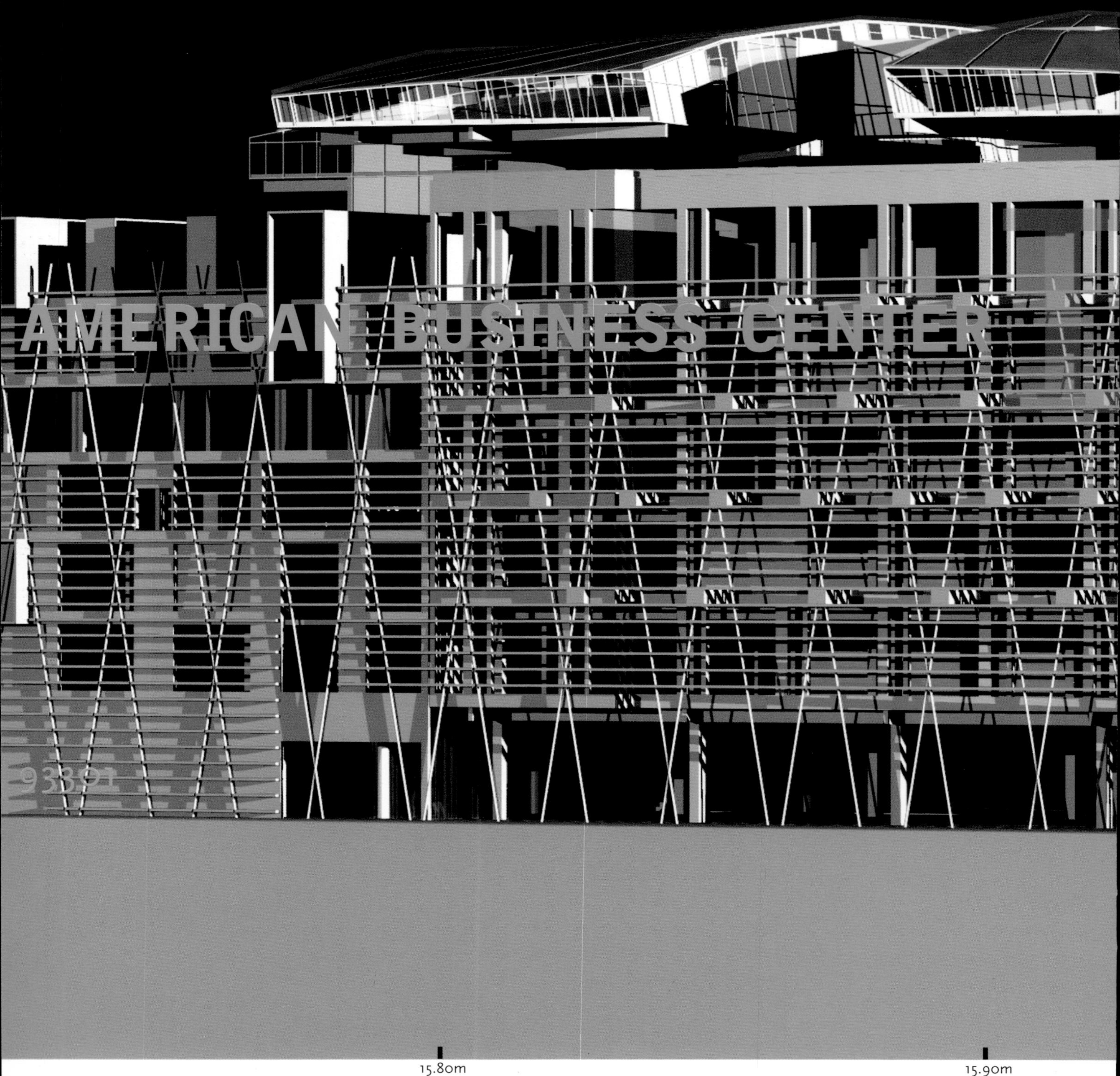
AMERICAN BUSINESS CENTER
93301
15.80m
15.90m

BERLIN, SITE
BERLIN
GERMANY
APPENDIX
II.16 ABOUT THE WORK
LOOKING
NORTHWEST
16.00m
16.10m

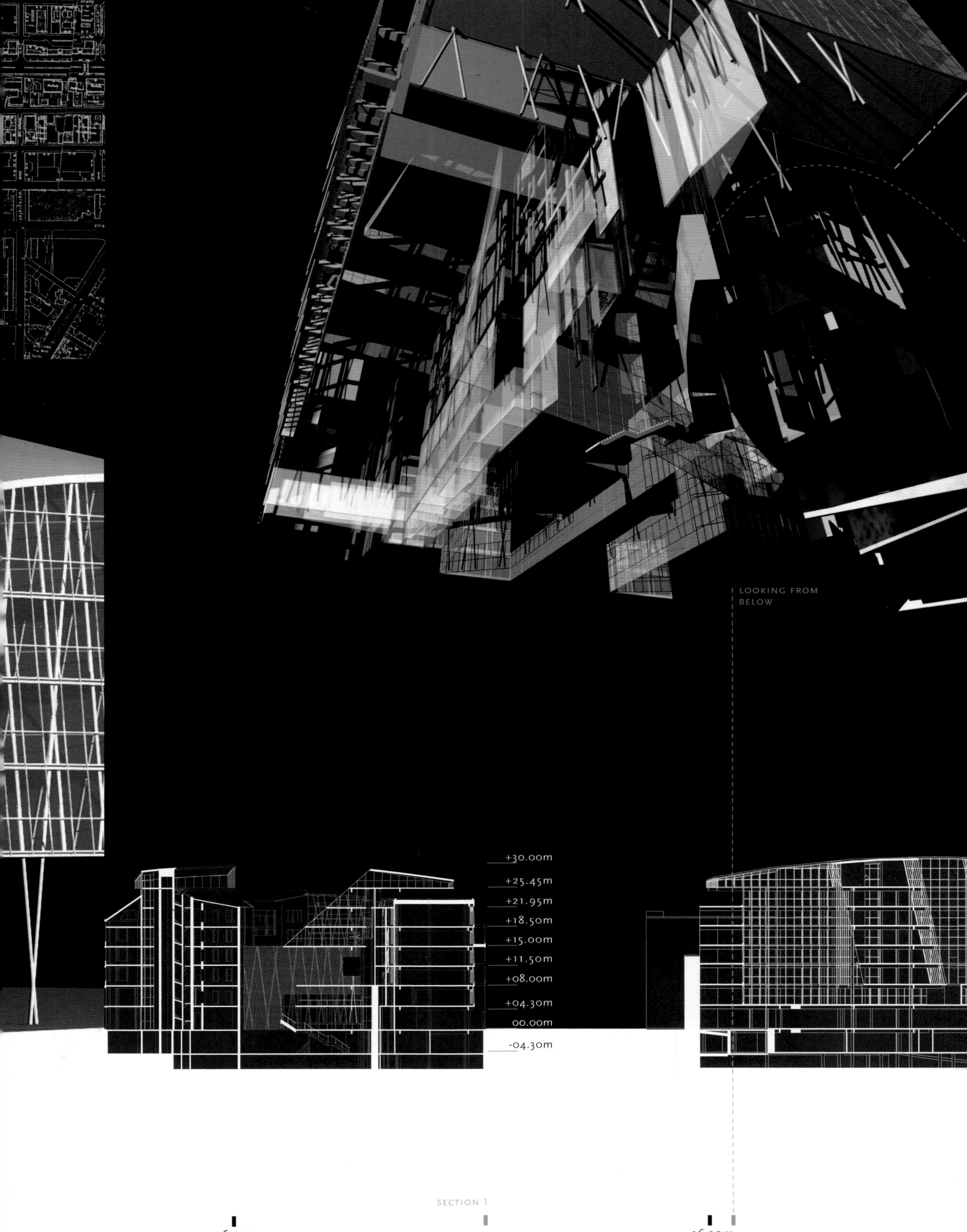

LOOKING FROM BELOW
+30.00m
+25.45m
+21.95m
+18.50m
+15.00m
+11.50m
+08.00m
+04.30m
00.00m
-04.30m
SECTION 1
16.20m
16.30m

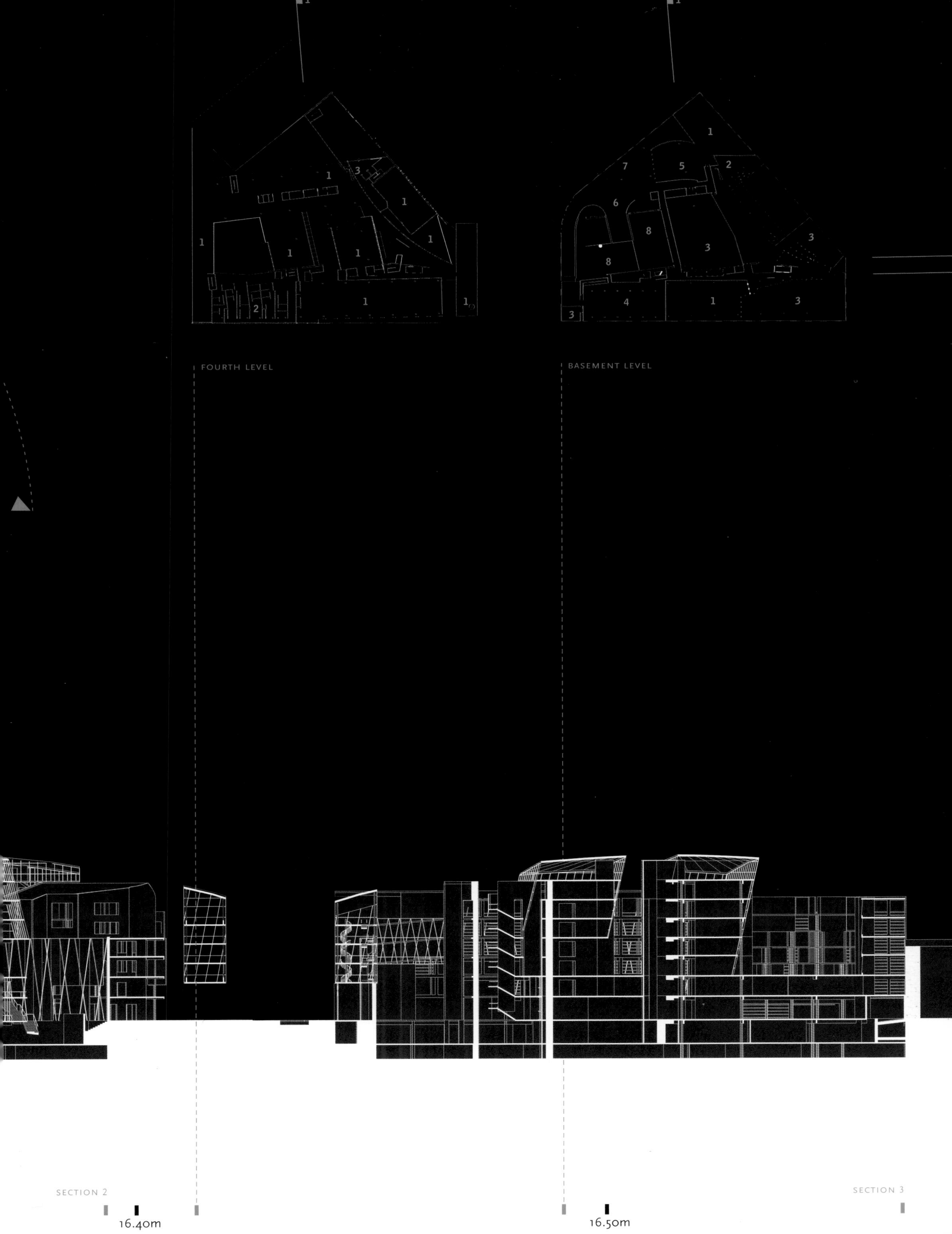

1
1
3
1
1
1
1
1
1
2
1
1
1
7
5
2
6
8
3
3
8
4
1
3
3
FOURTH LEVEL
BASEMENT LEVEL
SECTION 2
16.40m
16.50m
SECTION 3

1

1

2

3

1

1

1

2

1

1

08.00m

00.00m

GROUND LEVEL

1

2

PARKING LEVEL

FOURTH LEVEL 1. Office Space **2.** Apartments **3.** Lobby **GROUND LEVEL 1.** Public Offices **2.** Courtyard **BASEMENT LEVEL 1.** Archive **2.** Lobby **3.** Public Offices **4.** Storage **5.** Kitchen **6.** Delivering **7.** Ramp **8.** Mechanical **PARKING LEVEL 1.** Ramp **2.** Parking

16.60m

16.70 m

LOOKING WEST

m

16.90m

17.00m

LOOKING WEST
17.10m
17.20m

17.30m
17.40m

LOOKING WEST
17.50m
17.60m

17.70m 17.80m

PROJECT DATA

AREA OF SITE

EXISTING BUILDING

Instrumental Building: 14.732sf / 1369.18m^2
Social Building: 26.231sf / 2437.83m^2
Storage Building: 11.835sf / 1099.91m^2
Office: 9.996sf / 929.02m^2

PROGRAM

NEW BUILDING

Administration: 48.420sf / 4500m^2
Shops: 96.840sf / 9000m^2
Parking: 193.684sf / 18000m^2
Storage: 59.180sf / 5500m^2
Social: 37.660sf / 3500m^2
5 Apartments: 5.380sf / 500m^2
TOTAL 378.375sf / 35.165m^2

HUMAN POPULATION

Staff: 400

PARKING

Cars: 230
Trucks: 180

MECHANICAL SYSTEM

Heat Pump

STRUCTURAL SYSTEM

Steel Frame

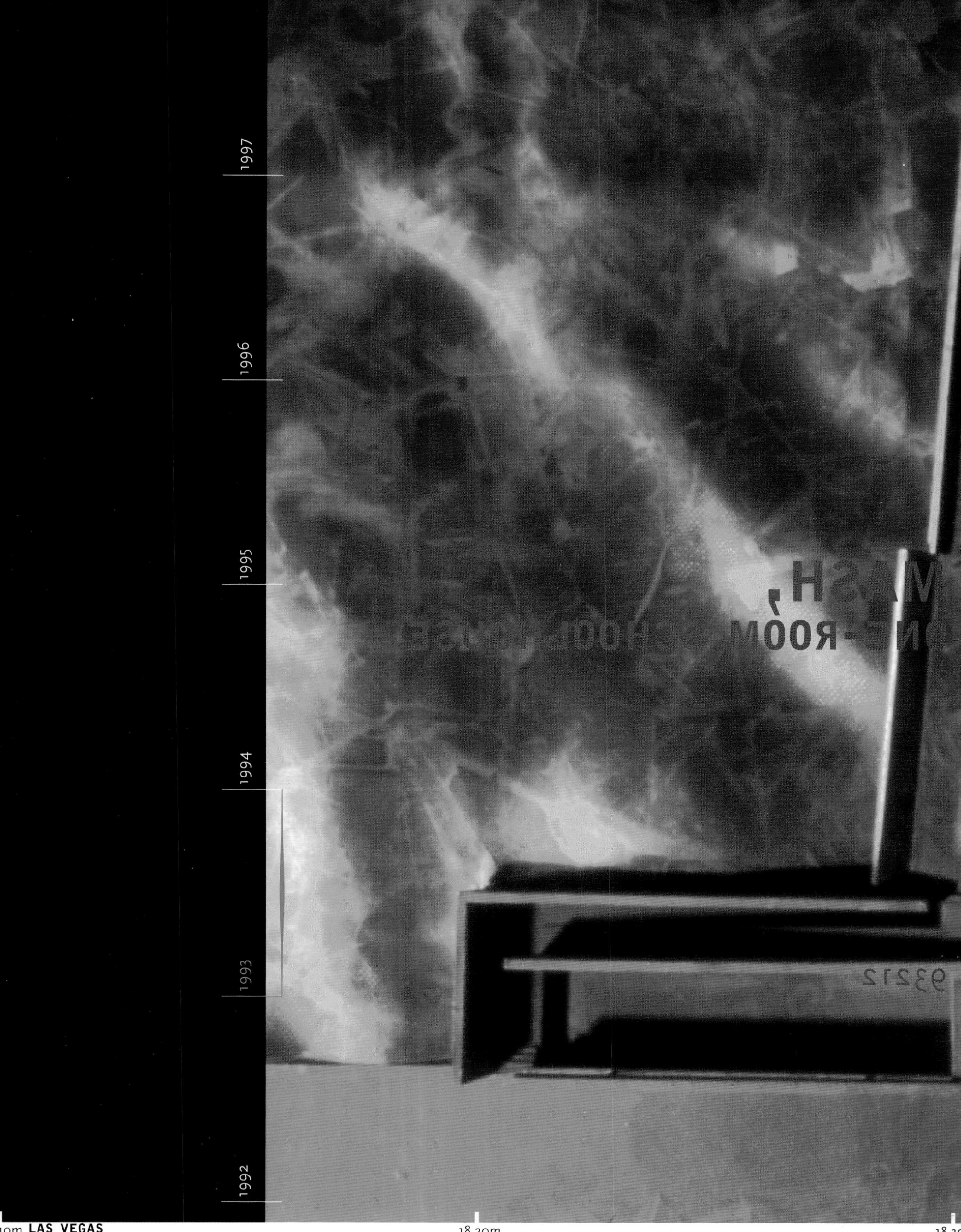

MASH,
ONE-ROOM SCHOOLHOUSE

93212

PROJECT FROM
ABOVE

18.40m

18.50m

LAS VEGAS
NEVADA

APPENDIX
II.18 **ABOUT THE WORK**

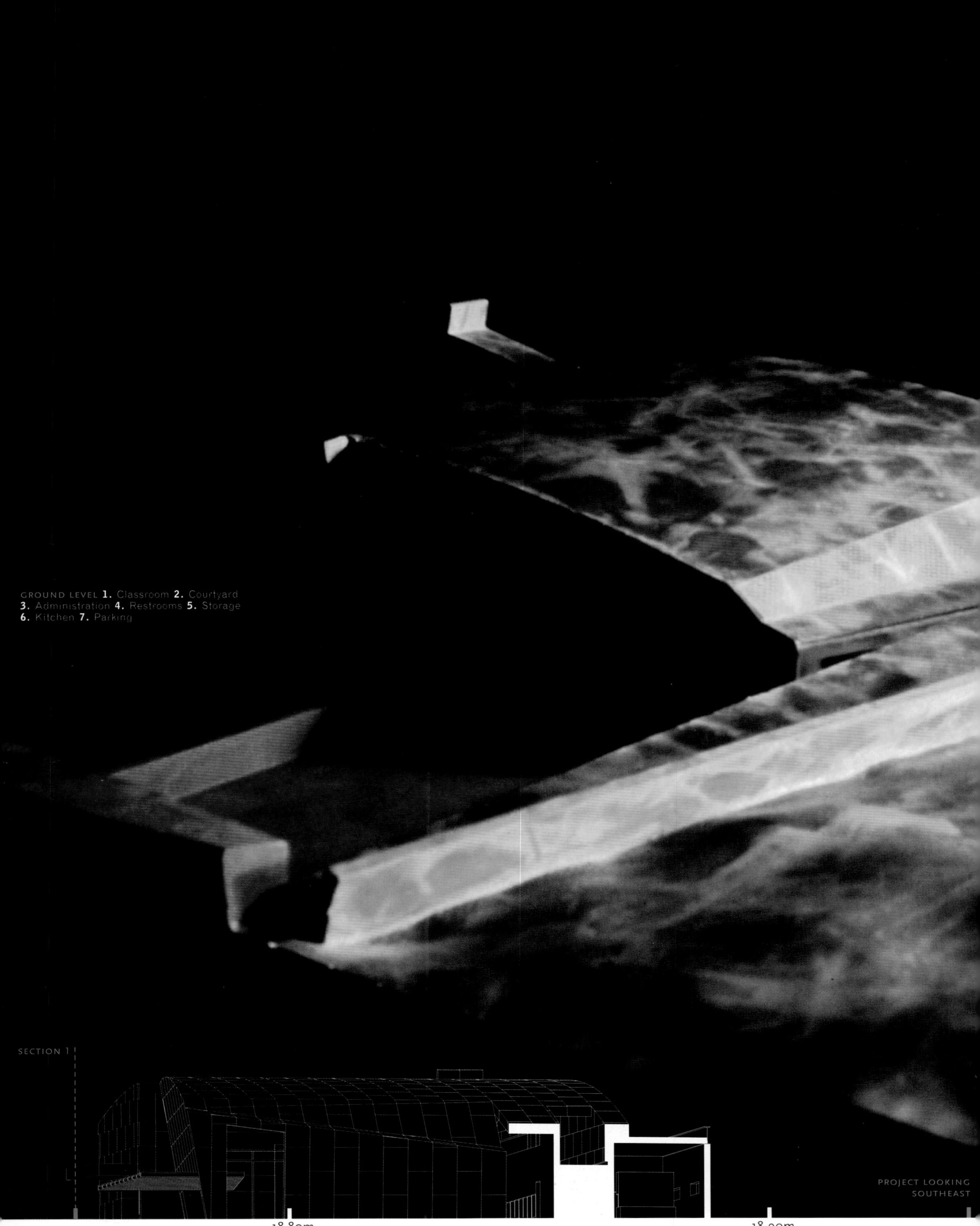
GROUND LEVEL **1.** Classroom **2.** Courtyard
3. Administration **4.** Restrooms **5.** Storage
6. Kitchen **7.** Parking
SECTION 1
PROJECT LOOKING SOUTHEAST
18.80m
18.90m

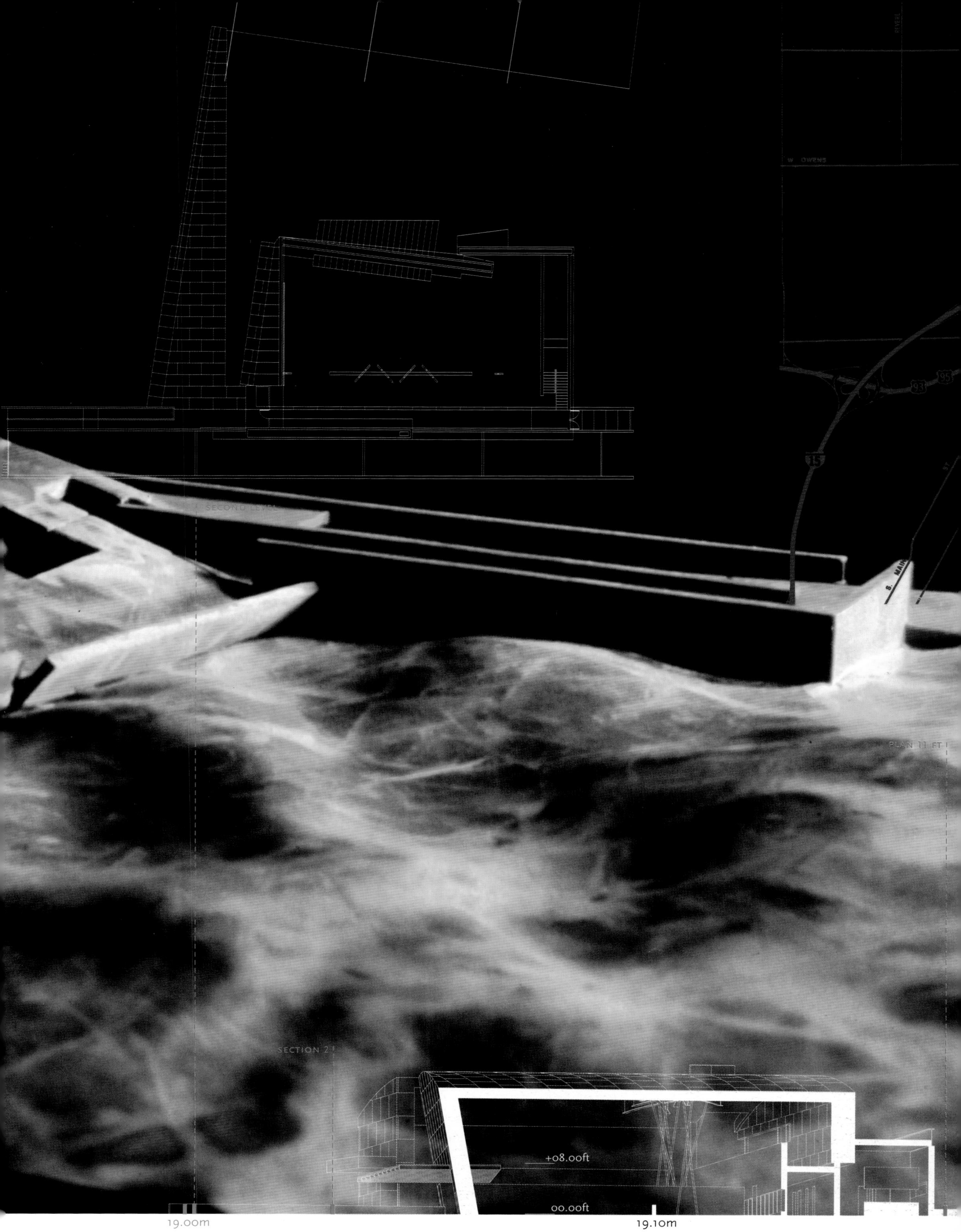
W. OWENS
93
95
15
S. MAIN
SECOND LEVEL
PLAN 11 FT
SECTION 2
+08.00ft
00.00ft
19.00m
19.10m

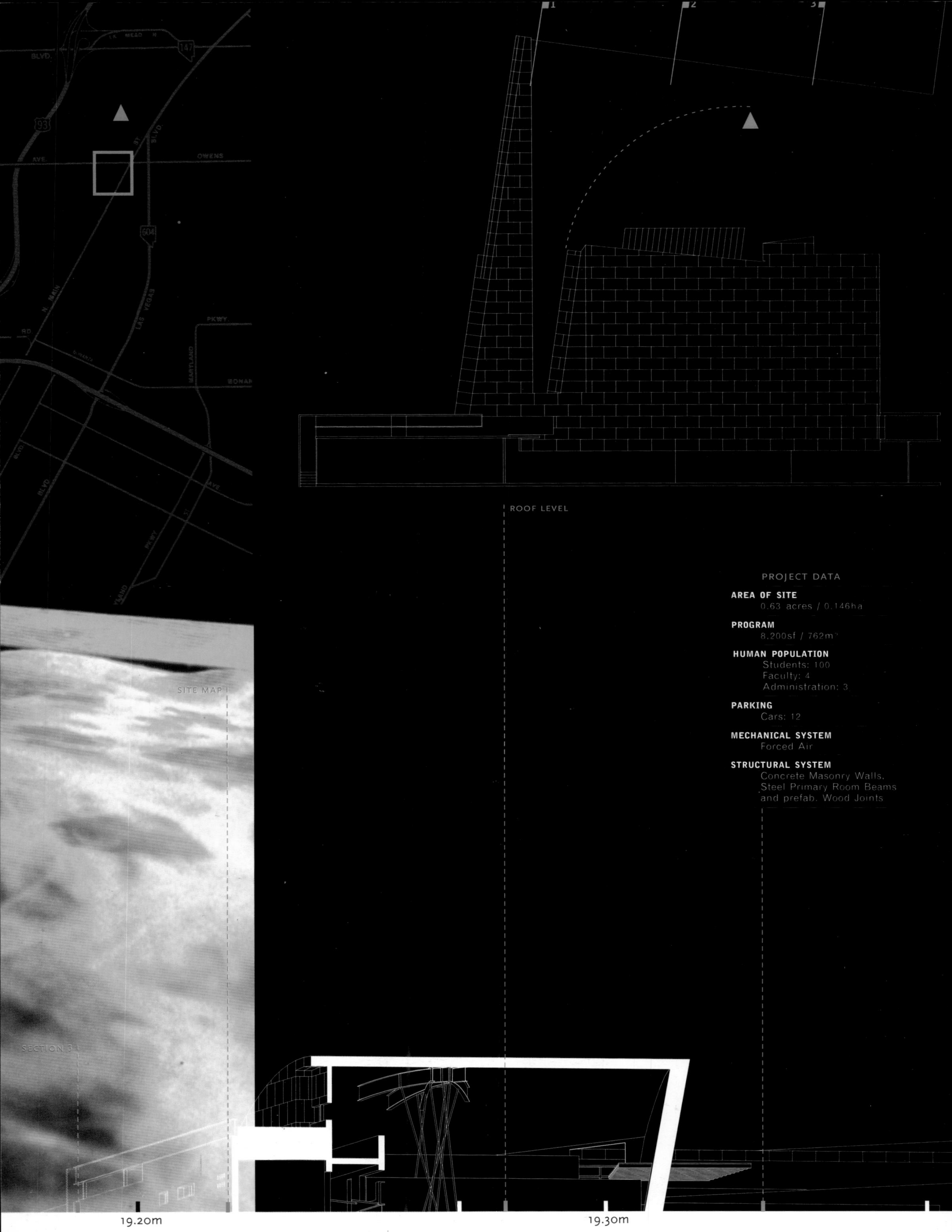

PROJECT DATA

AREA OF SITE
0.63 acres / 0.146ha

PROGRAM
8,200sf / 762m²

HUMAN POPULATION
Students: 100
Faculty: 4
Administration: 3

PARKING
Cars: 12

MECHANICAL SYSTEM
Forced Air

STRUCTURAL SYSTEM
Concrete Masonry Walls, Steel Primary Room Beams and prefab. Wood Joints

썬 타워

SUN TOWER

95300

1995

1994

1993

1992

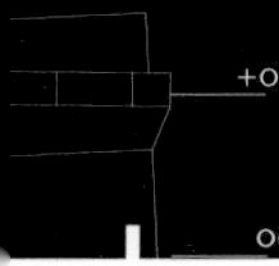

+08.00ft

00.00ft

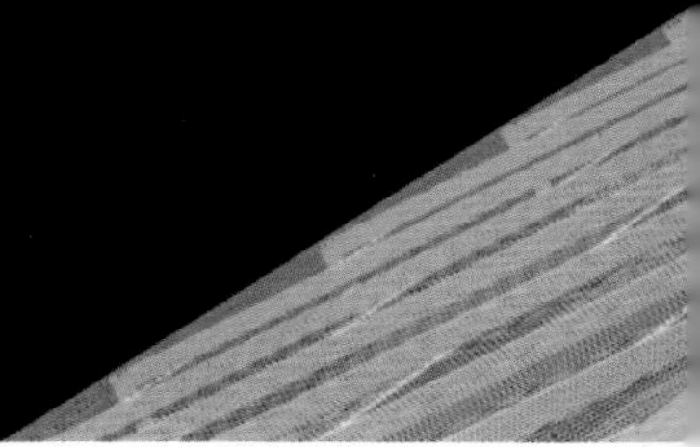

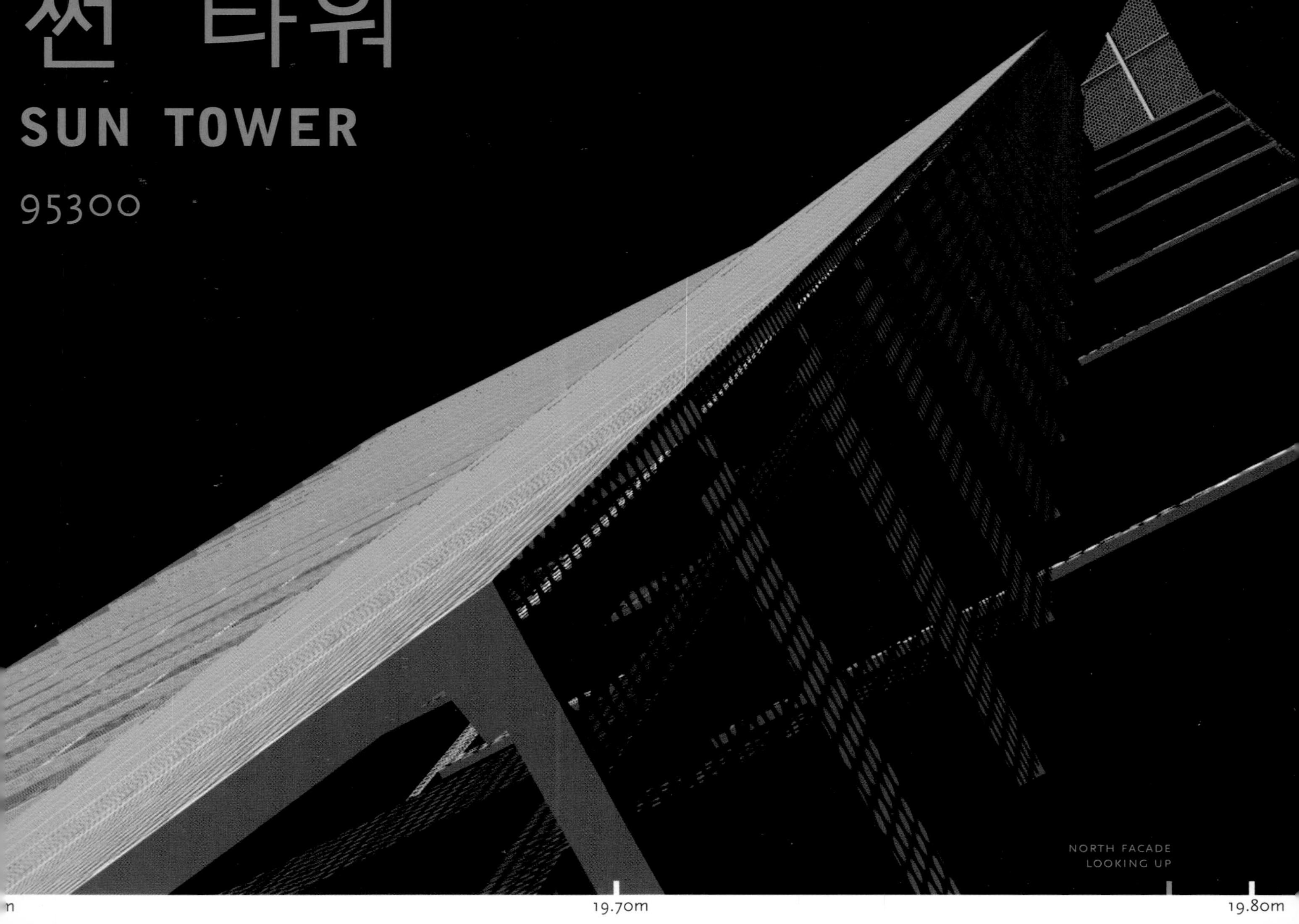
썬 타워
SUN TOWER
95300
NORTH FACADE
LOOKING UP
n
19.70m
19.80m

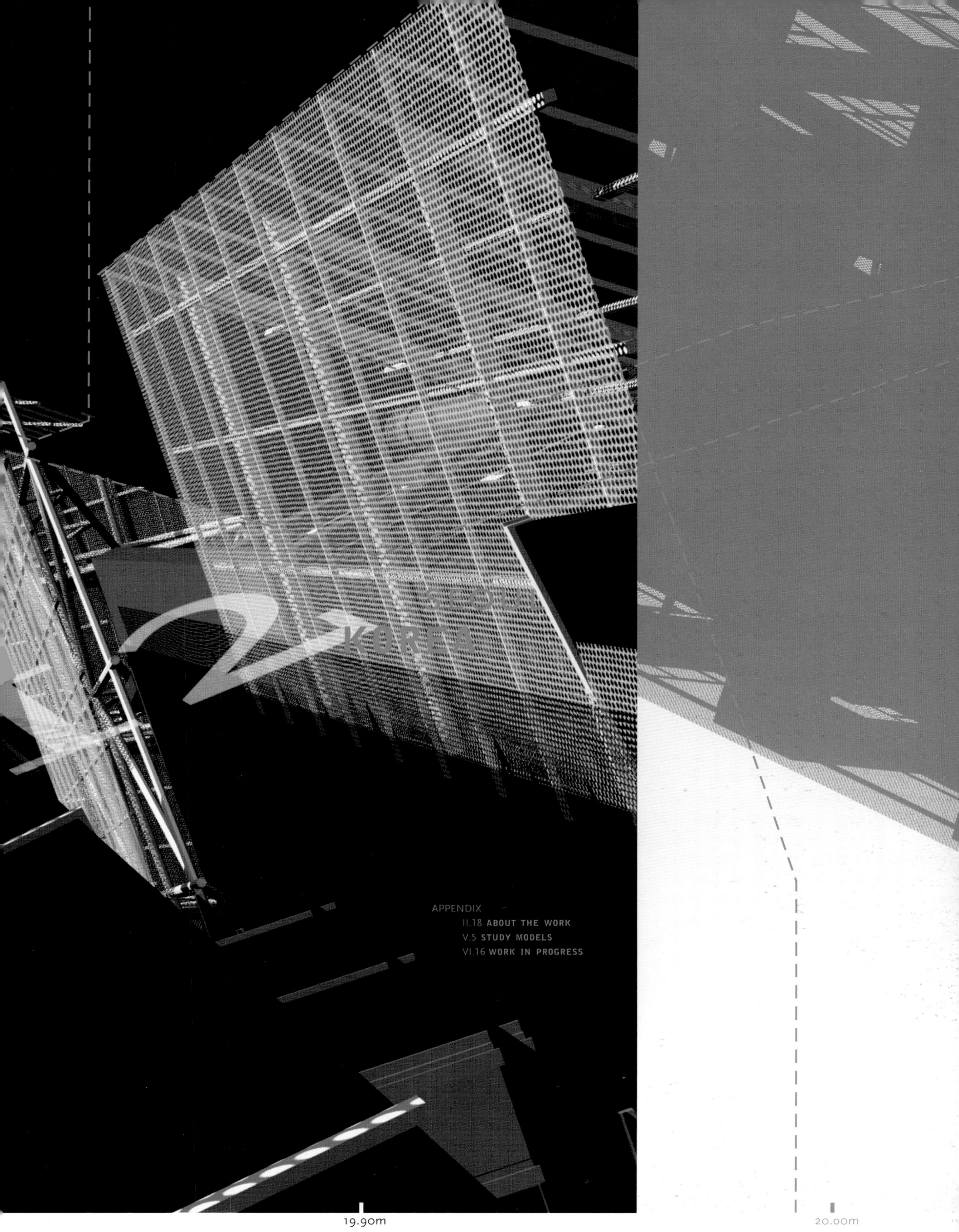

APPENDIX

II.18 ABOUT THE WORK
V.5 STUDY MODELS
VI.16 WORK IN PROGRESS

LOOKING SOUTH
DOWN
20.10m
20.20m

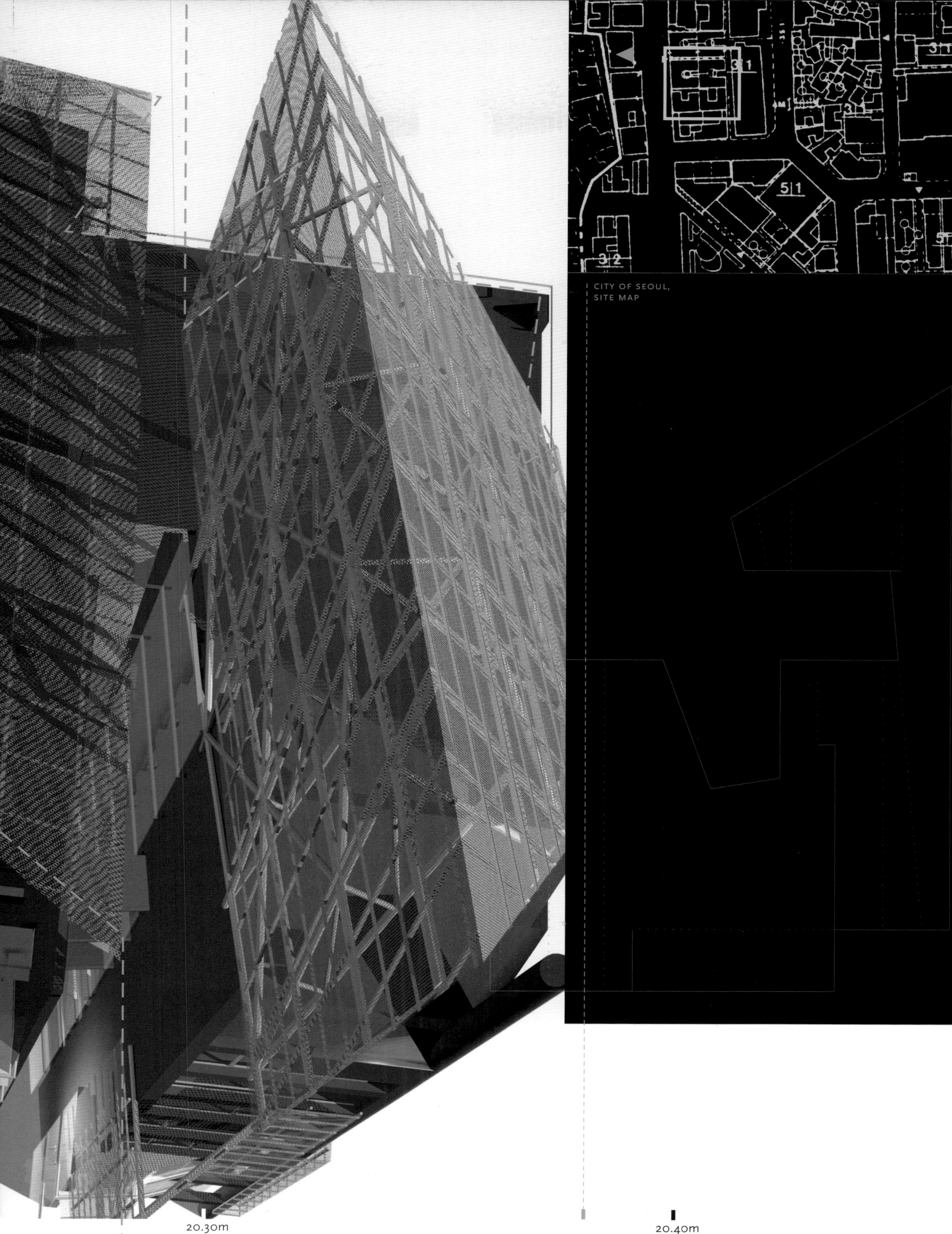

CITY OF SEOUL,
SITE MAP

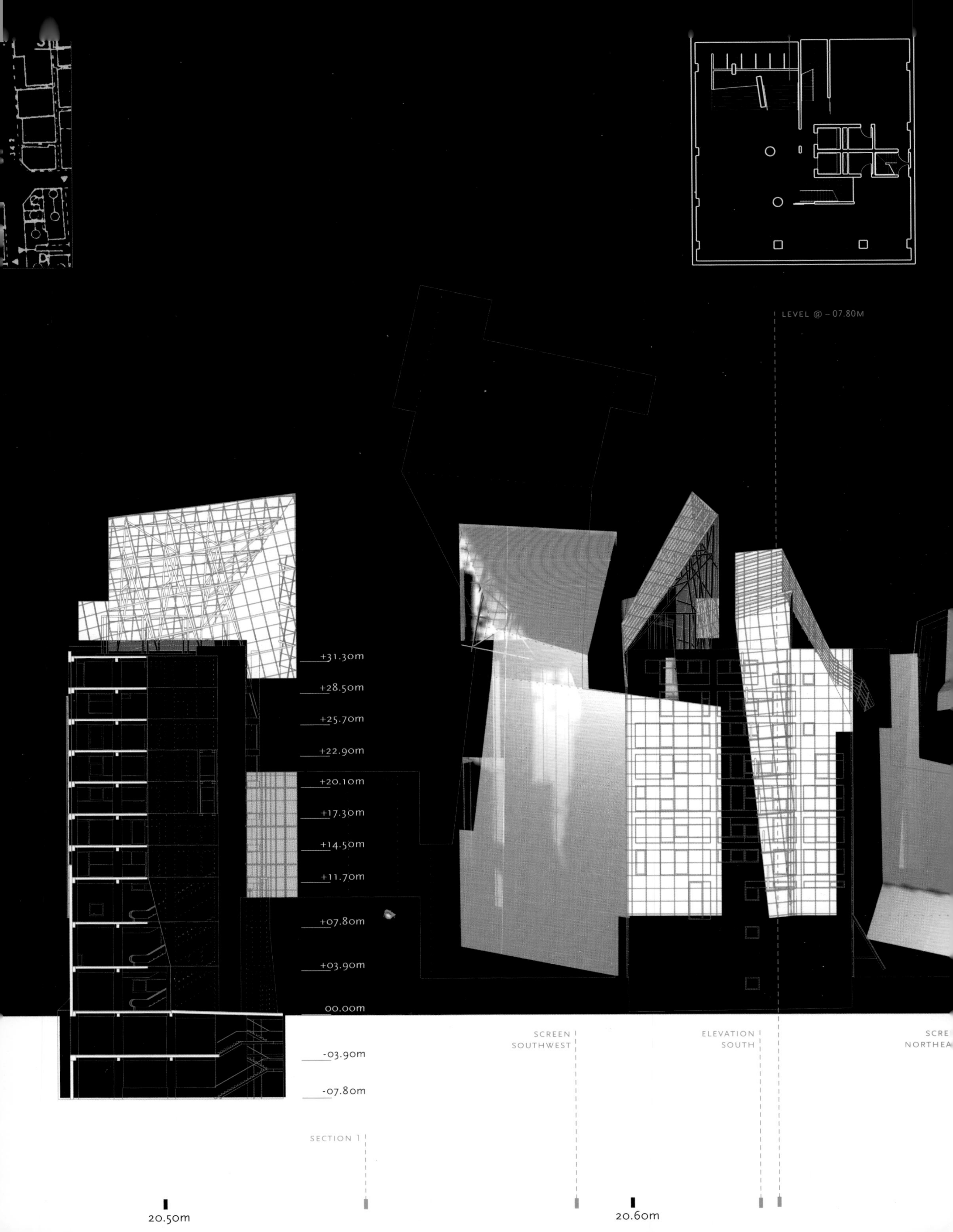
LEVEL @ – 07.80M
+31.30m
+28.50m
+25.70m
+22.90m
+20.10m
+17.30m
+14.50m
+11.70m
+07.80m
+03.90m
00.00m
-03.90m
-07.80m
SCREEN
SOUTHWEST
ELEVATION
SOUTH
SECTION 1
20.50m
20.60m

1
1
1
2
1
1
3
4
5
4
5
1
1
01.20m
00.00m
GROUND LEVEL
LEVEL @ +03.90M
ROOF LEVEL
GROUND LEVEL 1. Retail 2. Court
3. Lobby 4. Elevator 5. W.C.
ELEVATION
WEST
SCREEN
SOUTHEAST
ELEVATION
EAST
20.70m
20.80m

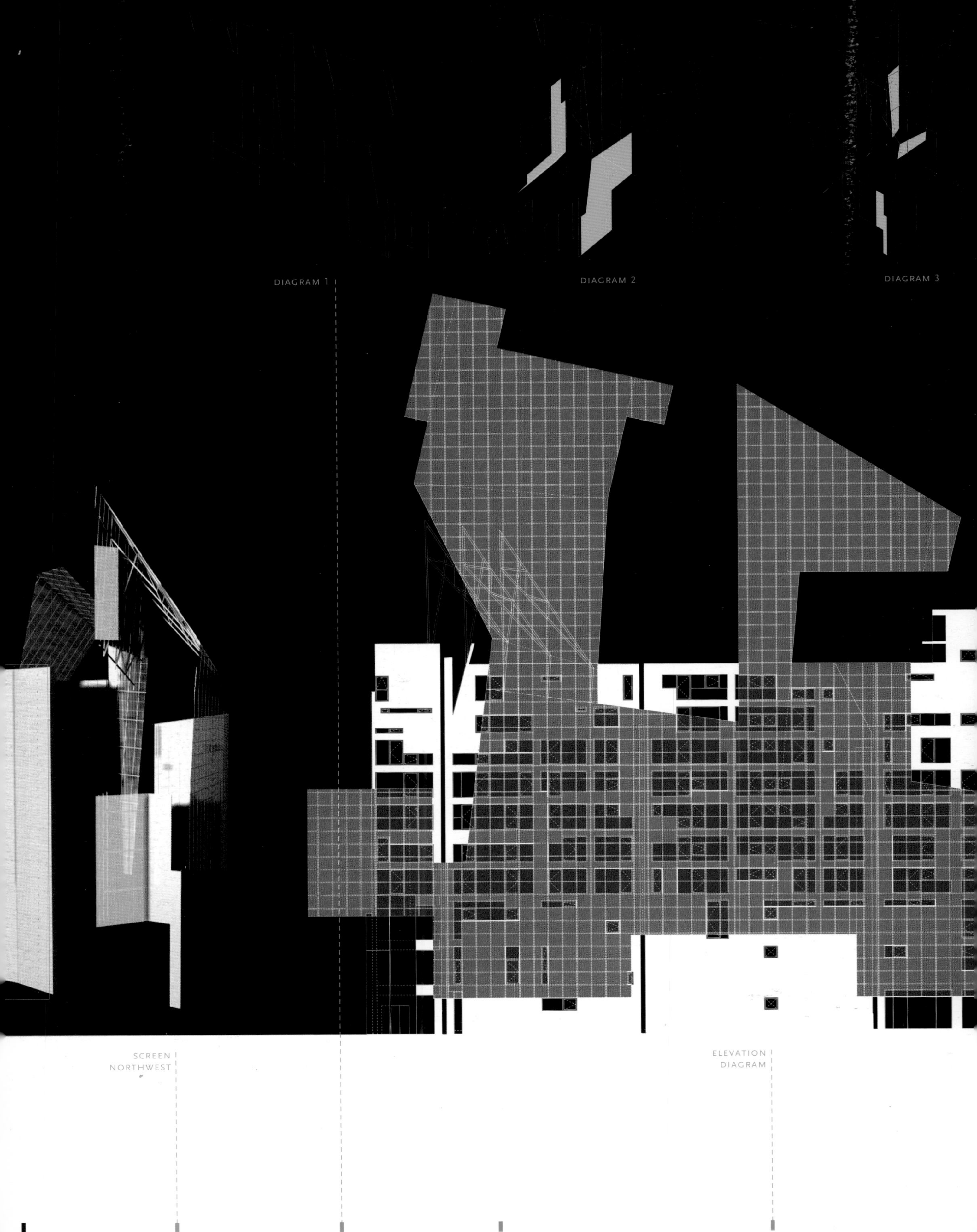

DIAGRAM 1
DIAGRAM 2
DIAGRAM 3
SCREEN
NORTHWEST
ELEVATION
DIAGRAM
20.90m
30.00m

UNFOLDED ELEVATION

30.20m

30.30m

SCREEN DIAGRAM
DIAGRAM 7
C 40
F 39
102.8°
C 41
12.8°
F 42
12.8°
C 43
F 44
5.3°
115.6°
C 45
F 46
17.2°
C 47
8.3°
8°
C 33
F 32
97°
F 31
21°
77°
93.5°
13.3°
F 1
C 48
6395
C 49
4590
C 50
7170
C 51
4648
4686
12080
9998
6752
1500
C 1
F 2
F 3
F 5
F 7
F 12
B
NORTH
A
3
WEST
8
A
SOUTH
G
8
LOOKING SOUTHEAST
30.40m
30.50m

88°
C 27
C 26
104°
C 25
10902
C 24
5442
1730
8448
F 18
C 19
C 20
9°
C 16
C 13
400
200
7100
2b
G
NORTH
E
LOOKING
SOUTHWEST
30.60m
30.70m

30.80m 30.90m

DETAIL VIEW OF SCREEN

31.00m

31.10m

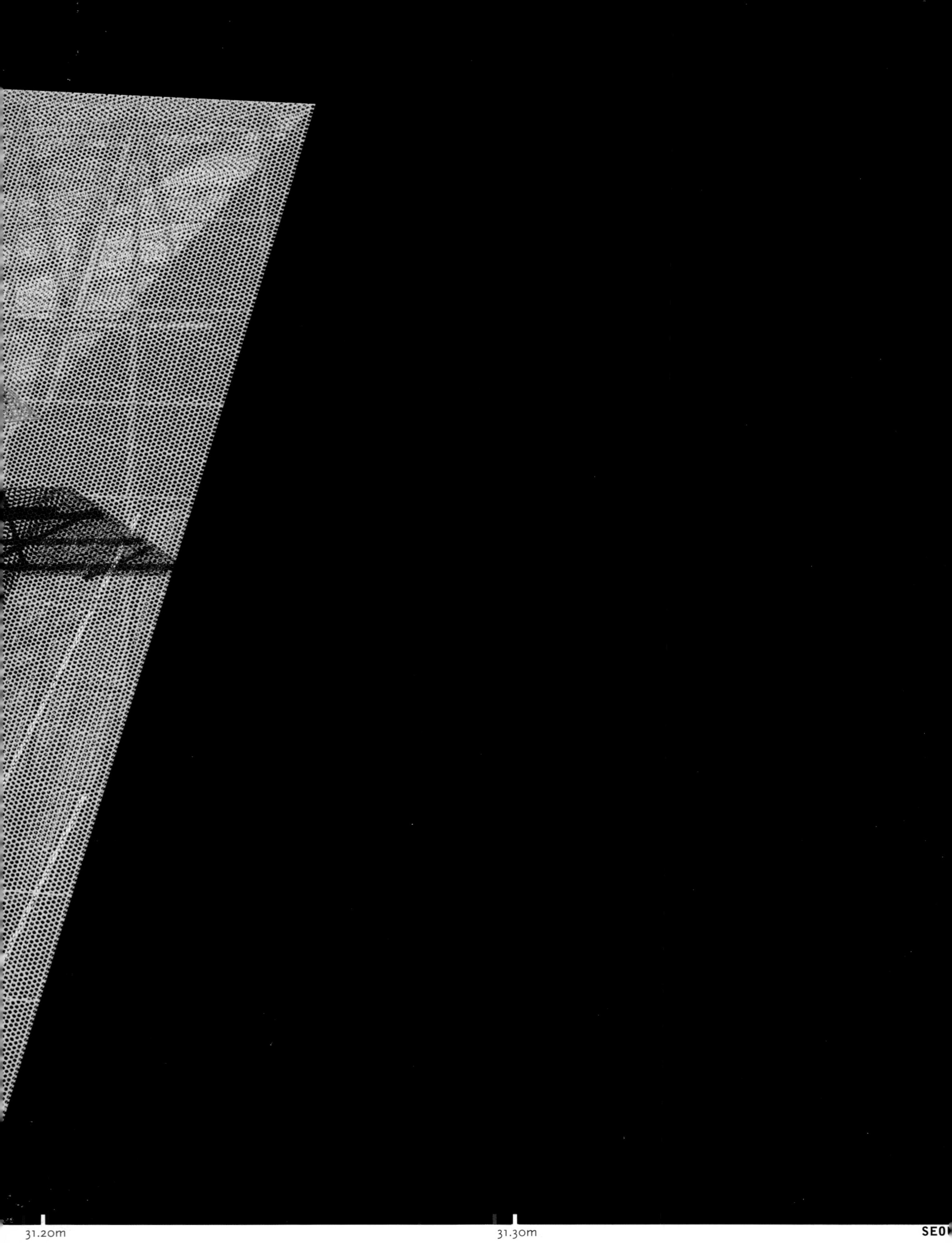
31.20m
31.30m
SE0

1997
1996
1995
1994
1993
1992
31.50m
31.60m

95200
日月光 主題活動區
A.S.E. VISITOR CENTER
PLAN A
31.70m
31.80m

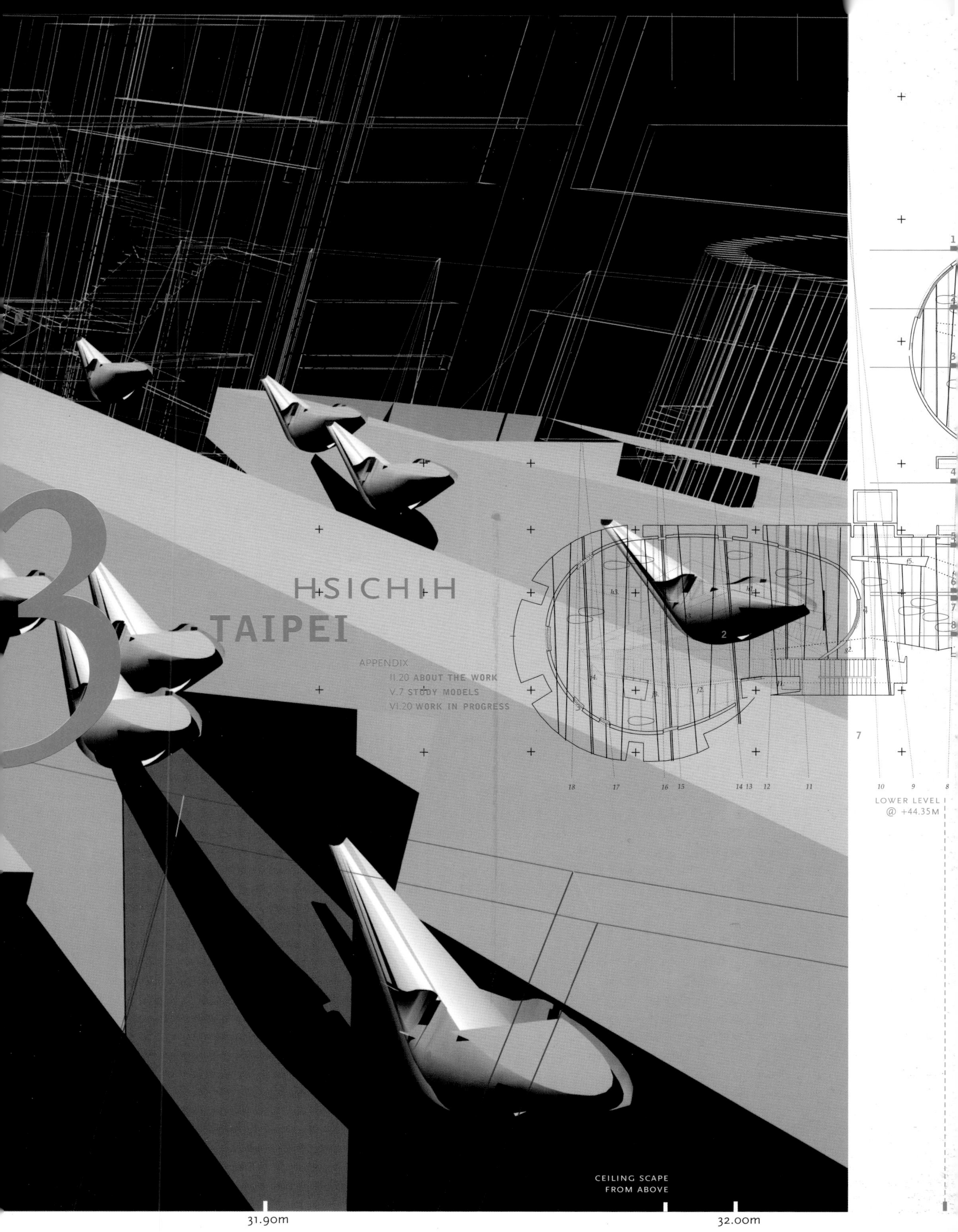
3
HSICHIH
TAIPEI
APPENDIX
II.20 ABOUT THE WORK
V.7 STUDY MODELS
VI.20 WORK IN PROGRESS
LOWER LEVEL
@ +44.35M
CEILING SCAPE
FROM ABOVE
31.90m
32.00m

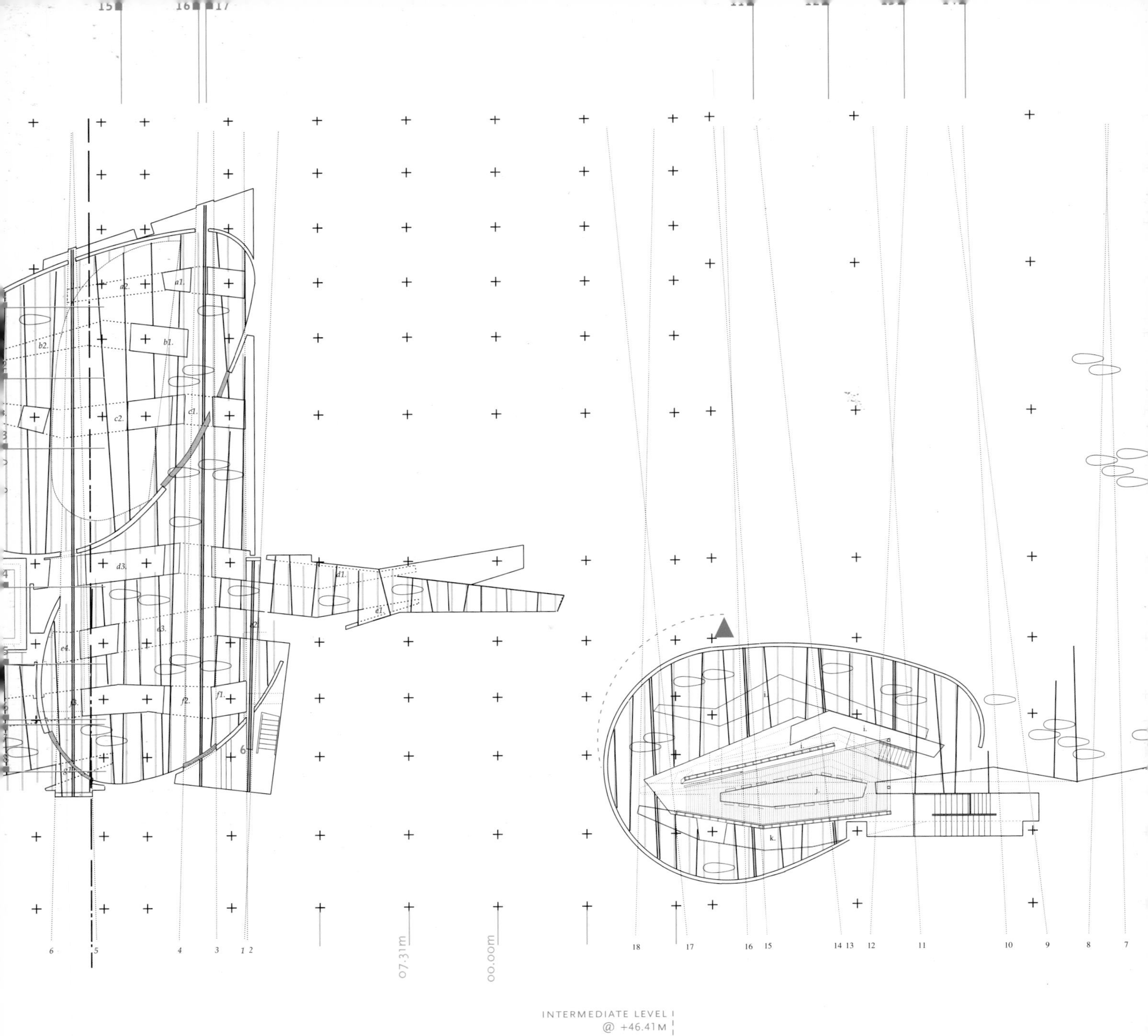

INTERMEDIATE LEVEL
@ +46.41M

LOWER LEVEL **1.** Cafe Area **2.** Storage **3.** Exhibition Area **4.** Food Prep Area **5.** Lecture Area **6.** Entrance **7.** Gallery INTERMEDIATE LEVEL **1.** Private Dining Room UPPER LEVEL **1.** Restaurant **2.** Storage **3.** Food Prep Area **4.** Service Bar Area **5.** Cocktail Area **6.** Gallery **7.** Display Niche

32.10m

32.20m

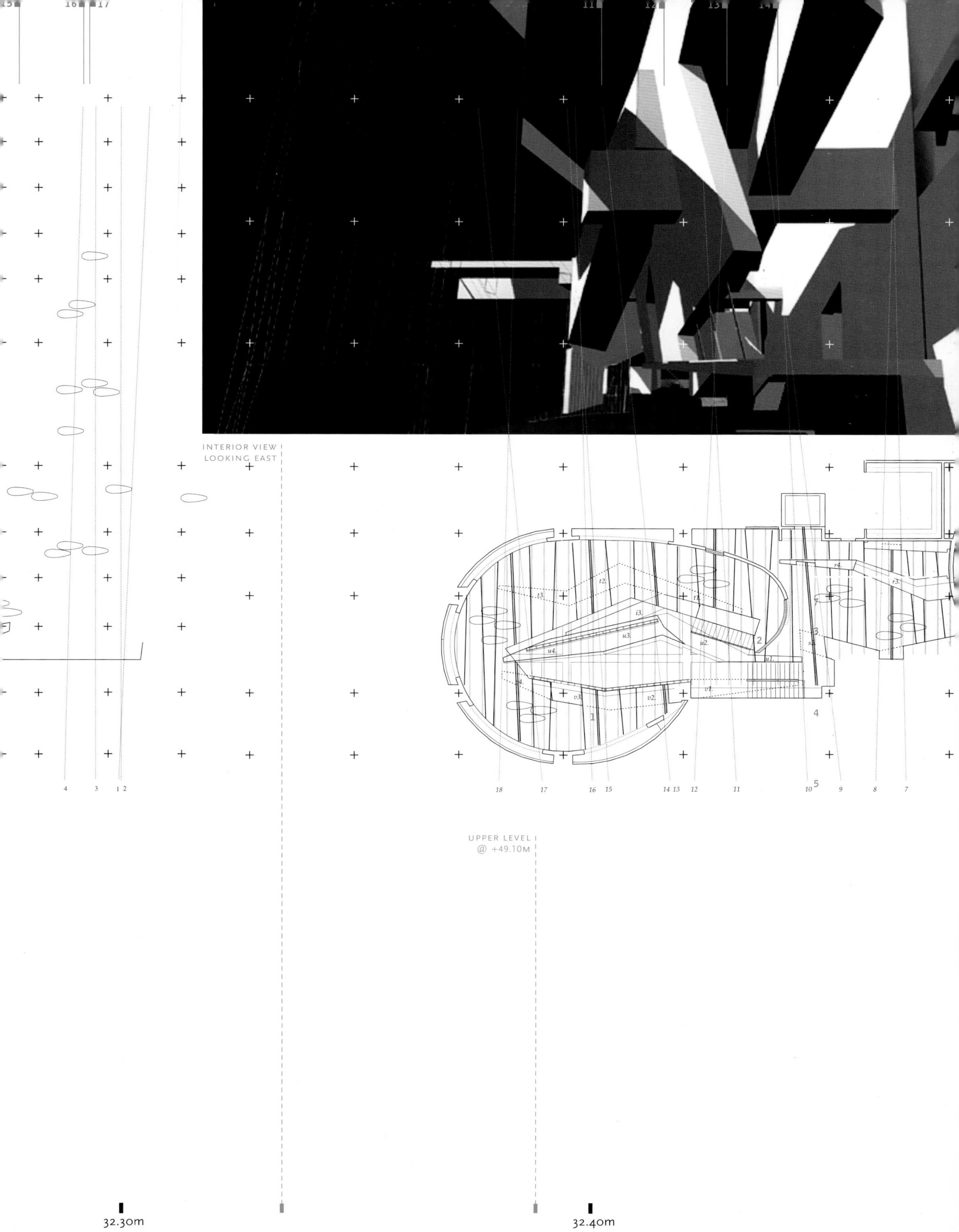

INTERIOR VIEW
LOOKING EAST
UPPER LEVEL
@ +49.10M
32.30m
32.40m

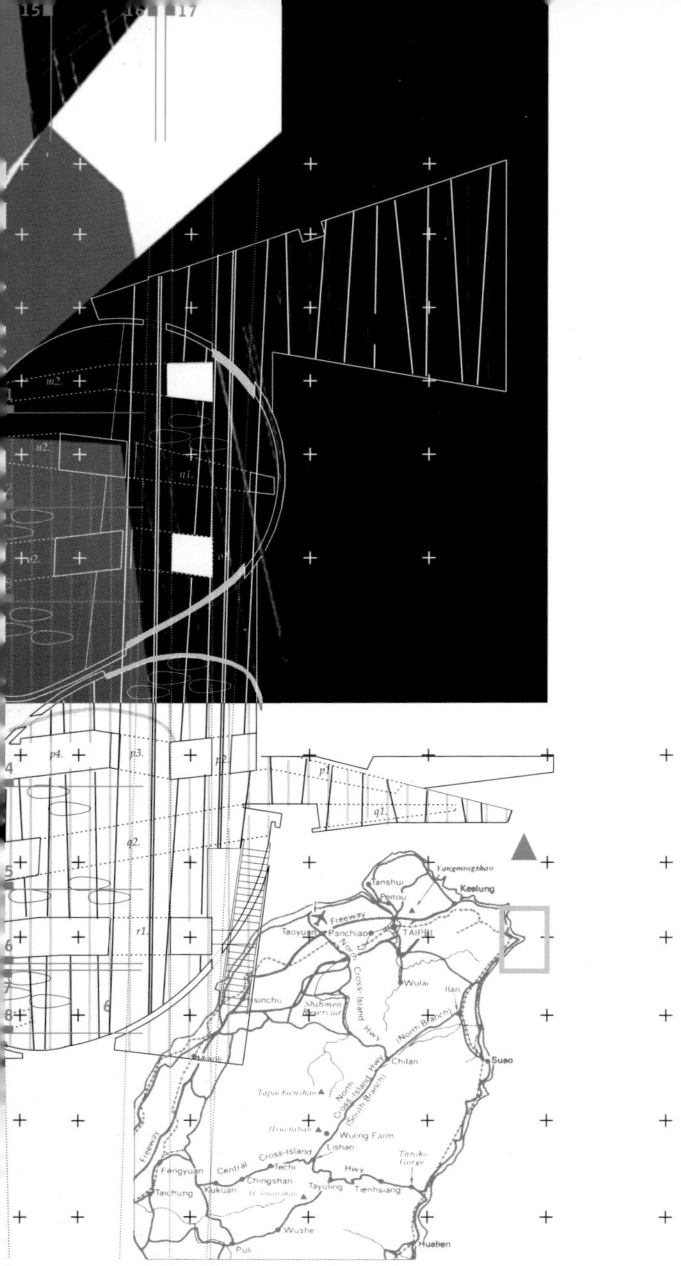

SITE MAP

EXISTING AREA WITH COLUMNS

IMPOSITION/STEEL RADII

USABLE AREA

IMPOSITION/SHARDS

IMPOSITION/TRANSVERSE SPEARS

RESOLUTION

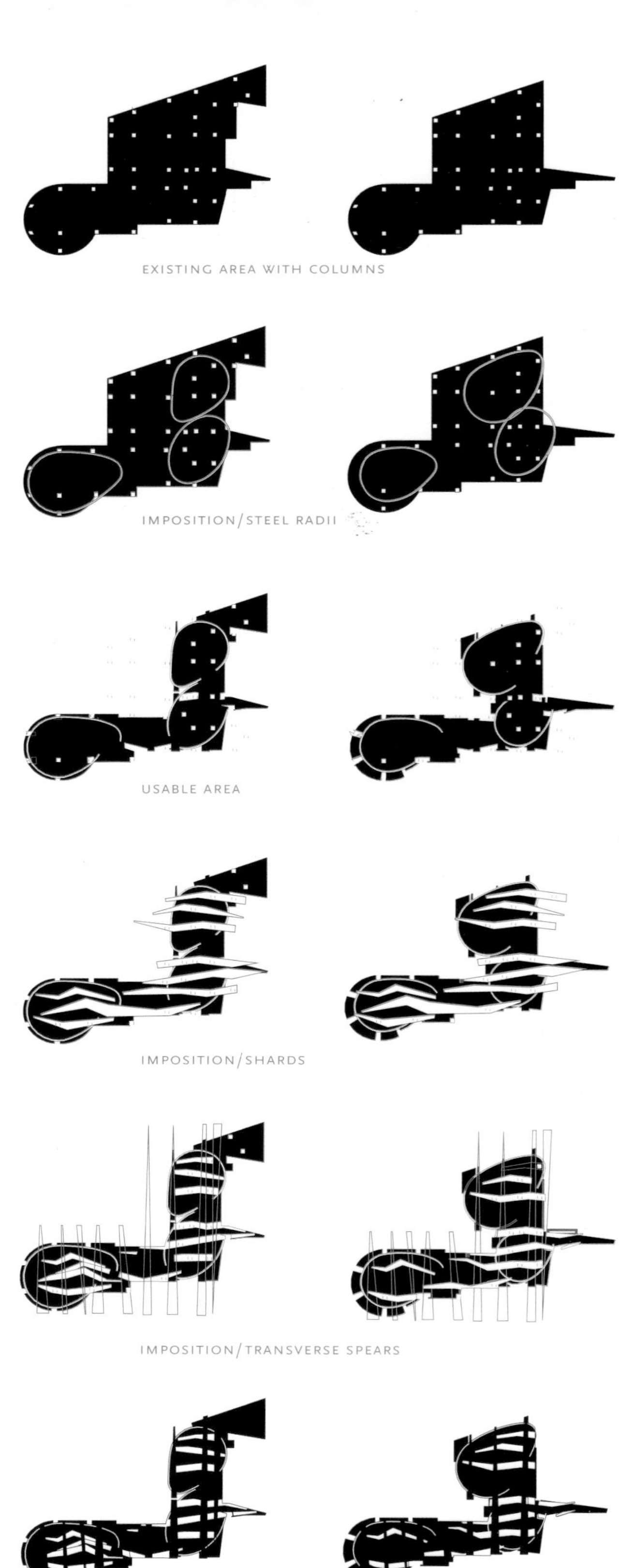

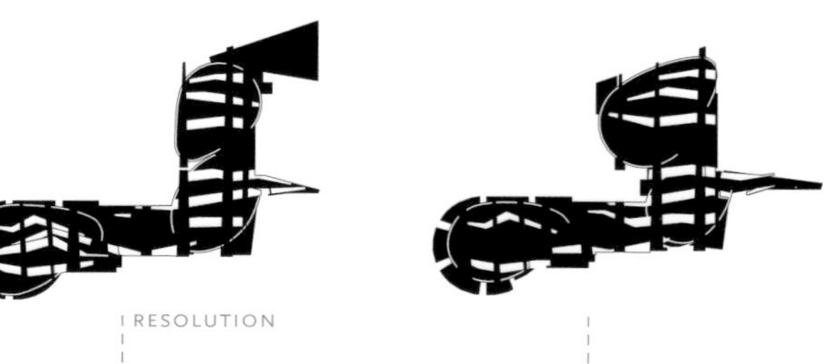

DIAGRAMS 1-6
@ +44.35M

DIAGRAMS 1-6
@ +49.10M

32.50m

32.60m

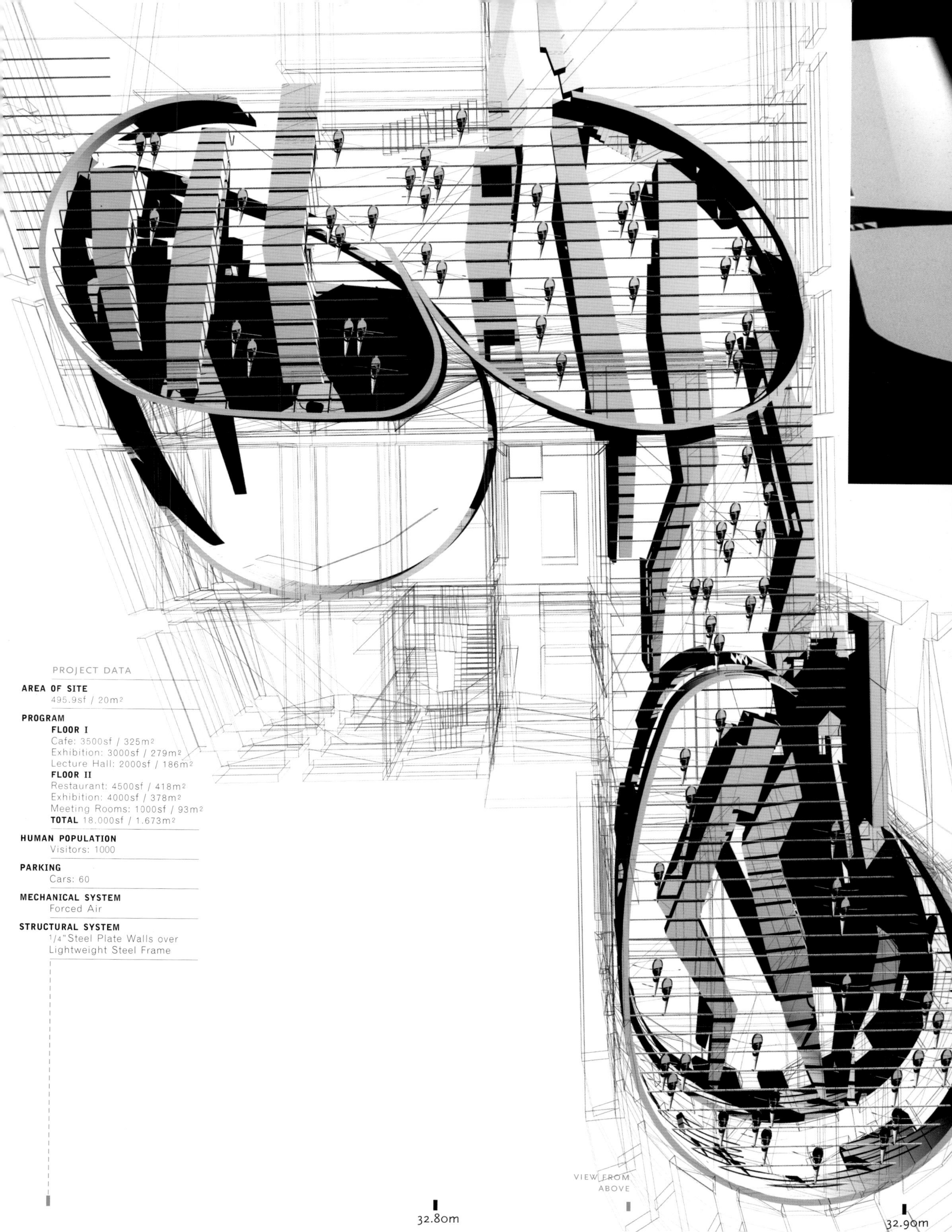
PROJECT DATA
AREA OF SITE
495.9sf / 20m2
PROGRAM
FLOOR I
Cafe: 3500sf / 325m2
Exhibition: 3000sf / 279m2
Lecture Hall: 2000sf / 186m2
FLOOR II
Restaurant: 4500sf / 418m2
Exhibition: 4000sf / 378m2
Meeting Rooms: 1000sf / 93m2
TOTAL 18.000sf / 1.673m2
HUMAN POPULATION
Visitors: 1000
PARKING
Cars: 60
MECHANICAL SYSTEM
Forced Air
STRUCTURAL SYSTEM
1/4" Steel Plate Walls over
Lightweight Steel Frame
VIEW FROM
ABOVE
32.80m
32.90m

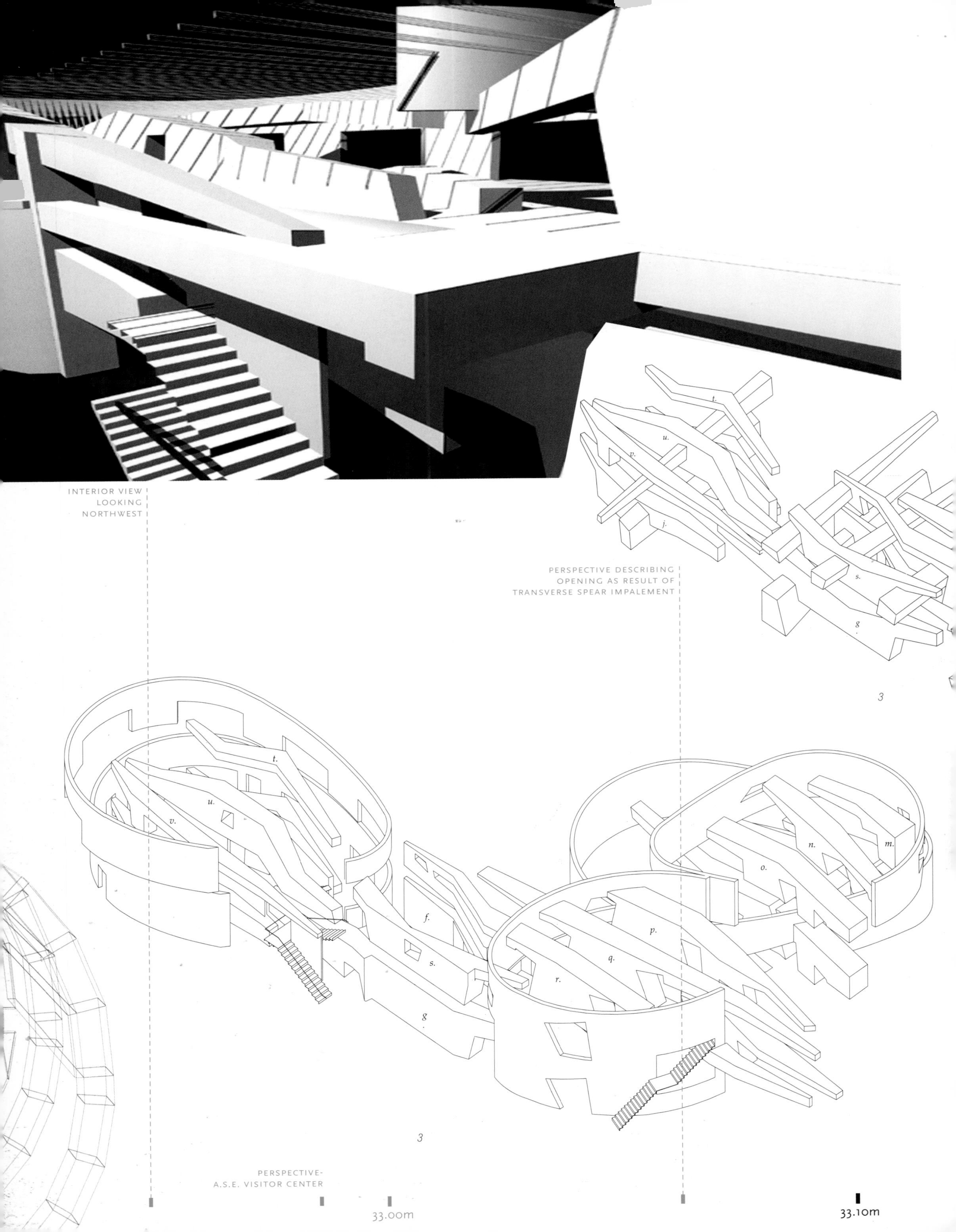
INTERIOR VIEW
LOOKING
NORTHWEST
PERSPECTIVE DESCRIBING
OPENING AS RESULT OF
TRANSVERSE SPEAR IMPALEMENT
t.
u.
v.
j.
s.
g.
3
t.
u.
v.
f.
s.
g.
n.
m.
o.
p.
q.
r.
3
PERSPECTIVE-
A.S.E. VISITOR CENTER
33.00m
33.10m

+49.10m
m.
a.
+44.35m
+53.85m
+49.10m
n.
b.
+44.35m
o.
c.
p.
d.
q.
e.
t.
r.
h.
f.
SECTIONS 1-8
v.
i.
u.
+53.85m
+49.10m
i.
+44.35m
33.20m
33.30m

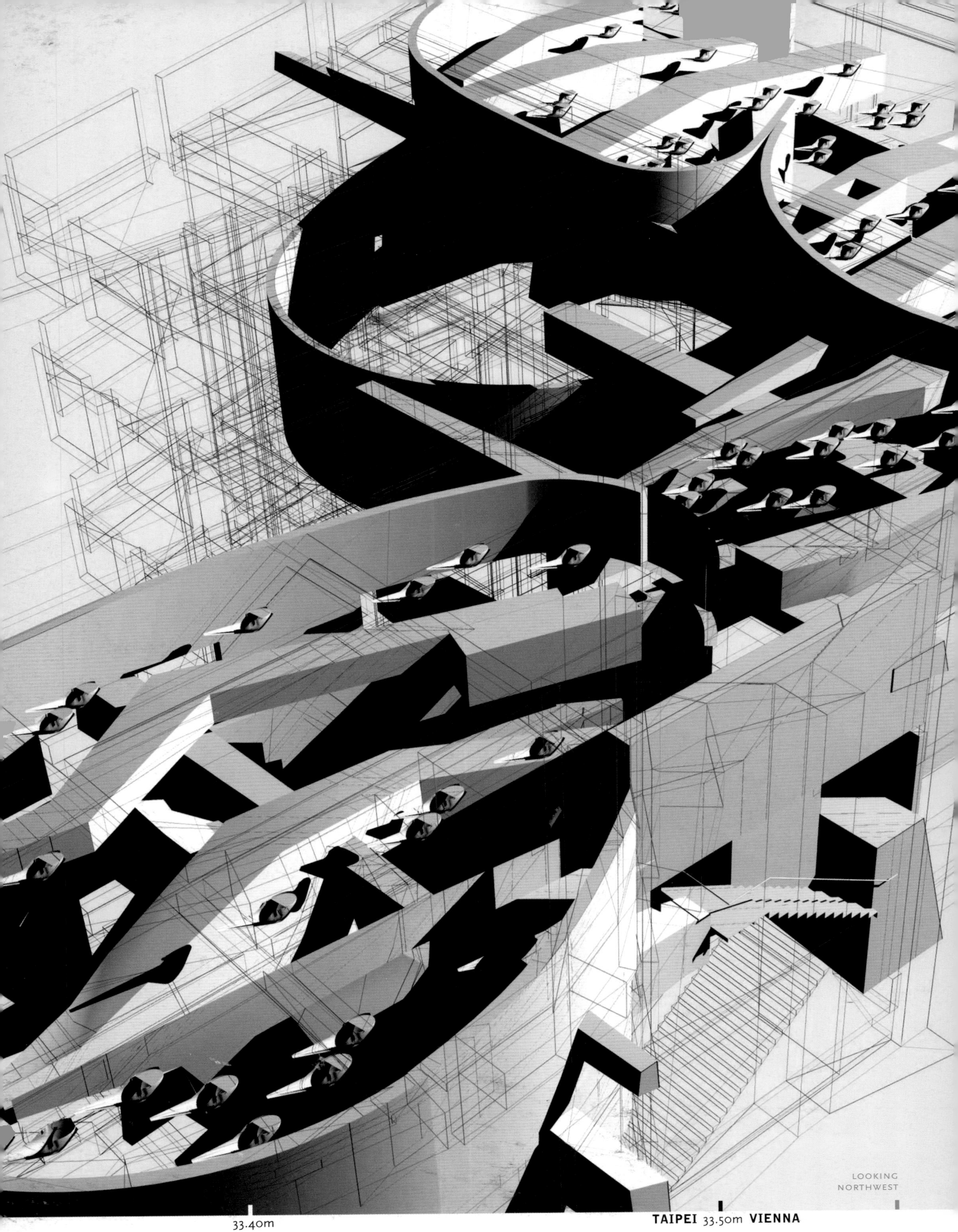
LOOKING
NORTHWEST
33.40m
TAIPEI 33.50m VIENNA

WOHNBAU WAGRAMER STRASSE
VIENNA HOUSING
1997
1996
1995
1994
1993
1992
33.60m
33.70m

WOHNBAU WAGRAMER STRASSE
VIENNA HOUSING

94444

PROJECT LOOKING NORTH

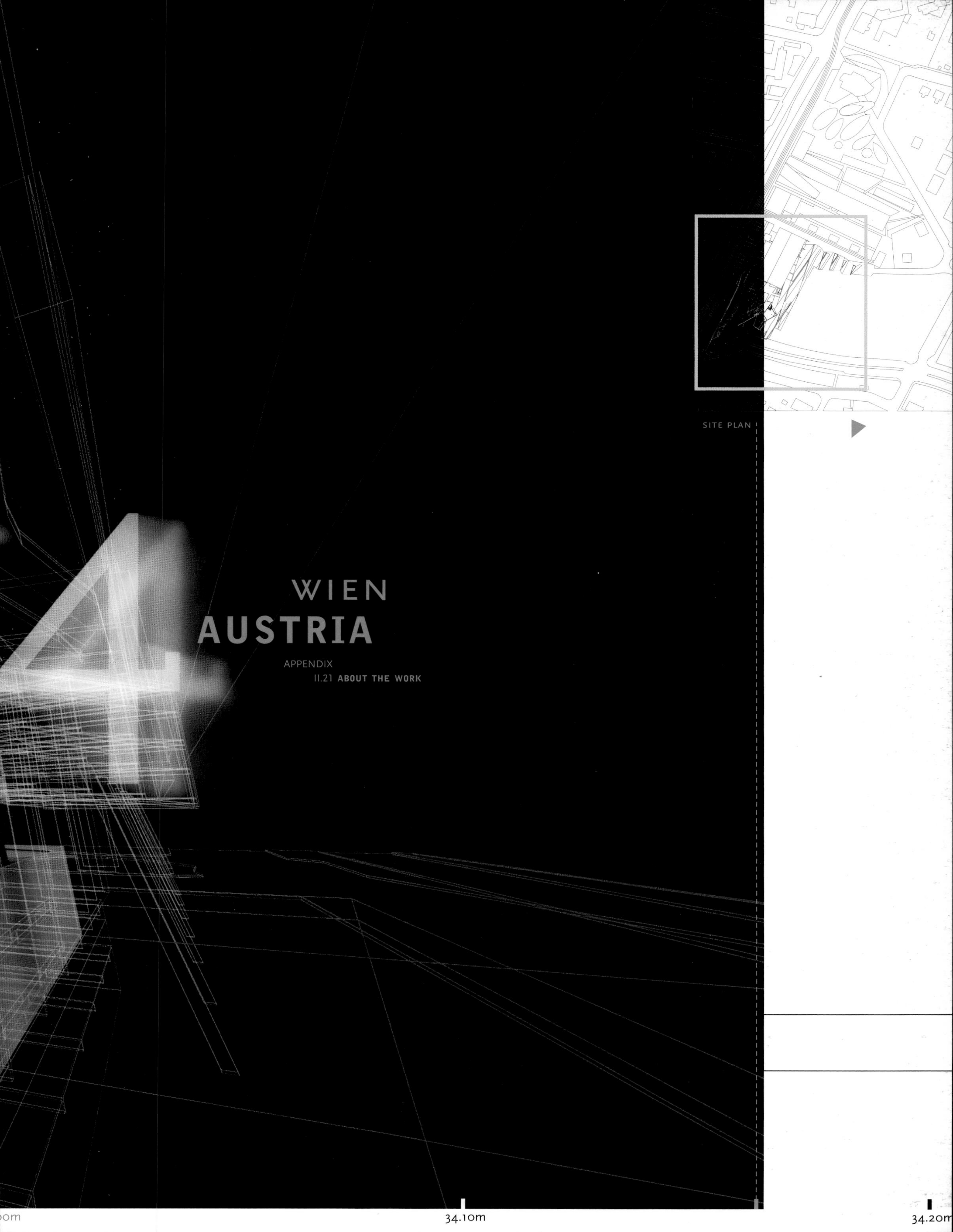
SITE PLAN
4
WIEN
AUSTRIA
APPENDIX
II.21 ABOUT THE WORK
34.10m
34.20m

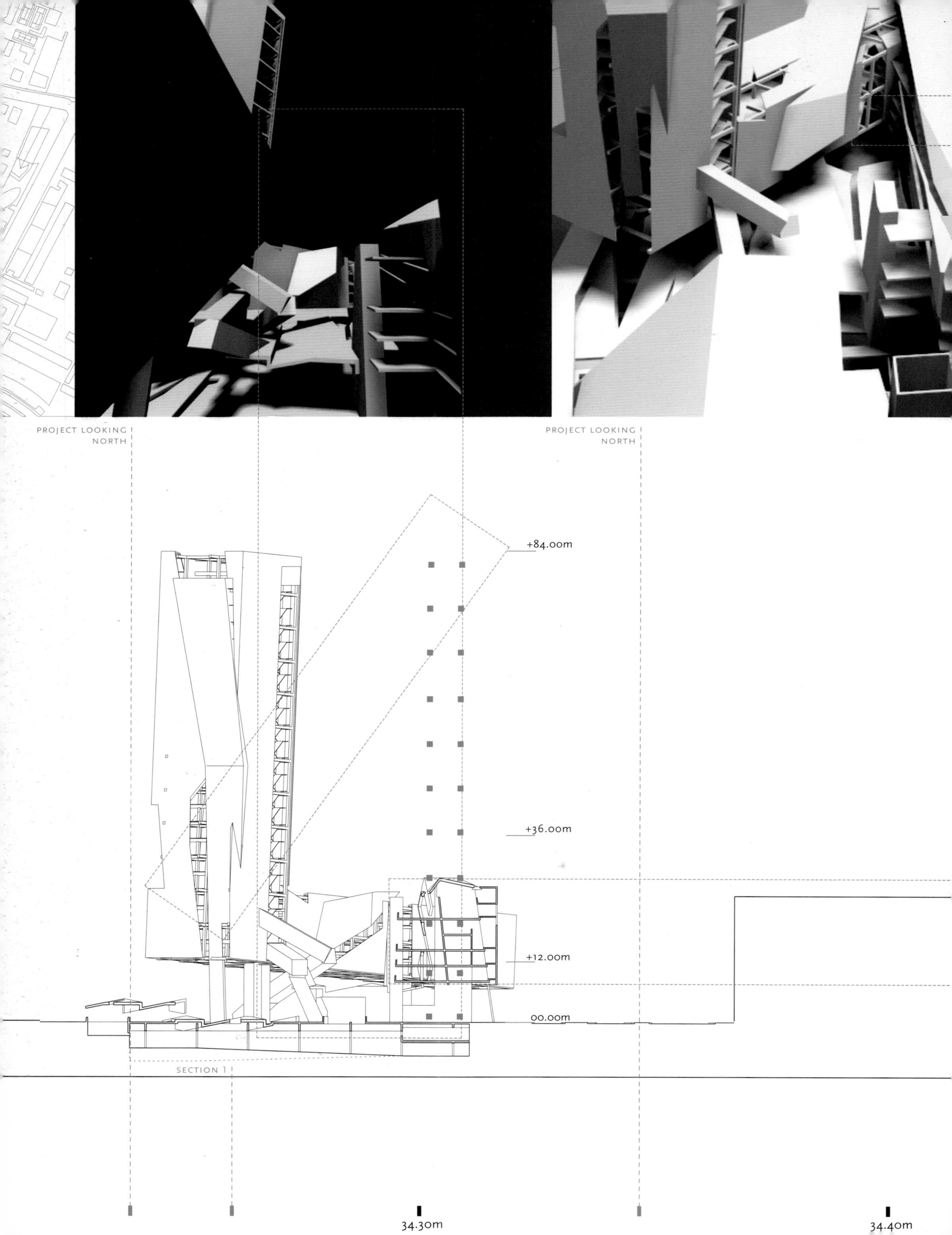
PROJECT LOOKING NORTH
PROJECT LOOKING NORTH
+84.00m
+36.00m
+12.00m
00.00m
SECTION 1
34.30m
34.40m

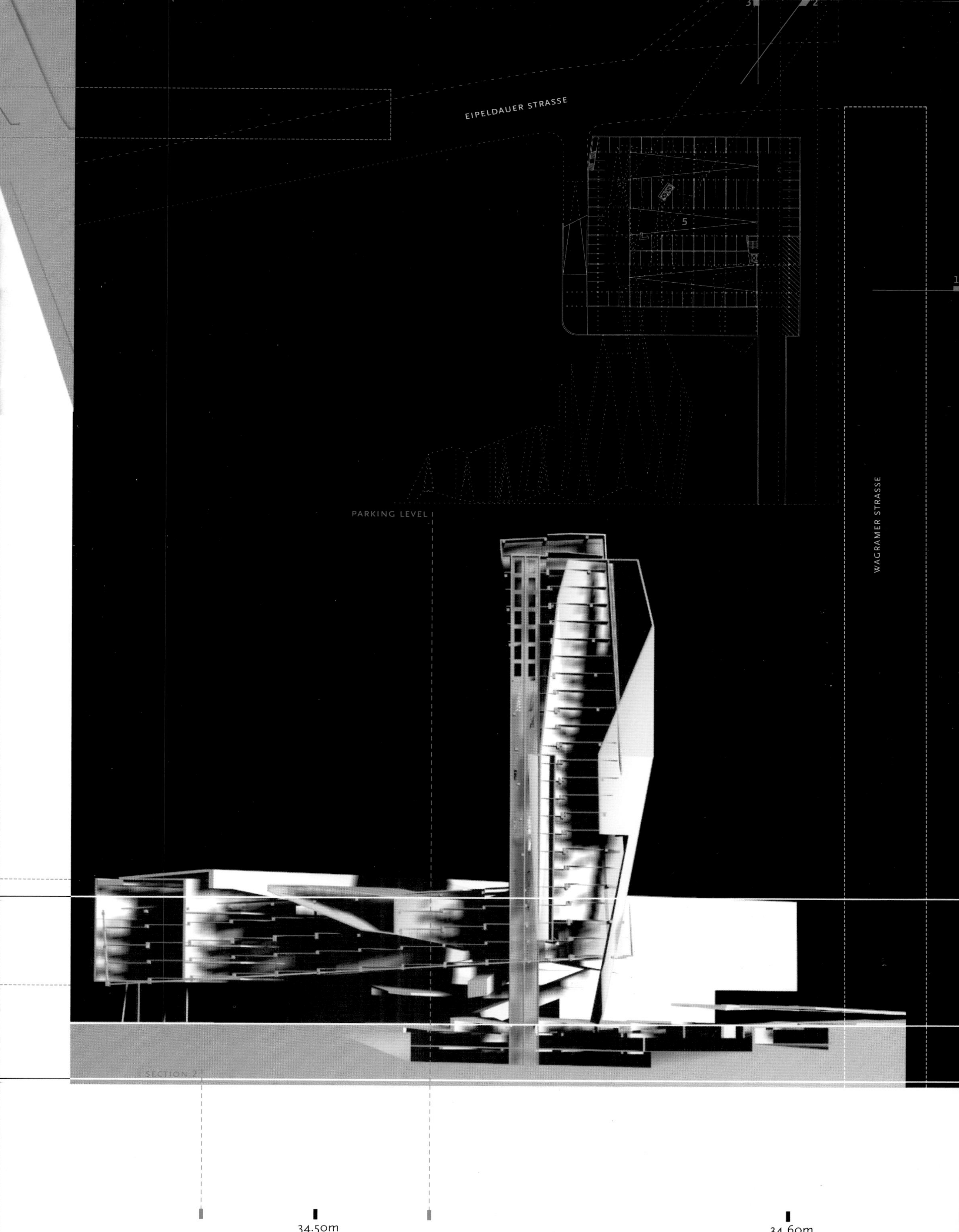

EIPELDAUER STRASSE
5
WAGRAMER STRASSE
PARKING LEVEL
SECTION 2
34.50m
34.60m

PROJECT LOOKING NORTHEAST

PARKING LEVEL – LEVEL @ +36M
1. Common/Public Use **2.** Landscape
3. Commercial **4.** Residential **5.** Parking

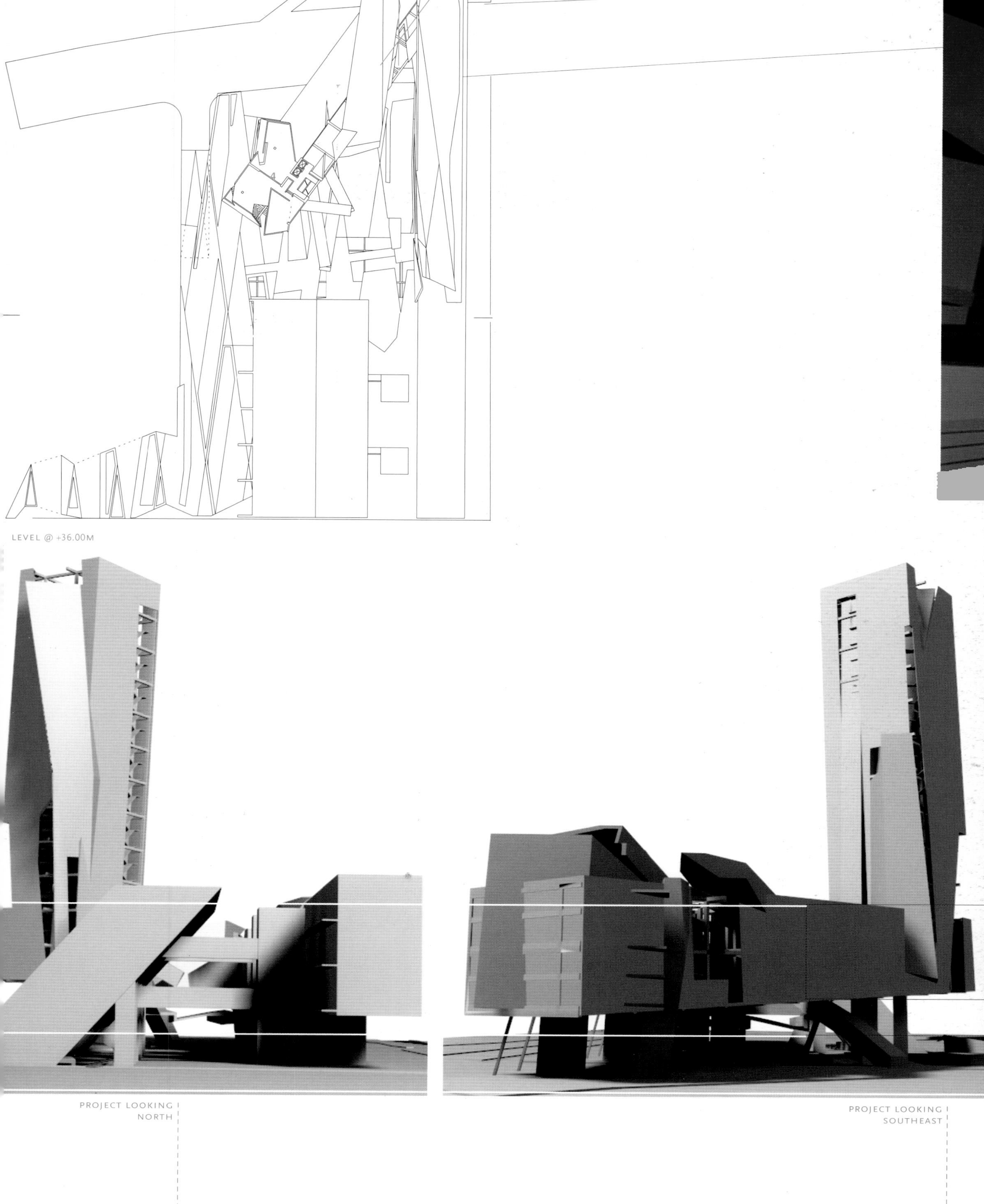

LEVEL @ +36.00M

PROJECT LOOKING NORTH

PROJECT LOOKING SOUTHEAST

34.90m

35.00m

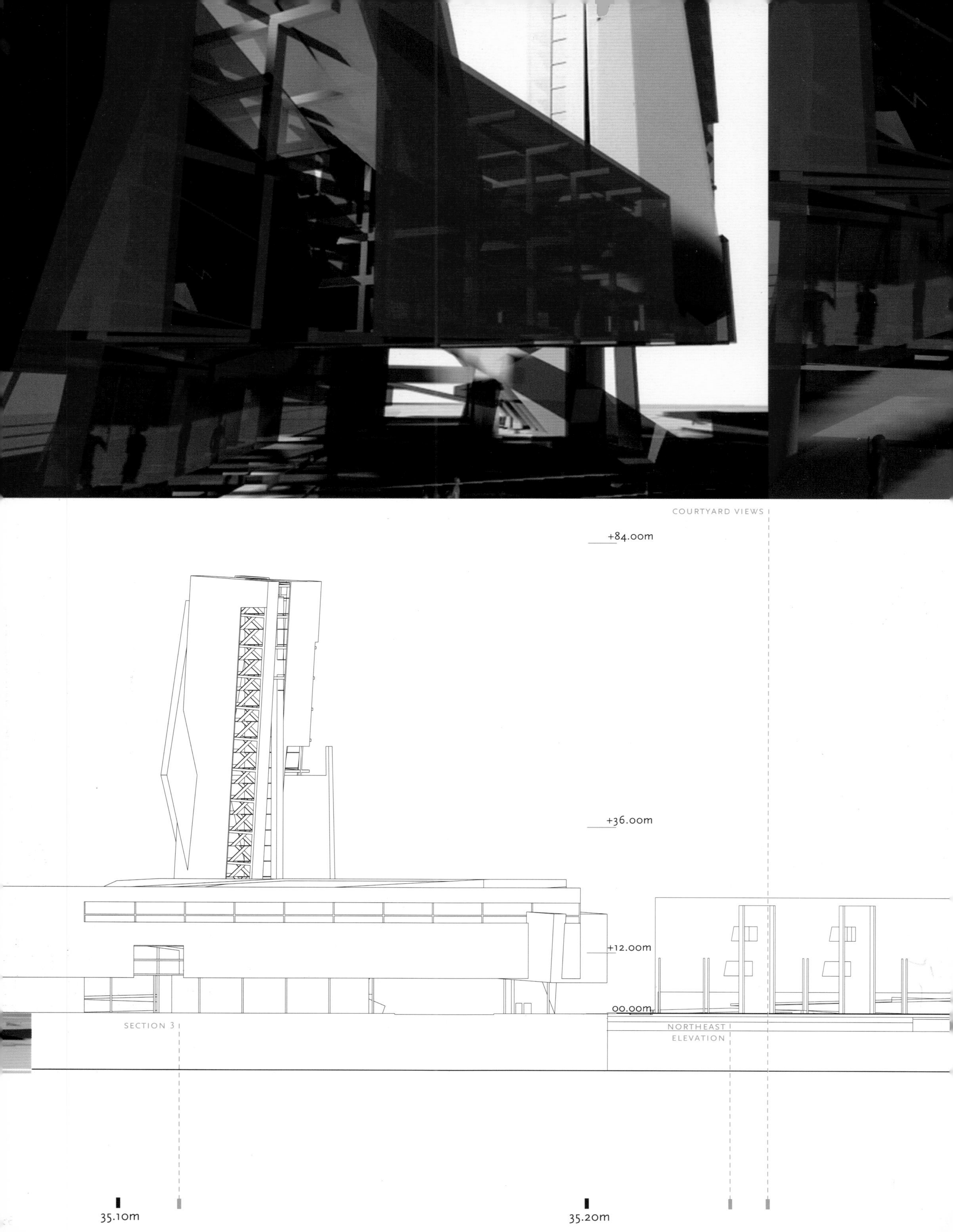
COURTYARD VIEWS
+84.00m
+36.00m
+12.00m
00.00m
SECTION 3
NORTHEAST
ELEVATION
35.10m
35.20m

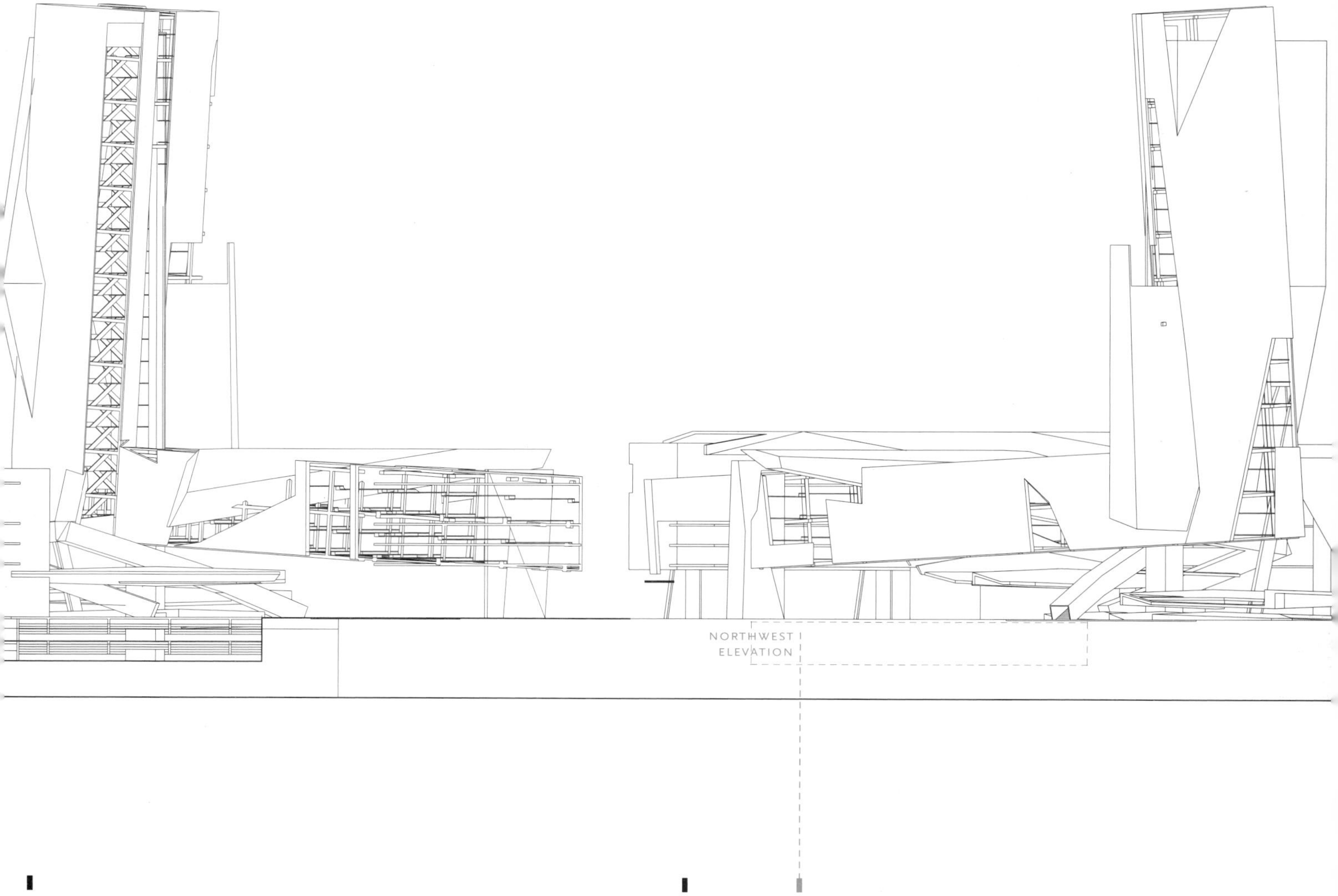

NORTHWEST
ELEVATION

35.30m

35.40m

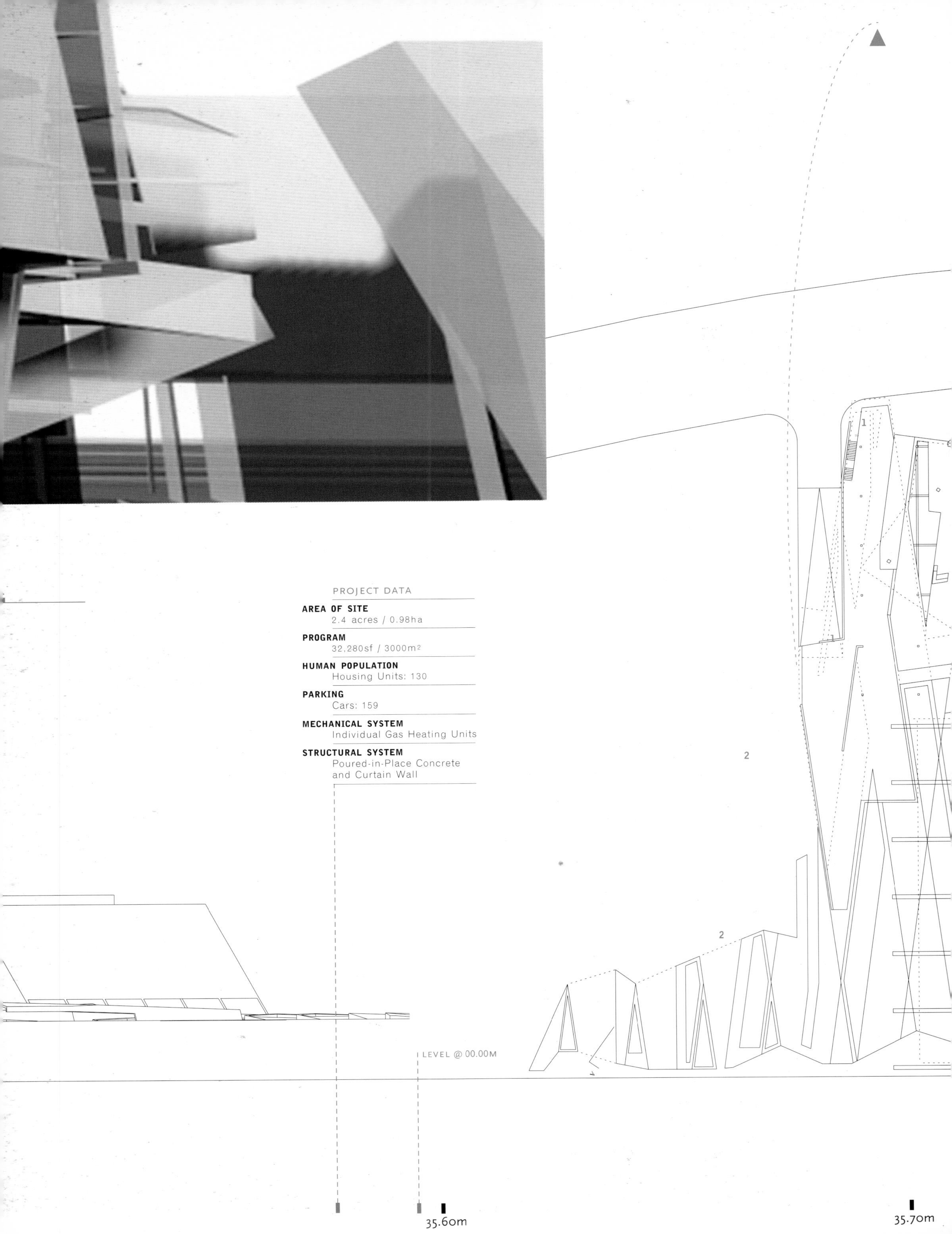

PROJECT DATA

AREA OF SITE
2.4 acres / 0.98ha

PROGRAM
32,280sf / 3000m^2

HUMAN POPULATION
Housing Units: 130

PARKING
Cars: 159

MECHANICAL SYSTEM
Individual Gas Heating Units

STRUCTURAL SYSTEM
Poured-in-Place Concrete and Curtain Wall

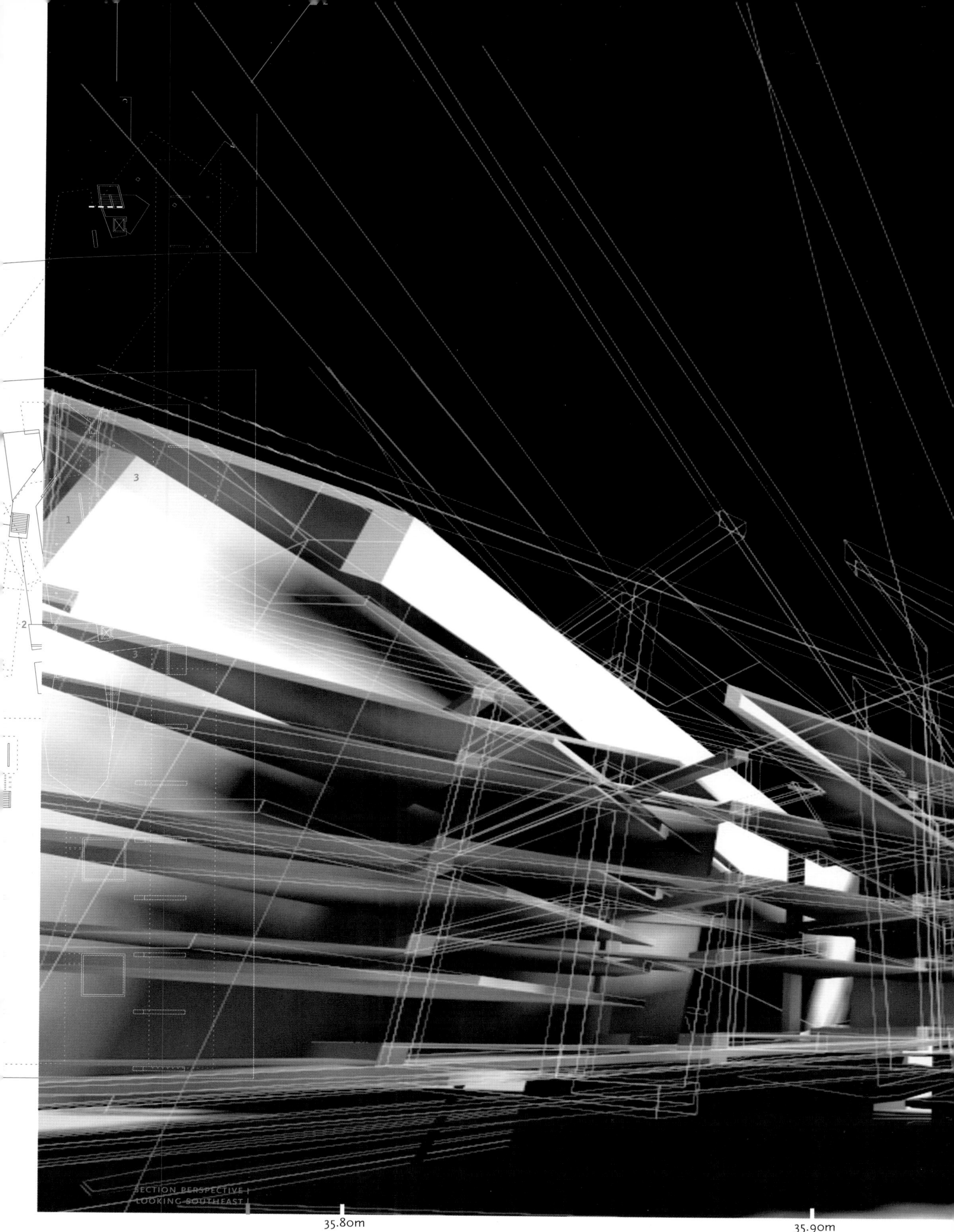
3
1
2
3
SECTION PERSPECTIVE |
LOOKING SOUTHEAST |
35.80m
35.90m

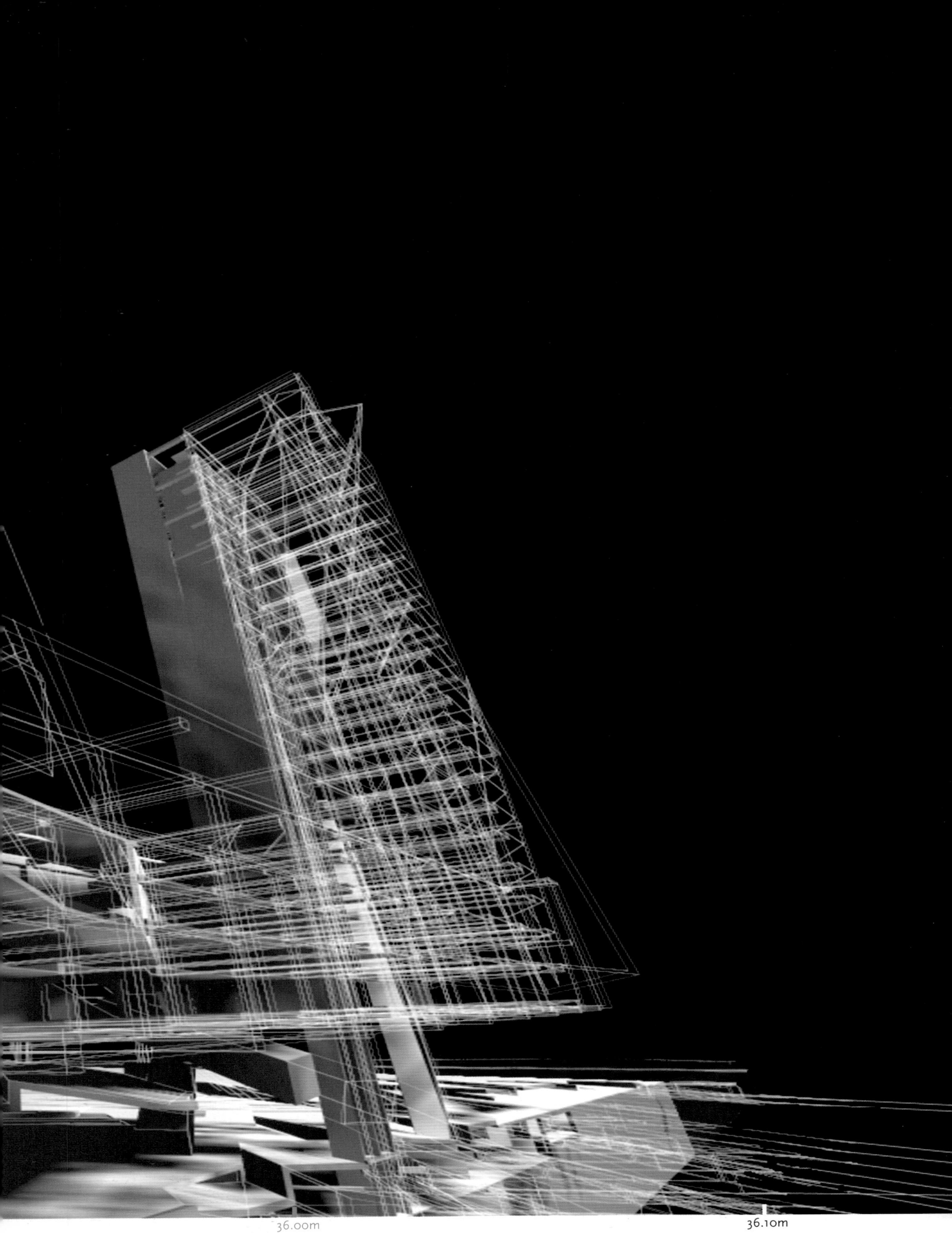
36.00m
36.10m

1997

1996

1995

1994

1993

1992

VIENNA 36.20m **POMONA**

36.30m

DIAMOND RANCH HIGH SCHOOL
I
93211
36.40m
36.50m

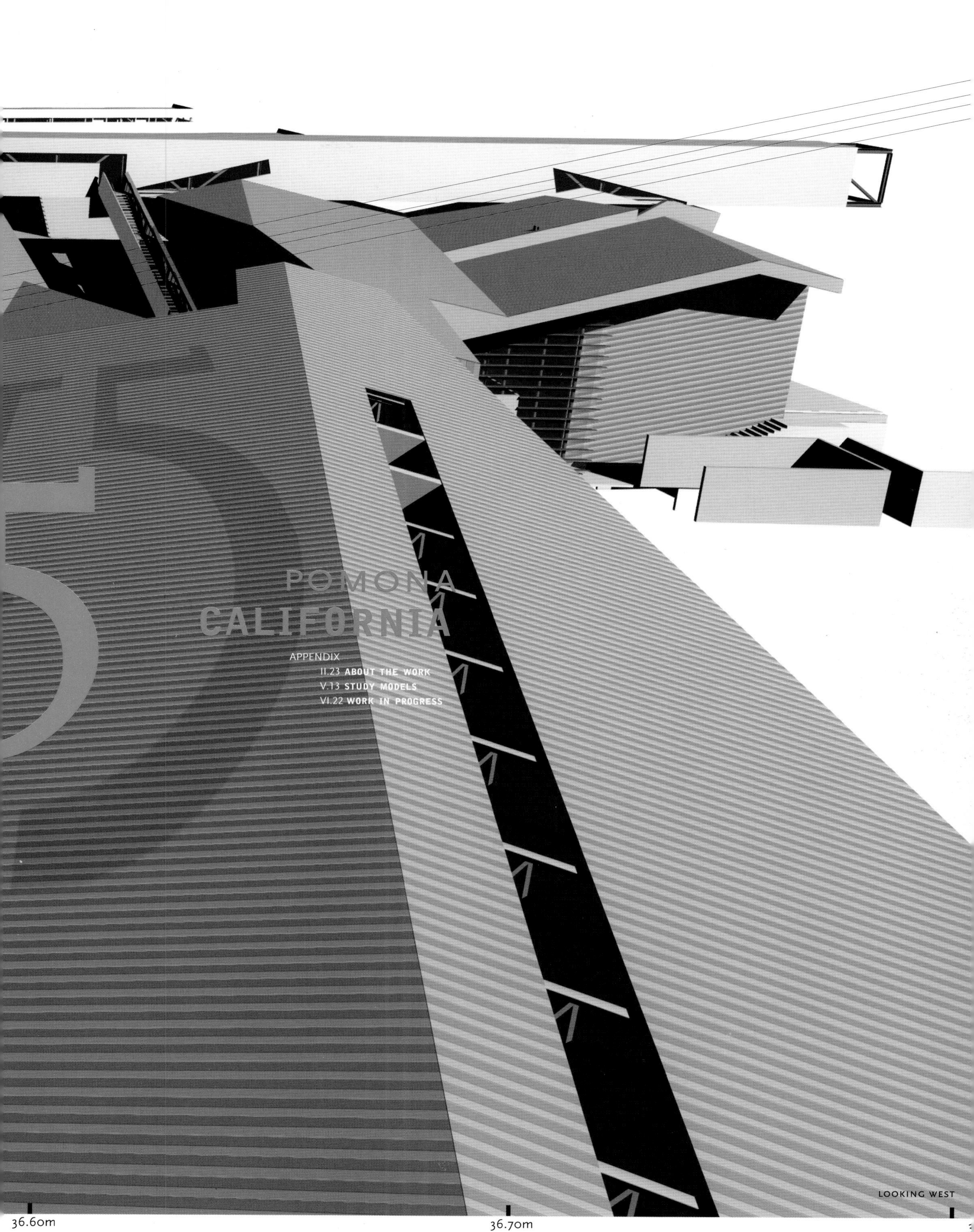
5
POMONA
CALIFORNIA
APPENDIX
II.23 ABOUT THE WORK
V.13 STUDY MODELS
VI.22 WORK IN PROGRESS
LOOKING WEST
36.60m
36.70m

1
2
3
4
5
SITE PLAN
LOOKING SOUTH

SITE, AERIAL VIEW
SECTION 1
+37.00ft
+31.00ft
+24.00ft
+12.00ft
00.00ft
37.10m

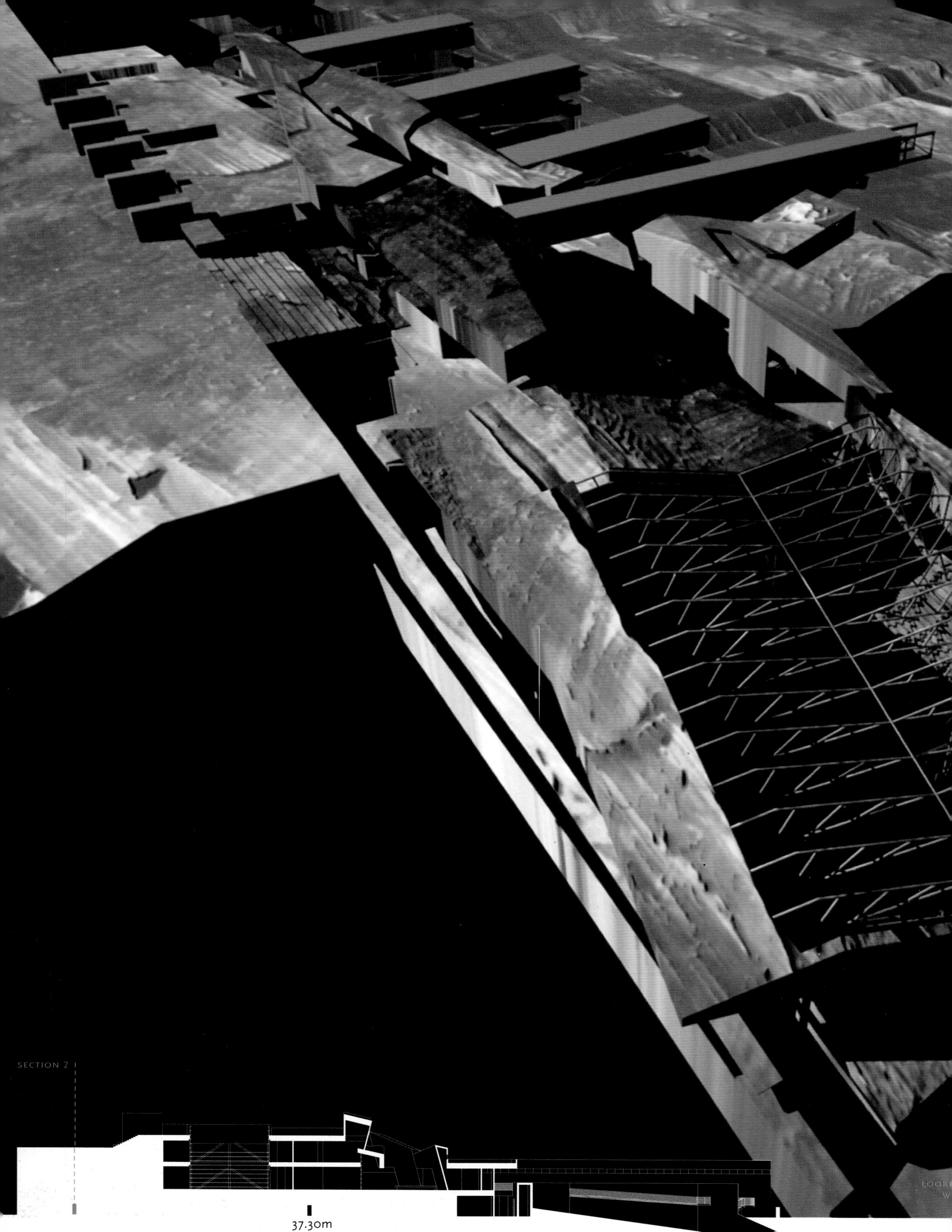
SECTION 2
37.30m

06 0708 09
27
26
2829 30
40 41 42 43
44
10 11 12 13 14 15 20 2122232425 34 35 36 37 3839
01 0403 02 05
31 32 33
45 46
CTION 3
+37.00ft
+31.00ft
+24.50ft
+12.00ft
00.00ft
37.50m

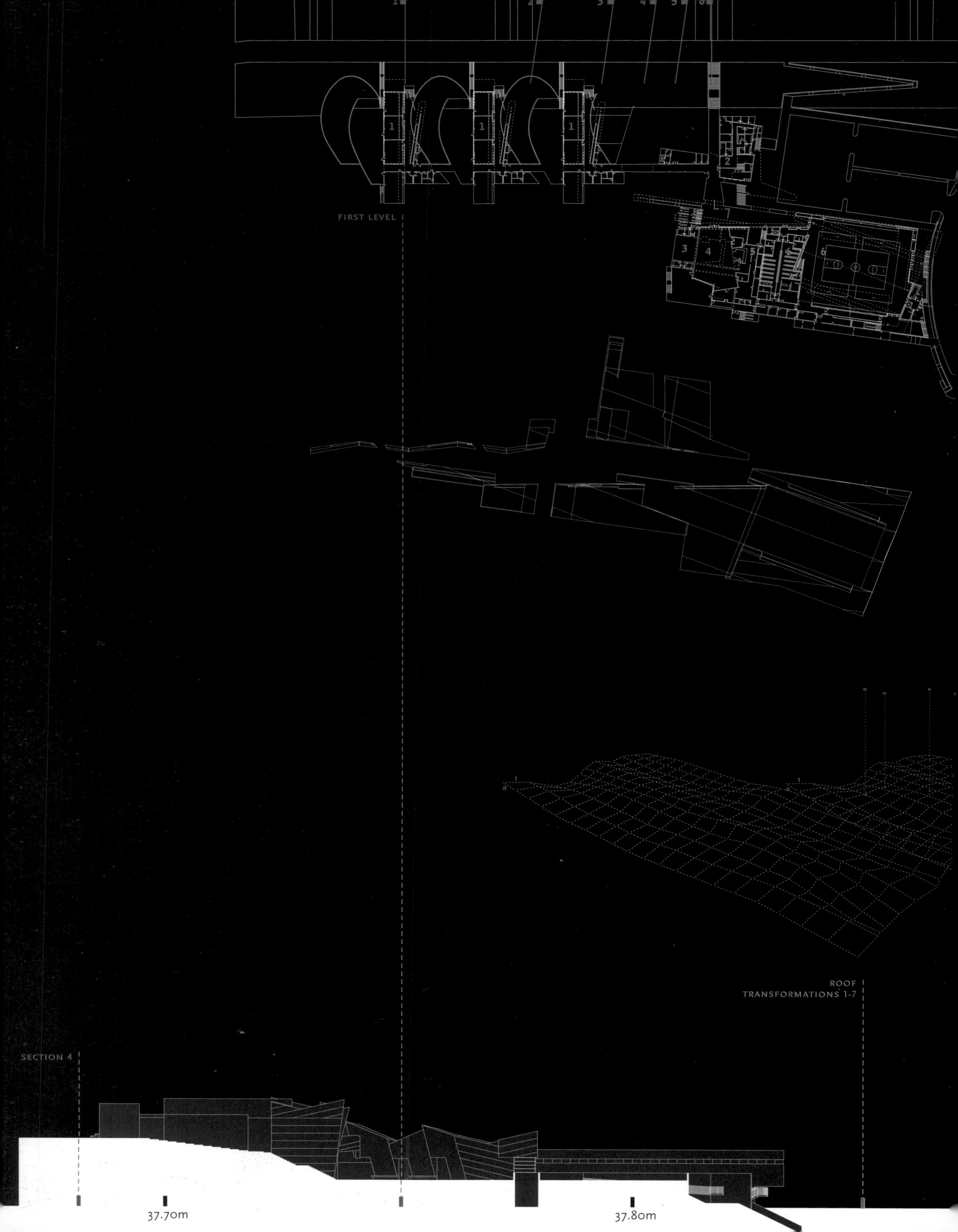
FIRST LEVEL
ROOF
TRANSFORMATIONS 1-7
SECTION 4
37.70m
37.80m

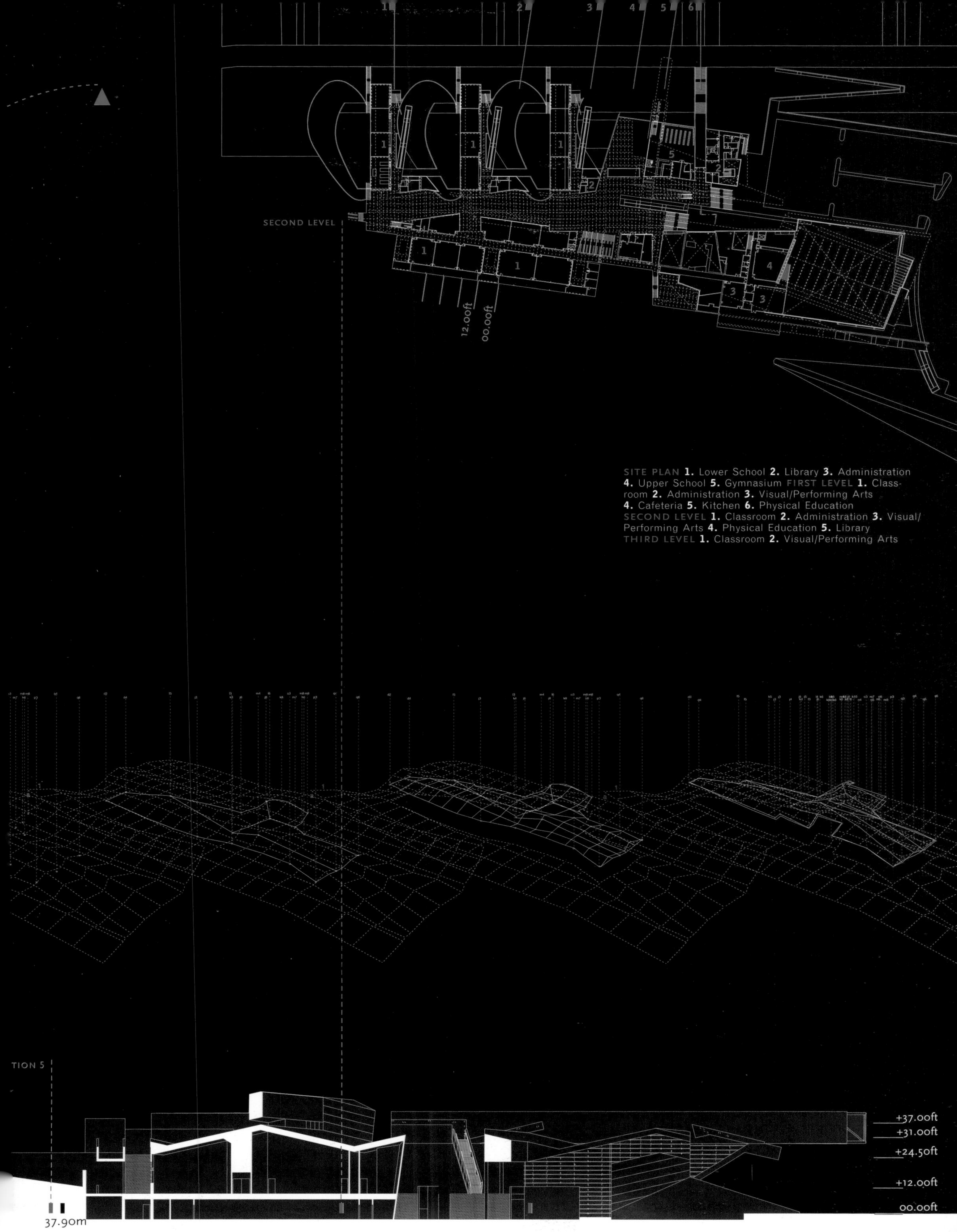

SITE PLAN **1.** Lower School **2.** Library **3.** Administration **4.** Upper School **5.** Gymnasium FIRST LEVEL **1.** Classroom **2.** Administration **3.** Visual/Performing Arts **4.** Cafeteria **5.** Kitchen **6.** Physical Education SECOND LEVEL **1.** Classroom **2.** Administration **3.** Visual/Performing Arts **4.** Physical Education **5.** Library THIRD LEVEL **1.** Classroom **2.** Visual/Performing Arts

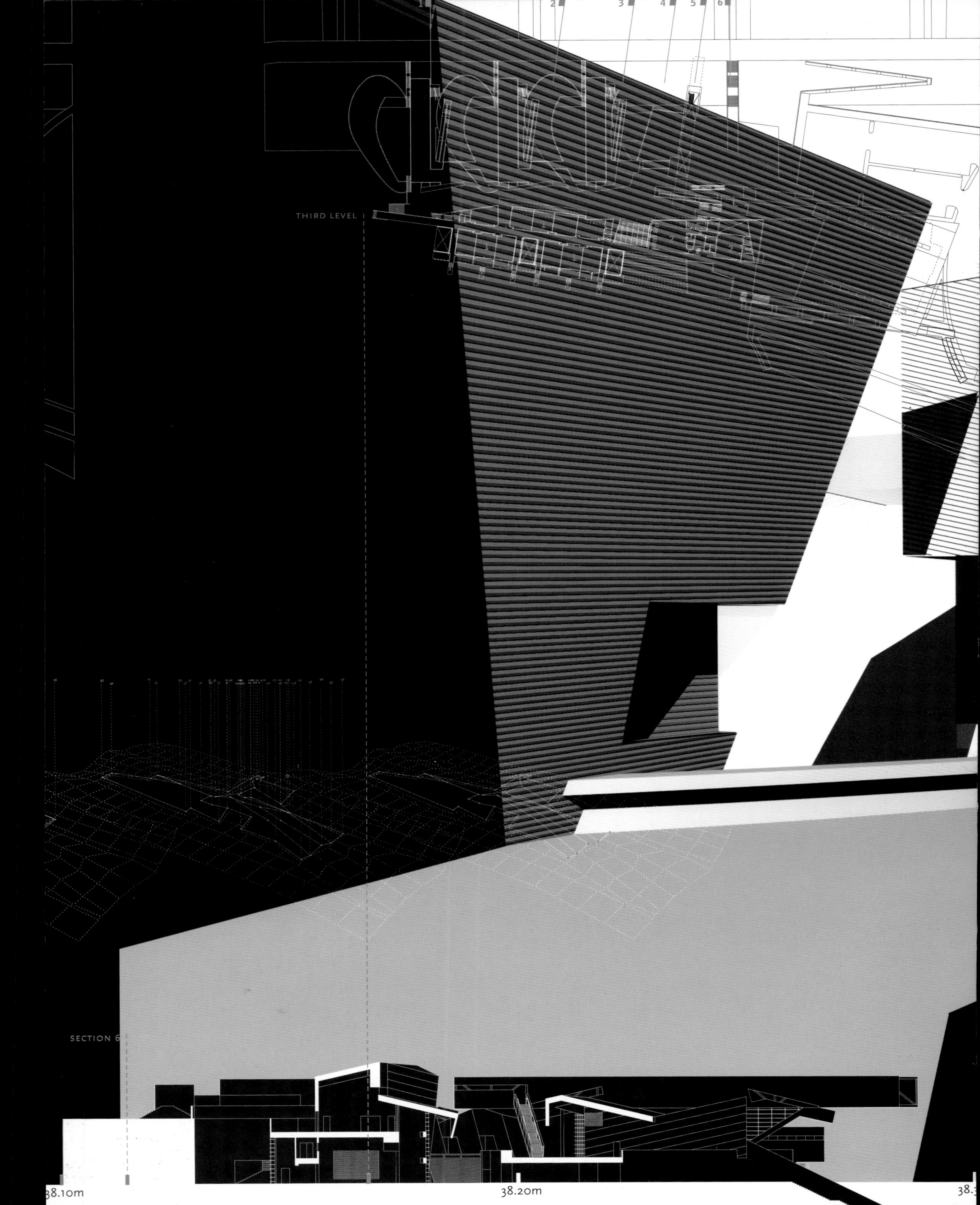
1
2
3
4
5
6
THIRD LEVEL
SECTION 6
38.10m
38.20m

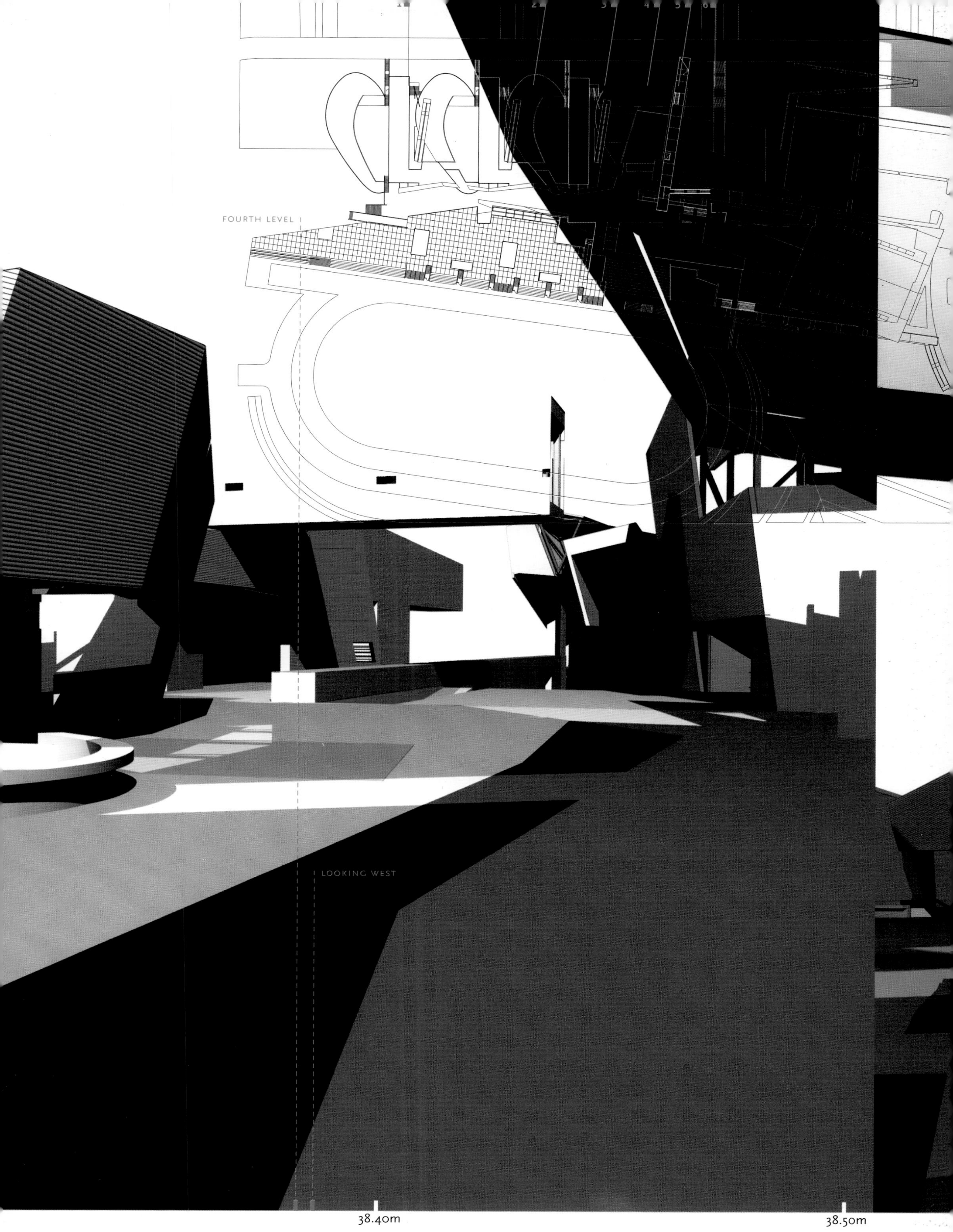
FOURTH LEVEL
LOOKING WEST
38.40m
38.50m

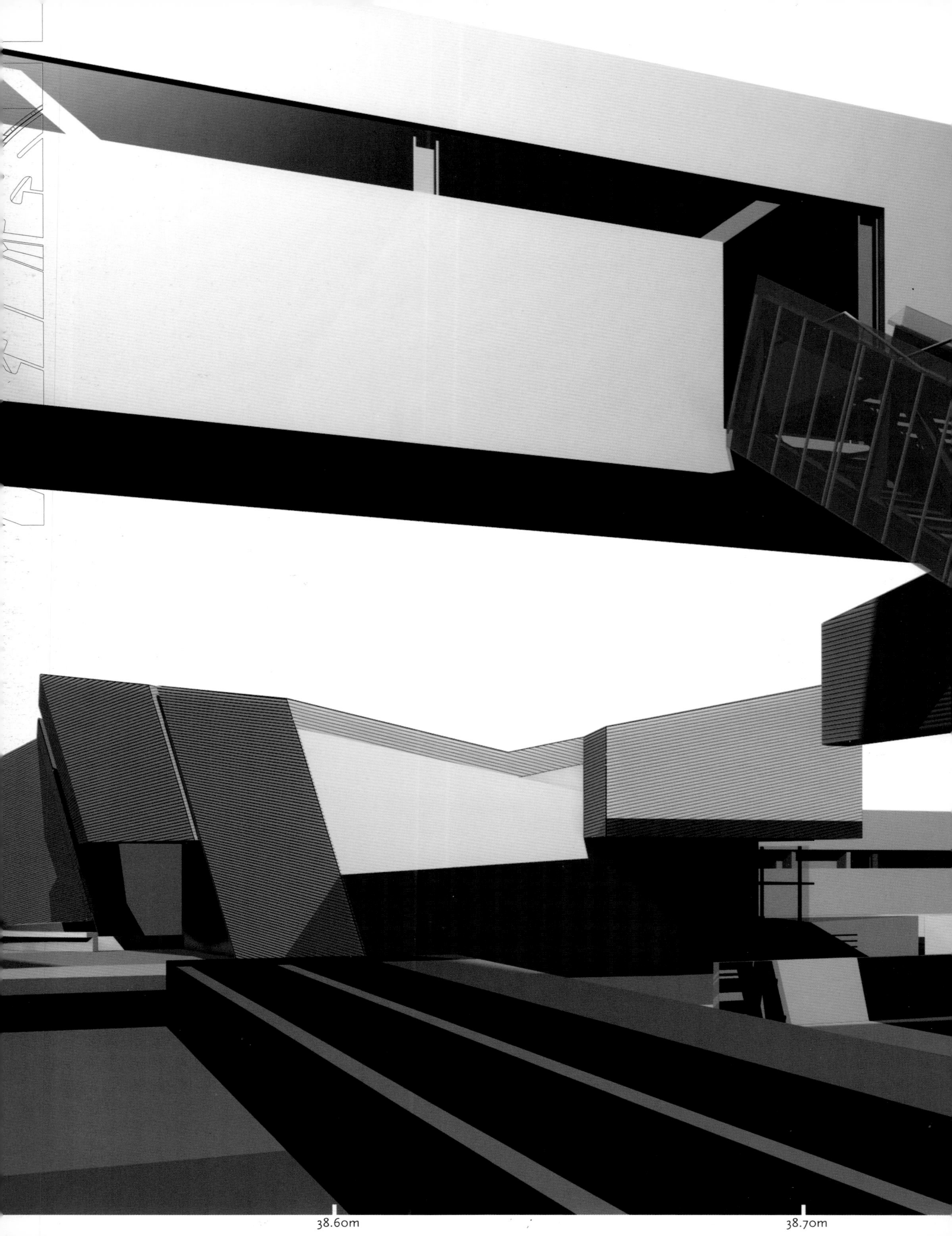
38.60m
38.70m

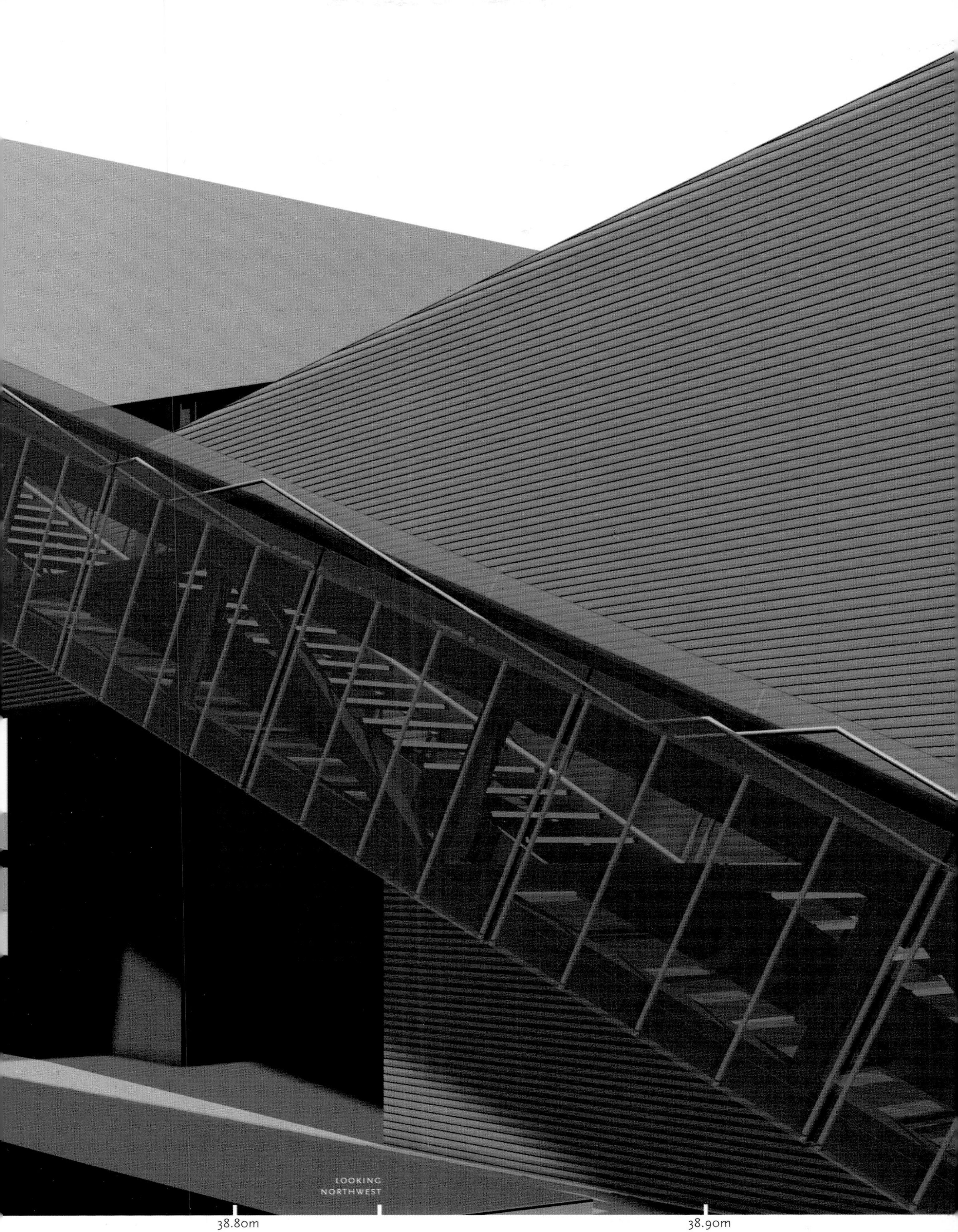
LOOKING
NORTHWEST

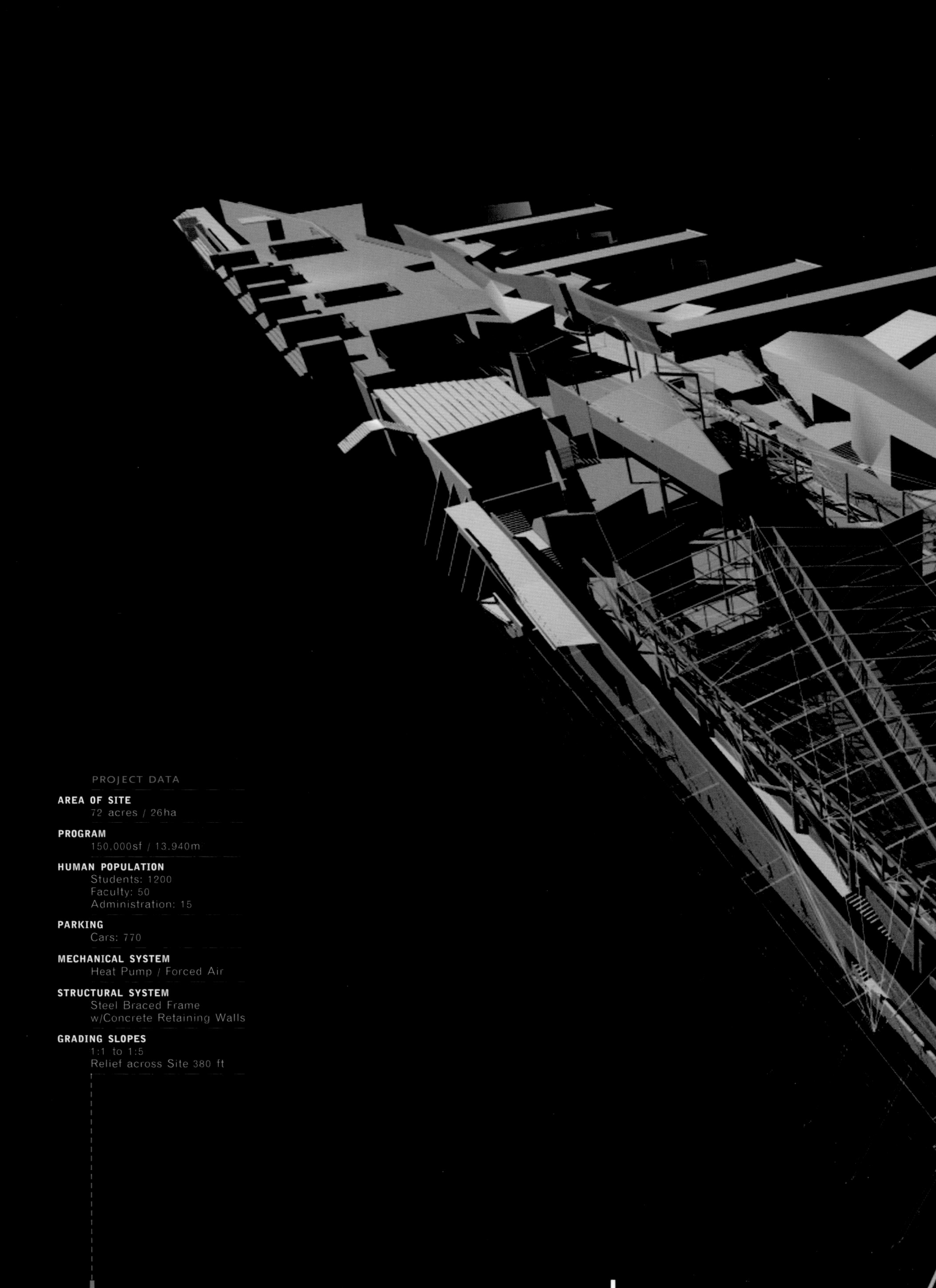

PROJECT DATA

AREA OF SITE
72 acres / 26ha

PROGRAM
150,000sf / 13,940m

HUMAN POPULATION
Students: 1200
Faculty: 50
Administration: 15

PARKING
Cars: 770

MECHANICAL SYSTEM
Heat Pump / Forced Air

STRUCTURAL SYSTEM
Steel Braced Frame
w/Concrete Retaining Walls

GRADING SLOPES
1:1 to 1:5
Relief across Site 380 ft

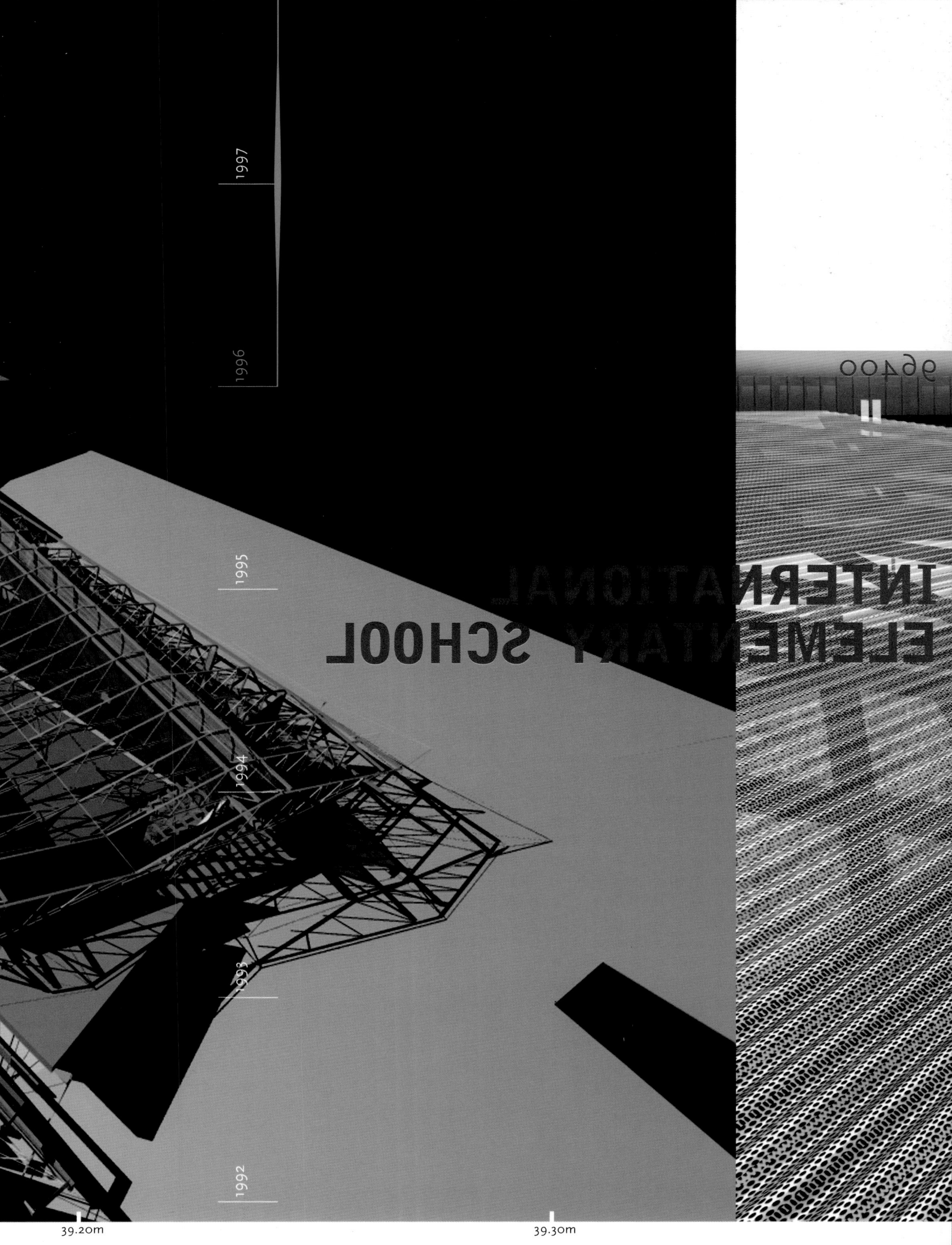
96400
INTERNATIONAL
ELEMENTARY SCHOOL
1997
1996
1995
1994
1993
1992
39.20m
39.30m

39.40m

39.50m

6 LONG BEACH CALIFORNIA

APPENDIX

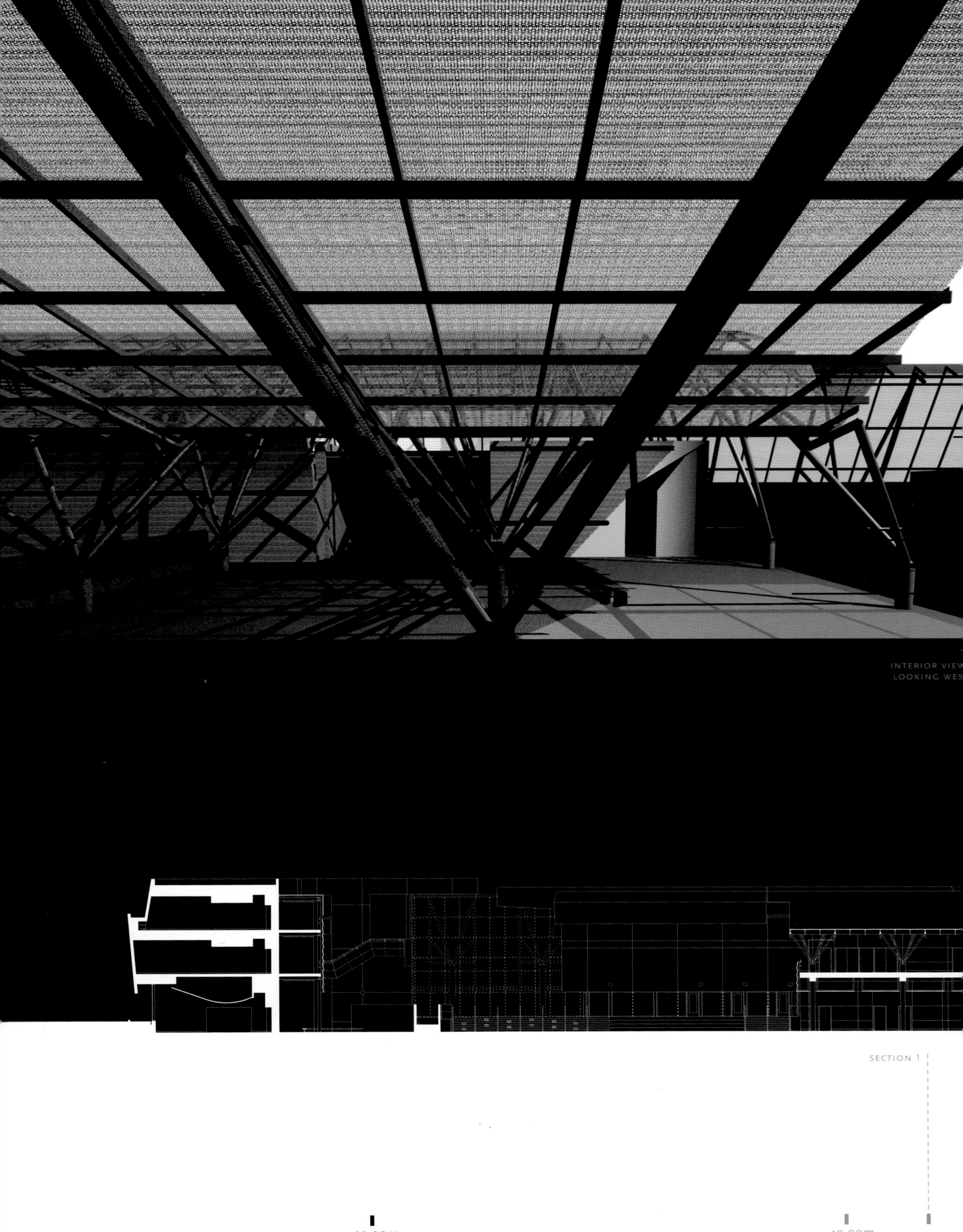

INTERIOR VIEW
LOOKING WES

SECTION 1

39.90m

40.00m

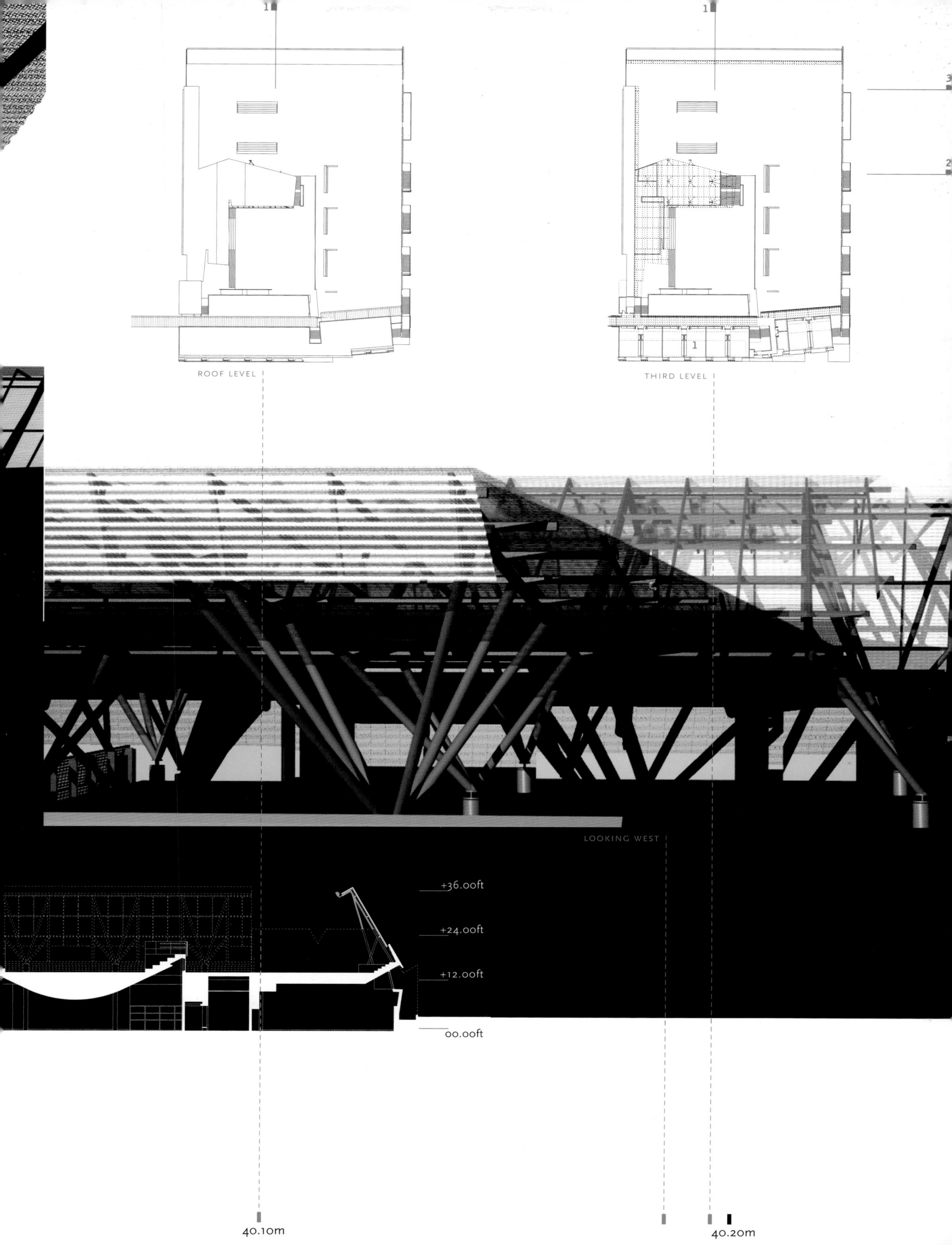
1
1
3
2
1
ROOF LEVEL
THIRD LEVEL
LOOKING WEST
+36.00ft
+24.00ft
+12.00ft
00.00ft
40.10m
40.20m

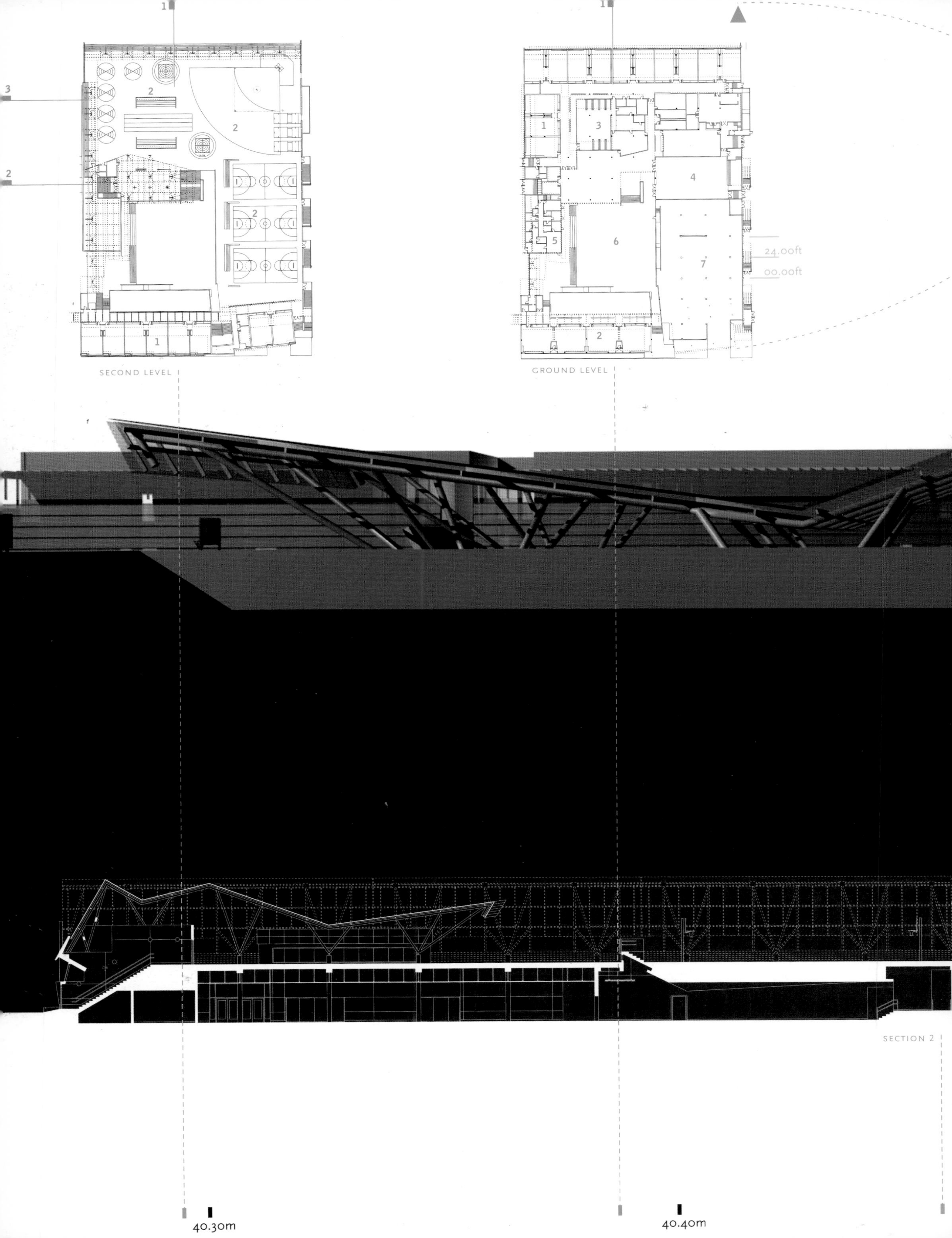

1
3
2
2
2
2
2
1
SECOND LEVEL
1
1
3
4
6
5
7
2
24.00ft
00.00ft
GROUND LEVEL
SECTION 2
40.30m
40.40m

GROUND LEVEL **1.** Classrooms **2.** Kindergarten **3.** Library **4.** MultiPurpose **5.** Administration **6.** Courtyard **7.** Parking SECOND LEVEL **1.** Classrooms **2.** Playground THIRD LEVEL **1.** Classrooms

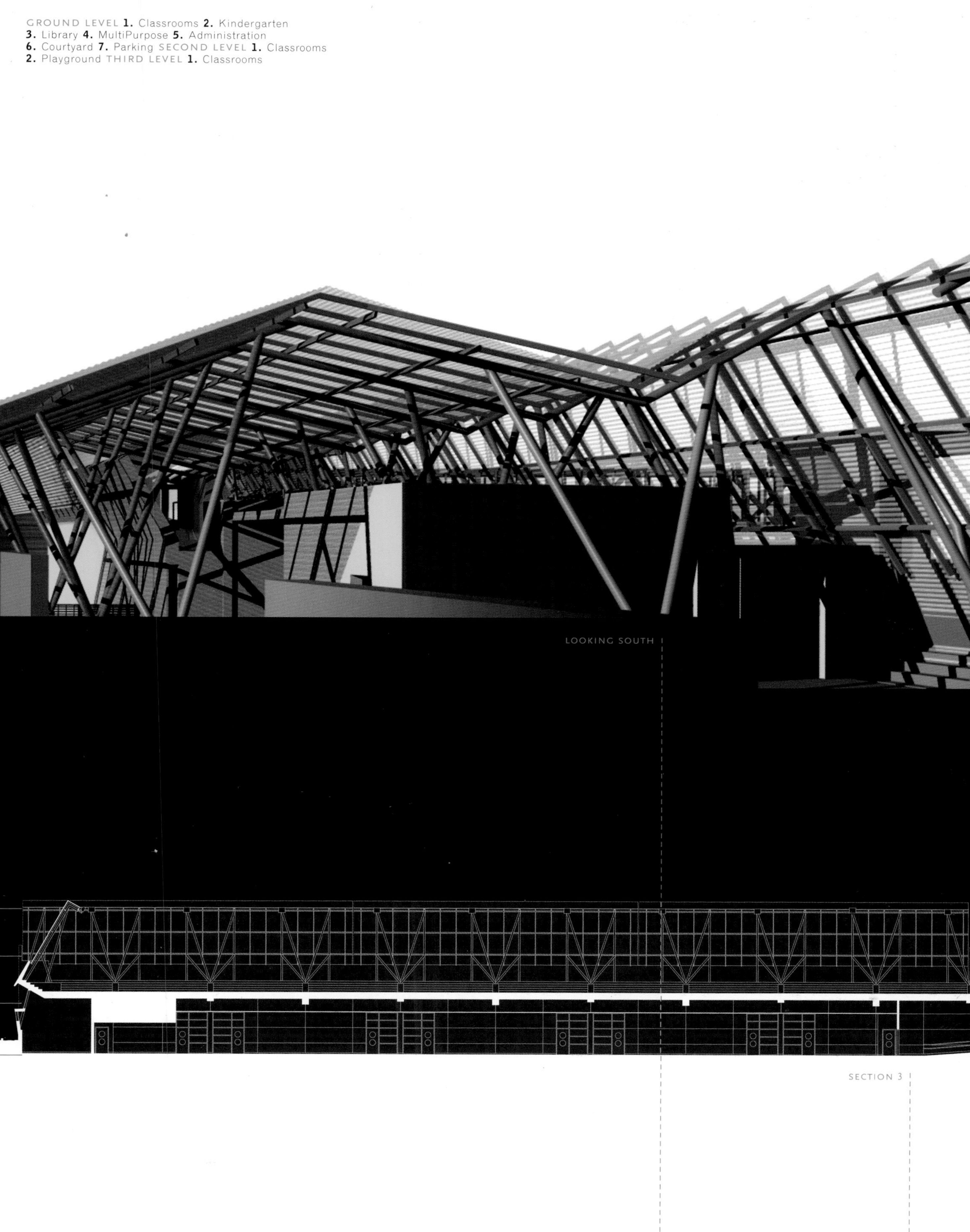

40.50m

40.60m

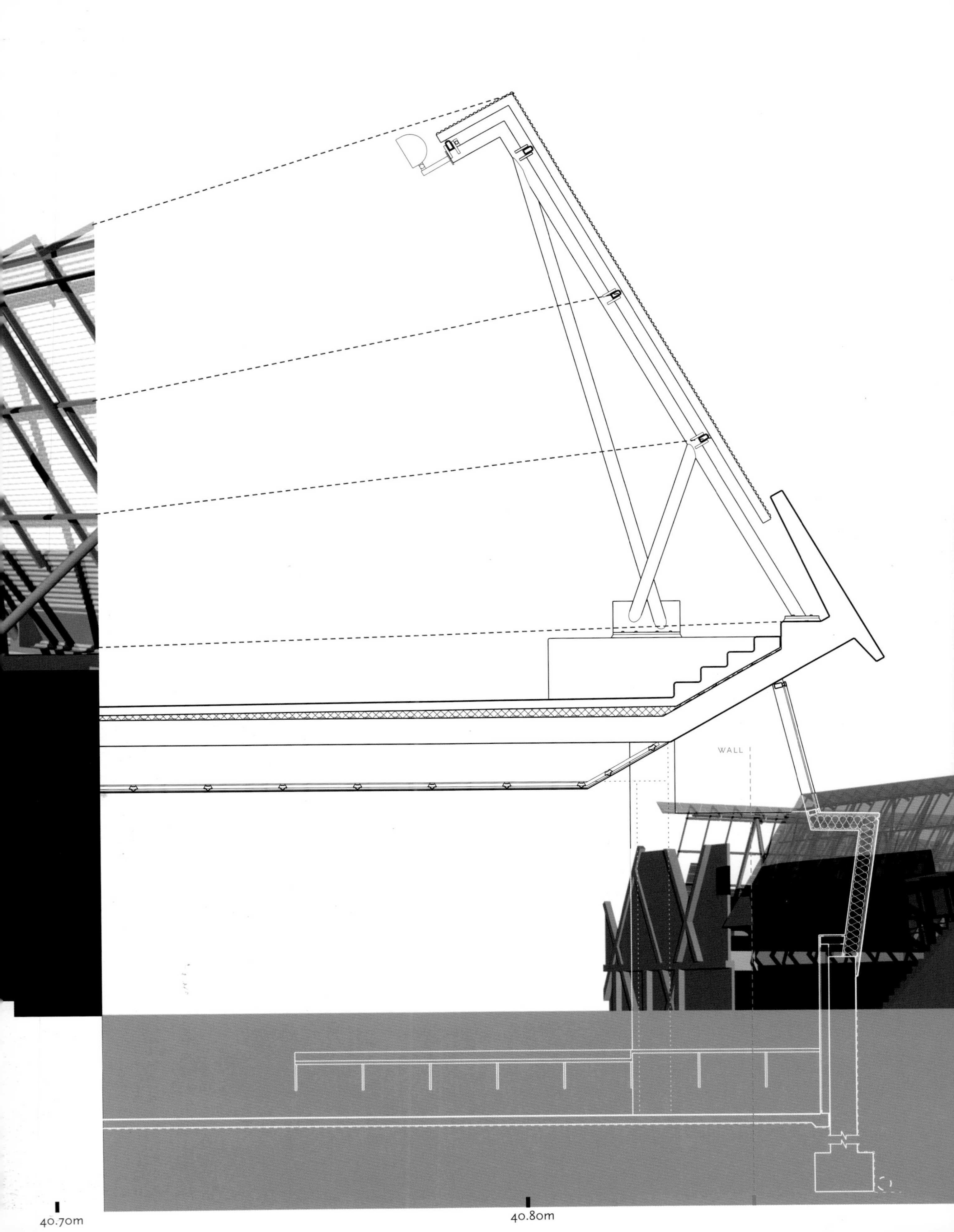
WALL
40.70m
40.80m

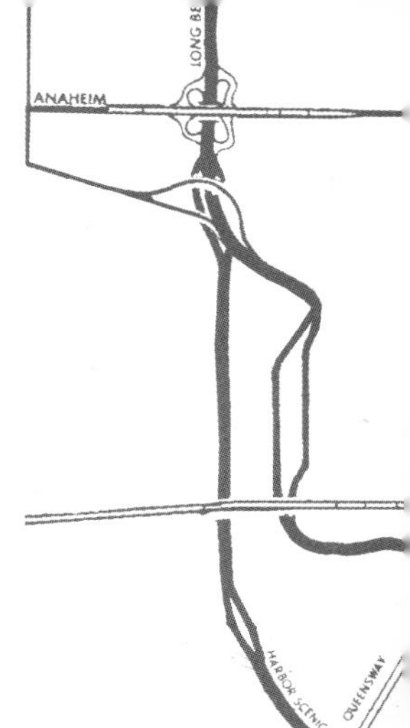

LOOKING NORTHEAST

SITE MAP | DETAIL OF SOUTH FACADE

PROJECT DATA

AREA OF SITE
2.5 acres / 1.02ha

PROGRAM
91,270sf / 8,482m²

HUMAN POPULATION
Students: 1000

PARKING
Cars: 60

MECHANICAL SYSTEM
Heat Pumps

STRUCTURAL SYSTEM
Concrete and Structural Steel

LOOKING WEST

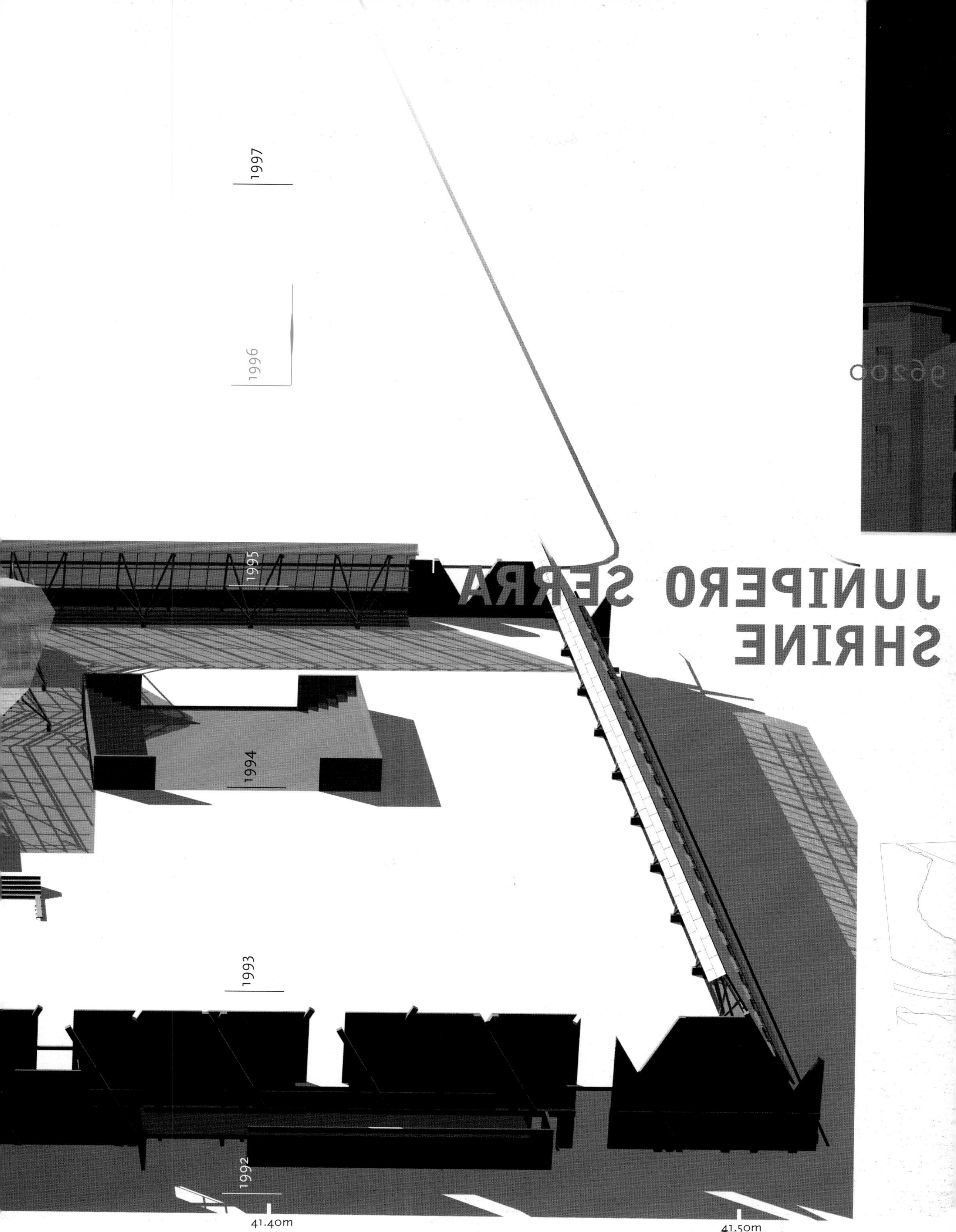

JUNÍPERO SERRA
SHRINE
1992
1993
1994
1995
1996
1997
41.40m
41.50m

JUNIPERO SERRA SHRINE

APPENDIX
II.27 ABOUT THE WORK
LOS ANGELES
CALIFORNIA
SECTION 2
DOWNTOWN
LOS ANGELES
41.80m
41.90m

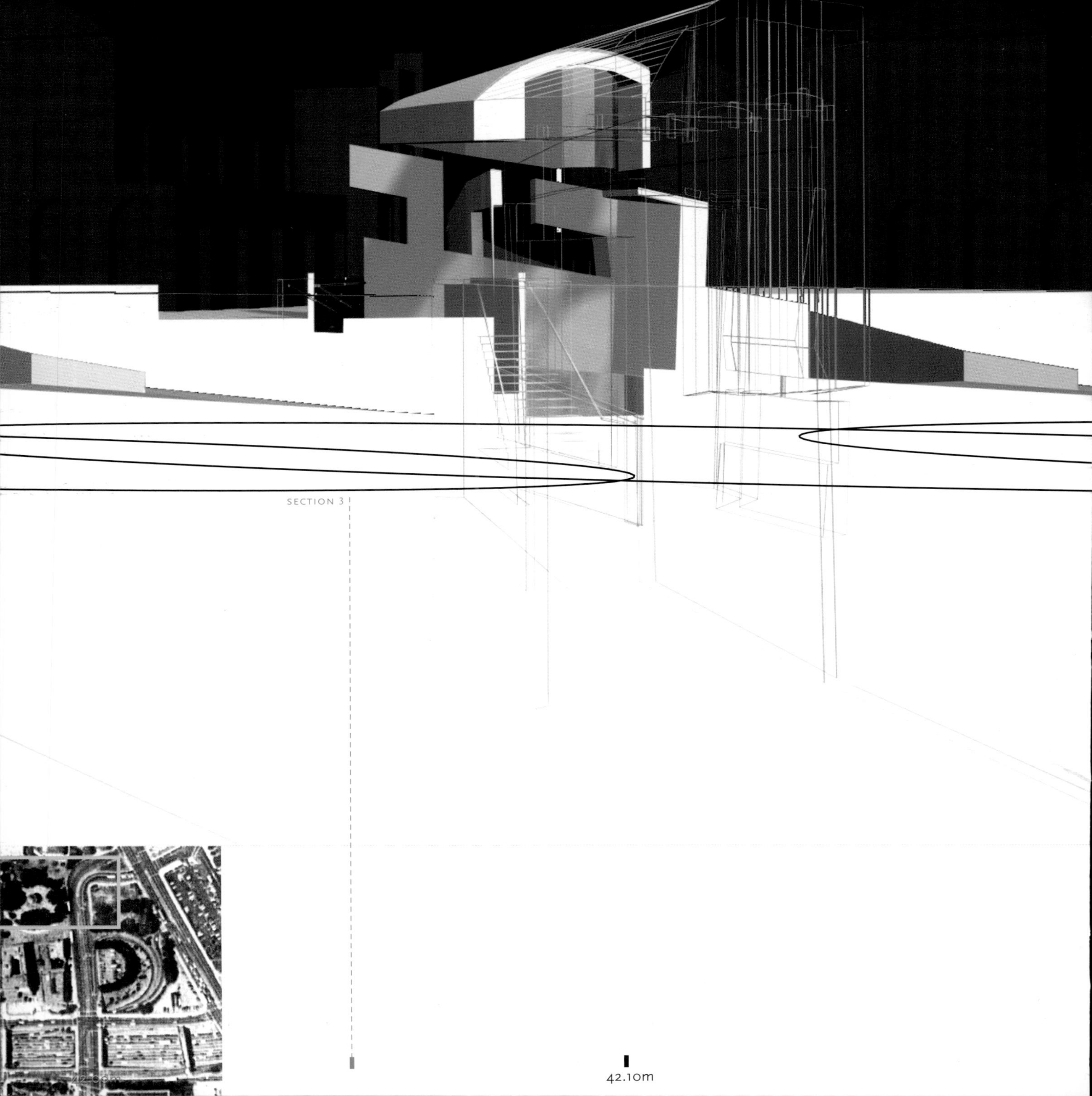
SECTION 3
42.10m

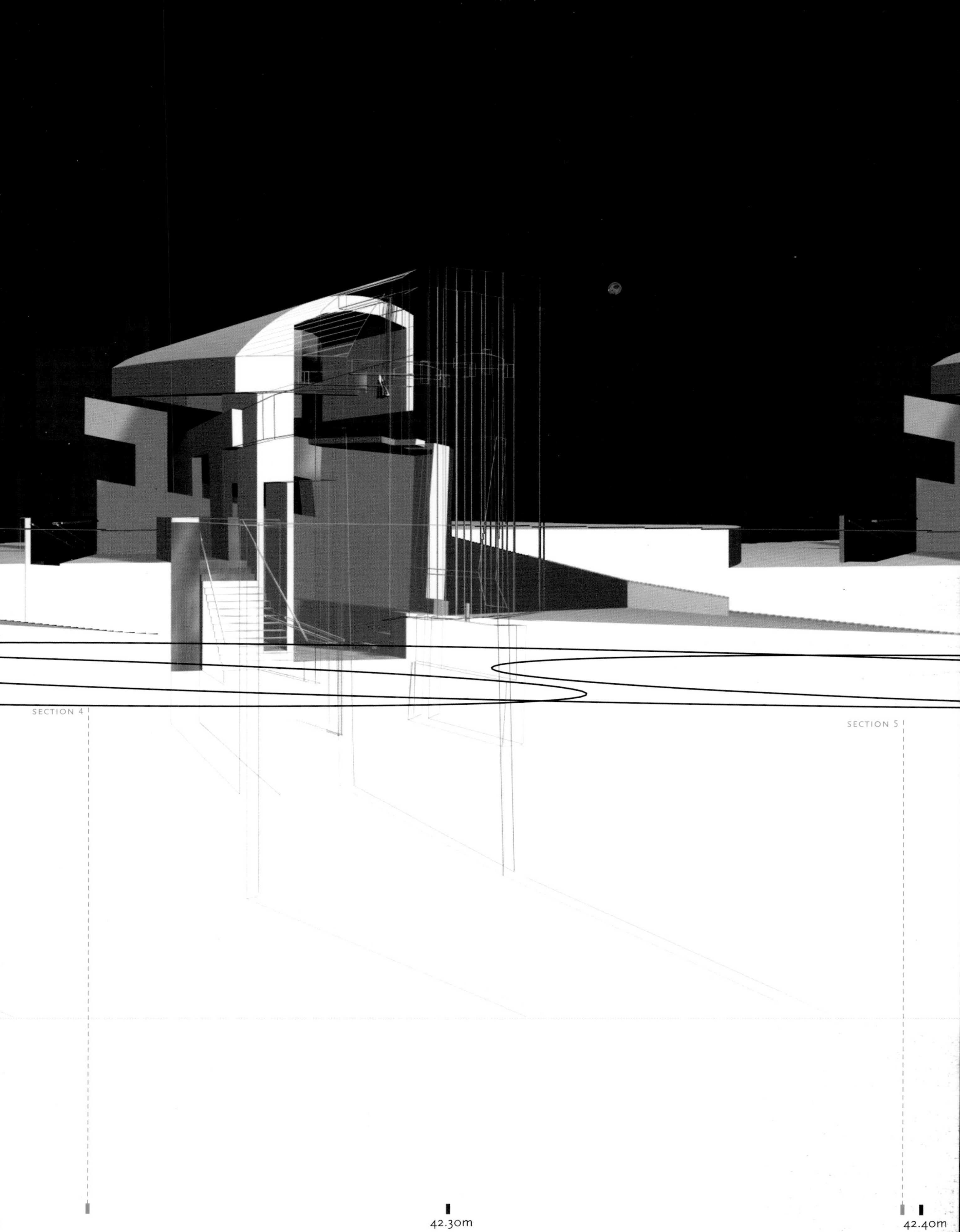
SECTION 4
SECTION 5
42.30m
42.40m

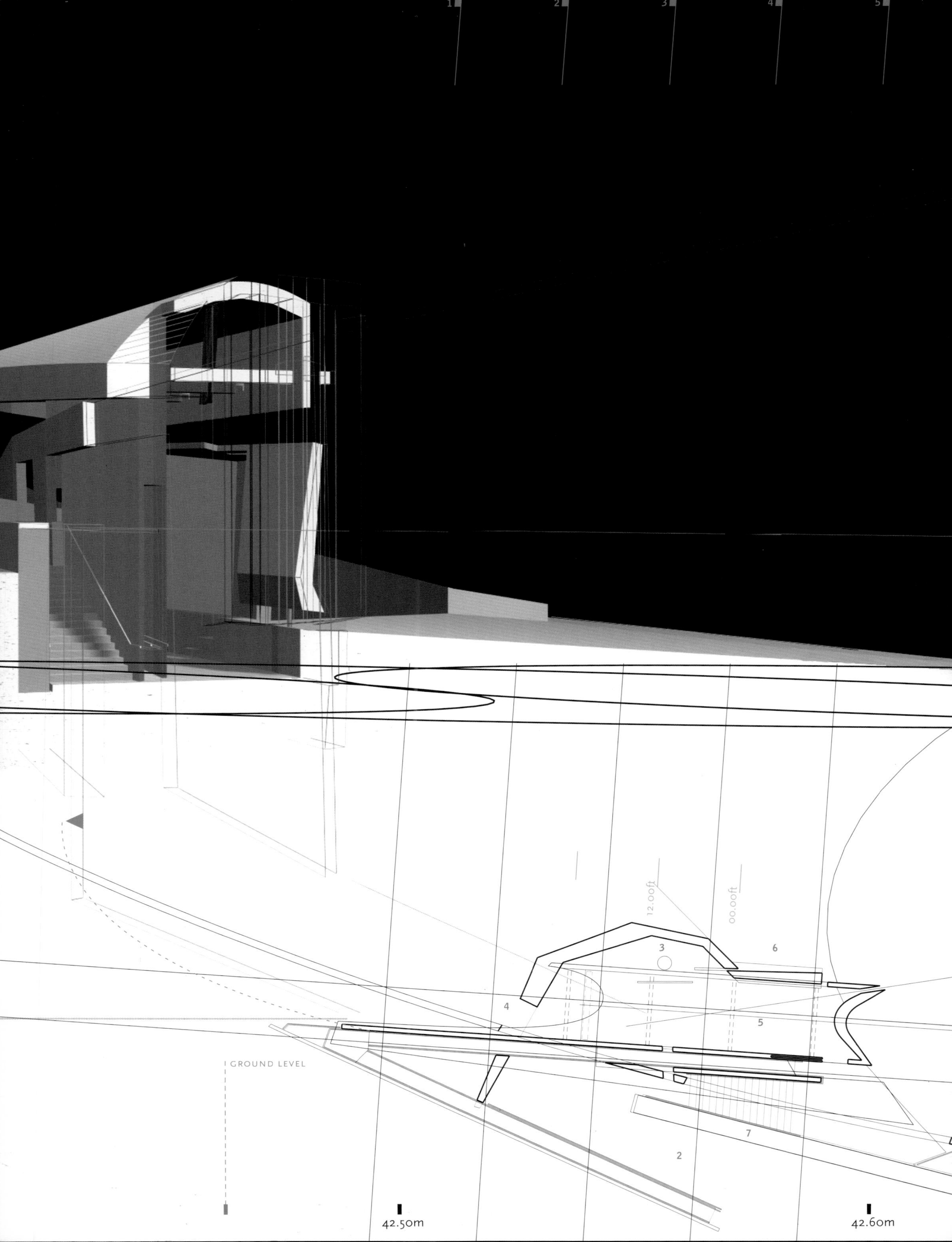
1
2
3
4
5
12.00ft
00.00ft
3
6
4
5
GROUND LEVEL
7
2
42.50m
42.60m

8

MADRID
SPAIN

APPENDIX
II.29 **ABOUT THE WORK**

PROJECT FROM ABOVE

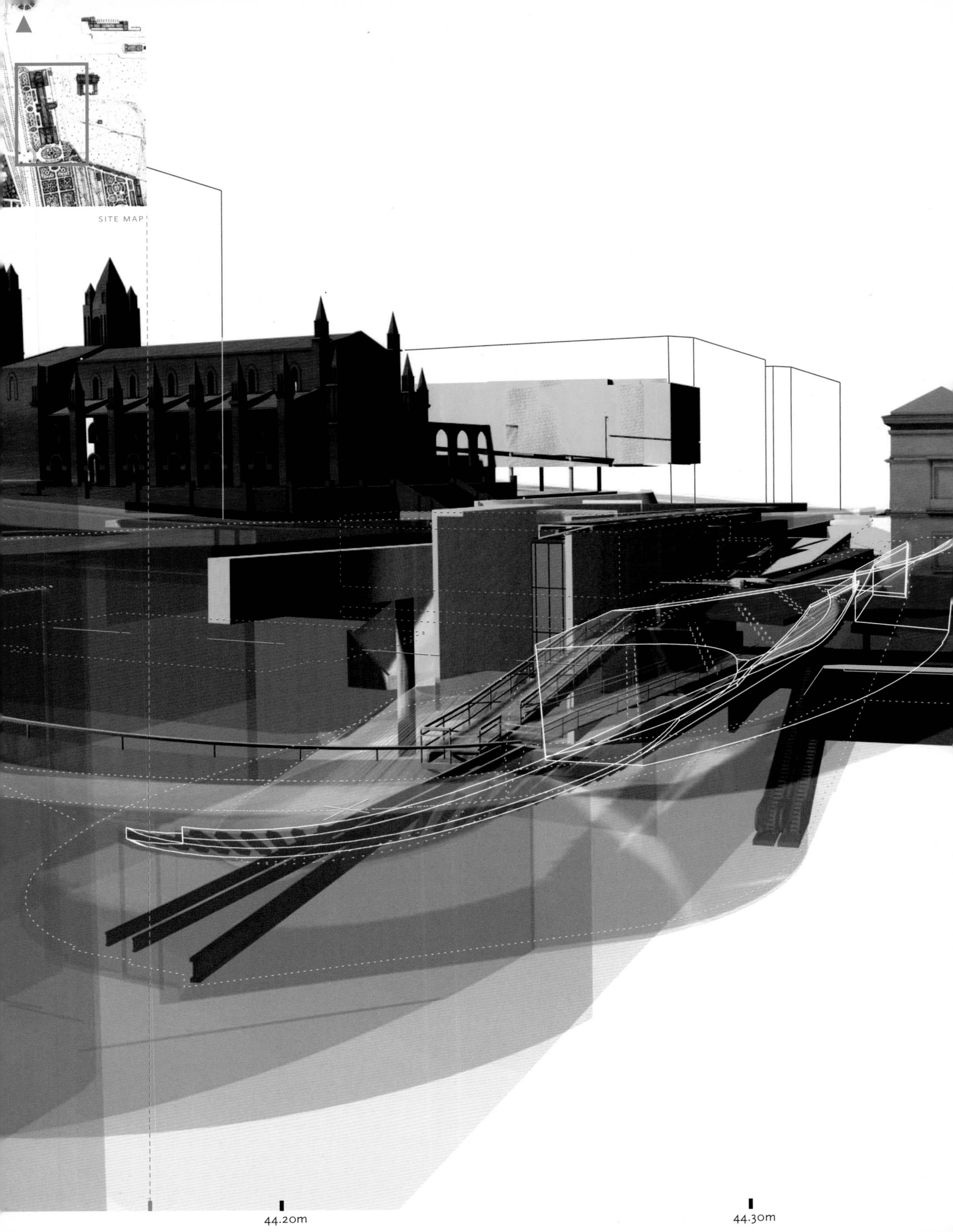
SITE MAP
44.20m
44.30m

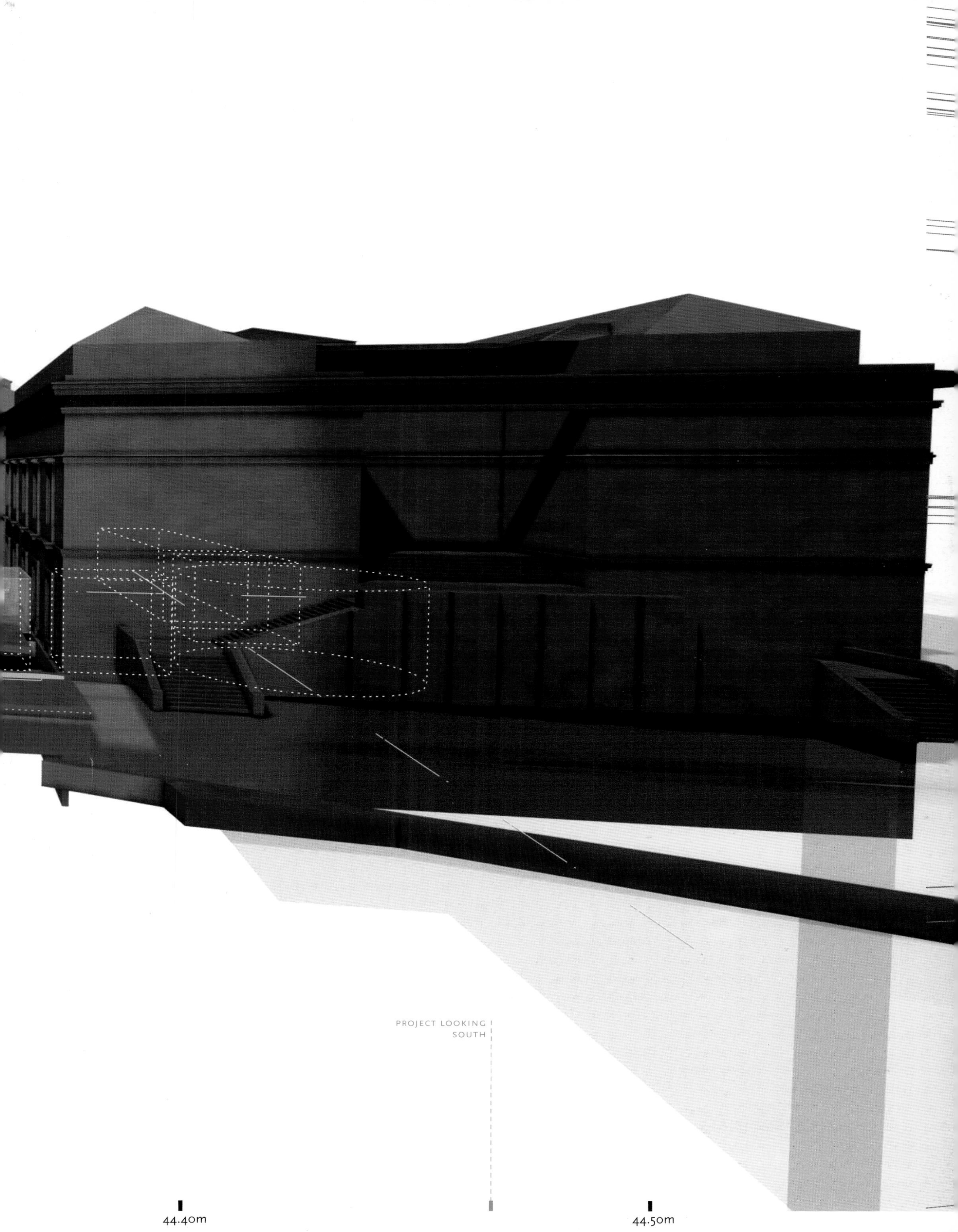

PROJECT LOOKING
SOUTH
44.40m
44.50m

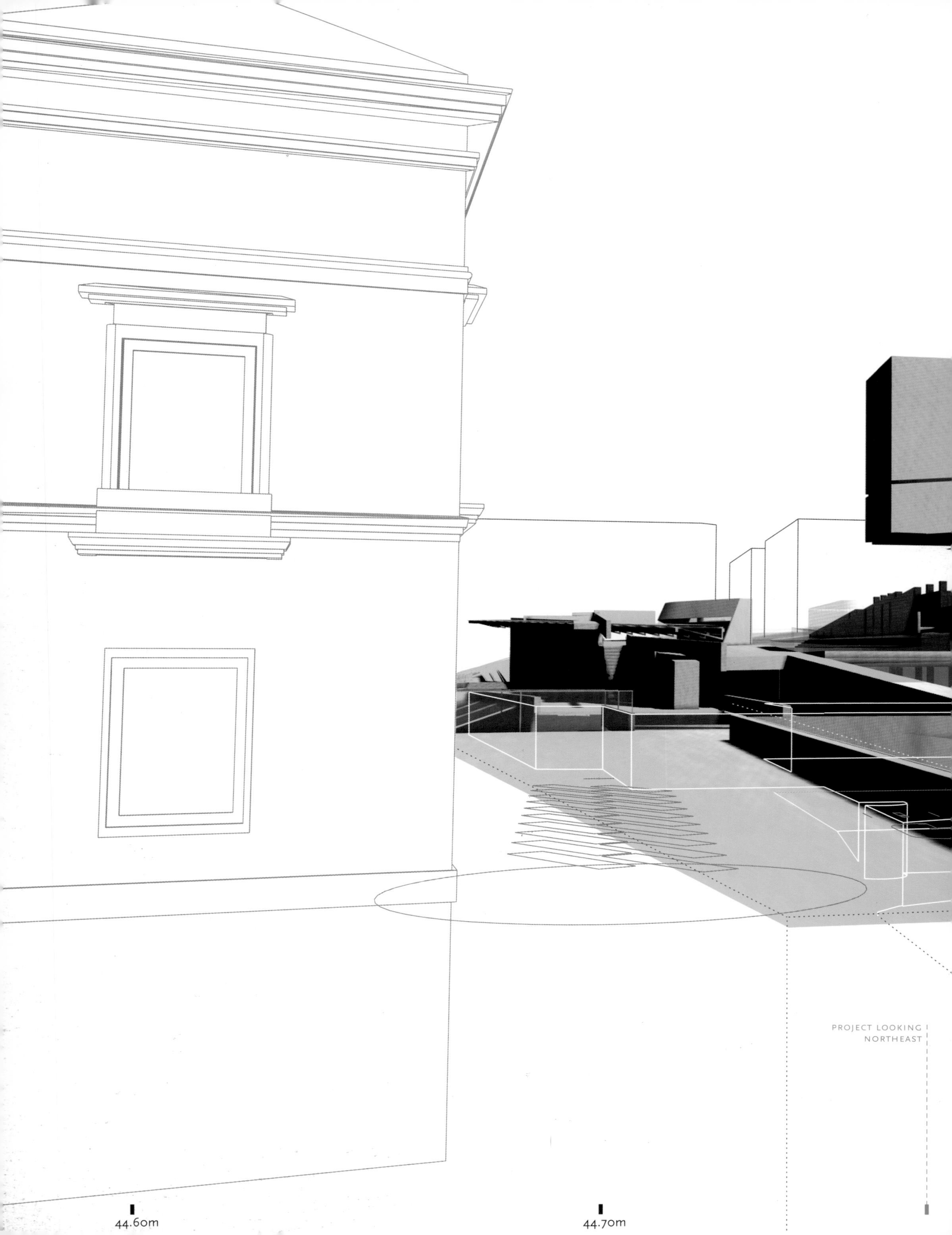
PROJECT LOOKING
NORTHEAST
44.60m
44.70m

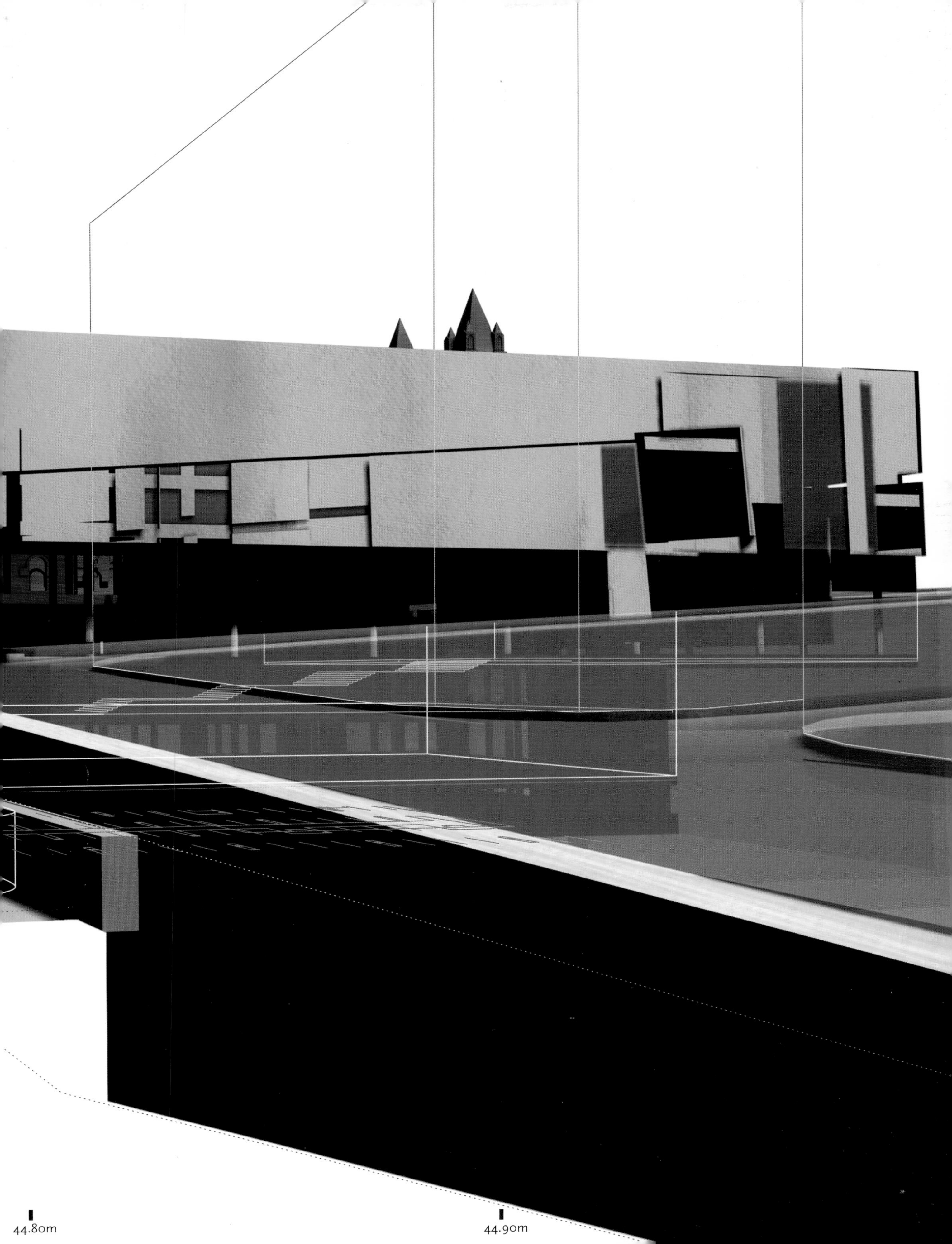
44.80m
44.90m

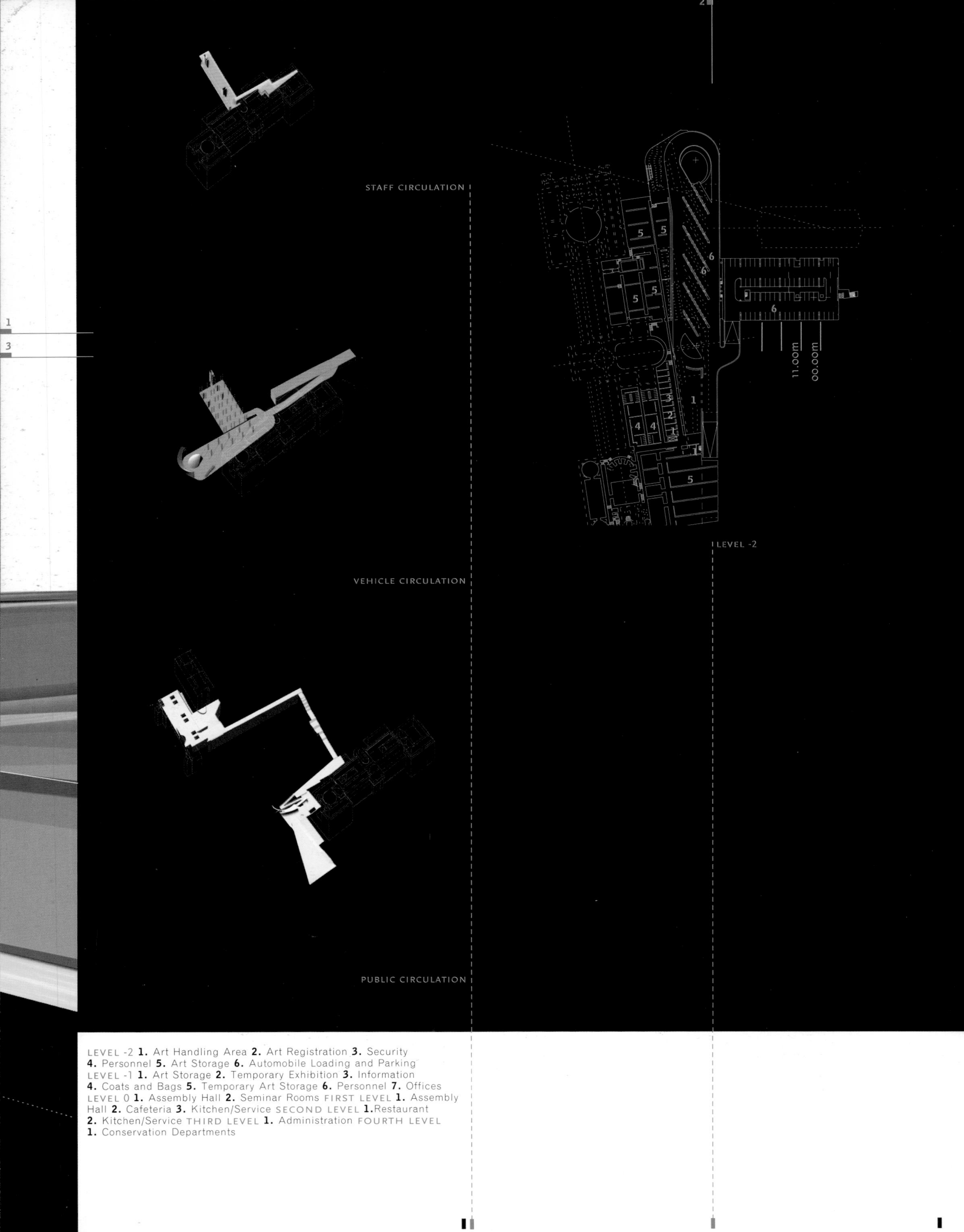

LEVEL -2 **1.** Art Handling Area **2.** Art Registration **3.** Security **4.** Personnel **5.** Art Storage **6.** Automobile Loading and Parking LEVEL -1 **1.** Art Storage **2.** Temporary Exhibition **3.** Information **4.** Coats and Bags **5.** Temporary Art Storage **6.** Personnel **7.** Offices LEVEL 0 **1.** Assembly Hall **2.** Seminar Rooms FIRST LEVEL **1.** Assembly Hall **2.** Cafeteria **3.** Kitchen/Service SECOND LEVEL **1.**Restaurant **2.** Kitchen/Service THIRD LEVEL **1.** Administration FOURTH LEVEL **1.** Conservation Departments

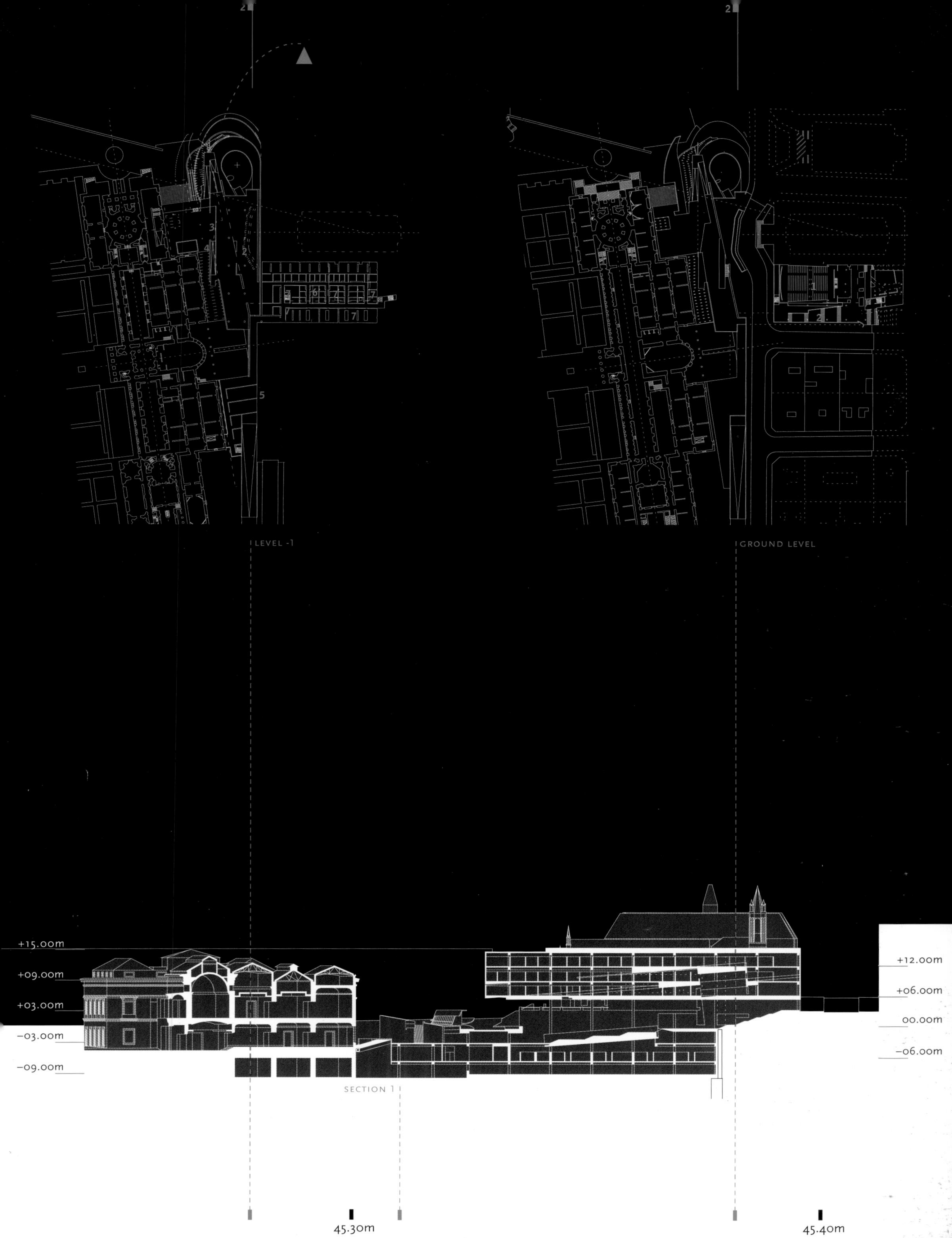

LEVEL -1
GROUND LEVEL
+15.00m
+09.00m
+03.00m
-03.00m
-09.00m
SECTION 1
+12.00m
+06.00m
00.00m
-06.00m
45.30m
45.40m

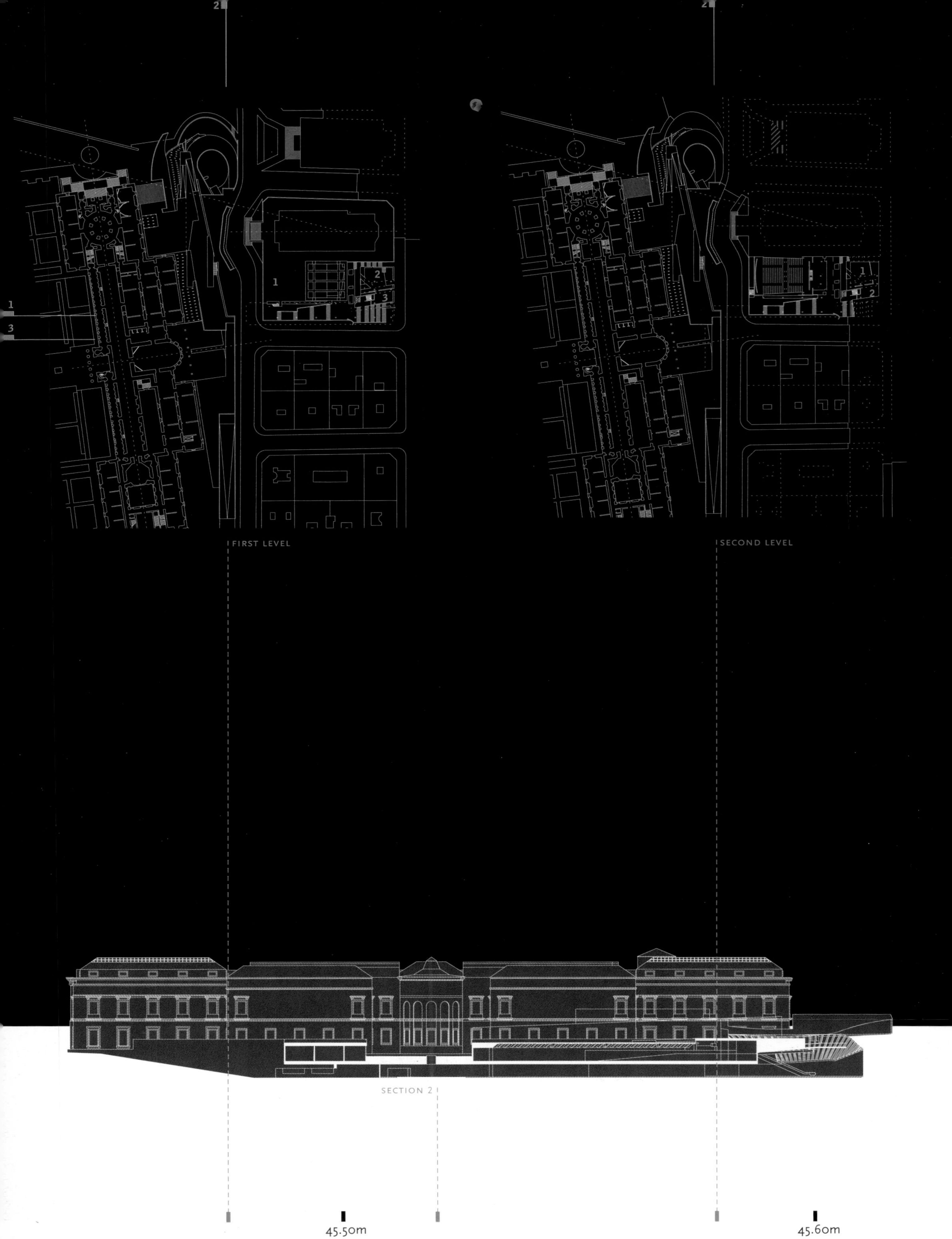
FIRST LEVEL
SECOND LEVEL
SECTION 2
45.50m
45.60m

1
THIRD LEVEL
PROJECT DATA
AREA OF SITE
18.7 acres / 7.56ha
PROGRAM
Exhibition Space: 16,140sf / 1500m^2
Total: 50,539sf / 4697m^2
HUMAN POPULATION
Visitors per Year: 2,000,000
Visitors per Day: 6,390
PARKING
Cars: 70
Bus Drop Off Areas: 4
MECHANICAL SYSTEM
Forced Air
STRUCTURAL SYSTEM
Cast In Place Concrete
+15.00m
+09.00m
+03.00m
-09.00m
+12.00m
+06.00m
00.00m
-06.00m
SECTION 3
45.70m
45.80m

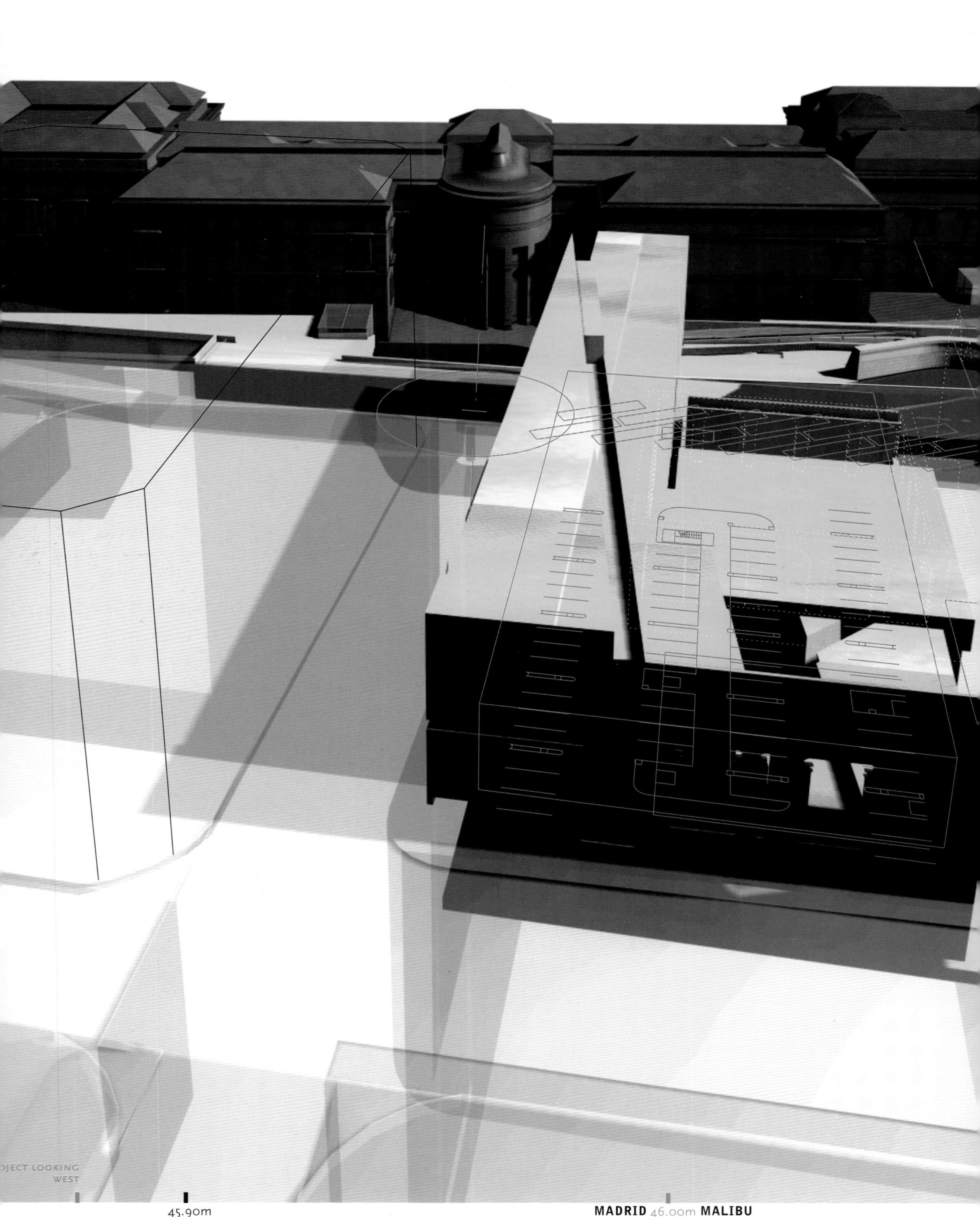

OJECT LOOKING
WEST

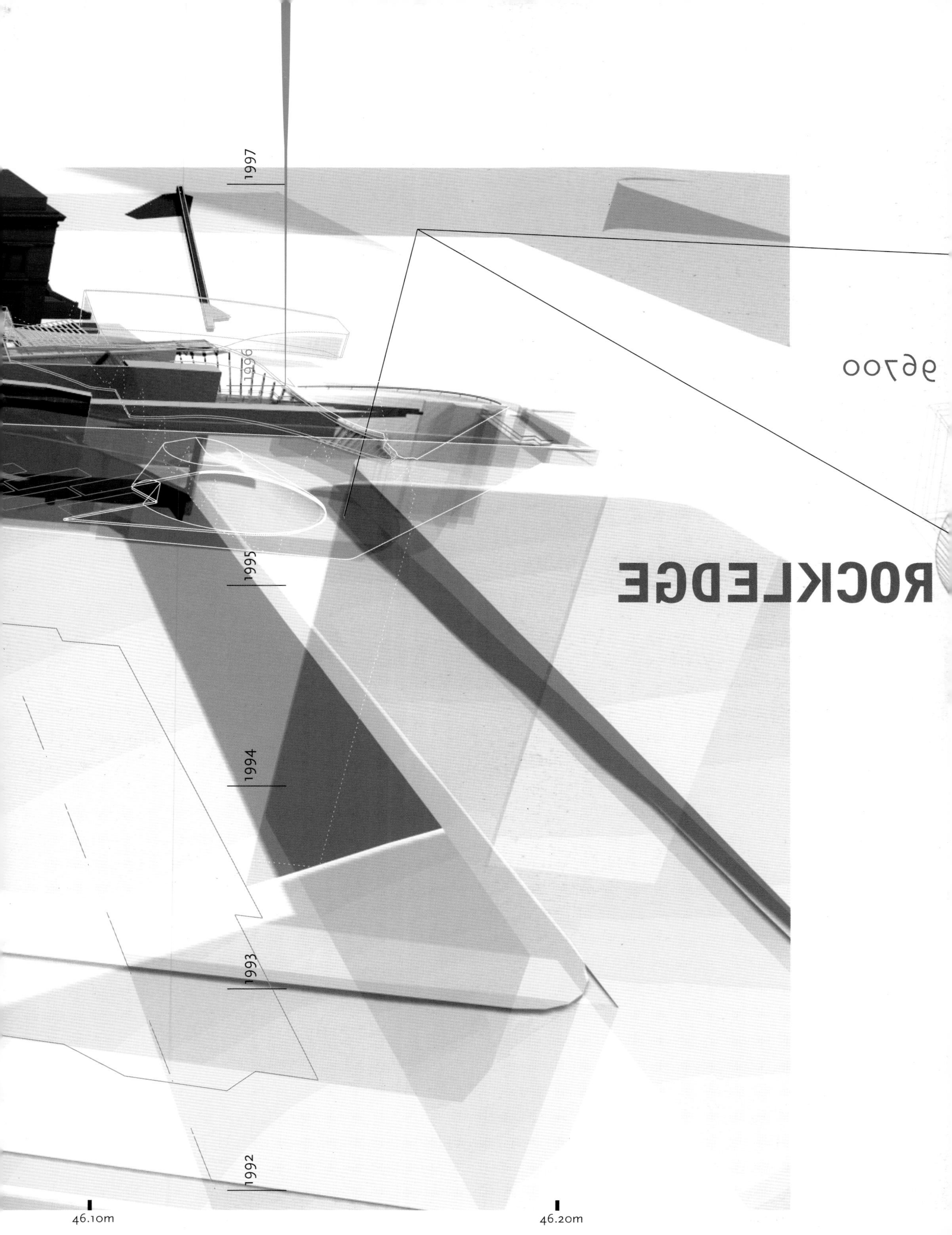

1997
1996
96700
ROCKLEDGE
1995
1994
1993
1992
46.10m
46.20m

96700

ROCKLEDGE

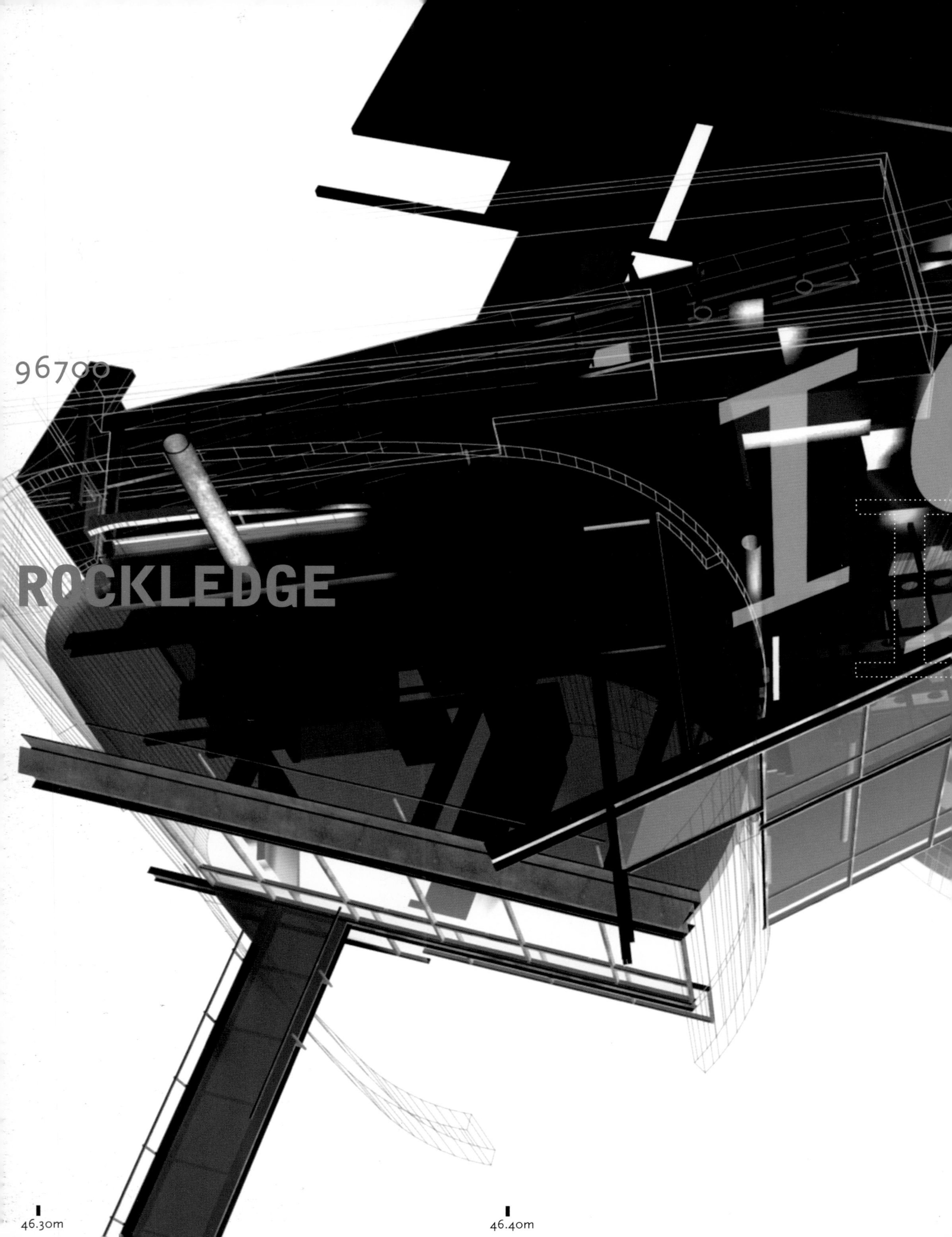

46.30m

46.40m

MALIBU
CALIFORNIA
APPENDIX
II.31 ABOUT THE WORK
V.19 STUDY MODELS
SCHUEREN
CANYON
RD
FLORES
RAMBLA
LAS
PACIFICO
LOOKING NORTH
FROM ABOVE
SITE MAP
46.60m
46.70m

1
5 3 2 4
6
6
5
4
3
LEVEL @ +1664FT
2
1
7
DIAGRAM SHOWING
VIEW AXIS
46.80m
46.90m

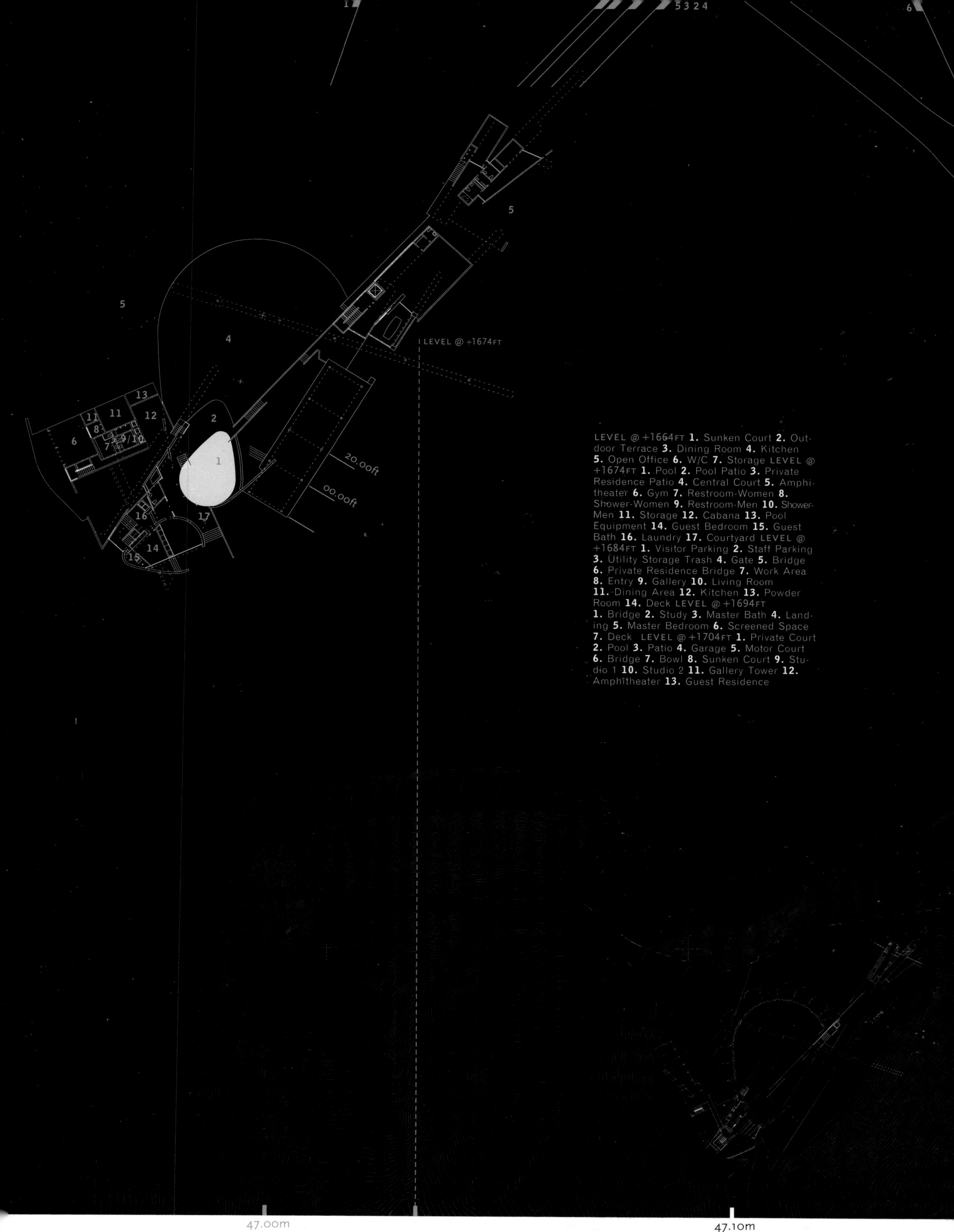

LEVEL @ +1664FT **1.** Sunken Court **2.** Outdoor Terrace **3.** Dining Room **4.** Kitchen **5.** Open Office **6.** W/C **7.** Storage LEVEL @ +1674FT **1.** Pool **2.** Pool Patio **3.** Private Residence Patio **4.** Central Court **5.** Amphitheater **6.** Gym **7.** Restroom-Women **8.** Shower-Women **9.** Restroom-Men **10.** Shower-Men **11.** Storage **12.** Cabana **13.** Pool Equipment **14.** Guest Bedroom **15.** Guest Bath **16.** Laundry **17.** Courtyard LEVEL @ +1684FT **1.** Visitor Parking **2.** Staff Parking **3.** Utility Storage Trash **4.** Gate **5.** Bridge **6.** Private Residence Bridge **7.** Work Area **8.** Entry **9.** Gallery **10.** Living Room **11.** Dining Area **12.** Kitchen **13.** Powder Room **14.** Deck LEVEL @ +1694FT **1.** Bridge **2.** Study **3.** Master Bath **4.** Landing **5.** Master Bedroom **6.** Screened Space **7.** Deck LEVEL @ +1704FT **1.** Private Court **2.** Pool **3.** Patio **4.** Garage **5.** Motor Court **6.** Bridge **7.** Bowl **8.** Sunken Court **9.** Studio 1 **10.** Studio 2 **11.** Gallery Tower **12.** Amphitheater **13.** Guest Residence

1
5 3 2 4
6
1
2
3
4
13
14
12
13
10
LEVEL @ +1684FT
PERSPECTIVE
RESIDENCE
SECTION 1
47.20m
47.30m

LEVEL @ +1694FT
1
2
4
5
6
SECTION 2
+1704ft
+1694ft
+1684ft
+1674ft
47.40m
47.50m

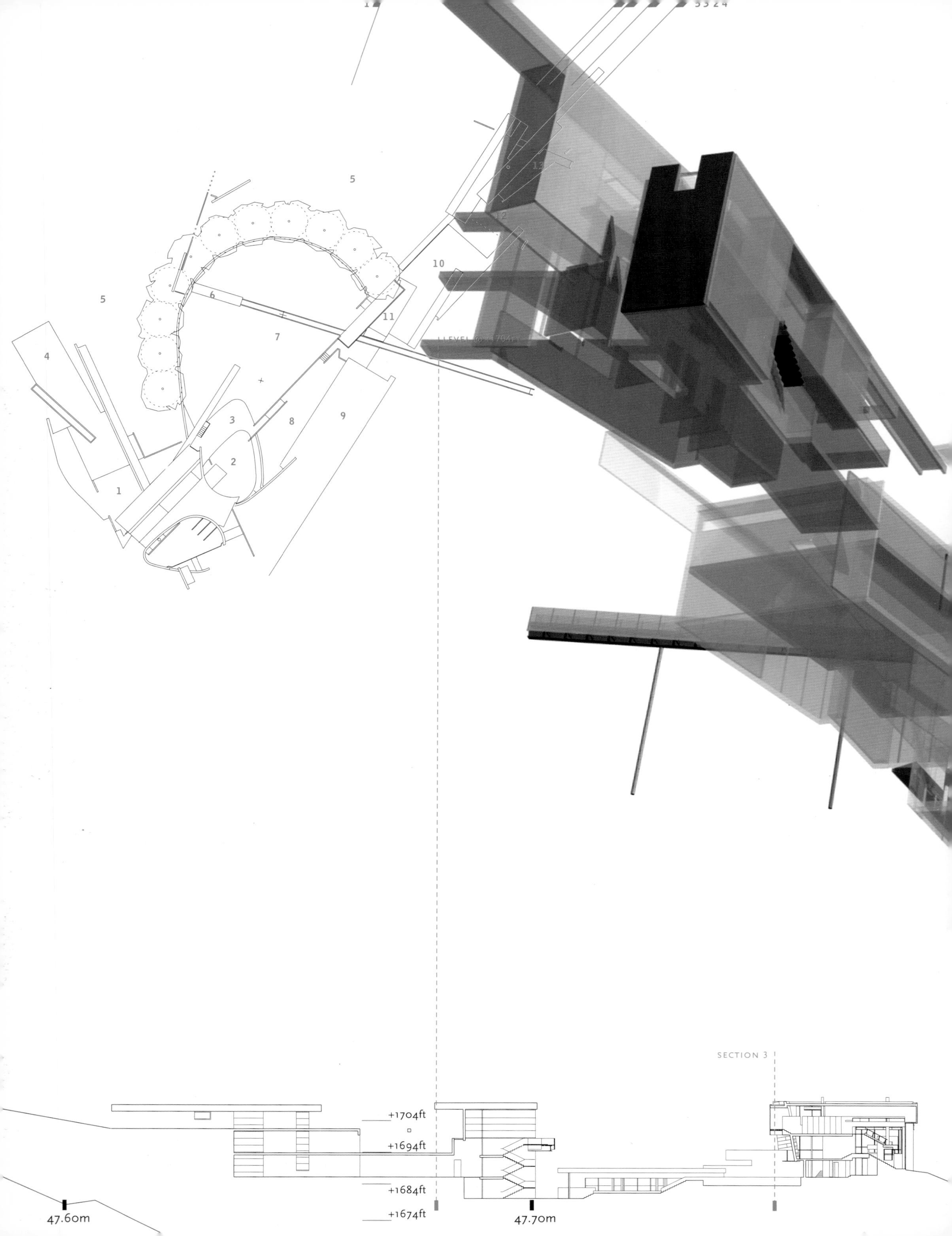

1
5
5
4
6
7
3
2
1
8
9
10
11
12
13
LEVEL @ +1704ft
SECTION 3
+1704ft
+1694ft
+1684ft
+1674ft
47.60m
47.70m

SECTION 4
47.90m
48.00m

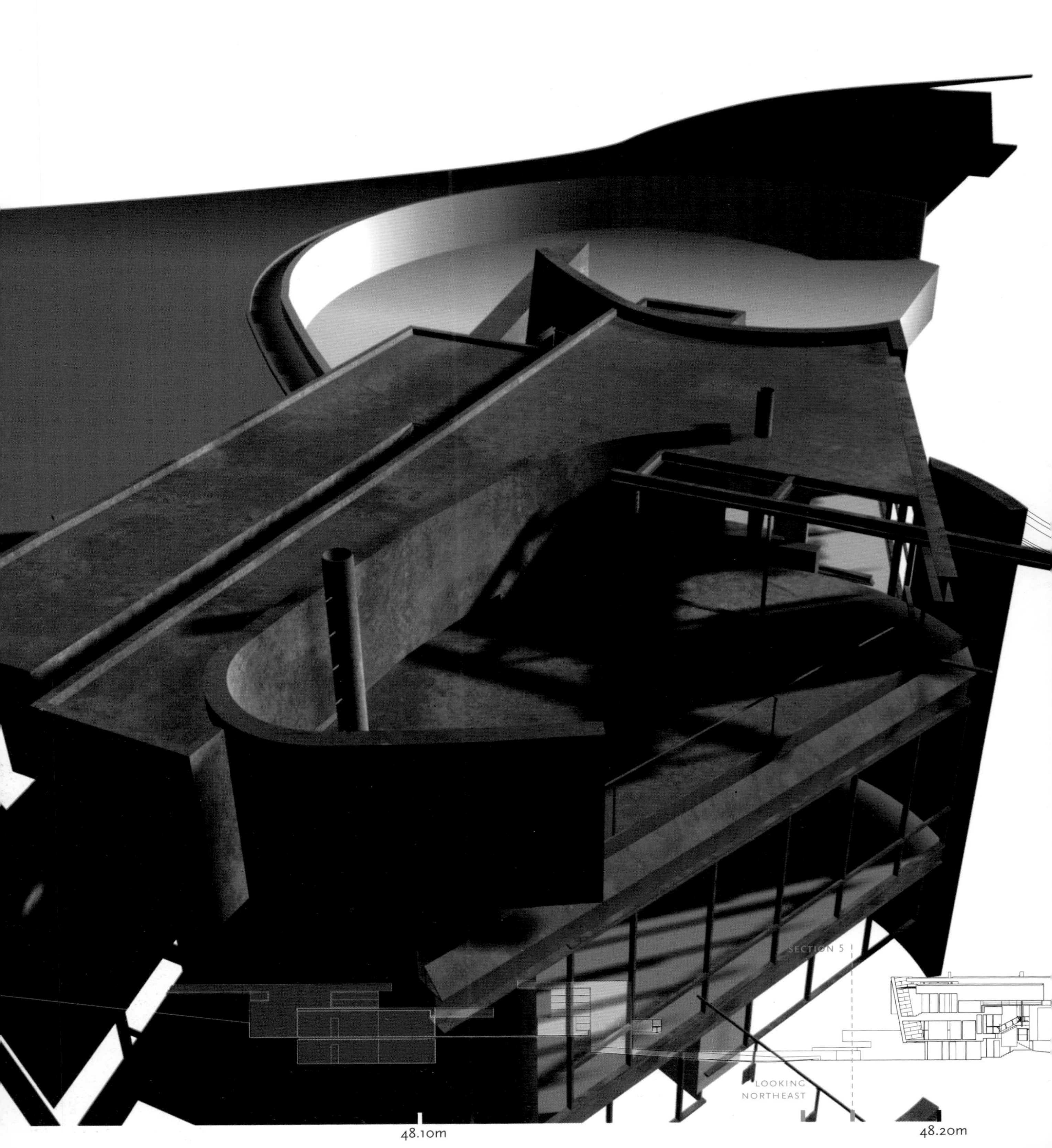
SECTION 5
LOOKING
NORTHEAST
48.10m
48.20m

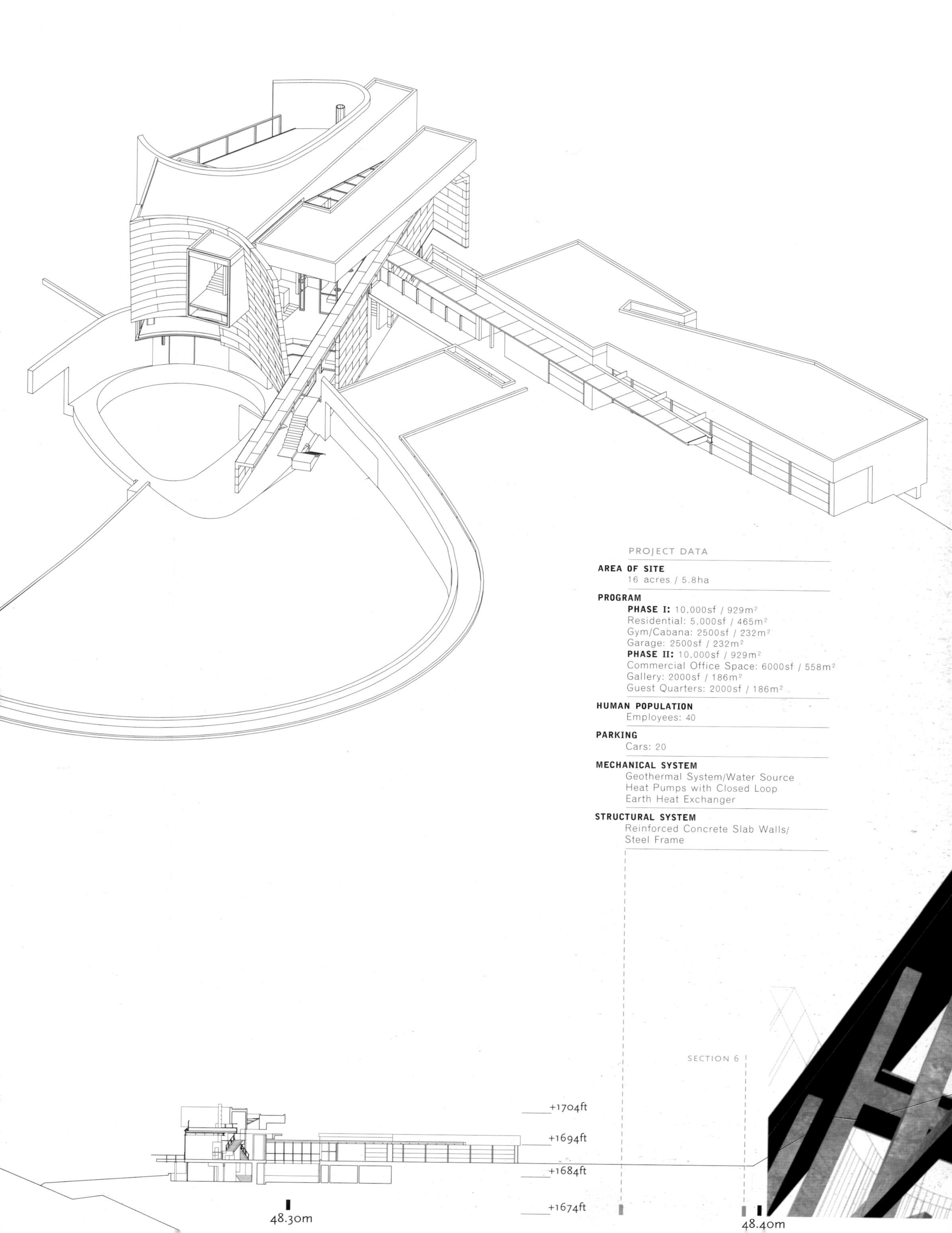

PROJECT DATA
AREA OF SITE
16 acres / 5.8ha
PROGRAM
PHASE I: 10,000sf / 929m²
Residential: 5,000sf / 465m²
Gym/Cabana: 2500sf / 232m²
Garage: 2500sf / 232m²
PHASE II: 10,000sf / 929m²
Commercial Office Space: 6000sf / 558m²
Gallery: 2000sf / 186m²
Guest Quarters: 2000sf / 186m²
HUMAN POPULATION
Employees: 40
PARKING
Cars: 20
MECHANICAL SYSTEM
Geothermal System/Water Source
Heat Pumps with Closed Loop
Earth Heat Exchanger
STRUCTURAL SYSTEM
Reinforced Concrete Slab Walls/
Steel Frame
SECTION 6
+1704ft
+1694ft
+1684ft
+1674ft
48.30m
48.40m

48.50m
48.60m

97800

1997

1996

48.70m

MALIBU 48.80m **SHERMAN OAKS**

97800
MACK HOUSE
48.90m
49.00m

SHERMAN OAKS,
CALIFORNIA

SHERMAN OAKS
CALIFORNIA

APPENDIX
II.31 **ABOUT THE WORK**
V.25 **STUDY MODELS**

LOOKING
NORTHWEST

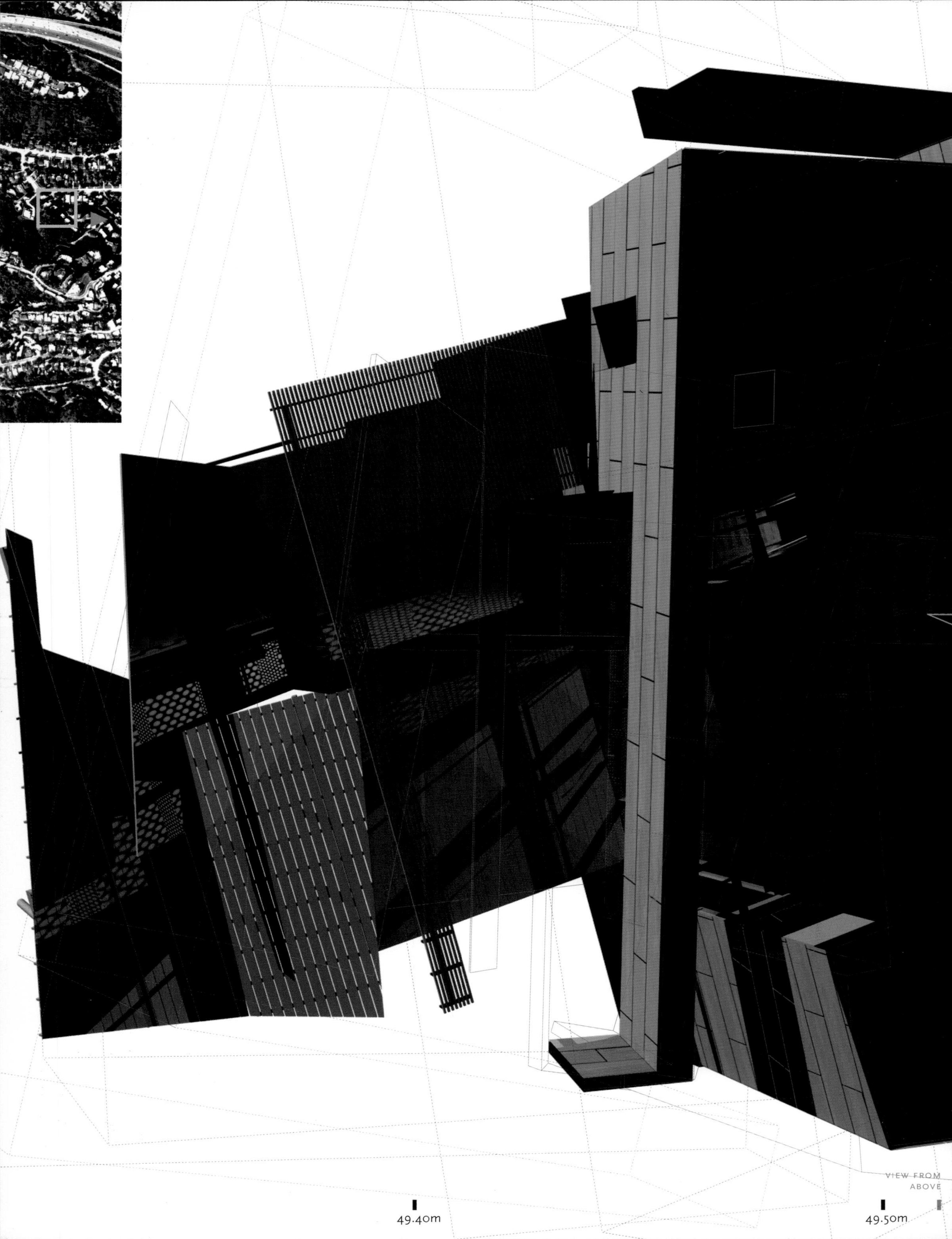
VIEW FROM
ABOVE
49.40m
49.50m

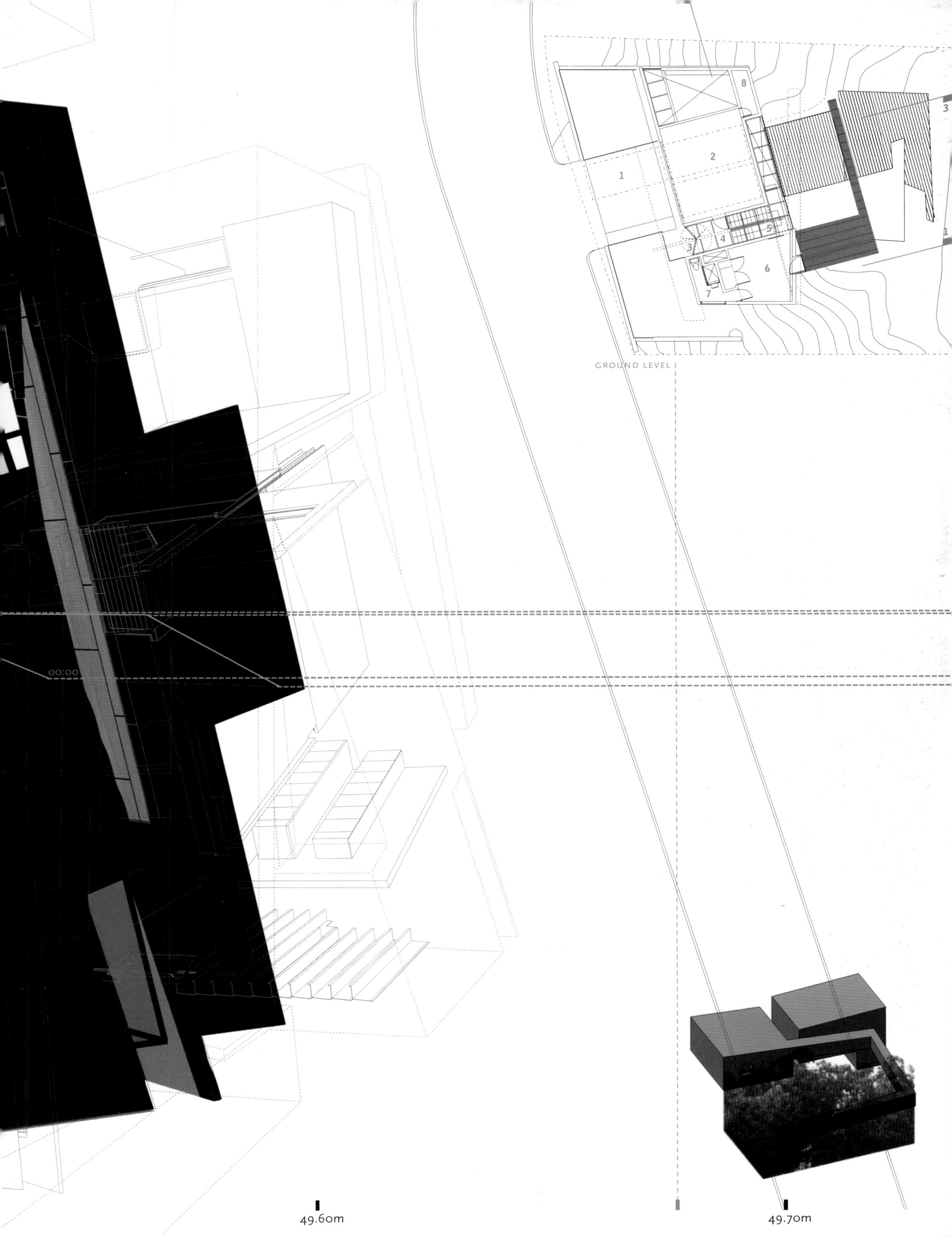
GROUND LEVEL
1
2
3
4
5
6
7
8
00:00
49.60m
49.70m

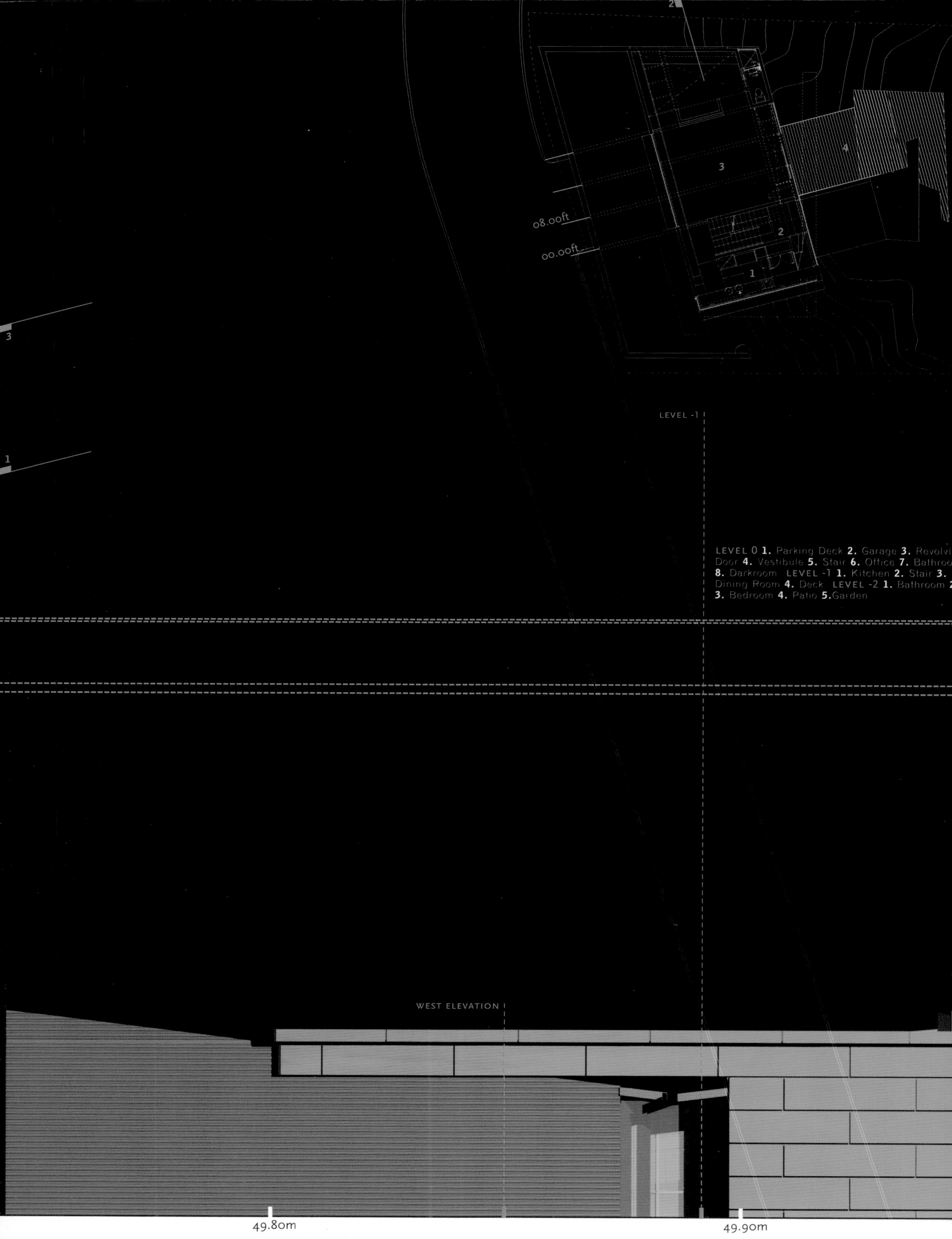
08.00ft
00.00ft
LEVEL -1
LEVEL 0 1. Parking Deck 2. Garage 3. Revolvi
Door 4. Vestibule 5. Stair 6. Office 7. Bathroo
8. Darkroom LEVEL -1 1. Kitchen 2. Stair 3.
Dining Room 4. Deck LEVEL -2 1. Bathroom 2
3. Bedroom 4. Patio 5.Garden
WEST ELEVATION
49.80m
49.90m

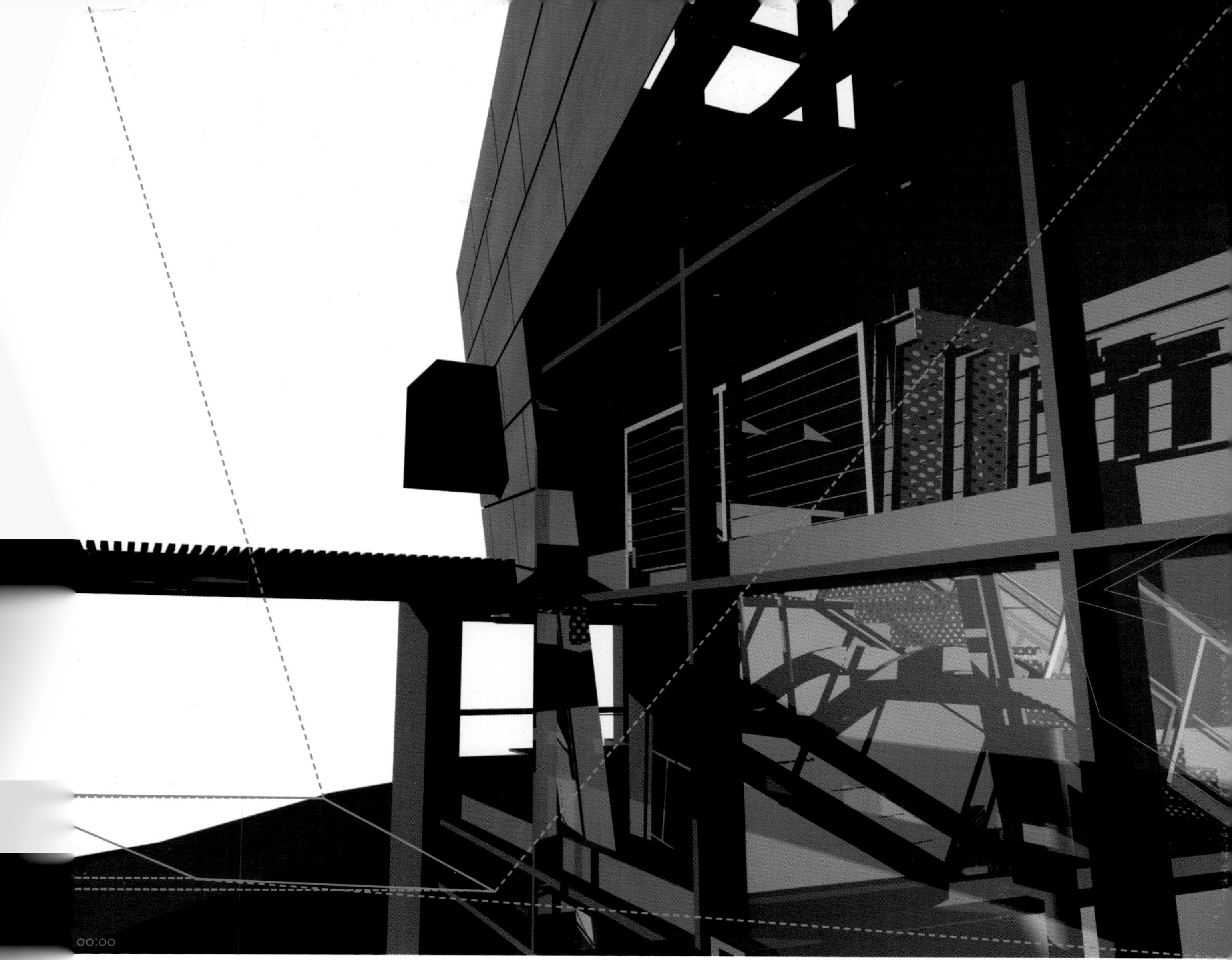

00:00

LOOKING SOUTH

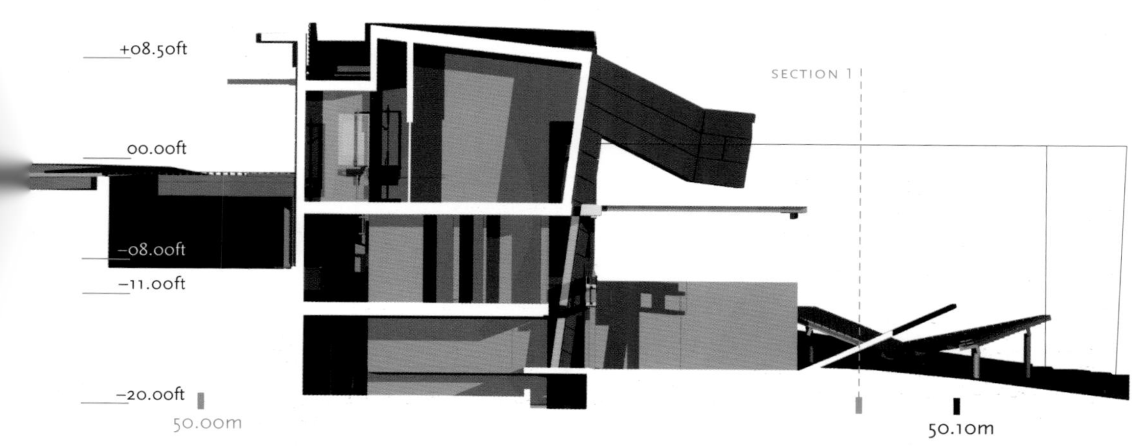

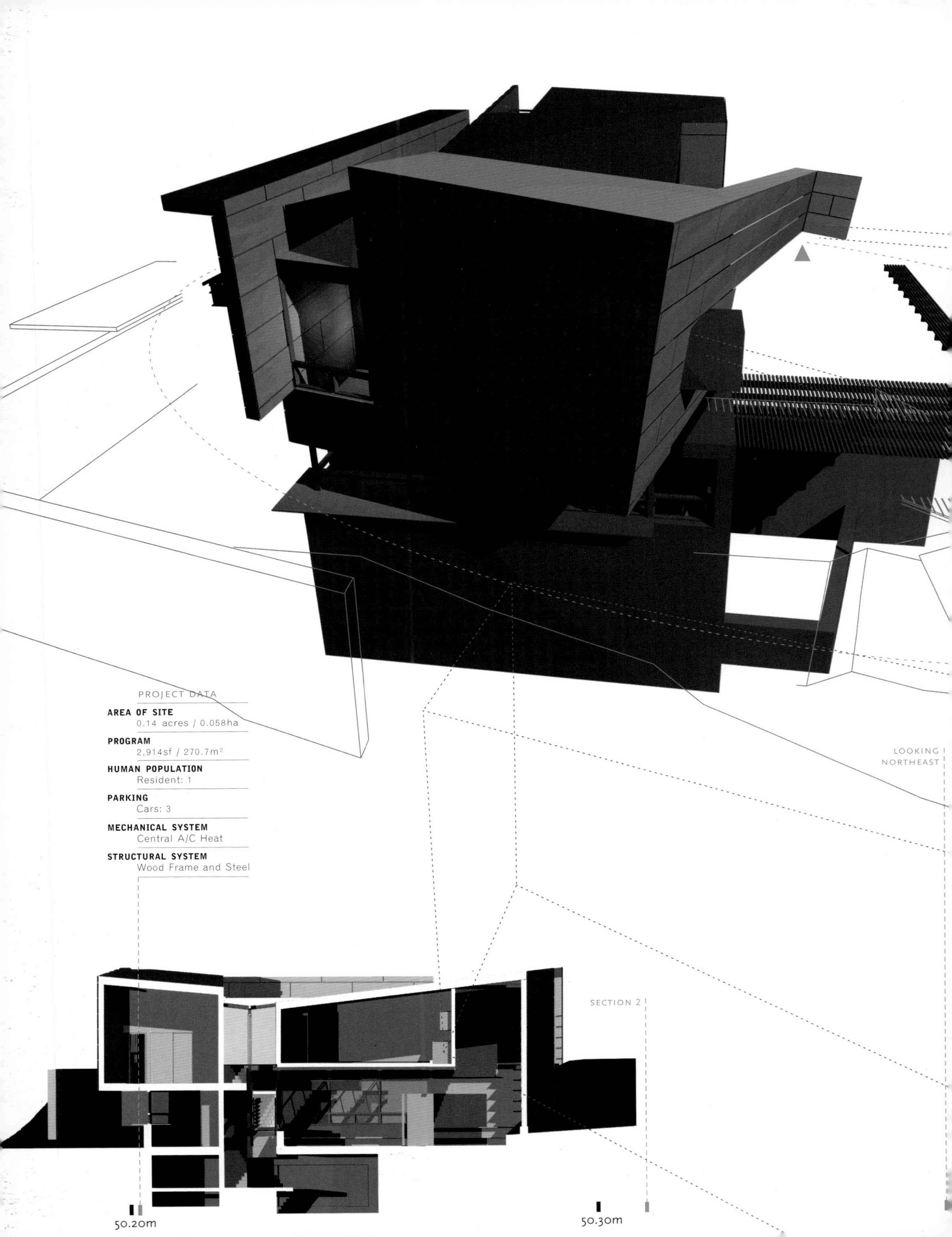

PROJECT DATA
AREA OF SITE
0.14 acres / 0.058ha
PROGRAM
2,914sf / 270.7m²
HUMAN POPULATION
Resident: 1
PARKING
Cars: 3
MECHANICAL SYSTEM
Central A/C Heat
STRUCTURAL SYSTEM
Wood Frame and Steel
LOOKING NORTHEAST
SECTION 2
50.20m
50.30m

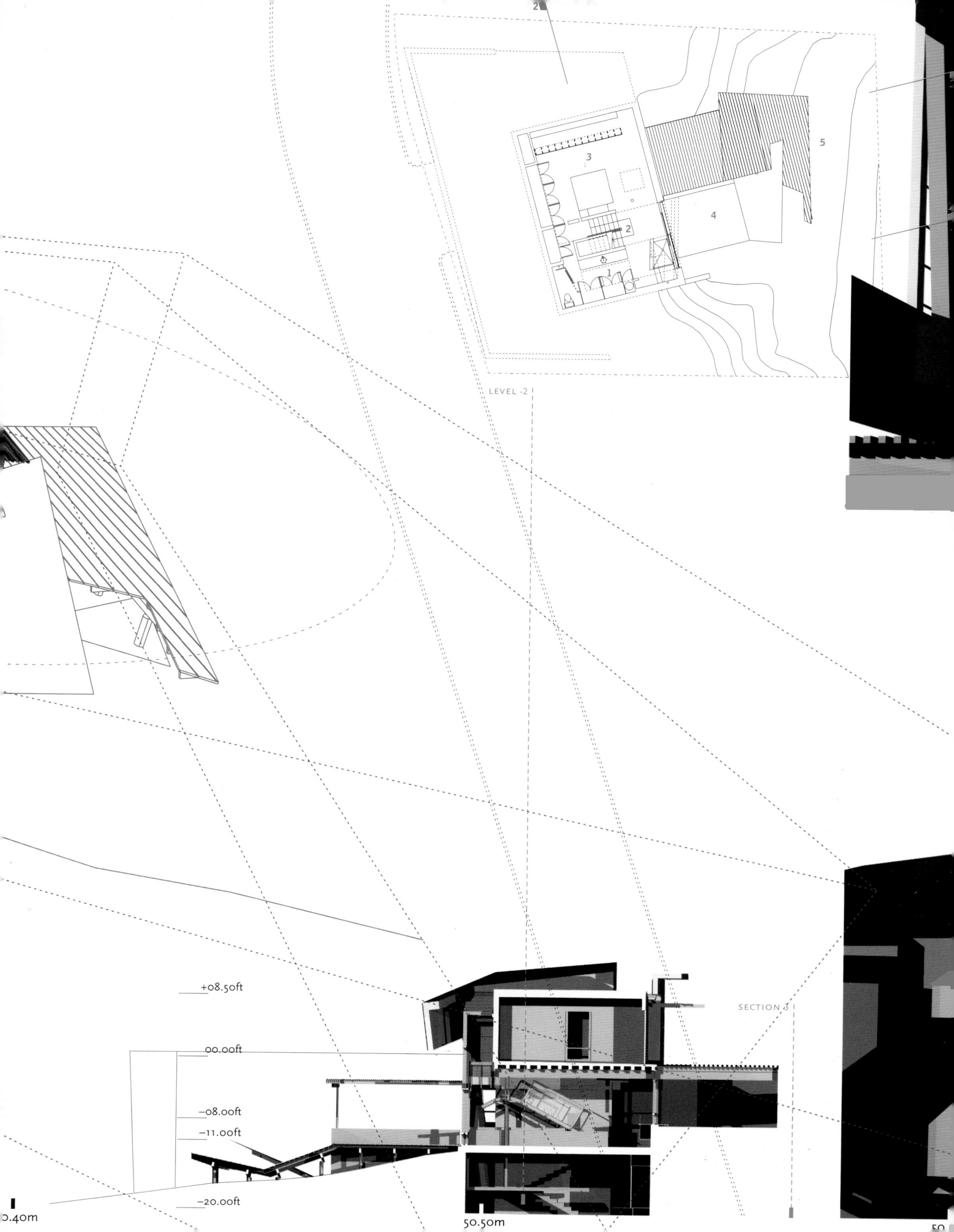

2
3
2
1
4
5
LEVEL -2
+08.50ft
00.00ft
–08.00ft
–11.00ft
–20.00ft
SECTION 3
50.50m

INTERIOR VIEW
m
50.70m
50.80m

1997

1996

1995

1994

1993

1992

97011
S.H.R. PERCEPTUAL MANAGEMENT
INTERIOR VIEW
51.10m
51.20m

21

SCOTTSDALE ARIZONA

APPENDIX

II.32 ABOUT THE WORK
V.27 STUDY MODELS

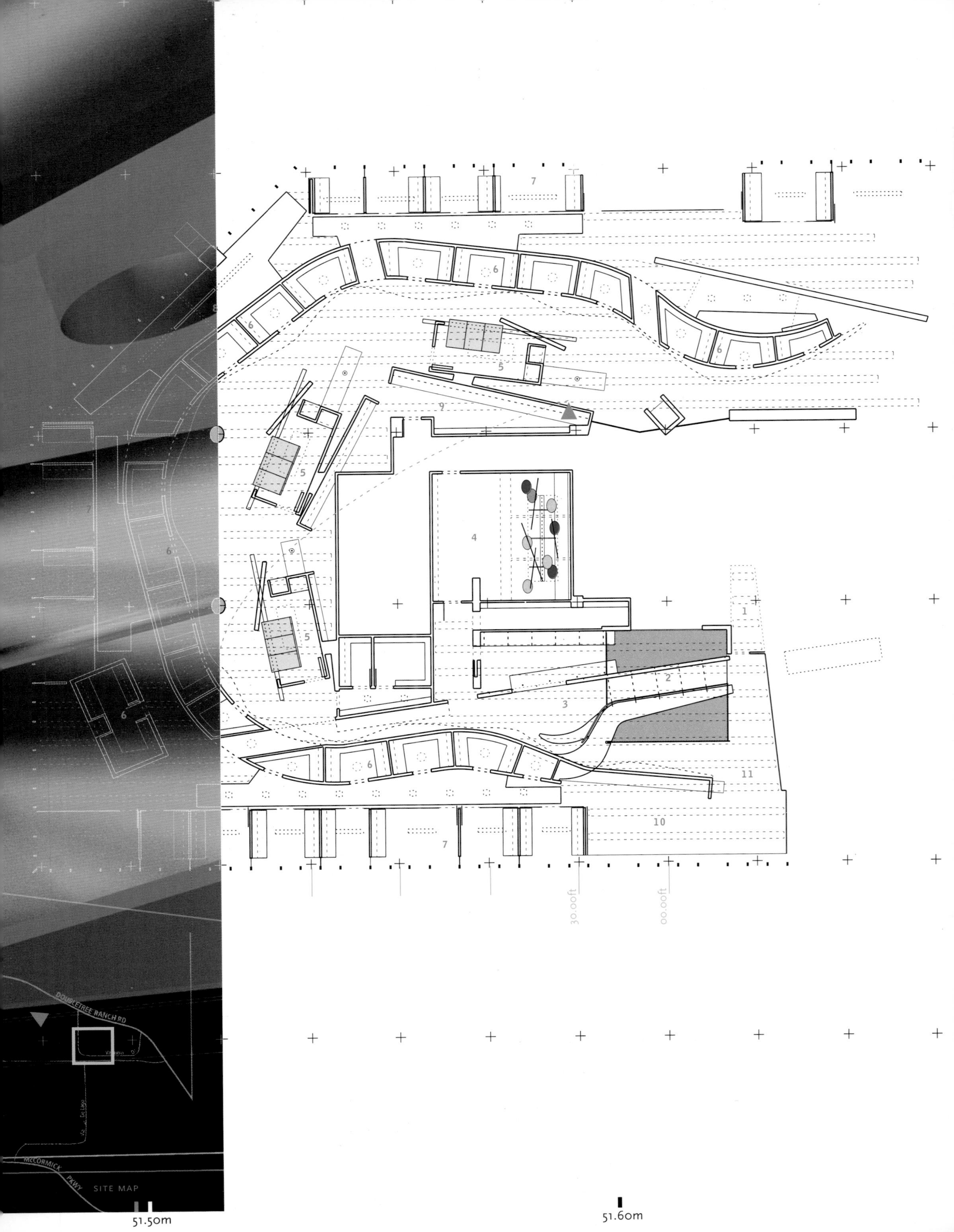
DOUBLETREE RANCH RD
MCCORMICK PKWY
SITE MAP
30.00ft
00.00ft
51.50m
51.60m

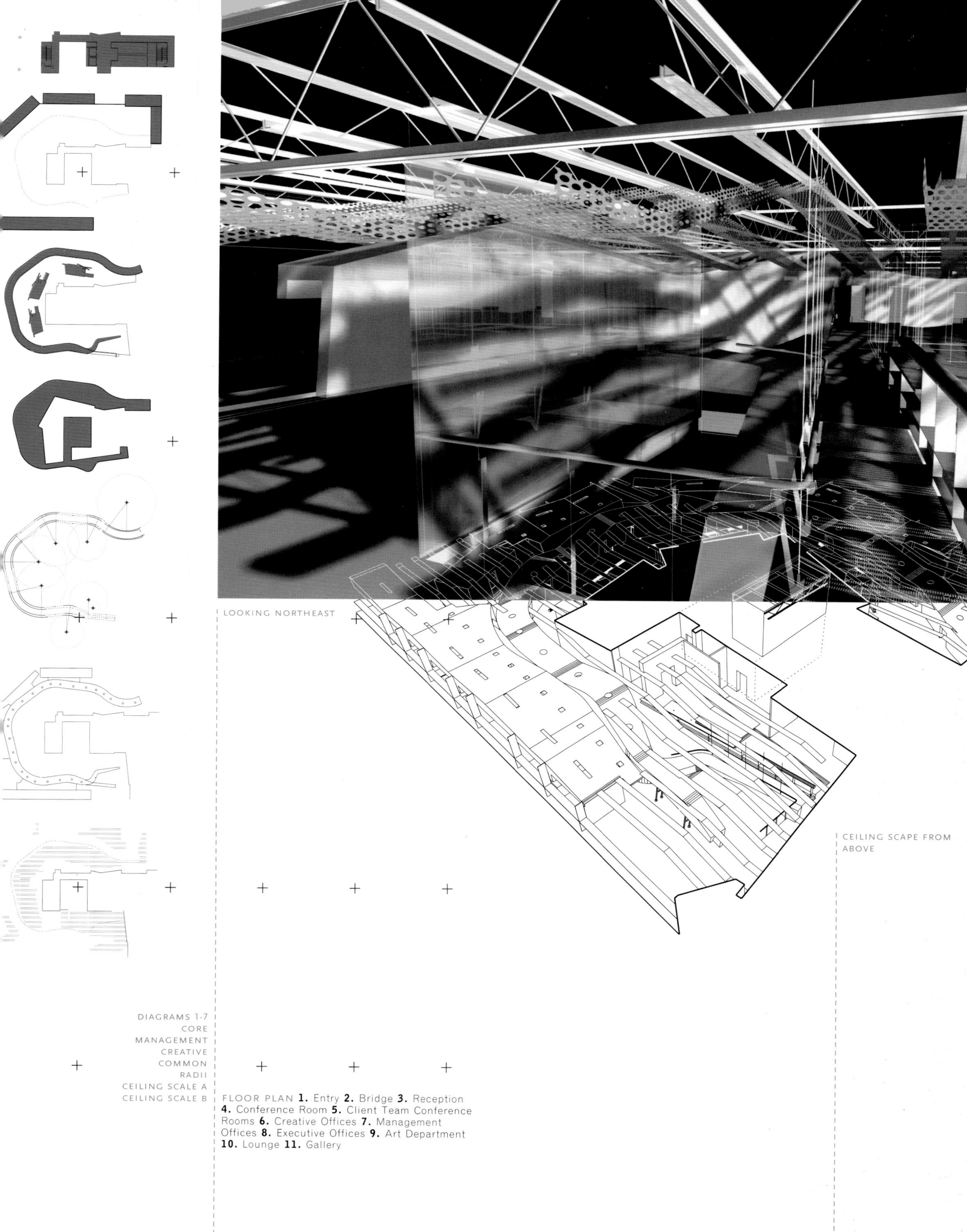

LOOKING NORTHEAST

CEILING SCAPE FROM ABOVE

DIAGRAMS 1-7
CORE
MANAGEMENT
CREATIVE
COMMON
RADII
CEILING SCALE A
CEILING SCALE B

FLOOR PLAN **1.** Entry **2.** Bridge **3.** Reception **4.** Conference Room **5.** Client Team Conference Rooms **6.** Creative Offices **7.** Management Offices **8.** Executive Offices **9.** Art Department **10.** Lounge **11.** Gallery

LOOKING FROM BELOW

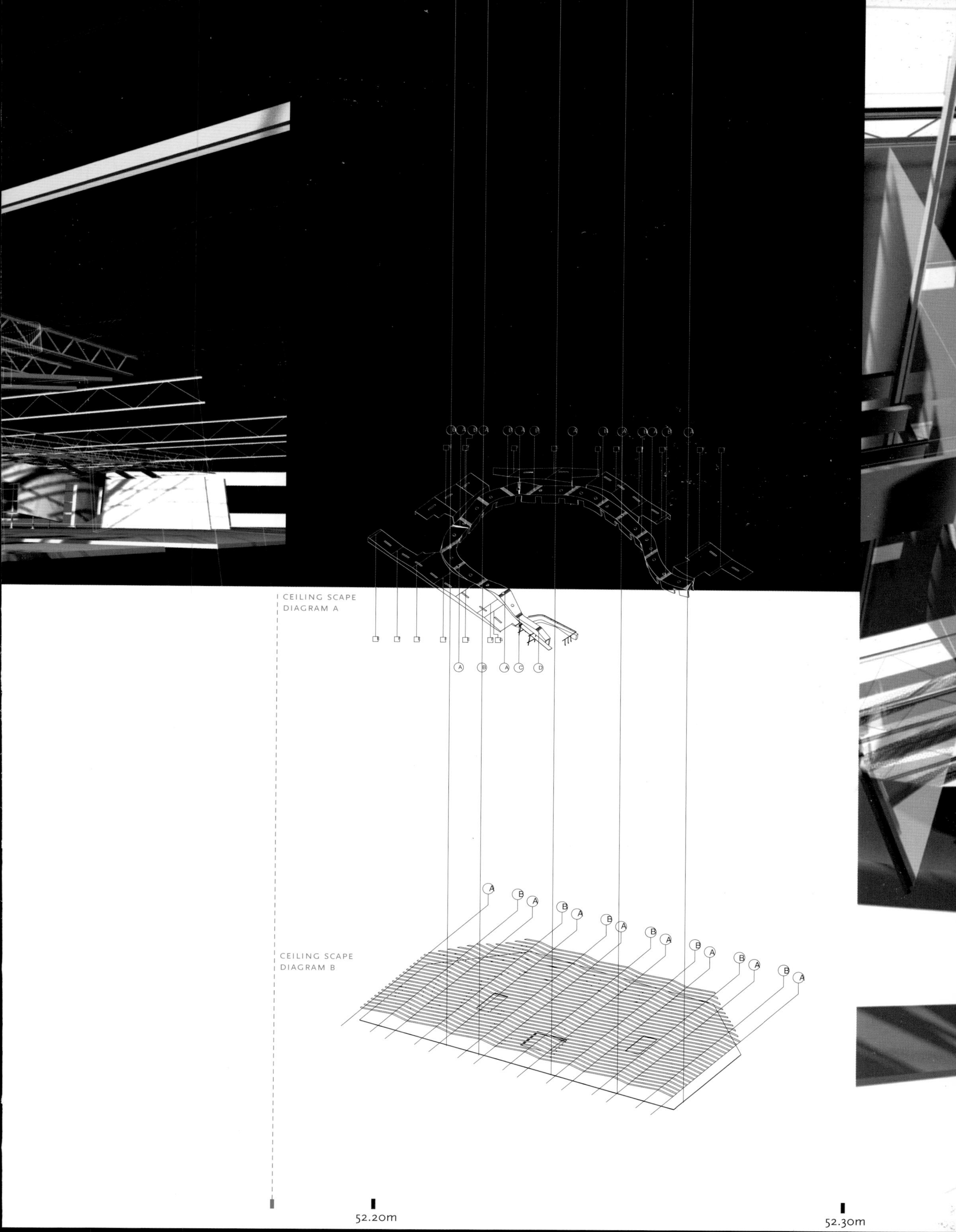
CEILING SCAPE
DIAGRAM A
CEILING SCAPE
DIAGRAM B
52.20m
52.30m

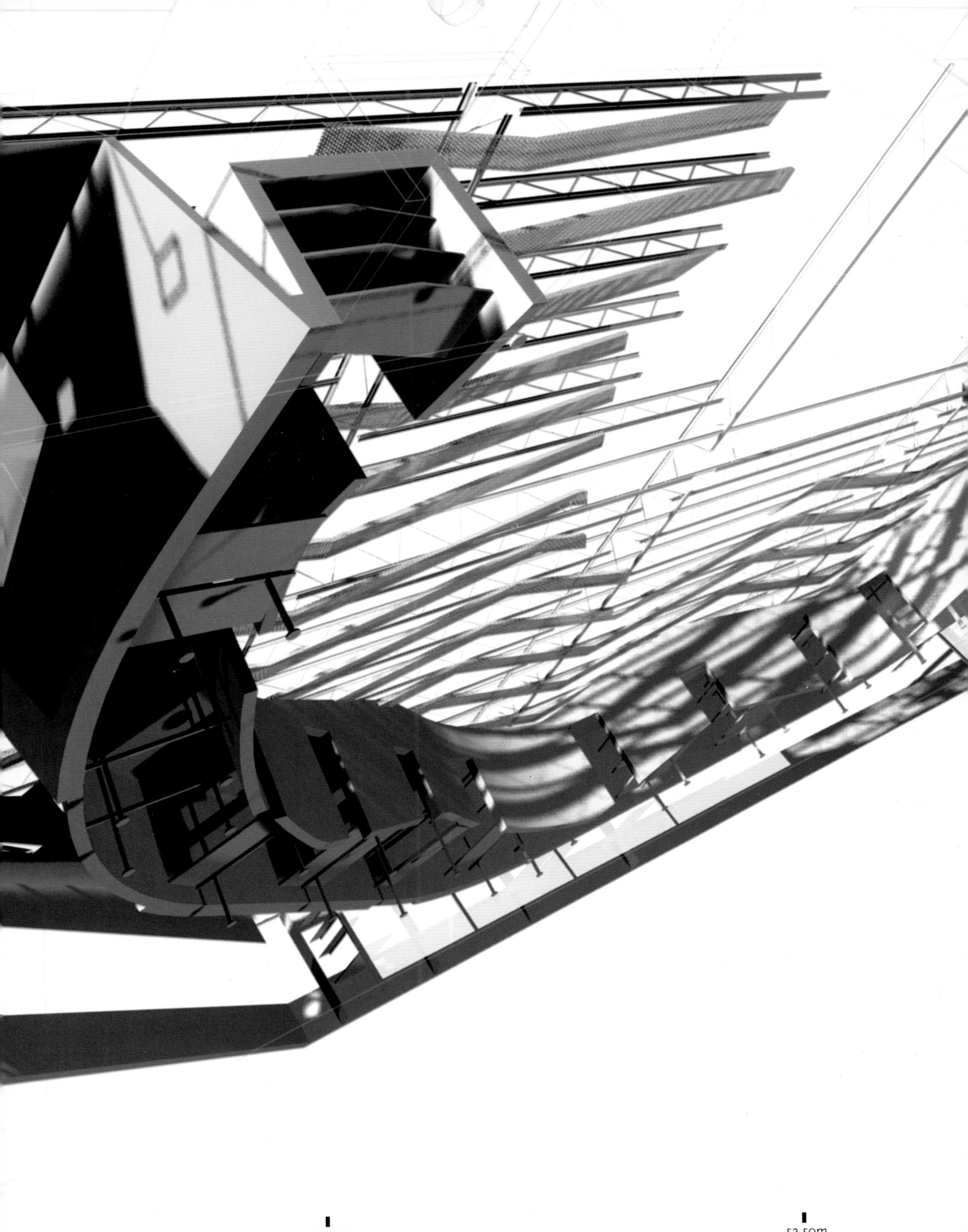

52.40m 52.50m

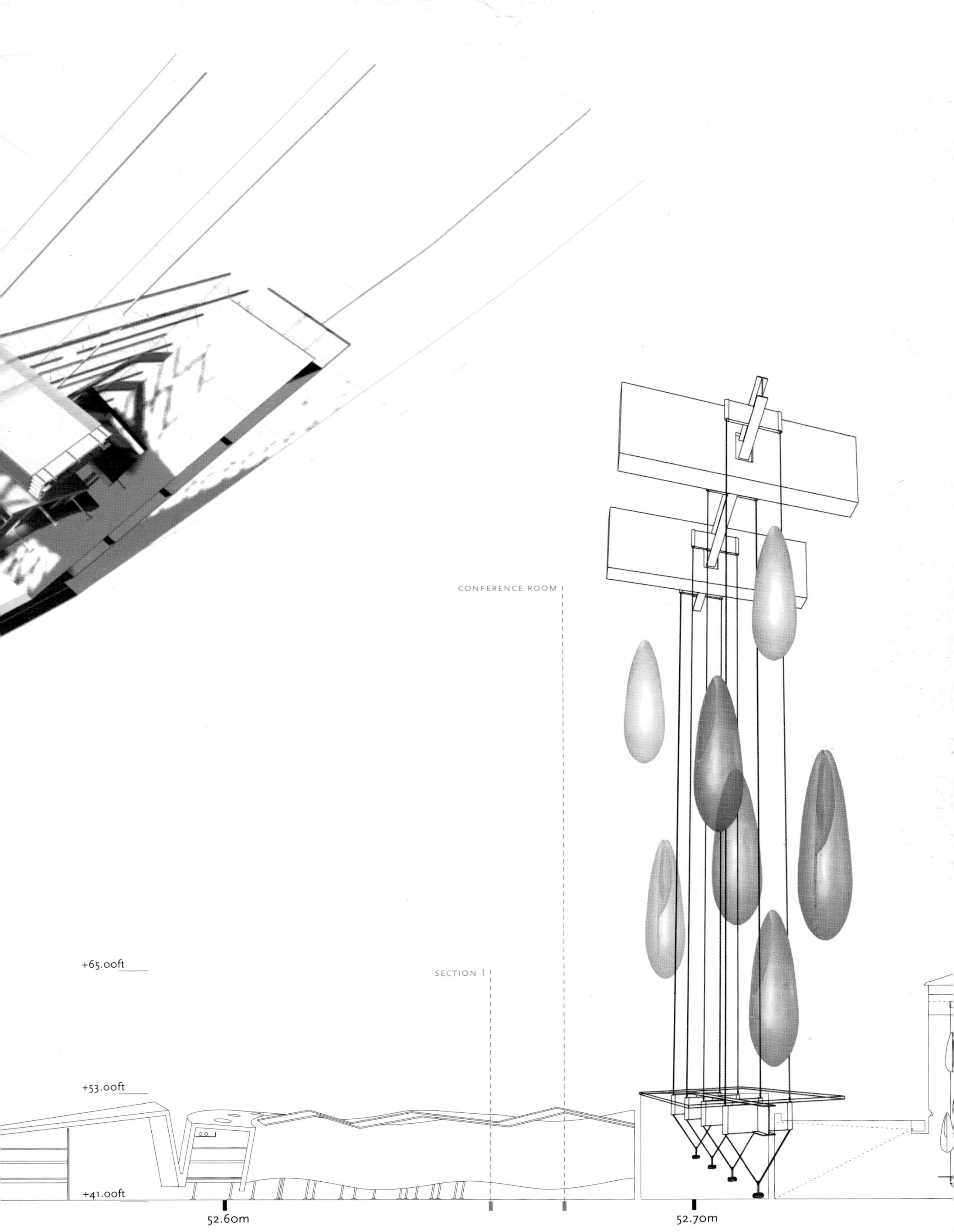
CONFERENCE ROOM
SECTION 1
+65.00ft
+53.00ft
+41.00ft
52.60m
52.70m

PROJECT DATA

AREA OF SITE
Tenant Improvement

PROGRAM
14,960sf / 1390m²

HUMAN POPULATION
Staff: 50

PARKING
Cars: 30

MECHANICAL SYSTEM
Forced Air

STRUCTURAL SYSTEM
Lightweight Steel Frame

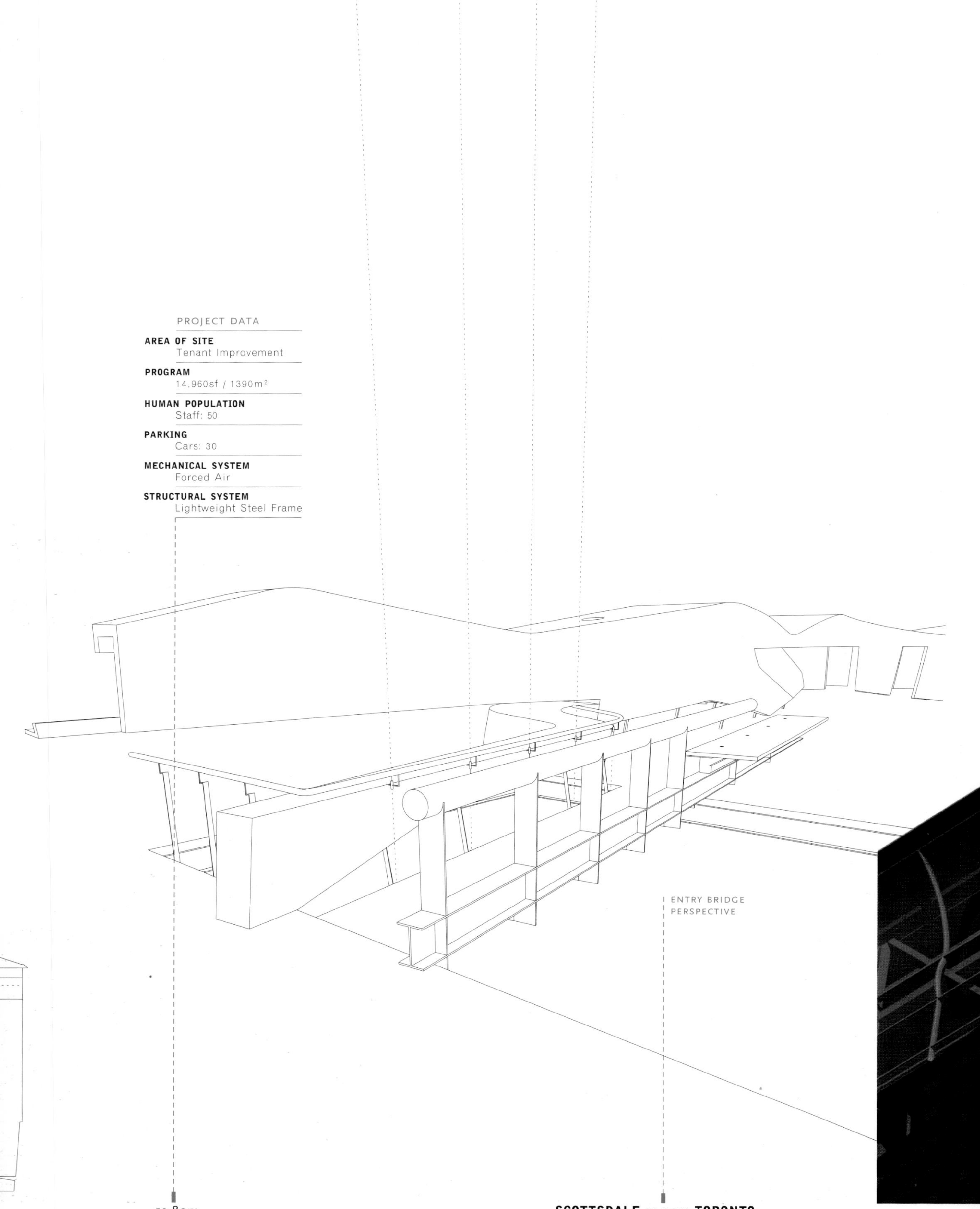

ENTRY BRIDGE PERSPECTIVE

97021
UNIVERSITY OF TORONTO
GRADUATE HOUSING
1997
1996
1995
1994
1993
1992

97021

UNIVERSITY OF TORONTO GRADUATE HOUSING

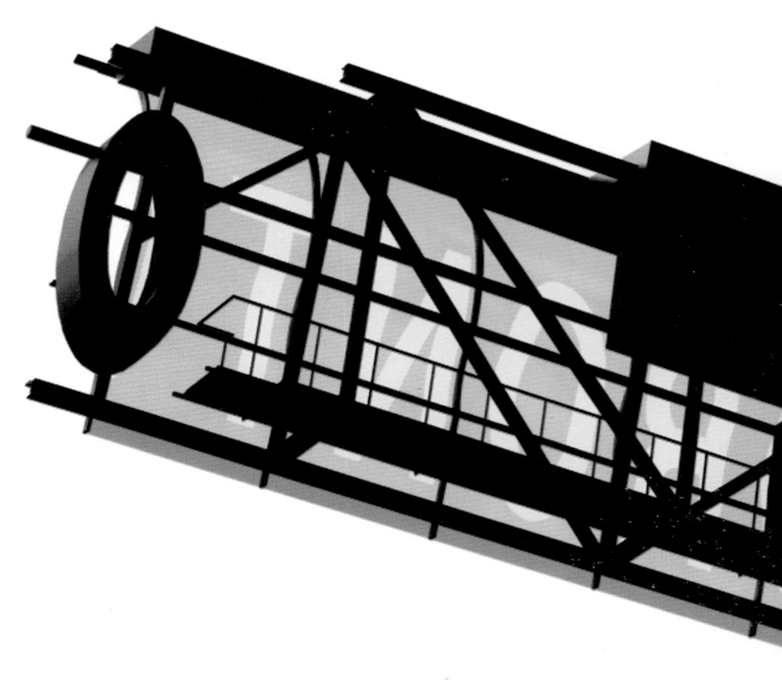

CITY OF TORONTO,
SITE PLAN

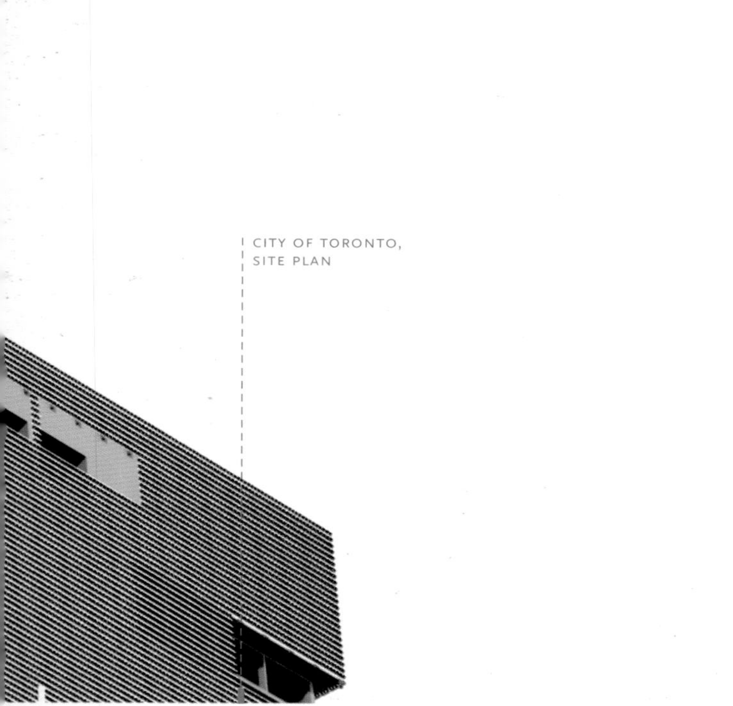

TORONTO
CANADA

2

APPENDIX
II.32 ABOUT THE WORK
V.31 STUDY MODELS

LOOKING NORTHWEST

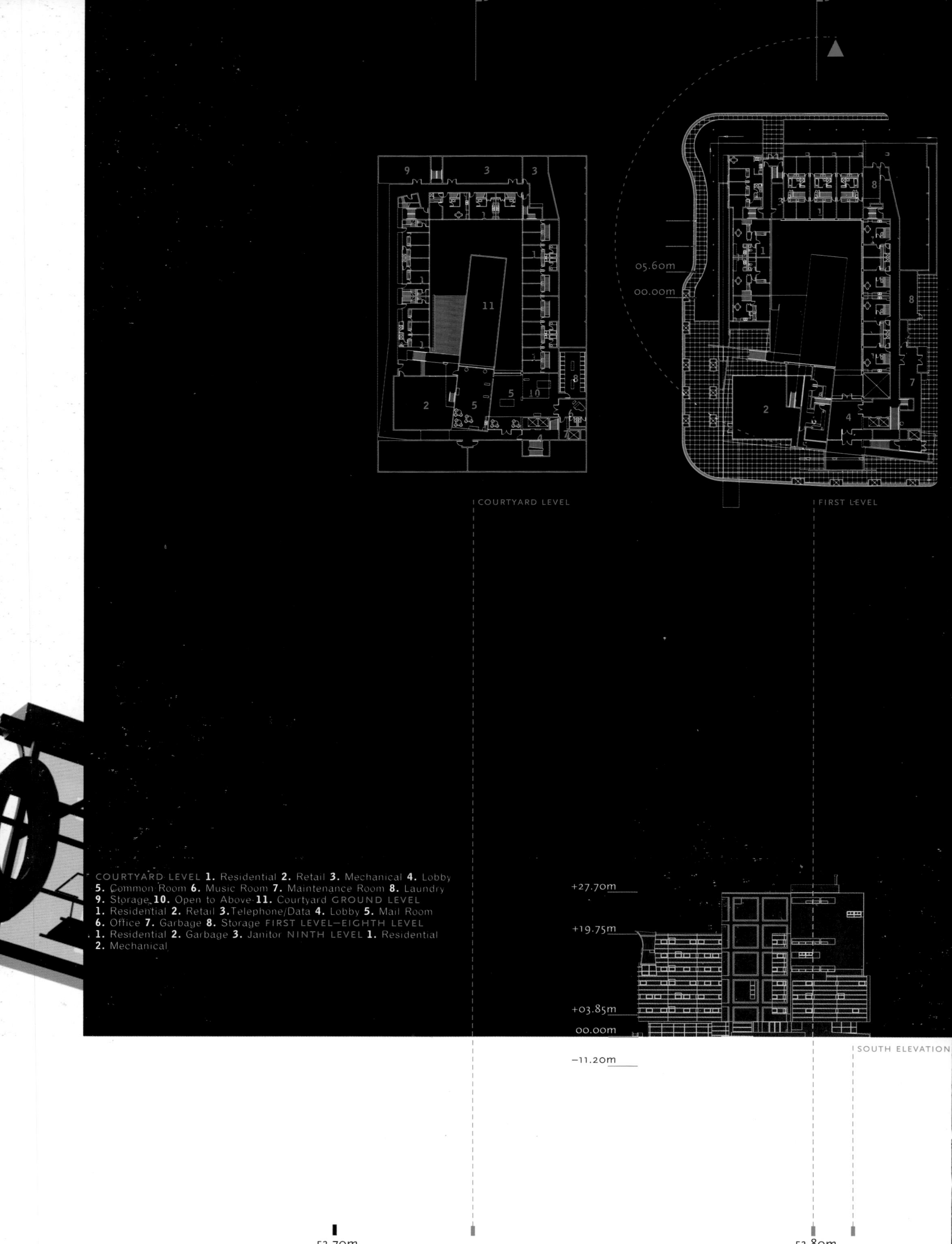

9
3
3
11
2
5
5
10
8
7
05.60m
00.00m
1
3
8
8
7
2
4
COURTYARD LEVEL
FIRST LEVEL
COURTYARD LEVEL 1. Residential 2. Retail 3. Mechanical 4. Lobby 5. Common Room 6. Music Room 7. Maintenance Room 8. Laundry 9. Storage 10. Open to Above 11. Courtyard GROUND LEVEL 1. Residential 2. Retail 3.Telephone/Data 4. Lobby 5. Mail Room 6. Office 7. Garbage 8. Storage FIRST LEVEL–EIGHTH LEVEL 1. Residential 2. Garbage 3. Janitor NINTH LEVEL 1. Residential 2. Mechanical
+27.70m
+19.75m
+03.85m
00.00m
–11.20m
SOUTH ELEVATION
53.70m
53.80m

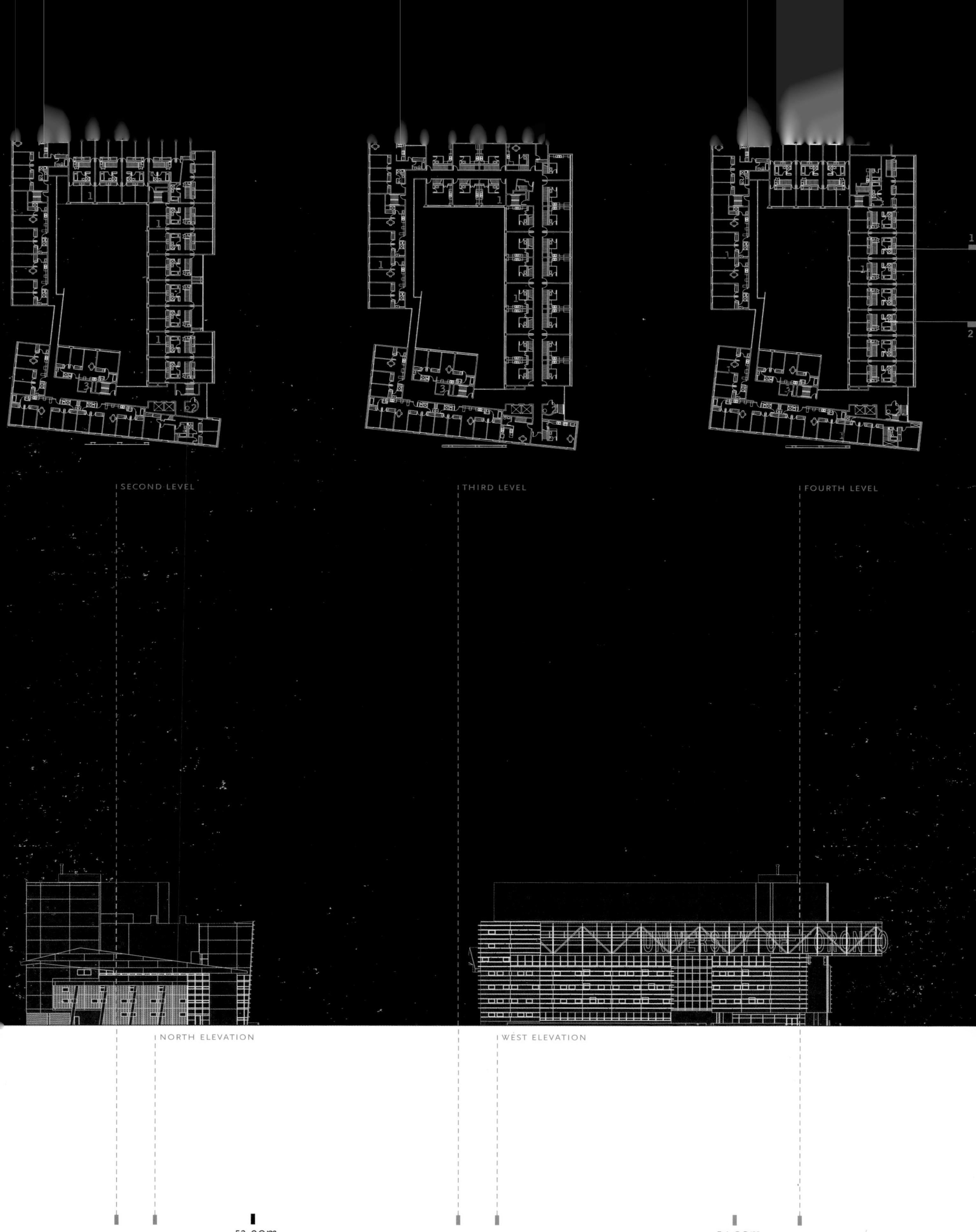
1
2
SECOND LEVEL
THIRD LEVEL
FOURTH LEVEL
UNIVERSITY OF TORONTO
NORTH ELEVATION
WEST ELEVATION
53.90m
54.00m

FIFTH LEVEL
SIXTH LEVEL
SEVENTH LEVEL
+27.70m
+19.75m
+03.85m
00.00m
-11.20m
EAST ELEVATION
SECTION 1
54.10m
54.20m

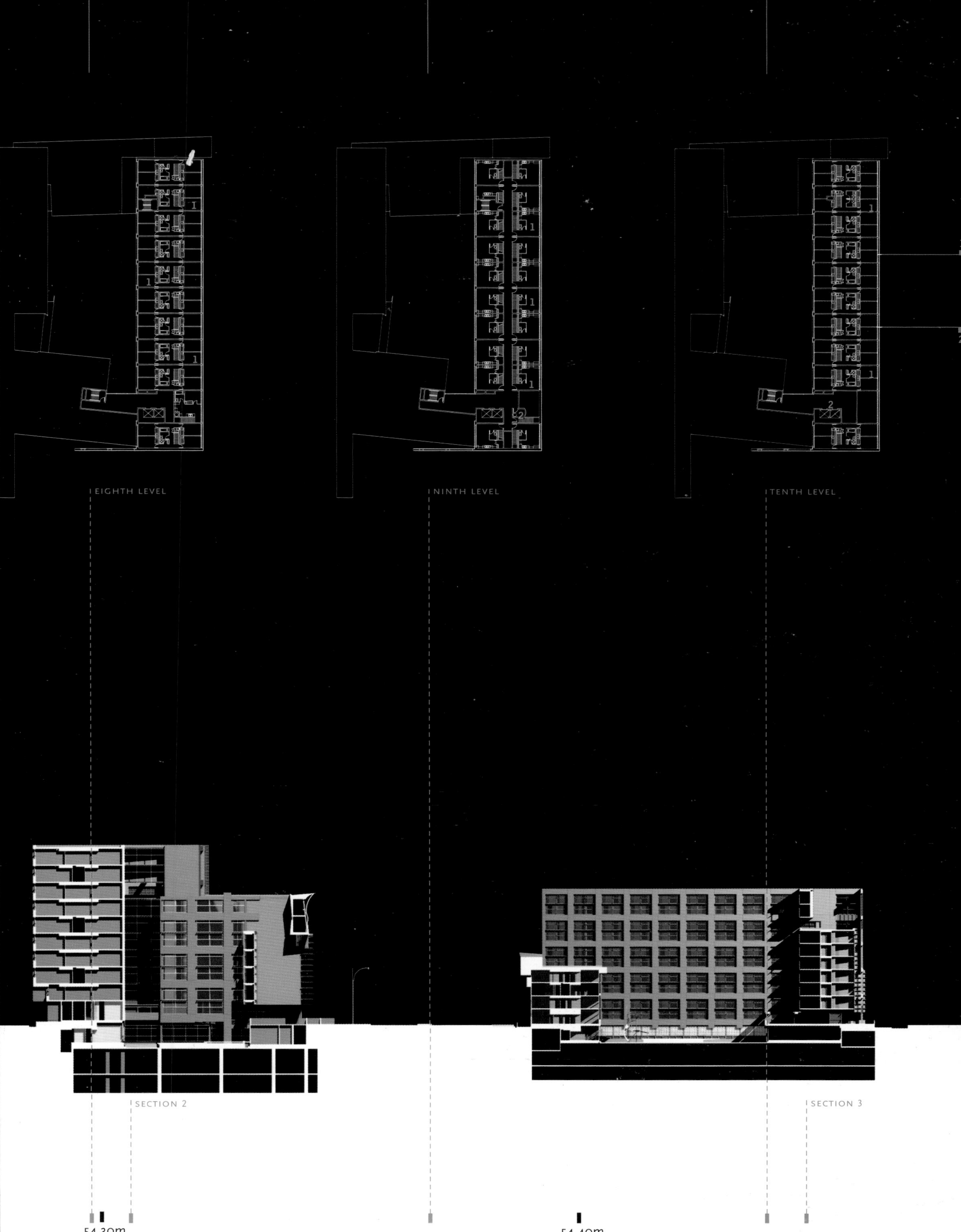

EIGHTH LEVEL
NINTH LEVEL
TENTH LEVEL
SECTION 2
SECTION 3
54.30m
54.40m

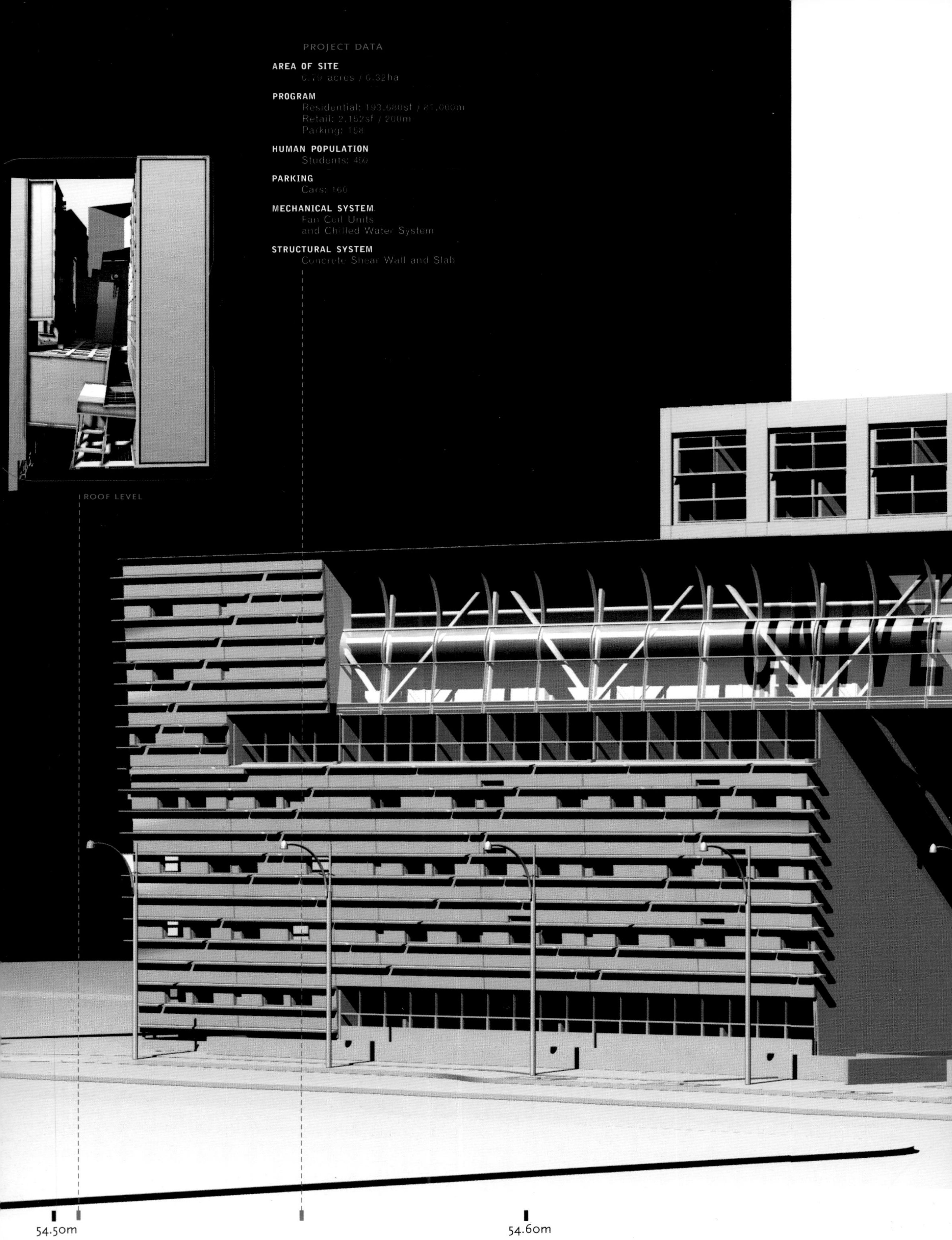
PROJECT DATA
AREA OF SITE
0.79 acres / 0.32ha
PROGRAM
Residential: 193,680sf / 81,000m
Retail: 2,152sf / 200m
Parking: 158
HUMAN POPULATION
Students: 450
PARKING
Cars: 160
MECHANICAL SYSTEM
Fan Coil Units
and Chilled Water System
STRUCTURAL SYSTEM
Concrete Shear Wall and Slab
ROOF LEVEL
54.50m
54.60m

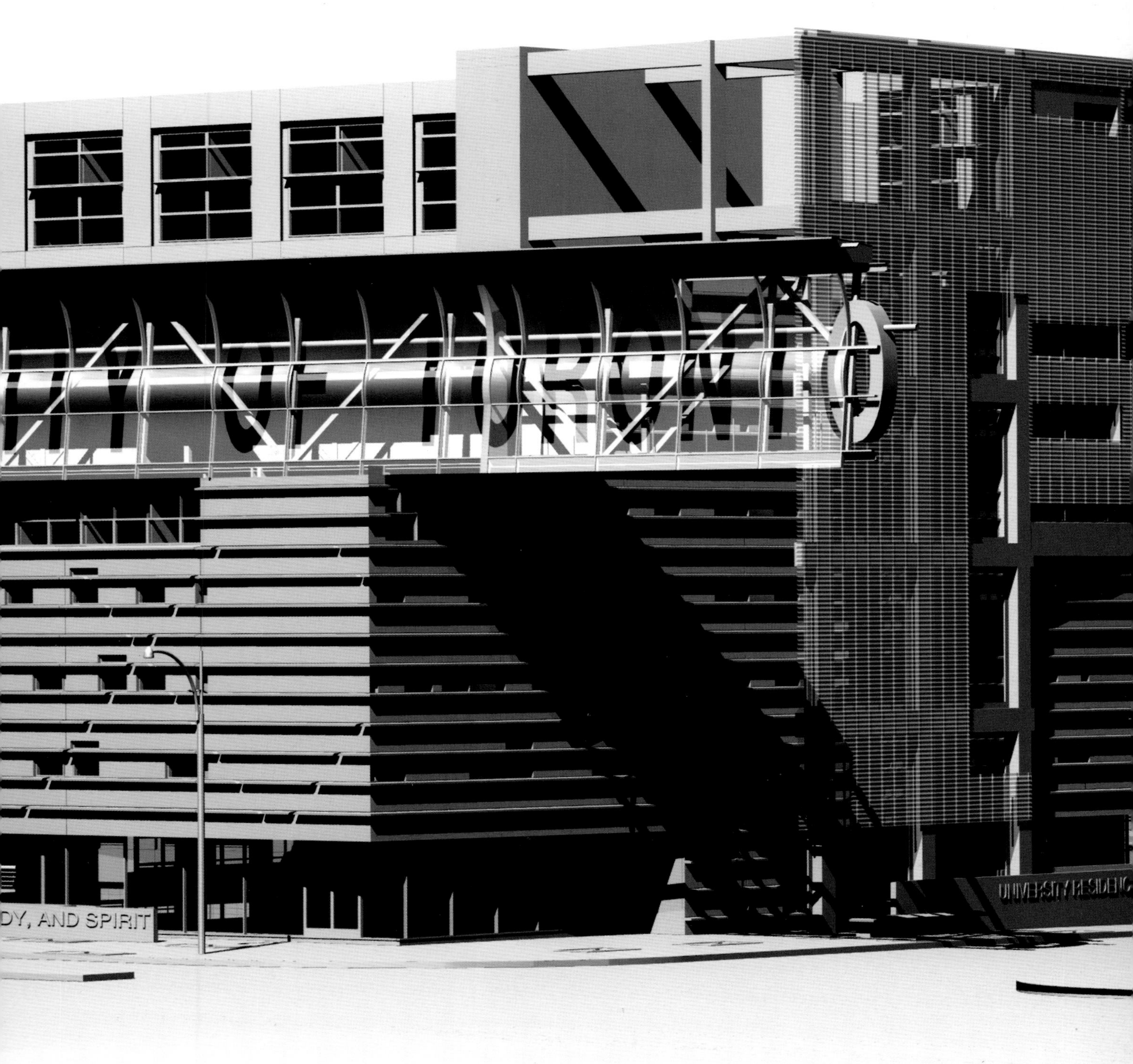

54.80m 54.90m

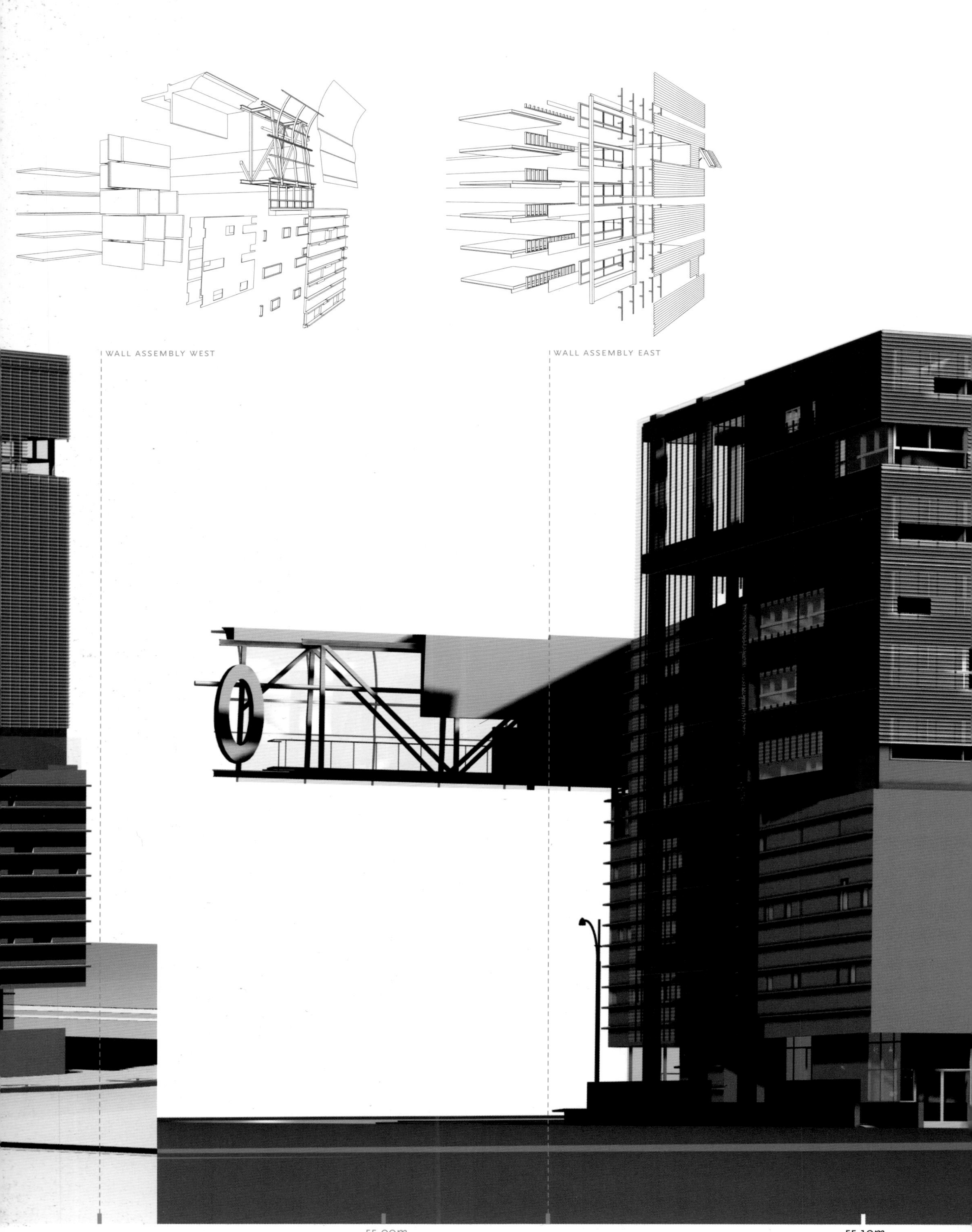
WALL ASSEMBLY WEST
WALL ASSEMBLY EAST
55.00m
55.10m

1997
1996
95900 COMPETITION
HYPO ALPE ADRIA CENTER
1995
1994
1993
1992
EAST ELEVATION
TORONTO 55.20m KLAGENFURT
55.30m

HYPO ALPE ADRIA CENTER
2
LOOKING WEST
55.40m
55.50m

3 KLAGENFURT AUSTRIA

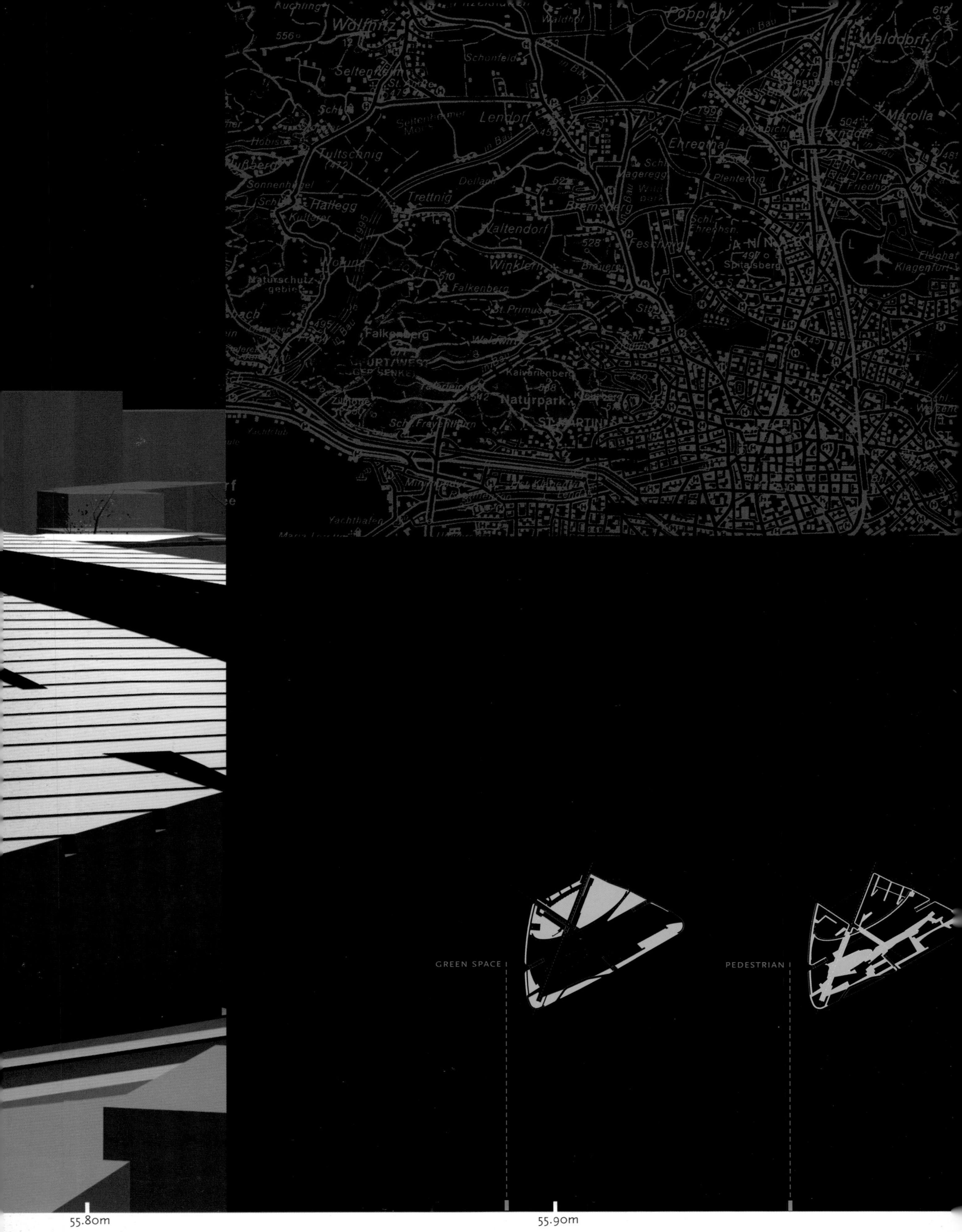
GREEN SPACE
PEDESTRIAN
55.80m
55.90m

Sechziger B.
St. Thomas
Matzendorf
Zeiselberg
Kreuzbichl
Gundersdorf
Nessendorf
Gottesbichl
Eselsberg
Drasendorf
Reigersdorf
Portendorf
Zinsdorf
Schl. Krastowitz
Hollern
Jägergedenkstätte
Farchern
St. Margarethen
Blasendorf
Hortendorf
Oberhaidach
Rain
Pokeritsch
Gutendorf
Perkonigg
Haidach
Limmersdf.
Schloß Ra
St. Jakob
a. d. Straße
Niederdorf
Kropp
Oberfischern
KLAGENFURT, SITE
SITE PLAN
HASE 1
PHASE 2
PHASE 3
ARKING
om
56.10m
56.20m

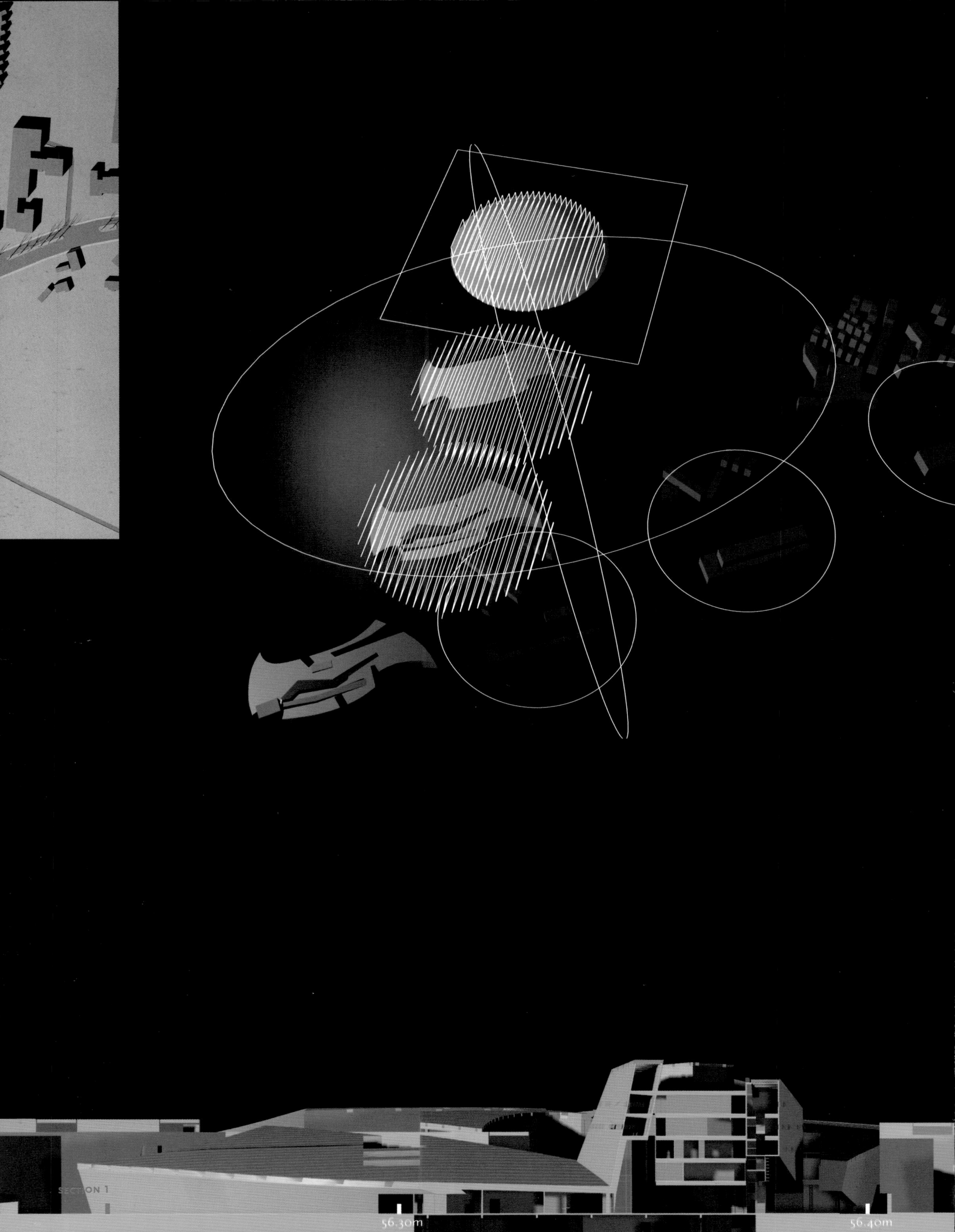
SECTION 1
56.30m
56.40m

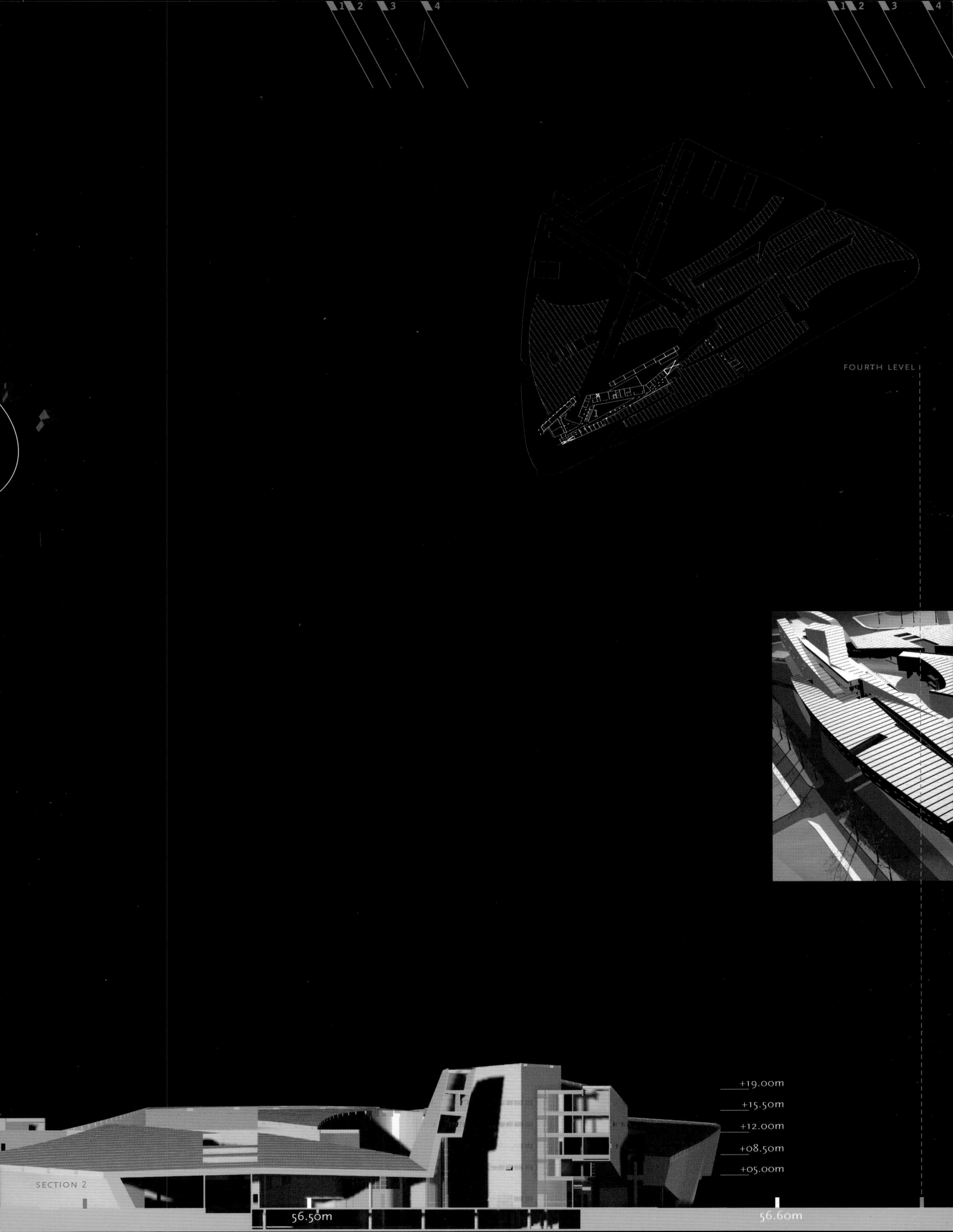
1
2
3
4
1
2
3
4
FOURTH LEVEL
+19.00m
+15.50m
+12.00m
+08.50m
+05.00m
SECTION 2
56.50m
56.60m

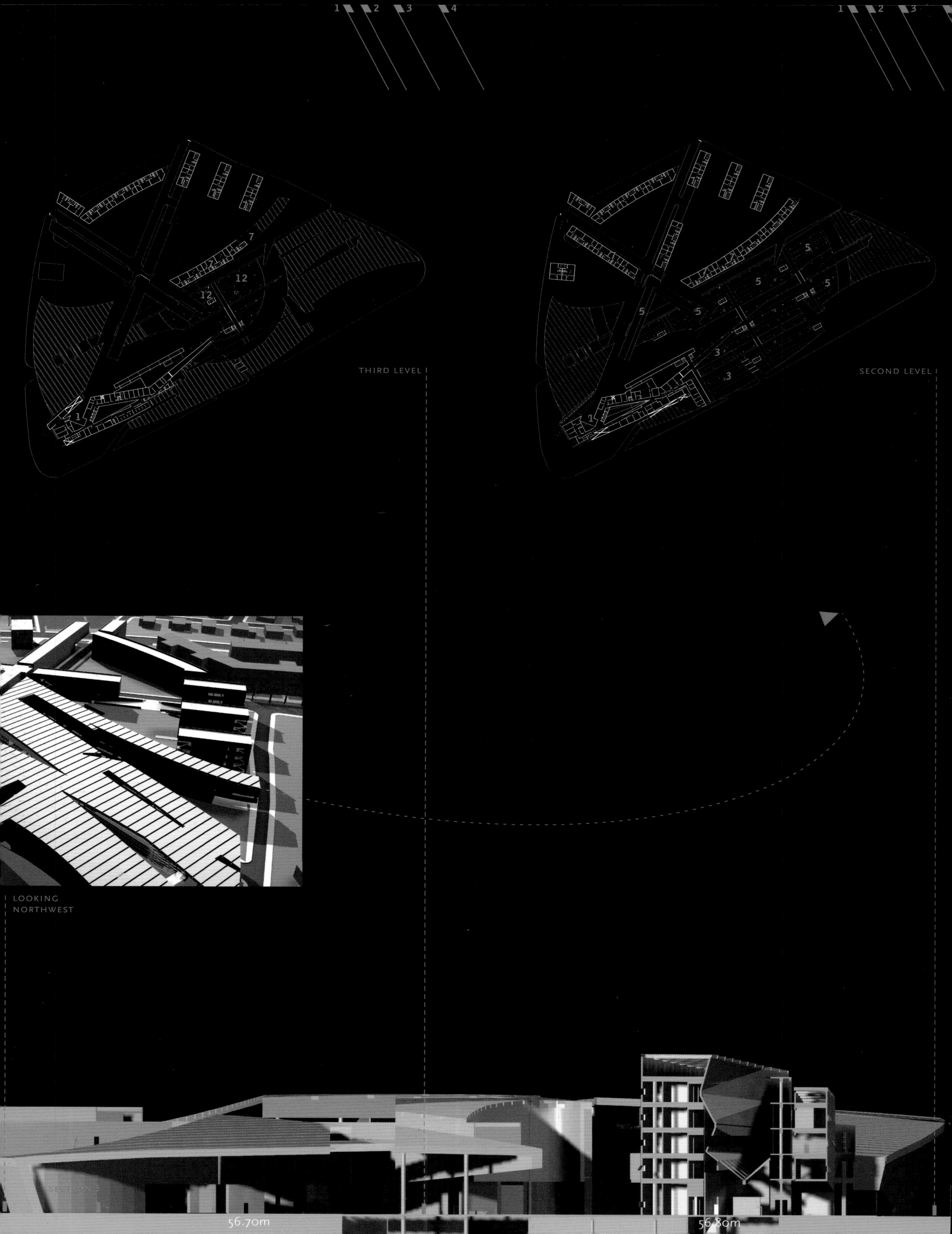

1
2
3
4
1
2
3
7
12
12
1
THIRD LEVEL
5
5
5
5
5
7
3
3
1
SECOND LEVEL
LOOKING
NORTHWEST
56.70m
56.80m

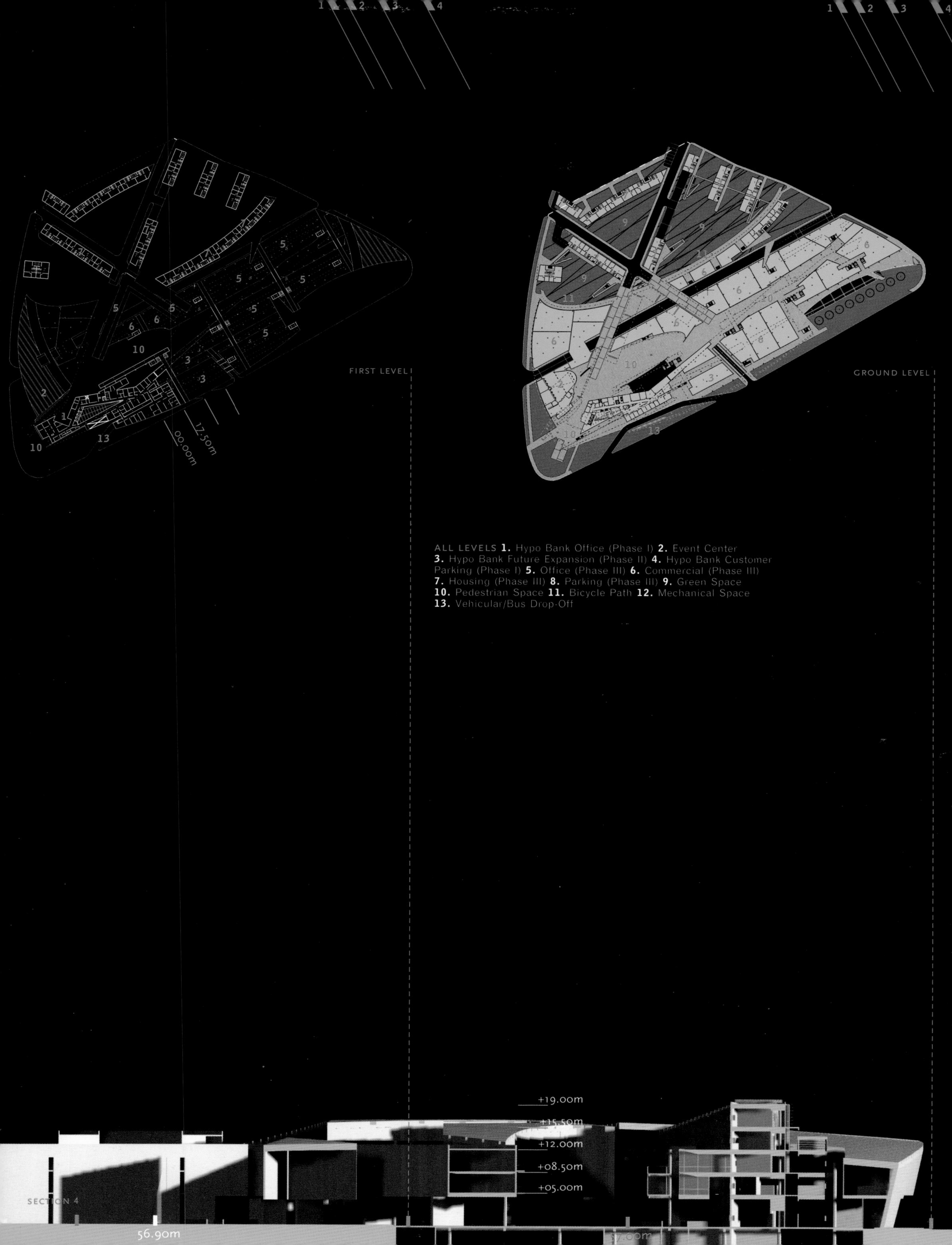

ALL LEVELS 1. Hypo Bank Office (Phase I) **2.** Event Center **3.** Hypo Bank Future Expansion (Phase II) **4.** Hypo Bank Customer Parking (Phase I) **5.** Office (Phase III) **6.** Commercial (Phase III) **7.** Housing (Phase III) **8.** Parking (Phase III) **9.** Green Space **10.** Pedestrian Space **11.** Bicycle Path **12.** Mechanical Space **13.** Vehicular/Bus Drop-Off

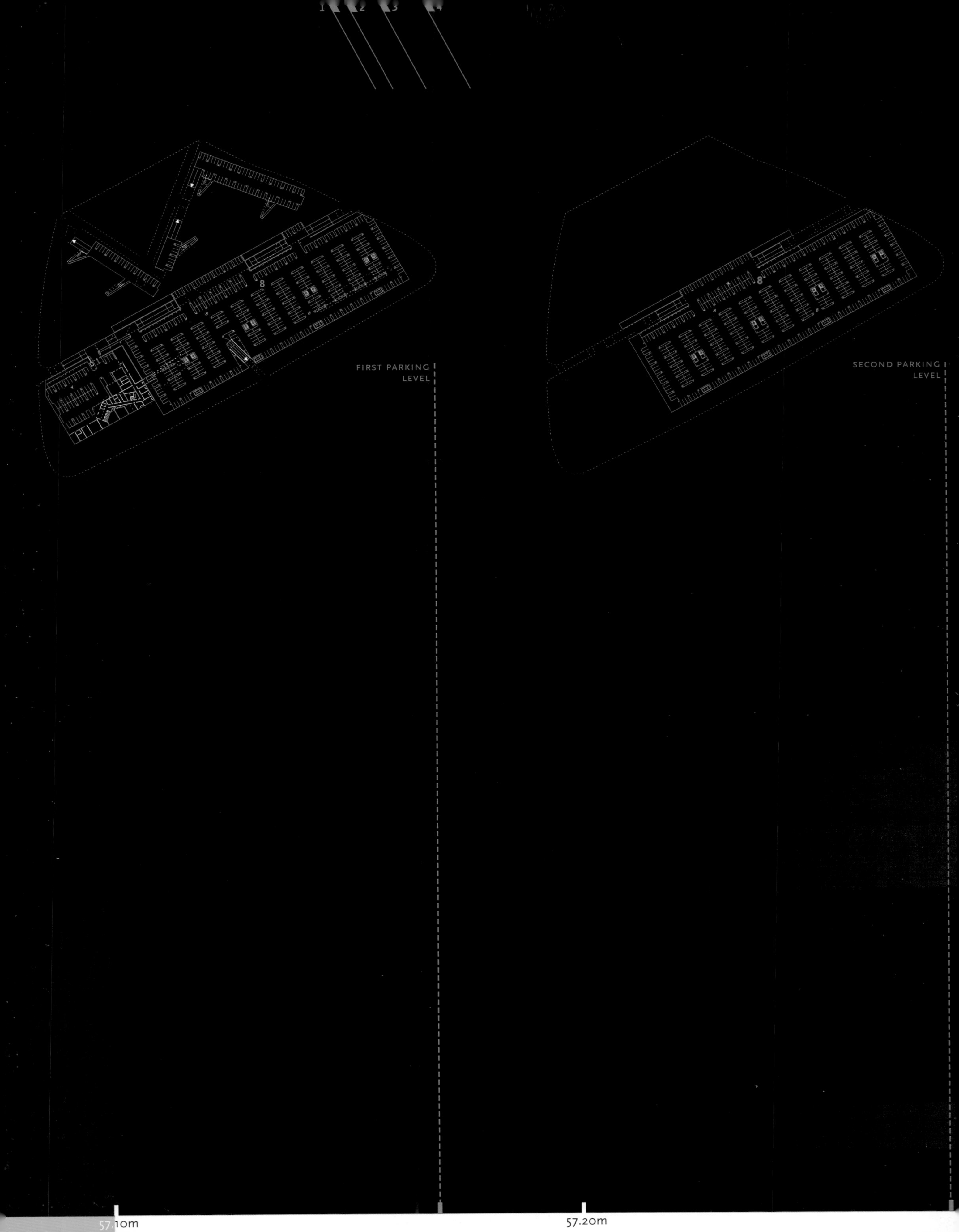

1
2
3
4
8
FIRST PARKING LEVEL
8
SECOND PARKING LEVEL
57.10m
57.20m

1997

1996

HYPO ALPE ADRIA CENTER

1995

PROJECT DATA

REA OF SITE
9.91acres / 4.01ha

ROGRAM
PHASE I: 107,600sf / 10,000m²
PHASE II: 61,332sf / 5700m²
PHASE III: 90,384sf / 8400m²

UMAN POPULATION
General: 1000

ARKING
Cars: 983

ECHANICAL SYSTEM
Heat Pump

TRUCTURAL SYSTEM
Cast in Place Concrete Frame
w/Steel Roof

1994

1993

1992

.30m **KLAGENFURT** 57.40m **KLAGENFURT** 57.50

97778 PHASES I, II & III

HYPO ALPE ADRIA CENTER 2

4 KLAGENFURT AUSTRIA

APPENDIX

NORTH ELEVATION

57.80m

57.90m

KLAGENFURT, AUSTRIA

LOOKING NORTHEA

58.00m

58.10m

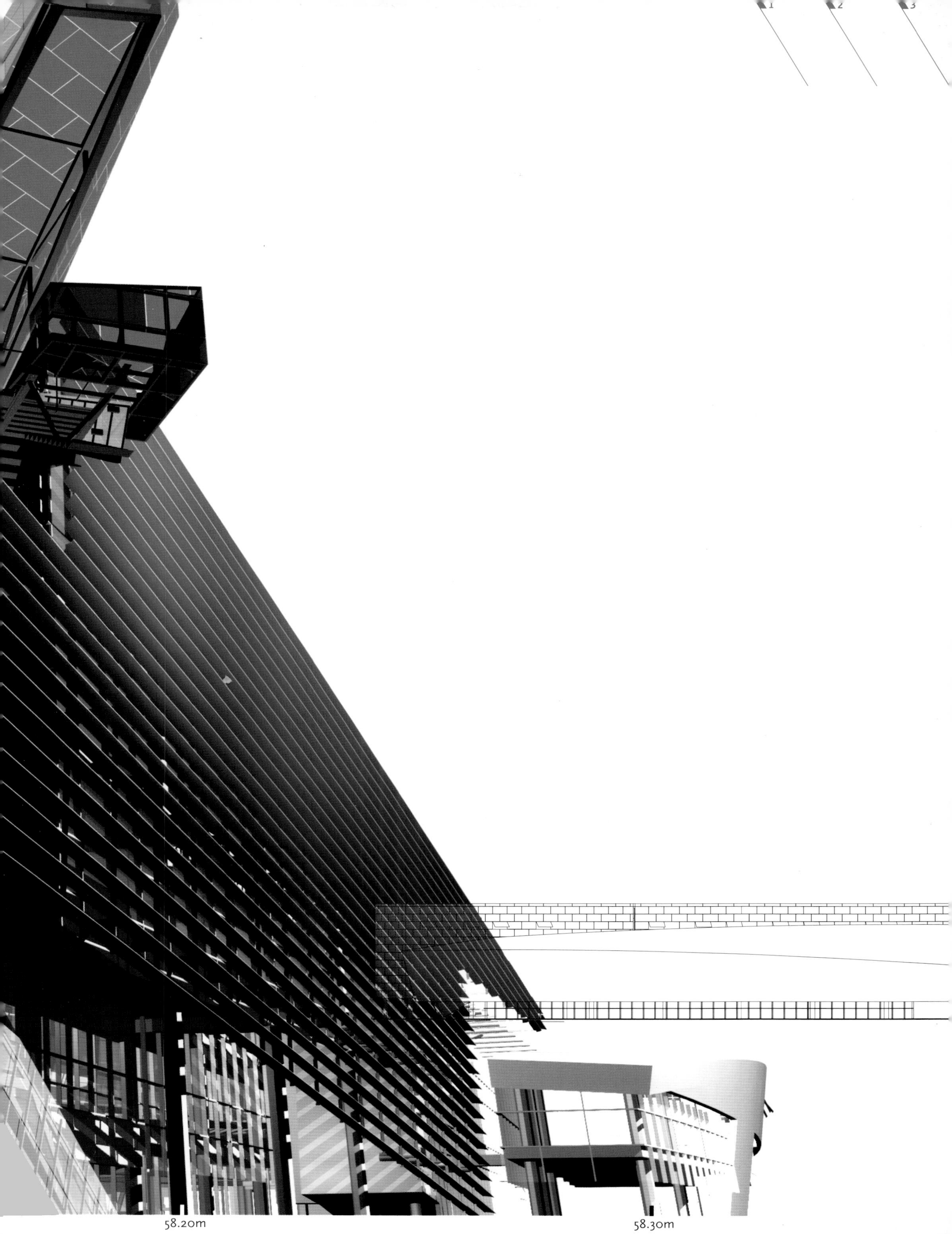
1
2
3
58.20m
58.30m

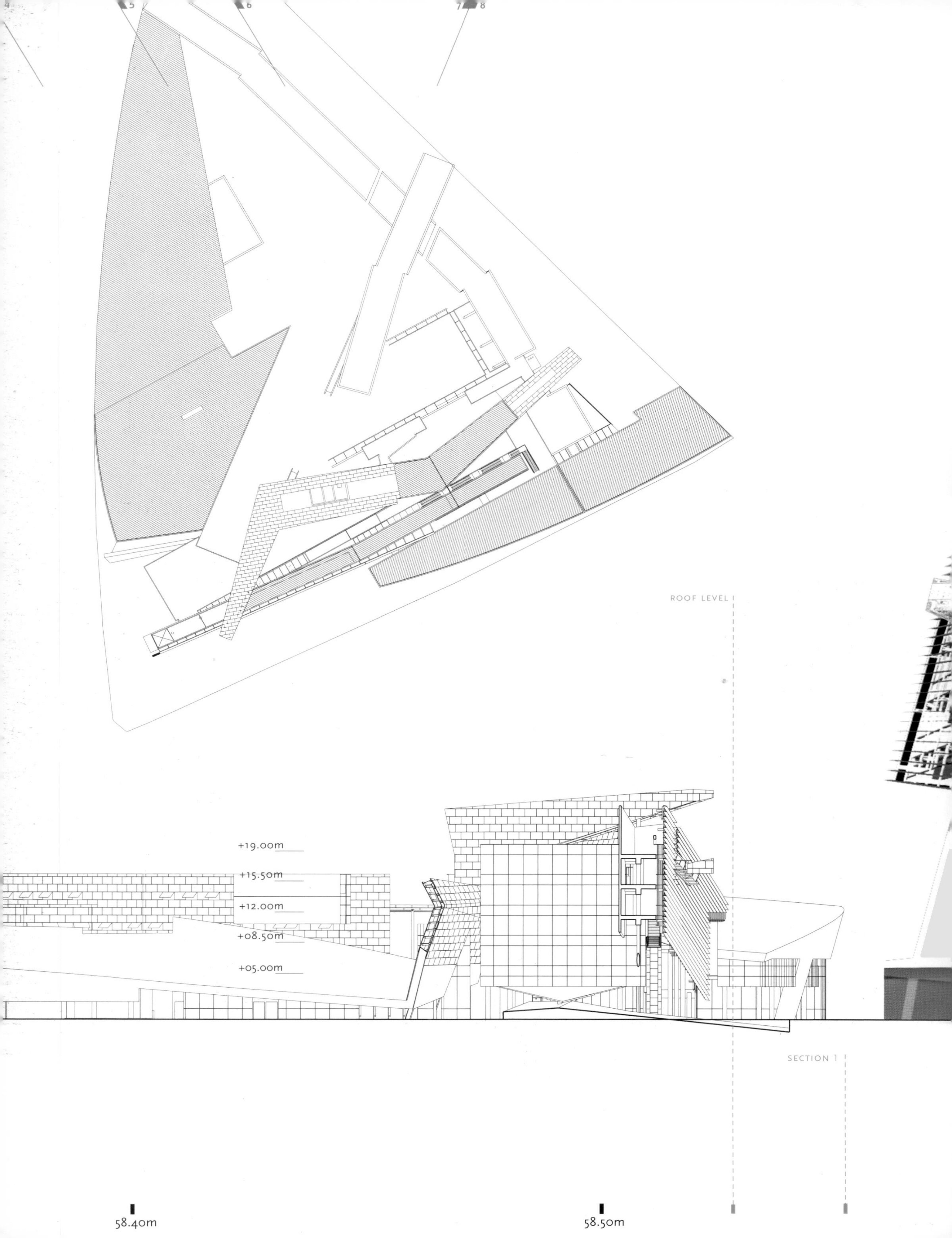
4
5
6
7
8
ROOF LEVEL
+19.00m
+15.50m
+12.00m
+08.50m
+05.00m
SECTION 1
58.40m
58.50m

LOOKING WEST

58.60m

58.70m

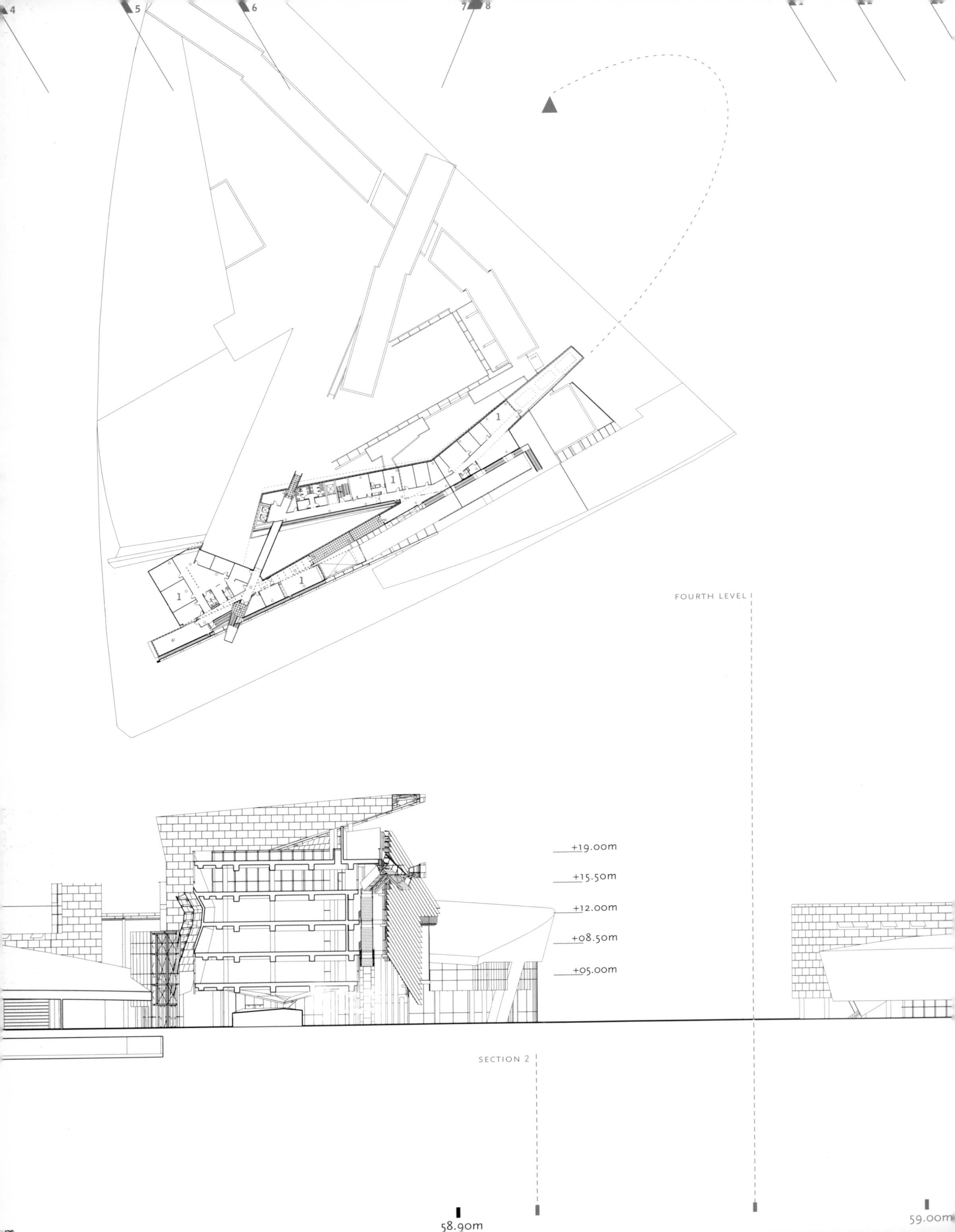
4
5
6
7
8
1
1
1
1
FOURTH LEVEL
+19.00m
+15.50m
+12.00m
+08.50m
+05.00m
SECTION 2
58.90m
59.00m

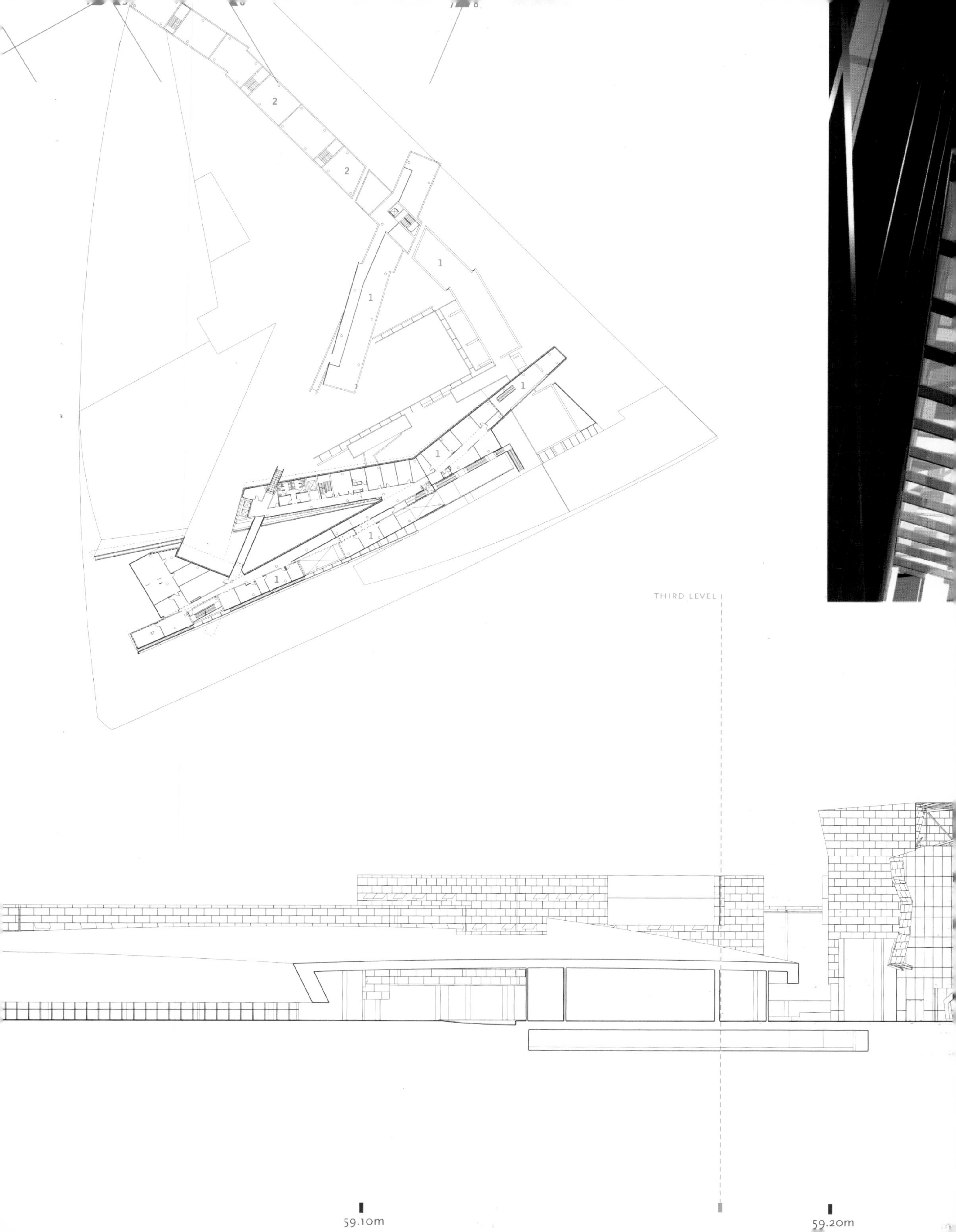
2
2
1
1
1
1
1
1
THIRD LEVEL
59.10m
59.20m

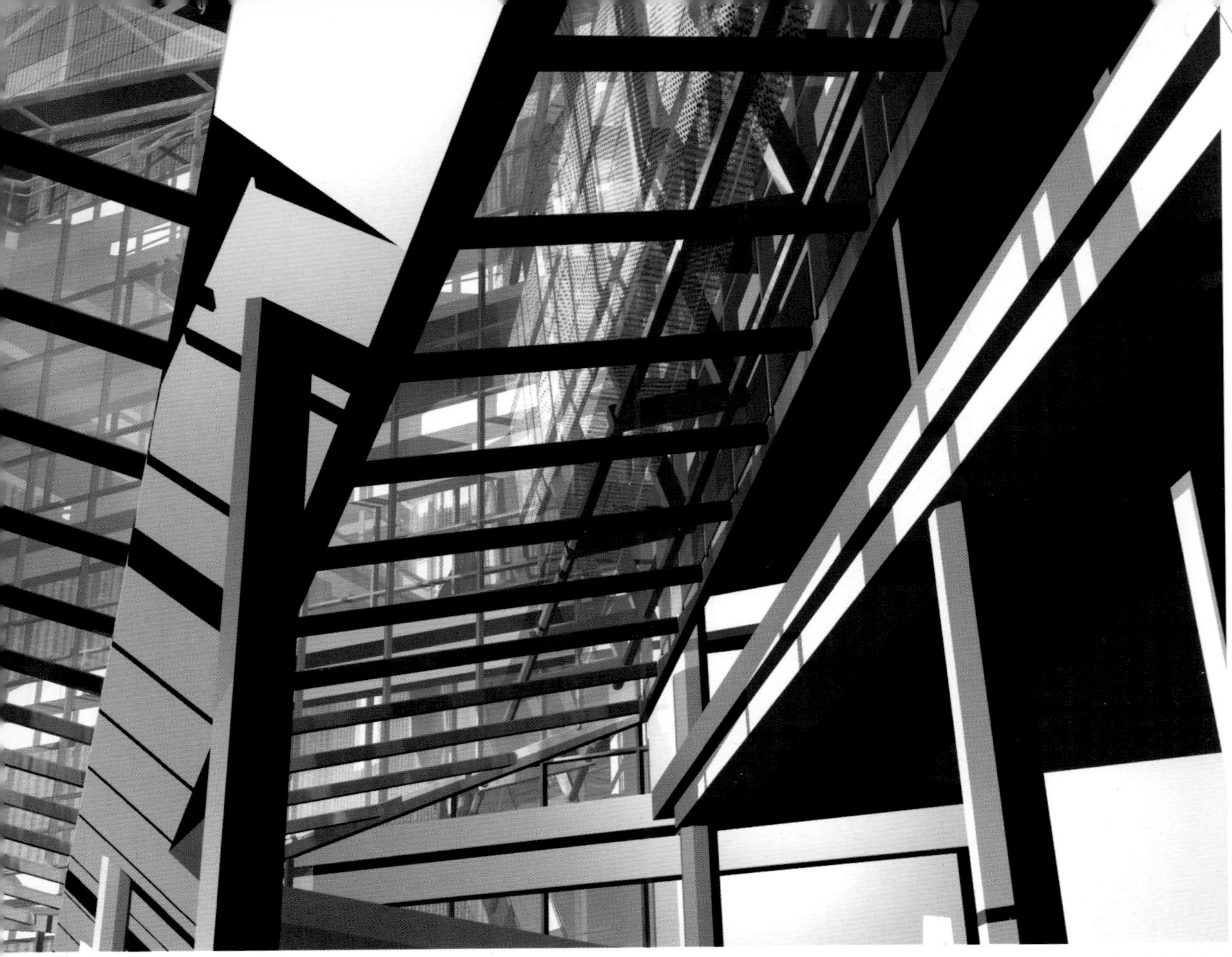

INSIDE ATRIUM

FOURTH LEVEL **1.** Offices THIRD LEVEL **1.** Offices **2.** Housing SECOND LEVEL **1.** Offices **2.** Housing FIRST LEVEL **1.** Offices **2.** Retail **3.** Housing GROUND LEVEL **1.** Branch Bank **2.** Offices **3.** Event Center **4.** Courtyard **5.** Retail **6.** Parking **7.** Kindergarten PARKING LEVEL **1.** Parking **2.** Storage/Offices **3.** Mechanical

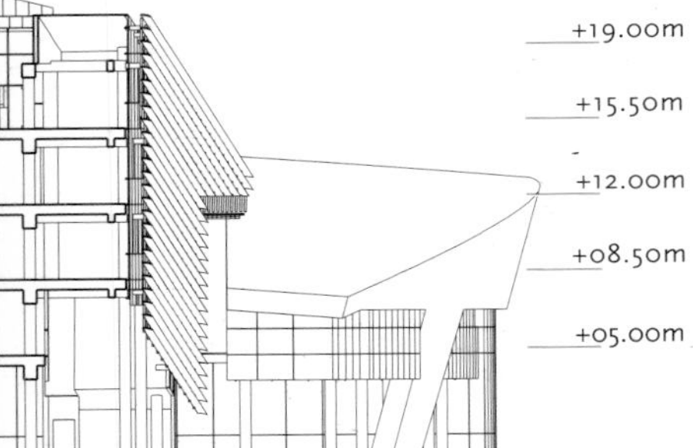

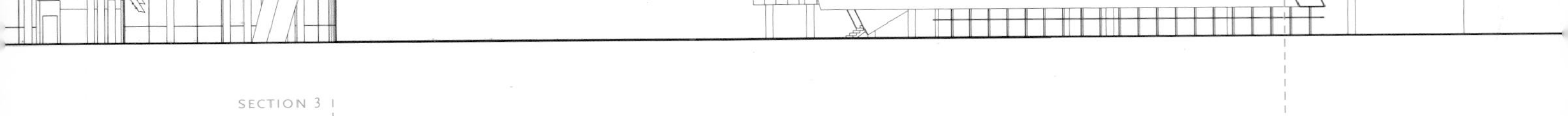

SECTION 3

59.30m

59.40m

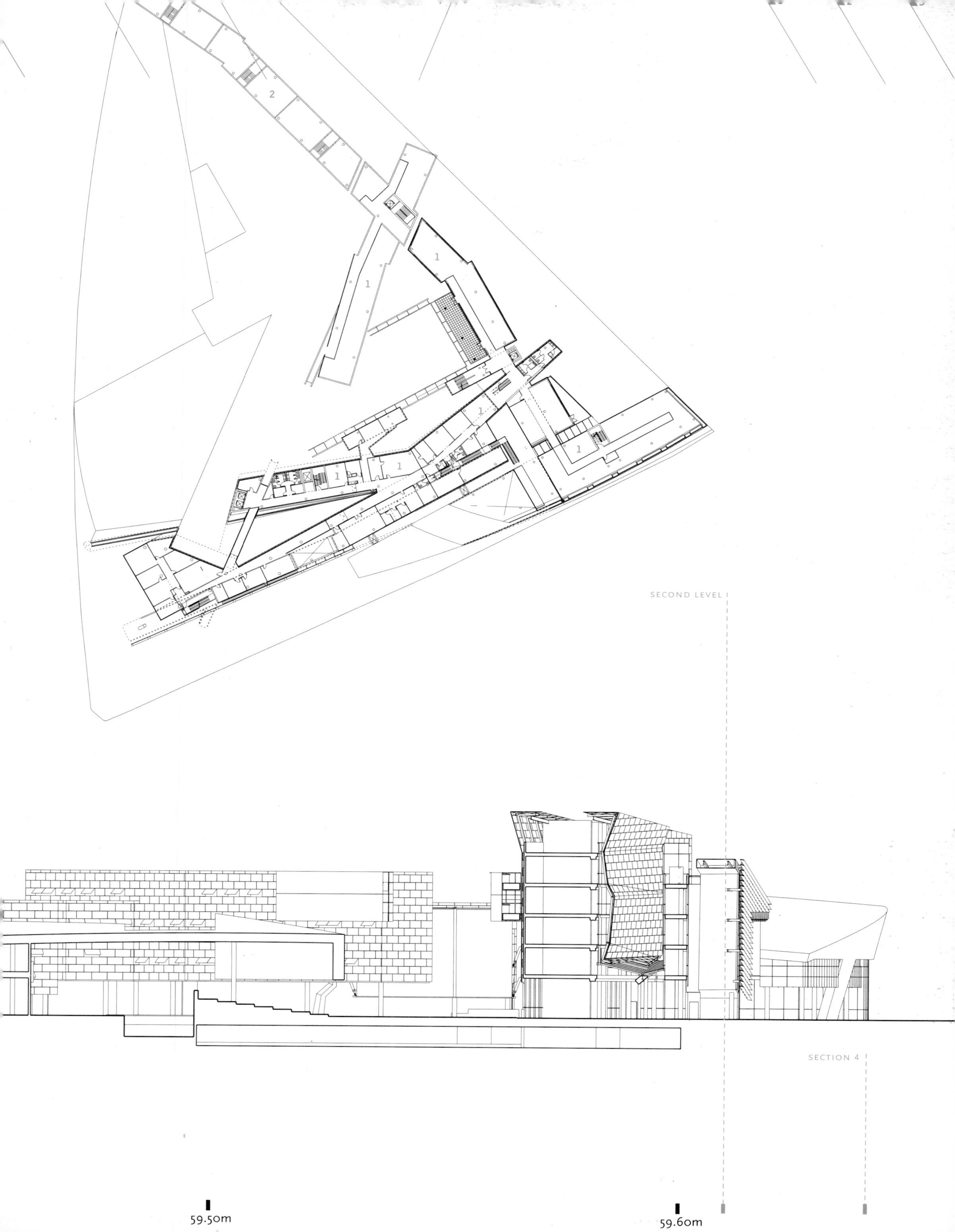
2
1
1
1
1
1
1
1
SECOND LEVEL
SECTION 4
59.50m
59.60m

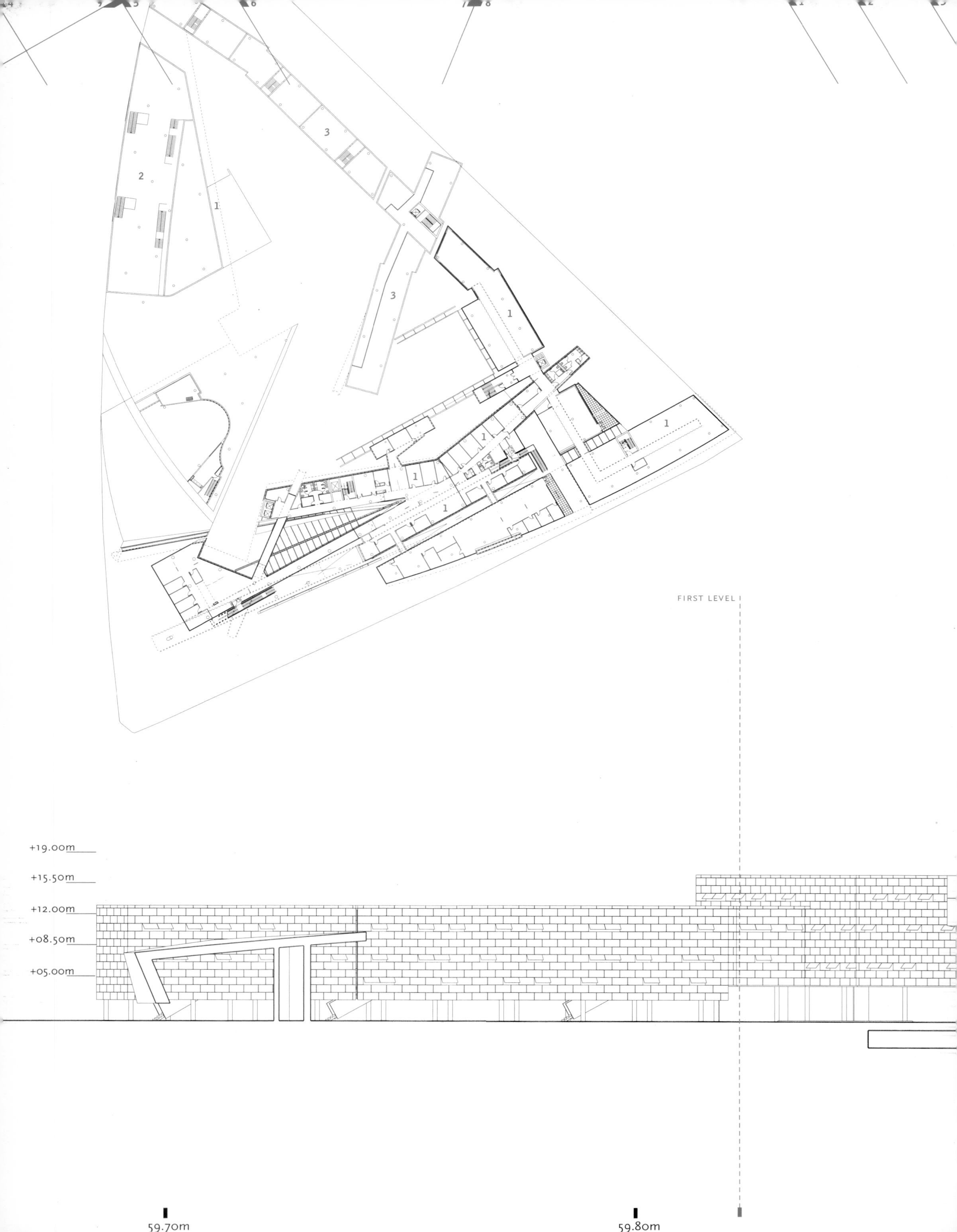
3
2
1
3
1
1
1
1
1
1
FIRST LEVEL
+19.00m
+15.50m
+12.00m
+08.50m
+05.00m
59.70m
59.80m

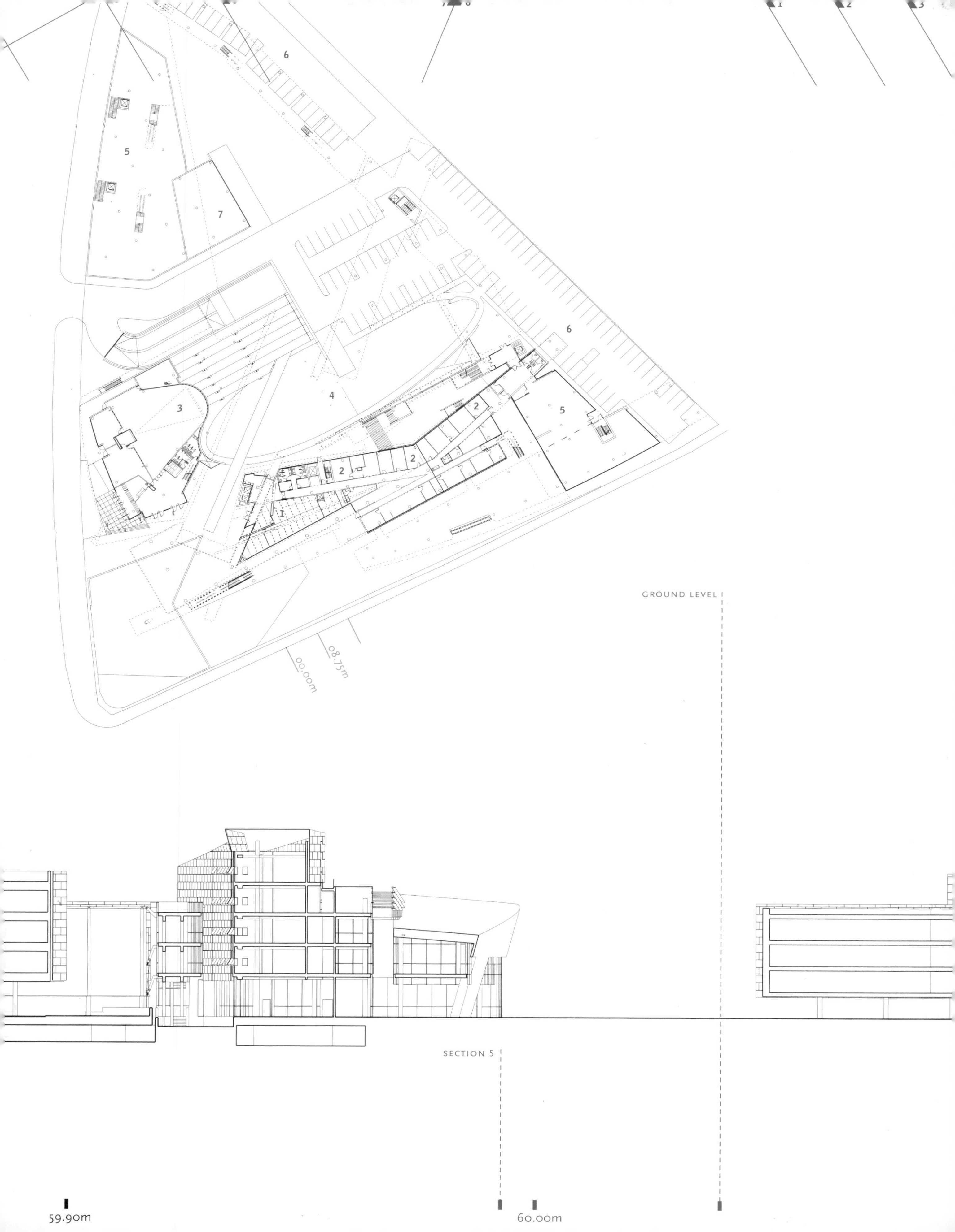
6
5
7
6
4
3
2
2
2
5
1
GROUND LEVEL
00.00m
08.75m
SECTION 5
59.90m
60.00m

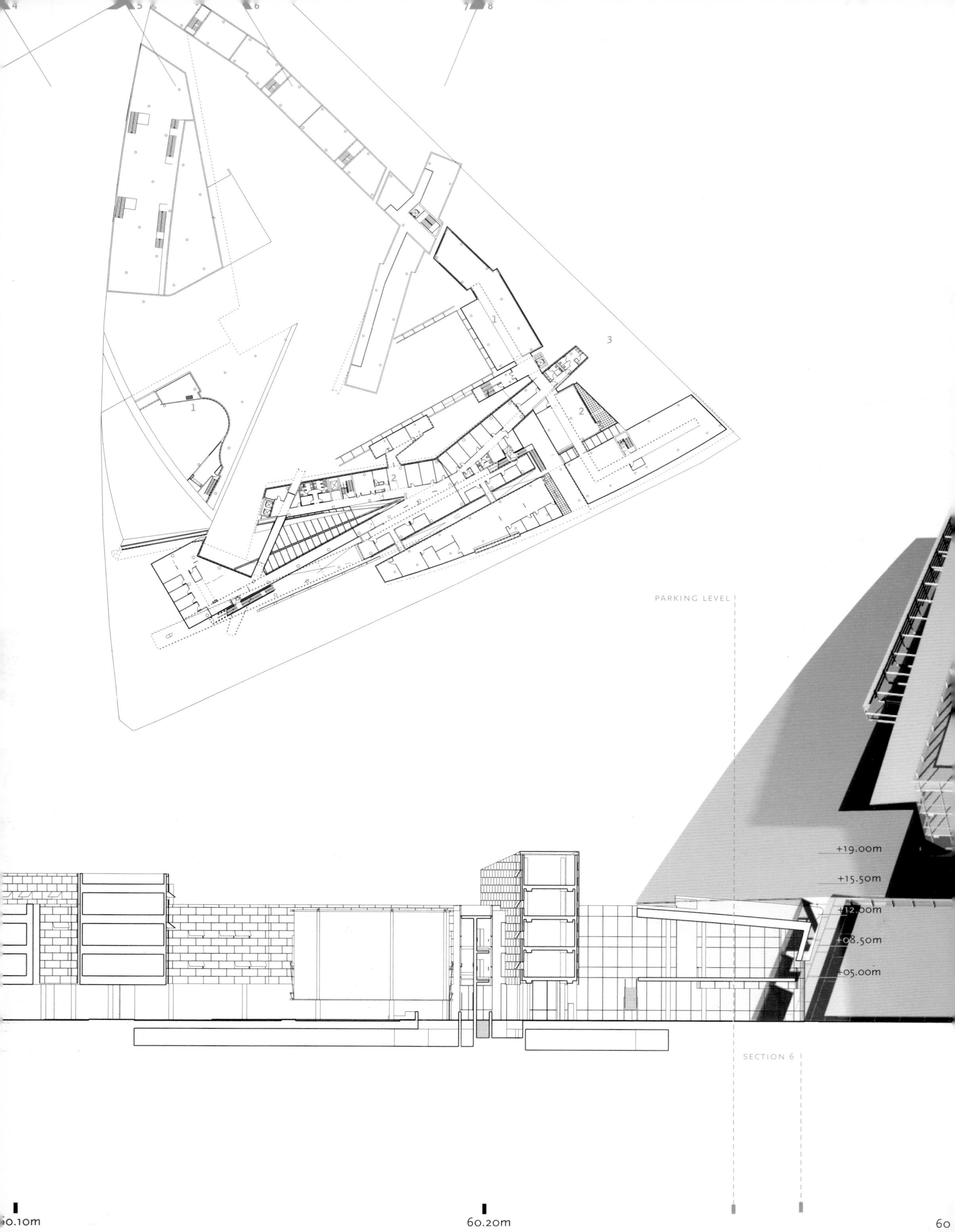
1
2
3
PARKING LEVEL
+19.00m
+15.50m
+12.00m
+08.50m
+05.00m
SECTION 6
0.10m
60.20m

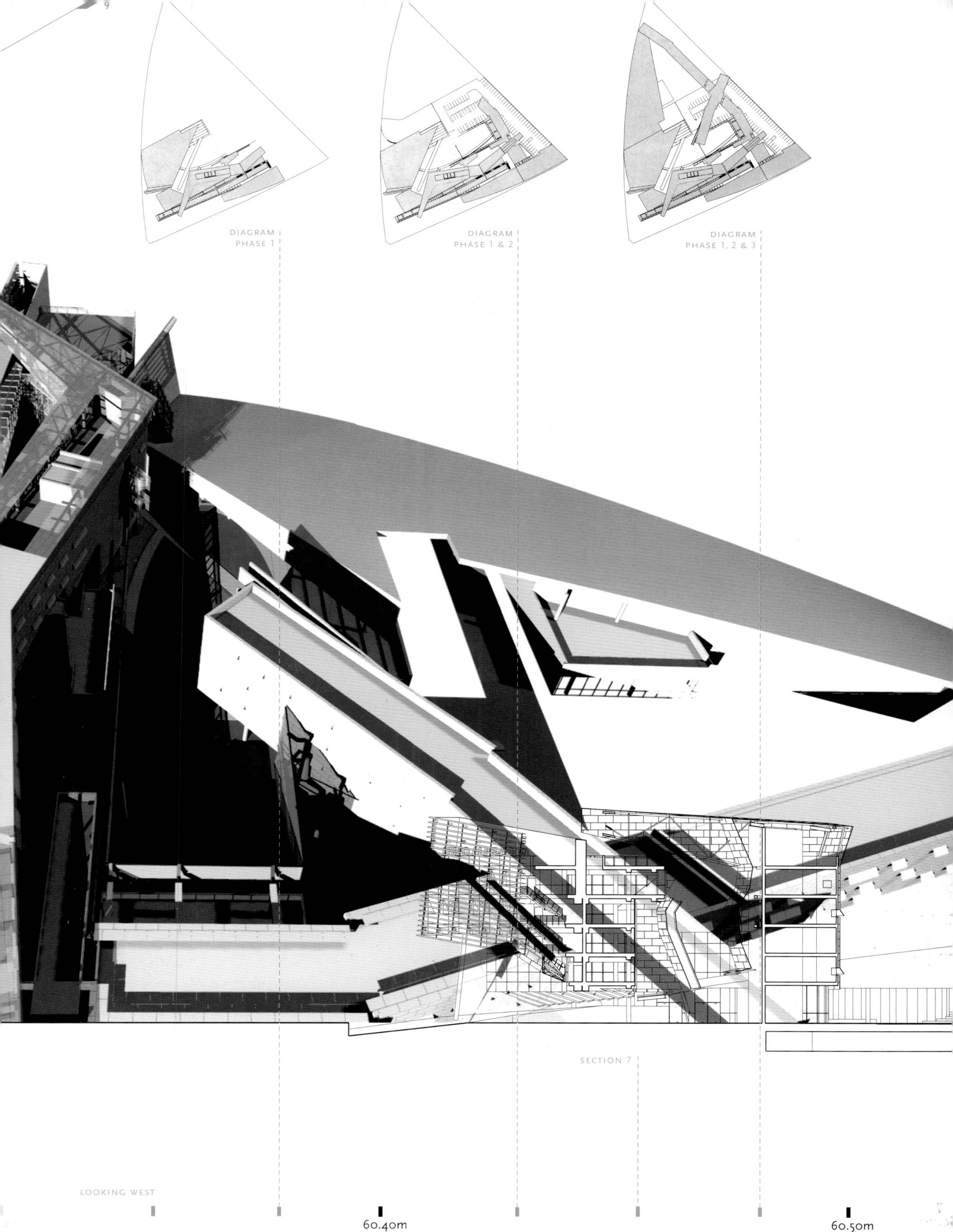
9
DIAGRAM
PHASE 1
DIAGRAM
PHASE 1 & 2
DIAGRAM
PHASE 1, 2 & 3
SECTION 7
LOOKING WEST
60.40m
60.50m

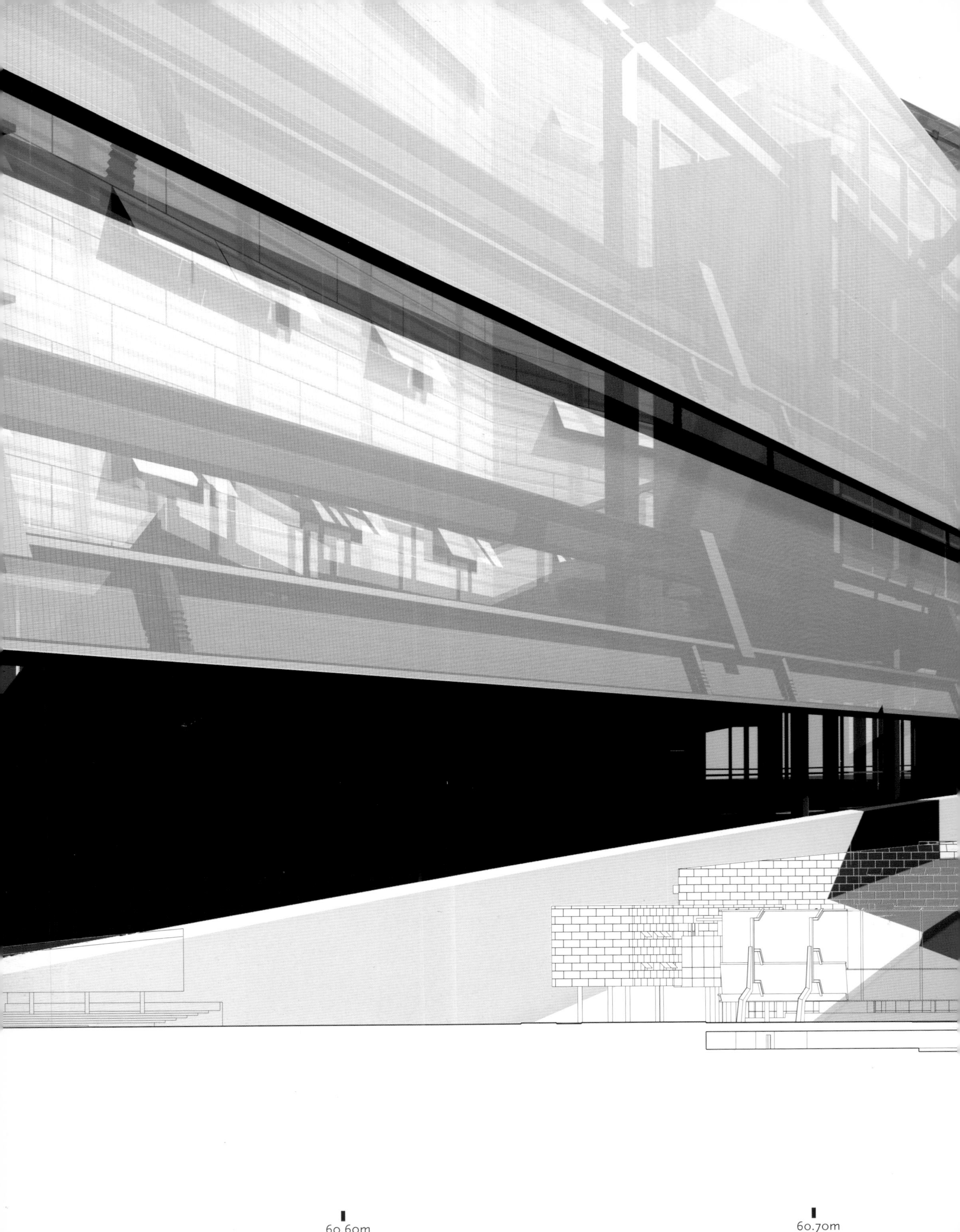
60.60m
60.70m

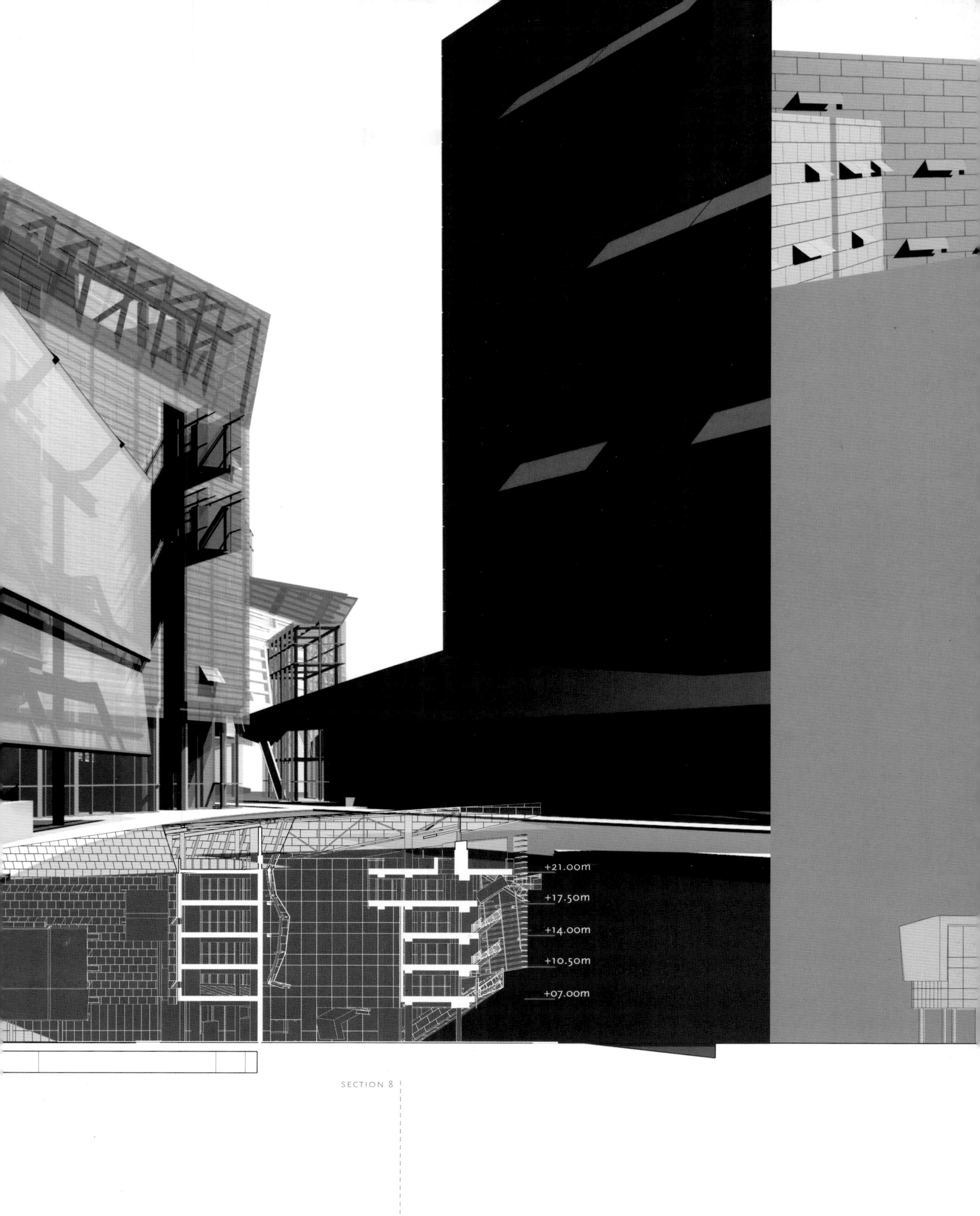
+21.00m
+17.50m
+14.00m
+10.50m
+07.00m
SECTION 8
LOOKING WEST
60.80m
60.90m

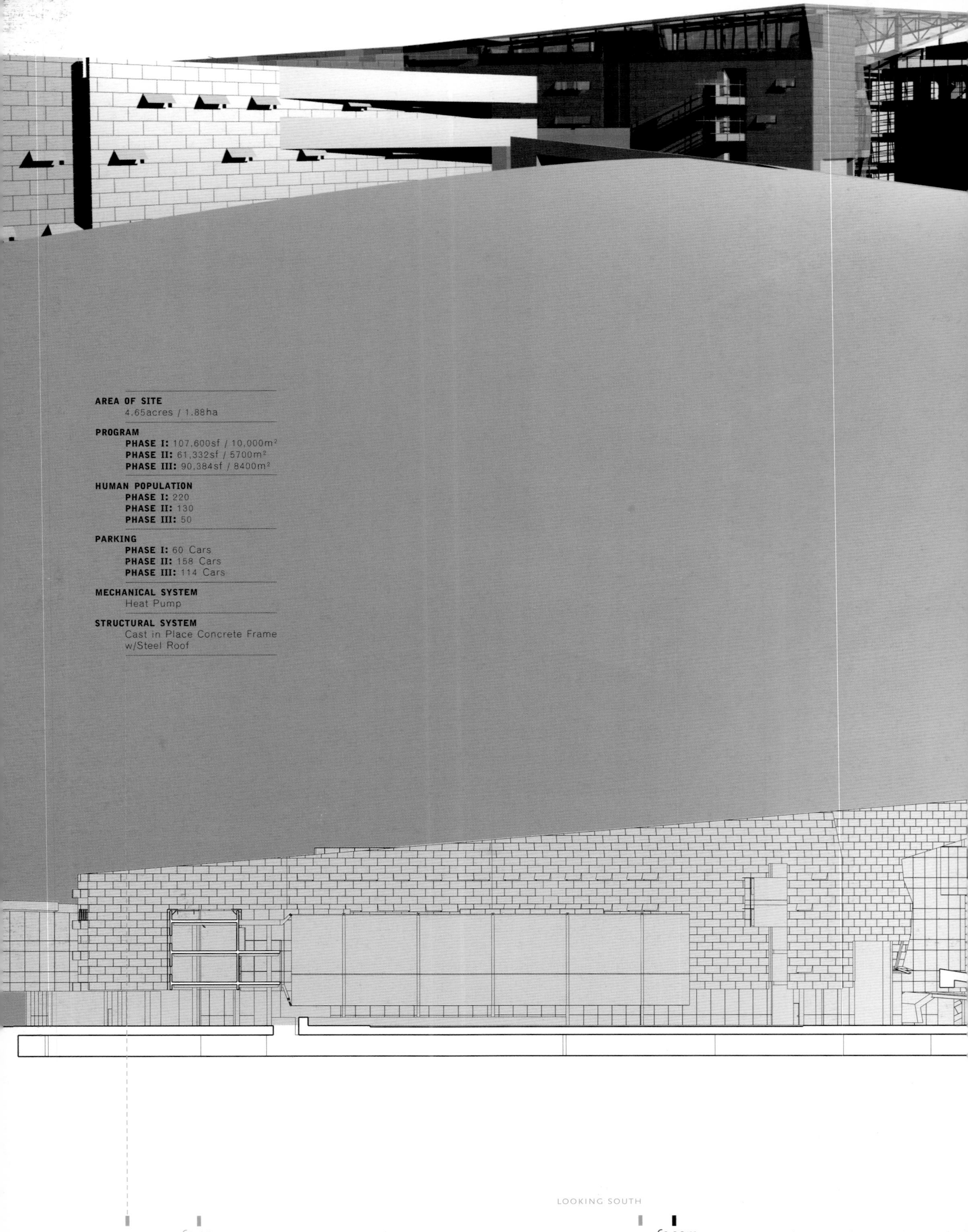

AREA OF SITE
4.65acres / 1.88ha

PROGRAM
PHASE I: 107,600sf / 10,000m²
PHASE II: 61,332sf / 5700m²
PHASE III: 90,384sf / 8400m²

HUMAN POPULATION
PHASE I: 220
PHASE II: 130
PHASE III: 50

PARKING
PHASE I: 60 Cars
PHASE II: 158 Cars
PHASE III: 114 Cars

MECHANICAL SYSTEM
Heat Pump

STRUCTURAL SYSTEM
Cast in Place Concrete Frame w/Steel Roof

LOOKING SOUTH

61.00m

61.10m

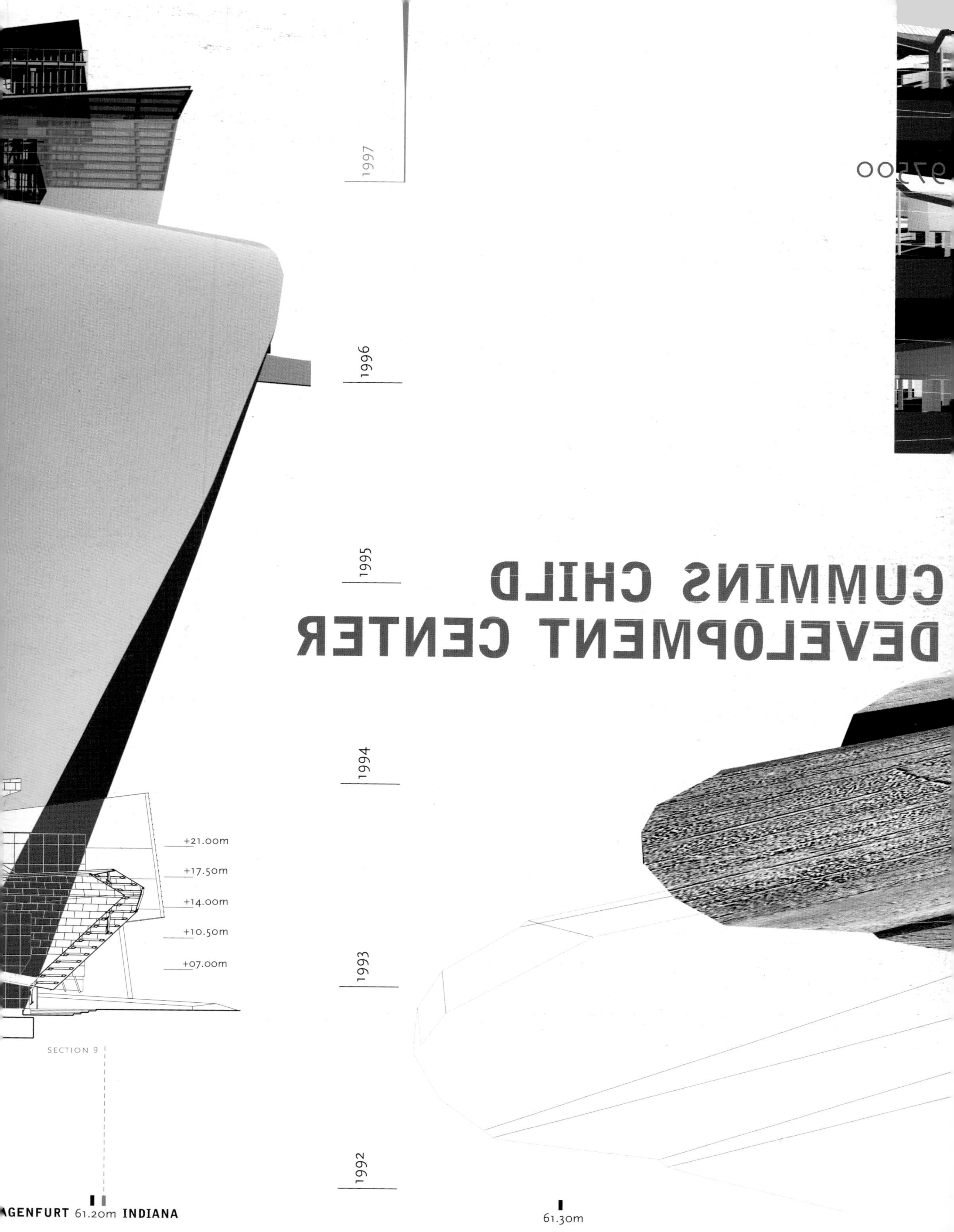
97500
1997
1996
1995
CUMMINS CHILD
DEVELOPMENT CENTER
1994
+21.00m
+17.50m
+14.00m
+10.50m
+07.00m
1993
SECTION 9
1992
AGENFURT 61.20m INDIANA
61.30m

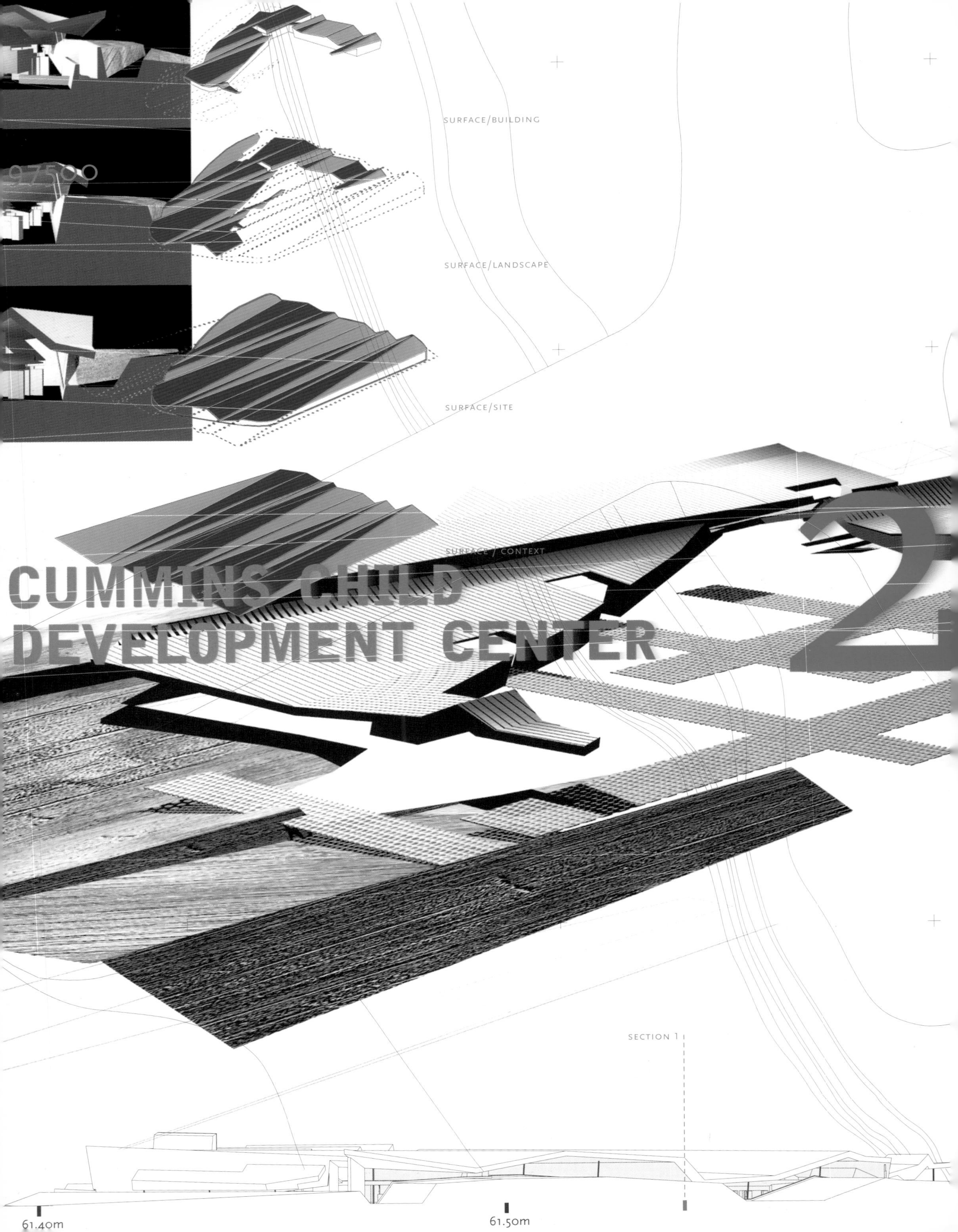
97500
SURFACE/BUILDING
SURFACE/LANDSCAPE
SURFACE/SITE
SURFACE / CONTEXT
CUMMINS CHILD DEVELOPMENT CENTER
2
SECTION 1
61.40m
61.50m

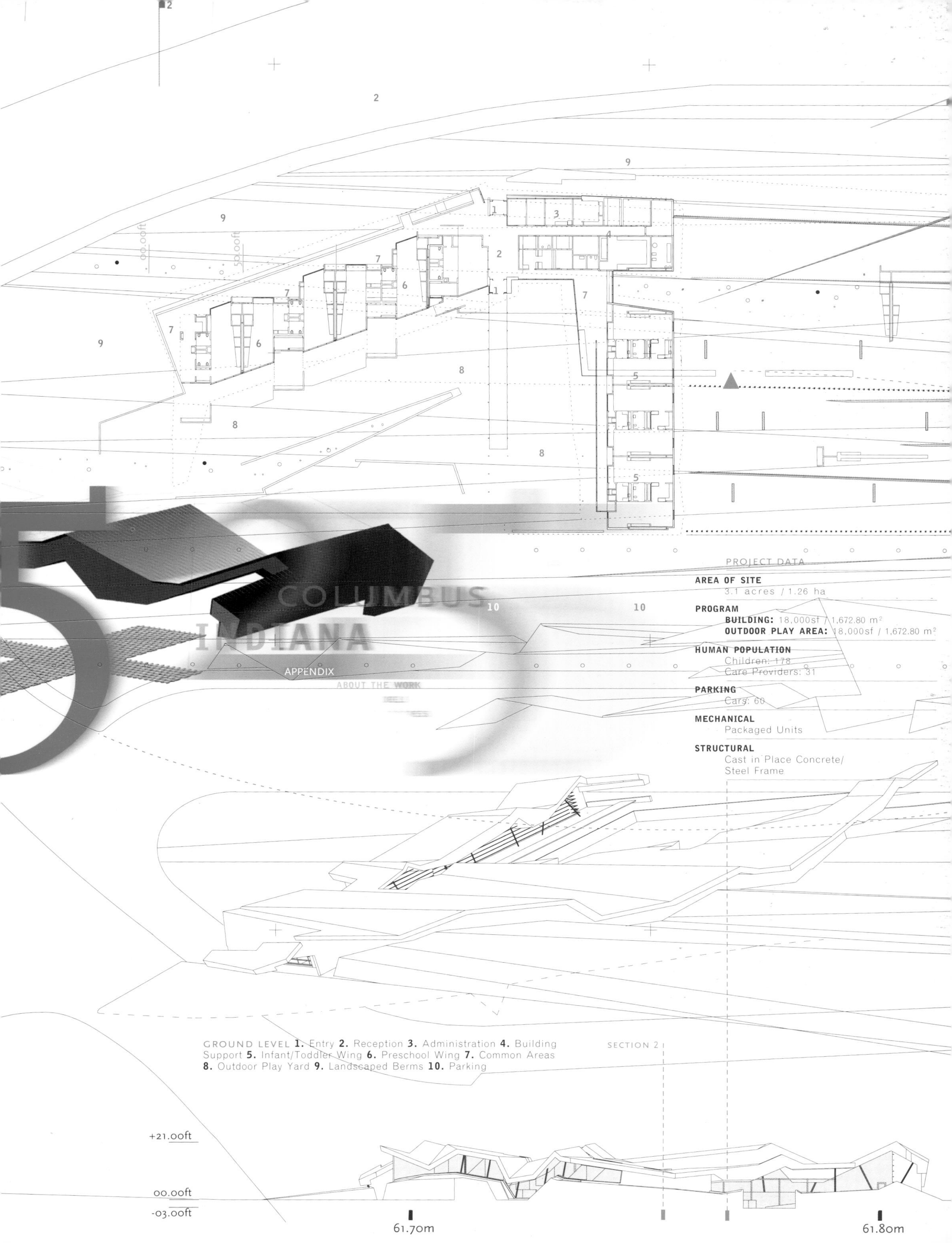

COLUMBUS
INDIANA
APPENDIX
ABOUT THE WORK
PROJECT DATA
AREA OF SITE
3.1 acres / 1.26 ha
PROGRAM
BUILDING: 18,000sf / 1,672.80 m²
OUTDOOR PLAY AREA: 18,000sf / 1,672.80 m²
HUMAN POPULATION
Children: 178
Care Providers: 31
PARKING
Cars: 60
MECHANICAL
Packaged Units
STRUCTURAL
Cast in Place Concrete/
Steel Frame
GROUND LEVEL 1. Entry 2. Reception 3. Administration 4. Building Support 5. Infant/Toddler Wing 6. Preschool Wing 7. Common Areas 8. Outdoor Play Yard 9. Landscaped Berms 10. Parking
SECTION 2
+21.00ft
00.00ft
-03.00ft
61.70m
61.80m

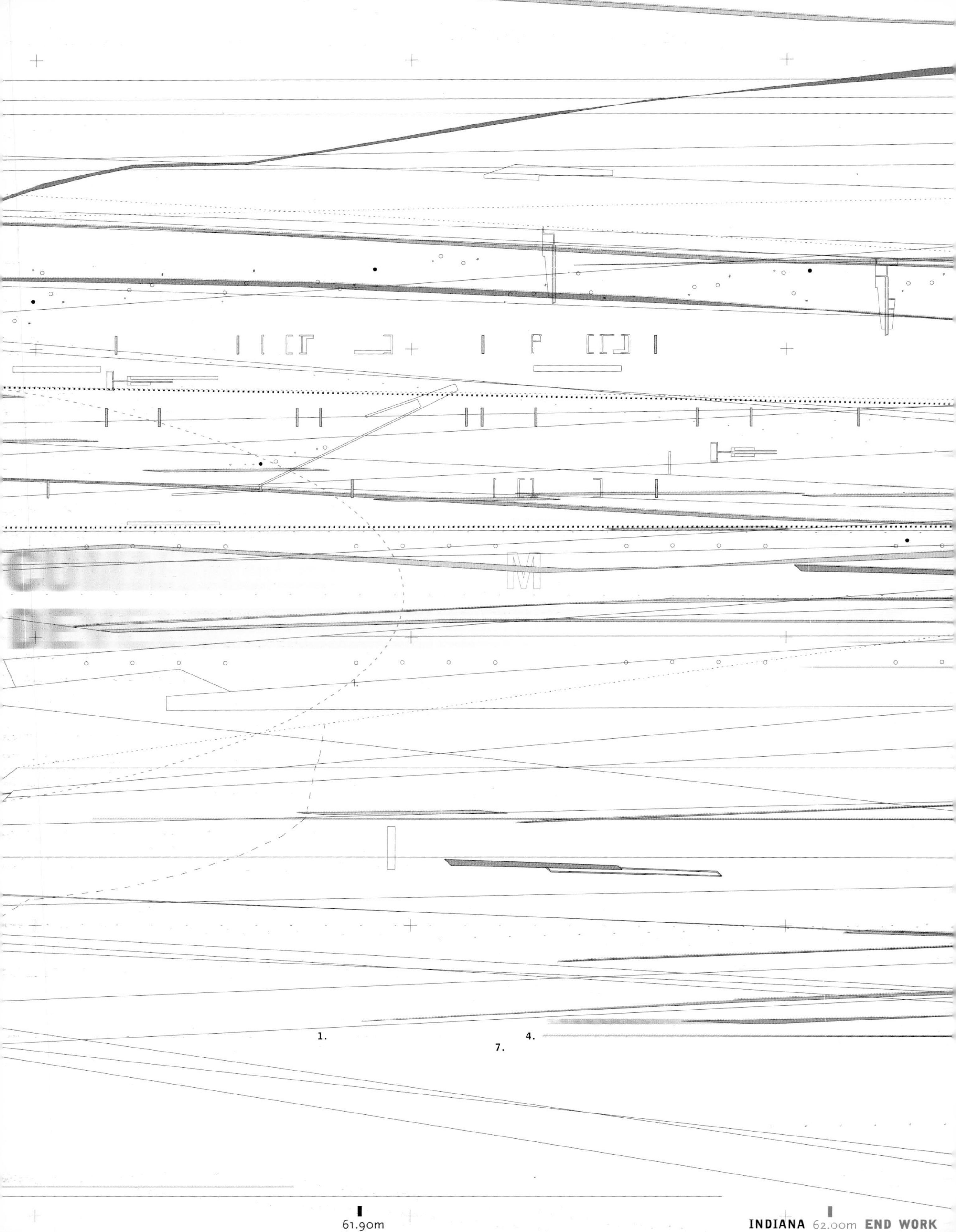
1.
1.
4.
7.
61.90m

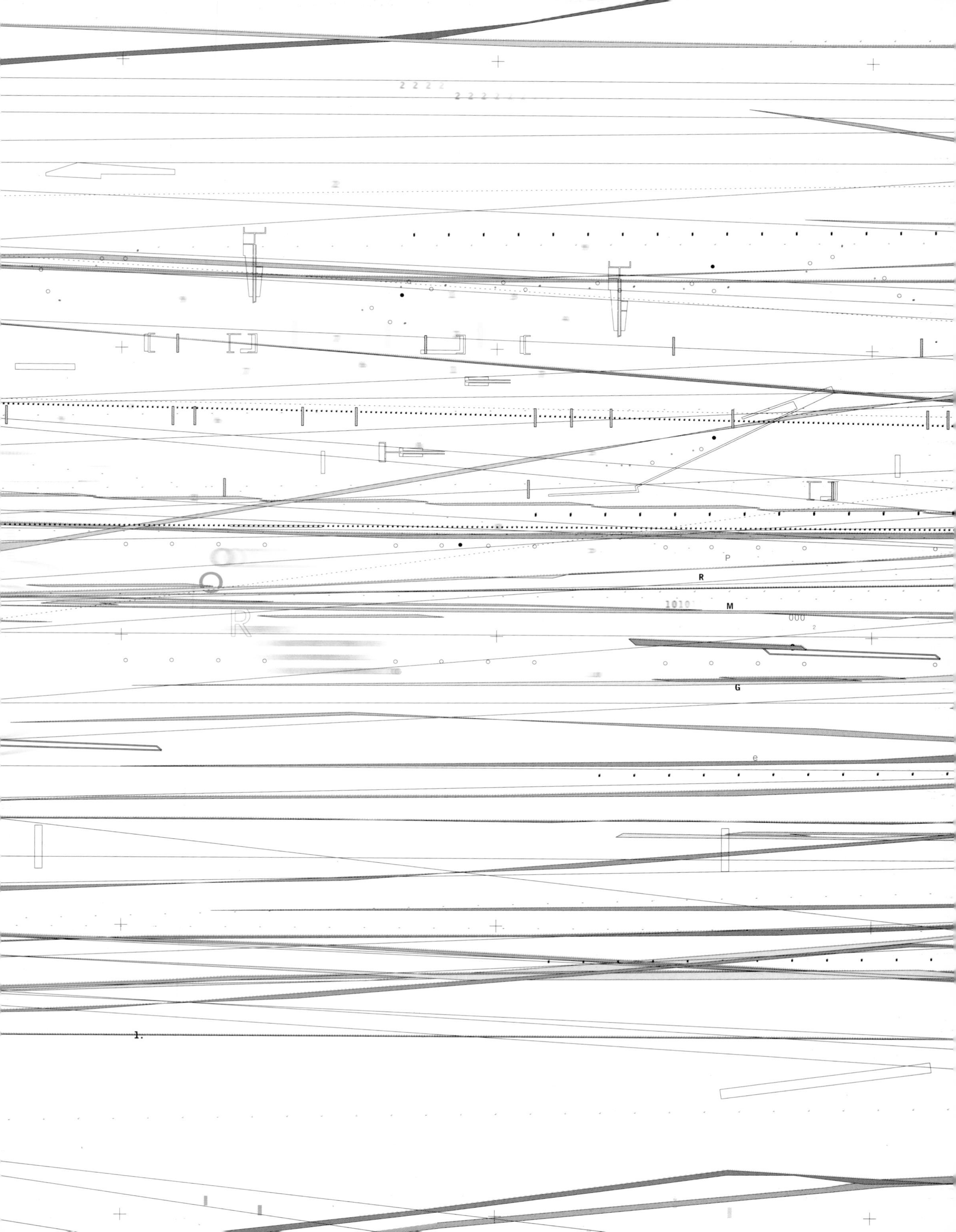

E
g
t / T
g 7. C
8. O
a 9.
k

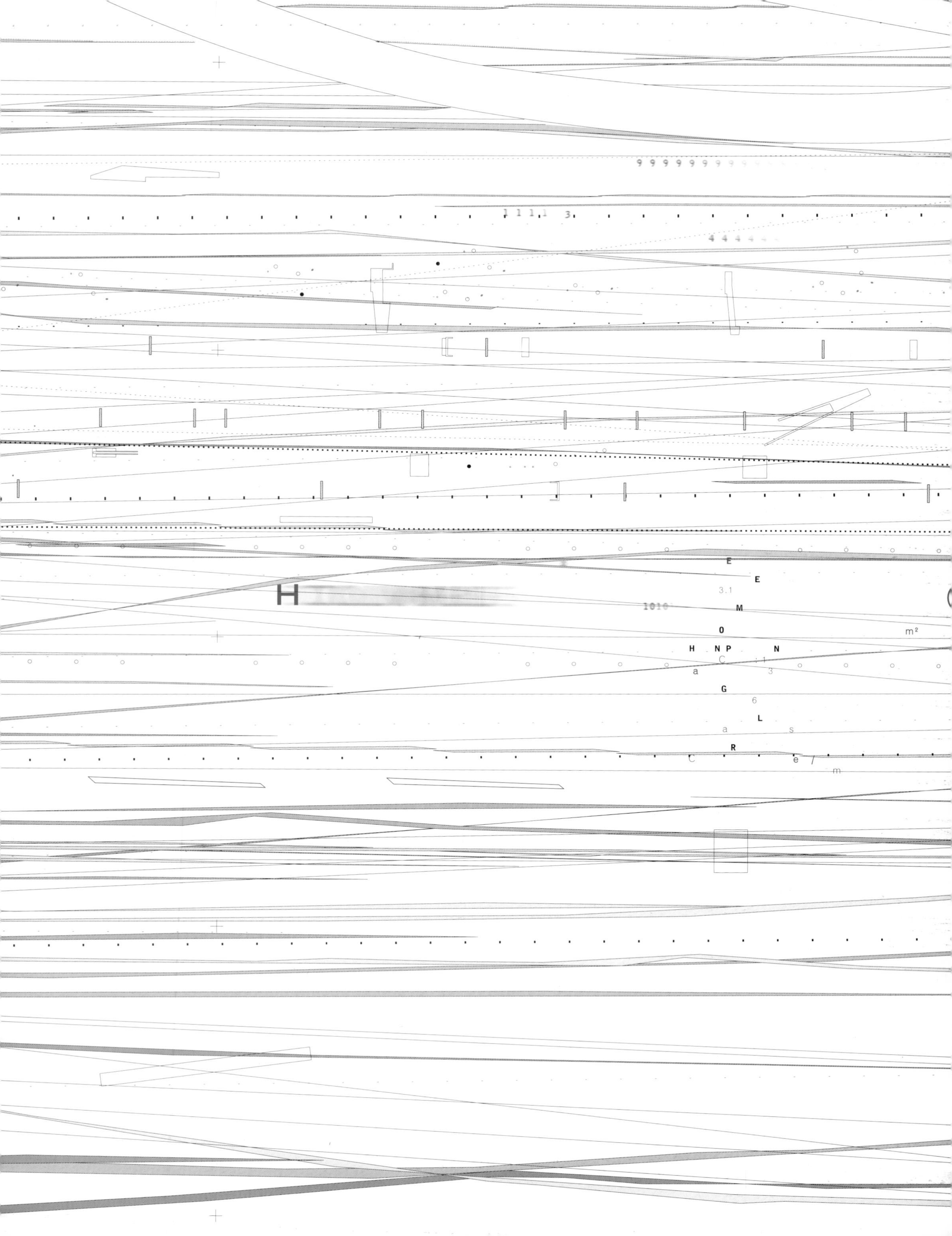

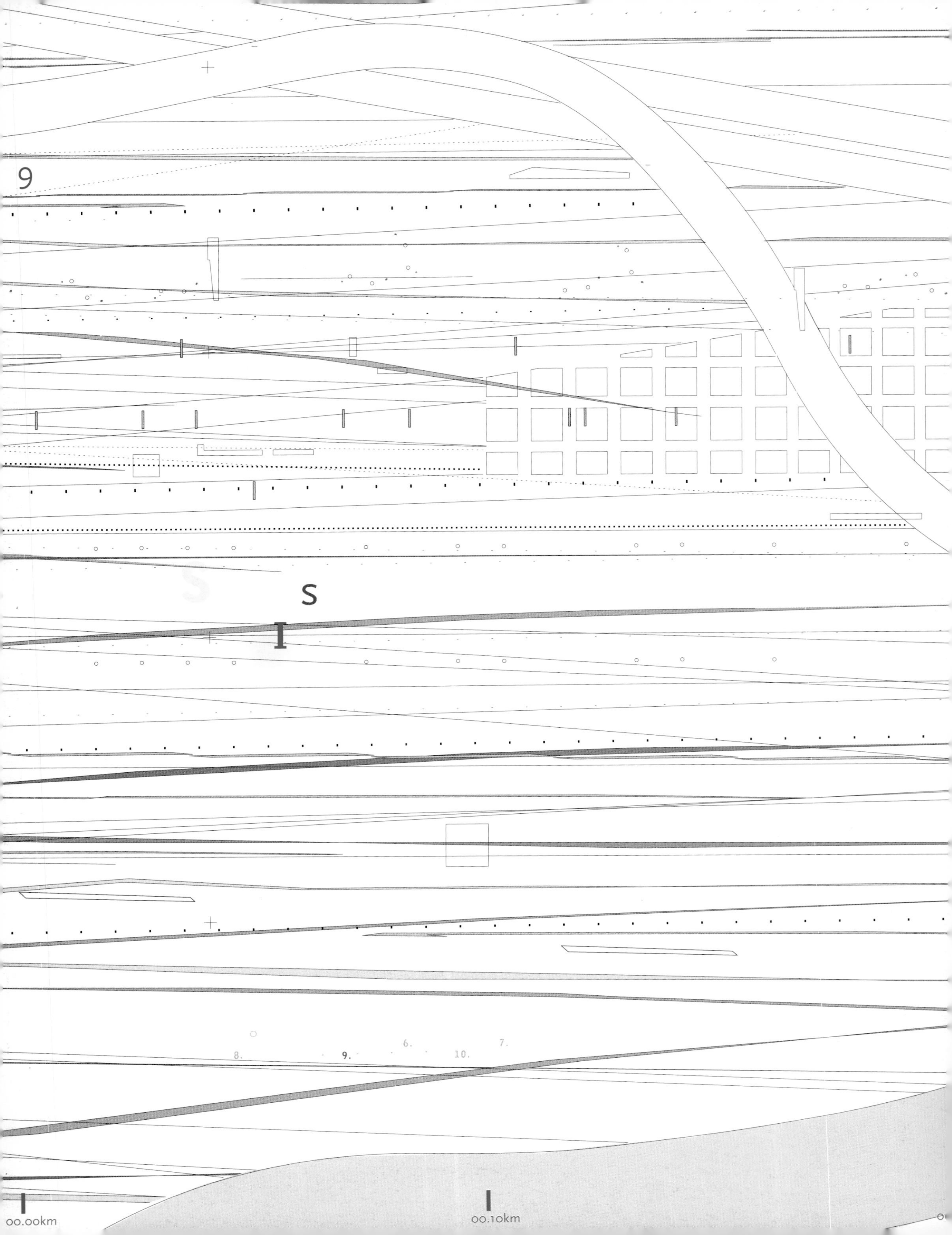
9
S
I
8.
9.
6.
10.
7.
00.00km
00.10km

10
SPREEBOGEN
INTERNATIONAL DESIGN COMPETITION
00.00 m — 02.70 m
APPENDIX II.1 ABOUT THE WORK
CENTRE CULTUREL DU TOURS
TOURS CULTURAL ARTS CENTER
04.80 m
APPENDIX II.6 ABOUT THE WORK
V.1 STUDY MODELS
04
00.30km
00.40km

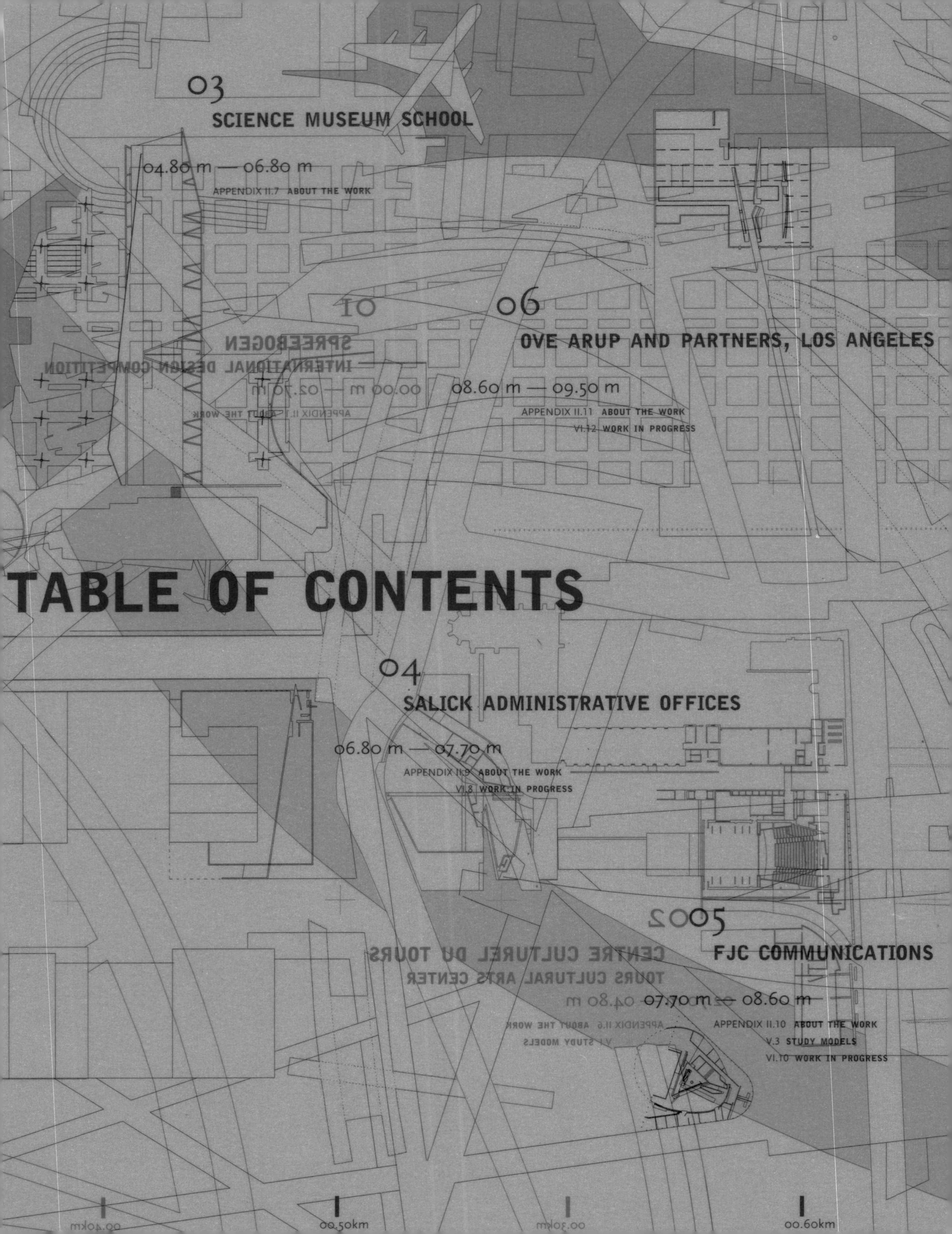

TABLE OF CONTENTS

07
LANDA HOUSE
09.50 m — 11.60 m
APPENDIX II.12 ABOUT THE WORK
VI.14 WORK IN PROGRESS
11
MASH, ONE ROOM SCHOOL HOUSE
18.10 m — 19.50 m
13
A.S.E. VISITOR CENTER
31.40 m — 33.50 m
APPENDIX II.20 ABOUT THE WORK
V.7 STUDY MODELS
VI.20 WORK IN PROGRESS
09
MÜLLAUFBEREITUNGSANLAGE FRANKFURT
FRANKFURT WASTE MANAGEMENT FACILITY
13.30 m — 15.50 m
APPENDIX II.14 ABOUT THE WORK
08
BLADES HOUSE
11.60 m — 13.30 m
APPENDIX II.13 ABOUT THE WORK
VI.1 WORK IN PROGRESS
14
WOHNBAUEXPERIMENT WAGRAMER STRASSE
WAGRAMER STRASSE HOUSING
33.50 m — 36.20 m
APPENDIX II.21 ABOUT THE WORK
12
SUN TOWER
19.50 m — 31.40 m
V.5 STUDY MODELS
10
AMERICAN BUSINESS CENTER
15.50 m — 18.10 m
APPENDIX II.16 ABOUT THE WORK

11
MASH, ONE ROOM SCHOOL HOUSE
18.10 m — 19.50 m
APPENDIX II.18 ABOUT THE WORK
13
日月光 主題活動
A.S.E. VISITOR CENTER
31.40 m — 33.50 m
APPENDIX II.20 ABOUT THE WORK
V.7 STUDY MODELS
VI.20 WORK IN PROGRESS
12
SUN TOWER
19.50 m — 31.40 m
APPENDIX II.18 ABOUT THE WORK
V.5 STUDY MODELS
14
WOHNBAUEXPERIMENT WAGRAMER STRASSE
WAGRAMER STRASSE HOUSING
33.50 m — 36.20 m
APPENDIX II.21 ABOUT THE WORK

15
DIAMOND RANCH HIGH SCHOOL
36.20 m — 39.10 m
APPENDIX II.23 ABOUT THE WORK
V.13 STUDY MODELS
VI.22 WORK IN PROGRESS
16
INTERNATIONAL ELEMENTARY SCHOOL
39.10 m — 41.30 m
APPENDIX II.26 ABOUT THE WORK
V.15 STUDY MODELS
VI.24 WORK IN PROGRESS

17
JUNIPERO SERRA SHRINE
41.30 m — 43.40 m
APPENDIX II.27 ABOUT THE WORK
18
MUSEO DEL PRADO
EL PRADO MUSEUM
43.40 m — 46.00 m
APPENDIX II.29 ABOUT THE WORK

20
MACK HOUSE
48.80 m — 50.90 m
APPENDIX II.31 ABOUT THE WORK
V.25 STUDY MODELS
22
UNIVERSITY OF TORONTO GRADUATE HOUSING
52.90 m — 55.20 m
APPENDIX II.32 ABOUT THE WORK
V.31 STUDY MODELS
19
ROCKLEDGE
46.00 m — 48.80 m
APPENDIX II.31 ABOUT THE WORK
V.19 STUDY MODELS
21
S.H.R. PERCEPTUAL MANAGEMENT
50.90 m — 52.90 m
APPENDIX II.32 ABOUT THE WORK
V.27 STUDY MODELS
01.60km
01.70km

23/24
HYPO ALPE ADRIA CENTER
55.20 m — 61.20 m
APPENDIX II.35 ABOUT THE WORK
V.35 STUDY MODELS
VI.26 WORK IN PROGRESS
25
CUMMINS CHILD DEVELOPMENT CENTER
61.20 m — 62.60 m

APPENDIX

I. SILENT COLLISIONS

When architects write about their work—and they probably shouldn't—they are often quick to make distinctions between projects and buildings. Projects are incomplete, schematic, and trapped in the midst of their production. They are often optimistic investigations that, were it not for some undefined tragedies of reality, would be granted more pictures in the oeuvre, more words, and a longer life. Buildings, on the other hand, are finite, resolved, and liberated from all scars of their production. They are guaranteed *long lives,* having already acquiesced to a few of the undefined tragedies of reality. Projects are left to engage only other architects and students of architecture. Buildings have the opportunity to engage architects, students, the public for whom it was meant, and the subsequent publics who could never have been anticipated.

We find it necessary to consider everything we produce, and everything in this book, to be a project. Regardless of how much concrete has been poured and of the presence of (exhilarated?) inhabitants, we find ourselves reluctant to give up the investigations undertaken in each project, reluctant to surrender the optimism, and unwilling to erase the traces of our productive impetus.

Perhaps it is because, from the beginning, we have been engaged in reconsideration of the *problems of authorship* in architecture that we prefer to see our work as a series of projects, since a project is closer to the process of its making than a "building" might be. We have made a conscious effort to produce works that do not communicate with a singular voice, but that instead seem to emanate from a number of sources (sometimes like a choir, sometimes like a brawl). It is not our task to give form to our own individuality, but to give form to the individuality of things. We would never wish to eliminate the reader—every work is offered with the intention of being read—but we hope that by using an expanded, plural form of authorship we can fold aspects of understanding into aspects of production; we can combine the phenomena of reading with the processes of authoring; we can keep the design process intellectually animated; and we can produce works that address their audiences with a multivalent resonance.

As one facet of developing this resonance in our work, we have attempted to unite two prevalent ideas regarding the production of architectural form, ideas that are generally considered to be mutually exclusive. The first considers architecture to be based on certain universal and homogeneous systems and principles. The second values those forms that are specific to cultural, local, and historic precedents. Taken alone, each approach exacts a price. The universal, for example, often finds its sources for global dissemination in specific technological, sociological, or metaphorical "truths" (like nature, the human body, and so on). The drive to universalize tends to lead one to overinvest in regularizing this singularity, failing to address the necessities of the human world, its symbolic, emotional, and subjective urges. At its worst, a universal architectural theory might be based on the dispersal of a personal vision—egocentrism. Universal theories of architecture, by their very nature, suppress the idiosyncratic, a key source of architectural ideas. On the other hand, theories that focus on the particular lead one to sift through local conditions in search of a set of rules, resulting in works that are, ideally, culturally appropriate. But this type of formal theory is out of touch with global forces, potentially perpetuating provincialism while maintaining the social stratifications and prejudices that lie dormant within traditional forms. In isolation, each approach leaves the architecture bifurcated and incomplete. The union of these two ideas allows for work that responds to a need for "monumentalized existence," while making room for expanding impulses that are imperative for confronting architecture's relationship to a radically defined idea of the city.[1]

The work in this volume utilizes the richness of juxtapositions found in our global culture[2] and therein finds potential, not to mention the obligation, for generating infinite and productive complexities. It is ultimately an architecture that is diverse in both knowledge and information. Each work has its own unique presence, its own underlying architectonic ideas. New opportunities abound, as we feel free to borrow from art, cinema, and the sciences in our search for the forms that might support these complex relationships.

[1] Today, there are vast differences in the architectural strategies applied to the problem of the city. The dominant discourse on urbanism in the U.S. is informed by nostalgia. Promoted as the only cultural value capable of finding a viable constituency in the public realm, nostalgia is imbued with the hope that the social relationships and accompanying values, the simplicity and security that took place in some historic context, can be evoked again. One senses a distaste for the messiness of heterogeneous urban existence. This reasoning is flawed. First, it introduces the false notion that form has a constant relationship to context and meaning. Second, it reflects a romanticized and radically one-sided view of the past which posits that we can only reach the desirable qualities of the past by manifesting it literally in the present. There is little confidence that the direction of the future, if left to develop freely, would ever be as safe and desirable (let alone possibly better) as something that is known from the past.

A counterargument rejects the prescriptive role of history and its repression of the present. It tends to promote a dystopian view based on a loss of confidence in principles of order as a means of shaping the city. It builds reductivist theories based upon the confusion of the contemporary condition, and upon the tradition of aesthetic detachment and autonomous form, both reductionist in nature. This architecture no longer aspires to be civic. It has an ambivalent relationship to the relevance of the physical environment. It explores substituting the digital and virtual for the physical and real.

Our argument, or a third point of view, embraces the complexity and sheer size of the new urban condition. (Cities today are countries—Los Angeles is two Swedens, Mexico City is one-and-a-half Hollands). Cities are a place of unlimited engagement, saturation, and simultaneity.[A] We accept the methodologies that arise from the erosion of the conventions of order as a natural consequence of the radical transformation that cities have undergone over the last half century. We work in the midst of this uncertainty, lacking any viable consensus, looking for a means to, in Clement Greenberg's words, "keep culture moving despite ideological confusion and violence." We no longer idealize either the conventions of history, nor the traditions or conventions of the tabula rasa and the abstraction of modernity. Each has been judged by its inadequacy to address our current circumstance. We accept the need for continuity with the past while acknowledging a necessity for a more expanded set of procedures which are capable of addressing the multi-faceted problems we face.

Like complex ecosystems, cities should support and nurture the diverse character of complex, relational, interacting organisms. Our architecture must address civic culture to clarify what is desirable, to aim at some good. Architecture must exhibit a sense of place. The conflict and the compatibility of the multiple physical and cultural forces develops into cities which elaborate their own distinctiveness. We accept the mandate of playing a role in discerning values, making people reach, making people think beyond.

[1A] As captured in Damien Hirst's *I Want to Spend the Rest of My Life Everywhere, with Everyone, One to One, Always, Forever, Now!*

[2] "A new Mongolia is evolving. Its religion, a Tibetan type of Buddhism, is reviving, along with a reverance for Genghis Khan, the 13th Century conqueror whose cult was suppressed by the Soviets. (Khan's face now graces the currency, displacing a Soviet era revolutionary hero). The country's historical isolation is breaking down fast: the traditional evening entertainment of slurping fermented mare's milk in a neighbor's tent has given way to nights in front of a television set—'Baywatch' is a hit—with a six pack of Coca-Cola." *Time,* September 1, 1997

The loss of craft traditions[3] which were so evident in our early work, is offset by the availability of new technical means. The work in this volume is digital and in that respect represents a marked departure from the work of our two earlier volumes. Computers were incorporated in our studio with some skepticism and were quite literally put to work as tools to further the reach and scope of our hands. We made no attempt to make the work look digital but rather we set to work to harness the energy of the computer to continue established procedures.[4] We intend to continue to investigate the material world through digital means, both in reassessing the processes (or generative forces) of our architecture and as a means of representation.

Our methodology proceeds through a constant oscillation between what exists and what could be, realism and idealism.[5]

[3] "Craftsmanship is a mediation; its forms are not governed by the economy of function but by pleasure... In craftsmanship there is a continuous movement back and forth between usefulness and beauty." Octavio Paz, *Convergences: Essays on Art and Literature* (New York: Harcourt Brace Jovanovich, 1987), p. 59.

[4] The inherent workings of the computer were compatible and transitional to the operational methods of reiteration and layering which we used during our first twenty years. Over the last five years there has been a gradual shift in the formal language and in the organizational and structural possibilities which seem quite "natural" for digital programs. At a generative level, we have worked with Form-Z, PowerDraw and MicroStation, Photoshop, Quark Express, 3-D Studio (Max), and Electric Image. In most of these projects we have started with exploring space and 3-D object organizations in Form-Z, in an attempt to understand the implications of the various programs. These studies develop at a later stage into the conventions of plan, section, elevations, and, later, into representative drawings.

[5] "There are two kinds of art, that which you can do, and that which you can't do." This statement was related to me by Gladson de Rocas in Brasilia from a conversation with his four-year-old son about life and art. All of us are propelled by the latter, of course.

We establish intentions and then attempt to penetrate and even subvert the rationale of those intentions, confident that specific, external systems of thought (theory) cannot be a generative force in producing a work. We are interested in the idea that a formal "intelligence" arises out of the synthesis of simplicities, and it therefore does not have to come from somewhere else. In the beginning, there are questions, hunches, and tentative solutions that are challenged and tested. The work often begins from scratch, propelled by its own internal energy, an attempt to make something from nothing. In many cases the direction indicated by these explorations is invalidated, and we are led through an examination of our missteps to more developed solutions.[6] This is an iterative methodology that aims to synthesize an architecture. The continuity apparent from project to project is a result not of stylistic qualities, but of the consistent use of this method over twenty-five years of practice.

We are proceeding provisionally. We are no longer embarrassed by form. The work in this volume is an outgrowth of these interests.[7]

[6] Karl A. Popper, *Conjectures and Refutations: The Growth of Scientific Knowledge* (New York: Harper and Row, 1963), p.36, summarizes seven conclusions of scientific theory: "The criterion of the scientific status of a theory is its falsifiability, or refutability, or testability."

[7] We began our work with an obligation to science "without bias," a concern with facts. The early work from 1973 to 1988 *(Morphosis: Buildings and Projects)* began with a focus on infrastructure. Program and the dynamic forces of nature were the primary variables in the creation of an architecture celebrating incompleteness, change, and flexibility, "neutral" architecture (Sequoyah School or the Medical Office Building) committed to a belief in the logic of the engineer—Prouvé was the model. There was, at that time, an ambivalence to the "formal." This was a dynamic and turbulent period in the U.S. We worked intermittently. There seemed to be so many diversions within the political/cultural landscape. Our preoccupations soon turned toward the city. In the 1970s and early 1980s neorationalism maintained a strong influence, providing solutions to the questions of the time having to do with the conflict of modernism in its relation to memory, tradition, and the physical and dreamlike reconstruction of the city. With the Venice houses we started exploring the connection between building and context, idealiz-

CONSISTENCIES (GLUE)

Not Getting Lost. Architecture is the product of a continuing investigation of strategies of organization and construction which have the capacity and the intention to make the complex coherent. The expansion of this thinking nurtured ideas favoring differentiation, a concept I encountered in 1965, during my third year of undergraduate studies at the University of Southern California. Through the exploration of organizational structures capable of adapting interrelationships of natural phenomena[8] we are led directly to a perspective of the complexity of the city. From this condition emerges a "unity of disunity,"[9] ing the idiosyncratic characteristics specific to each problem, interested in exploring an architecture reflexive of what appears to so many as conflict, so much a part of the pluralistic culture of L.A. Our interest in the generation of a language that grew out of these circumstances was partnered by a fascination with communicating the process and activity of construction and the inherent qualities of material—a presence that located a type of undeconstructable "authenticity," an attempt at locating value. We were conscious of the apparent overinvestment of energy that was expended on these small-scale projects and the artifacts (models/drawings) that were part of this effort. Later work, 72 Market Street and Kate Mantillini, pursued more confrontational strategies, interventions into existing buildings, and were to instill in us the value of relational systems within the work, which would later become more dominant. The larger-scale projects (ending in the Amerika-Gedenkbibliothek) explore a more overt, explicit manifestation of urban strategies based on ideas of a coherency of disbursement and fragmentation. The "knitting and fitting" operations so much at the heart of the urban proposals of people like James Stirling (Cologne and Düsseldorf) and Matthias Ungers entered our work, as it did with so many other architects, with the discourse started by Colin Rowe and Fred Koetter's Collage City, celebrating the dialectical process with reality as found. The city offered the material for endless interpretations. By the end of this period I was no longer an apologist of form.

The works from 1989 to 1992 *(Morphosis: Buildings and Projects 1989–1992)* explored larger scale projects, more explicit in their reliance on operational strategies, promoting the relational nature of their constituent parts. Paris Utopie, Expo '95, and the Nara Competition are all examples of this effort. We were becoming increasingly aware of a territory between the collective role of planning problems versus the more specific, immediate potentialities of architecture.

The enhanced role of the natural site emerged within this period. The Crawford House was our first freestanding work outside of the (sub)-urban context and was instrumental in forcing us into new trajectory organizations. The collapse and disbursement of the object, the shift from central to peripheral organizations, the obfuscation of boundary, and the enhancement of the accidental were all part of this work. This new relativism between site and building led to a heightened awareness of the role of movement and systems of repetition as primary organizing devices. The idea of marking a site (as at Nazga) and of utilizing subtraction as a constructional technique became possibilities. The Chiba Golf Club project more fully explored these ideas. At the same time these strategies were beginning to influence the urban projects. Paris Utopie and Vienna Expo '95 initiate the use of an "augmented" ground surface to accommodate programmatic material and begins a process of perceiving building and site as a singular problem—the site is now an active, dynamic component of the architectural construct. The figure-ground is insufficient as a framework for comprehending the city.

[8] Ralph Knowles, who was heading the third-year curriculum, was experimenting with new concepts of order and differentiation very much at odds with the notion of typology prevalent at this time. An architecture of simple order characterized by symmetry and formal homogeneity was being replaced by organizational systems capable of responding to the dynamic influences of external events. The work focused on the morphological characteristics of form and could be seen as an extension of the method of Cartesian deformation that was developed by D'Arcy Thompson to describe the transformations of natural forms within a dynamic environment. Geometry was no longer a static measure, but dynamic systems of descriptions very much a part of the "exact" geometry described by Husserl.

[9] Marshall Berman in *All That Is Solid Melts into Air* (New York: Penguin, 1988), p.15, writes: "Modern environments and experiences cut across all boundaries of geography and ethnicity, of class and nationality, of religion and ideology: in this sense, modernity can be said to unite all mankind. But it is paradoxical unity, a unity of disunity: it pours us all into a maelstrom of perpetual disintegration and renewal, of struggle and contradiction, of ambiguity and anguish. To be modern is to be part of a universe in which, as Marx said, 'all that is solid melts into air.'"

or a system of relations responsible to the heterogeneity of our existence, which is both normative and idiosyncratic. We are making the rules that govern our work within a society of laws. The rules are in a constant state of transformation and evolution.[10]

Imperfections. We introduce an element of contradiction into our projects to provide an opportunity for the exploration of faults within a continuity of form. The work aspires to promote heterogeneity, value diversity, evoke sensuality, respect differences, and ultimately have the ability to come to terms with discontinuity. In this post-Freudian era, we have come to understand ourselves as composites, often contradictory and internally incomplete. In our work, this conception is manifested in fragments and aggregates (the unfinished) that reveal idiosyncracies, allude to a tomorrow, and challenge the occupant to

[10] Rupert Sheldrake writes of the possibility that the laws of nature evolve in *The Presence of The Past* (New York: Vintage, 1989), p.18: "In the context of the new cosmology, all physical reality is evolutionary. But the old idea of eternity lives on in the conception of eternal laws that transcend the physical universe. If we question this assumption we find that it is very deeply held. But is there any persuasive reason, other than the power of tradition, why we should accept the idea of central physical laws? In an evolutionary universe, how can we rule out the possibility that the laws of nature evolve, or that there is memory in nature and that the regularities of nature are habitual? Even to entertain such notions involves a radical break with tradition. It means contemplating the possibility of a new understanding of the nature of nature. It would involve carrying forward towards completion the change of paradigm which has already gone so far; namely, the change from the idea of physical eternity to an evolutionary conception of the cosmos."

engage with the work. "Imperfections" are sometimes elicited by getting lost;[11] free association is used as a strategy for finding our way back and is valued as a method that will periodically counter the weight of the rational, which, by the nature of the discipline, can tend to dominate the work.

Talking Back. Our methodology promotes self-criticism and regularly summons the muse of doubt as part of our success. While it may sometimes seem to reveal an apprehension of concretizing the text, it more aptly describes a strategy for overcoming the potentially destructive nature of doubt (inactivity) by providing recurrent opportunities for a return to coherence. It is in the very early gestational phase of a project that there is the most danger of lapsing into a fixed position (whether it be a bias toward the historical, the technological, the pragmatic, and so on). To counter this condition, we've become increas-

[11] On my way to the studio this morning, driving my son, Cooper, to school, he started talking about the color of the mud splattered on the side of the car next to us at a stop light. "I really like the color of that mud, look at how white it is, isn't it dope [great]? Where do you think it comes from?" So much of our work is derived from this type of spontaneous, nonlinear, seemingly nonsequential musing.

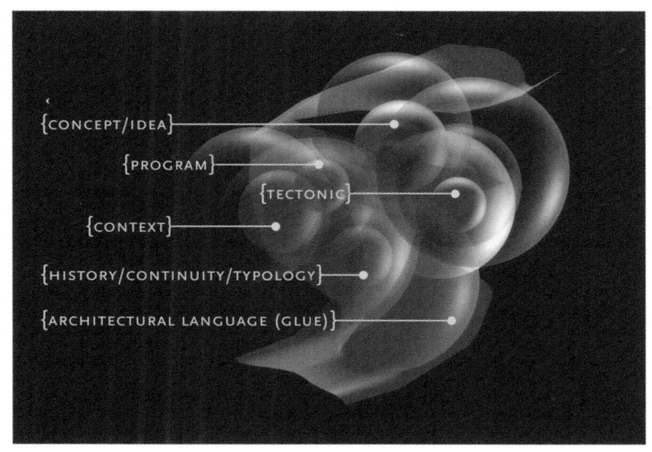

ingly interested in developing a provisional strategy that requires a flexible position as to the role and the degree of influence of the generative sources such as those diagrammed below. Groupings of assumptions evolve in two ways. First, and most typically, an autonomous discipline is favored and then consistently applied a priori to the solution of the problem. An architect, for instance, may favor program or history as the primary generative force. The work consistently proceeds from that perspective and shares commonalities across projects and even entire careers that reveal that particular approach. The second method is committed to a changing role in the types and degrees of a variety of generative sources, and depends entirely on the relationship of these factors that arise when addressing a specific problem. All of the possible generative sources are given equal weight at inception. What develops is a plurality of solutions—a wide spectrum of architectural interpretations. Instead of proposing a single ideal, a catalogue of inclusive solutions is made available. We believe in this second method.

II. ABOUT THE WORK

1. SPREEBOGEN Landscape elements, pieces of urban infrastructure, and elements of the newly proposed "buildings" were combined to create a balletic, expository architectural performance. In this project we proposed a new genus of space for the city of Berlin,[1] one that contrasts with the statist approach to creating ceremonial public urban spaces stocked with revered objects in which freestanding buildings serve as cultural icons. Historically, architects of the state used symbolic geometries to organize various buildings, creating the optical equivalent of a national identity. For the buildings themselves, these architects used a courtly language of classical forms with powerful symmetries meant to emphasize the moral authority of the State.

For us, the goal was to question this view of the singular state, and to dispute the unifying role of central government. Our project suggests a view of government in which national identity is a complex assemblage and not a hierarchical ordering, a parti-colored quilt of multiple interests, groups, and regions.

The project took its point of departure from the topographic sweep of the Spree River running through the center of Berlin, anchored by the existing locations of the Reichstag, Humboldt-hafen, and former Platz der Republik. These key buildings provided the urban site with a generative geometry that was used to inscribe a series of arcs. These arcs were then used to define the lyrical form of the river edge to contrast with the idea of an ordered garden, as is the case with the historic Tiergarten to the south.[2] The

[1] In 1991, the German Bundestag chose the city of Berlin as the new seat of parliament and government, with the Reichstag as the location for parliament sessions. The Spreebogen area again became the subject of discussion as a new parliamentary and government quarter, which in turn led to a competition in 1992 for conversion of the Reichstag building into the German Bundestag and to the *International Spreebogen Urban Design Ideas Competition* for this future quarter as a whole. The brief outlined the concept of finding ". . . exemplary solutions to the problem of bringing together the two halves of the city at this place marked by the deep historical division between East and West Berlin. The new quarter in the Spreebogen should become an integrated part of the unified city of Berlin. For this to happen, not only must the Spreebogen's urban texture and urban spaces acquire meaningful links with the adjacent neighborhoods, but the architectural expression of its new building must also be convincingly integrated into the Berlin cityscape. Integration of the parliamentary quarter along these lines would also correspond to the self-awareness of the German Bundestag as an open and accessible parliament close to the people."

[2] Just before World War I, two large planning projects affected the Spreebogen area and the design of an appropriate "forum" there: a competition for a new opera house on the Konigsplatz (1910) and an urban design competition for Greater Berlin (1908–1910). The opera house participants included Arnold Hartmann, Ludwig Hoffman, and Otto March, who eventually prevailed as the winner in 1912. His scheme proposed an additional major public building (a War Ministry) and the enclosing of the entire public space with colonnades, forming a "patriotic forum." The urban design competition had three main goals: the creation of a "residential city," a "working city," and an urban center in the form of a "monumental city." This latter was to be an assemblage of "institutions of higher education, museums, churches, concert halls, theaters, exhibition buildings, administrative buildings for national and local government authorities or large private companies, urban palaces." Martin Machler presented a scheme which he continued to work on after the war with the active support of Max Berg and Hugo Häring. While dealing with a number of comprehensive issues such as transportation, he proposed the Konigsplatz as "the most suitable location for the offices of central government," including a new Government Council and Imperial Chancellery with embassies along the riverbanks. This project was displayed in 1927 at the Berlin Art exhibition together with plans by Hugo Häring, Peter Behrens, Ludwig Hilberseimer, Hans Poelzig, and Max Heinrich. Häring's scheme was noteworthy for his addition of an east-west axis to the standard north-south axis from the historical city through the Tiergarten. This axis ("Strasse der Republik") would have been lined on both sides by government ministries within the curve of the Spree and with the Reichstag as the dominant urban element. This hierarchy was altered two years later with the addition of a large open-air theater—a republican forum for political events—that extended towards the Reichstag. In the same year, a competition for the expansion of the Reichstag took place, re-working a competition from 1927 in which 278 architects had entered, but in which the terms of the brief were deemed incomplete. Included in this later, invited competition

project knits together a series of building "walls" and landscape "walls." For example, building walls are used along the edge of the Spree River, while landscape walls—made of paths and garden elements—are introduced in order to structure the internal spaces of the site.

Buildings for government usually accept the normative view of the symbolic centrality of government and its institutions. They become isolated buildings, conceived and constructed as segregated edifices. We began, then, with a relatively simple concept: attack the detached singularity of such an "object building." We offered a strategy for resituating the idea of government in the context of an "active" society. Rather than representing government as a symbolic center reflecting a hierarchy of decisions and policies, and ultimately focusing on a central hub, we understood government as a weaving of ideas and influences across a permeable border or divide.[3]

Early in the process, we decided we would not use the body of the site for buildings; instead we decided to focus on the periphery as the location for new building elements and to use the body of the site to represent this process of weaving. The internal landscape of the site was untouched, dotted only with monuments used as generative centers for a sequence of arcs that form the site diagram. This produced an image of serpentine flow, a diagrammatic energy field that we proposed as the actual "government center," a coalescing riverine/government center given a material form.

were Emil Fahrenkamp and H. de Fries, Hans Poelzig, Peter Behrens, Eduard Jobst Siedler, Wilhelm Kreis, and Paul Schmitthenner. The winning scheme of Fahrenkamp and de Fries reconstructed the Alsenplatz square with new ministry buildings on the north-south axis. An honorable mention was given to the Poelzig scheme which took out the Alsenviertel and attempted to integrate the city and the landscape of the Tiergarten with new open construction in the Spreebogen, alternating with Tiergarten greenery brought right out to the banks of the river. This was one of the first proposals to attempt an integration of the powerful landscape and cityscape aspects of Spreebogen.

In 1936, Albert Speer, acting as architect for the Third Reich, was commissioned to design a new monumental boulevard leading into an enormous central square around Königsplatz, modeled on Machler's original design. This scheme was the central element in the new National Socialist urban plan for Berlin, re-named "Germania." Dominating this symbolic boulevard and square (which incorporated the Reichstag building) was a domed "Great Hall," with a capacity of one million, placed on axis at the arc of the Spree. Speer also realized the importance of incorporating traffic planning ideas that consolidated street traffic, and pursued the construction of new north and south train stations.

After the war, in 1946, Walter Moest and Willi Gorgen brought forward their Zehlendorf Plan, incorporating all existing structures into a plan for expansion of the main street network, with the main intervention being a reduction of the major axes planned by Speer. In the same year, Hans Scharoun proposed a kind of linear city made of four east-west city "belts"(core, cultural, residential, and work), based on a traffic pattern that defined the limits of each zone. For Scharoun, this was a response to the destruction of Berlin during the war, which created the opportunity for a "new urban landscape."

In 1958, West Berlin held the Berlin Capital Competition, which attracted 150 entries who ignored cold war political boundaries and proposed schemes oriented to automobile traffic and consisting of isolated high-rise buildings in a Radiant City setting. The construction of the Berlin Wall in 1961 effectively put the Spreebogen area into a peripheral realm, and plans for the area remained dormant until a new land use plan for the Central District of Berlin came into being. This led to yet more competitions for the area, including one in 1985 for an urban quarter in the Spreebogen area. Three different approaches were premiated: Petzold/Hansjakov, Halfmann/Zillich with FPB, and Hans Kollhoff. At the same time, a proposed German historic museum was won in competition by Aldo Rossi, but was abandoned with the city's later re-unification.

[3] The theme for this work came from an earlier project we did that was very close in spirit; toward the end of the cold-war era, we entered a competition to link east and west with a "mending wall," which under current conditions we tend to think of as a "healing wall."

This energy field is like ballet in the sense that it causes the viewer to suppress some aspects of ordinary perceptual vigilance. In ballet, one is brought into a hall, the house lights dim, the stage lights rise, and the dancers' gestures make one progressively less conscious of the limits of body weight and balance; if the effort and control required for the dance is evident, the dancer has not yet succeeded in binding perception to movement patterns or in using gestures that lift the spirit as they defy the laws of gravity. If the architecture, like the ballet, presides over the space of the stage, there is an awareness that the vacancy at the center of the site was choreographed to allow this energy field to build, shifting the focus to the dynamics of the edge condition where building efforts have been intensified.

This presented us with a chance to engage in a complete rethinking of the idea of infrastructure. Our approach was based on the notion of flow: there is no singularity of building; instead, a continuous matrix architecture collapses the boundary between that which is building and that which is landscape, between that which is man-made and that which is "found earth." The Spree River has been changed many times over the years, for example, and we came upon it as a concrete channel, not exactly a piece of raw untouched nature. Despite its containment, and one might even say its denatured character, it still evokes allusions to depth, darkness, and the chthonic forces of the unknown. We added to this concrete channel numerous computer generated lines of flow, each representing a series of placements that the river took over its historic evolution. These images resemble ribbons, a series of stop-action photographs of the invisible river, making visible its underlying primal forces; like a delta, it inexorably keeps carving out different linear spaces. The diagrammatic description of this force field is in fact a description of the flow of the river over time. Multiple positions are combined as these riverine strands are moved through the site.

Similarly, because we were framing a government center for an "active society," as opposed to a formal ceremonial culture, we saw our efforts as an attempt to create a system of liquid spaces, a series of interstitial areas between landscape and city, water and hardscape.[4]

[4] This "active society" component is operating in many of our subsequent projects. For example, the Hypo-Bank is still working with and developing aspects of this idea. We realized (first in the Vienna project) that we were no longer dealing with and could be released from the standard conventions of figure-ground, building and site. We came to see the site as the focus of the work. We found ourselves operating at the same time on both the site and on the object as we took the site to be a dynamic condition, part of the flow, as opposed to the idea of dynamic object defined against the stable background of a static site. We used the metaphor of surfing vs. skiing, where both the site and the floating object are in motion. In surfing, the site is moving and changing in relation to the object; in skiing the site can be treated as a fixed condition.

The idea of center has been replaced by these ribbons, as they form a continuous field; the ribbon architecture is neither object nor context. The ribbons are penetrated by pieces of the urban grid that extend the existing city. They become part of the weaving of connections between the landscape and the city; the government itself connects to this fluid landscape language as opposed to the orthogonal language of the "royal state." They also make reference to the weaving together of past and present, the repercussions of the reconnection of east and west, and the likely relocation of the capital from Bonn to Berlin.

In the end, this is an example of an alternative architecture. Rather than an hierarchical system with clear boundaries and internal structural forms, fluid systems crop up from the force fields that are present below the ground. Governmental offices, rather than being seen as eternal institutions, have a built-in type of obsolescence that causes them to disappear and be replaced as the underlying dynamics change. The primary organizing mechanism is horizontal. Every year the core institutions are replaced by new vertical expressions of the fluid underground forces.

This is an architecture that deals with migrating, mutually repelling and transforming border cultures. It involves a weaving of new hybrid fabrics between realms that are defined in opposition to one another. In this case, the focus of this wandering identity is the Spree River, which is also the mythic source of much of German culture. Berlin Mitte is the equivalent of Île de la Cité (the founding core of the city). The river is the genesis of the city and the German culture around it, manifest in the lives of individual citizens and communities.

The primary idea of the design is to decentralize the governmental and institutional aspects of the work. We designed a linear bar with a series of pavilions: one for the Ministry of Finance, one for the Ministry of the Interior, and so on. This produced a continuous band that was woven together with elements of the city, so that some of the pieces exist on the orthogonal system—the grid of the city—while others are within the band. The key to the project is its continuous flow of energy. There is no need for a new Reichstag (the old one is left as a part of history), for the various departments of the federal government are now parts of this continuity. The continuity itself represents an integration that is inextricably linked to the site, the historical site,[5] (which is the Tiergarten), the historic city, and the Spree (which is already a boundary condition integrating east and west, past and present).

The project builds upon a broad notion of boundary, a boundary that—like the river—acts as an isolating device while also serving as a connecting device, never singular in its character. We have an abiding interest in the ambiguity of this kind of boundary. As the pieces move through, this porous boundary literally brings you across the Spree River on a series of pedestrian bridges.[6] Parts of the buildings span across as well. The boundary is always both a connecting device that bridges across and a qualifier that differentiates between.

Our architecture attempts to operate as a critique of the limitations of traditional methods of translating the social and institutional sphere into built form. The devices we have inherited for organizing large human settlements have evolved little since the early Roman architecture of the grid. We felt that given the hybrid structure of most cities, there is a no longer a normative surface that can be used as a connecting matrix. We are left with a series of lines as connective gestures as opposed to the traditionally reliable continuous surfaces (street edges, for example, or the setback lines that Haussmann imposed on Paris). Since we are no longer using objects as tools, we are able to use surfaces as a source of continuity and connective tissue.[7]

The lines in Spreebogen are continually connecting and reconnecting, but the idea was to represent an intentional/causal understanding of the relationships between the departments that constitute the government as if they were interactions between client groups or constituencies. The lines also represent the everyday life of the city as it intersects with government. All of this challenges the isolation, autonomy, and monumentalization of government.

The Reichstag is left as an historic emblem of the statist past. The Tiergarten is the opposite, an open landscape. In the end, both the site and the city beyond are not singular systems, but rather complex organisms. One can see the city from Berlin Mitte outward, or from the Tiergarten inward. They are ambiguous in their hierarchy. One does not

[5] The Spreebogen area began as undeveloped land outside Berlin's city gates, containing recreational miscellaneous villas, restaurants, and festival halls, which coexisted with buildings and exercise fields of the Prussian military. The military abandoned the site in the first half of the nineteenth century, and Peter Joseph Lenné, who had just completed the Tiergarten as a landscaped park, proposed an urban design scheme for the area in 1839. This was followed a year later by a proposal from Karl Friedrich Schinkel, only a year before his death. Both schemes modified the bend in the Spree River to a nearly exact semicircle, imposed upon it a north-south axis, and transformed the former military field into a parade ground formally lined with buildings on either side. The two schemes differed in that Schinkel gradually blurred the distinction between the landscaped Tiergarten and the proposed urban construction to the north of the Spree's arc, whereas Lenné conceived a new urban quarter inside this curve forming a hard edge to the Tiergarten's landscaped area. This scheme was modified in 1842–43 to accommodate increased shipping and rail traffic volume, corresponding with a surge of public building that occurred there, with projects by Ludwig Persius and Heinrich Strack. A new harbor, the Humboldthafen, was created by Lenné in the 1850s on the north-south axis of the Spreebogen planning area and connected to the top of the arc with a short canal. With a greater number of buildings and additional landfill, the old exercise field was slowly transformed into a major urban center with official commemorative names for streets and squares. By the end of the nineteenth century, the area had become a main seat of government with embassies, government institutions, and honorary residences for members of all wings of political and military life. The Reichstag was completed on the western side of Königsplatz in 1894 by Paul Wallot, an achievement which formally initiated the continuous architectural debate about the appropriate design for this highly symbolic space representing state and society in one of the world's great cities.

[6] The river is a chthonic source with its own life-giving qualities. It is like a primordial spring that emerges out of the earth. It is uncontrollable, irresistible, filled with dangerous libidinal impulses. Beneath the surface rationality is the potential for being swept up into a spell of culture, or the charismatic voice of a powerful leader. The State (bureaucracy) attempts to control those impulses and subdue these chthonic forces through its civilizing processes.

[7] In the past, as in Venice III, we used repetition of elements as an architectural device for establishing an autonomous beat that drew the energy of the surrounding area toward the interior of the project. These primary organizational themes are gradually receding from prominence in our projects, even though they are still present in some (for example, in certain elements of the Exposition Park School).

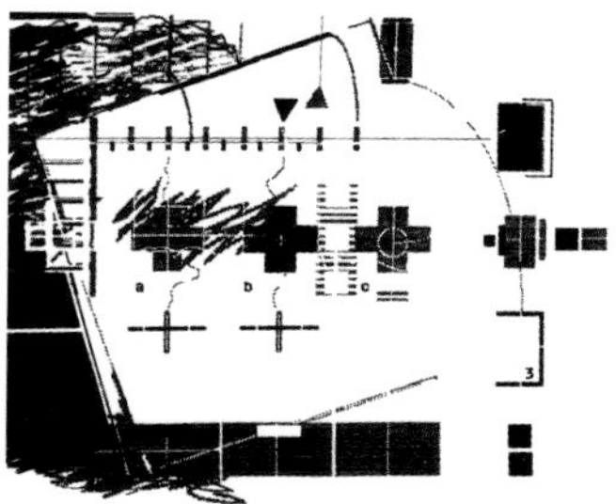

suppress the other. The park comes through, and the site that remains is a park. Nature survives! The statuesque and revered Reichstag building sits forward in this new Garden. On the ground plane, the walls are open, raised on *pilotis,* deferring to the honorific condition of the public space. The individual fragmentation of these permeable and incomplete walls into discrete pieces is intended as a manifestation of active democracy and decentralized power; they are porous, flexible, and constantly re-defining the central shared goals of the urban public realm.

TOURS CULTURAL ARTS CENTER This project required fitting a large program of new construction into a small, medieval historic site.[8] The intention was to reinforce the traditional techniques of making public space in European medieval towns, which are based on the concepts of edge and middle. The edge, or wall, creates the street, while the hollow middle of the dense urban blocks creates the court. These two arenas of civic space have nurtured the public life of the citizenry throughout history. 2.

The design approach is a continuation of a strategy we had initiated in 1989 with the Amerika-Gedenkbibliothek. It was a strategy that could be called "contingent planning," in which each architectural gesture makes up the whole in a reflexive response to a specific condition found on the site.[9] The street edges are reinforced by the position of the two major program elements—the theater and the gallery—at the two boundaries of the site. Each of these honorific volumes is enclosed at the street by a wall-like building that complements the tradition of the existing historic structures. The public spaces of the streets on the site's exterior are thereby reinforced, and a court is configured on the interior employing both new and existing buildings, becoming the focal point of activity

[8] The area Francis Poulenc is located at the south periphery of the ancient walls in the center of the historic city of Tours. The site is surrounded by a number of important historic religious monuments (the cathedral Saint Gatien, the cloister "de la psalette," etc.) and a remarkable architectural inheritance. The project reorganizes an assembly of activities which will include the High School Paul Louis Courier, the National Conservatory of the Region (c. seventeenth century), the School of Music (c. eighteenth century) and the proposed Center of Contemporary Art.

9

for the whole complex. This primary gesture provides the framework for secondary events that have been developed to function with greater flexibility.[10]

These secondary events include the placement of classrooms and offices within an extention of the existing building volume at the southwest corner of the court. These smaller rooms are connected to similar spaces belonging to the theater administration and support the west edge of the theater volume. To the south of the main gallery volume is a smaller bar of space that mediates between the gallery itself and the apse of the adjacent church, forming a small entry square near the street and establishing a layer between the gallery and the court. In the middle of the court is pedestrian access to the shared underground parking, so that those arriving by car might experience the civic presence and civil activity of the court before entering any of the main facilities.

Despite its large size, this new arts complex is easily woven into the architectural fabric of the town because its "primary level of definition" has been determined by the urban characteristics of the site, including street, court, and the "found objects" of the existing historic buildings. This approach allowed the specific forms and materials of each architectural element to be expressive of and about contemporary life, while maintaining the contextual paradigm of the medieval town.

3. **SCIENCE MUSEUM SCHOOL** The Science Museum School distorts and transforms the urban school typology by letting the natural world enter the daily life of the students, who are for the most part subject to an intense urban experience (Los Angeles) and deprived of a direct experience of nature. For this project, the existing Armory was taken down, and the school becomes the third building around the Rose Garden, accompanied

[10] This is a method indebted to the ideas of O.M. Ungers, "Planning Criteria" *Lotus #11* (Milan, 1976), pp.13–14. In discussing his own work, he says:

"The first criterion of my design is the dialectical process with a reality as found . . . The impulse of the design comes usually from a permanent confrontation with the environment as it exists as well as the acceptance of specific economic, social and historical conditions. . . . The design is determined by the specific building task, by the integration into an existing context and also by the intensification of the place. The architectural concepts are based upon the reinforcement of the genius loci out of which they grow and of which they are a part. . . .

"The second criterion which all the designs have in common has to do with the problem of planning and accident in several ways. First, that accidents are sometimes turned into planning intentions or to put in better terms into an architectural event. Secondly, that the plan has at least two levels of definition, a primary and a secondary. The primary level determines the framework or the basic structure which organizes the space for a secondary event which can be more accidental, spontaneous and if necessary temporary. Part of it is also the necessity to create planning-fields for a more individualistic architecture within a set of fixed rules, or to develop a design strategy for every specific solution.

"The third criterion that I want to demonstrate with the design is the plurality of solutions or the wide spectrum of the architectural interpretation of one and the same element. As far as it is possible the spectrum is conceived as a continuum of interpretations which represent steps in between two extremes. Implicit in this criterion is a catalogue of alternatives, in contrast to the usual attempts at an ideal solution. The projects are better characterized as fragments and partial solutions of a very specific area, than ideal realizations of a platonic idea. They can be seen as an attempt to get away from the myth of the perfect plan. Pseudoideological criteria like flexibility versus fixidity or objectivity versus subjectivity, process versus object, form versus content or whatever antagonisms do exist as an ideological hang-up become relative in this 'continuum-concept' as I call it. Or put it in other terms, they are treated as complementary factors. . . ."

by the new Science Museum and the Natural History museum. This is also the corner site of Exposition Park, which serves as part of the entrance sequence. The program is a prototype for an elementary school in a district in Central Los Angeles, woven together in this instance with the Science Museum. By taking advantage of its adjacency to the Exposition Park Rose Garden, the architecture of the garden extends directly into the structure of the school, providing places that are more Arcadian than one could find in a typical urban school. In our project, the Rose Garden became the formal catalyst.

The primary architectural gestures are (1) a layered three-story bar of space, and (2) a horizontal garden-like trellis structure. The first contains classrooms, administrative space, and open-air teaching decks in a long structure that stretches from the edge of the Aerospace Museum (by Frank Gehry) at the southern end of the park to the oval athletic field to the north, engaging the field by overlapping its boundary. As the land lifts up, this very simple bar building protrudes from it, thereby avoiding the turbulence that might have occurred if we tried to define a transitional element that bridged between Gehry's form-language and our own. From the front of the site, the building has been dug into the ground to create an architecture that is about privacy, protection, and sanctuary. It also reveals the discrepancy between this protected zone for children and the surrounding streets, noted for violence and drive-by shootings[11]

[11] The building demonstrates a more comprehensive attitude about architecture, science, and site. In the news every day there is some discussion that causes us to rethink the relationship of science and the forms of knowledge that we had come to accept as stable and given. Science is no longer solely concerned with "explanation" in an abstract sense; it has become part of the everyday field of information that is vital to the way we live and make critical decisions. It can also be said that science, once buoyed by maintaining theoretical distance from everyday life, set up since the Renaissance to focus on theoretical empirical observations and permanent fields of knowledge, is now also changing with context. More and more theoretical studies address the complexity of living systems rather than trying to create them from simple atomistic foundations.

A figure around which this project could be framed is Rupert Sheldrake. Putting aside for the moment the more controversial aspects of his theories, he is clearly one of a multitude of scientists interested in self-organizing natural systems. In his case, he deals with the cause of form, in organizing fields, form-shaping fields, which he calls morphic fields. The original features of forms of societies, ideas, crystals, and molecules depend on the way that previous generations of that kind have been organized. There's a kind of built-in memory in the morphic fields of each type of thing. So the regularities of nature are more like habits than things governed by eternal mathematical laws that somehow exist outside nature. What are such fields made of, electromagnetic fields, or gravitational fields? Nobody knows, even in the case of the known fields of physics. The magnetic field around a magnet, for example, is not made of air, and it is not made of matter. When you scatter iron filings, you can reveal this field, but it is not made of anything except the field. In the same sense, we see the building as a way of revealing the field.

In the past, there were similar ways of revealing the knowledge field; for example, in the orderly system of a rose garden, a Victorian invention, based on taxonomies and types as opposed to momentary and changing patterns. We used the park as an opportunity to reinterpret its operations and its underlying structure; the system of the rose garden is going from surface to depth to volume, the volume of a park. This is similar to Parc Guell as a park that has been dealt with spatially; it is not merely a level field or a two-dimensional organization representation.

The project is also inevitably about the relationship between science and mysticism. Freud represents science, albeit radically intuitive, isolating the human psyche, translating the landscape of the human character through the auspices of science. Freud tried to control and civilize the unconscious. We are looking forward to a new kind of science, perhaps one with an Eastern aspect, which can engage non-linear, complex problems that were impossible in the first atomistic phase. It is paradoxical to use a science building to create a mystery, to represent the search for those edge conditions from which issues of emergence will erupt, rather than to focus on the known and the knowable. Why doesn't science captivate society with all its mysteries and compelling directions? A subtext of the work is that there is mystery just below the surface of the rational investigation of a complex project. The anthropology of plants in relation to climate and region, as well as culture, forms an interaction between the species, native science, the tie between ethnobotany and medicine. We have become obsessed with stabilization and control of nature rather than merging with the energy of nature.

The territory that is of most interest to me ties observation and intuition to hypothesis testing, defining new relationships of language and logic. The virtual aspect of these explorations would never have been possible without the mental journeys of Freud and Joyce, who opened up new dimensions of experience. Within these virtual spheres we can navigate through space and time in ways that are essentially closer to the reality of how the mind operates.

It is hard to imagine the limitations of narrative chronological time as the only framework within which to novelize or conceive of our own personal autobiographical development. We now know that our lives are always being reconstructed in relation to context and the content of our experience. In this sense, the artist is drawn closer to science, to examine the internal process and express it in the extended product. The school is about that kind of revealing process, as in the idea of the folded landscape, which becomes evident as the spatial condition, and leads to the emergence of other properties. Also, the work is always operating within an open architecture, concerned with how the work will respond to changes in the future.

This is one of the buildings in which we are using the "skin" as an organizing device. The building is sheathed on the east side with a skin held away from the body of the building, and on the garden side by a garden-trellis structure that wraps the side of the building, creating depth and indoor/outdoor volumes in various spatial layers.

The man-made grid is extended over the surface of the earth until it becomes a trellis, creating an outdoor space for the young children. We essentially removed the third building element and left only the entrance piece of the historic building (the roof, two columns, and a piece of the pediment). The trellis structure houses a series of rooms that require more flexible spatial arrangements than the bar of space will allow, including the kindergarten play area, library, multipurpose space, eating area, and several courtyards and outdoor student garden spaces. The overhead trellis is, at various times, the roof of an enclosed volume, a cover for shaded outdoor space, and a profile of outdoor spaces open directly to the sky. This garden structure has a direct connection with the public rose garden, in both a literal and a metaphorical sense; it is an artificial extension of the landscape, anchoring the classroom bar physically to the site and phenomenally to the world of the cultivated urban garden. Bringing this element into the school is an example of how a typology can be transformed and enhanced by the opportunities and potentials of its context, weaving institutions more poetically into the collaged fabric of the city.

4. **SALICK ADMINISTRATIVE OFFICES** The architectural device of the non-load-bearing "curtain wall" has been the subject of reconsideration for architects throughout the late twentieth century. Although celebrated by the members of the "heroic" period of modern architecture,[12] the situation has changed nearly three quarters of a century later: the universal gridded modulation that is economical and readily available has become a popular symbol of corporate anonymity and the shortcomings of the modern movement. Just such a standardized grid was replaced with this design for a new building that utilizes the infrastructure of an existing, prosaic three-story office building of the 1960s, one thought to be lacking distinction and character. The problem was approached in the same manner and with the same spirit as other more "macro" programs. That is, we looked to exigencies of the site to provide inspiration for design. In this case, the "site" was the existing infrastructure of the building and its immutable architectural events: the

[12] Ulrich Conrads (ed.) *Programs and Manifestos on 20th Century Architecture* (MIT Press, 1977), p. 75. Mies van der Rohe, writing in 1923, described the frame building in his typical laconic manner: "Reinforced concrete buildings are by nature skeletal buildings. . . . That is to say, buildings consisting of skin and bones." Ibid., p. 100: In 1926, Le Corbusier produced his declaration, *Five Points towards a New Architecture,* in which two of the points, "The horizontal window" and "Free design of the façade," describe the curtain wall in liberative terms.

rhythm of the existing structural bays, the mechanical service components, and the position of the entry.

At the northeast corner, the new surface membrane is fractured into a vertically canted volume that rises out over the roof, interrupting the visual datum of the glass and granite cladding system. This fracturing gesture is then juxtaposed against a structural element that expresses its pragmatic functions and simultaneously provides an ordering geometry. This system, expressed on the ground plane as a truncated triangular plane, is carried up through the building as a series of fragments, and is finally resolved as an object on the roof that serves as the building's penthouse mechanical shed. The building's prior formal aspirations summarized by a universal anonymity have been redirected into an elaboration of the specific. In the careful making of this corner of the building into an architectural gesture, the nature of surface and volume inherent in retrograde modernism is simultaneously revealed and critiqued.

FJC COMMUNICATIONS The creation of an identity within the ubiquitous non- 5.
place of the speculative office building is one of the most difficult challenges confronting architects today. This challenge is often further complicated by the contingency that it be accomplished within a rapid time frame and with minimal funds. Friedland Jacobs Communication, a merger of two companies to form an advertising/production company, was no exception. Within their workplace, the conference/screening room was identified both as the nucleus of activity and its metaphorical heart. A strong geometric figure—a fragment of an elliptical cone—was conceived as enclosing this representational center of the workplace. With its spatial and figural presence, it clearly marks an identifiable place within the larger context of this normative generic office environment.[13] Inside of this

[13] Although altered, this technique for delineating spatial boundaries and "place" is closely allied to the work of architectural theorist and historian Christian Norberg-Schulz. In *Intentions in Architecture* (MIT Press, 1977), pp. 134–136, he states: "As an architectural 'mass-element' we denominate a body which is separated from its environment in such a way that its extension can be described by means of a Euclidean co-ordinate system. The first qualification of a mass, hence, is topological concentration. As a criterion for the concentration of a mass (its 'figure-character'), we will take its ability to join other masses. We have seen that the straight line stems from the operation 'to aim.' A straight line and a plane surface, therefore, define directions which point outside their origin. The closed curve, instead, returns to its starting point. The sphere, hence, has a maximum of concentration, while the upright cylinder may be extended (joined to other masses) in one direction, and the lying cylinder in two. A cone standing on its base comes close to the sphere in concentration, while the pyramid, because of its plane bounding surfaces, is more easily joined to other bodies. A mass which is defined in a purely topological way by accidental curves may in principle be adapted to adjacent bodies by changing the contour. The figure-character (Gestalt quality) is therefore in general stressed through geometrization. . . . We may say that the mass-element is characterized by its topological-geometrical form. Rather than considering the numerical relations one might discover on measuring a mass, we maintain that the pregnant Gestalt is decisive. Thus we distinguish between a semi-sphere and a cube, etc. It is essential that the form should be *pregnant.* Psychological experiments show that we tend to overlook or stress irregularities. A deviation from the symmetrical or regular form has to be distinct to be formally active. The character of an element is hence determined by its degree of concentration, or by its ability to join other elements. The topological *isolation* is of course also decisive for its independence. An element appears as an independent *figure* if it stands out against a continuous, undisturbed ground. We have also seen that the treatment of the bounding surfaces determines the character of the mass-element." [see note 14]

white, curved, embryonic wall, the space embraces and nurtures the creative process. The social intention of the geometric heart of this volume is to provide a collective holding space within the open office area. From this geometric/functional center, regulating lines radiate outward directing the geometry of the secondary interior events. Maximizing the visual and tactile contrast with the smooth curved walls of the interior shell, these smaller scale and functionally specific gestures are faceted angular constructions.[14] In opposition to the amorphous surface of the shell, secondary interior events express their materiality through layers of surfaces and planes: glass and steel horizontal surfaces, canted plywood planes, and a long cantilevered spine of glass and fluorescent light linking the central nucleus to the outer work areas and metaphorically out to the entertainment world of Hollywood beyond. The exposed metal studs of the ceiling further emphasize the figural quality of the elliptical shell by creating a regular visual surface datum. Individual offices are placed at the edges of the shell, occupying the interstitial space between its wall and the exterior glass wall. These offices have various relationships with these two boundaries, with some inside the shell, some outside, and some intersecting the shell's spatial boundary. Their angled walls allow these spaces to borrow from one another by sharing "borders."[15] In this way, a simple, expedient set of architectural events provides a distinct place for each required function without losing the sense of belonging to—and being inside of—a larger organic whole.

6. OVE ARUP & PARTNERS The existing volume of this warehouse conversion contained two distinct volumes: one 25 feet high, spanned with three bowstring trusses; the other lower in height without expressive structure. Three architectural strategies provide the basis for this professional office within the various spaces: two distinct strategies appropriate to the division of spaces within each of these two volumes and a third strategy that intersects the others.

In the taller space a set of three interior walls responds formally to the three bowstring trusses. These folded-plane walls of perforated metal move through the space,

[14] Again, from Norberg-Schulz: "Illumination, colour, and texture are other important means to the definition of the mass-elements. While one texture, such as a polished and reflecting surface, can make the mass dissolve, another may stress its concentration."

[15] Rudolf Arnheim, *The Dynamics of Architectural Form* (University of California Press, 1977), pp.73–74, discusses this phenomenon: "In Aristotle's presentation, neighboring objects share their borders peacefully. In perception, however, boundaries are the precarious products of opposing forces. Psychologists speak of 'contour rivalry' which comes about in the two-dimensional plane when two adjacent surfaces each attempt to annex the common contour as its own boundary. . . . Perceptually, a disturbing contradiction is created when an interface belongs to two different boundaries but is only one thing nevertheless. In such a case the interface is related dynamically to two different vectorial centers and is therefore torn in opposite directions. While these antagonistic pulls and pushes make for balanced borderline conditions when the interface is a straight line, they create asymmetries in all other cases—for example, when curves generate convexity on the one side, concavity on the other. The resulting difference is so strong that the identity of the common shape is not recognized perceptually.

geometrically deviating from the truss while spatially modulating open workstations and the reception area. Functionally, they are engineered to simultaneously reflect both artificial and natural light from skylights while modulating the acoustics within the large open volume. In the smaller volume, which also contains "team" stations for collaborative work, smaller metal planes hover above, inflecting individual spaces within the office layout and again supplying acoustic control throughout the room.

The third gesture—a frameless glazed "bar" of smaller spaces—stretches across both studio volumes, binding the entire office into a single whole. This elongated transparent box containing private offices, a kitchen, and small conference rooms, both divides and binds the spaces together while keeping the support staff, entry reception, and library separate from the open work areas. Its presence in both studio volumes gives dramatic visual, functional, and spatial continuity to the workplace.

Services for the mechanical systems are incorporated within the raised concrete tile floors of both studio areas, creating a floor plenum for distribution of power and communication cables as well as conditioned air. A vertical glass duct inside the glass "bar" reveals the flow of air between clerestory returns and floor diffusers with visible fan impellers that resemble the traditional wheels and gears of the engineer's art.

This strategy sets up an organic architectural position within the office interior: a particular interior place can have its own language that need not rely on the ubiquitous office syntax of normative work environments.

LANDA HOUSE This project is a reminder of the opportunities the design of a small house contains for the exploration of profound architectural issues. In this particular case, techniques of establishing and expanding volumetric boundaries are juxtaposed with methods of vertical spatial organization. Each of these has, in turn, its own relationship to the modified existing house and its site. Volume is the primary means of defining boundaries in this house, as opposed to a project like 6th Street House (1987), where surface was extensively used.[16] 7.

16

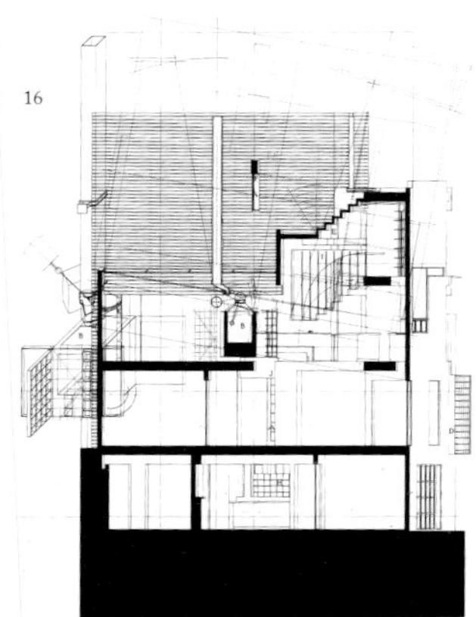

The architectural devices explore ideas of surface, volume, and boundary conditions, maintaining a tenuous dialogue between the existing house and the new intervention. A distorted cube hovers above the existing plinth of the first-floor volume. It acts as a primary site/volume boundary for the new addition, acknowledging the limits of the given property. This splayed orthogonal wall surface of concrete panels wraps around three sides of the newly enclosed second and third floor volume, with a single piece folded down for the main entrance. A second surface element—a fragment of a truncated cone—also sits above the first floor, inside the splayed surface boundary. This element, a distorted cylinder, provides another layer and type of enclosure, intersecting and penetrating the splayed walls of the cube, thereby creating voids of natural light and ventilation in the rooms below. Its geometric construction begins with a center point shifted from the axis of the site, suggesting a boundary beyond that of the legal property description.

An awareness of this extended boundary critiques the legal definition of the site, expanding into physical topographic boundaries and social concepts such as neighborhood. The interior truncated cone is the more pure of the two geometric figures, and, as such, provides a platonic internal world for the house, in opposition to the specific contingent surfaces imposed upon each side of the distorted cube by the delimited site.

Two vertical elements occupy the confines of both surface structures: a wall of steel shelving along the centerline of the cone, and a stair. The shelving wall divides the studio from the stair and bedroom above, while the stair is itself a hybrid tower incorporating fragments of foundation, HVAC, structure, and storage. At the third floor, it expands as a horizontal plane to become a bedroom loft. These two elements anchor the new surface volumes to the body of the existing house below, thereby linking the exigencies of daily life to the modified idealism of this contemporary villa in which strategies of connection and of randomness produce a series of idiosyncratic moments.

8. BLADES HOUSE Unlike nearly all other world cultures, the typical American house has been unable to establish a private exterior domain within the undifferentiated suburban landscape. Within these suburbs, it has been traditional to give the house a figural position in the neutral "ground" of the site, in which the "building/machine" is active and the "site/nature" is passive. With the Blades House, the intention was to transcend this limited concept, attempting a work that assimilates and activates the site as a whole. The distinction between exterior and interior space was blurred in order to expand the typical suburban boundaries and make the landscape habitable. The space of the garden—the fragment of the site that forms the basis for this work—is meant to be experienced and understood as a dominant component within the overall composition. This elliptical outdoor room is the primary domain of the site; the enclosed volume of the house is subordinate to this gesture of occupation in the earth.[17]

[17] This project is in many ways a critique of the Crawford House, which occupied a middle ground between our interests in exploring the site, and an architecture based on the traditional iconography of "house-ness," where the site is seen as passive and the building as active. We started this in our Paris project (1989), where approximately 70 percent of the program was embedded in a manipulated ground plane, transcending the typical figure-ground opposition between site and building. With Paris, and later the Vienna Expo (1991), both the ground and the object are manipulated to the point of equivalency. The Blades House anticipates our current work, all of which is predicated on working very literally with the ground itself as opposed to objects on the ground.

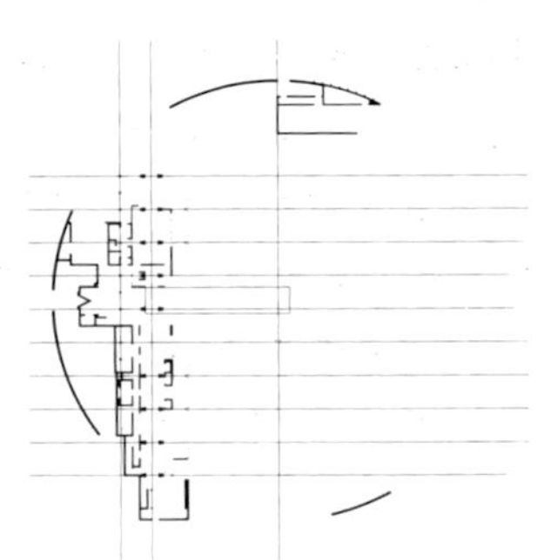

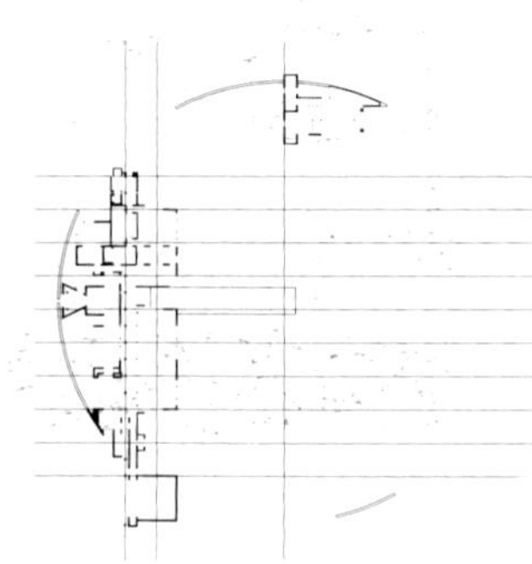

Two types of walls are used to create outdoor spaces. One set is orthogonal and responds to both the geometry and the community of houses in the neighborhood. The other, elliptical set of walls defines and extends the space of the outdoor room. Walking through the house, walls move inside and out as voids in the exterior walls. The house itself is a fragment or vertical slice of segmented space that extends laterally across the site, engaging the landscape elements in an architectural dialogue between exterior and interior space. A curved roof begins at the road outside the elliptical boundary wall, rises to an arc at its highest point near the center of the outdoor room, and lowers again at the opposite end of the site, outside the boundary wall. At the two extreme points of departure for this enclosed volume, separate elements anchor the house as it bridges from the road to the inner site domain. The street end contains an inconspicuous garage and gallery, a modest statement deferring to the character of the neighborhood. At the further, unoccupied edge of the site is the bedroom, straddling the boundary wall, a part of both worlds, confined and unconfined. Breaking out of the singular gesture of the main volume, this set of more intimate spaces fractures, tilts, and opens to the natural landscape beyond. In this way, the house moves from the order of the street to the freedom of the natural landscape, with the indoor/outdoor living/landscape space as the mediator between the two conditions. By augmenting and reshaping the natural landscape as a boundary, a place of habitation has been created.

FRANKFURT WASTE MANAGEMENT FACILITY As in nearly all twentieth-century urban industrial areas, the site for this project—within the city of Frankfurt[18]—is idiosyncratic. It sits within an industrial archeology of found objects with differing histories, configurations, and scales.[19] A site order for the project establishes a continuous boundary along Schiele Strasse with a long, narrow "ribbon" building housing the administrative offices—those that are most appropriate for the street. This building ends at the north with an existing historic building and at the south in what is proposed to be a large public 9.

[18] E.A. Gutkind, *Urban Development in Central Europe* (Free Press, 1970), pp. 266–270. The ancient commercial town of Frankfurt had become, by the thirteenth century, one of the most important commercial towns of Western Europe. It occupies a site beside a convenient river crossing connecting northern (ancient) and southern Germany. The original Roman town developed in successive layers moving outward from the original *Pfalz*, or royal castle, and its immediate market square.

[19] From the competition brief, *Neubau Hauptbetriebshof für das AMT für Abfallwirtschaft und Stadtreinigung* (Stadt Frankfurt am Main, Der Magistrat–Hochbauamt): "The original site for the Frankfurt Gasworks was obtained in 1909, in what was then the growing Eastharbor industrial district on the Schielestrasse. The architect Peter Behrens was commissioned for the main buildings of the complex, while the company of Berlin-Anhaltische Maschinenbau AG was hired for the design of the furnace and cleanerhouses. These latter buildings were standardized industrial structures of their time, related to the Behrens designs only by the predominant use of a similar exterior material: a dark violet iron clinker brick. A building permit was applied for in November 1910, and construction began in the spring of the following year, with completion of the Ofenhaus in the fall of 1912, allowing for gas production to begin. The four towers so prominent in the scheme were reservoirs for ammonia, water, tar, and process water. In each case, their form was determined by the required capacity, structural capabilities of the

park. The Workshops occupy the compound's remaining area inside the set of buildings by Peter Behrens.[20] This factory building is an "L"-shaped block consisting of two distinct parts: to the north, a modest rectangular element with smaller individual spaces; and to the west, a large-scale, honorific open volume, in which most of the physical work is performed. This main volume is spanned with a series of folded plates, skewed to the geometry of the plan in order to achieve the required north-facing clerestory light.

The expressive tectonic quality of this structure is revealed in the room's interior and in the vast exterior "landscape" of the roof. The character of this folded roof is that of a re-configured ground plane, reducing the perception of the new building as an inserted "object" competing with the existing buildings on the site.[21] At its southern end, this volume penetrates the narrow Administration building, revealing its nature to the street and directly connecting these two pivotal elements of the program. The east wall is made as a series of openings for vehicles, while the west wall is a translucent glazed membrane, augmenting and balancing the natural light from the roof monitors above.

In the tradition of bringing industrial buildings into the realm of architecture, these buildings both articulate their purpose and create an identifiable domain, or "campus," within the larger urban landscape. At the same time, the ensemble gives back to the city the historic Behrens buildings with a revitalized working life, a new public open space, and a distinctive and noble site for one of the city's major industrial facilities.

ring-structures, and functional heights for distribution of material. At the same time, the towers clearly had a symbolic role, addressing the traditional historic forms of the Nürnberger Fortress. The housing, administration, and social buildings were planned along the street, as traditionally these formed a link between the world of the factory and the world "outside" the plant. The two-story director's house marked the northwestern edge of the site."

[20] The history of Peter Behrens's work is complex, and architectural historians find the Frankfurt Gasworks buildings to occupy a position in his oeuvre that is somewhat transitional. Leonardo Benevolo, *History of Modern Architecture* (MIT Press, 1977), pp. 382–384, in his comprehensive history of the Modern Movement, describes them relative to his more famous work for the A.E.G. in Berlin: "[Peter] Behrens built various industrial buildings for the A.E.G. in Berlin and, even in such works, he never abandoned his attitude of artist-decorator, whose intention was to accommodate the functional elements with dignity and even a slightly outdated grace, Wagnerian in flavour. The general tone was sober and ponderous, with a vaguely literary allusion to the gloomy atmosphere of the traditional factory, while various salient episodes were treated in a distinctly decorative fashion, which concealed the functional nature of the structures: for instance . . . the cylindrical volumes of the reservoirs [of the Frankfurter Gasgesellschaft], expressionistically accentuated, like menacing towers."

Stanford Anderson, "Peter Behrens," in *Macmillan Encyclopedia of Architects* (Free Press, 1982), pp. 165–169, views this work as indicative of Behrens as a classicist: "The gas works of the Frankfurter Gasgesellschaft are differently conceived [than the A.E.G. buildings in Berlin]. Here Behrens deployed a few, relatively small, typical building units, to form a functional complex around the central coal storage. The Gas Work constructions employ a brick technology and forms that again go back to German medieval usage, but now it is a robust, fully plastic construction that does justice not only to the medieval precedents but also to the revived interest in these works by the early 19th Century classicists whom Behrens admired: Friedrich Gilly and Karl Friedrich Schinkel. . . ."

[21] Compare with similar roofscape/landscape drawings of the Diamond Ranch and Vienna Housing projects.

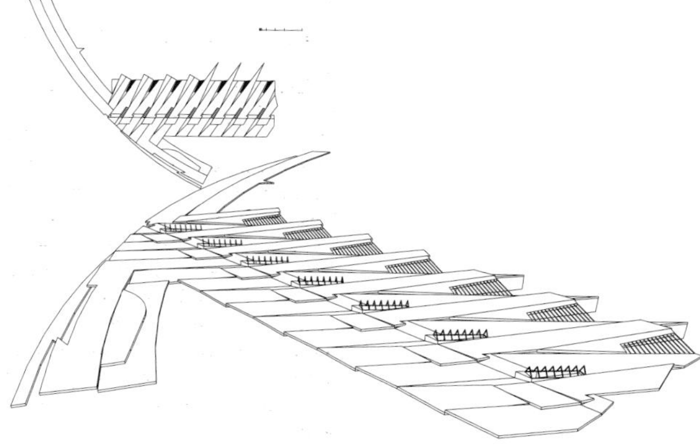

AMERICAN BUSINESS CENTER The competition site for the American Business Center was on four adjacent blocks along the Friedrichstrasse,[22] which was one of the great commercial avenues of South Friedrichstadt in pre-war Berlin.[23] We were invited to make a proposal for block 105, at the historic intersection of Zimmerstrasse and Mauerstrasse, the famous gateway in the Berlin Wall formerly known as "Checkpoint Charlie." Great importance was placed on the urban characteristics of the development of this site, vis-a-vis its significance in the history of this specific city[24] as well as its symbolic connotations with regard to the overall post-war German-American relationship.[25] 10.

At the corner of this large, irregularly shaped block in Berlin, the project transforms a traditional perimeter block strategy in order to incorporate a greater density of (mostly office) space than this nineteenth-century typology would allow. The idea of the perimeter block—a single building element wrapping the site exterior while leaving a hollow interior—is transformed in two major ways. First, each exterior edge condition produces a distinct vocabulary of architecture, dependent upon the character of the street or intersection. The perimeter building element along the Mauerstrasse, for example, reinforces the existing architectural scale and language of this street, while the edge of Zimmerstrasse bounding the site to the west is defined by a building of predominantly horizontal components, emphasizing the layers of walls that occur along this street (including the former Berlin Wall, a fragment of which is reassembled here). A third, smaller transparent/translucent fragment stands at the intersection of these two more opaque street facades, expressing the language of the internal structure while marking the main entry to the Center, and reinforcing the site's tan-

[22] Francesca Rogier's article, "Growing Pains: From the Opening of the Wall to the Wrapping of the Reichstag," in *Assemblage #29* (MIT Press, 1996), p. 54:

"The project [American Business Center], totaling about eleven thousand five hundred square meters on four blocks, was the brainchild of Ronald Lauder and Mark Palmer, who formed the Central European Development Company (CEDC) shortly after reunification. They soon acquired permission for development from the city, but were left on their own to negotiate settlements with former owners. More than one lawsuit arose in the process, which took about two years, but the courts narrowly interpreted the special restitution laws promoting rapid redevelopment and found in favor of the company. . . . The invited competition for the entire project included sixteen firms from both Germany and the United States, as a symbol of German-American cooperation."

[23] From the architectural competition brief, *American Business Center at Checkpoint Charlie: Architects' Brief* (CEDC, Berlin, 1992):

"When the Berlin Wall was constructed in 1961, Friedrichstrasse was divided into a northern area (East Berlin) and a southern area (West Berlin), and the intersection of Friedrichstrasse and Zimmerstrasse was the site of the famous border crossing known as Checkpoint Charlie. This division in some way paralleled an architectural boundary that already existed between the area of the Inner Friedrichstadt of the 17th century and the southern expansion by Philip Gerlach in 1734, characterized by a Baroque axial layout of streets and buildings. In 1987, several buildings for the International Building Exhibition (IBA) were constructed as part of an urban renewal project of 'critical reconstruction.' This included projects by OMA, Peter Eisenman, John Hejduk, and Raimund Abraham. To the west of the competition site is an open area exhibit, 'Topography of Terror': a memorial on the former site of a Gestapo facility. Adjacent to this is the Martin-Gropius-Bau, a museum, the former Prussian Parliament (renovated to contain the Berlin House of Representatives), and the German Ministry of Aviation (containing the Federal Trust) which in 1992 was the largest office building in Europe. North of the Checkpoint Charlie site is a planned Government District, the renowned Schauspielhaus by K. F. Schinkel, and the Friedrichstadt Arcades, a mixed-use development with buildings by Jean Nouvel; Pei, Cobb, Freed; and O. M. Ungers.

"Other landmarks in the immediate area of the competition site are the 'House at Checkpoint Charlie,' by OMA, a mixed-use building by Bohigas, Martorell and Mackey, a planned project by J. P. Kleihues, and an open-air Wall Museum with several remnants of the border crossing (a gate, fragments of the Wall, anti-tank barriers, electric fences, a guard post, a watchtower, etc.)."

[24] From the architectural competition brief, *American Business Center at Checkpoint Charlie: Architects Brief* (CEDC, Berlin, 1992):

"The site of the American Business Center lies in the heart of the Friedrichstadt in the historical city center Berlin-Mitte. The development of the Friedrichstadt is to be viewed in the context of the competitive situation since the end of the last century between the historical center of Berlin and the middle-class center in the West around the Kurfürstendamm. With the overcoming of the city's division, this bipolar structure has been rejuvenated and will remain determinant for the further development. While very little potential for increased density is perceivable in the City West, the main new building projects are concentrated in the district Mitte. In the list of planned building projects, the Ameri-

15.50m

gential relationship to Friedrichstrasse and the former Checkpoint landmark.

The other transformation of the perimeter block occurs within the interior of the site. Replacing the traditional static idealized courtyard is an interstitial glazed structure that pushes out against its internal boundaries, colliding with the perimeter edge buildings. In this way, the interior of the block has both the negative open space traditionally found in this location—two large courts (one at either end) with a smaller one in between—and a positive "built" space containing office space. Of the larger courts, one is open to the street at Mauerstrasse as a public atrium for entry, orientation, and circulation, while its counterpart is more private, used primarily to provide a double exterior orientation for the housing units between the atrium and Zimmerstrasse. The smaller, middle court provides light and air to the offices. This glazed interior "building" presents itself to Zimmerstrasse only on the top floor, which contains the Archives; here, its dual curved volumes reach beyond its physical internal boundary and onto the horizontal block below.

The exploitation of these various site relationships through the transformation of an existing Berlin typology allows for high density commercial development inflected by contemporary expression of the eccentricities of the particular site. At the same time, the configuration remains responsive to the strongest traditional urban values of Friedrichstrasse and historic Berlin: the public aspect of the city street, and the interior semi-public character of the court.[26] Here, the conceptual order converges with the analytic order, responding to our own initiatives as well as to our examination and confrontation of precise, localized circumstances.

can Business Center assumes an important position.

"With the building project of the American Business Center and following the competition for the 'Friedrichstadt Arcades,' the last large open areas of the Friedrichstadt will be filled. The American Business Center will make an essential contribution to the reconstruction of the city at this site and will represent a link between the previously divided sections of the city. . . .

"The primary goal is to develop, in the sense of a critical reconstruction, buildings and structures which may [be] integrated into this urban site."

[25] Taken from the architectural competition brief, *American Business Center at Checkpoint Charlie: Architects Brief* (CEDC, Berlin, 1992):

"In no other city is the German-American friendship so evident as in Berlin. From the airlift of 1948 to the speech by John F. Kennedy on to the efforts of Ronald Reagan for Berlin, the Americans have constantly demonstrated their unwavering engagement for the freedom of this city. As gifts of the American people to the city of Berlin, the Congress Hall and American Memorial Library were built in the period of reconstruction in the 1950s. An essential symbol of the American commitment to Berlin was the presence of the American forces at Checkpoint Charlie. Now that the military is withdrawing and in their stead business partners have announced their interests, this historical site can again become the symbol of German-American friendship. American enterprises desire to establish themselves in Berlin, and they will participate in the development of the new German states and Central Europe.

"These diverse functional [program] offerings are to contribute to the Friedrichstrasse regaining its former status as the main thoroughfare of the cosmopolitan city Berlin. . . . The image of the new buildings should consciously avoid any historicism and should correspond to the *Zeitgeist;* they should furthermore express the tension between old and new."

[26] From the competition brief by Josef Paul Kleihues, *Urban structure plan, Southern Friedrichstadt,* Report (July 1984), ed. Building Exhibition Berlin:

"There is no prescription for the Southern Friedrichstadt. A general plan cannot recapitulate or exceed historical conditions in a Baroque manner, and it cannot be satisfied with the idea of an aesthetic dialect with the rest of the murdered city. New and old have bequeathed a situation which provokes a third way. . . .

"The constituent elements of the historical city do not permit themselves to be prescribed or to be imitatively or nostalgically utilized. Yet the urban plan poses an obligation even if its reconstruction is impossible. It remains the starting point for the idea of a new entirety that is more than ever dependent on individual areas whose functional and design quality demands a correspondence that includes the fragmentary and improvisation."

11. **MASH, ONE-ROOM SCHOOLHOUSE** The roof is one of the most powerful elements in the language of architecture, imparting both symbolic meaning as well as fundamental ontological value as shelter. Here, in a school for the homeless community, the roof is used as a discrete architectural gesture, invoking both its literal and metaphorical connotations of shelter. In its social context, the building proposes a lucid and identifiable place for indigent children in a city (Las Vegas) that is often characterized by its complicated and confused social values that are accompanied by some of the greatest material excess in the country. A prime generative aspect of the scheme was to provide a sense of simple shelter for these children, intimately connected to the natural world.

The sheltering roof gently rises from a low retaining wall, marking playgrounds in the earth. A fragment of the roof ascends along the entire length of the wall, reinforcing the boundary of the school and providing shade to the upper level of the playground. Where the schoolhouse volume begins, the roof slowly curves upward, draping the large volume of the schoolhouse. The ground plane of this room is a continuation of the outdoor playground area, encouraging the indoor/outdoor activities of the school. A low terrace-wall continues from the playground into the open side of the schoolroom where it separates the activities of two of the children's areas while allowing them all to be within the single protective gesture of the roof.

A complementary gesture is provided by an orthogonal linear structure that contains the entry, offices, infant area, and services for the building. This low wall-like element extends beyond the limits of the roof, anchoring the entry of the school more firmly into its site with a series of overlapping walls.

The roof has a double role in this project: as transformed artificial landscape, and as a symbol and provider of protection and shelter. This double-functioning roof engages the playground terraces made in the earth, creating an indoor/outdoor place of interaction, shelter, and connection to the natural world for children who have often had none of these experiences in their lifetimes.

SUN TOWER The requirements for this tower included five floors of retail 12. (including two in the basement) and penthouse offices for the international corporate headquarters of a clothing manufacturer. These were combined with a very constricted site condition, a mandate to maximize the zoning envelope, and a restricted budget.

The site of the Sun Tower was divided between two neighboring property owners acting in concert to build a single building. This schism provided a duality that would be carried through the project and ultimately challenge the typology of the tower in both plan and elevation. The conflict between the two owners of the building was articulated by vertically severing the building, creating two articulated elements with a public entry—a fragment of space—in between. The ten-story height would produce an awkward proportion as a single mass, and so was modified into what might be perceived from the street as two slender towers.

With this initial gesture, the typology of the standard office tower was manipulated both in plan and in elevation. The regular outline of the square plan has an open, wedge-shaped volume intersecting it, providing the place of entry at the street level while defining the position of the elevator core and marking the division of space between the two building owners. The nature of this narrow fragment results in a compressed, indeterminate, ad-hoc space between the two blocks; additionally it suggests a reinterpretation of the city code, which requires 25 percent of the site to be open area.

The second architectural idea involves the separation of the formal necessities of the surface from the pragmatic requirements of the body, a direct response to economic requirements as they confronted the restrictions of planning and zoning. The concept of "wrapping" is explored, along with the possibilities of producing forms that would define an architecture in isolation from the constraints of the body. The terms and definitions of the wrapper have their own logic, distinct from the pragmatic concerns of the internal body of the tower.[27] Origami and the pattern-making of garments—recalling the client's role in the design and manufacturing of clothing—suggested the manner in which the wrapper was developed. The volume of the building was enclosed with a "second skin" of perforated aluminum "fabric" set 20 cm beyond the face of the concrete enclosure. This clothlike membrane, freed of the pragmatic constraints of a standard building surface, responds in a more lyrical and abstract way to various forces: on the interior, it acts as a *brise-soleil,* with the flexibility of adapting to different conditions of light on each facade; on the exterior, this same translucent layer reinterprets city setback constraints, wrapping and folding its way up the height of the tower. This membrane ultimately encloses a penthouse with a set of three-story trusses containing mechanical space while alluding to the "top" articulation of the traditional tower typology, as in the work of Louis Sullivan.

This space between the surface of the body and the surface of the skin—the interstitial territory bounding interior and exterior—allows each face of the building to be altered as the light conditions change with the movements of the sun across the sky and pedestrians along the street. At night, this translucency is reversed as the building is illuminated from the interior, suggesting an oversized urban billboard of light and shadow.

[27] This is reminiscent of Jim Dine's work on the "robe" and the "body" and the challenge it makes to the assumption that they are inextricably related.

The final result is one of ephemerality as the facade creates optical effects that cause the building to dissolve under certain light conditions. Paradoxically, while the folded plane, "origami" characteristics of this screen wall refer to one of the more intricate handcraft traditions, here it is a direct result of the use of the computer. Just as paper has been replaced by perforated aluminum, the complex plane geometry of this structure could only have been generated with contemporary computer technology.[28]

A.S.E. VISITOR CENTER The "context" here is a place of "no context": a vast undifferentiated development of approximately two million square feet of gridded interior space, within which the Design Center required individual places of specific identity and use. To achieve this, two primary architectural paradigms are juxtaposed, each a transformation/distortion of one aspect of the existing "context." Further sub-systems then add character, depth, and consistency to the spaces. This technique is employed in order to create spaces of "controlled irregularity," as in a forest: complex systems in opposition to traditional methods of spatial ordering, using the regularity of a repetitive organization. The overlay of these systems results in the "controlled irregularity" of a series of spaces and vistas, resulting in an impression of great variety.[29] 13.

[28] The computer has, of course, completely altered the manner in which our office is able to function. In the past, projects came about by the intentional juxtaposition of different ordering systems that we knew were incompatible. We used our own drawing conventions to "work our way out" of conflicts that we ourselves had established; we resolved to use these collisions and contradictions as a basis for developing our designs. In this case, the datum, the drawing or model, is now also part of the process of change. In the same sense that figure-ground relations have been transposed into something else, the relationship of the drawings or models to the project is changing rapidly. There has been a definite shift in the mental process. We are interested in surprise and emergence. We do not use an aleatory model to cause us to generate new forms. In the end, we use a series of well-tried techniques that we have developed over time for producing these surprise phenomena in a reliable manner. Previously, when we were working with drawings, they were based largely on right angles, and our responsibility as architects was to anticipate the impact of changes in section and plan on the three-dimensional spaces. The section was always the most interesting view for us, and it became more and more interesting to interrelate plan and section, for example, to define plans that are also sections and sections that are also plans. This was one of our time-worn strategies.

[29] This is an exploration that was begun with the overlay of systems in the Crawford House involving the juxtaposition of architectural elements as grids, lines, and points.

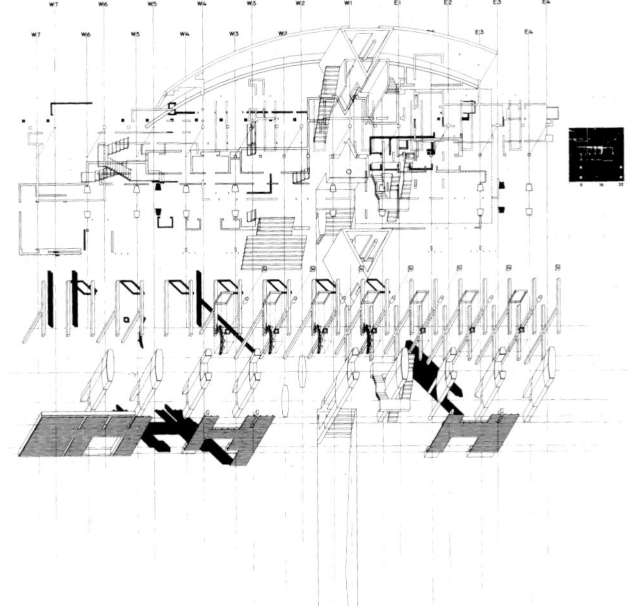

The first major system establishes a set of curved boundary walls within the undifferentiated volume of space. These walls take the form of distorted ellipses, a transformation of existing found boundary conditions. This biomorphic planar shell system is constructed of steel. The second major system consists of a series of thickened lines that traverse the entire space, cutting across, into, and through the primary walled boundaries. These distorted lines transform while unifying the existing irregular structural piers of the building, creating smaller zones of space within the three elliptical territories.[30] This linear system is constructed of a lightweight steel framework clad in white plaster, accomplishing the dual function of providing runs for all the mechanical systems and serving as backdrops for display and exhibition. This system is given its three-dimensional shape by the forces within the project as they require specific accommodation.[31]

The "sub-systems" include the set of voids that are discovered running perpendicular to the thickened lines, the set of lines in the roof construction, the set of skewed lines in the floor, and the many elliptical fiberglass elements distributed throughout the spaces (the "field") which serve as visual/spatial counterpoints to the dominant harmonic structure of the primary architectural devices.

14. **VIENNA HOUSING** This is an "edge city" project, exploring the middle ground between the housing typology of the perimeter block and the high rise.[32] A reconfigured ground plane and a continuation of Carl Prucha's block building create the context for this

[30] The role of the computer was important in this project. One of the symbols of the office had been the repetitive sectional drawings that established the beat or base note of the project. With computers, it became easy to generate sections closer and closer together and to develop them in more and more detail. We were always working x-y-z, with primary emphasis on the z-axis. With hand drawings, we had very early begun to distort the Platonic geometry of the plan-section, and the interconnections of systems of geometry. It was a method of distorting as well as a method of inventing, searching for this moment of surprise. It allowed us to produce complex new entities that satisfied the requirements of program, site, etc. With the computer, we found that you could set up a series of departure points from different positions and with different built-in assumptions. The computer has the capacity to make connections among those lines, no matter how incompatible they may seem at first. Suddenly, we were not limited by the simplicity of drafting techniques for connecting plan, elevation, sections. The computer synthesizes them more or less automatically. If you put down a system of lines, you can study their consequences as an organizing device. All of our work started from some abstract conceptualization, as an *a priori* idea—a laying down of lines, a forming of background rhythms in the material structure of the project. It never came to us as a complete idea; it evolved step by step, and never really arrived anywhere. In essence it is still part of an extended process. For example, in Columbus, the last project in the book, we started by laying down a series of lines, eleven lines in fact. We connected these lines in a certain way and studied the relationships between these lines generated when they were converted into surfaces.

[31] This theory of form generation was best expressed by D'Arcy Thompson, *On Growth and Form* (ed. J. T. Bonner, Cambridge University Press, 1971), p.11: "... the form of an object is a 'diagram of forces,' in this sense, at least, that from it we can judge of or deduce the forces that are acting or have acted upon it: in this strict and particular sense, it is a diagram . . . of the forces which have been impressed upon it. . . ."

[32] On the initiative of Carl Pruscha (Vienna) and Michael Sorkin (New York), eight architects were invited to participate in a social housing project for the Sagramer Strasse in the 22nd district of Vienna. The architects were: Raimund Abraham, Coop Himmelblau, Mark Mack, Thom Mayne, Eric Moss, Carl Pruscha, Martha Schwartz/Jennifer Luce, and Michael Sorkin. The proposed new quarter was 32,500 square meters of land situated directly on the axis of a Viennese town development on the planned north extension of the underground line U1. Conditions for the architects included: a closed front on Wagramer Strasse (because of the nearby tram line); building heights from 18 to 26 meters; and a 50 percent built area occupation

proposal, which uses an interactive language with platonic geometry as the starting point of a methodology for organization and articulation.[33] A social goal was to stress the individuality of the housing units—the geometric and typological differences make for nearly 150 different units for each of the 150 families.[34] There are three distinct types of housing, providing alternative ways of living and connection to the ground: 1) conventional (towards the street), 2) hybrid "bridge" consisting of the connecting piece between the tower and grid-pieces derived from the artificial landscape, and 3) the tower itself.

The artificial landscape at the ground-plane level—folded and cut with interwoven horizontal planes—initiates the project's spatial geometry.[35] These landforms work, in an abstract sense, to provide borders of demarcation and delineation.[36] They become the generative materials for the formation of the architecture while programmatically accommodating parking requirements for the complex. An internal courtyard—a vestige of the perimeter block typology—is accessible through a "bridge" that moves through the void of one of the cutouts. This lattice of artificial landscape allows natural light into the parking structure below, frames civic open spaces for community functions, and acts as a transitional element for the adjacent architecture. The internal courtyard has many conditions of movement within it, including access to the elevators for the tower housing. The entire scheme is connected underground with a vehicular entrance accessed via Eipeldauerstrasse, with a subterranean street parallel to Wagramerstrasse servicing the retail spaces and giving access to parking.

The traditional housing block responds to the street edge and forms one wall of the courtyard, while the bridge housing is more integrated with the artificial landscape.

of the sites. The group of eight architects divided the entire area into seven lots of equal size: three projects with two building sites each (Moss, Sorkin, Mack); two projects with oblong, narrow building sites (Coop Himmelblau, Abraham); and two compact sites (Pruscha, Mayne). The free space was specified as the link between the shared projects (Schwartz/Luce). The shared subterranean car park, entered via Eipeldauer Strasse, was agreed upon by the architects. The brief requested 506 housing units, with shops, a cinema, two coffee shops, a gym, a kindergarten, offices, spaces for cultural and trade use, and conference facilities. The Morphosis site at the corner of Wagramer Strasse and Eipeldauer Strasse had the greatest density allowed, since it would not cast shadows on adjoining lots.

[33] The tentative dividing line between the Morphosis project and that of Carl Pruscha is ruptured and overlaid by buildings from both adjacent schemes.

[34] Our project included an additional "overflow" of housing units that were not accomodated in the Coop Himmelblau scheme.

35

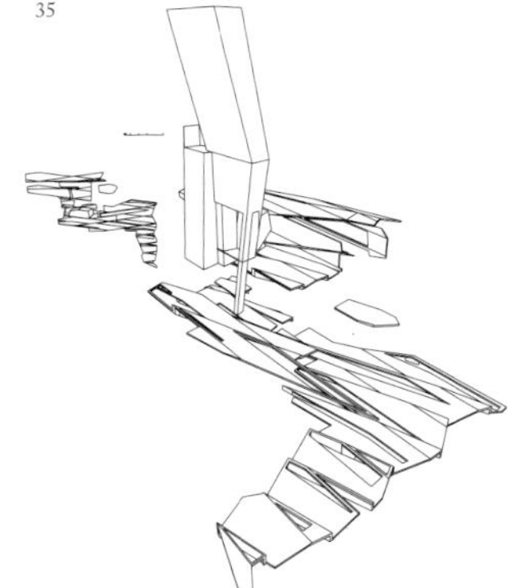

[36] The forms for the artificial landscape and the tower were generated by computer; in fact this was one of the first projects in the office done entirely on computer. It couldn't have been produced without it as we were no longer working in plan. With this project we were able to establish a system of rules which determined an outcome, allowing a broader set of possibilities for a real framework of exploration. The plans are a result of a three-dimensional process, not the other way around. The plan of this building, as a generator, never existed; it is the result of a series of very specific connections between two systems—pragmatic constraints and intuition. For the computer to have real value, it must be located in the processes by which we define our architectural problems. It doesn't take long to recognize the possibilities of working in three dimensions—there are no sections, no elevations, no plans—the plan is now secondary.

This ribbon-like band—a variation of the typical pre-twentieth-century Viennese perimeter building type—intersects the lattice, turning upward and forming the framework of the tower housing. The tower augments the horizontal plane of the reconfigured landscape with a vertical urban object.[37]

15. DIAMOND RANCH HIGH SCHOOL Fusing landscape and building into a single organic unity, the Diamond Ranch High School design concerns building as topography, with a majority of the architectural program contained within the reshaped site.[38] The proposal focuses on three major areas: (1) the complex's conceptual attitude toward the site, (2) social organization, and (3) educational flexibility. The first is the desire to take advantage of the site's natural beauty by integrating the play fields and buildings into the surrounding hillside. The second goal was to create a dynamic built environment to foster maximum social interaction between students, teachers, administration, and the community. Finally, the proposal attempts to facilitate a flexible teaching environment with a solid foundation core curriculum for grades 9–10, and numerous specific program majors for grades 11–12.

The steeply sloped seventy-two-acre site—considered "unbuildable" and donated to Pomona Unified School District—provided an opportunity to create a place where architecture and environment continually exchange places. The idea of grading the hillside to accommodate the program gave way rather quickly to a more interesting concept in which the land was shaped in conjunction with the architecture rather than in preparation for it. Minimizing the displacement of earth for budgetary and environmental rea-

[37] This is an extension of our thinking done first in the Yuzen Vintage Car Museum of 1991 and carried on in the Hypo-Bank project.

38

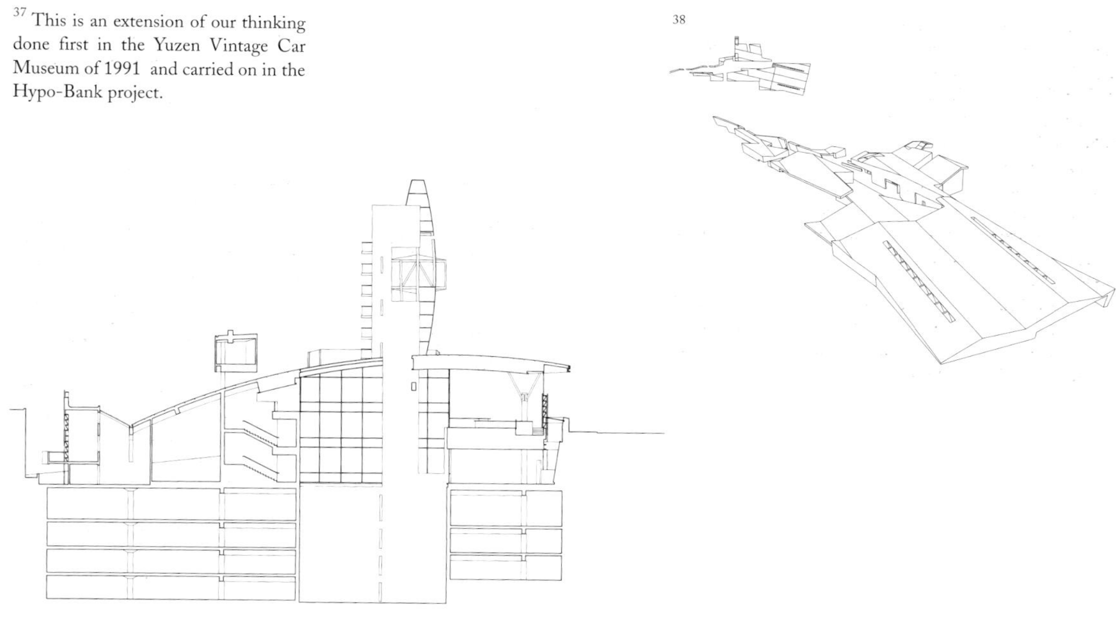

sons, the siting of the project took advantage of a natural bowl for the playing field and primary football field, embedding them in the sloped earth at the south of the site to create an economically efficient hillside seating area. The gymnasium to the east mimics the hillside with a pitched roof that undulates with the terrain. The folded roof plane reconfigures the surface, oscillating between plane and volume.[39] Rising from a low retaining wall while inscribing the playgrounds in the earth, this adaptive strategy incorporates the majority of the programmatic and ancillary elements.[40] As with the Mash One Room Schoolhouse, part of the roof rises along the length of the retaining wall, underscoring the boundary of the school while shading the upper playground.

From the parking court at the side of the gymnasium, the landscape/building events of the school weave together with a pedestrian street that unites the entire complex, a physical manifestation of the school's sense of community. One of the major focal points of the scheme is a monumental stairway (reminiscent of that at the Metropolitan Museum of Art in New York City) that allows movement from the main school areas to the roof terrace and football field above, while creating a student amphitheater. This element also serves as outdoor seating for the performing arts classroom—its exterior walls lift and transform this drama space to a stage. To the south of the pedestrian street, against the retaining wall edge, one finds the upper school, while the flexible space of the lower school classrooms erupt from the earth, anchored by the elliptical courtyards carved into the ground. The "floor" of this space is a continuation of the outdoor playground area, encouraging the school's indoor/outdoor activities.

From the major access road to the east, one is greeted by a curved wall that connotes a path of entry. The administration building is conceived as an extension of this entry sequence: it is a gateway and control point to the school. The first floor contains general administrative offices with student services above. Past the administration building, the school opens up to form the "pedestrian street." This pedestrian system is the pri-

[39] Again, the computer was an essential ingredient in the design of this landscape/roofscape element. In earlier models and drawings, we were operating completely at the edge of our drafting abilities. We did not have the mechanisms to draw and manipulate the models. The computer gives us more tools, allows us to expand the possibilities of our architectural languages. Intersections of oblique columns and trapezoids become almost irrelevantly simple problems. It is like the use of "casting" as a device. You can cast a cube or an intricate thing, and the system of casting does not care what the shape is, Platonic or random, as long as the rules of structure and thermal dynamics are observed. The computer can instantly provide computed double-curves, shapes we were not previously able to understand, manipulate, or work with. It has an immediate impact on the language of the work. The computer is a perfect tool for making architecture that is about connections. It makes this process of linking incompatibles extremely simple. You can take two forms and put them together, and you have an instant resolution, mathematically, formally rigorous. You can do in five minutes what it literally took up two or three weeks to do. Then the thinking changes, because it leads you to a different place.

[40] This strategy was explored at length in the *Paris Architecture et Utopie* Competition of 1989. In this project, the reshaped topography cut into the ground contained infrastructure and was a transitional element connecting the river to the interior of the city. The manipulated land surface was a dialogue between the land and the buildings that occupy that land—a critical view of the program as a series of collected objects sitting on the surface of the earth.

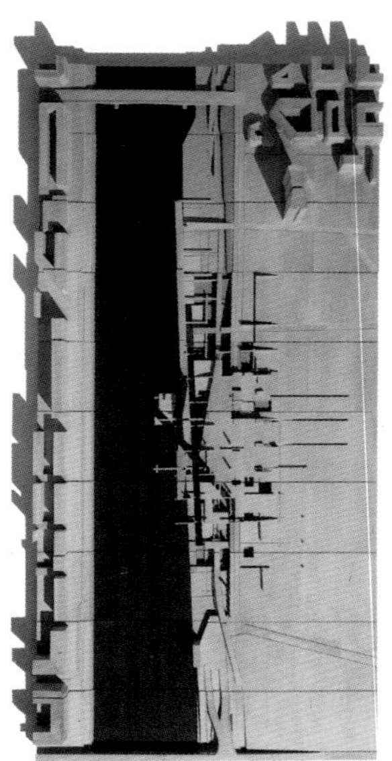

mary connector for the school, linking all spaces: academic, ancillary and support, social and meeting. The library, adjacent to the administration, is located on two floors with individual computer study cubicles above which an "information bridge" connects the north and south buildings of the school.

The gymnasium, adjacent to the entry, controls access from the parking to the stadium field above, and is centrally located for access/egress to and from the lower fields. The gymnasium's entire back wall is a repetitive "buttressed retaining wall." These buttresses penetrate through the roof terrace plane, providing support for shading devices and flexible seating for the stadium.

The main dining facilities adjacent to the gymnasium are organized around a large two-story volume open to natural sunlight and ventilation. It has access to a north-facing court along the main pedestrian street and the terrace above. Possibly the most compelling public gathering space is this rooftop terrace at the level of the football stadium offering a panoramic view of the school, the playing fields, and the city beyond.

The 9–10 grade clusters are positioned along the north side of the pedestrian street. These are conceived as small "schools within the school," articulated by separate two-story buildings that create a total of six clusters. Each cluster has its own outdoor gathering space, teacher's workroom, and guidance area, with the classrooms wrapping around a center, creating interstitial outdoor areas with views of the valley beyond. The classrooms are equipped with movable partitions that allow flexibility and expansion. Although the clusters are separate entities, they all open to the pedestrian street and are arranged in a split-level configuration maximizing access with stairs and ramps. An open space is left to the east for future expansion.

The bulk of the classrooms for grades 11–12 are placed to the south of the pedestrian street, arranged around open-air courtyards. The majority of the core curriculum classrooms are grouped around two courtyards on the second level, with shared computer labs and teacher workrooms integrated around these cores. The more specific curriculum areas (industrial technology, home economics, business, and so on) and the student center are on the first floor, with direct access to the pedestrian street. The amphitheater connects to the performing arts labs and dining facilities to the east. Use of the roof of the building is encouraged by the connection of the amphitheater and becomes another outdoor student gathering area. The entire building acts as a retaining wall to the hillside, while using a series of repetitive "buttress walls" to facilitate an economical retaining system.

INTERNATIONAL ELEMENTARY SCHOOL The desire to have children attend school within their neighborhood, combined with high urban real estate prices, drove this school district to explore alternatives to the typical sprawling Southern California elementary school typology.[41] The program for this school was very prescriptive, in terms of size, configuration, and organization. The challenge was to adapt this set of standards to the possibilities inherent within a constricted site. Our solution was to configure the open spaces of the program above the traditional classroom spaces, a vertical layering that reduced the site requirement for the program by 50 percent. 16.

Although the majority of the program is subterranean, it still required a fence or wall to protect the children. This wall is the primary visible element from the street, and it makes up three of the four facades—a boundary transformed into something three-dimensional, the skin without the body. What began as a vertical screen produced a boundary wall that developed into a horizontal surface, in turn producing a space that incorporates other functions, such as a covered play area and an area for mechanical equipment. The enclosed courtyard with its strong perimeter and the raised roof garden for athletics and play complement one another; the design of the protective boundaries promotes a redefinition of the building facade. With the facade's new functions surpassing the simple enclosure of volume, it is able to assume new forms: bleachers for seating, perforated screening for shade, and folded play structures for the children.

The section drawings indicate how the screen wall is an extension of the space of the classroom, occupying the periphery of the site. This provides the rooms with a maximum amount of natural light while maintaining the integrity of the play-deck above. The height of the classrooms at this outer edge and the studio-like fenestration help compensate for their underground position, a strategy used again at the interior of the playground where bleachers surrounding a small running track create the opportunity for natural light in the library below. The low-to-high variation of the school's section (from 7 to 17 feet) mediates between the institutional scale of this edge condition and the more personal, intimate scale of the interior.

[41] See, for example, the school typologies developed by Richard Neutra in Los Angeles in which indoor and outdoor space merged in large-scale one-story high school plans, known typologically as "open-air classrooms." This work of Neutra's, begun in 1928 with the Ring-Plan School, was a reaction to the existing public schools in Los Angeles, which tended to be without suitable contact with the ground and less than a reasonable amount of natural daylight. Neutra took his psychological/physiological/biological theories of design (e.g. the essays in *Design with Nature)* and applied them to school design. Further developed examples include the Corona Avenue School (1935) and the Kester Avenue Elementary School (1951), both in Los Angeles.

The plan wraps classroom and administrative space around the perimeter of the block, with meeting and support rooms such as the library and the multi-purpose room occupying the interior of the block. An outdoor courtyard provides light and air to the ground and second floor portions of the complex. On the roof, the playgrounds and outdoor athletic facilities are carved into the plane of the rooflike sculptural objects within a field. The angled glass facade again stretches over the building filling a variety of functional roles: covered outdoor space, protective enclosure, glass wall for enclosed volumes, and, to the south, a gateway for the school. Once inside the gate, the interior courtyard—created by the kindergarten play area, a mural wall, trees, and a shade canopy—is a gathering space, surrounded by the school's symbolic collection of international flags. In this way, a new world of three-dimensional space is created for the children, without ever having them lose contact with the ground or the sky.

17. JUNIPERO SERRA SHRINE This project has broad cultural implications related to the historic California region, with several major local cultures metaphorically converging in this proposal for a shrine on this site: the Catholic Church as it has been rooted in Hispanic society; Chinese culture and Japanese culture as manifest in neighboring Chinatown and Japantown; and the indigenous Native American culture. The design for the shrine is therefore based on powerful human forces. Although small in size, this project for a shrine extends its influence well beyond its immediate site, conveying broad urban implications.[42]

[42] This is similar to the strategy employed with the Cranbrook Academy Gatehouse of 1993.

The initial framework begins with the landscape, an embracing wall that invokes the qualities of a sanctuary (shelter, nurturing, stability, and loving embrace), and an earthen mound with its multivalent allusions to domed cathedral ceilings, Native American mounds, Buddhist *stupas,* and the fertile California landscape. The embracing wall clearly defines inside and outside as separate ontological and metaphorical places. At the same time it both protects the shrine and draws one toward it. Inside the wall is the earthen mound, planted with the magnificence and simplicity reminiscent of the land as Father Serra first found it: a simple mix of native California oaks, grasses, and poppies.[43] The mound has the added function of insulating the site from the distracting sounds of the adjacent freeway. Outside the wall is a densely planted combination of native and imported species, metaphorically integrating the European influence on the native landscape.[44]

The architectural language of the shrine itself reinterprets several aspects of the hybrid regional vocabulary that developed here. Among these are: thick walls (for thermal insulation and permanence), fountains and pools, desert cactus plantings around an "oasis," irregular shapes, tranquil sacred gardens, bells in a low *campanario,* and the indigenous materials and building craft of "crude perfection." The shape of the shrine's roof is derived from the traditional vaulted construction of basilical roofs. The shrine's main interior space is found below grade, unexpectedly coherent in the plan's figure of a generic rectangle.

Natural light illuminates the interior and also connects visitors to significant moments in time; shafts of light enter the space through apertures punctuating the wall at specific times and dates of Christian Feast days, major holidays, and days significant to the history of Serra (September 3, April 16, and the 19th of each month). In this way, light, earth, and a re-configured ground make the shrine a place both of the landscape and of the area's hybrid culture.

[43] Father Junipero Serra (1713–84) was a Spanish Franciscan priest who was beatified in 1987, the second step in becoming a saint.

Padre Juan de Ugarte, a Jesuit, of the mission San Xavier in Baja, was the first European to develop agriculture and irrigation in the New World. His efforts inspired Padre Junipero Serra, who brought many of the plants originally imported by Ugarte into Alta California. Heading north in May of 1769, the Franciscans found running streams lined with oaks, willows, cottonwoods, sycamores, and alders. In addition to the native trees, the Franciscans brought citrus trees, fig trees, dates, pomegranates, limes, grapes, almonds, quinces, raspberries, strawberries, plums, apricots, pears, walnuts, apples, pistachio, cypress, juniper, carob, peppers, and olives. Hedges of opuntia and agaves walled the mission gardens, demarking the cultivated from the original landscape of California.

[44] Father Serra celebrated his first mass at the site of the first mass in California. It was under a large oak tree near a ravine emptying into Monterey Bay. The oak was believed to be the same tree under which the Carmelites of the Vizaino sea expedition had offered the first mass in Alto, California, in 1602. The sea and land expeditions met here, singing hymns in their launch and received by the sound of the bells suspended from the oak. The standards of the Spanish Monarch and the Cross were both raised with the simultaneous sounds of bells, muskets and canons. This occurred at the time of the founding of the second mission, San Carlos de Borromeao in Carmel on Monterey Bay, on Pentecost Sunday, June 3.

18. EL PRADO MUSEUM The Prado National Museum in Madrid is one of Spain's most revered public institutions and an internationally renowned destination for vast numbers of tourists and scholars. The building is a traditional model of a museum—a palace for art—and one of the few museums in the world where the art and the building are considered as a single entity, much like the Louvre.[45] Over time, the open space around this palace has been slowly absorbed by the city, leaving only residual fragments. To make an expansion possible, the museum administration added a site directly behind the existing building, and adjacent to a cloister. The competition rules dictated that the cloister was to remain intact while the other two existing buildings were to be connected to form a large museum complex. Our approach was to reinforce the existing building rather than confront it, by focusing on landscape as a foreground for a construction that related to the original building. We also understood that the focal point of the addition would not be Goya,[46] but rather the prosaic tour buses by which so many of the Prado's visitors arrive each day.

Therefore, a strategy of excavation dominates the scheme, with the new components becoming a backdrop, or "non-building" enhancing the existing urban landmark structures.[47] Three primary elements make up the proposed intervention: 1) a new public

[45] From *AV Monograph #62* (November–December 1996), articles by Guillermo Solana (pp. 5–11) and Pedro Moleon (pp.13–21):

"On its opening day, the Prado Museum held 311 paintings, all by Spanish artists. Today it has more than 10,000 works including paintings, statues, sketches and decorative pieces from a range of periods and decorative pieces from a range of periods and countries. During this growth process, however, its collections have not lost their original profile, set by the Habsburgs' tastes, from Charles I to Philip IV: its backbone carries the great pictorial tradition of Venice, Flanders and Spain. . . .

"The Bonaparte family, which spoliated half of Europe to enrich the Louvre, also sowed the continent with museums in its image. In 1809, after the Brera Picture Gallery was opened in Milan to honour Napoleon, his brother Joseph decreed in Madrid that the paintings from the closed monasteries and royal palaces would also be collected in a museum. It was decided to prepare the [Juan de] Villanueva building, previously used for the Academy of Natural Sciences, to hold the collection. The Museum was opened officially on November 19, 1819, with 311 paintings hung in the rotunda and the north gallery. Works by Velázquez, Murillo, Ribera, Zurbarán and other old masters along with living painters such as Goya were hung in a not particularly rigorous order.

"The museum building is a synthesis of the paramount philosophical comprehension of classical tradition on one hand, and the finest renovating tradition of the Enlightenment applied to architecture on the other. Like very few others, it has a soul of its own that provides it with an outstanding memory, patent in the ancient Roman references of its moldings, a form of expression and poignancy, a character that is capable of externalizing what lies within with an emotional, atticist eloquence. Ultimately, as should be the case for all souls, it has a desire to be which at the same time is a project for the future, a principle of evolution or change that has regrettably been badly interpreted or ignored by those who were responsible for verifying it."

"After work on the museum was halted by the French invasion, no fewer than eighteen architects and their offices worked on finishing, remodeling, reconfiguring, and adding onto the Prado Museum from 1814 to 1995. The ownership and management of the museum also weathered major shifts during this time, from a royal property to a national one (1865), through the Second Republic, the Spanish Civil War, World War II, and the Franco regime, to its present organization under the Friends of the Prado Museum Foundation.

"The Museum—a magnificent ship, sometimes dismast and always insufficient for its immense cargo—has sailed through the troubled waters of history and the swamps of bureaucracy, it has undergone interminable repairs without entering port, and has been preserved almost by a miracle. It could well bear the motto of Paris—*Fluctuant nec mergitur*—'tossed by the waves and does not sink.'"

[46] The spaces for the paintings of Goya—the most renowned part of the collection—were, at the time of the competition, housed in the subterranean galleries of the building.

[47] The idea of the non-building was also developed, at a similar scale, in the Los Angeles Artspark of 1989, where the "building" elements were subservient to the garden, which was a series of connected landscape elements. In these explorations, we wanted to reverse the dominance of the building over nature, as in Renaissance planning, and make the building components subservient to nature; the building becomes negative space.

promenade connecting the museum buildings to one another and to the city; 2) a great elliptical rotunda at the urban scale excavated into the ground, and accommodating tourist bus traffic; and 3) a new "mirror" building south of the cloisters, with administrative and lecture spaces, connected to the Villanueva building by large-scale axial circulation elements.

The pedestrian promenade connects the Juan de Villanueva building with the Army Museum and Cason del Buen Retiro buildings and the church and cloisters of the Iglesia de Los Jeronimos. This open-air urban armature of public spaces connects the museum buildings to the fabric of Madrid. As an artificial landscape, these overlapping exterior spaces connect and weave together, forming an urban pathway used by the public independently from the museum.

Presently, the massive amount of tourist bus traffic destroys the entry sequence of this great museum. Our scheme's proposed elliptical rotunda/rotary to the north serves as a drop-off and parking area for these buses while creating a new center for entering the Prado buildings, with a grand scale appropriate for this major cultural urban landmark. The underground system, accessed by ramp from the south, also services the loading dock and staff parking, as well as the waiting area for twenty tourist buses. In this way, traffic congestion is dramatically reduced, while the roofs of these excavated areas are designed as public open spaces.

The new building proposed to the south of the cloisters contains spaces for the Prado's administrative and lecture facilities. The building's volume hovers over the public promenade on *pilotis,* while public stairs and elevators—biaxial to the Villanueva building—connect these spaces with the lower floors and the underground staff parking. The making of this new building continues the strategy of "background" intervention on the site: instead of introducing another architectural vocabulary, fragments of the Villanueva facade are recombined relative to the internal spaces, forming a new facade that is a three-dimensional "mirror" of the now amplified landmark building.[48]

The overall scheme is a "non-building": as a reconstructed landscape, it provides background and support for the existing buildings without adding volumes that would inhibit the "finished work" aspect of the Villanueva monument. The proposal for excavation re-aligns the entry sequence to the Prado, giving a new understanding to the original build-

[48] In our investigations into "non-buildings" there has been a social and political aspect to this architectural form—one of liberative individuality. We were inspired by Goya's own political mission, as described here by F.D. Klingender in *Goya: In the Democratic Tradition* (Sidgwick and Jackson Ltd, 1948): "The portraits, with their majestic progression from his first attempts to get away from the formalised aristocratic portrait of the baroque, through the brilliant works of the 1790s, to the ever more analytical, yet at the same time monumental, portraits of his old age, reveal an integral part of Goya's social and artistic personality. They are a true gallery of the men and women who made the history of his time, both statesmen and intellectuals. In a deeper sense they are documents of that liberation of individual personality which began, though it was not completed, with the bourgeois revolution. In that sense they are the necessary complement of Goya's main theme, the emancipation of the people."

ing, now appropriately about connections, arrival, and entry. The scheme weaves together the various public spaces as visitors move across and through the buildings, adjusting and reconnecting the series of buildings so that they all function coherently as a single complex.

19. **ROCKLEDGE** The architecture for this residential/business compound was determined by the topographic and geologic power of the site. Scarred by the ravages of a brush fire that destroyed the previous buildings, the topography is a rocky ledge with clear views to the ocean. Our initial response to the site was to create a large, terraced outdoor living room with an elliptical boundary wall open to the ocean view. This outdoor room reframes the natural world as an oasis in this harsh and arid landscape. The interior living room is situated at the outermost pivotal corner of the site and is a smaller version of the outdoor room, reversed to open entirely to the ocean view beyond. Both are constructed of heavy poured concrete as a signifier of permanent yet primal space while referring to the compound's temporal status. The programmatic spaces are located in the interstitial space between the interior and exterior living rooms.[49] The ancillary buildings of the compound are organized along the two outer edges of the outdoor room. On the southwestern edge, a straight concrete retaining wall accommodates circulation, and on the northeastern edge, a straight canopy acts as a boundary. A pool is both a cooling device and a landscape connector, flowing from beneath the main residence toward the studio courtyard, further blurring the boundaries between inside and outside.

MACK HOUSE The concept for this house involves the integration of architecture and topography through the alternate overlapping of built volume with open space. Conversely, it is about establishing boundaries, boundaries of a private realm within a dense suburban context that typically has no explicit public space and no clearly designated private space. The hedge—designed as a "wall"—creates a boundary for the main outdoor room, beginning with the interior edge of the property and working up and around towards the street. This "unbuilt" space is the primary volume of the project. Beginning at the street, the second spatial type occurs: a densely organized volume containing the programmatic elements of the house. As these spatial types intersect, the topographic bound- 20.

[49] In the Chiba Golf Club of 1991, we explored the idea of placing building elements between other landscape/building walls, open in character.

ary element is transformed first into a *brise-soleil* element, and finally at the upper level into an enclosed volume with the office portion of the program. Natural light fills the space between the office and the garage at this level, further emphasizing the two different strategies, one establishing private outdoor space within the infinite field of exurban development, and the other responding to the public community of the neighborhood and the street.

21. **S.H.R. PERCEPTUAL MANAGEMENT** This interior defines the different functional zones of a design firm with a set of distinct architectural gestures within a nondescript normative office environment. The existing building core, together with the existing (glazed) perimeter wall, form an overall "U" of raw office space. Within this area, the primary form is a thick wall of office partitions that three-dimensionally curves, bends, and folds its way in an arc from one end of the space to the other. The space enclosed by the concave arc of the tube and the orthogonal core block contains the flexible conference/work areas, singular architectural events of implied enclosure and material specificity. Between the outside edge of the tube and the existing exterior wall are the offices requiring complete privacy. The computer/conference area at the southwest corner is an isolated event. The bank of private offices is disrupted for the rotated platonic volume containing the computers and an interstitial conference/work area to occur at the glazed wall.

Secondary themes—both material and spatial in nature—simultaneously confront, oppose, and reinforce the primary gesture of demarcation. Each of the three conference/work areas inside the white "tube" of workstations is an oasis of distinct material presence. The office entrance from the generic elevator lobby is a dynamic and complex procession with a double-height volume from below and a material/spatial axis sliced through the "tube" toward the computer volume and the outdoors beyond. Linear, folded screens of perforated metal float above the interstitial work areas. Attached to the bottoms of the existing trusses, they reveal the architecture of the generic shell within which this particular *genius loci* is established.

UNIVERSITY OF TORONTO HOUSING Located at the northwest entry of the University of Toronto's St. George campus, the graduate student housing building is configured as a perimeter block, providing a large open courtyard. This courtyard is not only a traditional place of identity, meeting, and gathering within a college campus, but it also provides light and air to the student rooms that open onto it. The massing of the building and its exterior articulation responds to contingent site characteristics as well as to its intense programmatic needs. Each of the four elevations has a distinctive massing that cor- 22.

responds to the scale of the adjacent neighborhood. The two main components are a ten-story block to the east, or rear, of the site, and a seven-story block on the west, or front, of the site. The elements engage one another by wrapping around the southern corner, forming the resultant south facade. To the north, a smaller four-story block with a distinctive roof addresses a more intimate scale of housing. The larger ten-story block has a "skip-stop" plan,[50] allowing for a higher density within the building envelope than one could obtain with a standard double-loaded corridor. This block is screened with a series of irregular openings that furnish a counterpoint to the regularized rhythm of the housing within. The lower block is primarily a single-loaded corridor system, which salutes the city in a glazed, occupiable "human cornice" on its sixth and seventh floors. This main street facade uses the glass cornice for circulation as well as a monumental sign for the campus as a whole, addressing the city, rather than just the street. A large retail space at the southwest corner of the complex forms an active urban node precisely at this point one enters the campus.

23&24. HYPO ALPE ADRIA CENTER Two civic planning concepts belonging to the history of Western culture give urban order to this former agricultural land. First, a *cardo* and *decumanus,* derived from the existing street grid, are extended through the landscape. Secondly, a *forum,* or public space, is positioned along the *decumanus* and directly connected to the existing street intersection. Overlaid on these urban gestures is a third site idea that sets the denser, urban portion of the program to the south, along the busier Volkermarkter Strasse, and the less dense housing to the north, so that it might blend with the existing suburban context.

This is the headquarters for a bank in Klagenfurt, a medium-sized town in the southern part of Austria near the border of Italy and Slovenia, where the Slavic, Italian, and German cultures converge. The site is at the edge of Klagenfurt, where the city meets the neatly plowed fields of the farmlands. We wanted to preserve the rural space, to make it an integral part of the extended city. The program is a multi-use, generic piece of the town: it contains the headquarters for Hypo-Bank, office and commercial space, housing, and the public amenities that typically accompany a project of this scope. The building also had a restrained budget and a tight time schedule, contributing to its simplicity.

[50] The skip-stop plan was developed by the Association of Contemporary Architects in a response to the housing shortage in the mid-1920s. Adapted as a feature of communal housing, the skip-stop plan allowed for larger apartment sizes due to shared common facilities such as kitchens, libraries, and the like, and were featured in the Narkomfin Apartments in Moscow (Moses Ginzburg and I. Milinis, 1928). Roger Sherwood, *Modern Housing Prototypes,* (Harvard University Press, 1978), pp. 118–119, writes: "Narkomfin was an adaptation of two of the units [developed by the Association of Contemporary Architects], both of which were two-level, through apartments reached by a single-loaded corridor at every third floor. Stairs led up and down from this wide so-called 'interior street.' The single-loaded corridor was thought to be preferable to a double-loaded arrangement because of the natural light along one side."

The diagram we used was based on the typology of the city in one direction, and a typology of the country and landscape in the other direction. The design approach was one involving multiple generative sources, using existing infrastructure and building types to transform found elements into something new.[51] The urban structure, stretched east-west across the site, is made primarily of "reconfigured earth," giving back to the city a conceptual open landscape.[52] Over 50 percent of the program area is contained within this reconstructed fragment of rural topography, including an event center, commercial space (on the ground floor), offices, and housing.[53] Out of this pregnant, expectant form emerges another form representing the seismic shifts of tectonic plates: the bank headquarters itself, declaring its status as a major cultural and civic institution, connecting the public forum with the street. This is a five-story mass rising skyward in opposition to the two- and three-story curved roof "landscape" that lifts slowly from each corner of the site. Encountering it from behind are elements representing the normative, local building typologies: conventional intersections, and a series of simple, street-edge buildings that are treated quite conventionally as they address and engage various elements existing within the city.

[51] Our Nara Convention Center project of 1992 explored the dynamic conception of the landscape as a part of the project definition. At Nara, the ground surface was conceived as a membrane that was inflated, with the earth pushing up from below and becoming occupiable. The Disney plan is an earlier effort at planning using multiple generative sources. Both of these strategies were used at Hypo-Bank.

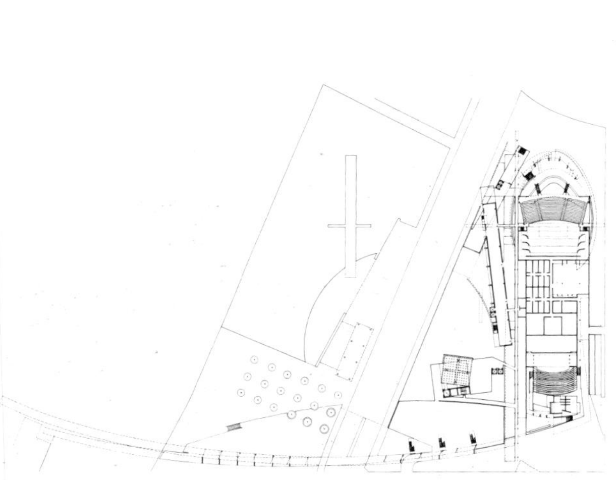

The public corner entry to the *forum*, at the end of the *decumanus*, is marked by the civic invitational gesture of a large open canopy, bringing the life of the city directly into the public realm of this new quarter: first with the immediate presentation of the bank and the event center, then onward into the network of pedestrian walks that are internal to the commercial and office space.

The northern portion of the site is a natural landscape, defined on the site as a covered elliptical pedestrian/bicycle path placed against the edge of the reconfigured landscape of the dense urban structure(s). This is a realm of greater light and air, gardens, and of connections to the surrounding suburbs. Here, the individual housing units find their various places, adapting to their immediate context: along the edges of the site, within the primary axial structures, or alongside the sweeping elliptical pedestrian path. In its making, this project is very ordinary, built for market value, and not as a canonic building made with culturally revered materials (like Gehry's American Center in Paris, or Meier's Getty Center). The Hypo-Bank project literally emerges from its context. It is not a freestanding institution, but an urban environment whose social roles can be discerned.

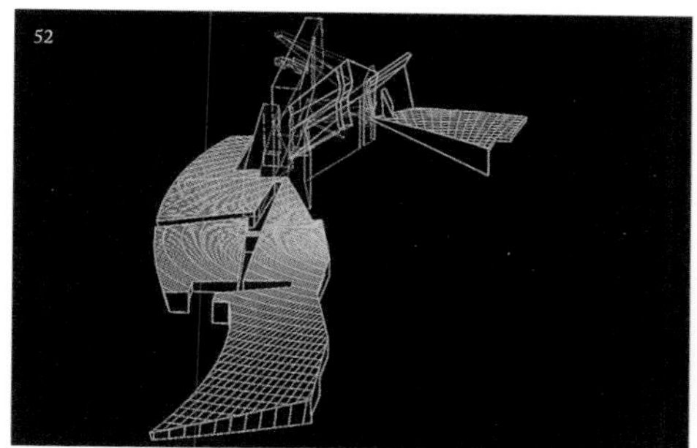

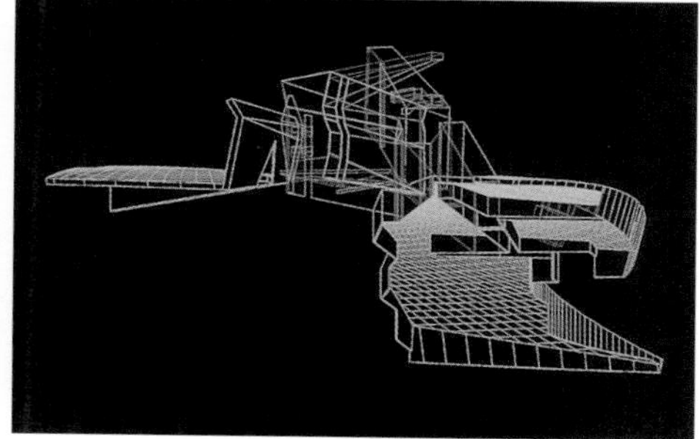

53 This reconfigured ground plane was used at a larger scale in our Vienna Expo proposal of 1990.

III. NEOFORMATIONS: METAMORPHOSES OF MODERNISM

It seems that the most modern functionalism more or less voluntarily reactivated the most archaic or mythical forms. Then, too, there is a mutual penetration of two bureaucracies, that of the past and that of the future (we're still at this stage today). Realizing this mixture, we can only distinguish the following as the two poles, ***archaisms with a contemporary function*** *and* ***neoformations.*** *It seems to us that Kafka was one of the first to recognize this historical problem.*[1]

[1] Gilles Deleuze and Félix Guattari, *Kafka: Toward a Minor Literature* (Minneapolis: University of Minnesota Press, 1986), 75–6.

DEATH CUBE K.

William Gibson, in his recently published novel *Idoru,* describes what he calls a "Franz Kafka theme bar" on the upper floors of a self-healing, bio-active building in the epoch after the postmillennial great Tokyo earthquake. Its first room, a "Metamorphosis" bar, constructed out of "acid-etched metal . . . of artfully corroded steel," sets the tone, with chairs molded from "some brown and chitinous resin" emulating insect backs, with sharp mandibles hovering over the heads of the drinkers. The light too is brown — "roach-light" — illuminating translucent walls that evoke wing-cases and "bulbous abdomens." Beyond, a stair, itself in the form of "glossy brown carapaces," leads to a disco — "The Penal Colony" — lit by "pulses of silent red lightning." Suspended from the ceiling is a machine with articulated arms "suggestive of antique dental equipment" and "tipped with sharp steel," the "pens" with which to engrave the sentence of guilt on the condemned victim's body. Finally, a second stair leads to "The Trial" room, with its low ceilings and "walls the color of anthracite."[2] In this description of the "Death Cube K." bar, Gibson neatly intersects the postapocalyptic tones of the cyberpunk "zone city" and the anticipation of catastrophe built into the modernist canon of the 1920s. Kafka, the ironic peddler of counterbureaucratic insects, is himself metamorphosed into a creature of millennialist consumption for the citizens of a world beyond hope in an architecture of deconstructive decay. Corroded metal, sharp steel, prosthetic instruments mimicking dental tools, insect-like interiors, dead-end black holes for judgement beyond the law — all seem images drawn directly from the recent past of 1980s architecture. While overly pictorial, and obviously undertheorized, Death Cube K. could stand for any one of a number of metallic, postcybernetic, and counter-postmodern environments of the last few years. On a purely imagistic level, indeed, one might think of connections to the restaurant interiors of

[2] William Gibson, *Idoru* (New York: G. P. Putnam's Sons, 1996), 3.

Morphosis, with their steel, clockwork-like contraptions and sharp-edged details, like so many "Penal Colony" writing machines. The literal evocation of *Metamorphosis* in Morphosis is hard to resist, and surely was not far from Gibson's own mind. And while the caricatural level of Gibson's architecture works against any sustained elaboration of the analogy with the elegant and abstract work of Morphosis, it would be wrong to assume that what seems to be an intuitive association of "K." with their work should be dismissed out of hand. Morphosis was obviously not the architects of Death Cube K., but, in more ways than one, Kafka's own architectural and spatial formulations of modern life might be brought to bear on an interpretation of their recent urban and institutional projects.

SCAPELANDS

Certainly from the air, as models are inevitably viewed, represented like so many frames from *Flight Controller 98,* angled and zoomed, they seem to be conceived as extensions of a William Gibson–inspired, postapocalyptic zonescape: fragmented, broken, twisted, and scored lines on the earth, perhaps marking the passage of multiple civilizations and the death throes of the last. From a lower perspective, Stealth-like and racing close to the contours, the models seem to meld with the earth's crust itself, heaving and breaking, splitting and opening up with seismic precision, as if mapping the fault lines of a once hot, now cooling culture. Inside, if we are allowed entry, the forms are all-enclosing, elliptical, ovoid, womblike, as if half-encased within the shell of a broken dinosaur egg. Projected along endless, Klein bottle–shaped corridors, the eye's perspective is canted with the planes that everywhere refuse the vertical, with nowhere to rest in the horizontal. The body, or rather its introjected projection, is relentlessly impelled forward at warp speed, as if suspended in the virtual frames of the computer game "Doom," with gravity-bending contortions that seem to defy Nietzsche's aphoristic invocation of the end of perspective: "we cannot see around our own corner."

At least, this would be one construction of the world constituted by Morphosis in its second iteration, a world no longer confined to the intricate filigrees of steel and concrete that mirrored the interior clockwork of the psyche in so many private restaurants and houses, but now, like the images in Gibson and Bruce Sterling's *Difference Engine,* exploded from the mechanical to the digital, and thus taking over the public realm by virtue of its conquest of matter as a whole, merging at once with the temporal moves of the population and the spatial shifts of the earth. The result may be compared to a "landscape" with all the characteristics invoked by Jean-François Lyotard to describe what he calls a "scapeland": displacement, estrangement, and, most importantly with regard to its implications for modern architecture, a kind of *dépaysement,* a shifting of location and judgement from the stable conventions of inside and outside to a realm where a kind of "systematic madness" reigns supreme. Not insanity, but "versanity," as Kant, cited by Lyotard, notes, "the soul is transferred to a quite different standpoint, so to speak, and from it sees all objects differently . . . just as a mountainous landscape sketched from an aerial perspective calls forth a quite different judgement when it is viewed from the plain."[3]

[3] Jean-François Lyotard, *The Inhuman: Reflections on Time* (Stanford, Calif.: Stanford University Press, 1991), 182. Citing Immanuel Kant, *Anthropology from a Pragmatic Point of View* (The Hague: Nijhoff, 1974): 54.

Lyotard extends Kant's characterization of the distance between subject and object implied by the visual experience of the landscape into a meditation upon all material that is transformed into landscape and its virtual character. However, there is nothing virtual about the morphosis accomplished by Morphosis. For the space that is transformed into a kind of landscape in these recent projects is not just any space, but a direct commentary on that kind of space peculiar to modernity, and, in particular, to modern architecture's rendering of modernity. And what is being exploded from inside to outside is not simply a representation, Caligari-like, of a fin-de-siècle soul in torment, an expressionist visualization of the neurotic psyche revamped for the end of the millennium, but a conscious reworking of a set of modern architectural prototypes, developed in the 1920s on behalf of a Taylorized and Fordized mass society, rendered lifeless from long complicity with corporate capital, but now seen as a possible source of late-twentieth-century modernism.

Here, Morphosis is enacting a complicated form of formal redemption. For, rather than jettisoning "modern architecture" in favor either of an ideological critique from the left, or of a nostalgic revival of "traditional" motifs from the right, Morphosis has chosen to identify a fundamental difference between "modernity" (and the spaces and socioeconomic forces that have supported its global extensions) and "modernism," with its sometimes critical, sometimes utopian architecture that has attempted, spasmodically throughout the century, to offer alternative spaces, other realms through which the posttechnological, postbureaucratic life might be framed and lived. That a critique of modernity might give rise to an architecture of modernism, that, in the words of Ibsen's master builder, Solness, "castles in the air" might, paradoxically, be built on "firm ground," has ever been an aspiration of the avant-garde — an aspiration that has often enough fallen into the unthinking service of modernity. But it is nevertheless on the basis of this sustained hope that Morphosis has attempted its own reframing of modernity's absorption of modernism, working with the language of the latter to construe a critique of the former.

MEN IN BLACK

The notion that a modernist critique of modernity might also harbor the premises of another kind of modernism has been a verity of avant-garde practice since the futurists. And yet the terms of this critique have often simply reduplicated the premises of modernity in avant-garde guise — hence the substitution of "war" and "violence" for bourgeois "accommodation" in futurism; the substitution of "rationalization" and "efficiency" for the uneven forms of capital development in the work of Le Corbusier and his contemporaries; the aesthetic idealization of manufacturing processes in the work of the constructivists; and so on. From the turn of the century, what might in retrospect be called "mainstream modernism" responded to the bureaucratic state with a rationalizing vigor and an implacable will to systematic downsizing that would have done honor to a late-twentieth-century venture capitalist. For every item on the corporativist agenda, modern architecture eagerly supplied a corresponding aesthetic alibi. What Max Weber saw as a loss of individual "charisma" was countered by an optimistic acceptance of what Walter Benjamin termed "loss of aura"; the economics of mass architecture were furthered by a rejection of ornament; the factory floor surveillance of a Bentham was extended into the secretarial pool with the techniques of Taylor; the drive for time and motion efficiency was sustained by a futurist ideology of speed, which also buoyed the inextricable relations of industrialization and war. Individual aspirations were contained within a rigid separation of private and public realms. The "men in black" of the turn of the century, in overcoats and bowlers, every bit as faceless as their contemporary, digitally manufactured counterparts, shuttled between their apartments and the elevators of *Metropolis* in anonymous silence. From Otto Wagner through Walter Gropius, Mies van der Rohe, and Ludwig Hilbersheimer, the new, endless, and all-encompassing city was stamped out in anonymous "bar-buildings" — rows of minimal offices served by double-loaded corridors cut with precision from seemingly endless strips like so many steel rails that have become the leitmotiv of modernist space.

Against this relentless production of rational space there was little resistance, save for the "charismatic" excesses of fascism on the one hand, or the individual psychic revolts of expressionism and Dada on the other. And, as Siegfried Kracauer noted, the complicity between the world of Dr. Caligari and that of *Metropolis* was hard to miss. Despite the formal explosions of film and theater, the stage sets of psychological disturbance were easily dismissed, and the traumas they expressed were all too easily pushed back underground, hunted like the murderer of *M,* lynched in secret underground trials by the "normal" mob. The psychic life of modernism, despite the efforts of psychoanalysis, was abandoned to the unconscious. Kafka's early nightmares of what he called "the horror in the merely schematic"[4] and Huxley's dystopian projections were no more than the parentheses within which the entire apparatus of twentieth-century shock, trauma, phobia, and neurosis were seen as the wastelands and unhygenic quarters of the metropolis, ripe for demolition and redevelopment rather than for architectural exploration.

[4] Max Brod, ed., *The Diaries of Franz Kafka 1914–1923,* Vol. 1 (New York: Schocken Books, 1949), 33.

The dream of a potentially liberating "space," more representative of the psychic and social fractures of modern life, has, however, been hard to resist: surrealists, situationists, and, lately, deconstructivists have cultivated the notion of an oppositional realm, partly introjected, partly projected, that will through the force of its ruptures and disjunctions force open the hermetically sealed vacuum of corporativism. The experiments of expressionism and constructivism, the biomorphisms of surrealism, the radical *informe* conceived by Bataille (recently revived under the sign of the amorphous "blob") have all offered formal vocabularies with which to counter the hermetic realm of business. Theoreticians of space have at the same time attempted to envisage a realm that might potentially be taken back by the public — or that might at least afford shelter from the pervasive forces of institutionalized capital. Lefebvre's call for the social "right to the city," Foucault's "heterotopias," and Deleuze and Guattari's "nomadisms" sought in different ways to characterize "other spaces," and such work has had important reverberations in gender and identity studies.

MORPHING THE TYPE

These various oppositional stances have led to much experimentation with architectural languages — either in the extension of modernist forms or in the invention of "other" forms. Yet despite the intense interest in the nature of institutional and formal "types" and "typologies" in the 1970s, which was sustained by the early studies of Foucault and his followers into the discursive structures of medical and penal institutions, few architects have sought to revise the structures of the fundamental building blocks of modernism: the office building, the apartment house, and their ancillary urban functions. Indeed the word "type" itself has, in the late 1980s and early 1990s, become an almost extinct term, as interest in expressive vocabularies and high technologies has displaced questions of urban and architectural "typo-morphologies." On the one hand this is explicable as a result of the quick absorption of typological concerns in the decorated sheds of postmodernism — a movement itself revealed as no more than the cosmetic pastelization of the corporate image. On the other, the waning of interest in type is paradoxical in the light of the present reaction against postmodern excesses, for the concept, emerging in the work of

Giulio Carlo Argan in the 1960s, and advanced by Joseph Rykwert, Alan Colquhoun, and Aldo Rossi, among others, was, at least initially, deliberately posed as a critique of the reductive containers of modernity, the empty shells that, in postwar development, had become the emblems of anomie, the visible frameworks of what Weber had understood as the "iron cage" of the bureaucratic state. Typology, in this sense, was an attempt to admit the macrostructure of the city into the microstructure of the individual building, at the same time as recognizing the individual building as a member of a "family" of types to which it, in general, belonged. While too quickly immersed in the postmodern fashion for stylistic traditionalism and aesthetic contextualism, typology, at its best, represented a hope for the continuation of the utopian and countercorporate ambitions of avant-garde modernism, couched in terms that remained committed to modernity and rejecting nostalgia.

It is precisely here, in this conjuncture of resistance and utopia, that Morphosis has returned to typological concerns. Initially identified with an aesthetic of expressive force and individual momentum that exemplified — in its embrace of the machine, of industrial materials and forms, of the broken and the fractured — the language of resistance to postmodern style in the 1980s, the work seems now to have gained in intellectual and formal strength by virtue of its contestation not only of corporate modern and postmodern style, but also of its basic organizing structures.

Thus, on a small scale, in the Friedland Jacobs Communications building, Morphosis introduced what the architects term a "transformation of generic office space" by inserting a "radius wall" to form an "embryonic shell." This principle of enclosure and individuation was also followed in the design for the Ove Arup in Los Angeles, where Morphosis developed an "organic language within the office interior" as a means of providing a degree of specificity — "the definition of a specific interior place" that dispensed with "the ubiquitous office syntax in normative work environments." Similarly, the A.S.E. Visitor Center in Tokyo is constructed of "elliptical territories" delineated by curved primary walls, forming a "biomorphic planar shell system" crossed through and striated with structure and linear volumes. On a larger scale, the Frankfurt Waste Management Facility, conceived as a kind of efficient "disposal campus," houses its administrative offices in a "ribbon" adjacent to the repair workshops. The American Business Center, located, ironically enough, at the site of the original Checkpoint Charlie, transforms the perimeter block into a high-density office space with a hollow, semipublic court within.

ELLIPSES

In what way, however, would these obvious formal metamorphoses of modern types be at once critical and prospective? Here we might return to our first model, that of a third architectural term, between the utopian and the realist, the modernist and the modern, one sketched most evocatively by Walter Benjamin in his remarks on Kafka. In a letter to Gershom Gerhard Scholem, written from Paris on June 12, 1938, Benjamin compared Kafka's work to "an ellipse" with its two foci far apart, the one "determined . . . by mystical experience (which is above all the experience of tradition)" and the other "by the experience of the modern city-dweller."[5] For Benjamin, ever caught between the same two foci, Kafka's prescience for the postapocalyptic century was that his understanding of modernity, of the plight of the "modern city-dweller," was precisely filtered through the lens of a traditional sense of disaster and redemption signaled by the "mystical." On the one hand, Benjamin poses Kafka's "modern citizen, who knows he is at the mercy of vast bureaucratic machinery, whose functioning is steered by authorities who remain nebulous even to the executive organs themselves, let alone the people they deal with," a figure well exemplified in *The Trial.* On the other is Kafka's equally powerful inner world, "frequently so serene and so dense with angels," through the frame of which he looked out at modernity. Kafka's "ellipse," then, was for Benjamin a kind of vertigo machine, drawing together worlds that could in no way be commensurate either on the level of reality or dream. Rather, Benjamin cites the poetic evocation of "reality" posed by the contemporary physicist Sir Arthur Stanley Eddington, whose book *The Nature of the Physical World* seemed uncannily to prefigure Kafka's vision:

> *I am standing on the threshold about to enter a room. It is a complicated business. In the first place I must shove against an atmosphere pressing with a force of fourteen pounds on every square inch of my body. I must make sure of landing on a plank traveling at twenty miles a second around the sun — a fraction of a second too early or too late, the plank would be miles away. I must do this while hanging from a round planet heading outward into space, and with a wind of ether blowing at no one knows how many miles a second through every interstice of my body. The plank has no solidity or substance. To step on it is like stepping on a swarm of flies. Shall I not slip through? No, if I make the venture one of the flies hits me and gives a boost up again; I fall again and am knocked upward by another fly; and so on. I may hope that the net result will be that I remain about steady; but if unfortunately I should slip through the floor or be boosted too violently up to the ceiling, the occurrence would be, not a violation of the laws of Nature, but a*

[5] Walter Benjamin to Gershom Gerhard Scholem (June 12, 1938), *The Correspondence of Walter Benjamin 1910–1940* (Chicago: The University of Chicago Press, 1994), 563.

rare coincidence. . . . Verily, it is easier for a camel to pass through the eye of a needle than for a scientific man to pass through a door. And whether the door be barn door or church door it might be wiser that he should consent to be an ordinary man and walk in rather than wait till all the scientific difficulties involved in a really scientific ingress are resolved.[6]

[6] Ibid., 564.

Out of similar components, Kafka constructed what Benjamin sees as a kind of "complementary world," one that "is the exact complement of his epoch, an epoch that is preparing itself to annihilate the inhabitants of this planet on a massive scale." Only Paul Klee, Benjamin concludes, of Kafka's contemporaries, had construed his life in so "solitary" a manner: "The experience that corresponds to that of Kafka as a private individual will probably first become accessible to the masses at such time as they are about to be annihilated."

Leaving to one side for a moment the significance of this last observation for our own fin-de-siècle epoch, what is interesting in Benjamin's observations is the spatial character he ascribes to Kafka's vision, and not so much that posited by the analogical ellipse (although the elliptical has often enough figured in countermodern formalisms under the sign of Klein and Lacan) but more that of the precarious, atomistic, fault-ridden universe posed by modern physics, with its slippages and unexpected empty spaces (also, in atomic diagrams of the period, we should remember, linked in intersecting elliptical trajectories). Here, Benjamin's model of Kafkanian space finds a contemporary echo in the schema traced by Deleuze and Guattari, who distinguish between two "states" of Kafka's architecture, the one linked to the old, traditional world of power, imperial and despotic — the world of "The Great Wall of China" — and the other, the new capitalist or socialist bureaucracy — the world of *The Trial.* In formal terms, these two states are complementary: Deleuze and Guattari identify them as (1) "infinite-limited-discontinuous-close and distant," and (2) "unlimited-continuous-finite-faraway and contiguous."[7]

[7] Deleuze and Guattari, 72–7.

The first state takes its model from the the Great Wall of China itself, imagined by Kafka as a structure of discontinuous blocks, a "system of piecemeal construction," as Kafka terms it, that would, according to Kafka's "scholar," provide the most secure foundations for a new Tower of Babel.[8] Deleuze and Guattari diagram this form as a sequence of broken arcs in a circle surrounding a spiral tower at the center. The second state, taking its cue from the spatial complexities of the bureaucratic and legal offices in *The Trial,* situates its furthest distances — those spaces that are furthest away from each other — in close contiguity. Thus, to cite Deleuze's example, K. will drive to see the painter Tintorelli "in a suburb which was almost at the diametrically opposite end of the town from the offices of

[8] Franz Kafka, "The Great Wall of China," in *The Complete Stories* (New York: Schocken Books, 1971), 238–9.

the Court," only to find that a second door leads from the studio into the judges' quarters.[9] Perhaps the most important aspect of Deleuze and Guattari's model, however, is not simply the formal identification of these two states, and their parallelism to the "two foci" of Benjamin's elliptical model, but the assertion that not only are the states complementary, but also essentially coexistent — that indeed they interpenetrate despite their distinct qualities. Deleuze and Guattari compare such intersection to that of the tower of Tatlin's Monument for the Third International, with its tipped and dynamic open-work spiral enclosing the traditional cubes, pyramids, and spheres that nevertheless are put into movement as they house the new bureaucracies of the Soviet state in mobilized forms of the old traditional orders — "the most modern functionalism more or less voluntarily reactivated the most archaic or mythical forms" in the "mutual penetration of two bureaucracies, that of the past and that of the future," in what Deleuze defines as a combination of the "infinite paranoiac spiral and the unlimited schizoid line."[10] Here is an ascription that precisely describes the spatiality of *The Castle* (height, hierarchy/contiguity of offices with moving boundaries) and not incidentally recalls the space of the paranoid/schizoid subject as delineated in Lacan's "The Mirror Stage," a virtually inaccessible "fortified keep" set in an arena of struggle surrounded by "marshes and rubbish tips."

[9] Kafka, *The Trial* (New York: Schocken Books, 1995), 141.

[10] Deleuze and Guattari, 75–6.

In this combination of avant-garde aspiration to invent the new, and the inevitable reliance on the form of the old, Kafka precisely outlined the spatial dilemmas of modernity as a whole, at the same time as pointing towards a possible form, not of their reconciliation or synthetic resolution, but of their uneasy, interpenetrating, and always broken coexistence. It is in this sense that we can see in the fractured blocks and arc-like forms of Morphosis's office complexes, and in the ovoid enclosures of their interior alignments, a bringing together of the distant and the close, and the faraway and the contiguous, in a setting that describes as it deconstructs the bureaucratic infinities and closures of modern life.

Thus the Spreebogen project for the Berlin Parliament competition establishes a symbolic "center" by setting up a symbolic periphery — a "large Platonic circle" that is then, like the Great Wall, "fractured and disjointed," its fragments reformulated to serve the different functions of the complex. Here the reference is evidently to the already demolished Berlin Wall, now standing only in "memorial" fragments, and its reassimilation into the fabric of a unified city. Morphosis's "piecemeal construction" here operates on the level of memory (the memory of the Berlin Wall is transformed into walls of memory) but also on the level of symbolic power. For even as the ambiguities of Kafka's China Wall allow for multiple hypotheses as to the Government's intentions — the Wall was in fact meant to be piecemeal, and therefore "inexpedient"; the Wall was the foundation for a new Tower of Babel; it symbolized the all-pervasive yet necessarily incomplete power of the vast Empire — so the breaks in Morphosis's Wall of Government register a fact and a desire: that, in their words, "government is now seen as dispersed and integrated into the urban fabric . . . it is fluid, open, transformable, and symbolic of the diverse culture it represents." Its form, however fragmented, has to be "coherent and rational in order for its constituents to know it." On another scale, the serpentine, fragmented "wall" of interior offices in the SHR Perceptual Management building functions in the same way to play individual location against collective identification.

TIPPING THE WALL

If the Great Wall of China is a metaphor for a modernist Babel structure, its fragmented and piecemeal character anticipating the discontinuities later to be celebrated in deconstructivism, the walls of Morphosis refuse even this stability of meaning. As if following the visual laws of Kafkanian space, they literally enact the forced perspective of the paranoid subject, always sloped and canted, fractured and broken. And while this has become a common signature for a certain school of post-postmodern form, in Morphosis the canted wall takes on a polemical quality, self-consciously posed against the "right angle" of modernity, the horizontality and verticality announced by the Domino House prototype. Perhaps, with *The Castle* in mind, we might see in these slopes an echo of the traditional fortification, the glacis, the pyramid, and yet more often than not the wall, again polemically, is removed from its support, floating in space, detached from any but a screening function. Canted walls, were, it is true, a leitmotiv of expressionism, where the complexes of a Freudian generation were exaggerated in perspective and shadow as so many psychic eruptions breaking the calm serenity of modern rationalism. But where the exploding walls of Coop Himmelblau might warrant such comparisons, the canted walls of Morphosis should rather be understood as an extension of their reflection on modernism.

Construing the complex formal gesture of the entrance wall at La Tourette, and observing its obvious departure from the transparent screens and horizontal ribbons characteristic of the earlier Domino House model, Colin Rowe seized on an apparently innocent remark in Le Corbusier's text, one ostensibly directed to an explanation of the effect of the interior of the Pompeii houses: "the floor which is really a horizontal wall."[11] This deceptively simple formulation, as Rowe points out, began to explain the apparent contradiction between the horizontally sliced space of Domino — the "sandwich" — and the vertically walled enclosures of the megaron volumes that appeared first in the Citrohan House. As

[11] Colin Rowe, "La Tourette," in *The Mathematics of the Ideal Villa and Other Essays* (Cambridge, Mass.: MIT Press, 1982): 196–7. Citing Le Corbusier, *Vers une architecture,* 150.

Rowe noted, "if floors are horizontal walls, then, presumably, walls are vertical floors; and, while elevations become plans, and the building a form of dice." Here we are presented with a far more complex condition of "wall" than simply the dialectical "return of the wall" characteristic of much postmodernism and countermodernism in the late twentieth century. Where this movement has insisted on the return of the wall, of the bounded space, of the recognizable place, in the face of the infinite horizontality of the modernist *"espace indicible"* and its pretensions to universality, the dialectic proposed by Le Corbusier between the horizontal and vertical elements of containment is completely lost. Further, the wall at La Tourette acts both as a surrogate "facade" and as a parallel container to the megaron volume of the chapel. This double function, itself mediated by the implied twisting of the wall, an illusion set up by the nonparallelism of the marks left by the "horizontal" shuttering, takes on a new significance in the light of the canted walls of Morphosis's modernist reprise. Here, the dictum "the floors are horizontal walls" would be reflected back in order to produce the interesting result, "the walls are canted floors," leading to the conclusion that all enclosing surfaces are destabilized, "sheared" and "fractured," to use Morphosis's own terms.

In this instability, we approach the condition implied by Kafka himself, of a spatiality that refuses gravity, that dissolves into a cosmic flux, at once microcosmic and macrocosmic, ceaselessly shifting from moment to moment according to the psychological drives of the moving and sensing subject, a space that, in the words of Javier Navarro de Zuvillaga, replicates a "cosmic space" that exhibits nothing but scorn for the concept of gravity:

> *K in all his characters moves in a cosmic space the fundamental characteristics of which are shown in the confrontation of various levels: the human level, the level of infinity and the absence of laws of gravity which . . . consequently produce a disorienting space on which Kafka's architecture is based.*[12]

This sense of cosmic anxiety, already noted by Benjamin, creates a virtual architecture in Kafka's novels and short stories that varies constantly "according to the mood of the character," that "changes together with the physiological momentum of the character . . . one recalls the endless corridors which offered K an ever-longed-for escape but simultaneously one notices that these long corridors could never be contained within the limits of perspective."[13] Such spaces would, in these terms, be perceived less through sight or even the senses, but rather through the anxious states of mind of the character — "eminently functional spaces," as de Zuvillaga notes, that stretch and shrink according to the character that moves within them. In this ascription, all Kafkanian spaces, as described, are banal and normal enough — offices, corridors, bedrooms, and the like — but are transformed

[12] Javier Navarro de Zuvillaga, "Kafka's Concept of Space," in *Architectural Association Quarterly* 7 (January–March 1975), 22.

[13] Ibid.

into a frightening abnormality by the projections and introjections of their inhabitants. The canted walls of Morphosis that slope and curve into infinity along canted floors that seem to allow no access, but that reveal ever receding horizons with the movements, actual and psychological, of the subject, would be in this sense the analog to Kafka's sense of space.

New, canted screens, as in the Salick Health Care Headquarters or the Village Fashion Building in Seoul, South Korea, are set up to break the rigid frames of existing buildings, creating interstitial spaces impossible to inhabit save by visual projection; these new "walls" are often visually permeable, translucent, and ambiguous. Angled walls frame the interconnecting spaces of the Friedland Jacobs Communications offices and the Ove Arup and Partners corporate offices, giving rise to perspectival distortions that "zoom" in from one zone to another.

THE BURROW

And if canted walls could be construed as so many sloped floors transposed into the "vertical," then the floors themselves would be so many slanted and inclined planes without vertical closure — above and below. Like the "mole" in Kafka's "The Burrow," Morphosis digs into the ground as if to imply that if there is no limit to height, neither is there limit to depth. Thus the Berlin projects are seen as so many "landscapes"; in the Mack house importance is given to the integration of the landscape into the house; in the Diamond Ranch High School, the building itself is conceived as a kind of "sitework," combining "reshaped topographies" and architecture to form a "primary space made with the earth and in the earth." The architect writes of "folds," "plates," and displays topographic folded grids in projects such as the M.A.S.H. (Mobile Assisted Shelter for the Homeless), a school and childcare facility that features a "reconfigured" earth. The Junipero Serra Shrine is formed of an embracing wall, an earthen mound, a shrine below ground, all set within a planted landscape. The project for the Prado Museum extension figures a sunken, artificial landscape, while the scheme for the offices of Dan Logan and Medical Planning Associates in Malibu has turf roofs as if to camouflage its architectural nature. Architecture indeed has here gone to ground, if not underground; the "burrow" has been literalized, but not, however, in an entirely Kafkanian sense. For, as Siegfried Kracauer noted of Kafka's conception of architecture, "the building that one generation erects after another is sinister, because this structure is to guarantee a security that men cannot attain. The more systematically they plan it, the less they are able to breathe in it; the more seamlessly they try to erect it, the more inevitably it becomes a dungeon." Kracauer cites Kafka's story "The Burrow," a cave-like construction built by "perhaps a mole or a hamster . . . out of fear of an invasion by all conceivable forces. Because this fear wants to eliminate those insecurities, inherent to creaturely existence, the burrow is a work of self-deception. It is no accident that its labyrinthine passageways and squares extend through subterranean night."[14] Morphosis, on the other hand, seems to celebrate the underground as simply another dimension of gravity-free space, moving at will around ground zero without recognizing the transition, without the sense of constriction given by the canonical modes of modernism and postmodernism.

[14] Siegfried Kracauer, "Franz Kafka: On His Posthumous Works," in *The Mass Ornament: Weimar Essays* (Cambridge, Mass.: Harvard University Press, 1995), 268.

In Morphosis, indeed, the paranoid "burrow" is recast as sanctuary: most notably in the Junipero Serra Shrine, where an angled, enclosing wall, bounding a "sacred" mound, finds its resolution in an underground shrine, forming a complex that is neither above nor below, a "hybrid" spatiality that is reinforced by the shafts of light that are calculated to touch the interiors at certain marked times of the year. Similarly, in the more secular context of the private dwelling — the projects for the Mack house, and in particular the Blades house — dig and reform the earth as if the "datum" of ground is entirely removed, forming a gravity-free space in which the various domestic functions are resited and staged in relation to already dramatic landscape sites. The public analog to these small "burrows" is found in the roofscapes of the Hypothenkenbank projects I and II, where the buildings rise up in great shallow curves, "mnemonic," as Morphosis puts it, "of the rural topography," creating a new, artificial landscape within the city, and intersecting with the old in broken and fragmented ellipses. The "building as garden" theme is continued in the Science Museum School, while in the crystalline cuts and fills of the Diamond Ranch High School, with its "folded surface" that moves easily above and below ground, the topography seems to respond to Deleuze's characterization of a Leibnizian space that refuses vertical and horizontal striation in favor of the continuous, folded, and Klein-bottle curves of monads in movement.

With these "earth moves," as Bernard Cache would term them, Morphosis has completed the morphological transition from modernism to a form of late-twentieth-century practice that, while recognizing the legitimacy of critical theory in its attacks on the bureaucratic, modern state, nevertheless refuses to abandon the quasi-utopian stance of the modernist avant-gardes. In the wake of what we might call "Kafka effect," and the attempt to reconstrue the terms of judgement for a modernity that has exceeded its own self-constructed rationales in its postnational and posthistorical conditions, Morphosis's "neoformations" begin to open up the territory of deterritorialization, without nostalgia, and also without false promises. In this space, as the projects in this book imply, there is freedom of movement, even if of a nomadic and fluid kind, for an architectural practice of global, but not globalizing, aspirations.

—Anthony Vidler

IV. MONTAIGNE'S ADDICTION

I am where I am not, therefore I am where I do not think.

— Jacques Lacan

6:42:21 A.M. Los Angeles.

The glow of the morning sun warms concrete and palms, turning vegetation into a vibrant anodized green. It shines, still low, through a haze that merges with distant hills, softening the edges of a diamond-clear foreground. Every morning the sun forgives and forgets, only to be violated by nightfall with the ravages of our new world — newly crippled sons, and women destined forever to wear rape on the quivering edge of a rare smile.

It will be another five minutes and thirty-nine seconds before the beginning of Montaigne's day. An exotic bird, with yellow and green plumage, sits in a tree outside the window. Occasionally there is a single loud squawk as it stretches its once-clipped wings. In the distance a dog (or is it a man?) overturns a garbage can and noses for food. In the farthest reaches of hearing a car alarm beeps incessantly.

The previous evening Montaigne had his wife hide three alarm clocks somewhere within the room. Acting like intravenous espresso, it is Montaigne's new substitute for coffee. This morning, as a discordant chorus of Brauns sends adrenaline rushing, he jolts upright. To his further shock, however, he finds his left foot somehow snagged, and ends up flat on his back on the cold wooden floor, legs in the air. A length of cord is wrapped round his ankle and secured to the rusted new steel of the bedpost.

His wife, Blush, enters the room, pleased with her trick. She is in control. Sliding the black silk of her negligee up her thighs, she straddles his chest as she lowers herself over him. Surrounding their wet kiss is a private screen of soft blonde hair.

"Armed response is on," says the woman who does not exist, in a voice with no intonation. Once the security system is switched on, Montaigne has ten seconds to leave and lock the door behind him. He does it calmly in five.

Now out of the door and feeling the warmth of day, he allows himself to think of his new passion. His addiction.

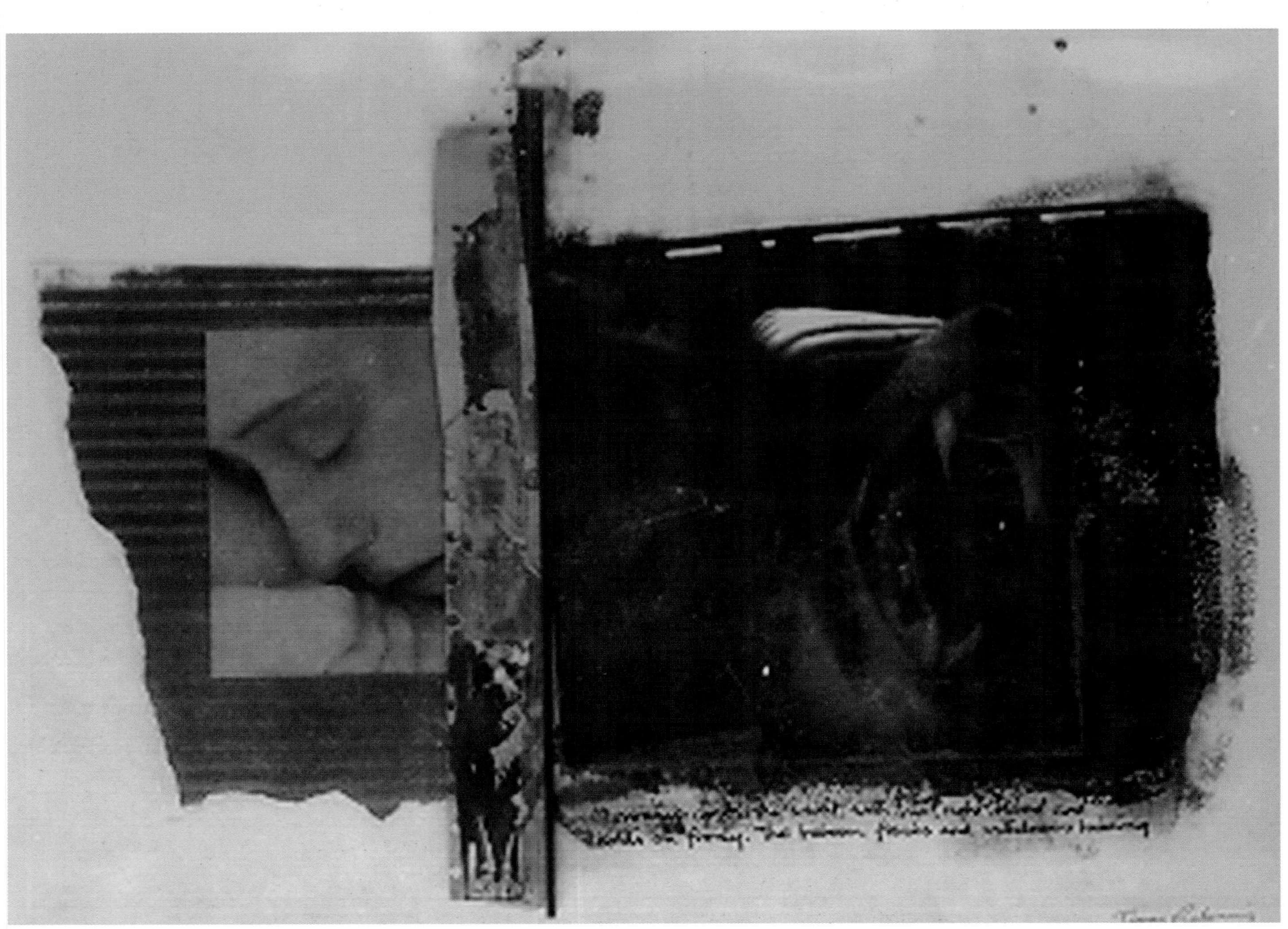

Montaigne is really pleased with himself. He has found a washroom in the nearby public library where he can take at least ten paces back from the mirror. It is perfect. Except for a janitor at the end of the day, Montaigne has never seen anyone else come in. He studies himself in the mirror by the cold glare of the overhead fluorescent light. Bohemian rough stubble covers his face and head evenly. He sees in front of him a map of all his experiences, four decades of laughter, lies, loves, and tears. A good rest at one time would have cleared up the lines that now are set there forever. Then there are the bruises. Three or four lay just below his hair line, of differing ages and colors. Montaigne has become familiar with the changes from reddish purple to a fading jaundiced yellow.

Blush sits alone in the house, delighting in the crisp crackle of the clear toffee wrapper that she unfolds with the tips of her fingers. The small brown candy is imprinted with the marks made by the cellophane folds. She places the candy in a dish overflowing with others identical to it, and then proceeds to cut the crystal wrappers in half neatly with scissors. It is one of those sounds that has no limit to its clarity. However closely the crackling plastic is placed to the ear, ever more pure sounds can be heard. Each half she halves again and then crushes all four segments into tight separate balls, which she then inhales sharply. The tingle maps her inner nasal cavity to an invigorating depth. She can almost sense her brain. She sits there, naked, undecided whether or not to do it again, then presses her thighs against the wet velour of the stool. It is hot, and the bird on the tree gives another piercing squawk.

Finishing his inspection, Montaigne slowly steps backward to the wall opposite the mirror. Everything in the room is hard and unforgiving, reminding him of hospitals. He glares at himself across the room, surrounded by shiny white tiles, and then runs as fast as he can. As he reaches the sink he leaps up at his image, which rises precisely as he does to meet him. With a resounding crack, Montaigne enters through the looking glass.

He finds himself sitting in a small room, on a floor of hand-cast concrete pavers blackened with graphite and age. The limits of the room are not clear at first. The floor opens up around one edge, and drifting into the abyss is a wall of glass and a heavy steel structure that appears to be cut off midair, supporting nothing. Above him a rusted steel arc slices the ceiling and sends his vision three stories to a skylit ceiling that floats in the middle of a room above. There is a thin slit in the wall to his right, which glows with halogen. He is sitting with an enormous mandrill.

He is shocked at the ape's size, and at the odor of damp hair between its legs that is both repugnant and grossly intimate. The baby blue snout belies its overwhelming ferocity. Montaigne grabs the snout with his right hand and holds on firmly. The ape freaks and withdraws, hissing and pulling its lips away from its intimidating teeth. Throughout this display of power it remains with its back legs loosely forward of its body in a vulgar stance. After a while it sidles calmly back to him. Still frightened, he grabs its snout again, which makes it growl ferociously. At this point he realizes that he can't let go without losing his hand.

Blush moves to the comfort of her bubble-filled tub, stretching her legs high out of the water onto the glass block enclosure. She is listening to the deep bass drone of Gorecki's Third Symphony through the echoed resonance of three inches of water, her hair and arms splayed out in Pre-Raphaelite decadence.

Montaigne is shaking, but after a few minutes the fierceness recedes and the animal seems to calm down. It starts a kind of humming out of the side of its mouth — a tune not far from "Good Vibrations" by the Beach Boys. Jolted by the strange humor, he mistakes this for a cue to ease his grip. Just as he does so, however, the mandrill throws Montaigne's hand off with a sudden and violent opening of its mouth and snaps at his fingers.

The fright wakes Montaigne from the floor of the washroom. He is relieved that the janitor hasn't found him there. He half expected to wake up in "outpatients" like the time before. There is blood on the mirror and he has cracked his elbow on the sink on the way down. It will be a few days before the pain takes second place to his addiction, and then he will return.

> *The work of Morphosis holds both the innocence of the morning and the memory of the night, it is the bird freed from its cage, the panic of several alarms, and the humor of a trick. It is the sexual encounter with a loved one, and the computer woman's "armed response." It is the orgasmic inhalation, and the white room with the power of steam running through the pipes. It is the mirror and the place beyond. It floats in the psilocybic drifting space between signifier and signified, standing with material surety and wallowing in the Lacanian "imaginary." It comes from a place of childlike naïveté yet glistens with the knowledge of a brutal world. We owe Morphosis. We have a debt. They are the harbingers, in full metal wrapper, of our own predicament. They bring us our chance at understanding the possibility of beauty in chaos, thrust from the unconscious and hung out on the sacrifice poles for us to see as we have not seen before.*

— Tony Robins

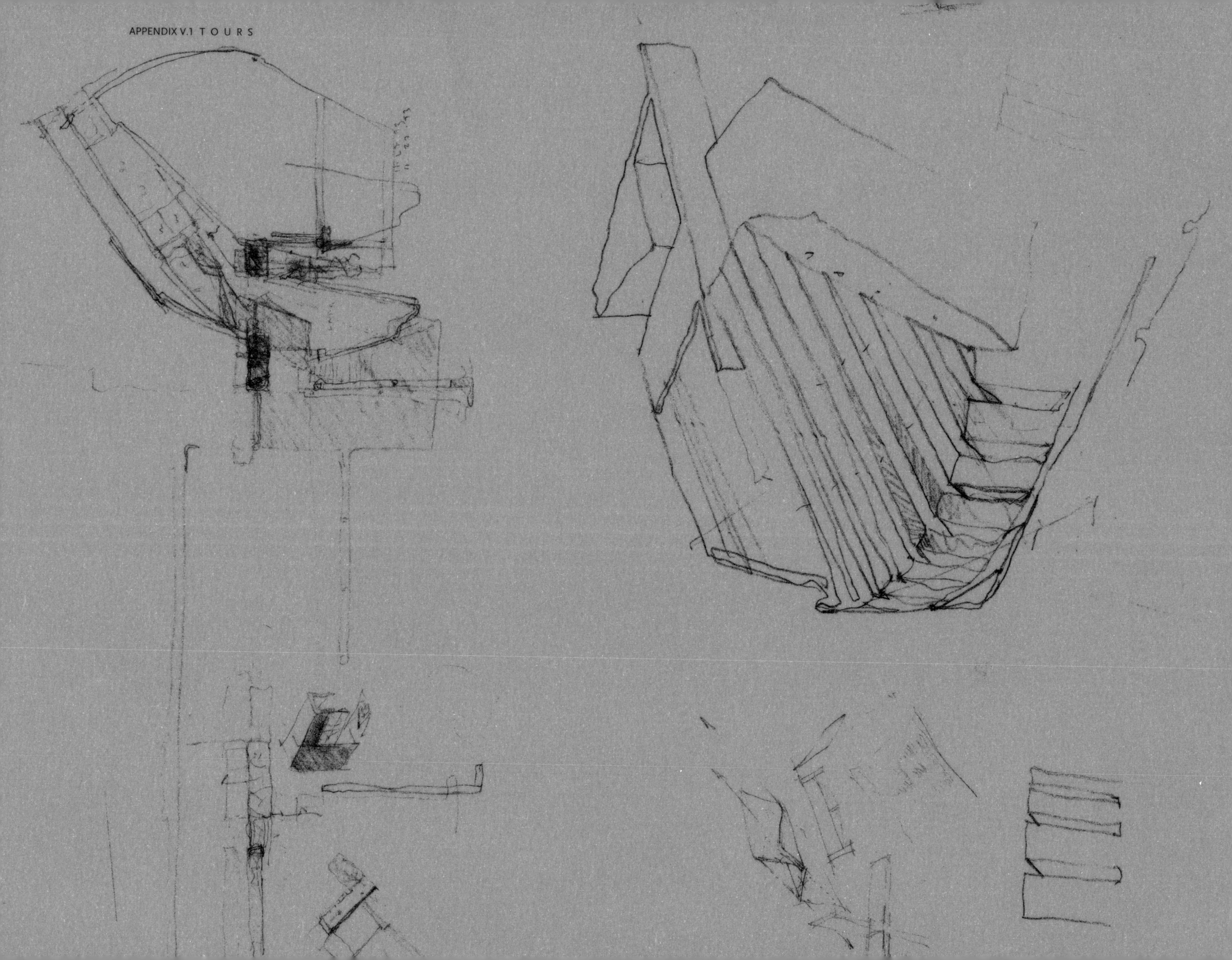

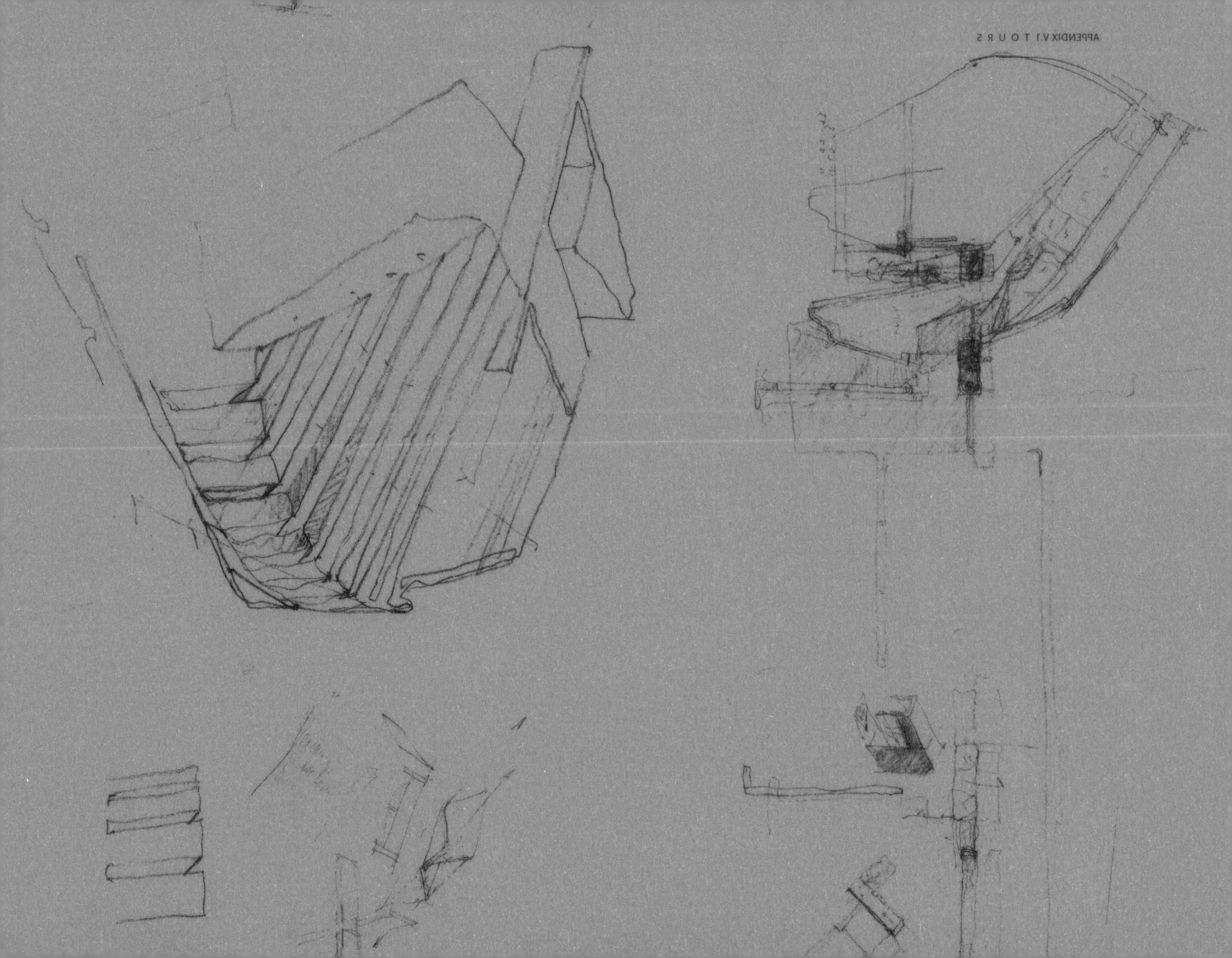

11.10.99

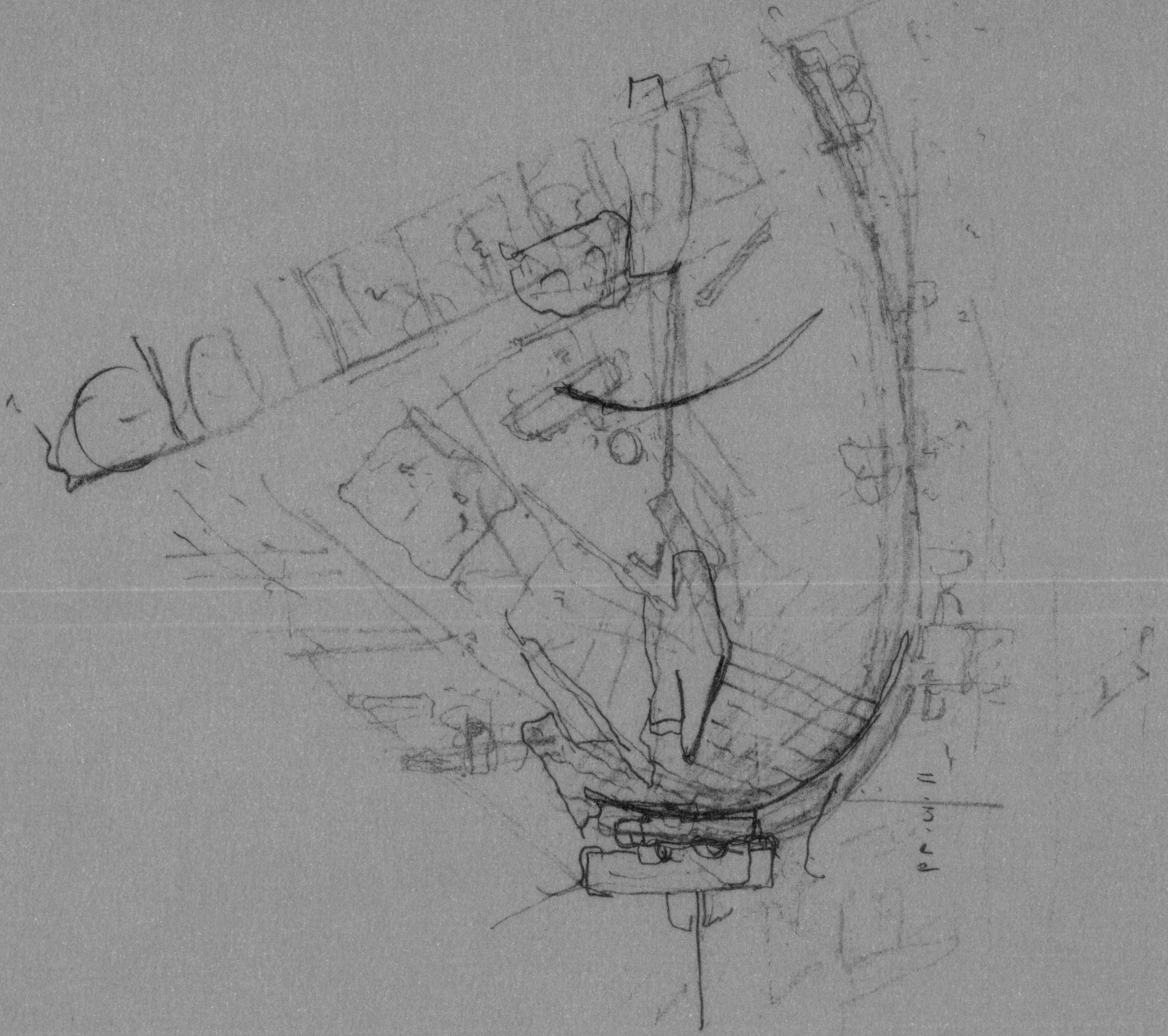

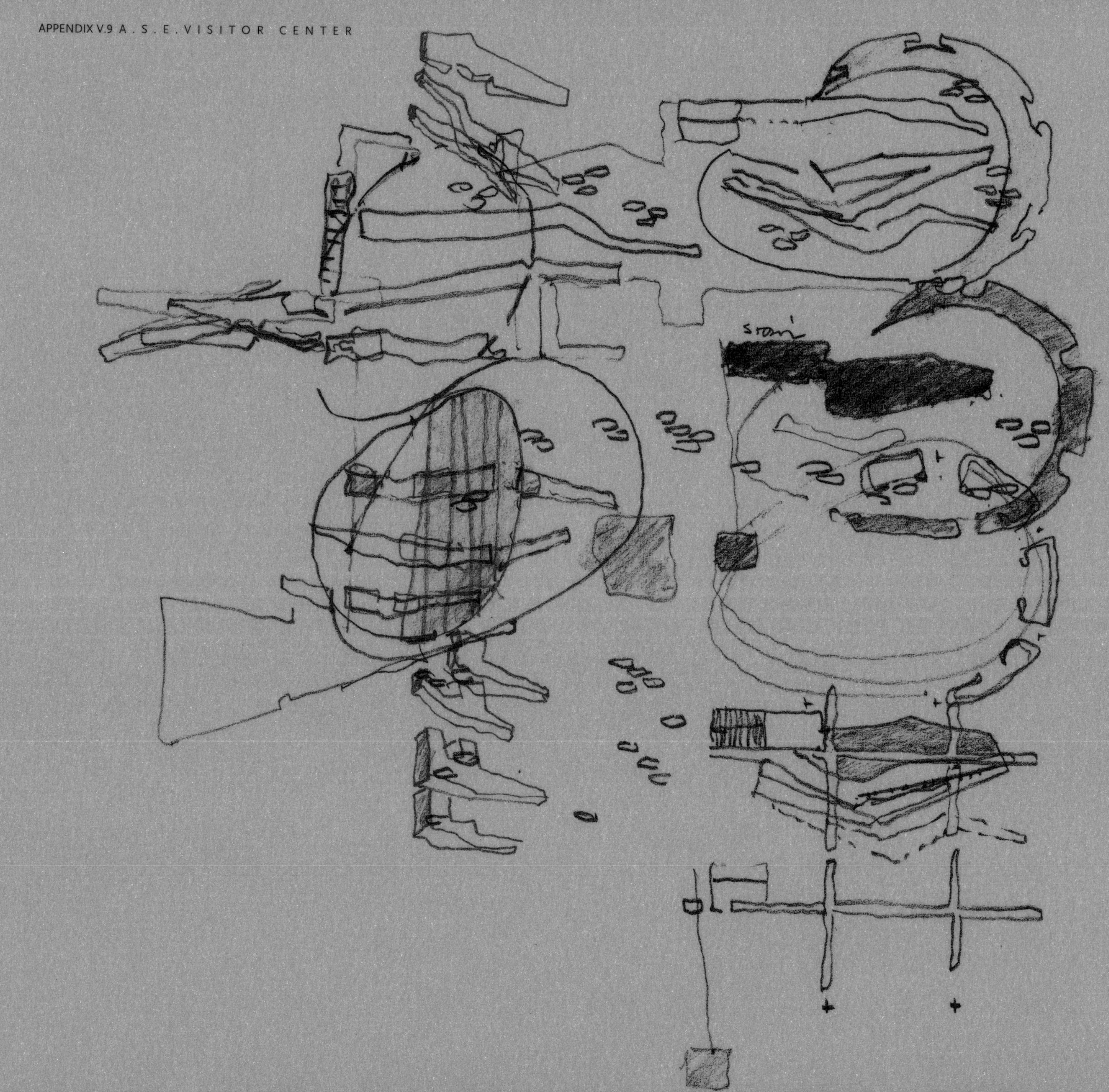
stair

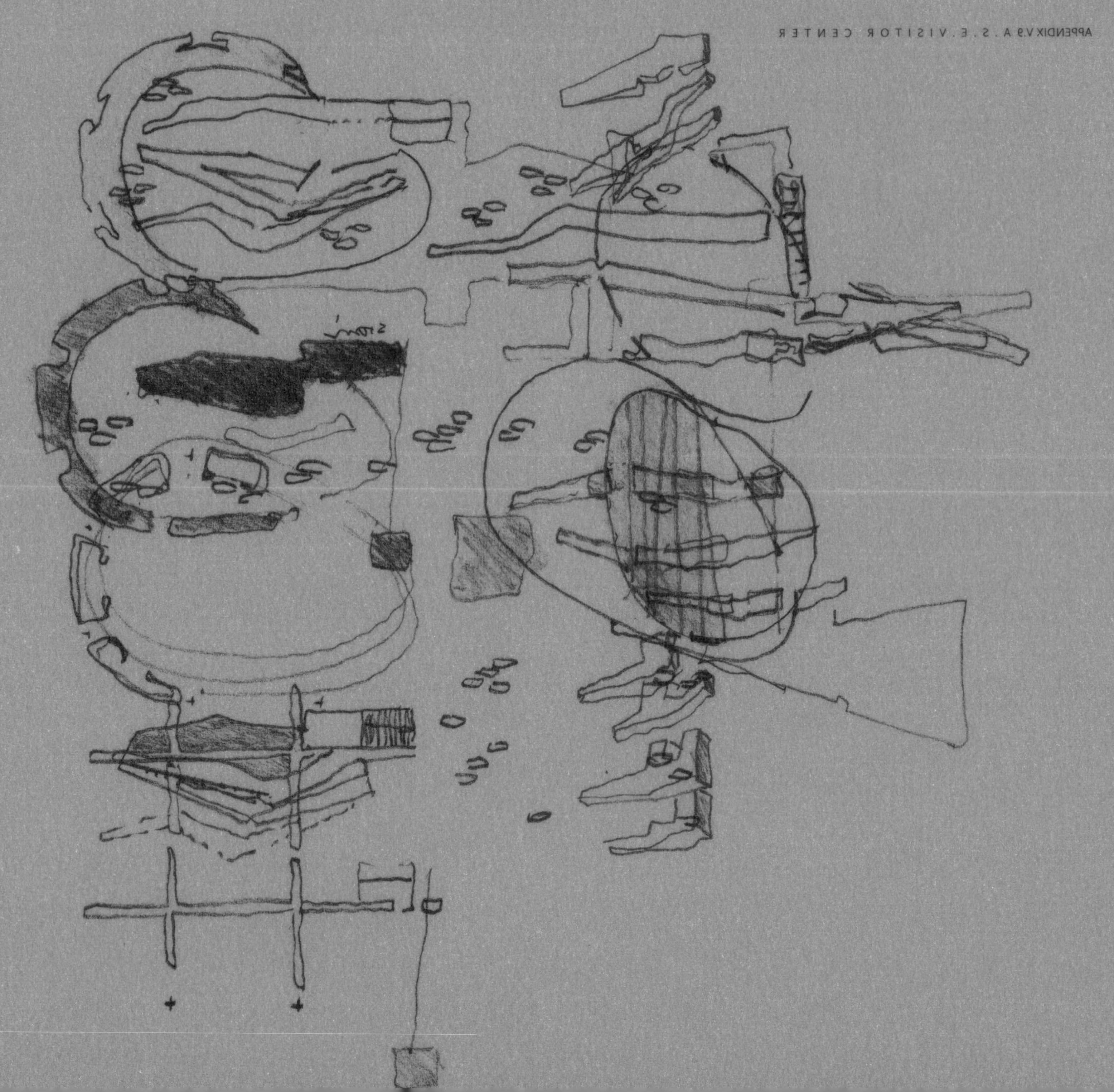

6.26.96
6.27.96

7.22.96

5.3.96

5.20.95

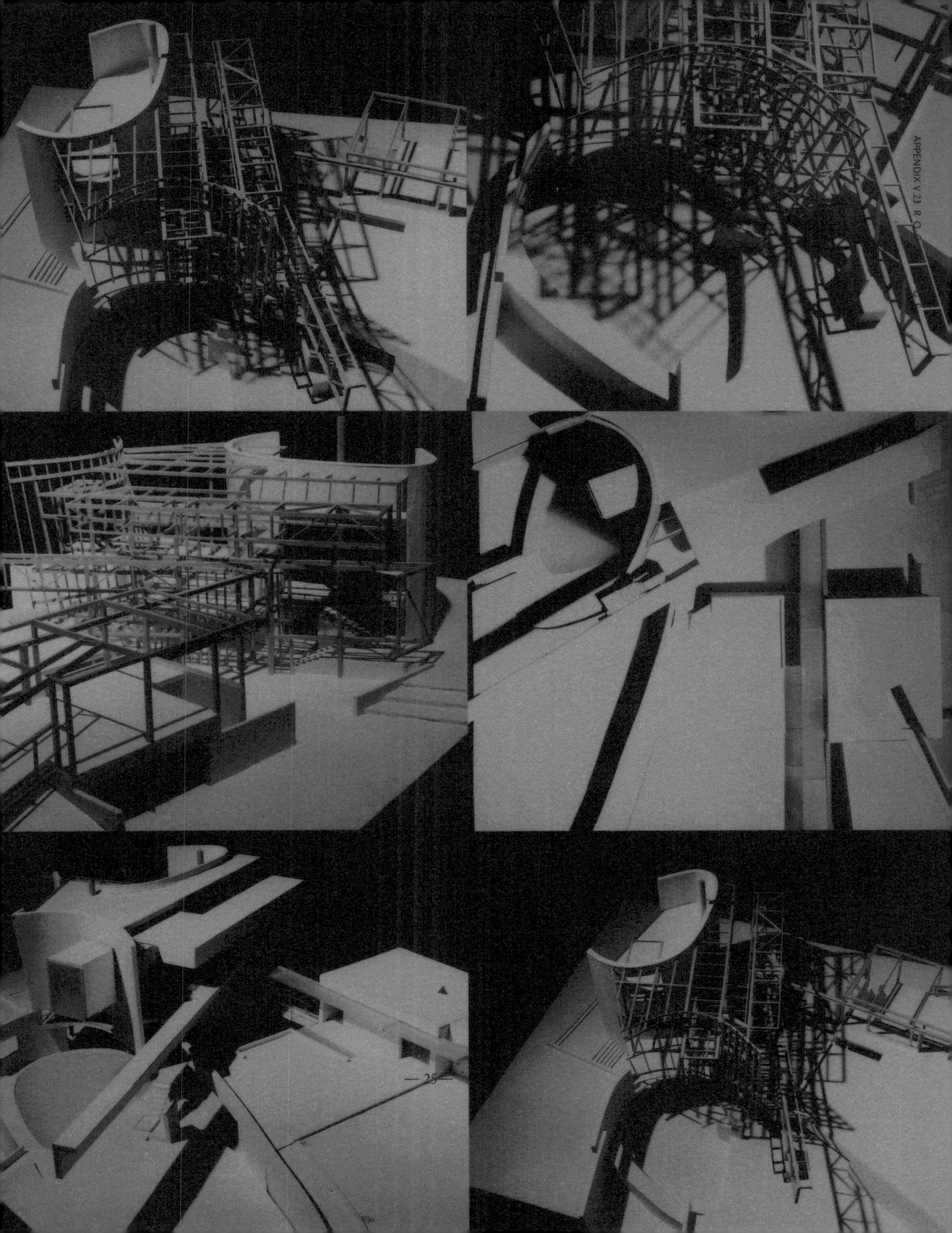

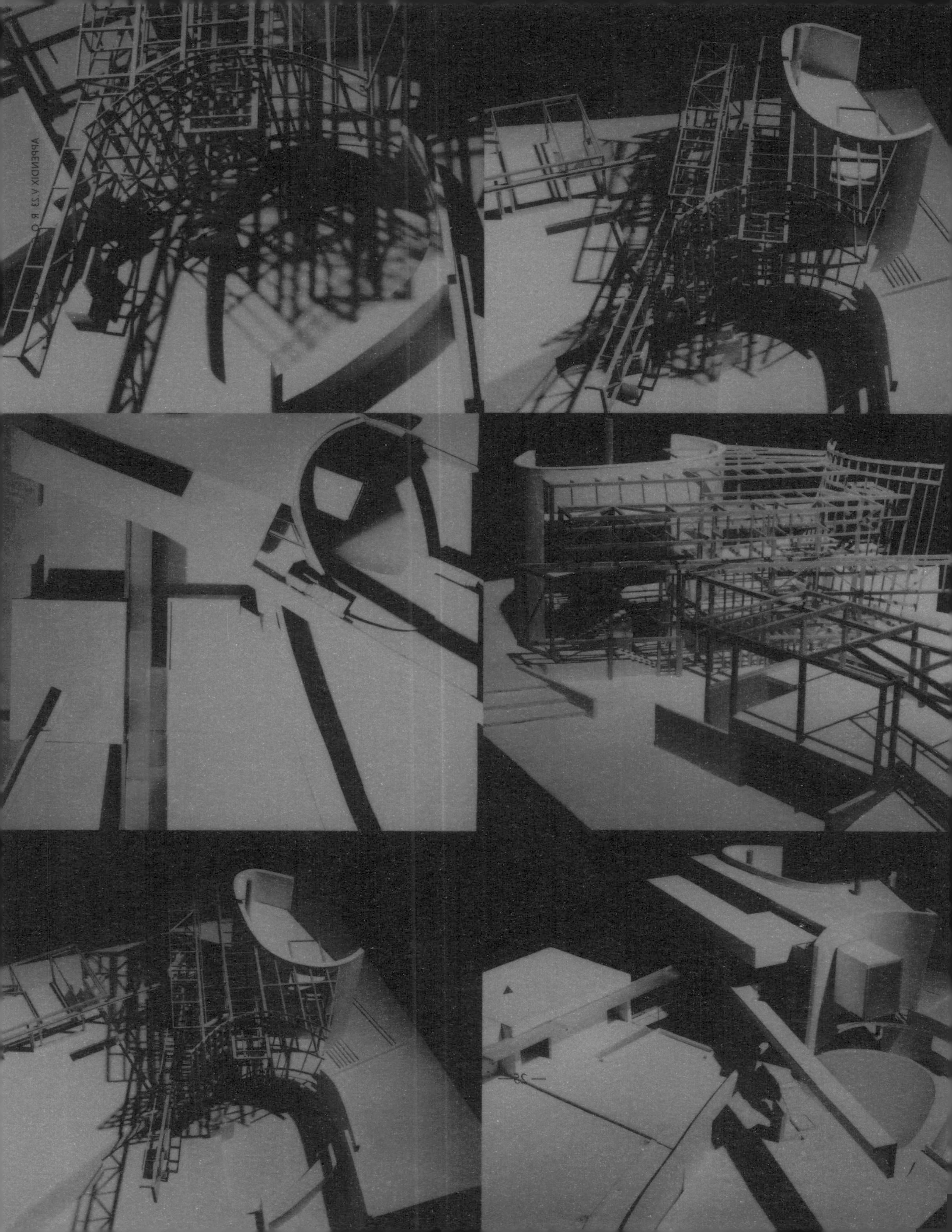

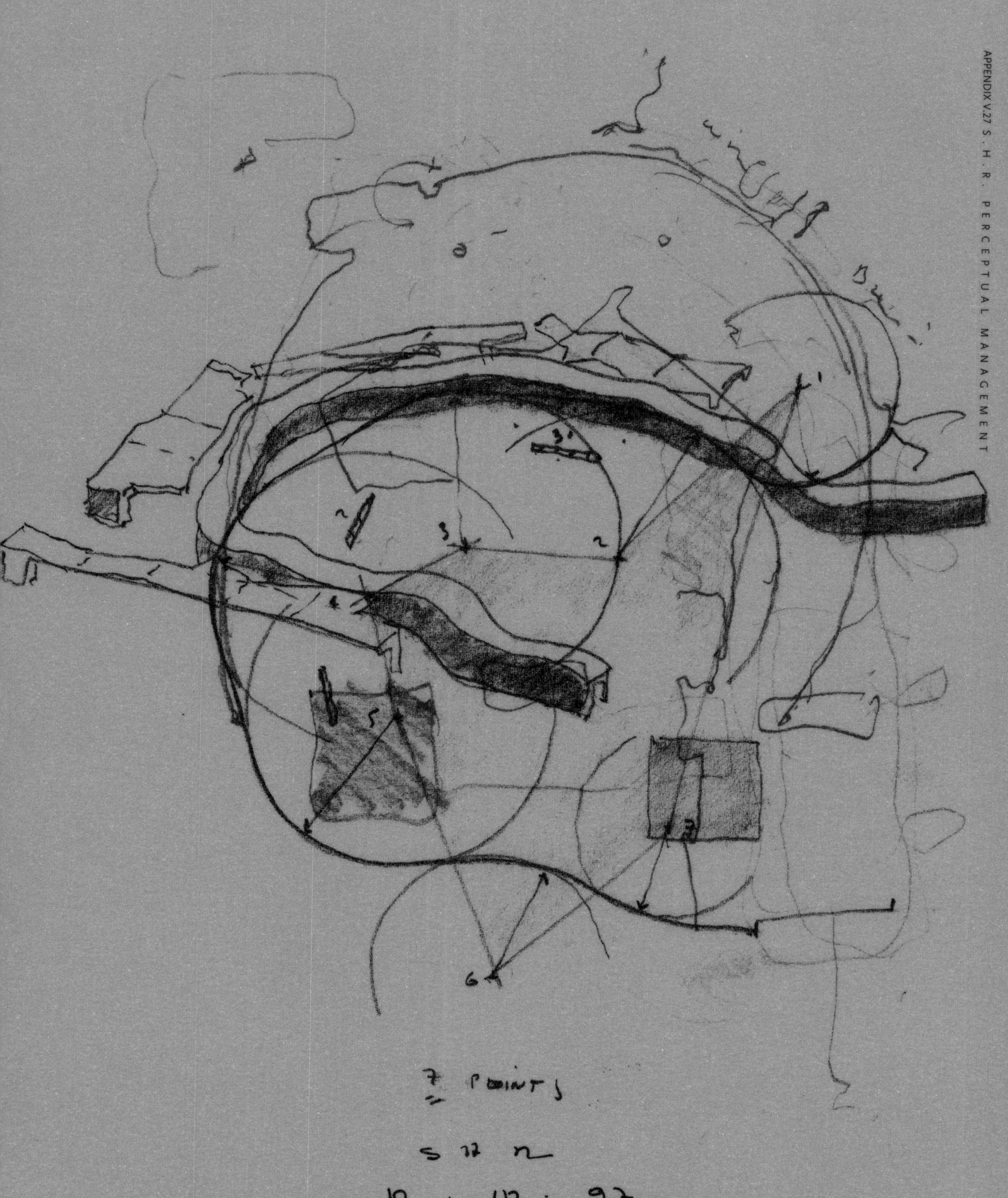
7 POINTS
S H R
10 . 10 . 97.

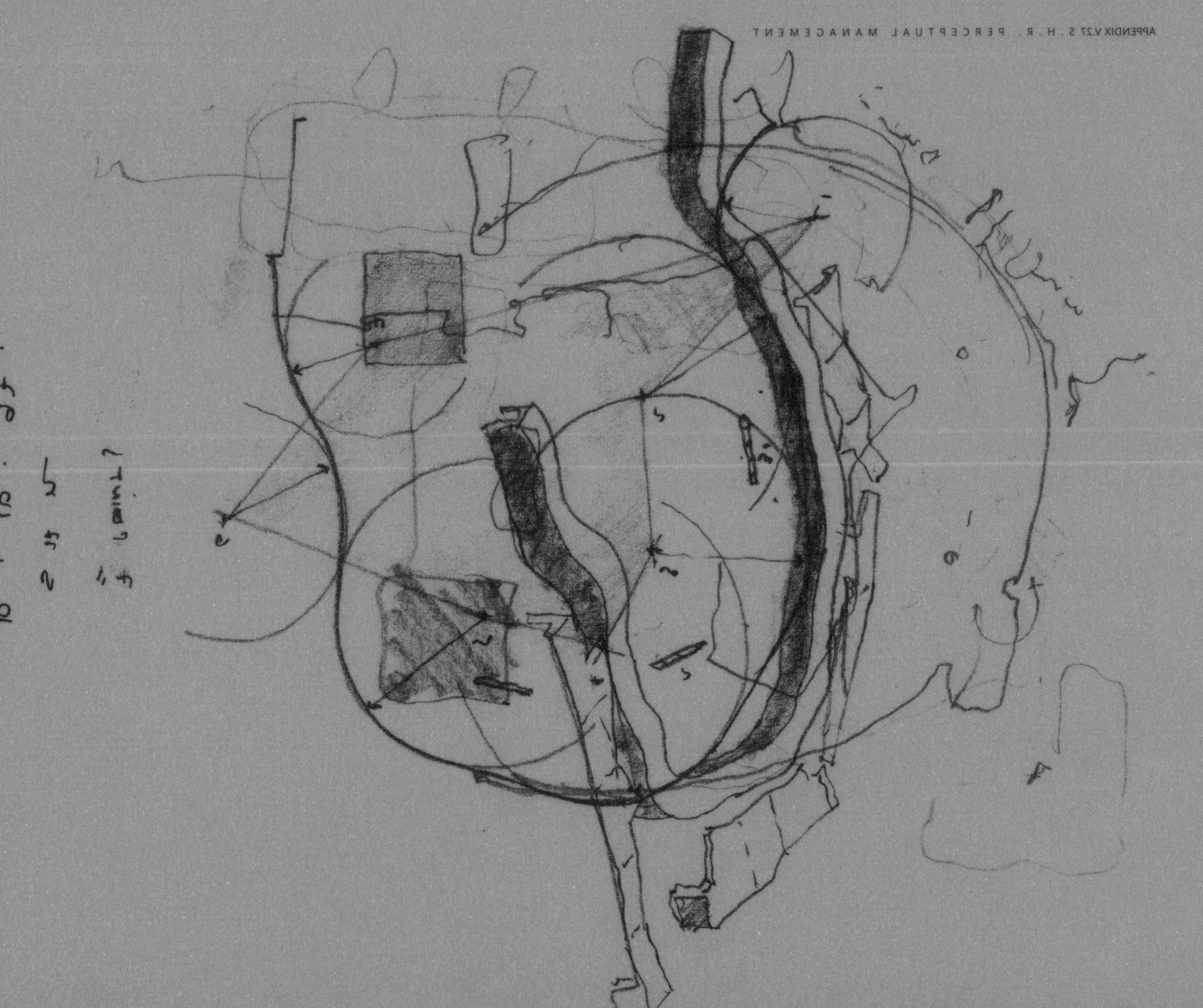

APPENDIX V.29 S . H . R . PERCEPTUAL MANAGEMENT

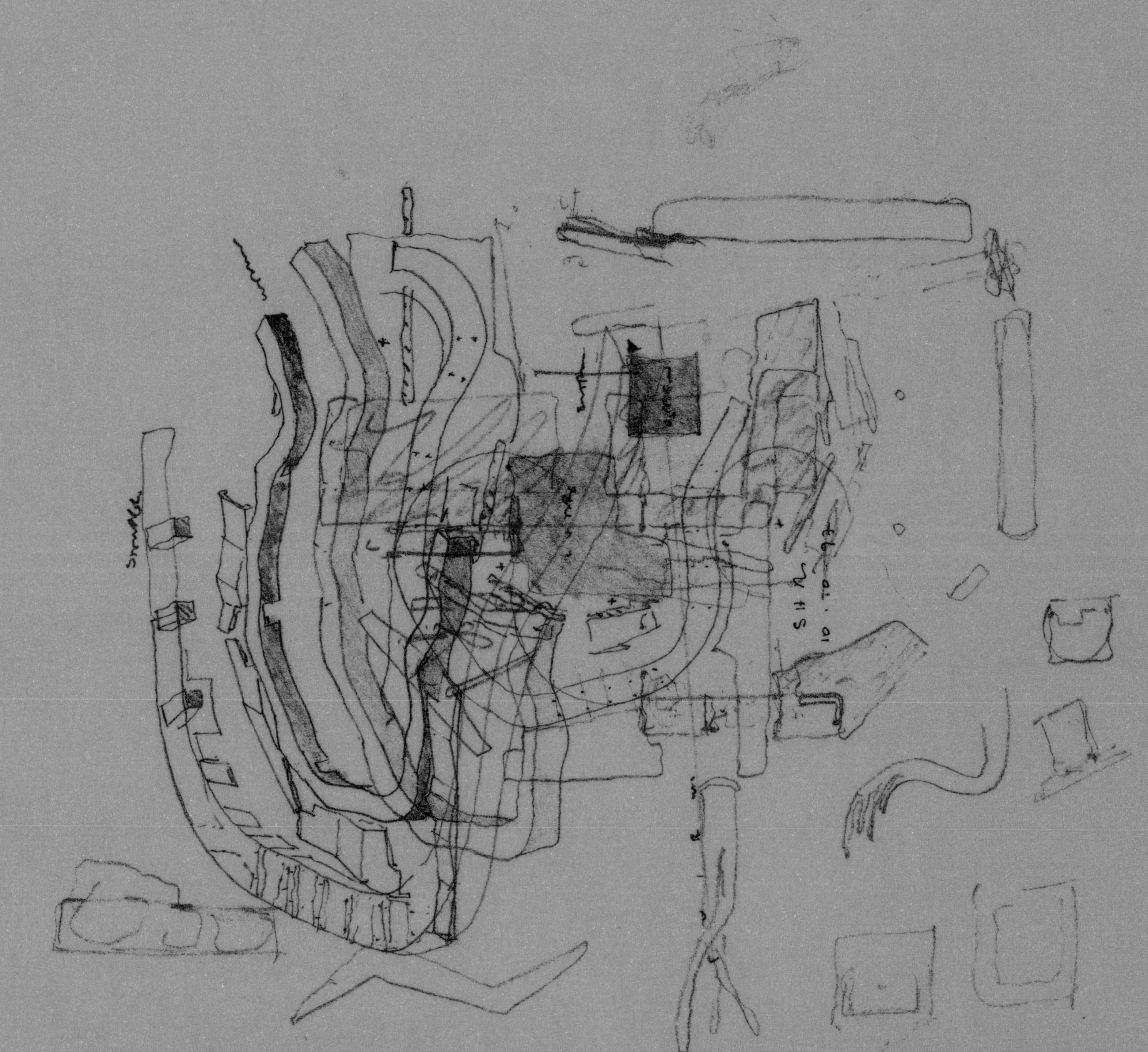

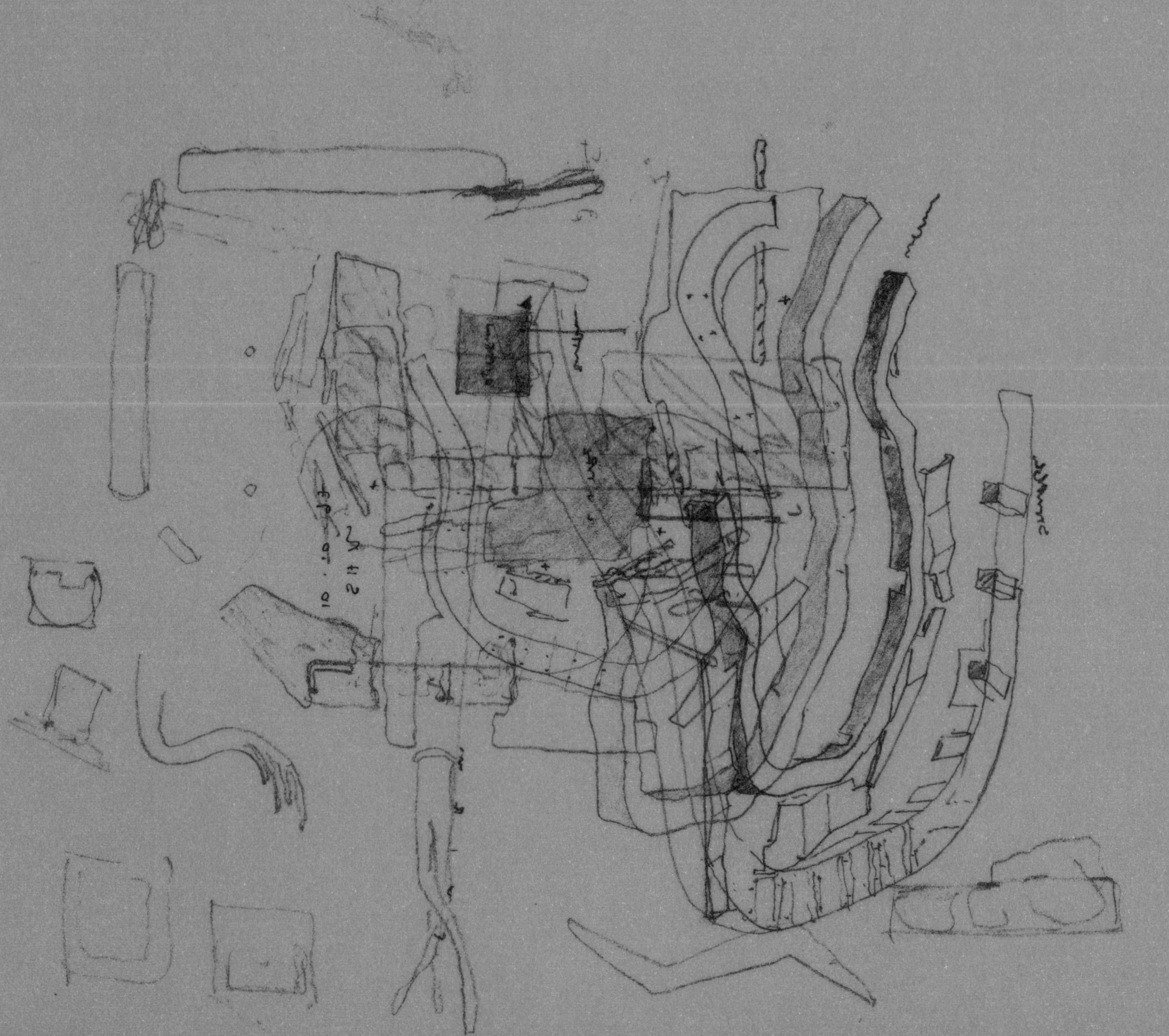

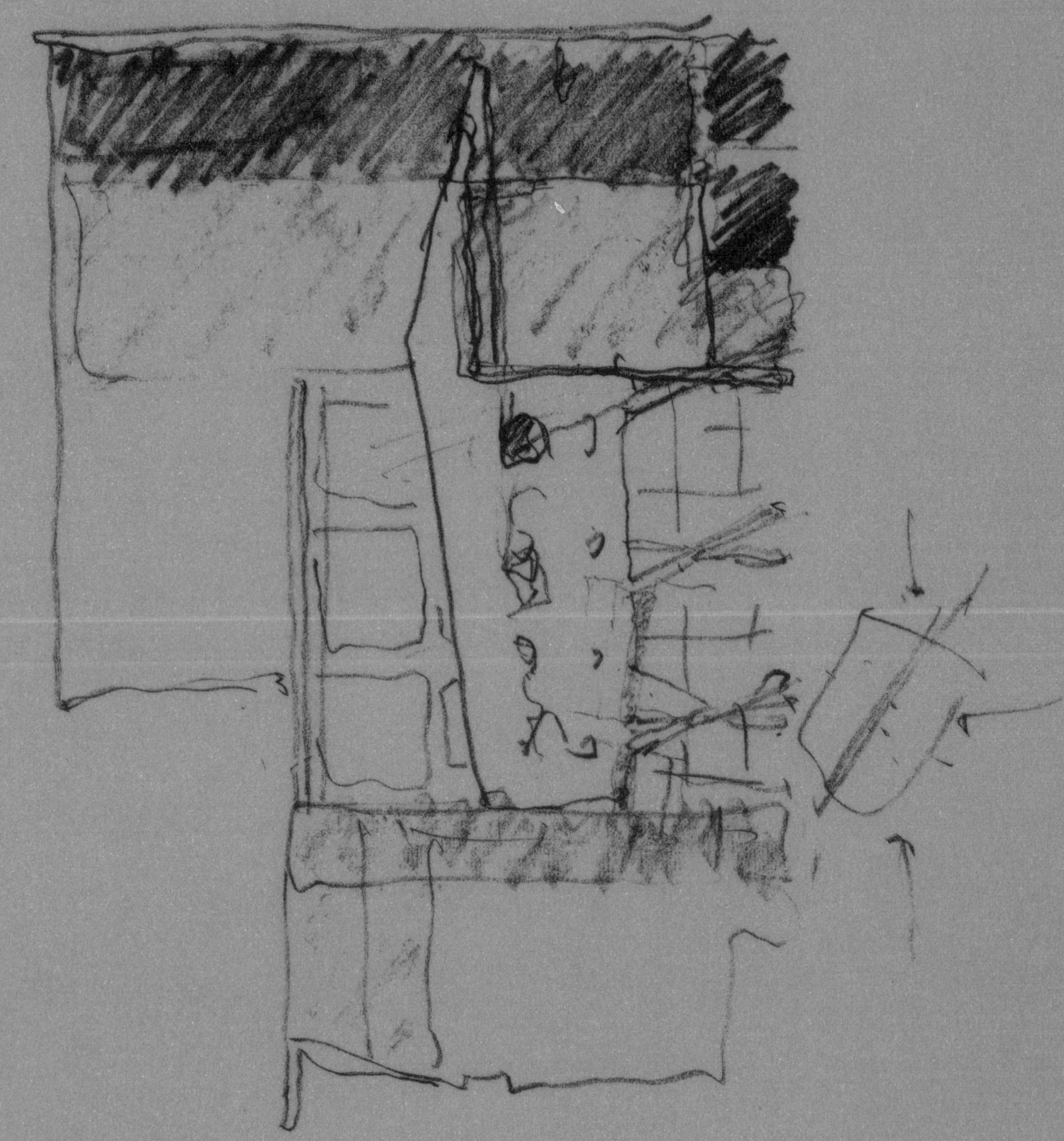

7 · 6 · 98

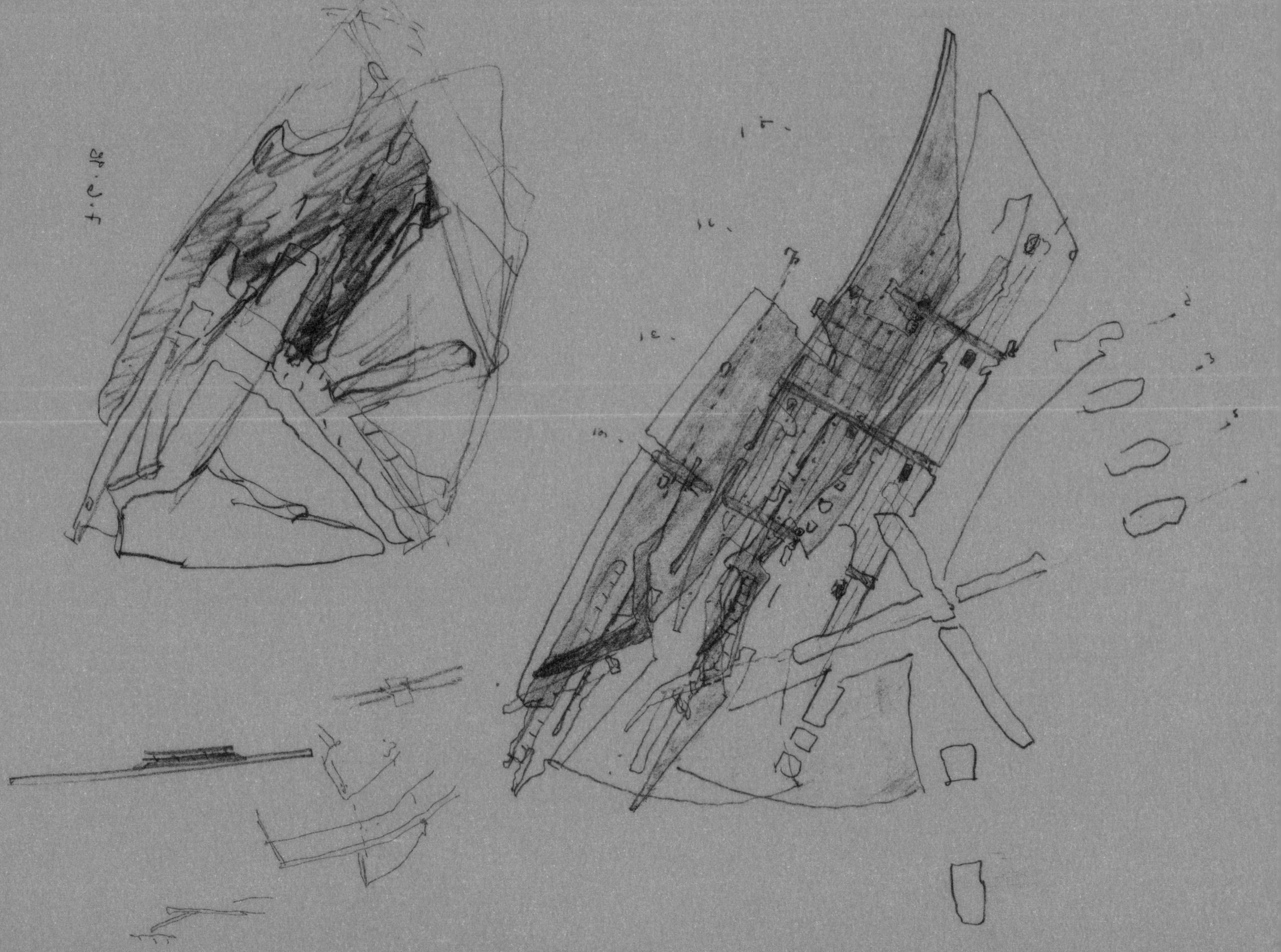

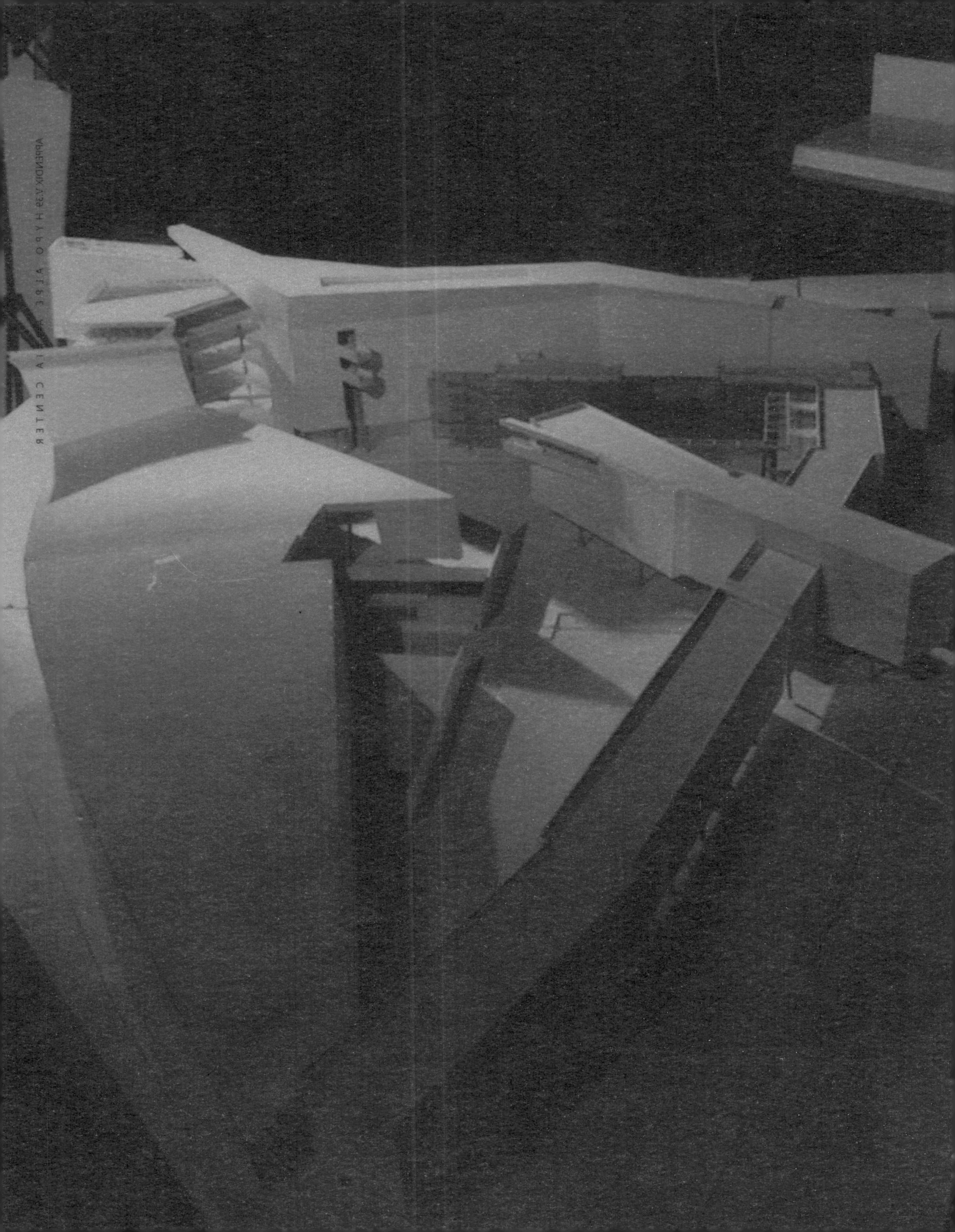

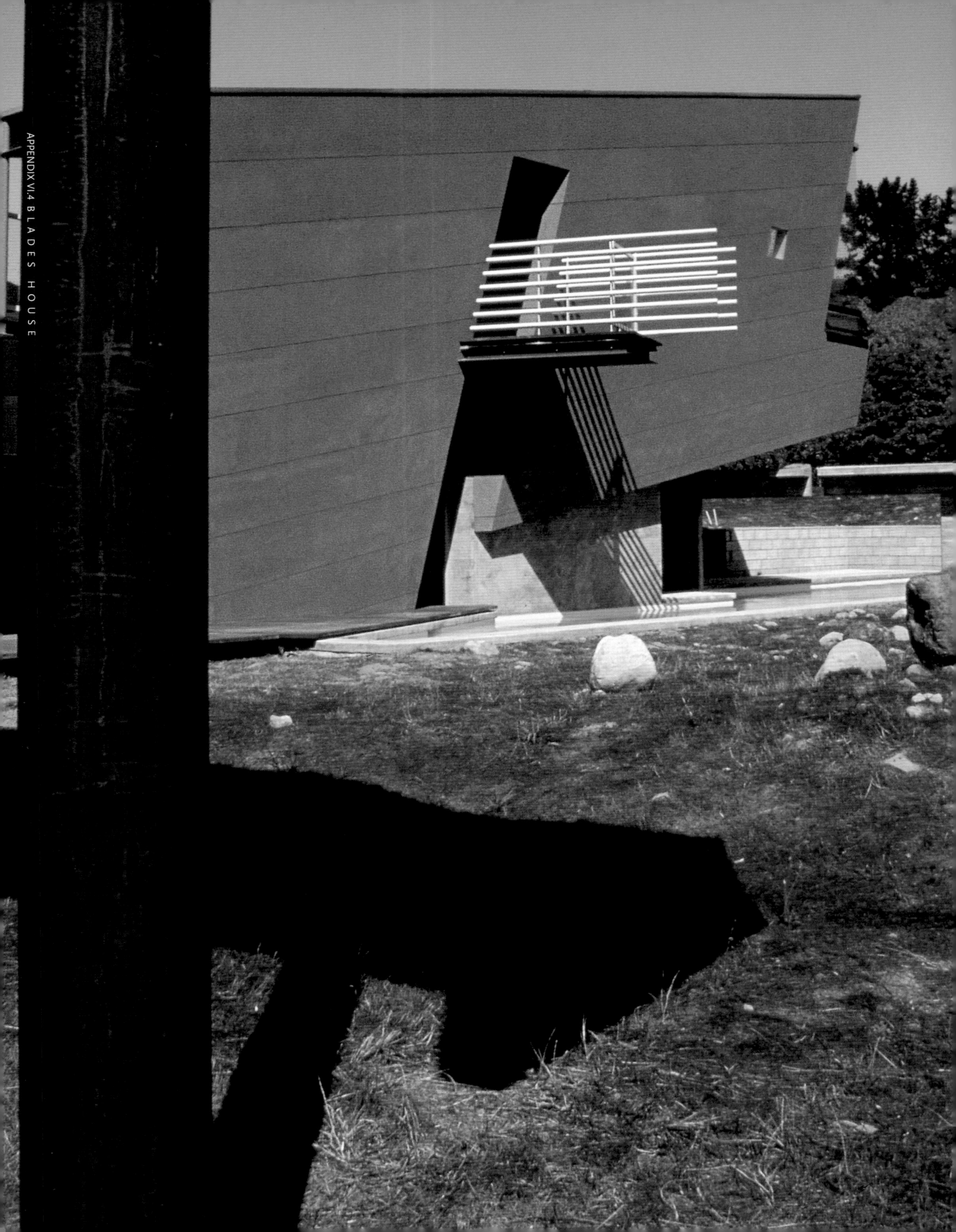

APPENDIX VI.12 OVE ARUP AND PARTNERS, LOS ANGELES

시오장헤어랜드
냉면
영진수선
옷수선
수선방

Pastel
TREND 20

APPENDIX VI.26 HYPO ALPE ADRIA CENTER

er-Bau
ELIN EBG
PFRIMER &
MÖSSLACHER

VII. SARAJEVO

December 8, 1997

Cities, like dreams, are made of desires and fears . . . even if the thread of their discourse is secret, their rules are absurd, their perspectives deceitful, and everything conceals something else.

— Italo Calvino, *Invisible Cities*

The bomb that destroys the house does not destroy a model of the body, but the body itself because the house is needed for the body to protect it. We are at once precipitated into a world of absolute danger and at the same time made to understand that this threat exists only insofar as we are in this world.

— Jean-Paul Sartre

I remember thinking that what at the time seemed to me somewhat risky and definitely outside of the bounds of my normal life must have been routine to the crew that piloted the C-141. I'm not sure I can remember all of the details. The flight was routine just like yesterday's or the one the day before. The British transport's payload consisted of four pallets of flour, a Canadian nun, a British journalist, and an architect who was full of questions as to what he was doing there. I had been pondering my role since I had accepted the invitation of Lebbeus Woods and Haris Pocovic. Why was I going to Sarajevo? Clearly we were not equipped to help in any tangible way. We were too early to aid with the rebuilding efforts; in the end it came down to not being able to say no. I had decided to travel to Sarajevo simply to lend my support to those who have not only lived in, but also studied, a city which was, for the last two years, being systematically and effectively

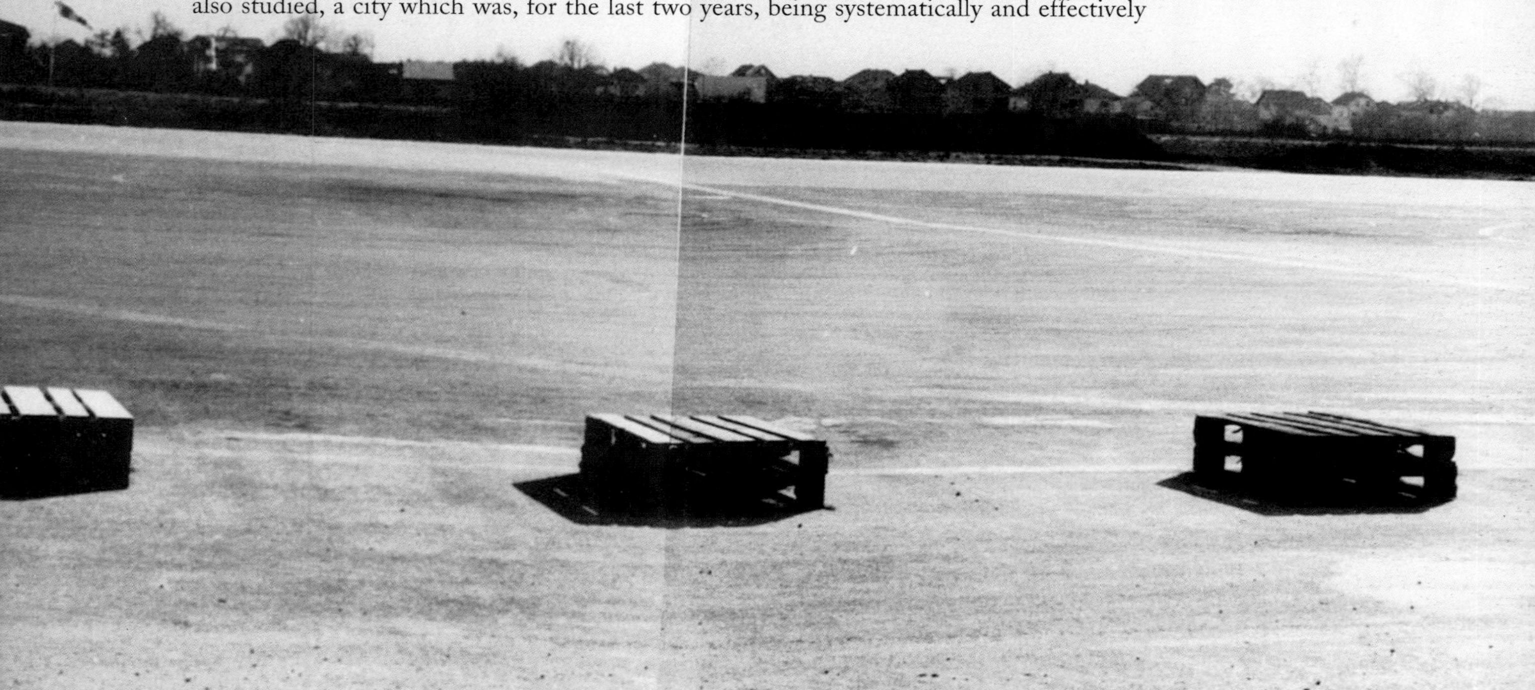

cannibalized. I was drawn there by a limited knowledge of a Sarajevo, one that was *presented* to me more or less constantly over the past two years via the press, and I was unable to truly grasp the situation. Being there immediately brought back these images, discussions, the feeling of dissociation.

Sarajevo was a place of enormous contrasts: on the one hand, the transformation of city to military camp was evident, while on the other hand, one was confronted with the power of the human spirit to aspire to normalcy at all costs — three women walking hand in hand, a cafe issuing the smell of espresso; children playing in a vestpocket park; women who had lost twenty percent of their body weight waiting in long lines for exorbitantly overpriced tubes of mascara — all the time aware of the tension of imminent danger, but determined to continue living. Much of the central part of Sarajevo had received so much shell fire that I couldn't find a place my vision could escape the scars of shrapnel or cannon fire. It is hard to convey the sense of total hatred you feel when you experience the extent of damage.

As a denizen of L.A., I have been tied up in the struggle to create an architecture that has meaning in our increasingly pluralistic world. I, like many of my peers, embrace the complexity that a heterogeneous population possesses. Homogeneity is no longer a viable paradigm for living. Yet I experienced a city which has found its plurality to be finally so disruptive that warring factions have chosen to obliterate not only people who are different, but all architecture which represents these differences as well. Living amidst the scale and ferocity of this destructive force reminded me of how little time and energy is required to decimate work that is produced by such an enormous effort. I think it was this, then, that made the most significant impression on me: that there are forces working to annihilate the intelligence, energy, and emotion invested accretively in the architecture of the city. This investment is the ultimate value of our work (that which provides a glimpse of people and how they live together). The distinction between architecture and building is

transcended while simultaneously made clear. It is here that I saw and appreciated the full power and yet vulnerability of architecture, the deep meaning buildings can have for people, and the vulnerability of such buildings: a sniper on a hill can attack a mosque, a library, a school with pinpoint accuracy. It's precise, systematic, building-by-building demolition.

For four days I was immersed in a world where I was faced with the sheer randomness of life. You sense the insanity, at an immense scale.

We spent three days in discussions, alternating anecdotes of recent history with the establishment of the terms of an architectural dialogue that would serve to reunite students who had been separated from their studies and from each other for over two years. Working without a studio or supplies of any kind (except for a box of 324s that I had brought among the 30 kilos of batteries, cigarettes, foodstuffs, etc.) we started out by sectioning off a third-generation map of the city with a grid, which was established by a stick of wood found in the park that served as our studio for the day. The stick's width defined the increment. The resultant grid system was numbered, the numbers were drawn from a hat, and thus each student's territory of exploration was determined. The next two days were spent in group discussions, which shifted between attempts to establish the terms of the proposal and to focus on personal histories that each of these people brought to the room. I left with a rather condensed sense of these individuals and of their initial instincts for ideas that reflected their response to the city of that moment.

It should come as no surprise that the collective tissue of the students' thoughts and ideas was dominated by notions of chance, entropy, and randomness, as well as interests in the most normative projects — restaurants, shops, business as usual. The resilience of these students is a tribute to the diverse and cosmopolitan life of a prewar Sarajevo. To the twenty-six young architectural students I worked with, thank you for the inspiration which came from your courage, perseverance, warmth, and openness.

VIII. THE PAST IS NOT WHERE I LEFT IT

This is how one pictures the angel of history. His face is turned to the past. Where we perceive a chain of events, he perceives a single catastrophe, which keeps piling wreckage and hurls it in front of his feet. The angel would like to say, "waken the dead and make whole what has been smashed." But a storm is blowing from Paradise; it has got caught in his wings with such violence that the angel can no longer close them. The storm irresistibly propels him into the future to which his back is turned, while the pile of debris before him grows skyward.

— Walter Benjamin, "Theses on the Philosophy of History" in *Illuminations*

In a dream, which I could remember clearly upon waking, I was falling in love with an exotically beautiful woman who continually eluded me as she made her way through the labyrinthian alleyways which were part of Old Havana. The dream was filled with the sensuality of the city itself, its warmhearted people, their openness, everywhere music and people moving to a slow, sensuous gait past beautiful buildings crumbling in a colorful riot of despair. Ancient, yet carefully maintained Chevies, De Sotos, and Packards were parked haphazardly along my way, and my senses were filled with the smell of the sea, of rum, of food, and sex. It was strange that I should have such a dream since I had never been to Cuba. I am precluded by laws in the United States from crossing borders such as these.

So it is that visiting Cuba, in my case to attend an architectural conference in Havana and contribute ideas toward the ongoing saga that is Cuba, is possible only to those who hold the correct passport. For some of us, understanding necessarily remains elusive. I offer these sketches as reflections of early impressions; abstractions of plant materials and the sea occupy the drawings, gestating in and inhabiting them, often as geometrical forms. These drawings are a record of my own incomplete process of immersion, questioning, erring. They reflect the complexity, elusiveness, and instability of the subject. The context does not exist for a smooth, seamless narrative. Coherence cannot be forced prior to experience or comprehension.

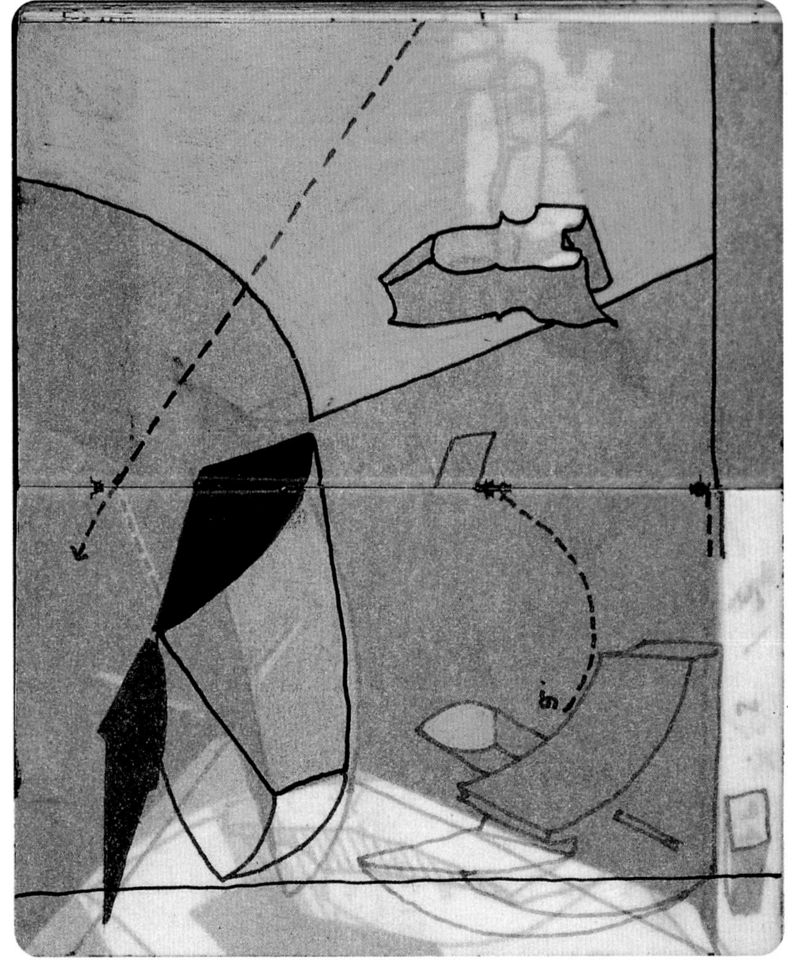

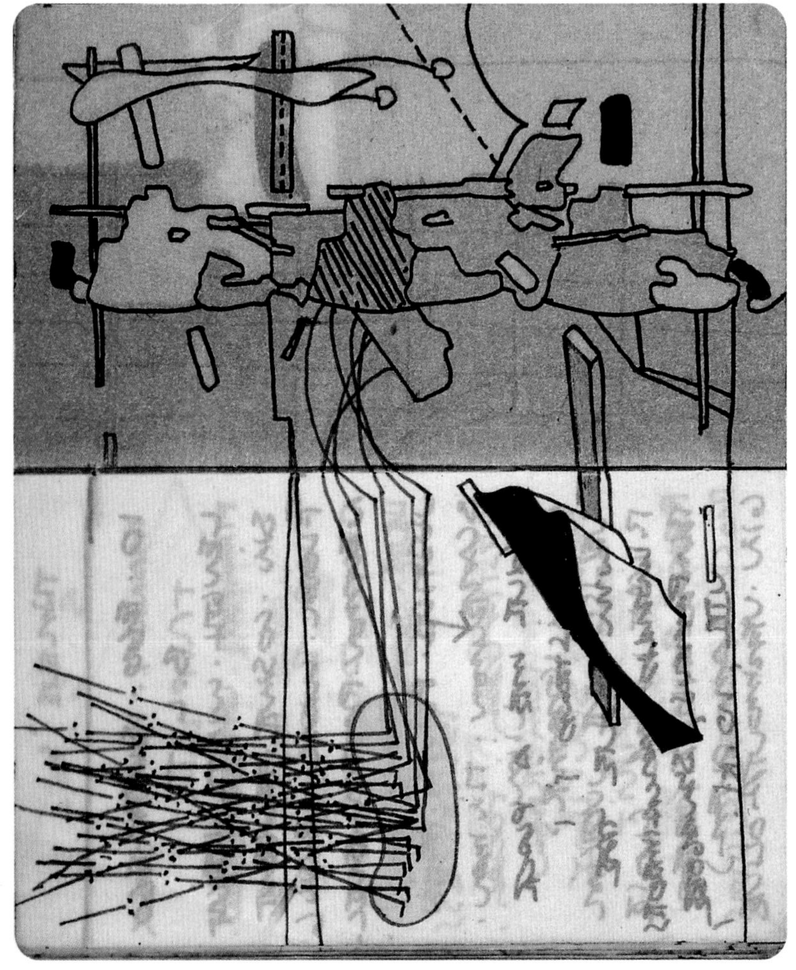

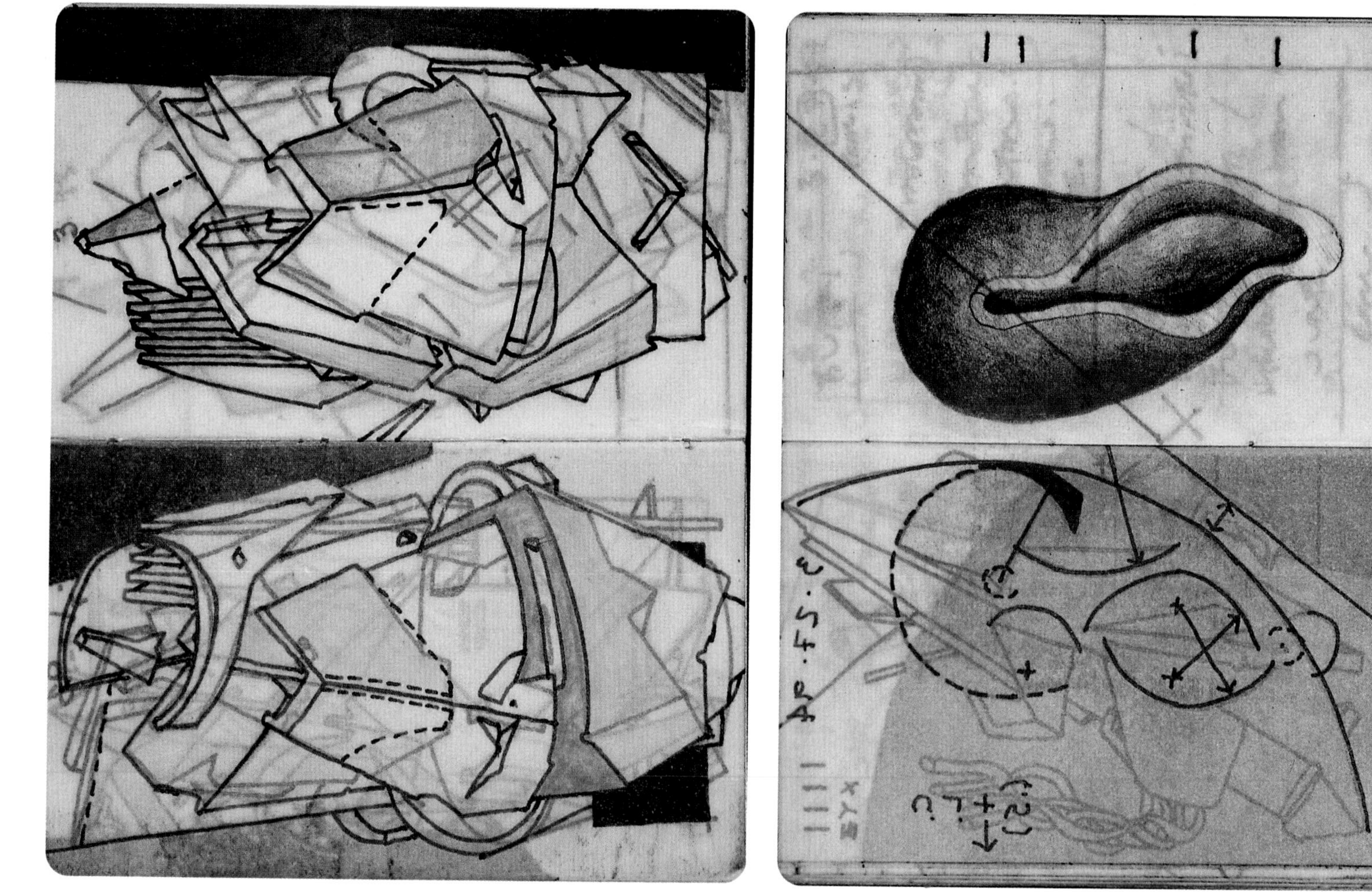

In most cases an architect approaches this kind of exploration with a relatively clear understanding of his/her subject, perhaps because he or she has been working or living there. For me, the comprehension would come via some other method — the dream maybe. I started with some understanding of the historical facts, but the facts of the past seem to have no bearing on the facts of the present. Disillusionment. I had always imagined that the key to understanding was a close observation of the details, moving beyond what Cocteau called the "eye of habit." The more accurate the scrutiny, the more successful the results. The implication is that the city can be understood, that beneath the infinite facades of building, street, and empty spaces there is finally a coherence, an order, a source of motivation. But after struggling to take in all these surface effects, I felt no closer to Cuba than upon my first arrival. I had been a denizen of La Habana, had walked at my pace, seen what I had seen, and the only thing I could feel was the city's impenetrability. Instead of narrowing the distance that lay between myself and the city, I had seen the city slip away, even as it remained before my eyes. Which Cuba was I occupying? The historical city? The current city? Regardless, an overriding sense of the immediacy and urgency of the problems hung over me.

When one is walking, the city comes to life, seething with possibilities, with secrets and contradictions. Since everything seen or said, even the slightest, most trivial thing, can bear a connection to the outcome of the overall impression, nothing must be overlooked. What I discovered in exploring this city was the sense of plenitude in its visual stimuli in conjunction with the economy of its delimited boundary. Heightened by being the consummate outsider (a *norteamericano),* this lent a surreal character to the entire endeavor. Everything became essence; the center of the city shifted with each event that propelled me forward. The center, then, is everywhere, and no circumference can be drawn until the journey is finished. La Habana was an inexhaustible space, a labyrinth of endless steps, and no matter how far I walked, no matter how well I came to know its neighborhoods and streets, I was always left with the sense of being lost in a dream. Lost, not only in the city, but within myself as well.

We architects, then, are those who talk, who look, who listen, who move through the morass of objects and events in search of thought, the idea that will pull all these things together and make sense of them. So how to proceed? I don't have answers, only questions. This is a society which has attempted "revolutionary" change: the system privileges the collective at the expense of the individual, and at the expense of the work of three of its finest architects (I'm thinking of Porro, Verate, and Vittare). Was this necessary?

To what end will architecture service the future of Havana? What future? What is being transgressed? In what manner does Cuba require new organizational and spatial configurations? Who is our client — this agent of society? A larger question emerges: How does architecture reconcile the individual and the collective? For nearly one hundred years all revolts and protests in Europe — whether left-wing or right-wing — were ideologically dependent on the idealization of the past, or at least upon the idealization of the simple and natural against the complex and artificial.

Speaking about Mexico, Octavio Paz has identified some of the salient issues which apply equally to Cuba:

> *I do not preach a return to the past, imaginary as are all pasts, nor do I advocate that we go back into the clutches of a tradition that was strangling us. I believe that Mexico, like the other Latin American countries, must find her own modernity. In a certain sense she must invent it. But she must start with the ways of living and dying, acquiring and spending, working and playing that our people have created. It is a task that demands not only favorable historical and social circumstances but an extraordinary imagination. The rebirth of imagination, in the realm of art as in that of politics, has always been prepared for and preceded by analysis and criticism. I believe that this duty has fallen to our generation and the next. But before undertaking the criticism of our societies, their history and their actuality, the Hispanic American writers must begin by criticizing ourselves. First, we must cure ourselves of the intoxication of simplistic and simplifying ideologies.*
>
> (*The Labyrinth of Solitude*, p. 398)

As Paz makes clear, it is for Cuba and Cubans themselves to begin the long and painful process that is required to reignite and reinvigorate their country. To be able to look at Cuba at all, I cannot forget that I am a citizen of the country with whom they have the most enmity. The work on these pages reflects the tension between my apprehension and my desire to make some contribution, to offer some hope to the city and its people. These sketches and the eighteen study models are part of a preliminary process exploring questions of landscape, edges, boundaries, and the cyclical nature of growth and decay within a territory along the Malecón — an isolated and deserted avenue which delineates the boundary between Havana and the sea.

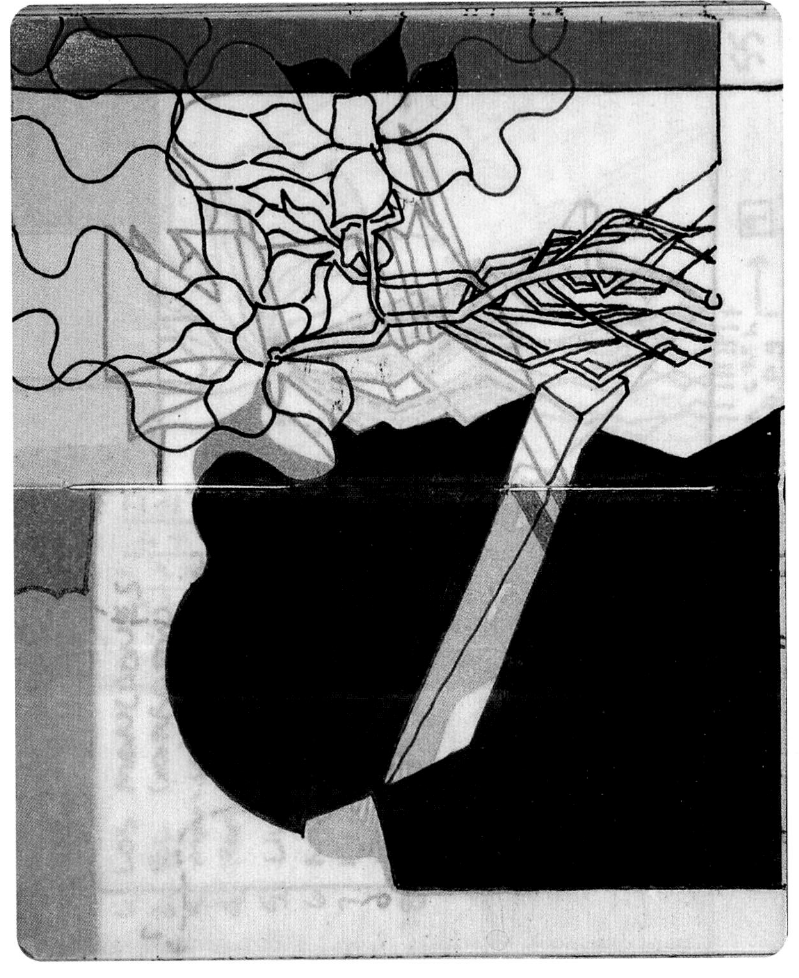

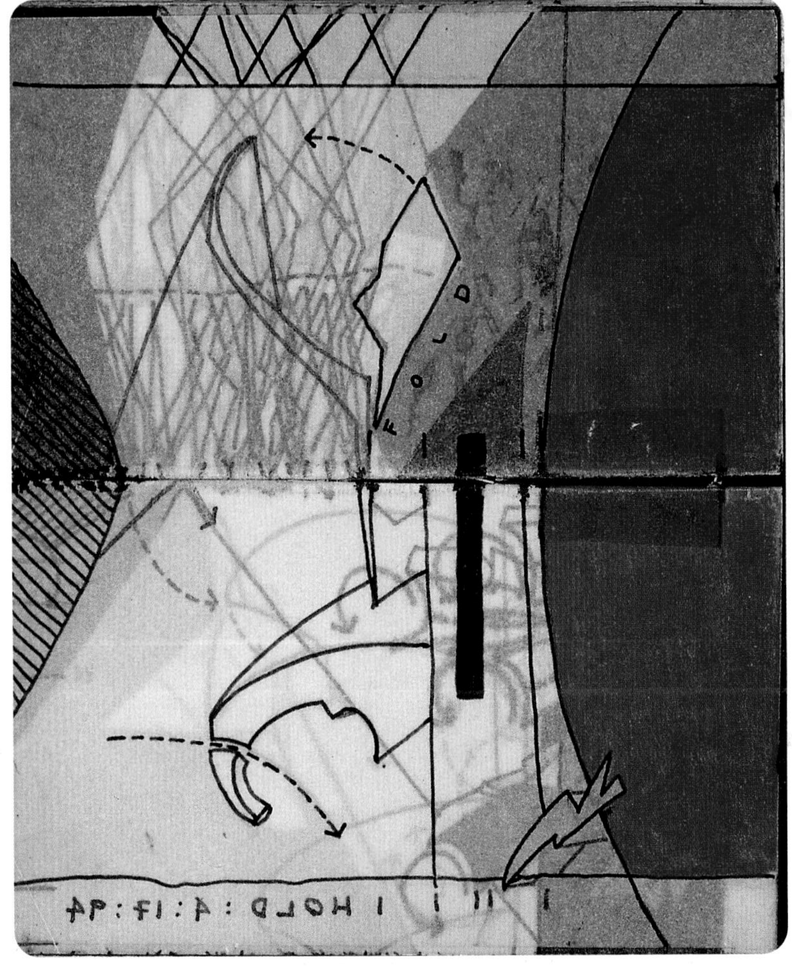
FOLD

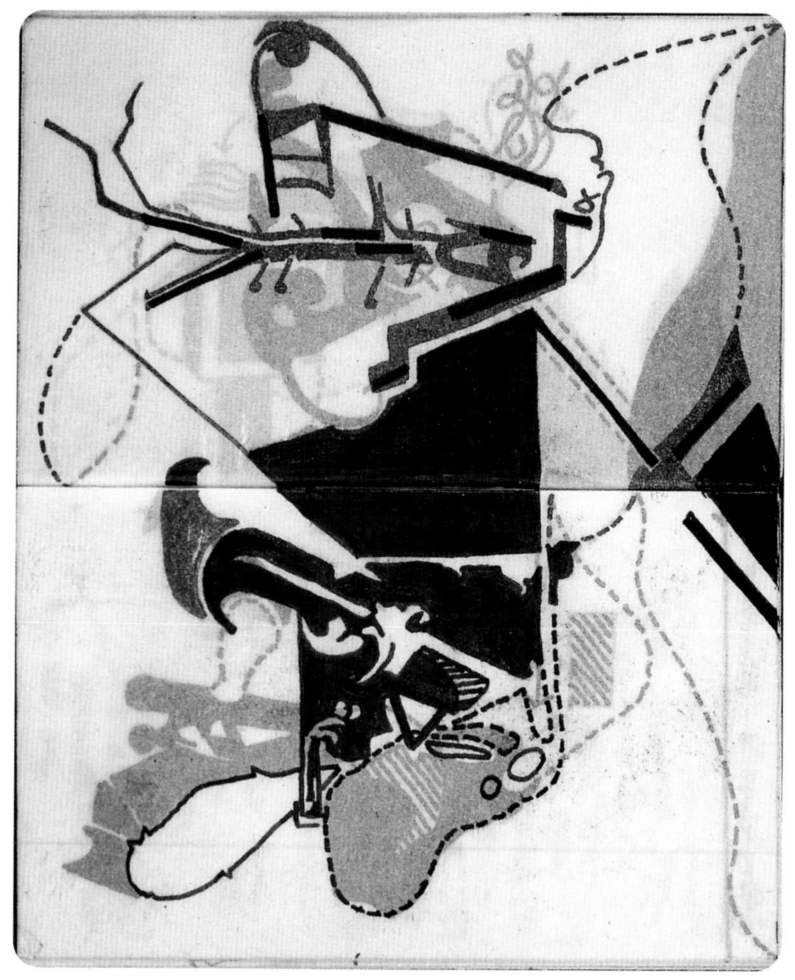

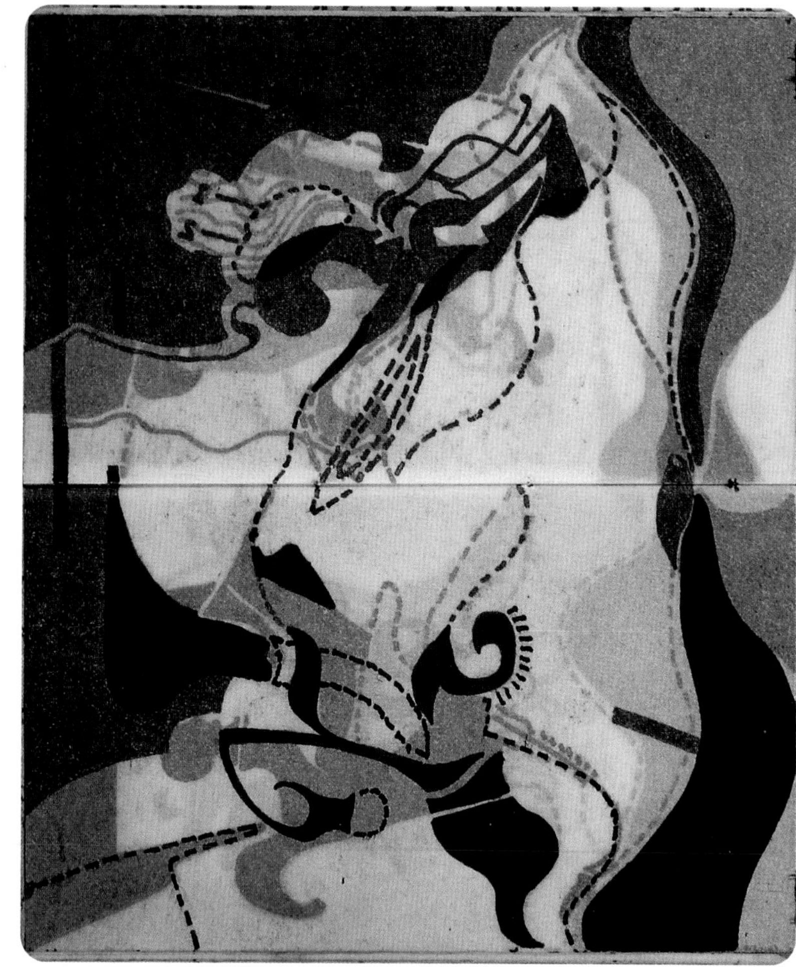

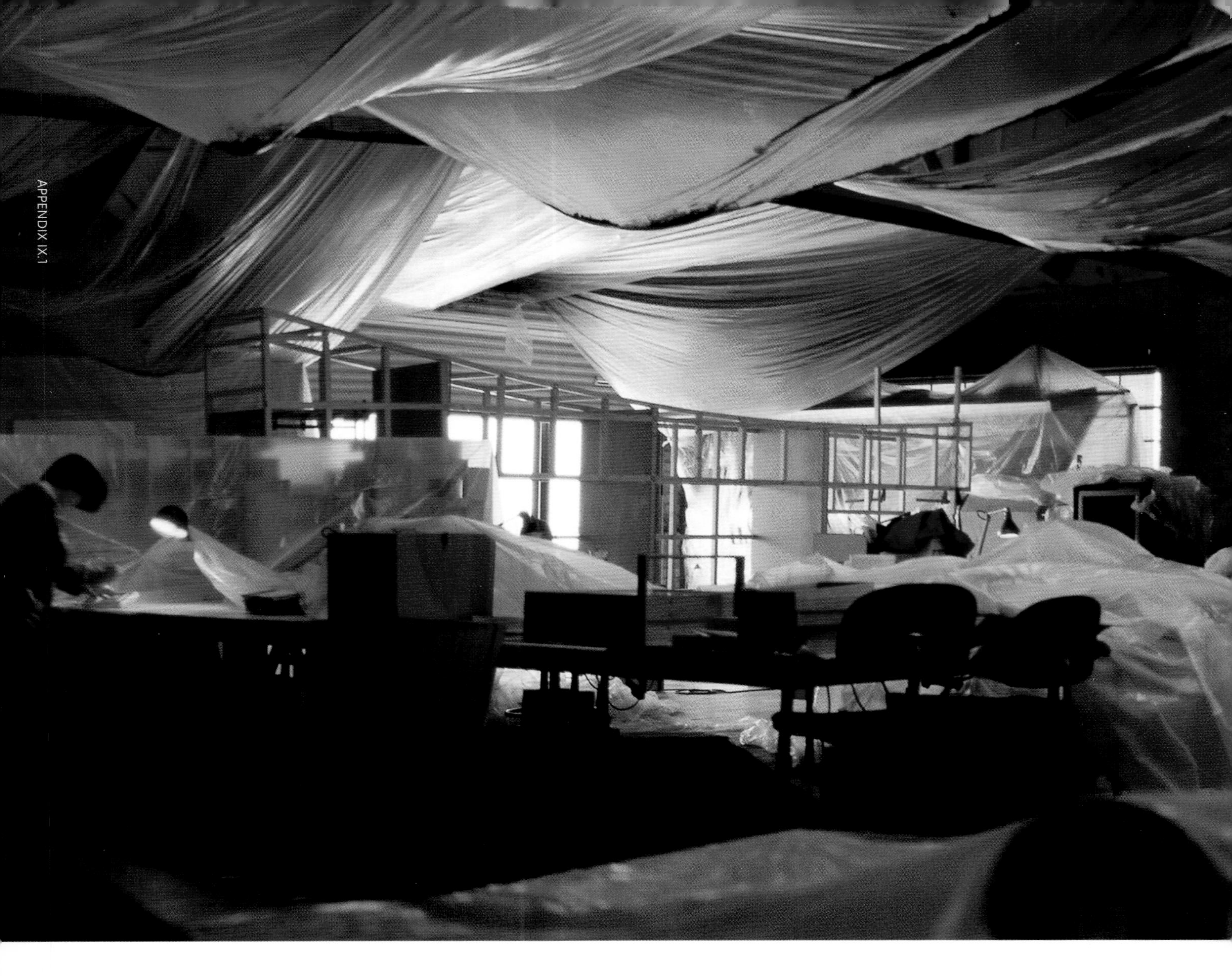

X. HIPPOCAMPUS

As he walked, Stillman did not look up. His eyes were permanently fixed on the pavement, as though he were searching for something. Indeed, every now and then he would stoop down, pick some object off the ground, and examine it closely, turning it over in his hand. It made Quinn think of an archeologist inspecting a shard of some prehistoric ruin. Occasionally after pouring over an object in this way, Stillman would toss it back onto the sidewalk. But more often than not he would open his bag and lay the object gently inside it. Then, reaching into one of his coat pockets, he would remove a small red notebook — similar to Quinn's but smaller — and write in it with great concentration for a minute or two. Having completed this operation, he would return the notebook to his pocket, pick up his bag, and continue on his way.

Other than picking up objects from the street, Stillman seemed to do nothing. Every now and then he would bump into someone and mumble an apology. Once a car nearly ran him over as he was crossing the street. Stillman did not talk to anyone, did not go into stores, did not smile. He seemed neither happy nor sad. Twice, when his scavenging haul had been unusually large, he returned to the hotel in the middle of the day and then reemerged a few minutes later with an empty bag. On most days he spent at least several hours in Riverside Park, walking methodically along the macadam footpaths or else thrashing through the bushes with a stick. His quest for objects did not abate among the greenery. Stones, leaves, and twigs all found their way into his bag. Once, Quinn observed, he even stooped down for a dried dog turd, sniffed it carefully, and kept it.

— from *City of Glass* by Paul Auster

Beyond the routine flashes of understanding, I see and see again the physical reality of the city — sometimes intentional or purposeful in some way, often totally random. The same place is never the same place but fragmented into always new aggregates, the consequence of collisions of other places, both interior and exterior, and always sooner or later provisional. Our understanding of the flow of past life into present subverts our senses. These cubic perceptions are time made apparent, juxtaposing reality and imagination. Chronological time is disrupted — a disruption asserting the subjectivity of our own memories and point of view, evolving an embryonic grammar of form.

Moving through Copenhagen, like Stillman, we translate the stream of time into a frozen field of space where things and events can be assimilated; we create narratives, linkages separate from current thoughts, and manipulate that which is not present. The model represents the received frozen elements into a singular memory event which fills the meat of the brain and gives rise to the spirit of the memory. Equivalent to the brain's hippocampus, the recollection is asystematic, not a record of events waiting to be unearthed as thought by Freud. Memory, above all else, is personal and subjective.

Samuel Johnson saw the difference between the mental behavior of humans and animals. He observed that animals have no equivalence of understanding, but have minds exactly adapted to their bodies. Humans, on the other hand, don't have their minds so efficiently matched. So few of the hours of life are filled up with objects adequate to the mind of man. We frequently lack present pleasure and employment, and so are forced to have recourse at any moment to the past and future for supplemental satisfactions. Memory becomes the ground from which human culture arises.[1] Johnson realized that memory not only recreates the past, but must be the source of the future as well. Memory makes us, consulting its table of facts; we project our future — what we expect it to look like.

As for the present, "It leaves us as it arrives, ceases to be present before its presence is well perceived, and is only known to have existed at all by the effects, more or less permanent, which it leaves behind. Therefore from the view before us or behind us."[2]

[1] Hilts, Philip J. *Memory's Ghost: The Nature of Memory and the Strange Case of Mr. M.* New York: Simon & Schuster, 1996.

[2] Ibid.

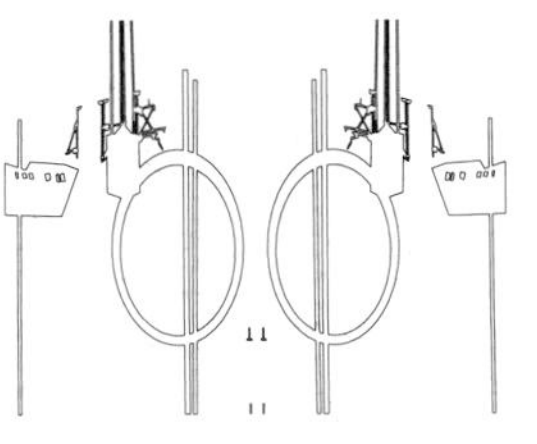

zx—010

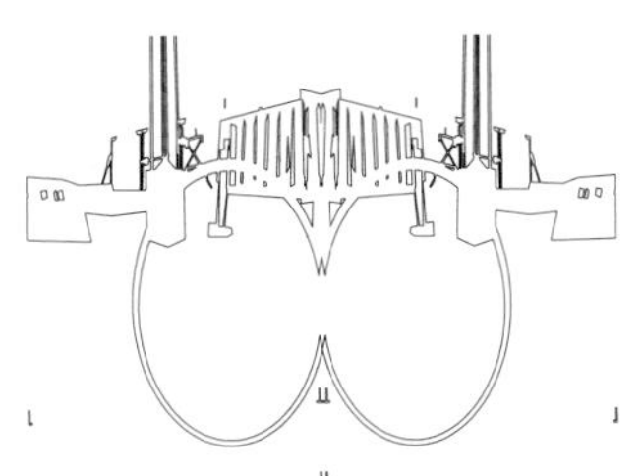

zx—020

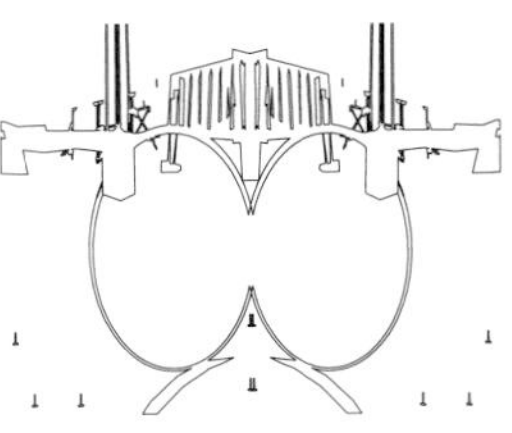

zx—030

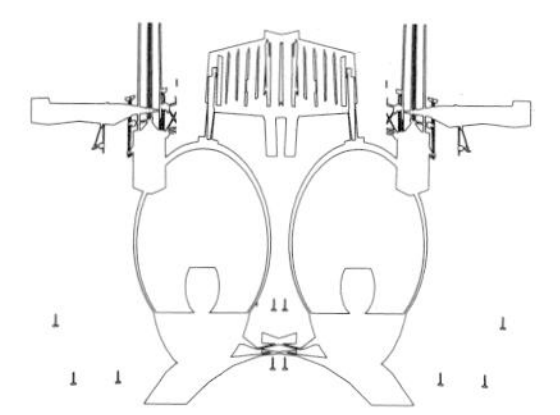

zx—040

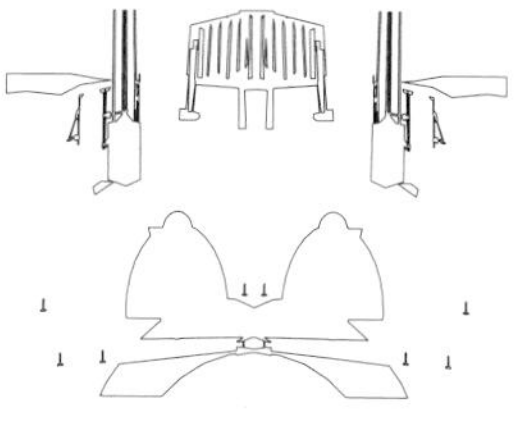

zx—050

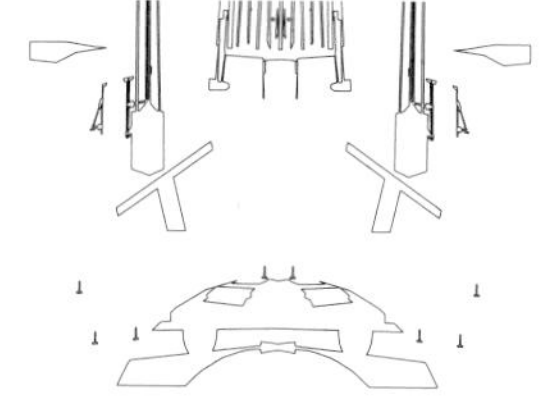

zx—060

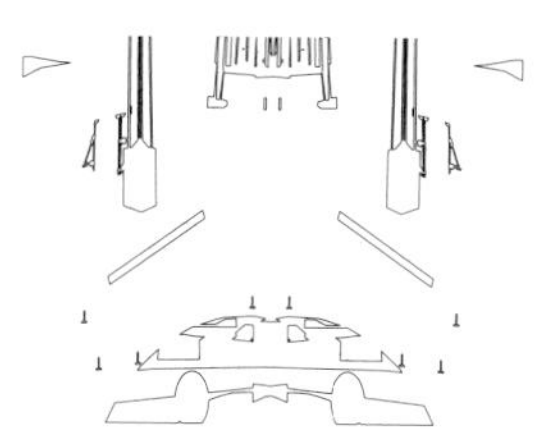

zx—070

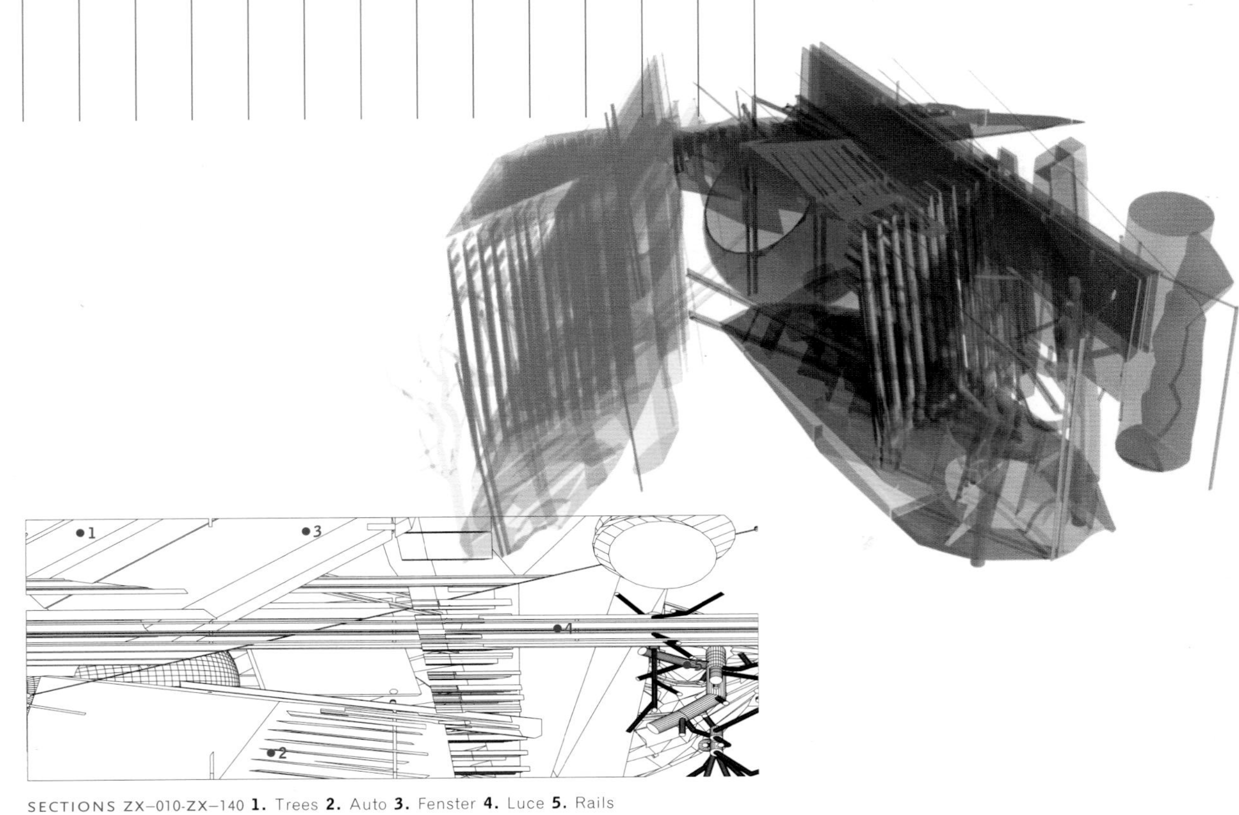

SECTIONS ZX–010-ZX–140 **1.** Trees **2.** Auto **3.** Fenster **4.** Luce **5.** Rails

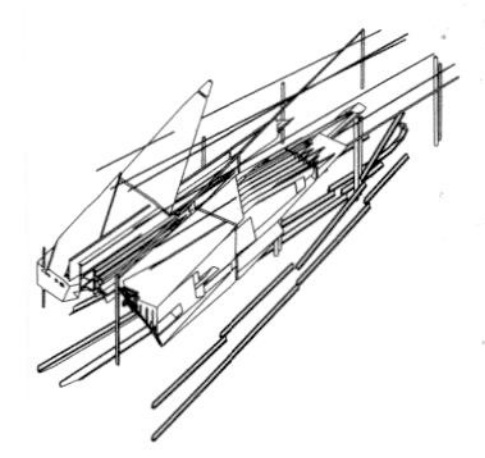

RAILS

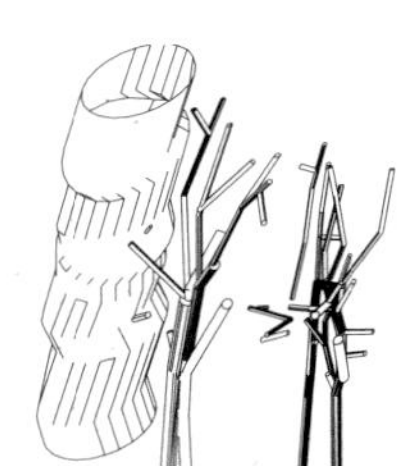

FLORA

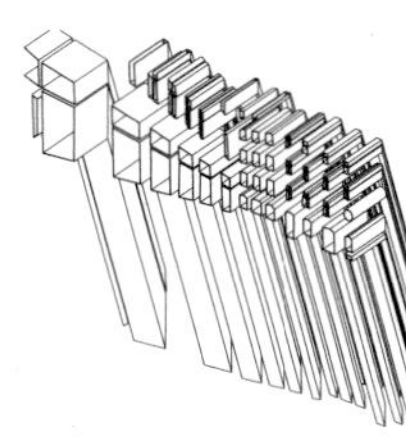

FENSTER

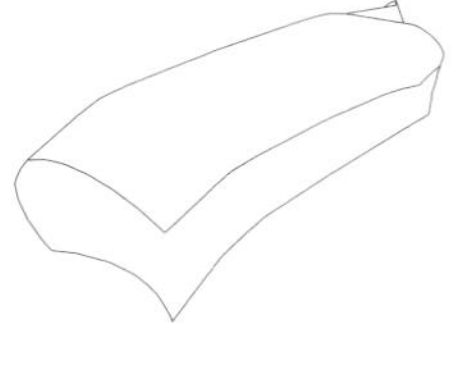

AUTO

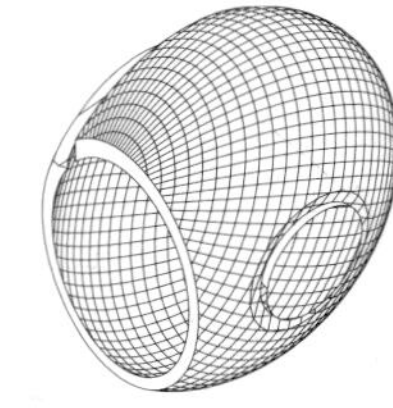

LUCE

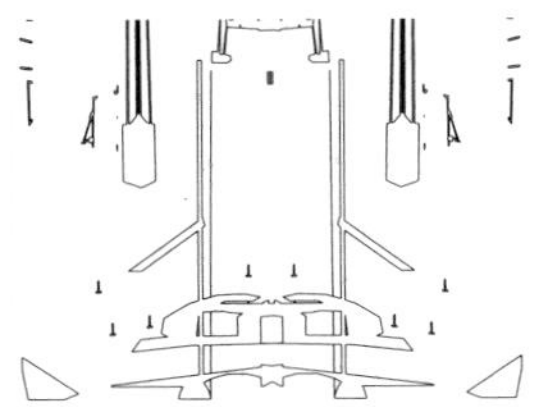

ZX—080

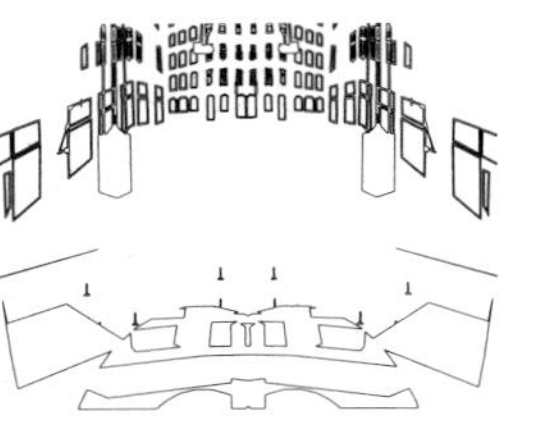

ZX—090

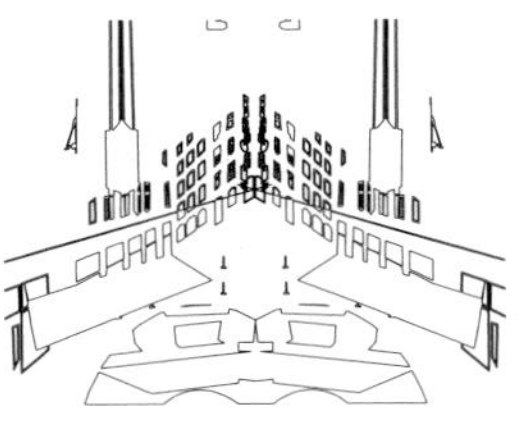

ZX—100

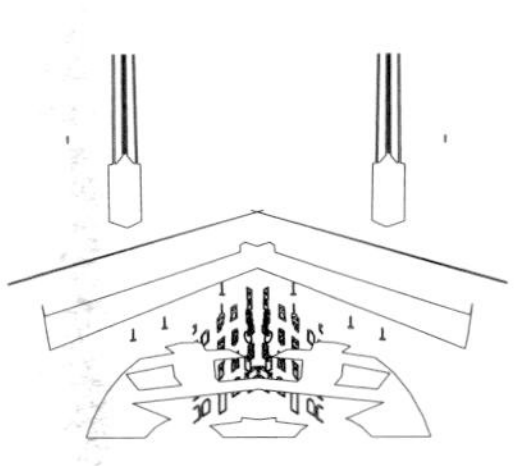

ZX—110

SECTIONS XY—010-XY—080 **1.** Tree **2.** Auto **3.** Fenster **4.** Luce

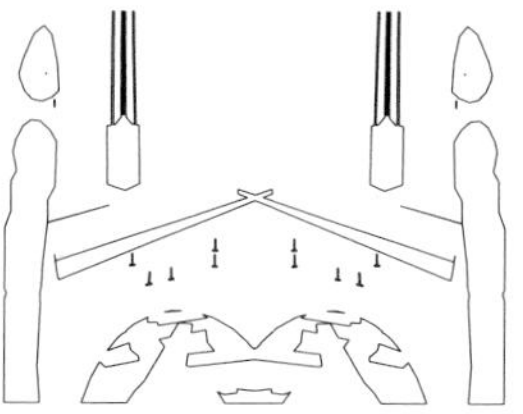

zx—120

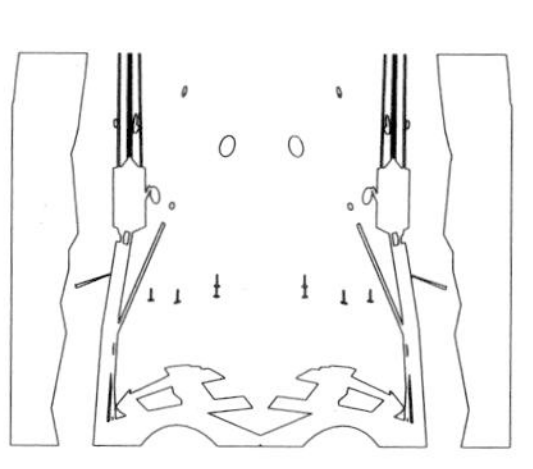

zx—130

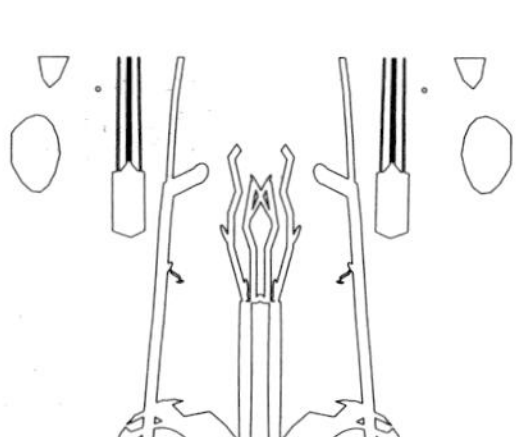

zx—140

{GUIDE WIRES}
{STEEL ARMATURE W/INSULATION}
{HORIZONTAL SLATS}
{RAIL (CURVED)}
{TREE SUPPORT}
{PEDESTRIAN WALKWAY}
{RAIL (MULTIPLE)}
{TREE (DECIDUOUS)}
{EXHAUST STACK}
{RAIL CROSSING}
{CIGARETTE BUTT(GAULOISE)}
{TREE (SMALL)}
{CARS(PARKED)}
{RAIL (MULTIPLE)}
{TREE (LARGE)}
{METAL PYLON (W/GRAFFITI)}

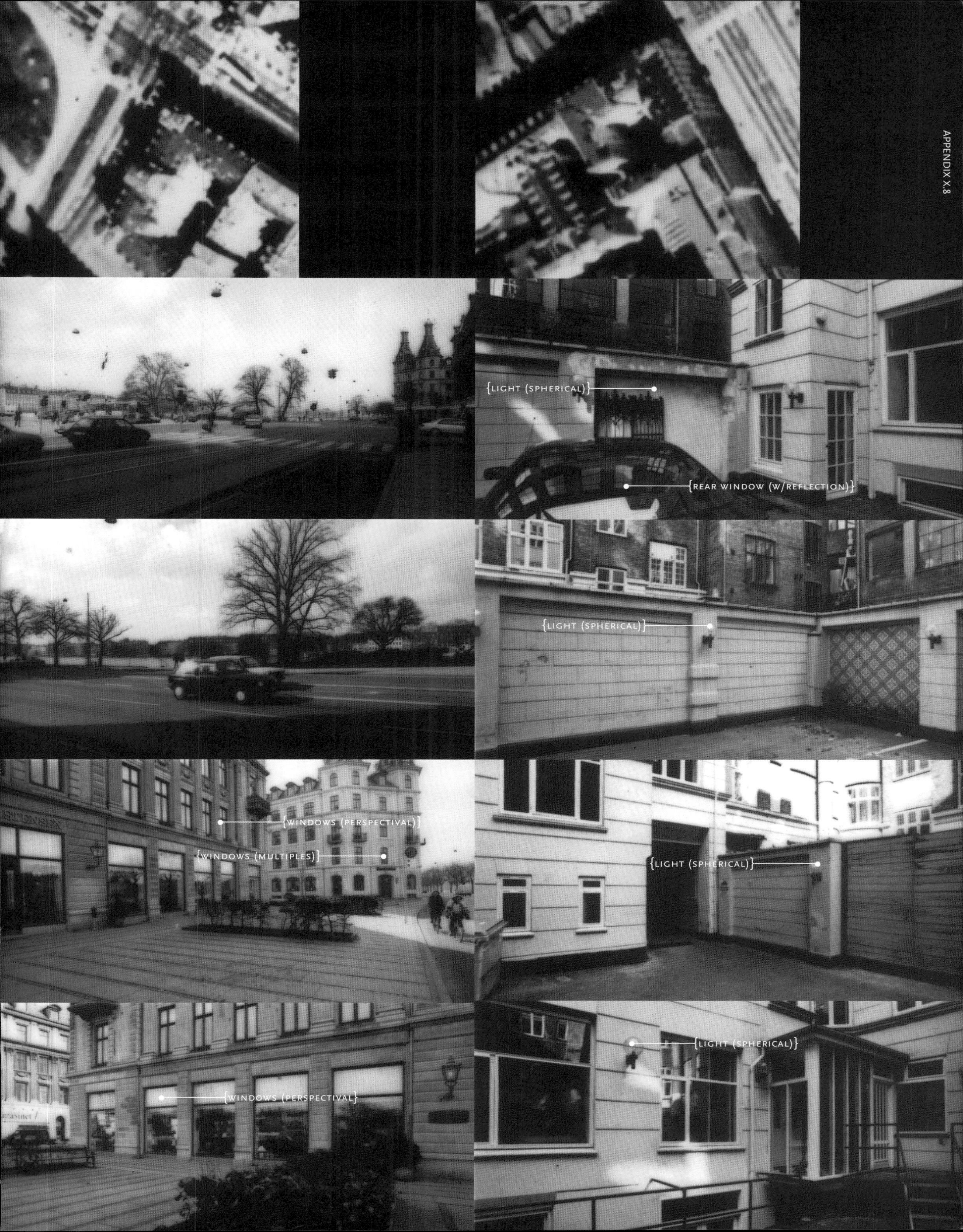
{LIGHT (SPHERICAL)}
{REAR WINDOW (W/REFLECTION)}
{LIGHT (SPHERICAL)}
{WINDOWS (PERSPECTIVAL)}
{WINDOWS (MULTIPLES)}
{LIGHT (SPHERICAL)}
{WINDOWS (PERSPECTIVAL}
{LIGHT (SPHERICAL)}

XY—010

XY—020

XY—030

XY—040

XY—070
XY—080

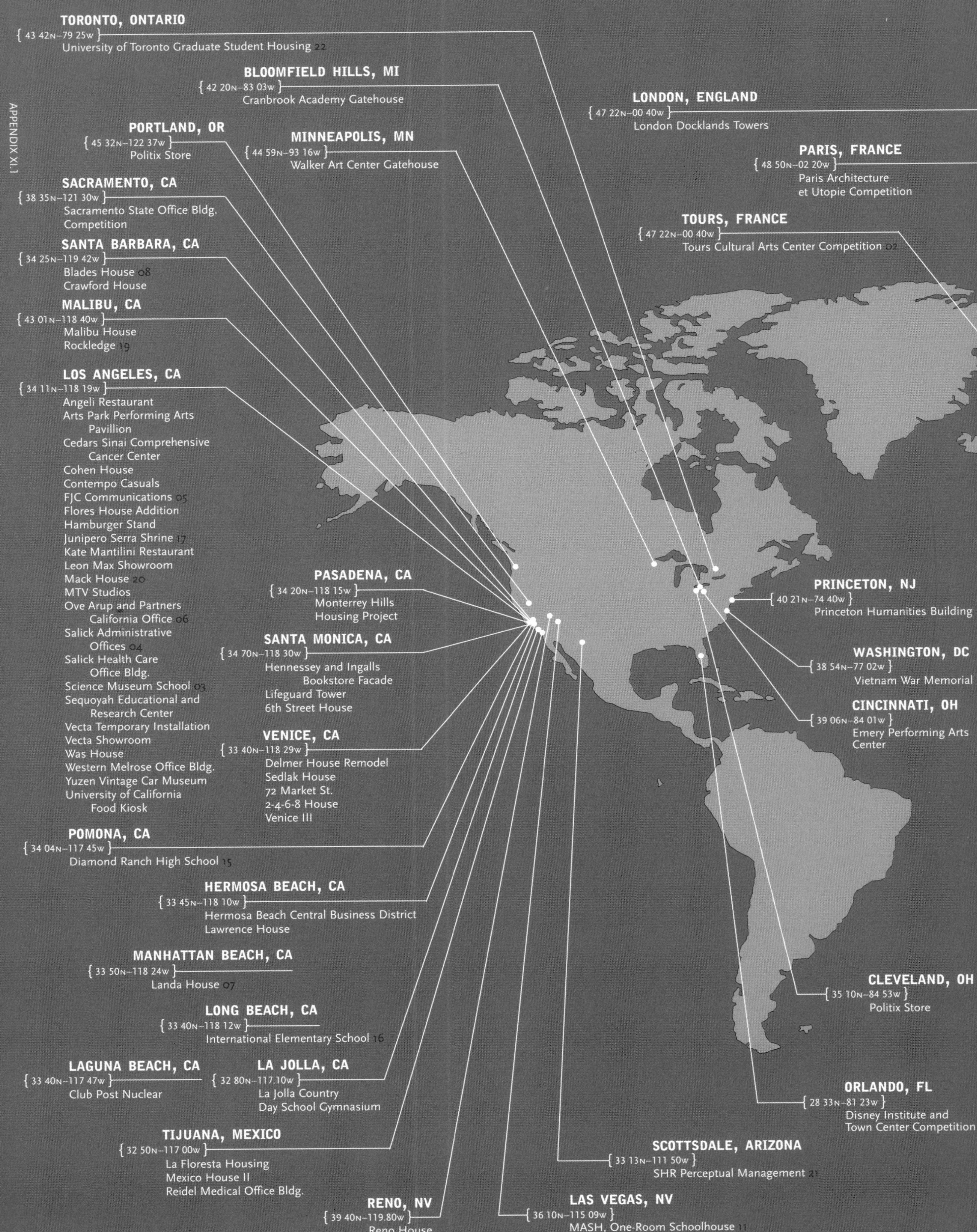

TORONTO, ONTARIO
{ 43 42N–79 25w }
University of Toronto Graduate Student Housing 22
BLOOMFIELD HILLS, MI
{ 42 20N–83 03w }
Cranbrook Academy Gatehouse
LONDON, ENGLAND
{ 47 22N–00 40w }
London Docklands Towers
PORTLAND, OR
{ 45 32N–122 37w }
Politix Store
MINNEAPOLIS, MN
{ 44 59N–93 16w }
Walker Art Center Gatehouse
PARIS, FRANCE
{ 48 50N–02 20w }
Paris Architecture
et Utopie Competition
SACRAMENTO, CA
{ 38 35N–121 30w }
Sacramento State Office Bldg.
Competition
TOURS, FRANCE
{ 47 22N–00 40w }
Tours Cultural Arts Center Competition 02
SANTA BARBARA, CA
{ 34 25N–119 42w }
Blades House 08
Crawford House
MALIBU, CA
{ 43 01N–118 40w }
Malibu House
Rockledge 19
LOS ANGELES, CA
{ 34 11N–118 19w }
Angeli Restaurant
Arts Park Performing Arts
Pavillion
Cedars Sinai Comprehensive
Cancer Center
Cohen House
Contempo Casuals
FJC Communications 05
Flores House Addition
Hamburger Stand
Junipero Serra Shrine 17
Kate Mantilini Restaurant
Leon Max Showroom
Mack House 20
MTV Studios
Ove Arup and Partners
California Office 06
Salick Administrative
Offices 04
Salick Health Care
Office Bldg.
Science Museum School 03
Sequoyah Educational and
Research Center
Vecta Temporary Installation
Vecta Showroom
Was House
Western Melrose Office Bldg.
Yuzen Vintage Car Museum
University of California
Food Kiosk
PASADENA, CA
{ 34 20N–118 15w }
Monterrey Hills
Housing Project
PRINCETON, NJ
{ 40 21N–74 40w }
Princeton Humanities Building
SANTA MONICA, CA
{ 34 70N–118 30w }
Hennessey and Ingalls
Bookstore Facade
Lifeguard Tower
6th Street House
WASHINGTON, DC
{ 38 54N–77 02w }
Vietnam War Memorial
CINCINNATI, OH
{ 39 06N–84 01w }
Emery Performing Arts
Center
VENICE, CA
{ 33 40N–118 29w }
Delmer House Remodel
Sedlak House
72 Market St.
2-4-6-8 House
Venice III
POMONA, CA
{ 34 04N–117 45w }
Diamond Ranch High School 15
HERMOSA BEACH, CA
{ 33 45N–118 10w }
Hermosa Beach Central Business District
Lawrence House
MANHATTAN BEACH, CA
{ 33 50N–118 24w }
Landa House 07
CLEVELAND, OH
{ 35 10N–84 53w }
Politix Store
LONG BEACH, CA
{ 33 40N–118 12w }
International Elementary School 16
LAGUNA BEACH, CA
{ 33 40N–117 47w }
Club Post Nuclear
LA JOLLA, CA
{ 32 80N–117.10w }
La Jolla Country
Day School Gymnasium
ORLANDO, FL
{ 28 33N–81 23w }
Disney Institute and
Town Center Competition
TIJUANA, MEXICO
{ 32 50N–117 00w }
La Floresta Housing
Mexico House II
Reidel Medical Office Bldg.
SCOTTSDALE, ARIZONA
{ 33 13N–111 50w }
SHR Perceptual Management 21
RENO, NV
{ 39 40N–119.80w }
Reno House
LAS VEGAS, NV
{ 36 10N–115 09w }
MASH, One-Room Schoolhouse 11

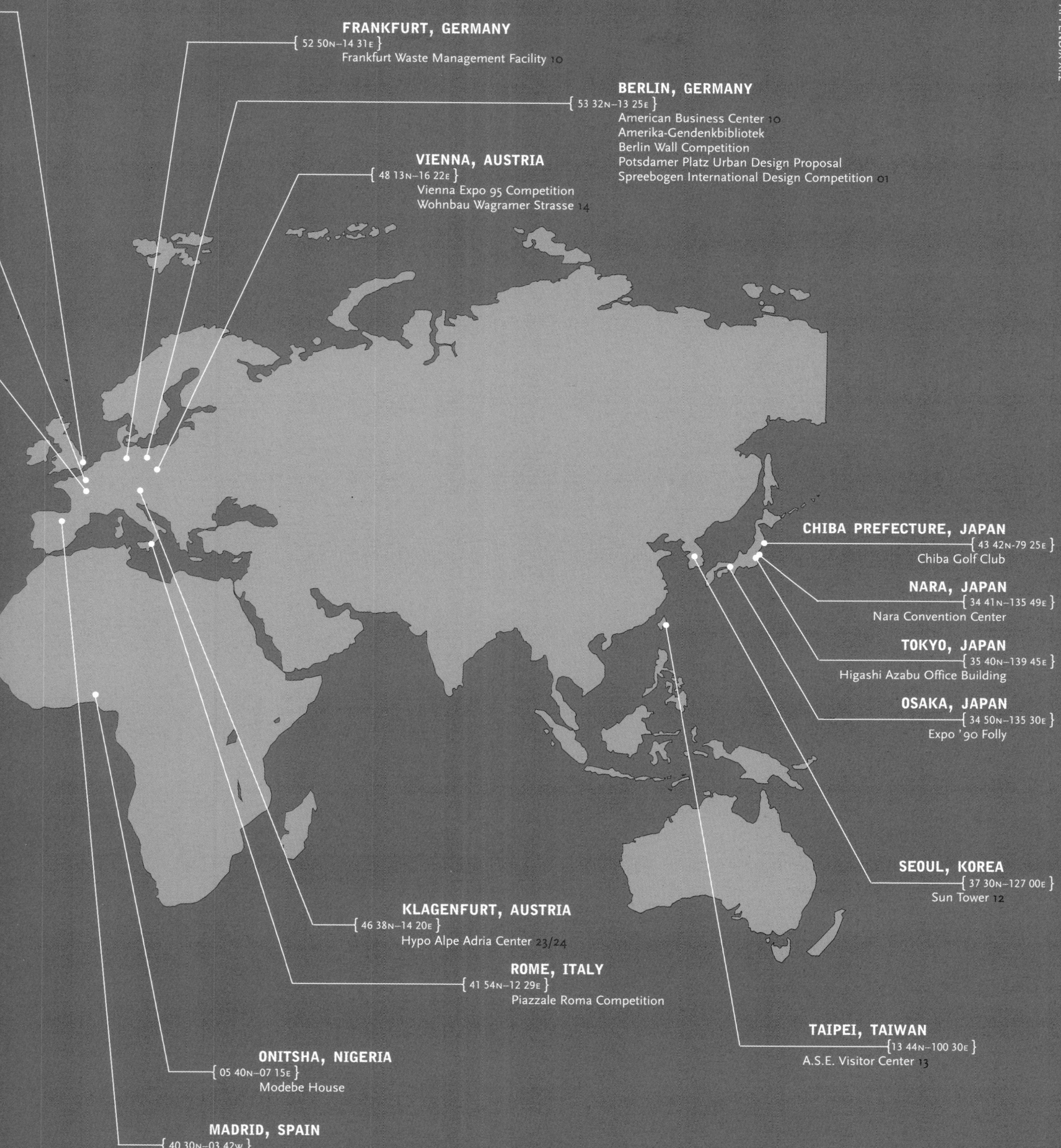
FRANKFURT, GERMANY
{ 52 50N–14 31E }
Frankfurt Waste Management Facility 10
BERLIN, GERMANY
{ 53 32N–13 25E }
American Business Center 10
Amerika-Gendenkbibliotek
Berlin Wall Competition
Potsdamer Platz Urban Design Proposal
Spreebogen International Design Competition 01
VIENNA, AUSTRIA
{ 48 13N–16 22E }
Vienna Expo 95 Competition
Wohnbau Wagramer Strasse 14
CHIBA PREFECTURE, JAPAN
{ 43 42N–79 25E }
Chiba Golf Club
NARA, JAPAN
{ 34 41N–135 49E }
Nara Convention Center
TOKYO, JAPAN
{ 35 40N–139 45E }
Higashi Azabu Office Building
OSAKA, JAPAN
{ 34 50N–135 30E }
Expo '90 Folly
SEOUL, KOREA
{ 37 30N–127 00E }
Sun Tower 12
KLAGENFURT, AUSTRIA
{ 46 38N–14 20E }
Hypo Alpe Adria Center 23/24
ROME, ITALY
{ 41 54N–12 29E }
Piazzale Roma Competition
TAIPEI, TAIWAN
{13 44N–100 30E }
A.S.E. Visitor Center 13
ONITSHA, NIGERIA
{ 05 40N–07 15E }
Modebe House
MADRID, SPAIN
{ 40 30N–03 42W }
Museo Del Prado 18

1971

Pablo Neruda is awarded the Nobel Prize in literatur
Bangladeshi war of independence
Greenpeace is founde
Apollo 14 lands on the moon
Woody Allen, *Bananas*
Bernardo Bertolucci, *The Conformist*
Jim Morrison
Peter Bogdanovitch, *The Last Picture Sho*
Werner Herzog, *Aguirre: The Wrath of God*
Stanley Kubrick, *A Clockwork Orange*
Sam Peckinpah, *Straw Do*
Luchino Visconti, *Death in Venice*
The Rolling Stones, *Sticky Fingers*
Chris Burden, *Sho*

1972

ɅORPHOSIS FOUNDED

U.S. planes bomb Haiphong and Hanoi

Polaroid camera is introduced

Apollo 17 becomes the last American mission to land on and explore the moon

Munich Olympics massacre leaves eleven Israeli athletes and five Palestinian terrorists dead

Harry S. Truman, and J. Edgar Hoover die

U.K. imposes direct rule on Northern Ireland

Ingmar Bergman, *Cries & Whispers*

Francis Ford Coppola, *The Godfather*

Herbert Ross, *Play it Again, Sam*

Luis Buñuel, *The Discreet Charm of the Bourgeoisie*

Alfred Hitchcock, *Frenzy*

Vito Acconci, *Seedbed*

David Bowie, *Ziggy Stardust*

Francis Bacon, *Three Studies of Figures on Beds*

Los Angeles Fine Art Squad (Terry Schoonhoven and Victor Henderson), *Isle of California*

Andy Warhol, *Mao II*

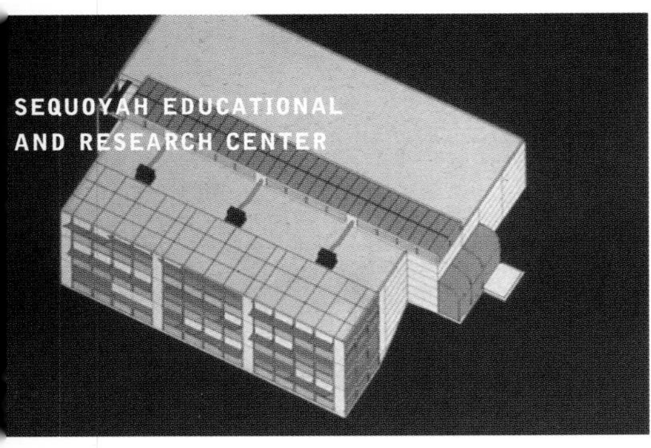

1973

Vice President Spiro Agnew resigns after pleading "no contest" to tax evasion charge

Manfredo Tafuri raises the issue of the relationship of class struggle to architecture

and defines the crisis of modern architecture as a crisis of the ideological function of architectur

Juan Péron is elected president of Argentina

U.S. troops leave Vietnam

Chilean president Salvador Allende Gossens is killed in a coup lead by General Augusto Pinoche

John Ford, Pablo Picasso, Robert Smithon, Edward Steichen

One hundred thousand people perish in Ethiopian famine

An eclipse of the sun lasts 195 minute

Push tab drink cans are introduced

Calf is born from a frozen embryo

Ingmar Bergman, *Scenes from a Marriage*

Bernardo Bertolucci, *Last Tango in Par*

Perry Henzell, *The Harder They Come*

Rainer Werner Fassbinder, *Fear Eats the Soul*

François Truffaut, *Day for Night*

Erica Jong, *Fear of Flying*

Thomas Pynchon, *Gravity's Rainbo*

E.F. Schumacher, *Small is Beautiful*

Kurt Vonnegut, *Breakfast of Champions*

Robert Smithon, *Amarillo Ram*

1974

President Nixon resigns over Watergate scandal
People magazine is launched
Patricia Hearst is kidnapped by Symbionese Liberation Army (SLA)
Stephen Hawking proposes his theory of black holes in space
"Four Days in May — White, Grey and Silvers" conference at UCLA
Ethiopian emperor Hailee Selassie is deposed
Louis Kahn, and Georges Pompidou die
Roman Polanski, *Chinatown*
John Cassavetes, *A Woman Under the Influence*
Ant Farm, *Cadillac Ranch*
Italo Calvino, *Invisible Cities*
Robert Pirsig, *Zen and the Art of Motorcycle Maintenance*
Joseph Beuys, *I Like America and America Likes Me*
Chris Burden, *Artist Crucified*
Gordon Matta Clark, *Splitting: Four Corners*
60 *Minutes*

1975

Pol Pot's Khmer Rouge capture Phnom Penh and establish control of Cambodi

Fall of Saigon: South Vietnam surrenders to North Vietnam

Generalissimo Francisco Franco dies at age eighty-two after thirty-six years of dictatorshi

First laboratory versions of antibodies usher in a new era in diagnostic and therapeutic medicine

Teamster Jimmy Hoffa disappears

Dimitri Shostakovich

Video Home Systems (VHS) is launched by JVC

Word processors begin to replace typewriters

Liquid crystal display (LCD) is introduced for calculator

Pier Paolo Pasolini is murdered

Robert Altman, *Nashville*

Milos Forman, *One Flew over the Cuckoo's Nes*

Keith Jarrett, *The Köln Conce*

1976

mmy Carter is elected president
Steve Jobs and Stephen Wozniak found Apple Computers
Fax machines cut transmission time from six minutes to three minutes per page
"Four Days in April — The Silvers" conference at UCLA
hn Cassavetes, *The Killing of a Chinese Bookie*
ritz Lang, Luchino Visconti, Howard Hughes Mao Zedong, Max Ernst, Alexander Calder, and Josef Albers die
Martin Scorsese, *Taxi Driver*
Lina Wertmuller, *Seven Beauties*
obert Wilson and Philip Glass, *Einstein on the Beach*
Christo, *Running Fence* (Sonoma and Marin counties, California)

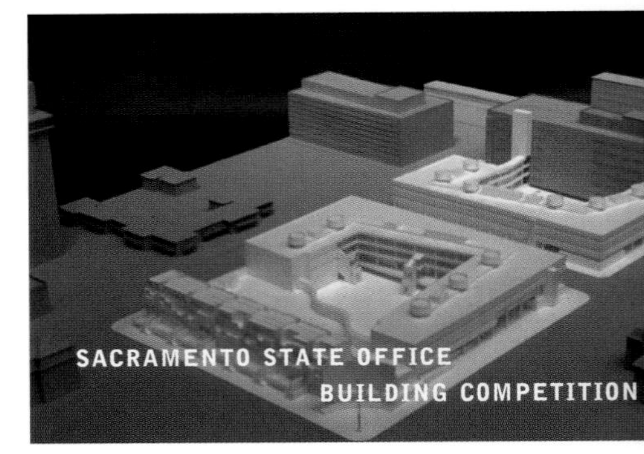

1977

Brezhnev becomes president of U.S.S.

Blue jeans sales at $500 million; Levi Strauss is market leader

Capital punishment in U.S. resumes after ten-year hiatu

Nicaraguan leftist guerillas seize the national palace in Managua and hold hundreds hostage for two days in a bid to oust dictator Anastasio Somoza Debayle

Charlie Chaplin, Groucho Marx, Vladimir Nabokov, Steve Biko, and Maria Callas di

Magnetic Resonance Imaging (MRI), a new diagnostic tool, is introduced

Bill Gates founds Microso

China lifts its ban on Beethoven and Shakespeare

Italo Calvino, *The Castle of Crossed Destinies*

Michel Foucault, *Discipline and Punishme*

Susan Sontag, *On Photography*

Woody Allen, *Annie Hall*

Wim Wenders, *The American Frie*

Luis Buñuel, *That Obscure Object of Desire*

John Kenneth Galbraith, *The Age of Uncertainty*

Alice Aycock, *The Beginnings of a Compl*

David Bowie and Brian Eno, *Low* and *Heroes*

Walter De Maria, *The New York Earth Room; The Lightning Field*

Jenny Holzer, *Abuse of Power Comes as No Surprise* (Times Square, New Yor

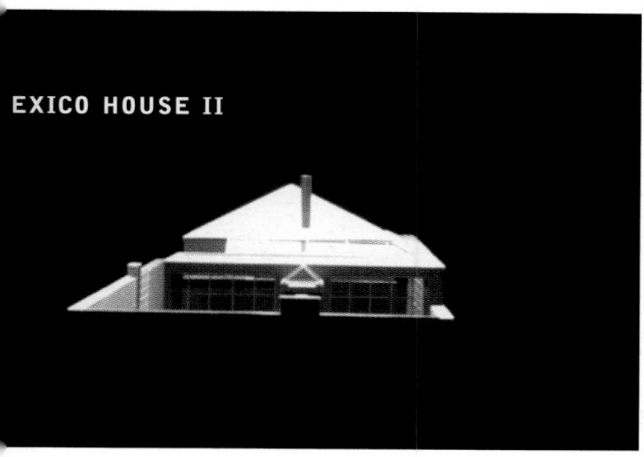

1978

enachim Begin and Anwar Sadat share Nobel Peace Prize

World's first test-tube baby is born

Ninety-eight percent of U.S. households own a television set

First recombinant DNA (human insulin) is produced in laboratory

First compact discs are developed

anco Brusati, *Bread and Chocolate*

Michael Cimino, *The Deer Hunter*

Brian Eno, *Ambient 1: Music for Airports*

John Irving, *The World According to Garp*

dward Said, *Orientalism*

Roland Barthes, *A Lover's Discourse: Fragments*

lian Schnabel, *The Patient and the Doctors*

1979

Ayatollah Khomeini returns to Iran following the exile of the sh

Partial core meltdown occurs at Three Mile Island power station

Sandinista rebels overthrow Nicaraguan dictator Anastasio Samoza Debayle

U.S. reports 21,456 murde

Cellular phones are invented in Sweden

Sony introduces the "Walkman"

John Wayne, Charles Mingu

Francis Ford Coppola, *Apocalypse Now*

Volker Schlöndorff, *The Tin Drum*

Hal Ashby, *Being The*

Manuel Puig, *Kiss of the Spider Woman*

Woody Allen, *Manhattan*

Paul Verhoeven, *Soldier of Orange*

Walter De Maria, *The Broken Kilome*

1980

Ronald Reagan is elected president
Solidarity is founded in Poland
U.S. spacecraft Voyager I and Voyager II (both launched in 1977) explore Saturn
El Salvador's leading human rights activist Oscar Armulfo Romero is murdered; civil war erupts and continues until 1992
In *Diamond v. Chakarabart,* court rules a man-made life form may be patented
Clyfford Still, Marshall McLuhan, Jean-Paul Sartre, Peter Sellers, Alfred Hitchcock, Henry Miller, and Roland Barthes die
Rollerblade, Inc. is founded
Leo Castelli solicits designs for private houses by international architects
John Lennon is shot to death in New York at age forty
Rainer Werner Fassbinder, *Berlin Alexander Platz*
Akiro Kurosawa, *Kagemusha*
David Lynch, *The Elephant Man*
Martin Scorsese, *Raging Bull*
Milan Kundera, *The Book of Laughter and Forgetting*
Laurie Anderson, *United States Part 1* (at the Orpheum, presented by The Kitchen)
Francesco Clemente, *He Teaches Emotions with Feelings*
Anselm Kiefer, *To the Unknown Painter*
Ted Turner launches CNN

1981

{THOM MAYNE MARRIES BLYTHE ALISON

Iran hostages are released January 20, the same day President Reagan takes offic

François Mitterand is elected president of France

Anwar Sadat is assassinated

AIDS is recognized as a distinct disease for the first time in the U.S

Columbia, the first reusable spacecraft, enters service

Bob Marley, Jacques Lacan

France's TGV train begins service from Paris to Lyon

World population reaches 4.5 billion, up from 2.5 billion in 195

IBM introduces the first personal computer

Eric Fischl, *Bad Bo*

Richard Serra, *Tilted Arc* (installed in NYC Federal Plaza)

MTV network is launche

1982

massive nuclear freeze demonstration in Central Park draws 500,000 to 1 million people

More than 25 million Americans smoke marijuana

irst artificial heart is implanted in a human

Paul Bartel, *Eating Raoul*

Peter Greenaway, *The Draughtman's Contract*

Ienry Fonda, Thelonious Monk, Ingrid Bergman, and Rainer Werner Fassbinder die

lan J. Pakula, *Sophie's Choice*

Ridley Scott, *Blade Runner*

Alice Walker, *The Color Purple*

Roland Barthes, *Empire of Signs*

aurie Anderson, *Big Science*

arbara Kruger, *You Rule by Pathetic Display*

1983

{SAM ALISON-MAYNE BORN

Arab suicide attacks on barracks in Beirut kill 241 American and 58 French personne

Israeli forces withdraw from Beirut

Drug traffickers develop crack (crystallized cocaine)

Computer "mouse" introduced by Apple

Nancy Reagan introduces "Just say No" sloga

Alain Robbe-Grillet, *La Belle Captive*

Paul Verhoeven, *The Fourth Man*

Luis Buñuel, Joan Miró, Buckminster Fuller

Phillip Glass score of Godfrey Reggio's *Koyaanisqatsi*

Jean-Jacques Beineix, *Diva*

Umberto Eco, *The Name of the Rose*

Paul Johnson, *Modern Tim*

1984

dira Gandhi is assassinated

Union Carbide leak in Bhopal, India, kills 2,000 people immediately, with as many as 10,000 deaths directly related to the incident; at least 200,000 and as many as 500,000 were injured

Reagan administration halts U.S. funding of birth control programs

'illiam Gibson coins the tern "cyberspace"

am Peckinpah, François Truffaut, Truman Capote, and Michel Foucault die

Laptop computers are introduced

Landmark Apple Macintosh commercial airs during Superbowl

Wim Wenders, *Paris, Texas*

Jim Jarmusch, *Stranger than Paradise*

hn Cassavetes, *Love Streams*

William Gibson, *Neuromancer*

ilan Kundera, *The Unbearable Lightness of Being*

1985

South Africa declares a state of emergency, giving police and the army almost absolute power in black townships; police may make arrests witho
warrants and hold people indefinitely without trial, but interracial marriages are legalized and some movie theaters are opened to patrons of all races
Mikhail Gorbachev becomes secretary of the Soviet Communist Party and calls for sweeping economic changes, indirectly criticizing his predecesso
Nicaraguan president Daniel Ortega Saavedra offers peace initiatives to contra rebels in February;
President Reagan responds that the contras are "the moral equal of our Founding Father
Ortega compares Reagan to Hitler, U.S. critics say Reagan is obsessed with Nicaragua, Marc Chagall, Orson Welle
and Congress votes to prevent Reagan from supplying the contras with anything but "non-lethal"
The world produces 1100 pounds of cereals and root crops per person, yet 800 million are malnourished
British scientists find a giant "hole" in the earth's ozone layer above Antarctica
A black hole is discovered at the center of the galaxy A series of earthquakes in Mexico City kills 5,000 to 10,000 peo
Lasers first used to clear clogged arteries Woody Allen, *The Purple Rose of Ca*
Akira Kurosawa, *Ran* Terry Gilliam, *Brazil* Lasse Halleström, *My Life as a D*
Paul Auster publishes the first story in his *New York Trilogy* (the three stories are published together in 199
Don DeLillo, *White Noise* The Starn Twins, *The Hor*

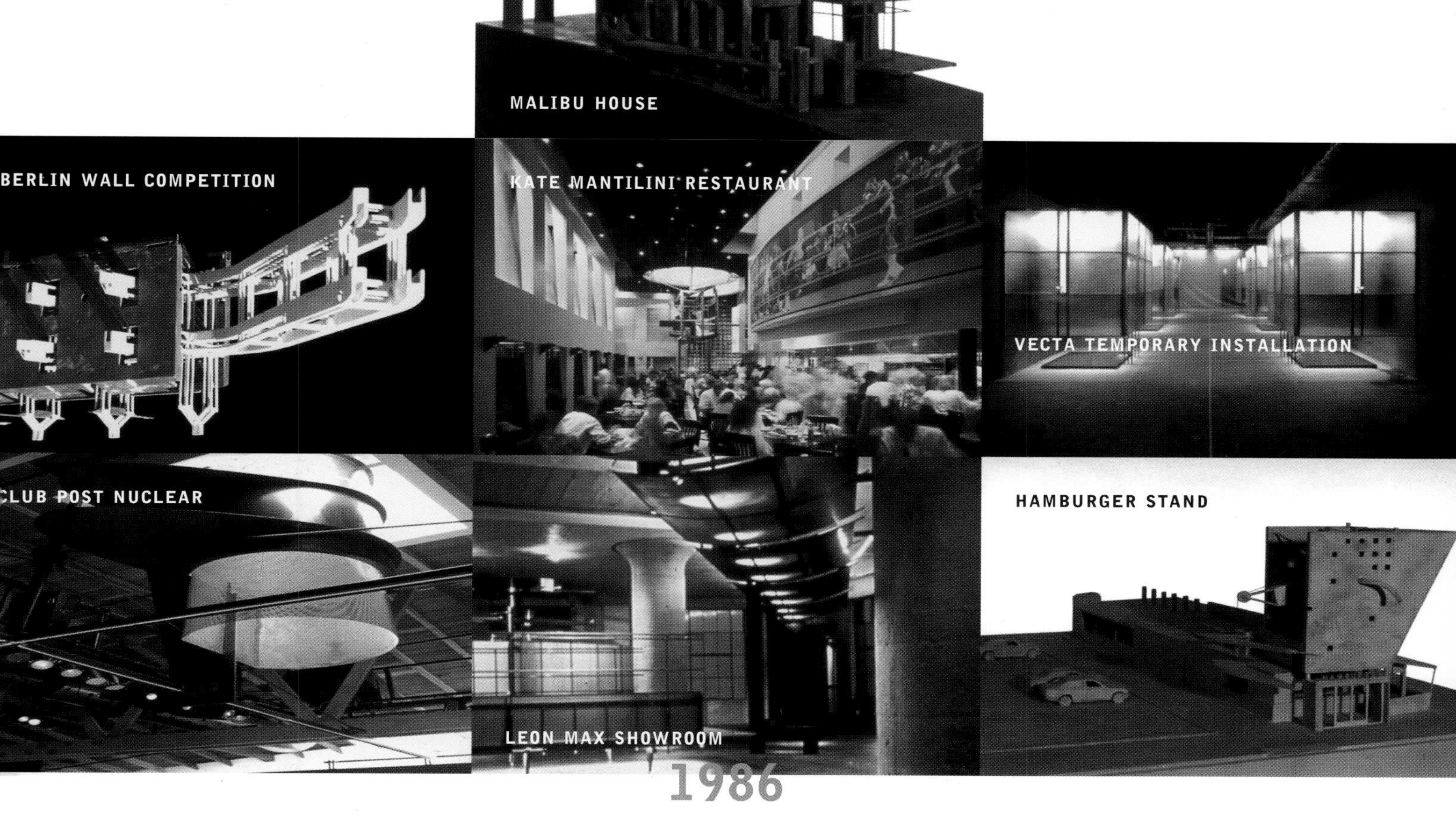

1986

The Iran-Contra Affair unfolds, beginning with the confession of American pilot Eugene Hasenfus after he was shot down on a covert mission over Nicaragua

The space shuttle Challenger explodes, killing all seven aboard

The U.S.S.R. launches the space station Mir

A meltdown occurs in a nuclear reactor at the Chernobyl power station near Kiev

Gorbachev introduces Glasnost

Joseph Beuys, Henry Moore, Jean Genet, and Andrei Tarkovsky die

Halley's comet is visible

"Joe Frank: Work in Progress" airs, KCRW Santa Monica

David Lynch, *Blue Velvet*

Andrei Tarkovsky, *The Sacrifice*

Woody Allen, *Hannah and Her Sisters*

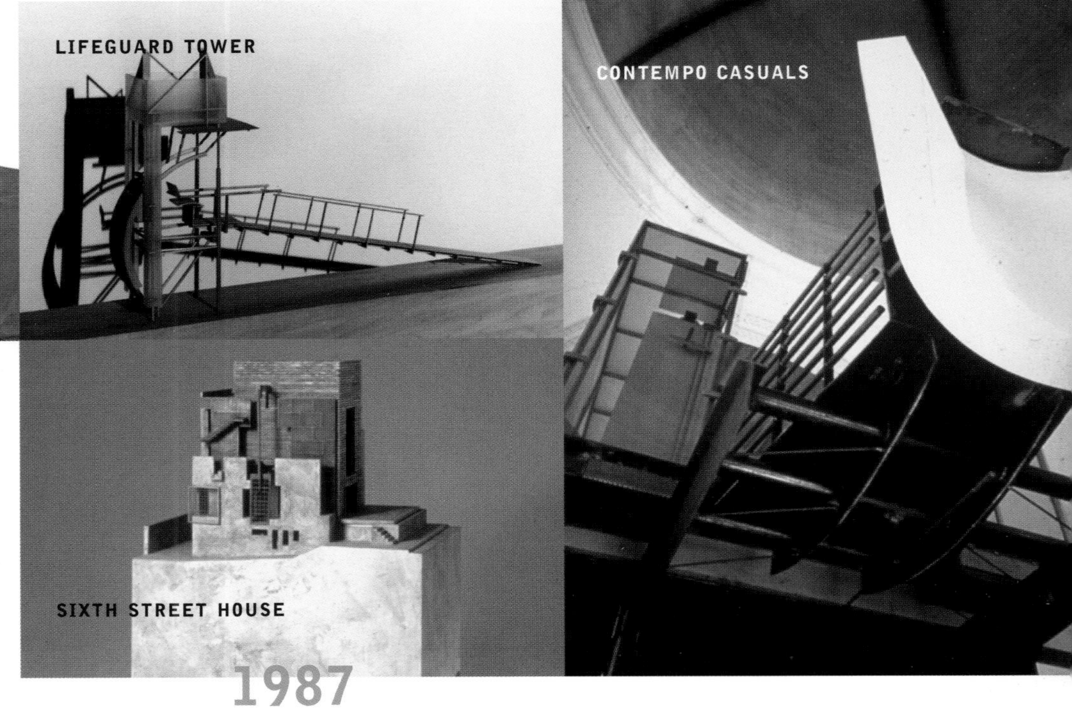

1987

{COOPER ALISON-MAYNE IS BORN}

Stockmarket crash of 1987 occurs on "Black Monday" (October 19)

Reagan and Gorbachev sign Intermediate Nuclear Forces (INF) treaty

Televangelists Jim Bakker and Jimmy Swaggert are publicly disgraced

Bernardo Bertolucci, *The Last Emperor*

Peter Greenaway, *Drowning by Numbers*

Andy Warhol dies

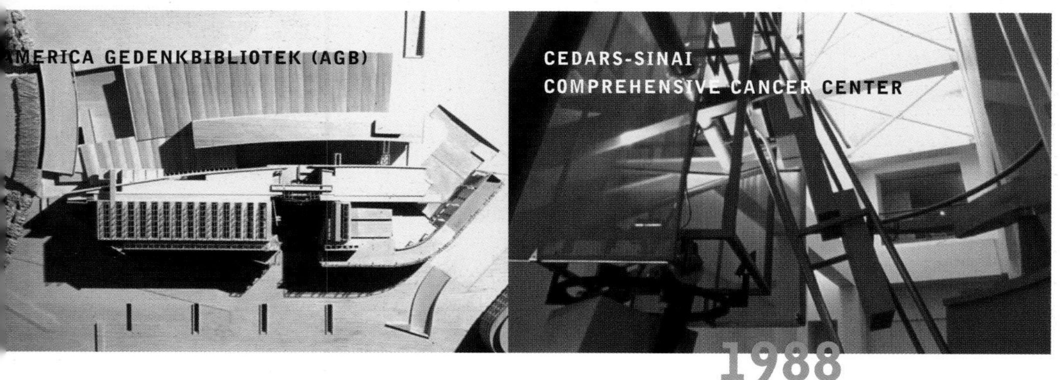

1988

eorge Bush is elected president
Afghan-Soviet war ends with the withdrawal of Soviet troops from Afghanistan
enile implants introduced
Lawrence Kasdan, *The Accidental Tourist*
Martin Scorsese, *Last Temptation of Christ*
Wim Wenders, *Wings of Desire*
om Wolfe's *The Bonfire of the Vanities* spends one year on bestseller list
Italo Calvino, *Six Memos for the Next Millennium*
ean Baudrillard, *America*

1989

Muslim extremists condemn Salman Rushdie's *Satanic Verses* as blasphemous and issue *Fatwa* against Rushdi

Demolition of the Berlin Wall begins November 9, Berlin's Brandenburg gate opens December 22

U.S. Supreme court rules five to four that burning the American flag is a right protected under the First Amendmen

Los Angeles Herald Examiner ceases publication after eighty-six years

The Exxon Valdez spills 240,000 barrels of oil into Prince William Sound, the worst U.S. tanker spill to dat

John Cassavetes and Salvador Dali di

Nicolai Ceausescu, president of Romania, and his wife, Elena, are execute by firing squad after being secretly captured and tried while attempting to flee the country

One hundred thousand people protest in Tiananmen Square; public executions follow

Guiseppe Tornatore, *Cinema Paradiso*

Edward Zwick, *Glor*

Peter Greenaway, *The Cook, The Thief, His Wife and Her Lover*

Woody Allen, *Crimes and Misdemeanor*

Sculptor Richard Serra's work *Tilted Arc* is removed from New York's Federal Plaz

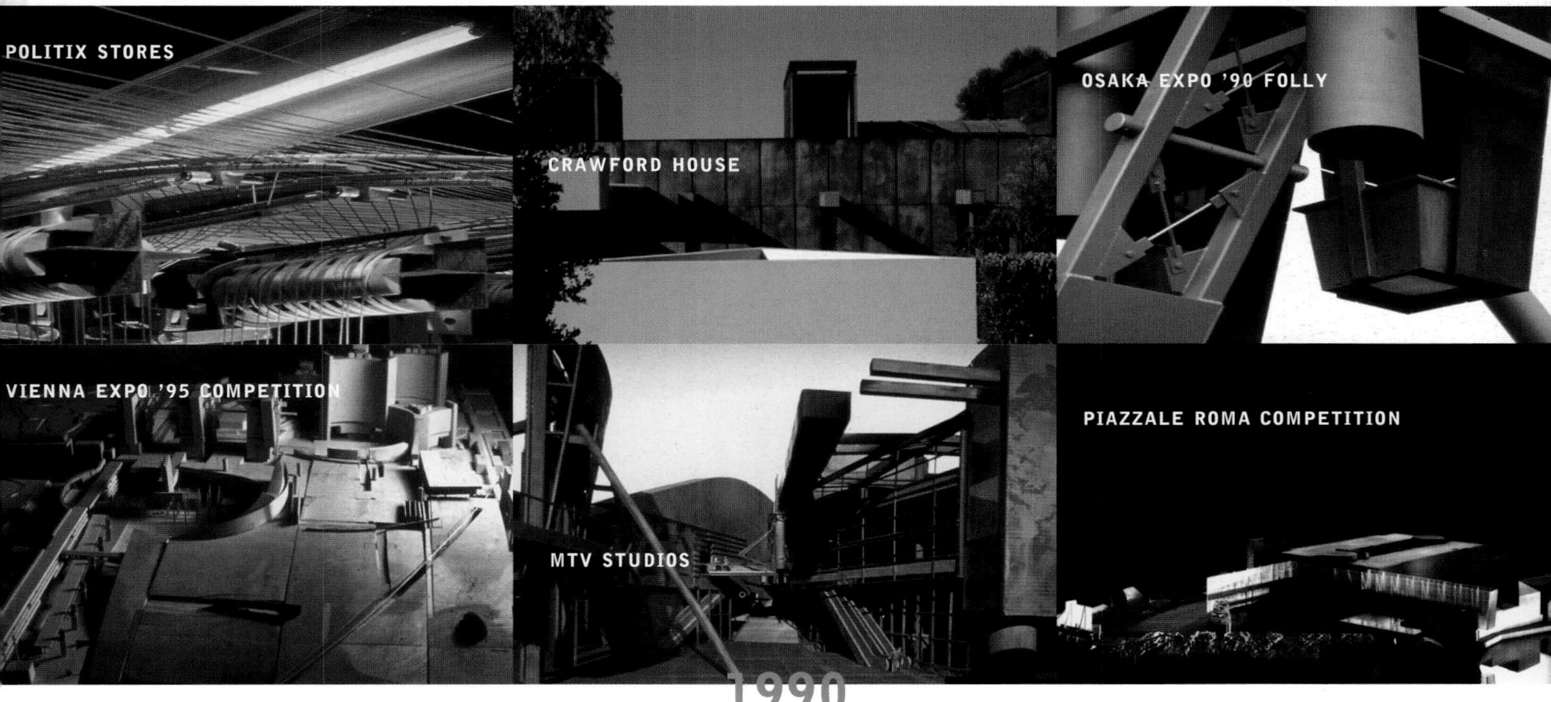

1990

Germany reunites after forty-three years of separation

Boris Yeltsin is elected president of Russian Republic

Nelson Mandela is freed after twenty-one years of imprisonment

Iraqi forces invade Kuwait after Kuwait refuses to pay compensation for allegedly drilling oil on Iraqi territory

In Nicaragua the Sandinistas are ousted in free elections after a decade of rule

Dr. Jack Kevorkian, "Dr. Death," performs his first assisted suicide, in his 1968 VW van

Canadian scientists determine that killer whales "speak" a number of different languages and dialects

Camille Paglia, *Sexual Personae*

Thomas Pynchon, *Vineland*

Mike Davis, *City of Quartz*

Rebecca Horn, *Buster's Window*

Anselm Kiefer, *Breaking of the Vessels* (at the Museum of Contemporary Art in Berlin)

Los Angeles Art Festival

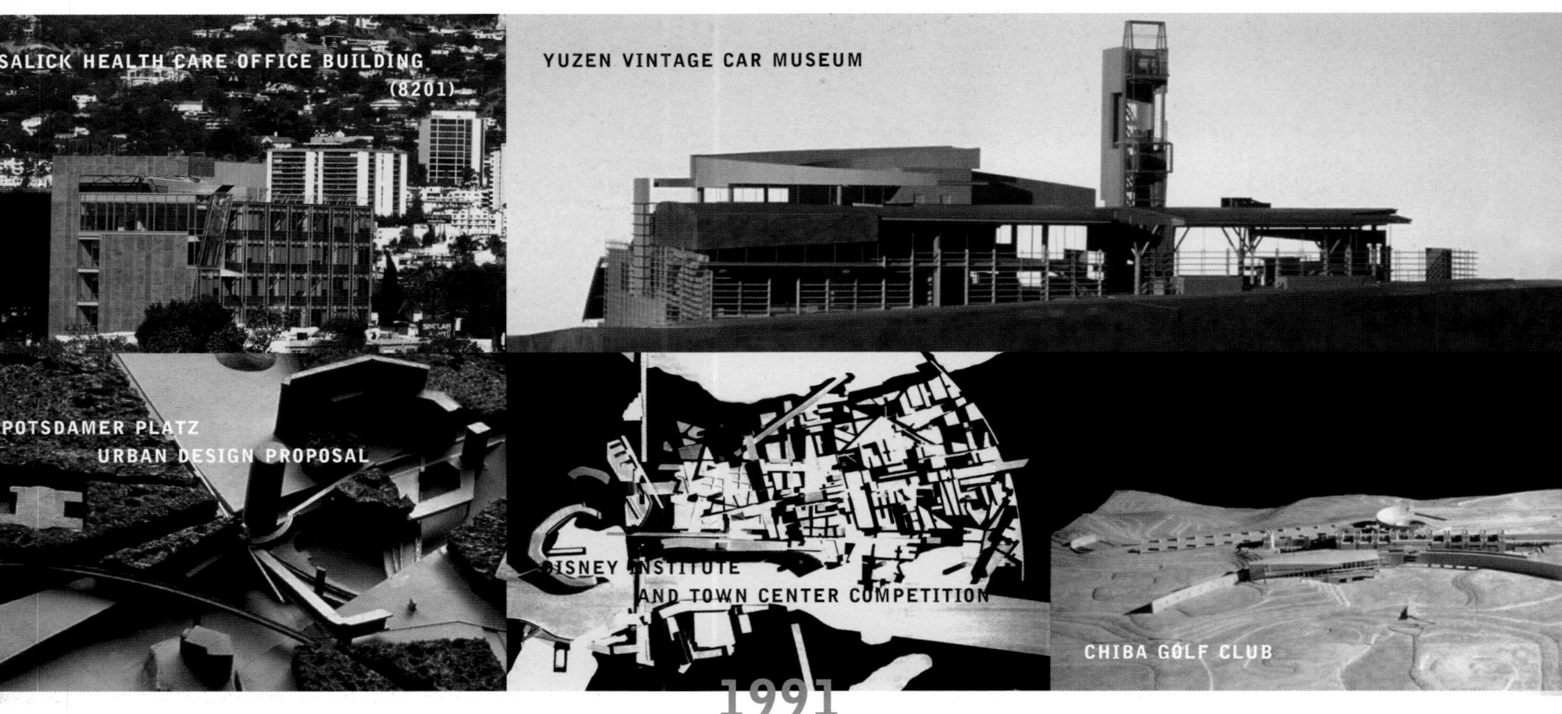

1991

Germany's Bundestag votes to move the nation's capital from Bonn to Berlin

Somali dictator Mohammed Siad Barre is deposed by rebel coalition forces; mass starvation and disease occur in large part because of factional blocking of international relief shipments

Operation Desert Storm culminates on February 24 and ends one hundred hours later as the world watches

Magic Johnson announces he has AIDS and is retiring from basketball

Robert Motherwell,

California has its fifth straight year of drought

World population reaches 5.5 billion

Gorbachev suspends Communist party, ending seventy-four years of Communist rule

Peter Greenaway, *Prospero's Books*

Ridley Scott, *Thelma & Louise*

Don DeLillo, *Mao II*

"High & Low: Modern art and Popular Culture" at the Museum of Modern Art in New York

Dennis Barry, director of Cinncinnati Art Center, is arrested for exhibiting photographs by Robert Mapplethorpe

André Serrano, *Piss Christ*

1992

Bill Clinton is elected president

South Africa's whites vote two to one to give President F.W. de Klerk a mandate to end white minority rule

Serbian "ethnic cleansing" against Muslims in Bosnia-Herzegovina continues

Los Angeles riots follow aquittal of police in Rodney King beating

Pope John Paul II says the Roman Catholic Church had been wrong to condemn Galileo 359 years earlier for claiming that the Earth revolves around the sun*

ames Stirling, and Francis Bacon die

* *Karl A. Popper, "Conjectures and Refutations: The Growth of Scientific Knowledge" (Harper and Row: New York, 1963), p.97*

"Once upon a time there was a famous scientist whose name was Galileo Galilei. He was tried by the inquisition, and forced to recant his teaching. This caused a great stir; and for well over two hundered and fifty years the case was continued to arouse indignation and excitement — long after public opinion had won its victory, and the church had become tolerant of its science."

Alfonso Arau, *Like Water for Chocolate*

Henryk Mikolaj Gorecki, *Third Symphony*

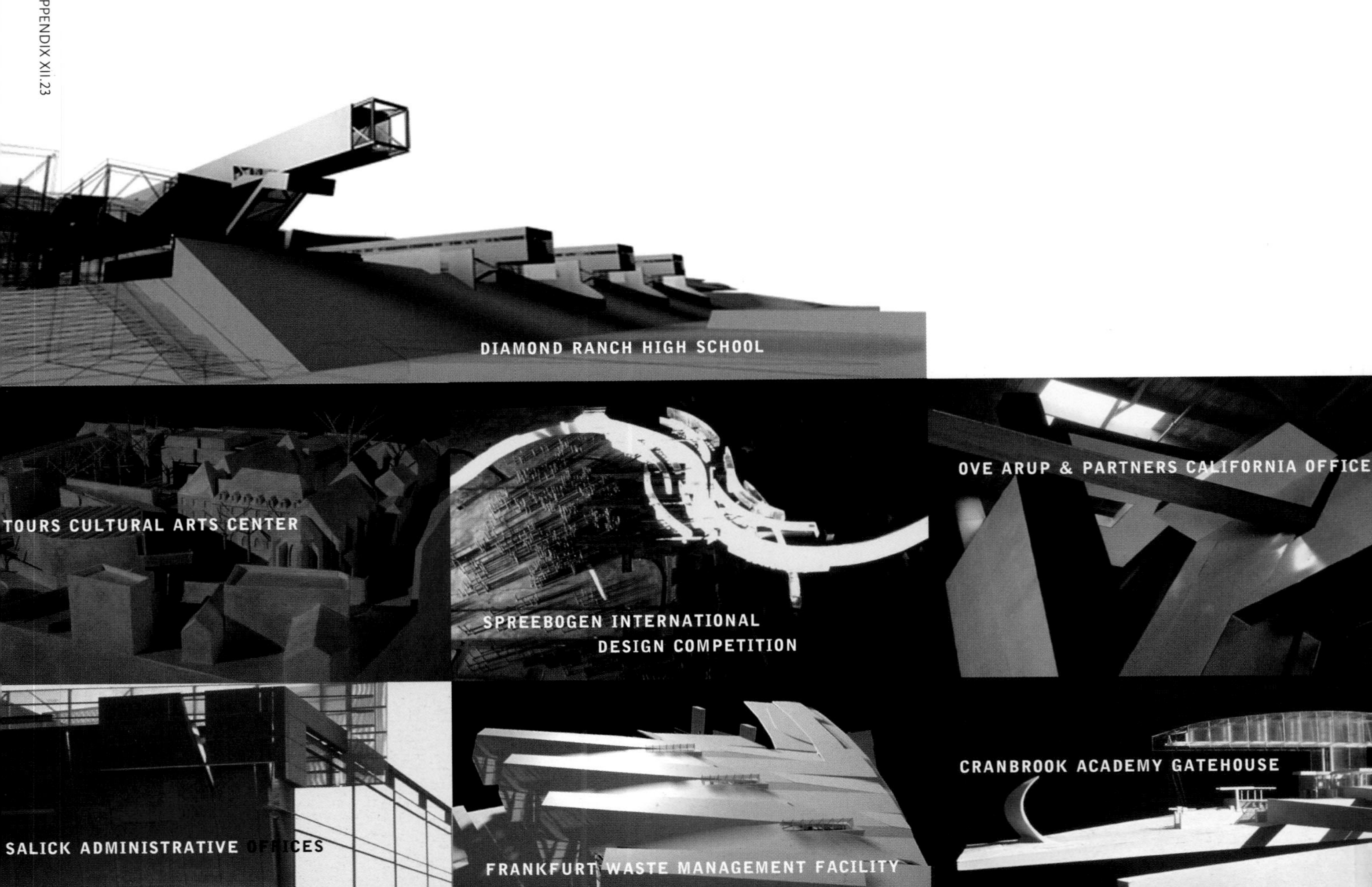

1993

After fifty-one-day siege, federal armed forces attack the Branch Davidian compound in Waco, Texas

Muslim terrorists bomb the New York World Trade Center

North American Free Trade Agreement (NAFTA) is ratified

Jane Campion, *The Piano*

Krzysztof Kieslowski, *Three Colors: Blue*; *Three Colors: White*

Richard Diebenkorn, Frederico Fellini

1994

RICHARD MAYNE'S THIRTIETH BIRTHDAY}

n Rwanda hardline Hutus kill 500,000 to 1 million minority Tutsis and moderate Hutus in retaliation against the deaths of Rwandan president Juvénal Habyarimana and Burundi president Cyprien Ntaryaira, whose plane was shot down over the Rwandan capital of Kigali

he Irish Republican Army announces a cease-fire

arl Popper, Elias Canetti, Jaqueline Kennedy Onassis, and Richard Milhous Nixon die

The number of people connected on the Internet (which had begun with a few linked computers in the 1960s) swells to 15 million

On January 17 an earthquake measuring 6.7 on the Richter scale strikes Los Angeles (see Appendix IX.)

uentin Tarantino, *Pulp Fiction*

Krzysztof Kieslowski, *Three Colors: Red*

an Baudrillard, *Simulacra and Simulation*

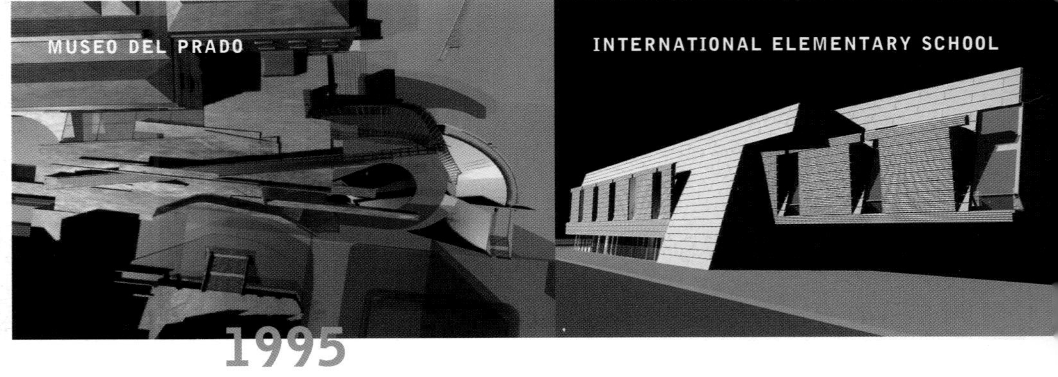

City Populations continue to expand: Tokyo-Yokohama Metropolitan area has 26.9 million people, Mexico City, 16.5; Sao Paolo, 16.
New York, 16.3; Bombay, 15.1; Shanghai, 13.5; Los Angeles, 12.4; Calcutta, 11.9;
Buenos Aires, 11.8; Seoul, 11.6; Beijing, 11.2; Osaka, 10.6; Lagos, 10.2; Rio de Janeiro, 10.1; Dehli, 9.9

Israel and the PLO sign a peace accord giving Palestinians self-determination on the West Bank

Opposing forces in former Yugoslavia sign a formal peace agreement after four years of fightin

Oklahoma City federal building bombing kills 167

Larry Clark, *KID*

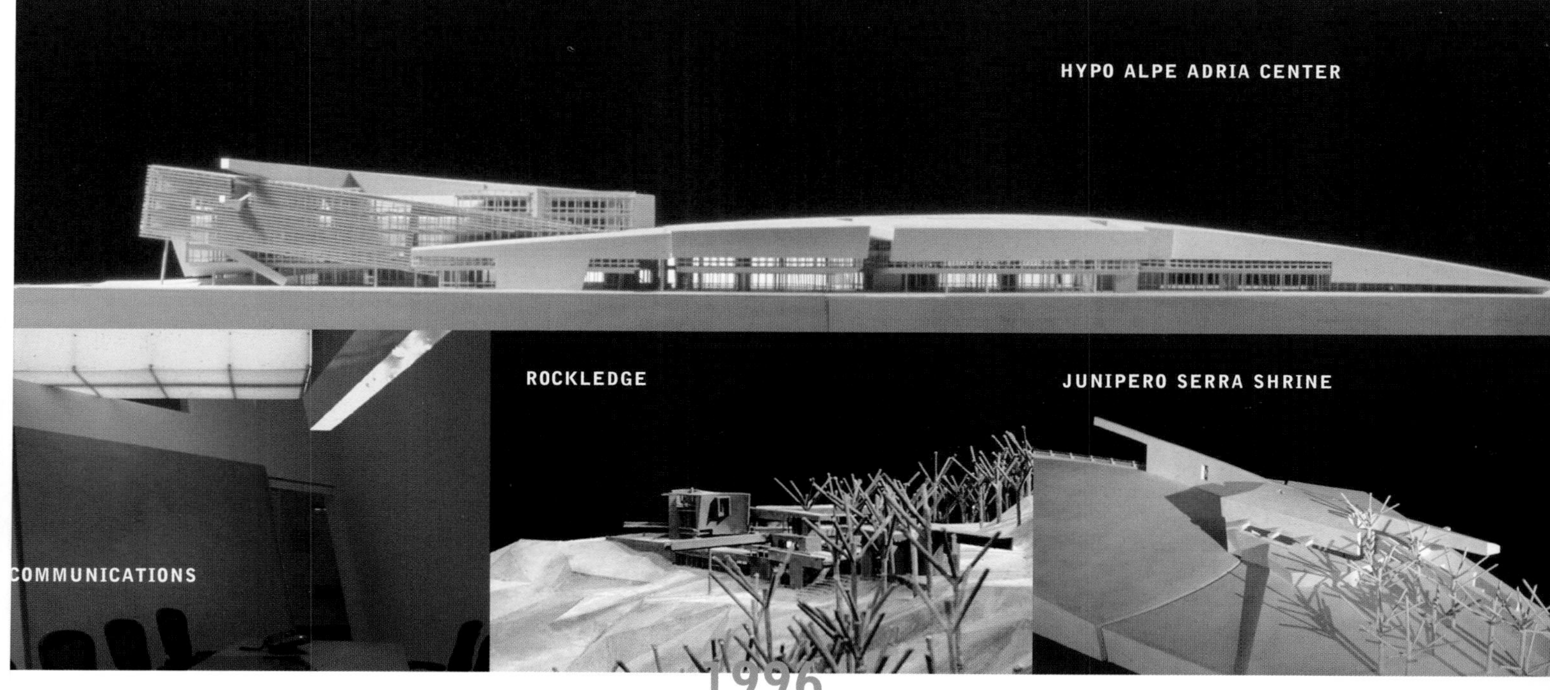

1996

non introduces the pocket-sized camera

Garry Kasparov, the world's greatest chess player that ever lived,

es a game of chess to an IBM computer called "Deep Blue"

Two federal appeals courts rule that Americans have a constitutional right to doctor-assisted suicide

nny Boyle, *Trainspotting*

Mike Leigh, *Secrets & Lies*

Lars van Trier, *Breaking the Waves*

François Mitterand dies

e Coen Brothers, *Fargo*

1997

"Pathfinder" gives earth first images of Mars topography

A sheep named Dolly becomes the first ever clone born from fully formed adult body parts:
Dr. Ian Wilmut takes a cell nucleus from a six-year-old ewe and duplicates it to create an identical twin

Peter Greenaway, *The Pillow Book*

Wim Wenders, *The End of Violence*

Allen Ginsberg, Mother Theresa, Paul Rudolph, and Aldo Rossi die

CUMMINS CHILD DEVELOPMENT CENTER

XIII. PROJECT CREDITS

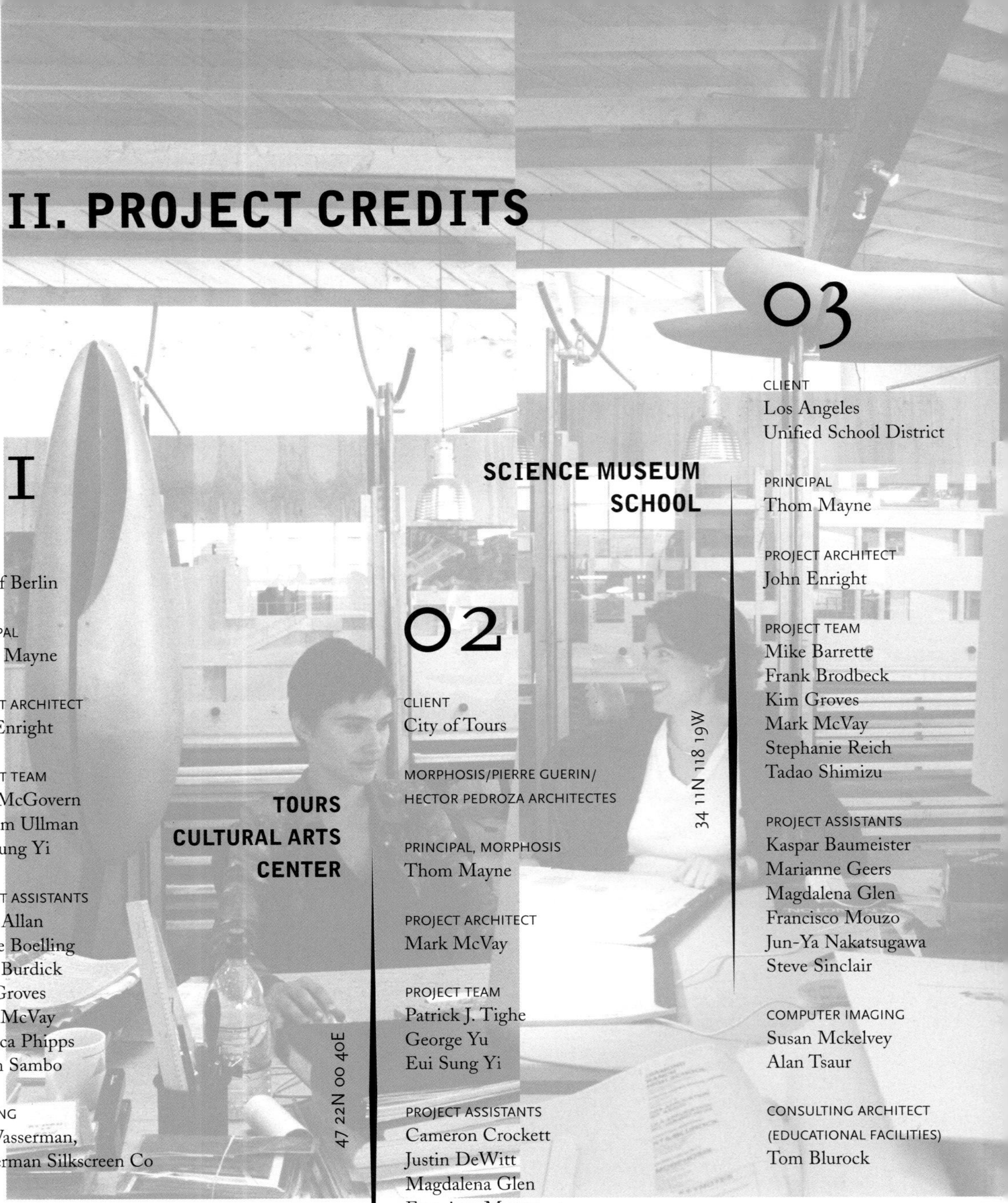

01

SPREEBOGEN INTERNATIONAL DESIGN COMPETITION

53 32N 13 25E

CLIENT
City of Berlin

PRINCIPAL
Thom Mayne

PROJECT ARCHITECT
John Enright

PROJECT TEAM
Peter McGovern
William Ullman
Eui-Sung Yi

PROJECT ASSISTANTS
Sarah Allan
Hanne Boelling
Craig Burdick
Kim Groves
Mark McVay
Rebecca Phipps
Robyn Sambo

PRINTING
Jeff Wasserman,
Wasserman Silkscreen Co

02

TOURS CULTURAL ARTS CENTER

47 22N 00 40E

CLIENT
City of Tours

MORPHOSIS/PIERRE GUERIN/
HECTOR PEDROZA ARCHITECTES

PRINCIPAL, MORPHOSIS
Thom Mayne

PROJECT ARCHITECT
Mark McVay

PROJECT TEAM
Patrick J. Tighe
George Yu
Eui Sung Yi

PROJECT ASSISTANTS
Cameron Crockett
Justin DeWitt
Magdalena Glen
Francisco Mouzo
Dave Neil
Kinga Racon
Ivan Redi
Robyn Sambo
Mark Sich

JOINT VENTURE

PRINCIPAL, PIERRE GUERIN/
HECTOR PEDROZA ARCHITECTES
Pierre Guerin & Hector Pedroza

CIVIL AND STRUCTURAL ENGINEERS
Hubert Debaille

LIASON
Dominique Jakob

03

SCIENCE MUSEUM SCHOOL

34 11N 118 19W

CLIENT
Los Angeles
Unified School District

PRINCIPAL
Thom Mayne

PROJECT ARCHITECT
John Enright

PROJECT TEAM
Mike Barrette
Frank Brodbeck
Kim Groves
Mark McVay
Stephanie Reich
Tadao Shimizu

PROJECT ASSISTANTS
Kaspar Baumeister
Marianne Geers
Magdalena Glen
Francisco Mouzo
Jun-Ya Nakatsugawa
Steve Sinclair

COMPUTER IMAGING
Susan Mckelvey
Alan Tsaur

CONSULTING ARCHITECT
(EDUCATIONAL FACILITIES)
Tom Blurock

ONYX (S.S.) R2STWO (K.L.) PETRA (J.M.)

04

SALICK ADMINISTRATIVE OFFICES

34 11N 118 19W

CLIENT
Salick Health Care
Dr. Bernard Salick

PRINCIPAL
Thom Mayne

PROJECT ARCHITECT
Kim Groves
Stephanie Reich

PROJECT TEAM
Frank Brodbeck
John Enright
Robyn Sambo
Patrick J. Tighe

PROJECT ASSISTANTS
Kaspar Baumeister
Ming Lee
Kinga Racon
Andreas Schaller

COMPUTER IMAGING
Lars Bleher
Mark Sich

STRUCTURAL ENGINEER
Joseph Perazzelli

MECHANICAL ENGINEERS
Mel Bilow & Associates

INTERIOR CONSULTANT
Denise Anton,
Salick Healthcare

CONSTRUCTION ADMINISTRATION
Cliff Muller,
Construction Management
and Supervision
Timothy Suita,
Salick Health Care

05

FJC COMMUNICATIONS

34 11N 118 19W

CLIENT
Friedland Jacobs
Communications
Scott Friedland
Ray Jacobs

PRINCIPAL
Thom Mayne

PROJECT ARCHITECT
Patrick J. Tighe

PROJECT ASSISTANTS
Laith Al-Sayigh
Mauricio Gomez
Towan Kim
Richard Koschitz
Ludovica Milo
Walter Ortiz

COMPUTER IMAGING
Cameron Crockett
Michael Mladenoff
Robyn Sambo

STRUCTURAL ENGINEER
Joseph Perazzelli

MECHANICAL ENGINEERS
Davar & Assoc.

ELECTRICAL ENGINEERS
V & M
Electrical Engineering

CONTRACTOR
Jamik Construction

TOAST

BLUE (M.B.)

WOODSTOCK (R.S.)

MESSY TEMPLE AKA HALO

07

LANDA HOUSE

33 50N 118 24W

CLIENT
Hans and Jutta Landa

PRINCIPAL
Thom Mayne

PROJECT ARCHITECT
John Enright

PROJECT TEAM
Frank Brodbeck
Brandon Welling

PROJECT ASSISTANTS
Lars Bleher
Frank Bohland
Cameron Crockett
Magdalena Glen
Martin Krammer
Ming Lee
Kinga Racon
Mark Sich
Stephen Slaughter

STRUCTURAL ENGINEER
Michael Ishler

CONTRACTOR
Michael Lee

STEEL FABRICATION
Tom Farrage/Co.

CUSTOM CABINETRY
Mauricio Gomez

06

OVE ARUP & PARTNERS, LOS ANGELES

34 11N 118 19W

CLIENT
Ove Arup & Partners
Peter Budd
Alan Locke

PRINCIPAL
Thom Mayne

PROJECT ARCHITECT
Kim Groves

PROJECT TEAM
Jay Behr
Steven Chen
John Enright
Ted Kane
Steve Sinclair

STRUCT./MECH./ELEC./PLUMB. ENGINEER
Ove Arup and Partners

CONTRACTOR
Limbrick A/A Construction

COCKPIT (DECEASED)

SINJIN (E.S.Y.)

FRONTIER (RETIRED)

XANADU AKA BUDAH

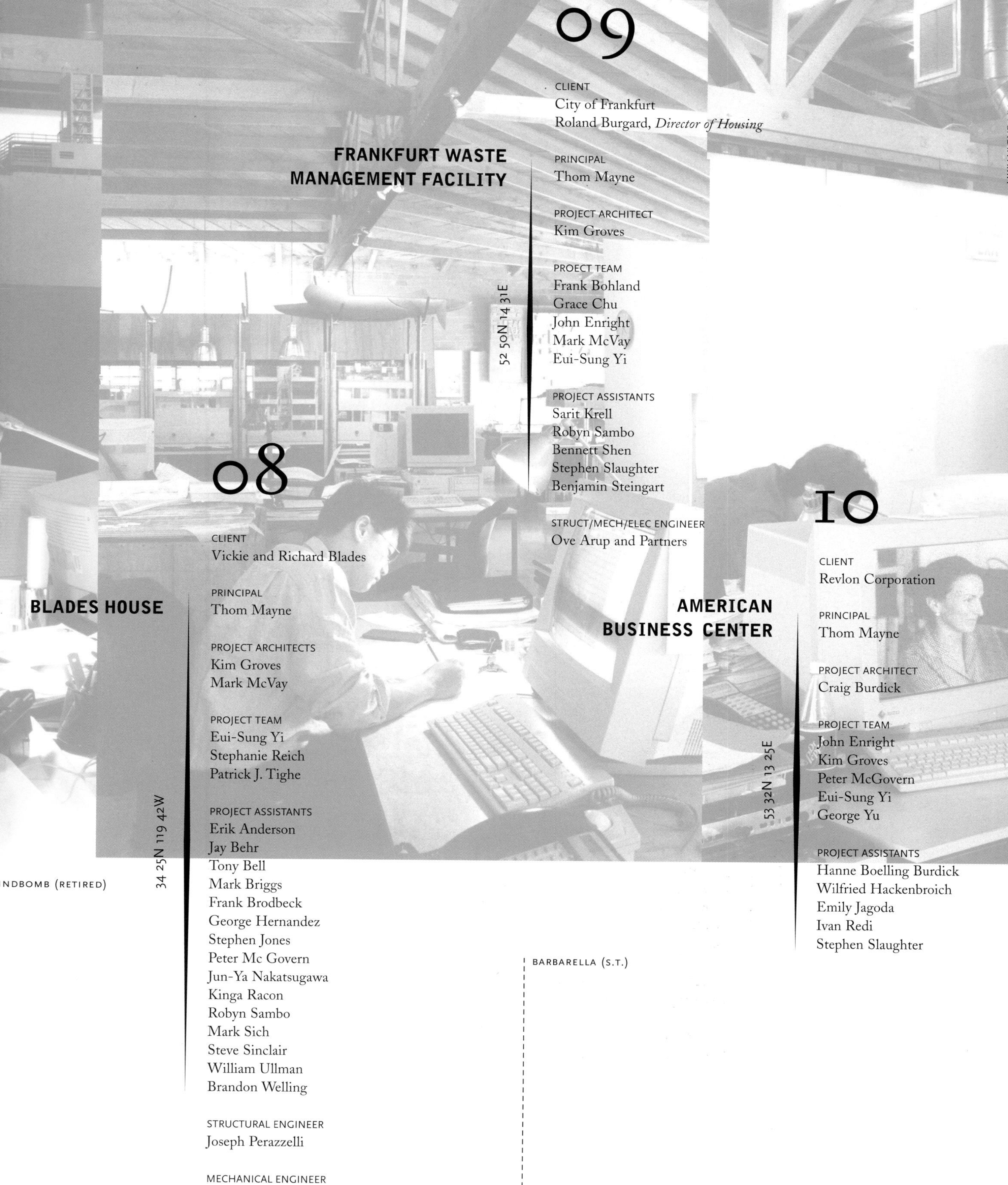

09

FRANKFURT WASTE MANAGEMENT FACILITY

52 50N 14 31E

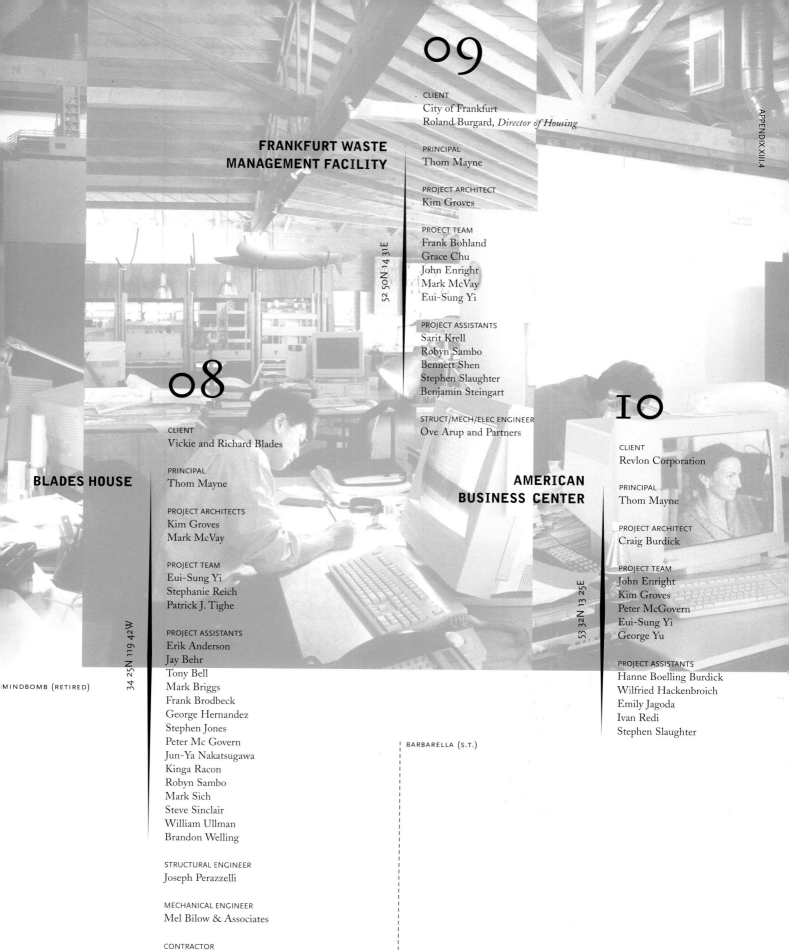

CLIENT
City of Frankfurt
Roland Burgard, *Director of Housing*

PRINCIPAL
Thom Mayne

PROJECT ARCHITECT
Kim Groves

PROECT TEAM
Frank Bohland
Grace Chu
John Enright
Mark McVay
Eui-Sung Yi

PROJECT ASSISTANTS
Sarit Krell
Robyn Sambo
Bennett Shen
Stephen Slaughter
Benjamin Steingart

STRUCT/MECH/ELEC ENGINEER
Ove Arup and Partners

08

BLADES HOUSE

34 25N 119 42W

CLIENT
Vickie and Richard Blades

PRINCIPAL
Thom Mayne

PROJECT ARCHITECTS
Kim Groves
Mark McVay

PROJECT TEAM
Eui-Sung Yi
Stephanie Reich
Patrick J. Tighe

PROJECT ASSISTANTS
Erik Anderson
Jay Behr
Tony Bell
Mark Briggs
Frank Brodbeck
George Hernandez
Stephen Jones
Peter Mc Govern
Jun-Ya Nakatsugawa
Kinga Racon
Robyn Sambo
Mark Sich
Steve Sinclair
William Ullman
Brandon Welling

STRUCTURAL ENGINEER
Joseph Perazzelli

MECHANICAL ENGINEER
Mel Bilow & Associates

CONTRACTOR
Froescher-Lewis Construction

10

AMERICAN BUSINESS CENTER

53 32N 13 25E

CLIENT
Revlon Corporation

PRINCIPAL
Thom Mayne

PROJECT ARCHITECT
Craig Burdick

PROJECT TEAM
John Enright
Kim Groves
Peter McGovern
Eui-Sung Yi
George Yu

PROJECT ASSISTANTS
Hanne Boelling Burdick
Wilfried Hackenbroich
Emily Jagoda
Ivan Redi
Stephen Slaughter

MINDBOMB (RETIRED)

BARBARELLA (S.T.)

HOMING PIGEON (E-MAIL)

11

MASH, ONE-ROOM SCHOOLHOUSE

36 10N 115 09W

CLIENT
Las Vegas Redevelopement Agency
Arnie Stalk

MORPHOSIS/
LUCCHESI GALATI ARCHITECTS INC.

PRINCIPAL, MORPHOSIS
Thom Mayne

PROJECT ARCHITECT
John Enright

PROJECT TEAM
Martin Krammer
Frank Brodbeck

PROJECT ASSISTANTS
Erik Anderson
Magdalena Glen
Blayne Imata
Brad Johnson
Jelena Mijanovic
Patrick J. Tighe
Kinga Racon

COMPUTER IMAGING
David Roberts
Robyn Sambo
Alan Tsaur

JOINT VENTURE

PRINCIPAL,
LUCCHESI GALATI ARCHITECTS, INC.
Chris Galati

PROJECT MANAGER
J. Denise Cook, AIA

PROJECT TEAM
Rudy Starks, Jr.
Dwayne Eshenbaugh

NOSERIDER (D.G.)

12

SUN TOWER

37 30N 127 00W

CLIENTS
Village Trading Co., LTD
Jae Kwon Kim

PRINCIPAL
Thom Mayne

PROJECT MANAGER
Eul-ho Suh

PROJECT DESIGNERS
Dave Grant
Kim Groves
Kristina Loock
Eui-Sung Yi

PROJECT ASSISTANTS
Min-Seok Baek
Jay Behr
Mark Briggs
Neil Crawford
Towan Kim
Richard Koschitz
Janice Shimizu

LOCAL ARCHITECT
Kyung Yeol Kim, Daisung

CONTRACTOR
Sejin-Tajima/
Dae Yoo Gong Young

STRUCTURAL ENGINEER
Ove Arup and Partners

BRAINDEAD (F.K.)

13

A.S.E. VISITOR CENTER

13 44N100 30W

CLIENT
A.S.E. Design Center
Eric Hsiang

PRINCIPAL
Thom Mayne

PROJECT ARCHITECT
Patrick J. Tighe

PROJECT ASSISTANTS
Towan Kim
Richard Koschitz
Eugene Lee
Ung Joo Scott Lee
Michael O'Bryan
Robyn Sambo
Steven Slaughter
Alan Tsaur
Bart Tucker
Oliver Winkler

DESIGN CONSULTANT
CY Lee

LIGHTING CONSULTANT
Patrick Quigley & Assoc.

CONTRACTOR
Taiwan Fuhbic Corporation

NEUROMANCER (J.E.)

15

DIAMOND RANCH HIGH SCHOOL

34 04N 117 45W

CLIENT
Pomona Unifed School District
Patrick Leier, *Superintendant*
Ron Young
Ed Walsh
Chris Butler

MORPHOSIS/THOMAS BLUROCK ARCHITECTS

PRINCIPAL, MORPHOSIS
Thom Mayne

PROJECT ARCHITECT
John Enright

PROJECT TEAM
Cameron Crockett
David Grant
Fabian Kremkus
Janice Shimizu
Patrick J. Tighe

PROJECT ASSISTANTS
Sarah Allan
Kasper Baumeister
Jay Behr
John Bencher
Mark Briggs
Frank Brodbeck
Takashi Ehira
Magdalena Glen
Ivar Gudmunson
George Hemandez
Martin Krammer
Ming Lee
Francisco Mouzo
Christopher Payne
Kinga Racon
Robyn Sambo
Andreas Schaller
Bennet Shen
Mark Sich
Craig Shimahara
Tadao Shimizu
Stephen Slaughter
Brandon Welling
Eui-Sung Yi

STRUCT./MECH./ELEC. ENGINEER
Ove Arup & Partners:
Bruce Gibbons, Structural Engineer
John Gautry, Mechanical Engineer
Gregory Morrison, Electrical Engineer
Anait Manjikian, Plumbing Engineer

CIVIL ENGINEERS
Andreasen Engineers, Inc.
Gary P. Andreasen

LANDSCAPE ARCHITECT
Fong & Associates

KITCHEN CONSULTANTS
K.I.A.

COST ESTIMATOR
Adamson Associates

CONSTRUCTION MANAGERS
Bernards Brothers Construction

JOINT VENTURE

PRINCIPAL
THOMAS BLUROCK ARCHITECTS
Tom Blurock

PROJECT ARCHITECT
Tom Moore

PROJECT TEAM
Mark Briggs
Kevin Fleming
Nadar Glassemlou
Chris Samuelian
Kristina Steeves
Jose Valentin
Wendell Vaughn
Lis Zuloaga

PROJECT ASSISTANTS
Gregory Ashton
Colleen Bathgate
Mike Blazek
Vince Coffeen
Karen MacIntyre
Kathy Sun
Brady Titus
Robert Trucios

14

WOHNBAU WAGRAMER STRASSE

48 13N 16 22E

CLIENT
City of Vienna
Hanns Swoboda, *Director of Housing*
Herbert Binder, *Coordinator*

PRINCIPAL
Thom Mayne

PROJECT ARCHITECT
Kim Groves

PROJECT DESIGNER
Kristina Loock

PROJECT TEAM
Dave Grant

PROJECT ASSISTANTS
Erik Anderson
Gavin Hutcheson
Richard Koschitz
Jelena Mijanovic
Ludovica Milo
Laith Al-Sayigh

COMPUTER IMAGING
Mark Briggs
Chris Peck

COORDINATOR
Markus Spiegelfeld

LANDSCAPE ARCHITECT
Martha Schwartz
Jennifer Luce

MORHOLT (P.T.)

NO FAILURE (S.L.)

CHAPULIN

CHILLINDRINA

16

INTERNATIONAL ELEMENTARY SCHOOL

34 40N 118 12W

CLIENT
Long Beach Unified School District
Tomio Nishimura, *Financial Director*
Lisa Dutra, *Director*
Falanai Ala, *Construction Manager*

MORPHOSIS/THOMAS BLUROCK ARCHITECTS

PRINCIPAL, MORPHOSIS
Thom Mayne

PROJECT ARCHITECT
Kim Groves

PROJECT DESIGNER
Silvia Kuhle

PROJECT TEAM
David Plotkin
Robyn Sambo
Stephen Slaughter
Brandon Welling

PROJECT ASSISTANTS
Rob Edmonds
Michael O'Bryan

STRUCT./MECH./ELEC. ENGINEERING
Ove Arup & Partners, California:
Andrew Tompson, Structural Engineer
Catherine Wells, Structural Engineer
Bronagh Walsh, Mechanical Engineer
Alistair McGregor, Mechanical Engineer
Fiona Cousins, Mechanical Engineer
Peter Balint, Electrical Engineer
Vahik Davoudi, Electrical Engineer

CIVIL ENGINEERING
Andreasen Engineering

LANDSCAPE ARCHITECT
Fong & Associates

KITCHEN CONSULTANTS
Dewco Food Facility Consultants

COST ESTIMATOR
Adamson Associates
Nick Butcher

CONSTRUCTION MANAGER
Pinner Construction

JOINT VENTURE

PRINCIPAL,
THOMAS BLUROCK ARCHITECTS
Tom Blurock

PROJECT ARCHITECT
Jim Moore

PROJECT MANAGER
Barbara Helton

PROJECT TEAM
Jose Valentin

17

JUNIPERO SERRA SHRINE

34 04n 118 15W

CLIENT
Archdioces of Los Angeles
Cardinal Roger Mahony
Monsignor Terrance L. Fleming

PRINCIPAL
Thom Mayne

PROJECT ARCHITECT
Kim Groves

PROJECT TEAM
Silvia Kuhle
Thomas Lenzen
Ingo Waegner

COMPUTER IMAGING
Jay Behr
Dave Grant
Jesse Seppi

PROJECT COORDINATOR
Janet Sager

LANDSCAPE ARCHITECT
Katherine Spitz Associates

CONSULTING ARTIST
Peter Erskine

STRATEGISTS
James Watt McCormick
Dr. George Rand

THEOLOGICAL AND LITURGICAL CONSULTANT
Stephen Lebowitz

GONZALES (S.K.)

HALO (B.W.)

MAVERICKS (B.T.)

S.S.MINNOW (J.F.)

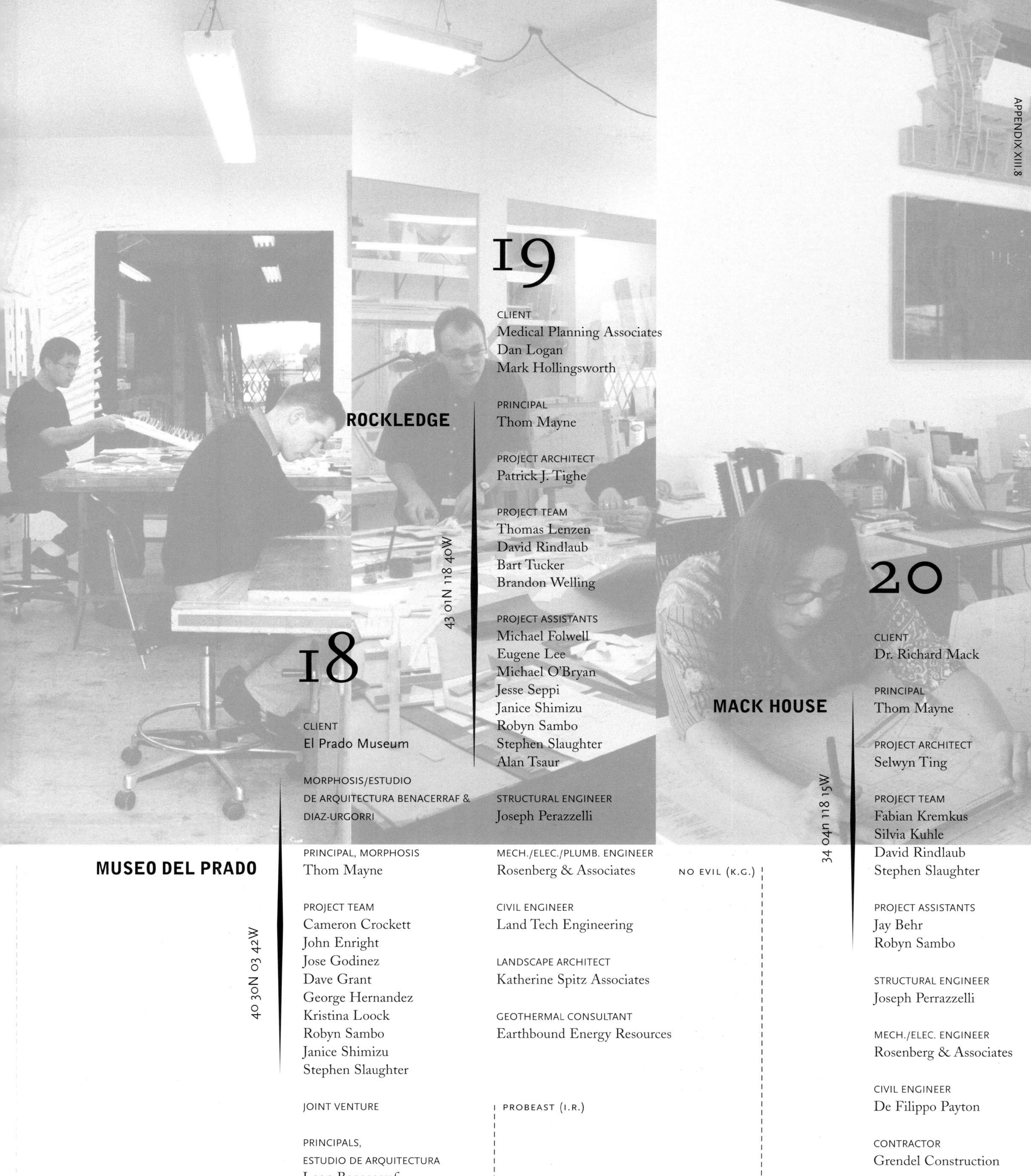

18

MUSEO DEL PRADO

40 30N 03 42W

CLIENT
El Prado Museum

MORPHOSIS/ESTUDIO DE ARQUITECTURA BENACERRAF & DIAZ-URGORRI

PRINCIPAL, MORPHOSIS
Thom Mayne

PROJECT TEAM
Cameron Crockett
John Enright
Jose Godinez
Dave Grant
George Hernandez
Kristina Loock
Robyn Sambo
Janice Shimizu
Stephen Slaughter

JOINT VENTURE

PRINCIPALS, ESTUDIO DE ARQUITECTURA
Leon Benacerraf
Begonia Diaz-Urgorri

19

ROCKLEDGE

43 01N 118 40W

CLIENT
Medical Planning Associates
Dan Logan
Mark Hollingsworth

PRINCIPAL
Thom Mayne

PROJECT ARCHITECT
Patrick J. Tighe

PROJECT TEAM
Thomas Lenzen
David Rindlaub
Bart Tucker
Brandon Welling

PROJECT ASSISTANTS
Michael Folwell
Eugene Lee
Michael O'Bryan
Jesse Seppi
Janice Shimizu
Robyn Sambo
Stephen Slaughter
Alan Tsaur

STRUCTURAL ENGINEER
Joseph Perazzelli

MECH./ELEC./PLUMB. ENGINEER
Rosenberg & Associates

CIVIL ENGINEER
Land Tech Engineering

LANDSCAPE ARCHITECT
Katherine Spitz Associates

GEOTHERMAL CONSULTANT
Earthbound Energy Resources

20

MACK HOUSE

34 04n 118 15W

CLIENT
Dr. Richard Mack

PRINCIPAL
Thom Mayne

PROJECT ARCHITECT
Selwyn Ting

PROJECT TEAM
Fabian Kremkus
Silvia Kuhle
David Rindlaub
Stephen Slaughter

PROJECT ASSISTANTS
Jay Behr
Robyn Sambo

STRUCTURAL ENGINEER
Joseph Perrazzelli

MECH./ELEC. ENGINEER
Rosenberg & Associates

CIVIL ENGINEER
De Filippo Payton

CONTRACTOR
Grendel Construction

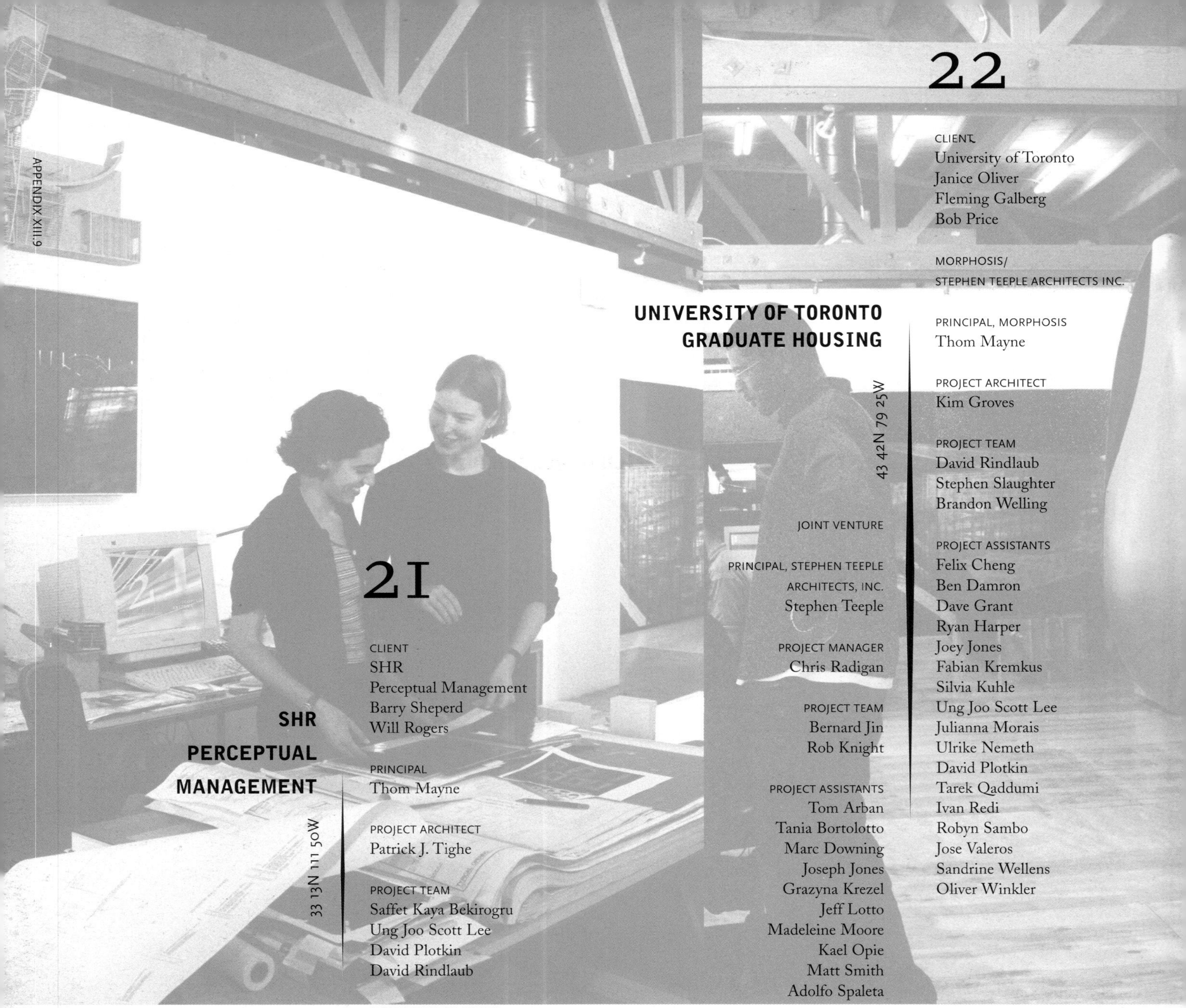

21

SHR PERCEPTUAL MANAGEMENT

33 13N 111 50W

CLIENT
SHR
Perceptual Management
Barry Sheperd
Will Rogers

PRINCIPAL
Thom Mayne

PROJECT ARCHITECT
Patrick J. Tighe

PROJECT TEAM
Saffet Kaya Bekirogru
Ung Joo Scott Lee
David Plotkin
David Rindlaub

STRUCTURAL ENGINEER
Caruso Turley Scott, Inc

MECHANICAL ENGINEER
MP Designs

ELECTRICAL ENGINEER
SW Engineering, Inc

CONTRACTOR
Hardison/Downey

22

UNIVERSITY OF TORONTO GRADUATE HOUSING

43 42N 79 25W

CLIENT
University of Toronto
Janice Oliver
Fleming Galberg
Bob Price

MORPHOSIS/
STEPHEN TEEPLE ARCHITECTS INC.

JOINT VENTURE

PRINCIPAL, MORPHOSIS
Thom Mayne

PRINCIPAL, STEPHEN TEEPLE ARCHITECTS, INC.
Stephen Teeple

PROJECT ARCHITECT
Kim Groves

PROJECT MANAGER
Chris Radigan

PROJECT TEAM
David Rindlaub
Stephen Slaughter
Brandon Welling

PROJECT TEAM
Bernard Jin
Rob Knight

PROJECT ASSISTANTS
Felix Cheng
Ben Damron
Dave Grant
Ryan Harper
Joey Jones
Fabian Kremkus
Silvia Kuhle
Ung Joo Scott Lee
Julianna Morais
Ulrike Nemeth
David Plotkin
Tarek Qaddumi
Ivan Redi
Robyn Sambo
Jose Valeros
Sandrine Wellens
Oliver Winkler

PROJECT ASSISTANTS
Tom Arban
Tania Bortolotto
Marc Downing
Joseph Jones
Grazyna Krezel
Jeff Lotto
Madeleine Moore
Kael Opie
Matt Smith
Adolfo Spaleta

STRUCTURAL ENGINEER
Yolles partnership Inc.
Barry Charnish
John Kooymans

MECHANICAL ENGINEER
Keen Engineering
Mark Mitchell
J. Michael Godawa

ELECTRICAL ENGINEER
Carincini Bart Rogers Engineering, Inc.
Corrie Burt
Michael Palmer

LANDSCAPE ARCHITECT
Janet Rosenberg & Associates

CONTRACTOR
Axor Construction Canada, Inc.

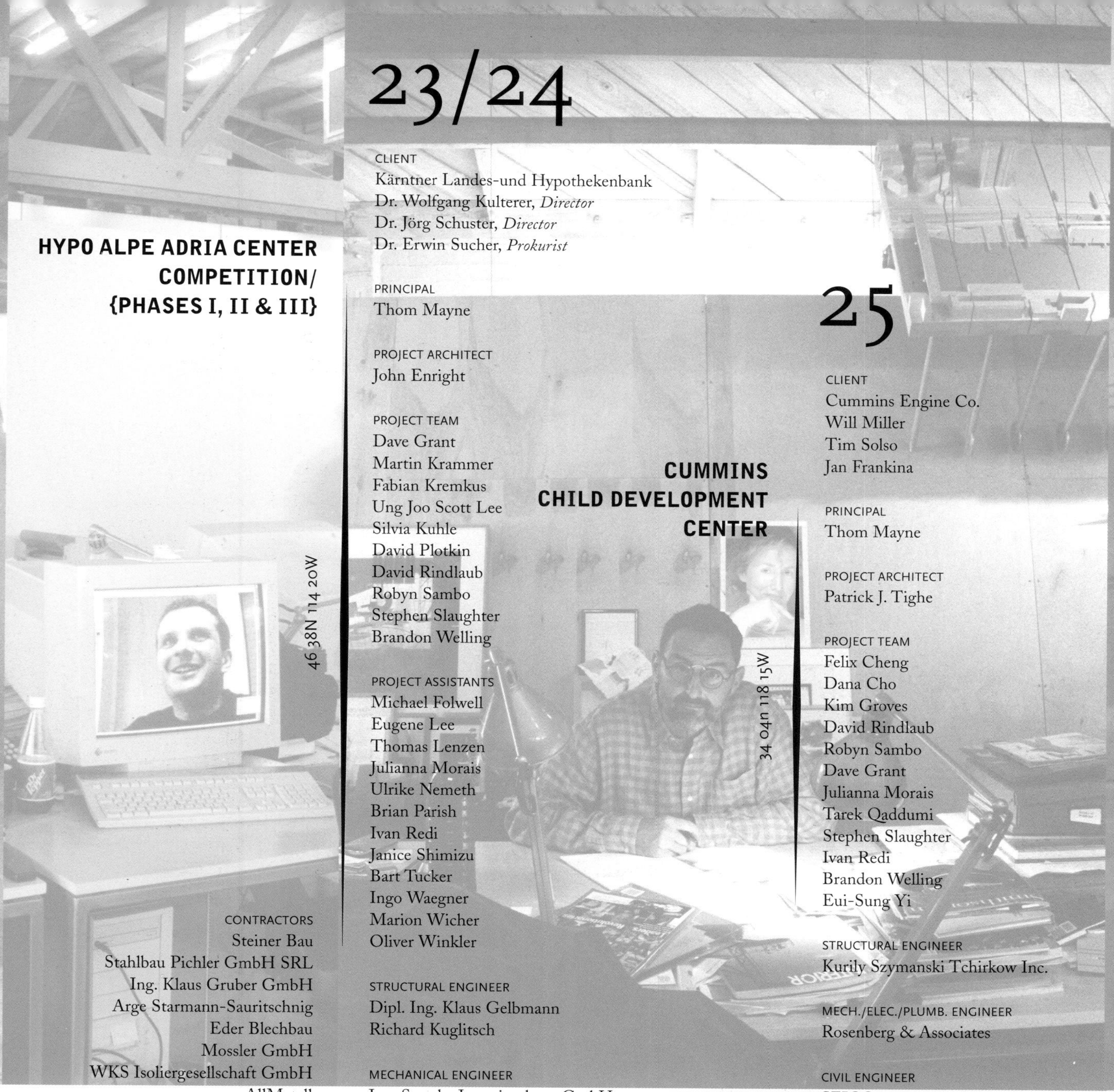

23/24

HYPO ALPE ADRIA CENTER COMPETITION/ {PHASES I, II & III}

46 38N 114 20W

CLIENT
Kärntner Landes-und Hypothekenbank
Dr. Wolfgang Kulterer, *Director*
Dr. Jörg Schuster, *Director*
Dr. Erwin Sucher, *Prokurist*

PRINCIPAL
Thom Mayne

PROJECT ARCHITECT
John Enright

PROJECT TEAM
Dave Grant
Martin Krammer
Fabian Kremkus
Ung Joo Scott Lee
Silvia Kuhle
David Plotkin
David Rindlaub
Robyn Sambo
Stephen Slaughter
Brandon Welling

PROJECT ASSISTANTS
Michael Folwell
Eugene Lee
Thomas Lenzen
Julianna Morais
Ulrike Nemeth
Brian Parish
Ivan Redi
Janice Shimizu
Bart Tucker
Ingo Waegner
Marion Wicher
Oliver Winkler

STRUCTURAL ENGINEER
Dipl. Ing. Klaus Gelbmann
Richard Kuglitsch

MECHANICAL ENGINEER
Ing. Smrcka Ingenieurburo GmbH
Ing. Ludwig Smrcka
Robert Sorz

ELECTRICAL ENGINEER
August Gregoritsch
Fritz Aufschlager

GENERAL COORDINATION
Zölestin Thomas Stich

BAUPHYSIC
Gerhard Tomberger

SPECIFICATIONS
Dipl. Ing. Reinhold Svetina
Werner Schusser

CONTRACTORS
Steiner Bau
Stahlbau Pichler GmbH SRL
Ing. Klaus Gruber GmbH
Arge Starmann-Sauritschnig
Eder Blechbau
Mossler GmbH
WKS Isoliergesellschaft GmbH
AllMetall
Wrulich
Elin Ebg
Pfrimer & Mosslacher

25

CUMMINS CHILD DEVELOPMENT CENTER

34 04n 118 15W

CLIENT
Cummins Engine Co.
Will Miller
Tim Solso
Jan Frankina

PRINCIPAL
Thom Mayne

PROJECT ARCHITECT
Patrick J. Tighe

PROJECT TEAM
Felix Cheng
Dana Cho
Kim Groves
David Rindlaub
Robyn Sambo
Dave Grant
Julianna Morais
Tarek Qaddumi
Stephen Slaughter
Ivan Redi
Brandon Welling
Eui-Sung Yi

STRUCTURAL ENGINEER
Kurily Szymanski Tchirkow Inc.

MECH./ELEC./PLUMB. ENGINEER
Rosenberg & Associates

CIVIL ENGINEER
SEICO

LANDSCAPE ARCHITECT
Pamela Burton & Company

Cost Estimator/Contractor
Sherman R. Smoot Co. of Indiana

JECKYL

BUDAH (T.M.)

HYDE

GRAPHIC DESIGN

Morphosis/Lorraine Wild
Thom Mayne
Lorraine Wild
with
Bele Ducke
Scott Lee
Ana Llorente-Thurik
Robyn Sambo

EDITING

John Cava
Blythe Alison Mayne
Dr. George Rand
Tony Robins
Val Warke

BOOK ORGANIZATION

Janet Sager

ACKNOWLEDGMENTS

The Morphosis office has been defined by a number of partnerships, formal and informal. Morphosis was founded in 1971-72 by Thom Mayne and Jim Stafford, parallel to the establishment of the Southern California Institute of Architecture, of which they were two of the six founding members. They were joined in 1973 by Michael Rotondi, formalizing a partnership lasting from 1980 through 1992. Kazu Arai worked in the studio through the 1980s, leaving his mark on individual projects and contributing to the energy and intelligence to the office as a whole. The 1990s have seen the emergence of John Enright and Kim Groves, without whom this work could not exist.

This book owes thanks to Lorraine Wild, who was responsible for the graphic design for the two previous Morphosis monographs published by Rizzoli, for her collaboration and patience in what seemed like an endless process always rich with obstacles.

I would like to thank Janet Sager for the initial assemblage and organization, and to John Cava for the massive editing required in gluing together the bits and pieces of project texts. George Rand, Blythe Alison Mayne, Tony Robins, and Val Warke provided valuable criticism of the text, and thank you to Sylvia Lavin for her general comments.

A special thanks to Chris Yessios of Form-Z for all his help and generous support with the myriad issues involving 3-D modeling and imaging. Also to Larry Crume of Kinetix and 3D Studio Max, Karen Raz of Electric Image, Inc., and D. J. Attfield of Treasure Mapper for all of their assistance and support.

APPENDIX PHOTOGRAPHY CREDITS Farshid Assassi: APPENDIX XII.16 (bottom middle), 19 (middle right), 20 (top left). Helene Binet: APPENDIX XII.20 (top right). Rainer Blunck: APPENDIX XII.14 (right), XII.15 (left). Tom Bonner: APPENDIX II.2, II.6 (right), II.24, II.29, 30, APPENDIX VI.12,13. APPENDIX XII.9 (right), 11 (all), 13, 14 (left), 15 (right), 16 (middle left, middle right, top center, bottom right), 17 (all), 18 (all), 19 (all, except middle right), 20 (bottom right), 21 (all, except bottom left), 22 (middle), 23 (middle left, middle right), 26 (bottom right). Steve Chen: APPENDIX II.27, APPENDIX XII.23 (bottom right). Yu-Hsien Chou: APPENDIX VI.20,21, APPENDIX XII.27 (middle right). John Enright: APPENDIX VI.14 (bottom), VI.15, VI. 26, 27, 28, 29. Young-Il Kim: APPENDIX VI.16, 17, VI.19. APPENDIX XII.27 (middle center). Nicole Koenigsberger: APPENDIX XII.20 (bottom middle). Duks Koschitz: APPENDIX V.5. Silvia Kuhle: APPENDIX VI.24/25 (all). Thom Mayne: APPENDIX II.6 (upper left), APPENDIX VII.1/2, 3/4. APPENDIX IX.1/2. APPENDIX XII.1, 9 (left), 20 (top middle). Mark McVay: APPENDIX VI. 1, 2/3 (bottom). Morphosis: APPENDIX XII.6, 7, 8, 20 (bottom left). XII.24 (right). Grant Mudford: APPENDIX VI.10 (upper right). Ferdinand Muller: APPENDIX XII.26 (middle). Tim Street Porter: APPENDIX XII.10, XII.16 (middle center). Kinga Racon/Magdalena Glen: APPENDIX XII.22 (right). David Rindlaub: APPENDIX V.25. Marvin Rand: APPENDIX XII.12. Janet Sager: APPENDIX II. 35 (bottom). Selwyn Ting: APPENDIX XII.21 (bottom left). Alex Vertikoff: APPENDIX XII.16 (bottom left). Paul Warchol: APPENDIX XII.14 (middle). Brandon Welling: APPENDIX V.7, 11, 13, 17, 23, 33, 37, 39, APPENDIX VI.8, 9, 10 (upper left, bottom), VI.11, 14 (top), VI.22/23. APPENDIX XII.22 (left), 23 (bottom left), 24 (left), 26 (bottom left, bottom middle), 27 (bottom middle, bottom right), APPENDIX XIII.1/15. Eui Sung Yi: APPENDIX VI.18, APPENDIX XII.23 (middle center). Daniel Zimbaldi: APPENDIX XII.5, 6 (right). Gerald Zugmann: APPENDIX VIII.1. Kim Zwarts: APPENDIX VI.4,5, 6, 7, APPENDIX XII.26 (top).

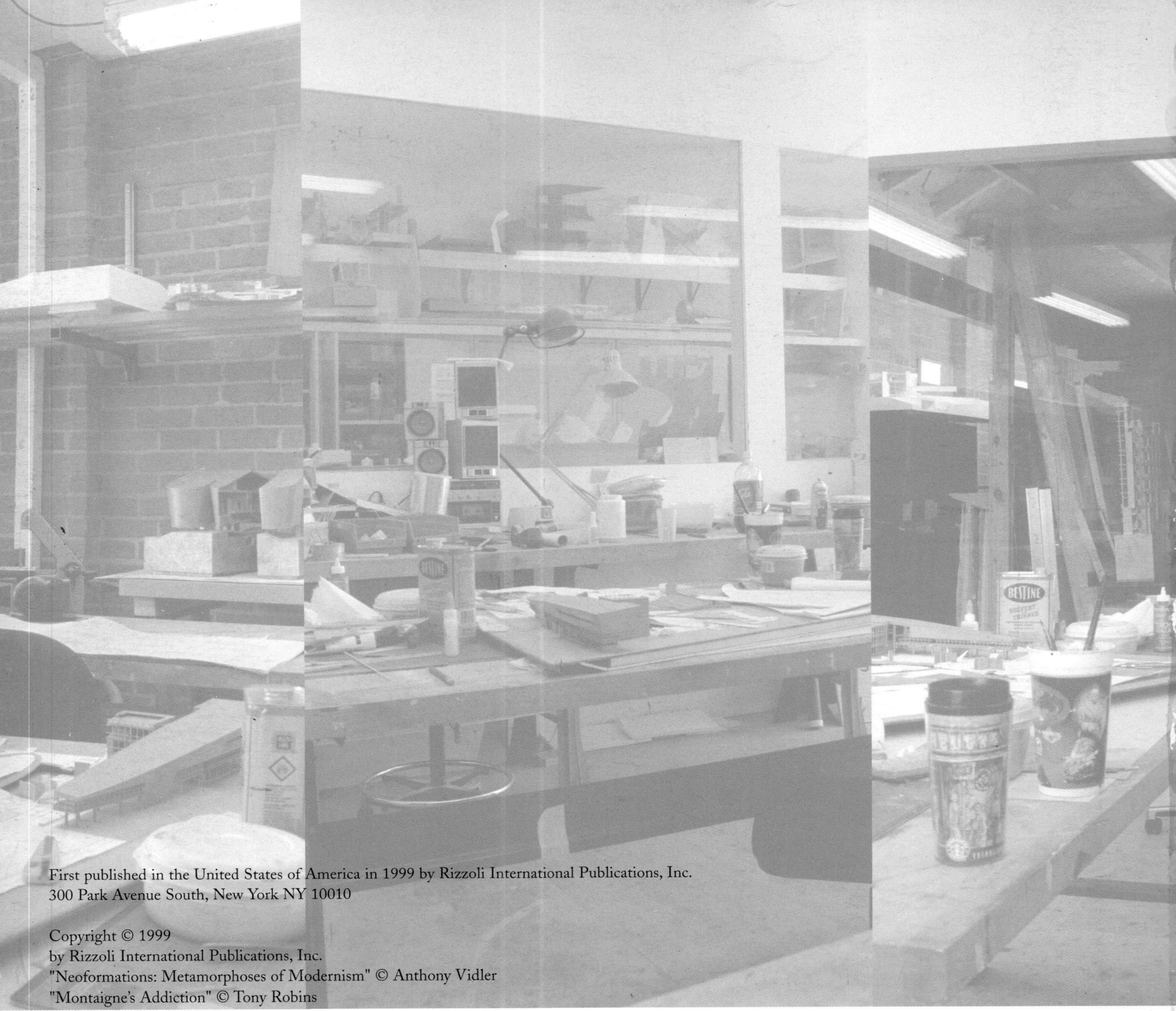

First published in the United States of America in 1999 by Rizzoli International Publications, Inc.
300 Park Avenue South, New York NY 10010

ISBN 0-8478-2074-2

LC 98-75231

Printed and bound in Italy